1968

This book may be kept

FOURTEEN DAYS

FROM SENSIBILITY TO ROMANTICISM

FROM SENSIBILITY
TO ROMANTICISM

Essays Presented to Frederick A. Pottle

EDITED BY

FREDERICK W. HILLES and HAROLD BLOOM

New York · OXFORD UNIVERSITY PRESS · 1965

TABLE OF CONTENTS

v

INTRODUCTION

For the past forty years Frederick A. Pottle has been a member of the Department of English at Yale. Sterling Professor of English, he is today the ranking member of the university faculty.

As a scholar he is best known for the books and articles that he has written about James Boswell, but a glance at his extensive bibliography indicates the wide range of his interests: from problems in Old English texts to modern fine printing, from the "respectability" of creeds and dogmas to the story of a hospital unit which operated in France during the first World War. Most of his published work deals with writers of prose, but his first book was a study of Shelley and Browning, and *The Idiom of Poetry,* though primarily concerned with literary criticism, testifies to his lifelong interest in English poetry.

A similar breadth of interest is reflected in the courses that he has taught. Naturally most of these have treated some aspect of English literature, but he has also been a teacher of language, of history, of economics, and of chemistry. Where he has perhaps been most influential with his students is in fostering a study of English poetry of the late eighteenth and early nineteenth centuries.

This volume gathers together essays written in his honor, and centers itself on a problem he has studied in *The Idiom of Poetry* and elsewhere, that of a "shift in sensibility" between two broadly defined literary periods. The transition studied here is the one that took place during the half-century following the death of Pope. Essays on this period, which has been called the "Age of Sensibility," are flanked in this volume by essays on Pope and on the Romantic poets, so as to provide a series of critical studies in depth of the main movement of English poetry between Pope and Keats.

F.W.H.

H.B.

June 1964
New Haven, Connecticut

FROM SENSIBILITY TO ROMANTICISM

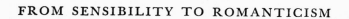

A NOTE ON PLATE I. The description of Pope's house in the text is based on the undated engraving shown in Plate I. It is entitled "An Exact Draught and View of Mr. Pope's House at Twickenham" and signed "Rysbrack delin. & pinx.", "Parr Sculp." It depicts Pope's house and a few neighboring buildings from across the river, several swans and boats in the river, a party of visitors landing on Pope's greensward with two small dogs scampering before them, and, in front of the grotto opening, a figure with a dog that plainly belongs to Pope's long line of Bounces. Below the picture are printed (without separation, as if they belonged to the same poem) *Imit. Hor.*, *Sat.* II i 123–4 and II ii 137–50. The artist in question is probably Peter Andreas Rysbrack, brother of the more famous Michael, who is known to have specialized in landscape and topographical views for engraving. (See M. I. Webb, *Michael Rysbrack, Sculptor*, 1954, pp. 19–20.)

This view of Pope's villa is apparently to be identified with the "Prospect of Mr. Pope's House, from the Surrey Side," which, according to his own account (*Mr. Pope's Literary Correspondence*, II, 1735, "To the Reader"), Edmund Curll had Rysbrack make for him on 12 June 1735, when he visited the villa in company with the artist, Pope being then in London. This "Prospect" afforded, Curll tells us, "a full View of our Bard's Grotto, Subterraneous Way, Gardens, Statues, Inscriptions, and his Dog *Bounce*," and "is now exhibited in a very curious Print, engraven by the best Hands." The gardens, statues, and inscriptions that Curll refers to do not appear in the extant Rysbrack "Draught and View." But Curll is not known for accuracy. He may have regarded Pope's parterre and hedges as sufficient to justify the term "gardens," since no view of the front of the house could possibly include the garden proper. He may during his visit have seen "sculptures" with "inscriptions" niched into the parterre hedge, which Rysbrack did not record in the painting. And he is careful to include later in the volume (pp. 221–2) a "Description of Mr. Pope's House," in which he makes it clear that he has penetrated the actual garden; learned from the gardener John Serle that he had "lived with Mr. Pope above Eleven Years," that "there were not Ten Sticks in the

Ground when his Master took the House," and that the master had been "annually improving the Gardens, to the Amount of above Five Thousand Pounds"; and taken note of several statues: "a fine Statue of a *Grecian Venus* Dancing (but it is in the leaden Taste)"; "at the End of one Walk . . . a *Busto* of *Sir Isaac Newton*,"; "in a little Summer-House, another of Mr. *Dryden*." He has also seen the obelisk and grotto entrance, whose Latin inscriptions he records. Over the grotto entrance: SECRETUM ITER / ET FALLENTIS / SEMITA VITAE. Around the obelisk: AH EDITHA / MATRUM OPTIMA / MULIERUM AMANTISSIMA / VALE. The first of these is one of the oft repeated grace-notes of the retirement theme, from Horace's *Epistles* (I xviii 103).

The Rysbrack "Draught and View" is the earliest view of Pope's house, and the only one published in his lifetime, with which I am familiar. How far Gibbs, if it was Gibbs, brought the villa to this appearance during the early alterations, how far it was modified by later ones, is perhaps now impossible to determine. In a letter to Digby that Pope dates 1 May 1720 (II 44), he refers to "my Tuscan Porticos, or Ionic Pilasters." This accords well with the Tuscan order featured by his portico and the Ionic order featured by his bow windows, as we see them in the Rysbrack "Draught and View." But there are references in 1732–33 to the building of a "portico," evidently designed by Kent and approved by Burlington; to his need of Burlington's counsel "about the Upper Cornish of my house, & the Moldings & Members of the Entablature" before going on with "Stuccoing"; and to a "New Room" before going on with "Stuccoing"; and to a letter to Fortescue in 1736 (III 322–3, 329, 341, 353, 356, 406). A letter to Fortescue in 1736 (13 April: IV 10) indicates that "improvement" is still going on.

The design of Pope's portico as depicted in the "Draught and View" stems from a formula found with some frequency in facades of Palladian inspiration. The seventeenth-century Villa Contarini near Padua shows an application of the formula that closely resembles Pope's (Giuseppe Mazzotti, *Ville Venete*, 2d ed., Rome 1958, Plate 291). So does the T. G. Simon house at 128 Bull Street, Charleston, S.C.

An Exact DRAUGHT and VIEW of Mr POPE'S HOUSE at TWICKENHAM.

A Poet in His Landscape: Pope at Twickenham

MAYNARD MACK

T HE subject of this essay is Pope's small estate at Twickenham.
There, in his famous garden and villa, he evolved over the
years a setting that expressed him and at the same time helped
nourish in his consciousness the dramatic personality who speaks
to us from the satires and epistles of the 1730's. This personality
is at once the historical Alexander Pope and type-hero of a highly
traditional confrontation between virtuous simplicity and sophisticated corruption. I have written on an earlier occasion of the
relations of this figure to the conventions of formal satire; and,
more recently, of the way in which the Twickenham situation provided a focus for that figure and those conventions in Pope's particular case, shaping a satirist's imagined counter-kingdom to the
kingdom represented by St. James's.[1] Here my purpose is more
specifically historical and biographical. I shall seek to reconstruct,
as far as evidence and space allow, a reliable account of the poet's
house and garden as they were when he frequented them between
1719 and 1744—without, however, abandoning the effort to understand what they may have contributed to the life of his poetic
imagination.[2]

I

It was in the late winter of 1719 that Pope settled at Twickenham, having leased on Thames-side a small house, together with
at first three, then five, acres of land, most of it divided from the
house by the main road between Hampton Court and Richmond.
He had been toying for some months with the notion of building
a *palozzotto* in London (his friend Bathurst's term for it), but

3

was at last dissuaded—we may suppose by several considerations of common sense. One no doubt was expense, of which Bathurst warns him in an amusing letter of August 1718, observing how "the noise of saws and hammers," then audible on his own estate at Cirencester, is "apt to melt money" in ways that the natural philosophy of neither Aristotle nor Descartes can explain.[3]

A further consideration necessarily was health. London, already complained of for "Sootie Ayre" in 1645,[4] and by this time in a fair way to assuming all winter long its "sea-coal canopy," as Byron would call it—

> A huge dun cupola, like a foolscap crown
> On a fool's head—[5]

was no place for a respiratory system like Pope's. Nor for his nervous system either, now that his reputation was made and his time beginning to be subject to all the vexations he would enumerate in due course in the *Epistle to Dr. Arbuthnot*. He could not command in London the privacy needed for a writing career; even Chiswick had failed badly on that count.[6] Besides, he had been reared among country scenes, needed them for exercise and relaxation; had grown up under a father who was a dedicated gardener, praised by his neighbors for his "Hartichokes";[7] and lately, when he had himself engaged, at the instance of wealthy friends, in the planning of plantations and buildings going forward on their estates, he had found in the work intense satisfaction. A letter to the Blount sisters from Lord Bathurst's in October 1718, where he had been enjoying this satisfaction for some time, shows clearly the impulses now prevailing with him to abandon his city "palace" for a residence where more gardening and life out-of-doors could be expected.

I write an hour or two every morning, then ride out a hunting upon the Downes, eat heartily, talk tender sentiments with Lord B., or draw plans for Houses & Gardens, open Avenues, cut Glades, plant Firrs, contrive waterworks, all very fine & beautiful in our own imagination. . . . I like this course of life so well, that I am resolved to stay here, till I hear of somebody's being in London that is worthy of my coming after.[8]

Some five months after this, he relinquished the ground Lord

Burlington was reserving for him in what is now Burlington Gardens behind Piccadilly and moved to the village on the Thames which has become inseparable from his name.

II

Twickenham in 1719 was an attractive spot. Far enough from London to be semi-rural, not so far as to be inaccessible, its cluster of houses and historic church rested gracefully on a broad bow of the river as it curled down through its "matchless vale" (the phrase is Thomson's[9]) from Hampton Court toward Kew and Chiswick, past what was then reputed one of the finest views in England, the prospect from Richmond Hill.[10] From Richmond— England's "Frescaty," as John Macky would misspell it in his *Journey Through England* in 1722,[11] alluding to the fashionable resort outside Rome—as far downstream as Chelsea, the riverside was "bespangled with Villages, . . . those Villages fill'd with [noble] Houses, and the Houses surrounded with Gardens, walks, Vistas, Avenues, representing all the Beauties of Building, & all the Pleasures of Planting." So reads the revised edition of Defoe's *Tour* in 1738.[12] In the opposite direction, upstream from Richmond to Twickenham, Teddington, Ham, and Petersham, the neighborhood where, to quote Thomson again, "the silver Thames first rural grows,"[13] the prospect was more open, comprising mainly field and wood as far as Hampton Court, between which and Twickenham John Macky could find nothing requiring notice.

At Twickenham village itself, the riverside was notably inviting. Across, on the curving Surrey shore, lay Hamwalks, a mixture of meadow and grove in which the Blount sisters "often walked" during the second summer of Pope's habitation in Twickenham, he no doubt with them; and which the following December, in time of severe flood, he looked out to see "covered with Sails."[14] In the river, just off the village, rose some picturesque islets or "aits." "Twickenham Ait" (better known to Victorians as Eel-Pie Island, mentioned by Dickens in *Nicholas Nickleby* and by Jerrold in *Mrs. Caudle's Curtain Lectures,* objective of many a cockney summer outing) was situated approximately opposite the church. Another ait lay at a few hundred yards upstream, where eventually the proprietor of Strawberry Hill would look out upon haymaking at sunset and be reminded of the coloring of Claude Lorrain.[15]

The village itself stretched along the Middlesex bank, flanked on either end by a succession of estates large and small, almost reaching in the upriver direction the site of the future Strawberry Hill and downriver as far as Marble Hill. Marble Hill, an elegant Palladian mansion, was erected in the fields toward Richmond a very few years after Pope's arrival by his friend Henrietta Howard, mistress to the Prince of Wales, whose own domicile lay across the river at Richmond Lodge.[16] It contributed "largely," according to Letitia Hawkins, "to give Twickenham the epithet of *classic*";[17] but there were other supporters of that reputation. Macky tells us that the villa of Lady Ferrers, Pope's close neighbor, whose summer-house may be seen in several of the engravings of his own villa, "would pass in *Italy* for a delicate Palace," and singles out for additional praise the house which in Pope's time belonged to James Johnstone, Pope's Scoto,[18] former Secretary of State for Scotland—which he describes as being "exactly after the Model of the Country-Seats in *Lombardy*," and as making— "for the Elegancy and Largeness" of its gardens, its *"Terrace* on the River," and its "Situation"—"much the brightest Figure" in "a Village remarkable for abundance of curious Seats."[19]

Pope's own venture in the Anglo-classic style was of course far more modest. Horace Walpole thought it "small and bad."[20] Yet one observer in 1747 found it "not of so large or magnificent a Structure, as of a lightsome Elegance and neat Simplicity in its Contrivance"[21]—terms which Pope would certainly have relished.[22] We do not know what the house was like when Pope leased it in 1719, but it emerged from his extensive alterations, some of which were designed for him by James Gibbs, a dwelling of three storeys and some ten or twelve rooms, whose plan and ornamentation recall in a general way the classicism of Inigo Jones, Palladio, and the north Italian villa.[23] It consisted of a central block, with slightly recessed and lowered wings, the north wing fitted with bow windows framed in Ionic pilasters, the center block rising from grotto-entrance in the basement storey to a balustraded platform at the level of the *piano nobile,* then rising again to a balustraded balcony supported on Tuscan pillars at the chamber-level, and so to a highly decorated cornice topped by a hipped roof.[24] Niched into the bank of the Thames, it had in front of it a handsome grass plot bounded by tall walls of verdure sloping to the Thames, and behind it, across the public road beneath which ran the Grotto, the famous garden. This last feature, partly through its owner's precepts and partly through his example, was to play a part in modifying the face of England and eventually half Europe.[25]

Such was Twickenham in the early 1720's, on the threshold of its fame. It had already literary associations: with Bacon, Donne, Suckling, Richard Corbet, and Clarendon of the great History.[26] But its reputation as an artistic and social resort, home of the Muses and Graces together, begins around the time of Pope's arrival and extends through Horace Walpole's lifetime, though by no means all of its renown was owing to them. For varying periods and at various dates during the next hundred years, Twickenham would be home not only to Pope, but to Fielding and Lady Mary Wortley Montagu; to Paul Whitehead and Sir John Hawkins; to Walpole and Richard Owen Cambridge, the former often visited by Gray, who said he knew no "more *laughing* Scene" in England than the neighborhood of Twickenham;[27] to Mrs. Pritchard and Kitty Clive the actresses; to the painters Godfrey Kneller, Thomas Hudson, Samuel Scott, and J. M. W. Turner; and to a host of lesser celebrities in the arts as well as many great celebrities in the world of fashion.[28]

Some sense of the coloration of the place at its peak of popularity in the century's middle years, when already Pope was becoming a legend, his house a shrine,[29] and Walpole's Strawberry Hill one of the great show-places of England, may be gathered from a pamphlet published anonymously in 1760 by Mrs. Henrietta Pye.[30] Mrs. Pye prefaces her *Short Account of the Principal Seats & Gardens in and about Richmond and Kew* with a brief discourse on Twickenham, which she calls "a little Kingdom on the Banks of the Thames," and describes as if she were a voyager bringing news of a far-off clime. "This Kingdom," she says, is

situated on the Banks of the *Thames;* its Soil Gravelly, its Air balmy, clear and healthful: The whole Place is one continued Garden. Plenty and Pleasure are the Ideas convey'd by its large Fields of Corn and its

verdant Meadows; tis govern'd by a King [here a footnote specifies that
the king is R. O. Cambridge], whom Arts (not Arms) recommend to the
Dignity, the Government not being Hereditary: He is proclaim'd by
a Muse, and acknowledged by the People. Their last Monarch [here
another footnote specifies that the "last Monarch" was Pope] was the
Terror of Fools and Knaves, and the Darling of the Learned and Virtuous: He reign'd long over them, belov'd and well-establish'd, and
was succeeded by their present Sovereign, whom God grant long to
reign! . . .

The Genius of the Inhabitants inclines not towards Commerce;
Architecture seems their chief Delight, in which if any one doubts
their excelling, let him sail up the River and view their lovely Villas
beautifying its Banks; Lovers of true Society, they despise Ceremony,
and no Place can boast more Examples of domestic Happiness. Their
Partiality for their Country [i.e., Twickenham, their "kingdom"] rises
to Enthusiasm; and what is more remarkable, there is scarce any Instance of a Stranger's residing for a few Days among them, without
being inspir'd by the same rapturous Affection for this Earthly *Elesium*.
Their Laws and Customs are dictated by Reason, and regulated by
social Love. Happy! thrice happy they, to whom it is permitted to spend
their Lives in such a Country, such Society, and under such a Government; possesst of

> An Elegant Sufficiency, Content,
> Retirement, rural Quiet, Friendship, Books . . .
> Progressive Virtue, and approving Heav'n.[31]

I quote Mrs. Pye at length, partly because her description is not
widely known, partly because it illustrates the extent to which
Virgil's great paean to the happiness of the Italian farmer in his
second *Georgic* is ever-present in the eighteenth century even to
the most ordinary sensibility. There were reasons for this which
had nothing to do with the veneration of Virgil as a classic. He
had evoked in the *Georgics* the simple virtues, the hardihood, and
the pieties joining man to man and man to nature, which had
brought Rome to its Augustan greatness. An evocation nostalgic
in tone, as if the verse already foretold the decline of these virtues
even at the instant of their triumph, it struck a sympathetic chord
in an age becoming conscious that Augustus's *Pax Romana* might
be paralleled by a Pax Britannica, and already anxious, at least in
some of its more sensitive minds, both Whig and Tory, lest the
post-Augustan chapters of Roman history be repeated too.[32]

III

Despite the reputation of Pope's garden with his friends and contemporaries, we have surprisingly little detailed information about it, still less about what it meant to him. We may properly say "what it meant," because as a number of recent studies have shown, gardens and the pursuits associated with them, could at this period "mean" a great deal.[33] They had been associated variously, during the hundred years from James I to George I, with the life of unspotted felicity, with ethical self-mastery, with "hortulan" saintship, with an innocent epicureanism, and with physicotheological "O-altitudinizing."[34] Garden imagery and garden situations, in poems of all genres by poets of all persuasions—Jonson, Herrick, Herbert, Waller, Denham, Cowley, Vaughan, Marvell, Milton, to mention only a few—had been made the vehicle for some of the deepest feelings of the age and some of its shrewdest comments on the human condition. Moreover, the relevant classical texts, all those passages in the Roman writers glorifying the retired life—its simplicity, frugality, self-reliance, and independence—had been so often culled, so often translated, paraphrased, and imitated that they had become part of the mind of England, and indeed of Europe. In mishmashes like Pomfret's *Choice*, where the fiber of Stoic tradition was replaced by sentimentality, they would soon become part of its fantasy life as well.

As if quickened by this tide of literary association, the English countryside itself brought forth ruins, arches, urns, obelisks, gods, goddesses, temples—all that "quarry above ground"[35] of which remnants may be seen in many an English park and garden today. It arranged itself in "scenes" to remind the traveler and virtuoso of Rome, Arcadia, and Elysium; of Praeneste, Daphne, and Tempe; of Poussin, Rosa, and Lorrain. It teased out "openings" on distant prospects, raised up hanging terraces and cascades, built mounts, grottos, theatres, canals. And since it was rarely forgotten in the eighteenth century for whom the earth had been (even if not exclusively) created, there was assigned to every romantic "view" a rustic bower or seat—"from whence," Pope writes of one such seat in Lord Digby's gardens at Sherborne, using a verb that might be more easily taken for granted a century later, "you lose your eyes upon the glimmering of the waters under the wood and your ears in the constant dashing of the waves."[36]

Altogether, landscape and garden at this period assume some of the functions of album and commonplace book, philosophical *vademecum* and *memento mori*. They serve as aids to reflection— or to recollection, introspection, and worship, giving us, says Addison, "a great Insight into the Contrivance and Wisdom of Providence" and suggesting "innumerable Subjects for Meditation."[37] They serve as memorials of friendship and virtue, secular incitements to holy living and holy dying, like the commemorative urns that line Shenstone's walks at The Leasowes[38] or the Temple of British Worthies at Stowe.[39] They present themselves to be read as epitomes of recent history, or psychological states, or human life in general, as by Marvell in *The Garden* and *Upon Appleton House;*[40] or of politics and the relationship of social classes, as by Denham in *Cooper's Hill;*[41] or of the *concordia discors* that ties the universe together, as in both *Cooper's Hill* and *Windsor Forest.* And sometimes they are felt as *horti conclusi*, enclosing, if not the tamed unicorn of the mediaeval tapestries, or even the lost footprints of the classical Astraea fleeing earth,[42] at any rate some lingering traces of that ancient animism whose ebbing before a new dispensation had so stirred Milton's imagination in his *Nativity Ode:*

> The lonely mountain o'er
> And the resounding shore,
>   A voice of weeping heard, and loud lament,
> From haunted spring and dale
> Edg'd with poplar pale
>   The parting Genius is with sighing sent;
> With flow'r-inwoven tresses torn
> The Nymphs in twilight shade of tangled thickets mourn.[43]

It is usually thought that by Pope's time the Nymphs have departed, leaving no addresses; but this judgment is not altogether correct: the "Genius" Milton sees "parting," Pope sees persisting as a "Genius of the Place,"[44] who continues to embody that intuition of a mysterious life in things which for another two hundred years his descendants will also embody, in a succession of changing forms, from ancient mariner and old leech-gatherer to scholar gypsy, Mr. Apollinax, and the cartoons of Charles Addams.

Though the weight of the Christian dispensation had tended to

despiritualize garden and landscape in this respect, it had helped
respiritualize them in another. The memory of the first garden
was never far away from the minds of those who worked in gardens, or wrote about them, in the seventeenth and eighteenth centuries. The individual gardener in his garden was acclaimed heir
to all the innocence and felicity of Eden, and to the pagan para-
dises that anticipated it. "Talke of perfect happiness and pleasure,"
says Gerard in his *Herbal* of 1597, "what place was so fit for that,
as the garden place, wherein Adam was sett to be the Herbarist?
Whither did the poets hunt for their sincere delights but into the
gardens of Alcinous and Adonis and the orchards of Hesperides?
Where did they dream that Heaven should be but in the pleasant
garden of Elysium?"[45] Addison writes less exuberantly in 1711,
but to the same effect: "A Garden was the Habitation of our first
Parents before the Fall. It is naturally apt to fill the Mind with
Calmness and Tranquility, and to lay all its turbulent Passions
at Rest."[46]

At the same time, it was never forgotten that the individual
gardener was Eden's heir in another sense, and faced therefore a
task of reparation and improvement, psychic and moral as well
as horticultural. Here again the continuity of the doctrine is impressive. Evelyn, in a letter to Sir Thomas Browne of 1658, announces his desire to form "a society of . . . *paradisi cultores*,
persons of antient simplicity, Paradisean and Hortulan saints";
he intends to show soon in print, he adds, "how caves, grottos,
mounts, and irregular ornaments of gardens do contribute to contemplative and philosophical enthusiasm; how *elysium, antrum,
nemus, paradysis, hortus, lucus,* etc. signifie all of them *rem sacrem
et divinam;* for these expedients do influence the souls and spirits
of men, and prepare them for converse with good angells."[47] In a
changed idiom, the professional gardener Stephen Switzer is still
saying much the same thing in 1715. "Paradise," he writes, in his
preface to *The Nobleman, Gentleman, and Gardener's Recreation:*

properly signifies *Gardens of Pleasure,* the Residence of Angelick and
Happy souls, unsullied with Guilt, and of Duration equal with Time:
And tho' the Original Compact between God and Man was after that
invalidated and broke, yet we may gather from After-History, how
great a Share Gard'ning and the Pleasures of the Country had in the

Minds and Practice of the most Virtuous in all the successive Centuries
of the World. . . .

And 'tis from the Admiration of these [i.e., "Rural Delights"] that
the Soul is elevated to unlimited Heights above, and modell'd and prepared for the sweet Reception and happy Enjoyment of Felicities the
durablest as well as happiest that Omniscience has created.[48]

Edward Young's inscription in his garden at Welwyn was presumably intended to remind him, and his visitors, of the Eden
situation at both its poles: *Ambulantes in horto audiverunt vocem
Dei.*[49]

IV

Seen against this context and habit of mind, certain aspects of
Pope's abode and life at Twickenham become luminous with implication. The site was obviously first chosen for its practical
advantages, being in the country but also near London; yet the
developments and improvements he carried out there over a period
of twenty-five years, and the increasing reference to one or other
aspect of it in the mature poems, suggest that it may have been
gradually transformed in his imagination by associations of the
kind we have been examining.[50] These were whimsical in part
no doubt. He drew amusement from considering himself a minus-
cule inhabitant of a world tailored to fit him. He is "Homer in
a nutshell," to use the phrase he appropriated from Bishop Atterbury, who had thus described his appearance when driving
his little "chariot."[51] He is "as busy in three inches of gardening,
as any man can be in three score acres . . . like the fellow that
spent his life in cutting the twelve apostles in one cherry stone."[52]
He is prepared, if need be, to live yet more diminutively than he
does, shrinking back to his "Paternal cell":

> A little House, with Trees a-row,
> And like its Master, very low.[53]

The Lilliputian scale of the poet's domain at Twickenham, reflecting his own proportions, became particularly a subject of jest
between him and Lord Bathurst, whose holdings at Cirencester
in Gloucestershire were vast. If you will agree to visit me, Bathurst
writes on one occasion in 1730, mixing playful bribe with threat:

I'll cutt you off some little corner of my Park (500 or 1000 acres) which you shall do what you will with, & I'll immediately assign over to you three or four millions of plants out of my Nursery to amuse yourself with. If you refuse coming I'll immediately send one of my wood-Carts & bring away your whole house & Gardens, & stick it in the midst of Oakly-wood [this was a part of Bathurst's estate] where it will never be heard off any more, unless some of the Children find it out in Nutting-season & take possession of it thinking I have made it for them.[54]

Pope alludes in the foregoing couplet on his "Paternal cell" to a favorite topos of the classical poets, which identifies a man's house with its owner. This analogy has relevance to his works at Twickenham as a whole, on which he impresses an image of himself as sharply as he impressed the head of Homer on the wax with which he sealed his letters. Horace Walpole gives a description of the poet's garden that is revealing in this respect. "It was a singular effort of art and taste," Walpole says, "to impress so much variety and scenery on a spot of five acres. The passing through the gloom from the grotto to the opening day, the retiring and again assembling shades, the dusky groves, the larger lawn, and the solemnity of the termination of the cypresses that led up to his mother's tomb"—Walpole means the obelisk erected in his mother's memory—"are managed with exquisite judgement."[55] We have only to retain Walpole's principal value-terms ("effort," "art," "taste," "variety," "exquisite judgement"), and substitute literary equivalents for the operations of gardening, to arrive at a statement that could be applied to the effects Pope achieves in his best poetry: packed couplets, graceful transitions, effective contrasts, and easy but diversified crescendoes leading to climaxes either small or large.[56]

Walpole's insistence on the amount of "scenery" Pope had managed to incorporate in his five acres is seconded by a remark of Bolingbroke's at the beginning of a philosophic letter addressed to Pope. There he says: "All I dare promise you is that my thoughts . . . shall be communicated to you just as they pass thro' my mind, just as they use to be when we converse together on these, or any other subjects; when we saunter alone, or as we have often done, with good Arbuthnot, and the jocose dean of St. Patrick's, among the multiplied scenes of your little garden."[57] Bolingbroke's "multiplied scenes" obviously refers to the poet's cunning disposition of the garden into areas and features—a grotto, three mounts (one of these quite large), some quincunxes, groves, a wilderness, an orangery, a vineyard, a kitchen garden, a bowling green, a shell temple, and an obelisk;[58] more especially, it must refer to his striking use of openings, walks, and vistas, each terminating on a point of rest, supplied by urn or statue.[59] With a curious foresight, Pope had discussed this practice and related it to poetry in his "Essay on Homer's Battles" in 1716. Defending Homer's bardic repetitions—for instance, the use of the same similes in the same words—he had protested: "But may not one say Homer is in this like a skilful Improver, who places a beautiful Statue in a well-disposed Garden so as to answer several Vistas, and by that Artifice one single Figure seems multiply'd into as many Objects as there are Openings whence it may be viewed?"[60] Pope's comment, like the intricate and ingenious garden he was soon to fashion on its principles, corresponds better with his own poetic practice than with Homer's. The artifice he praises in the disposition of a single figure to answer several points of view has more affinities with pun and zeugma than with bardic repetition, and is a species of economy and polysemousness wholly characteristic of his mode.

v

Walpole's description of the garden is interesting in a further respect. It indicates that the poet's obelisk to the memory of his mother was in fact the point of visual and emotional climax for the observer in the garden that it appears to be in John Serle's Plan. We need not read far in Pope's correspondence of any period to see that not only was he a very good son, but that good sonship occupied, in his case, a position of some importance in that more or less edifying conception of the self by which we all live; it was a salient point of reference for his imagination as well as for his daily life. After his mother's death, there was a picture by Richardson, now lost, showing "Pope in a mourning gown with a strange view of yͤ garden to shew the obelisk as in memory to his mothers Death,"[61] a picture one would give a good deal to recover.

Certainly the key position of the obelisk, as Walpole describes it, signalizes not only the gravity of his mother's loss but also, with an aptness of which Pope himself can hardly have been conscious, his repossession of her beyond "the solemnity . . . of the cypresses" —as the principal point of rest in a garden of memory and meditation, and, simultaneously, as one of the chief dramatis personae in that continuing drama about the meaning of his life which we may watch both the historical Pope and the figure who speaks to us from the poems of the thirties weave in his inner consciousness. "This," says the author of *The Short Account of the Principal Gardens in and about Richmond and Kew,* referring to Pope's obelisk and regard for his mother, "is a Circumstance of more Credit to him than all his Works; for the Beauties of Poetry are tasted only by a few, but the Language of the Heart is understood by all."[62] Today we incline to smile at such statements, and when we read in the poet's letters that he thinks he would rather be known for a good man than a good poet, we suspect him of posturing, or of a lack of self-knowledge. We may be wrong. Perhaps the will to virtue in Pope was genuine, only the act a slave to limit —as in many before and since. One of the strengths of the eighteenth century was that for all its superficial and sometimes genuine elegance it could not forget certain linsey-woolsey truths. This may have been one of the strengths of its best poet too.

Friendship was another factor which left its mark on the Twickenham design. Pope's capacity for making and keeping friends amounted to genius, as is clear from the forty years of his correspondence that we possess; and like the care of his mother, this also occupied a position of importance in his conception of himself. He likes to imagine his house "an inn," himself a patriarch living by the side of the road and "receiving all comers"[63]—a figure on the order of Menelaus in the *Odyssey,* whose capacity to welcome the coming, speed the going guest he claims for himself in his imitation of Horace's second satire of the second book.[64] Though he was not so indifferent as he liked to think to other sorts of eminence, he was right in believing that circumstances had fitted him peculiarly to cherish friends. "Nature, temper, and habit from my youth," he writes to Gay in 1730, "have made me have but one desire; all other ambitions, my person, education, constitution, religion, etc. conspir'd to remove far from me. That desire was to fix and preserve a few lasting dependable friendships."[65] Ten years later he had commemorated to a degree unmatched in literature every person he knew and loved: father, mother, Gay, Swift, Arbuthnot, Fortescue, Bathurst, Burlington, Ralph Allen, Martha Blount—the list could be extended indefinitely.[66]

This aspect of Pope's nature also attained to visible expression in the Twickenham estate. Though it seems unlikely that he ever actually placed over his gate the motto he told Fortescue would be suitable: *"Mihi & Amicis . . .* ; & indeed, *Plus Amicis quam Meipsi,"*[67] the effect of his lifelong orientation to friendship can be seen in the inventory of his goods taken after his death in 1744.[68] Apart from some expected and quite modest furnishings, his villa was like his poems a memorial to friends. On the bedroom storey, "in the Chince Room fronting the Thames," there were portraits of Wycherley, Betterton, Peterborough, his mother, and Martha Blount; in "the next Room fronting the Thames," portraits of Bolingbroke, Swift, Atterbury, Gay, Arbuthnot, Parnell, Prior, and Burlington; in "the Best Room fronting ye Thames," portraits of Martha Blount, Bathurst, Molly Lepell, Henrietta Howard, Lady Mary Wortley Montagu, Bolingbroke, and Dr. Garth. The *piano nobile* was furnished on the same lines. The "Little Parlor" had Lord Bolingbroke, and the Earl of Oxford; "m^r Pope's Room" had Hugh Bethel (a portrait Pope had obtained shortly before his death);[69] and "the Great Parlor" had (besides his father, mother, three aunts, and some likenesses of himself) Prior, Betterton, the Duchess of Hamilton, the Duchess of Montague, Lady Mary Wortley Montagu, Judith Cowper, and Martha and Teresa Blount. Besides these, there were in the best room at the third storey the Duchess of Buckingham, Craggs, Digby, Shrewsbury—

> Oft in the clear, still Mirrour of Retreat
> I studied Shrewsbury, the wise and great,[70]

and Walsh—"the Muse's Judge and Friend."[71] In no other small house of which we have records—as in no other poetry—can there be found such concentration on a single theme.[72]

VI

It is possible that Pope's house expressed him in other ways as well. During the years when the original alterations were being made, he was studying Palladio.[73] Here he would meet with an insistence on architectural responsibility, such as we see him inculcating later in his *Epistle to Burlington:* that an architect must not so much mind what his patrons "can afford to lay out as the quality of the building that is proper to them";[74] that the *pian terreno* of a dwelling should contain its "pantries, kitchens, servants-halls, wash-houses, ovens,"[75] not, as at Timon's villa (apparently), its master's study; that church buildings ideally should be round, to figure forth the divine strength, capacity, uniformity, equality, simplicity, and infinity,[76] and so become—if this may be legitimately taken as one meaning of the phrase in the *Epistle to Burlington*—"worthier of the God";[77] that where there are paintings in a place of worship, those "will not be proper, which by their signification alienate the mind from the contemplation of divine things,"[78] like the sprawling "Saints" on the ceiling of Timon's chapel.

Pope would also encounter in Palladio practices of mathematical proportioning in room design which have their ultimate theoretical basis in Pythagorean doctrine about the music of the spheres[79] and reflect the same theories of cosmic harmony that he had appealed to in his *Essay on Man.* These practices were still being warmly advocated as the great secret of the ancients by Pope's fellow townsman, the architect Robert Morris, in 1734.[80]

Nature has taught Mankind in *Musick* certain Rules for Proportion of Sounds, so *Architecture* has its Rules dependant on those Proportions, which are Arithmetical Harmony; and those I take to be dependant on Nature. The Square in *Geometry*, the Unison or Circle in *Musick*, and the Cube in *Building*, have all an inseparable Proportion; the Parts being equal, and the Sides, and Angles, etc. give the Eye and Ear an agreeable Pleasure; from hence may likewise be deduc'd the Cube and half, the Double Cube; the Diapason, and Diapenté, being founded on the same Principles in *Musick*.[81]

In *Musick* are only seven distinct Notes, in *Architecture* likewise are only seven Proportions, which produce all the different Buildings in the Universe, viz: The Cube—the Cube and half—the Double Cube—

the Duplicates of 3, 2 and 1—of 4, 3, and 2—of 5, 4, and 3—and of 6, 4, and 3, produce all the Harmonick Proportions of Rooms.[82]

We know that Pope was familiar with this kind of doctrine in its cosmological form. It was in fact a commonplace of the age:

> From Harmony, from heav'nly Harmony
> This universal Frame began:
> From Harmony to Harmony
> Thro' all the compass of the Notes it ran,
> The Diapason closing full in Man.[83]

Through Shaftesbury, if no one else, he must also have been familiar with its ethical extensions:

Shou'd a Writer upon *Musick*, addressing himself to the Students and Lovers of the Art, declare to 'em, "That the Measure or Rule of Harmony was *Caprice* or *Will*, *Humour* or *Fashion*"; 'tis not very likely he shou'd be heard with great Attention, or treated with real Gravity. For Harmony is Harmony *by Nature*, let Men judg ever so ridiculously of Musick. So is *Symmetry* and *Proportion* founded still *in Nature*, let Mens Fancy prove ever so barbarous, or their Fashions ever so *Gothick* in their Architecture, Sculpture, or whatever other designing Art. 'Tis the same case, where *Life* and Manners are concern'd. *Virtue* has the same fix'd Standard. The same *Numbers, Harmony*, and *Proportion* will have place in Morals; and are discoverable in the *Characters* and *Affections* of Mankind; in which are laid the just Foundations of an Art and Science superior to every other of human Practice and Comprehension.[84]

Was Pope familiar, like his fellow townsman Morris, with the long history of this doctrine in architecture? Had he applied the harmonic proportions in any of the reconstructions of his villa—in, say, that "great room" (a double cube room?) about which his friend Digby inquires in 1723?[85] or the "New Room" of which he tells the Countess of Burlington in 1733?[86] And did this sort of thing still carry with it an associative tingle? A man like Daniele Barbaro, Rudolf Wittkower suggests (alluding to the Venetian philomath and commentator on Vitruvius for whom Palladio built the magnificently "harmonic" Villa Maser at Asolo), could perhaps experience "under a Renaissance dome . . . a faint echo of the inaudible music of the spheres."[87] Could an eighteenth-century poet and Palladian experience, or imagine that he experienced, in the great salon at Marble Hill, or possibly in the interior of his own dwelling, if not so metaphysical an echo, at least an exhilarating access of confidence that all things are One? It is impossible to say. All we may safely say is that Pope and all the rest of the neo-Palladians shared their master's conviction (summed up in Wittkower's words) that "the practice of good architecture is . . . a moral faculty, and architecture . . . one emanation of the unity of the sciences and arts which together constitute the idea of *virtus.*"[88] It would not have surprised Pope to think that the pleasure of the eye in the proportions of a "Cube and half" or a "Double Cube" sprang from a principle of concord which also moved the sun and other stars, and might therefore be registered on that inner sense which is attuned to ditties of no tone.

> What tho' nor real voice nor sound
> Amid their radiant orbs be found?
> In Reason's ear they all rejoice,
> And utter forth a glorious voice. . . .[89]

This would not have surprised Pope, and it would have pleased him. Many things in his surroundings at Twickenham, like many things in his poems, indicate that his associative instinct was profound. In contemplating his "Tuscan portico" and "Ionic pilasters," he must have felt at the very least the same deep stirrings of identification with an admired tradition as those which impelled him to keep about him in his library the busts of Homer, Spenser, Shakespeare, Milton, Dryden, and to plan for his grass-plot at the river's edge the extraordinary ornament described by Spence in 1743.

VII

His design for this, Spence tells us

was to have a swan, as flying into the river, on each side of the landing-place, then the Statues of two river gods reclined on the bank between them and the corner seats or temples, with

> Hic placido fluit amne Meles

on one of their urns, and

> Magnis ubi flexibus errat

on the other. Then two terms in the first niches in the grove-work on the sides with the busts of Homer and Virgil, and higher, two others with those of Marcus Aurelius and Cicero.[90]

This is a more elaborate work of the associative instinct than at first appears. Like some of the allusions in Pope's verse, it spreads in circles of analogy that one hardly knows how far to follow. The first of the two inscriptions comes from Politian's *Ambra,* whose title is itself a reference to a villa by a stream at which Lorenzo the Magnificent and his circle, Politian being one, met to carry on their philosophical studies and conversations. Are we meant to see here an allusion to Bolingbroke and Pope, and "good Arbuthnot, and the jocose dean of St. Patrick's," who, as we have earlier seen, roamed the Twickenham garden engaging in similar pursuits? Probably not—yet it is difficult to be sure. As for the inscription itself, this is taken from a passage in the *Ambra* which describes the river Meles as follows

> Here softly flows the Meles, and silent in its
> deep grottos listens to its singing swans.[91]

This accounts for the stone swans Pope proposed, and reminds us of all those other "swans"—from Chaucer down—whose singing the Thames has heard, and in whose number Pope makes one. But the widening circle of analogy extends far beyond this. Politian's point in referring to the Meles is to introduce the particular poet with whom that river has immemorially been 'associated: "This region," the *Ambra* goes on,

first bore that excellent poet. A god, native of Ionia, patron of the dance and even able to contend on equal terms with Apollo, had filled beautiful Crathus with a secret child. Hence sprang that mighty genius—[92]

Homer.

Pope's other river-god to be assimilated to the Thames is that of Virgil's river, the Mincius. The inscription for *his* urn—"Where the Mincius wanders with great windings"—brings us once again to the *Georgics:* specifically to that famous passage in the third *Georgic,* where Virgil states a goal for himself which was to kindle many a Renaissance mind to like effort, but which Pope is the last major poet of England to take seriously: the goal of enlarging and enriching the national culture by causing to be poured into it the great works of classical antiquity. Dryden states the program with suitable resonance in his translation:

> I, first of *Romans,* shall in Triumph come
> From conquer'd *Greece,* and bring her Trophies home,
> With Foreign Spoils adorn my native place,
> And with *Idume's* palms, my *Mantua* grace.
> Of *Parian* Stone a Temple will I raise,
> Where the slow *Mincius* through the Vally strays . . .[93]

Thus, as by a conqueror, the Greek Muses are to be secured for Italy; Mantua is to flourish with Palestinian palms (as in Pope's *Windsor Forest* English oaks bear amber and balm); and a great temple is to be erected in verse, which in commemorating the victory will at the same time constitute it.

Here was a pattern, it must have occurred to Pope, which epitomized his own career. Had not he also brought home the Greek Muses for his country, adorned his "native place" with spoils from many literatures, and in the body of his work as a whole, nourished by the classics and dedicated to their honor, raised another votive temple beside another stream? Only some such thoughts, I am inclined to think, can have inspired his curious juxtaposition of the *Ambra* with the third *Georgic,* the Meles and the Mincius with the Thames, a passage on the birth of Homer with a passage on the conquest of Greece, and conceivably, though this may very well be pursuing the edge of analogy too far, Virgil's imaginary "temple in marble beside the water" with a Florentine villa beside a stream and a villa at Twickenham on the Thames. Horace Walpole spoke wittily, but also with a fine sense of what I suspect Pope's villa meant to its occupant, when he referred to it in a letter to Horace Mann as "that fragment of the rock Parnassus."[94]

NOTES

1. "The Muse of Satire," *Yale Review,* XLI (1951), 80–92; reprinted in *Studies in the Literature of the Augustan Age,* ed. R. C. Boys [1952]. " 'The Shadowy Cave': Some Speculations on a Twickenham Grotto," *Restoration and Eighteenth-Century Literature: Essays in Honor of Alan Dugald McKillop,* ed. Carroll Camden (1963), pp. 69–88.

2. Several works are referred to below by short-title or without the use of title: viz. George Sherburn, (ed.) *The Correspondence of Alexander Pope* (5 vols, Oxford, 1956); Wilmarth S. Lewis (ed.), *The Correspondence of Horace Walpole* (New Haven, 1937– ——); John Butt and others (eds.), *The Twickenham Edition of the Poetical Works of Alexander Pope* (1938–62). All quotations of Pope's verse are from this edition.

3. Pope's earliest mention of "building a house in town" in the surviving correspondence occurs in a letter to Caryll of June 1718 (I 475). Bathurst's objection on the grounds of expense comes in August of that year (I 488). On 11 October (I 516), Pope tells Burlington that the only reason he has not built this past summer "in that piece of ground behind Burlington house (which is the Situation I am fond of to the last degree)" is the expense of "Mr. Campbell's Proposal." This is Colin Campbell, author of *Vitruvius Britannicus* (3 volumes, 1715–25), whom Burlington was employing in 1718–19 to remodel Burlington House. In a further letter of February 1719, Pope informs Burlington that he is ready "to resign the piece of ground intended for me, as not being yet prepared to build, & absolutely unwilling to retard the progress of the rest who are" (II 2).

The first dated letter clearly directed to Pope at Twickenham is of June 1719 (II 6–7). February letters to Burlington and Broome suggest that by this date he has take the Twickenham house but is not yet living in it, doubtless owing to necessary renovations. In the autumn (9 November: II 18), he tells Thomas Dancastle that he has added "2 Acres of land last week." I infer this to be an enlargement of the plot across the London-Hampton Court road which divided the house from its future garden. That the total holding came to (approximately?) five acres is attested on several occasions by Horace Walpole. (To Mann, 20 June 1760, and 23 August 1781: XXI 417, and, for the second letter, not yet published in the edition by W. S. Lewis, Toynbee, XII 41. See also his *History of the Modern Taste in Gardening*, ed. I. W. U. Chase, 1943, p. 28).

4. Dudley North, *A Forest of Varieties* (1645), p. 68. See also Evelyn's *Fumifugium: or, the Inconvenience of the Aer and Smoak of London Dissipated* (1661).

5. *Don Juan*, X lxxxii.

6. George Sherburn, *The Early Career of Alexander Pope* (1934), p. 215. Cf. Pope's complaints to Caryll, 11 August 1718 (I 484): ". . . at my own house I have no peace from visitants, and appointments of continual parties of pleasure . . ."; and to Thomas Dancastle, 7 August 1716 (I 352): "I have been in a constant Course of Entertainments and Visits ever since I saw you. . . ."

7. Trumbull to Pope, 15 June 1706 (I 17).

8. 8 October [1718] (I 515).

9. *Summer*, 1425.

10. Often painted in the eighteenth and early nineteenth centuries—e.g., by Samuel Scott, Antonio Joli, and J. M. W. Turner. Pope refers to the view in his *Alley*, 53–4 (*T–E*, VI 44):

Ne Richmond's self, from whose tall Front are ey'd
Vales, Spires, meandring Streams, and Windsor's tow'ry Pride.

11. *A Journey Through England. In Familiar Letters from a Gentleman Here, To His Friend Abroad* (1722), 4th ed., 1724, p. 62.

12. I 238.

13. *Summer,* 1416.

14. Pope to Teresa Blount, 11 December 1720 (II 59). Two maps showing eighteenth-century Twickenham and its environs are by Jean Rocque (often referred to as John Rocques), *c.* 1746, and by Samuel Lewis, 1784.

15. Horace Walpole to Mary and Agnes Berry, 16 September 1791 (XI 351).

16. The design of Marble Hill is credited to Henry Herbert, ninth Earl of Pembroke, whose professional collaborator was Roger Morris. Swift's note to his amusing *Pastoral Dialogue between Richmond-Lodge and Marble-Hill* (*Poems.* ed. Sir Harold Williams, 2d ed. 1958, II 407) states: "Mr. *Pope* was the Contriver of the Gardens, Lord *Herbert* the Architect, and the Dean of St. Patrick's chief Butler, and Keeper of the Ice House." The house was said to be finished save "only for its roof" in a letter of 1724 (Pope to Fortescue, 18 September: II 257), but Roger Morris's bills for "finishing the principal story" and "for the finnishing all works done . . . at Marble Hill" are dated 1728 and 1729. The finishing obviously continued for some years after Mrs. Howard had taken up residence. (See James Lees-Milne, *Earls of Creation: Five Great Patrons of Eighteenth-Century Art,* 1962, pp. 80 ff.). Pope was engaged in planning and superintending work on the Marble Hill gardens from 1723 (Peterborow to Pope, undated: II 197).
Marble Hill still stands, though somewhat altered, and is open to the public.

17. *Anecdotes, Biographical Sketches, and Memoirs,* I (1722), 88–9. Peacock refers to Twickenham's "classic shores" in his *Genius of the Thames* (*Works,* ed. Brett-Smith, 1924–34, VI 147).

18. *Epistle to Cobham,* 158 ff. Johnstone was not one of Pope's favorites: see his *Alley,* 50 and note (*T–E,* VI 44–5); *Correspondence,* II 316, III 272 and note; and the reading of l. 363 in the first edition of the *Epistle to Dr. Arbuthnot* (*T–E.* IV 122).

19. Macky, p. 60. Johnstone's house was later called Orleans House, from the residence there of Louis Philippe during his first exile as Duke of Orleans (R. S. Cobbett, *Memorials of Twickenham,* 1872, pp. 214–15; *Victoria County Histories: Middlesex,* III, ed. Susan Reynolds, 1962, p. 150). Only the detached Octagon Room, said to have been built by Johnstone to entertain Queen Caroline, now stands.

20. To Mann, 20 June 1760 (XXI 417).

21. It is so described by "T", whose letter "To Mr. P— T— in Newcastle," dated 18 March 1747 and published in *The Newcastle General Magazine, or Monthly Intelligencer,* I (January 1748), 25–8, is the fullest account of Pope's house and garden by a contemporary that we possess.

22. Though Pope himself deprecates the house—"(which you know is noth-ing)"—in a letter to Ralph Allen (7 April [1736]: IV 9), this is hardly surpris-ing in view of the opulence Allen was used to and would soon start consolidating in stone at Prior Park.

23. A letter of Gibbs to Pope about "designes" in 1719 (?) may refer either to Pope's proposed house in London or to alterations of the Twickenham villa, as Sherburn remarks (II 4 and note). There is, however, in Gibbs's memoir of himself (now in the possession of Sir John Soane's Museum) an unamplified reference to his additions to "Alexander Pope's villa." (See Bryan Little, *The Life and Work of James Gibbs*, 1955, p. 85; and H. M. Colvin, *A Biographical Dictionary of British Architects, 1660–1840* [1954].)

Gibbs, who designed St. Mary-le-Strand, St. Clement Danes, St. Martin in the Fields, the Radcliffe Camera at Oxford, and many other public and pri-vate buildings of distinction, belonged to the circle of Pope's friend, Edward Harley, second Earl of Oxford, and was in general, as Summerson puts it, the "favorite architect of the Tory party" (*Architecture in Britain, 1530–1830*, 1954, p. 219). Though influenced by the fashionable Palladianism, which was to some extent a Whiggish phenomenon, he kept his balance and independ-ence—much like Pope himself.

24. See Plate I and the Note on Plate I.

25. Miles Hadfield, *Gardening in Britain* (1960), pp. 185–94.

26. Bacon had tenure of Twickenham Park during much of the 1590's and is said to have received Queen Elizabeth there. A later occupant of this seat was Lucy, Countess of Bedford, whose garden is celebrated in Donne's *Twicknam Garden*. Suckling had a house at neighboring Whitton. Bishop Corbet's father seems to have conducted a horticultural nursery in the area. York House, which still stands, belonged to Clarendon during the 1660's; according to Pepys (*Diary*, 6 December 1667), the morning after his escape to the Continent "his coach, and people about it, went to Twittenham, and the world thought that he had been there." Information on the residency of these and other prominent figures may be had from Edward Ironside, *The History and An-tiquities of Twickenham* (1797); Cobbett (cited above, n. 19); and the *Victoria County History* of Middlesex (also cited, n. 19).

27. To Wharton, 18 September 1754 (*Correspondence*, ed. Toynbee-Whibley, 1935, I 407).

28. F. C. Hodgson, *Thames-Side in the Past* (1913); G. S. Maxwell, *The Au-thors' Thames* (New York, 1924). Later, Dickens and Tennyson were short-time residents.

29. Pope's house remained a shrine until its demolition in 1807 by the Baron-ess Howe, who purchased it in that year, and is said to have demolished it on the ground that she was "tired of these intrusions on her privacy." (See "The Literary Suburb of the Eighteenth Century," *Fraser's Magazine*, LXI, 1860, 553). Even by 1760, however, Pope's successor in the property, Sir William Stanhope, had much changed the appearance of the house by adding wings, and in Horace Walpole's opinion had mutilated the garden past recognition

(to Mann, 20 June 1760: XXI 417). Most eighteenth-century views of the house show it with Stanhope's alterations.

30. London, 1760. It was also published with this title and a Brentford imprint, without date; as *A Short View of the Principal Seats and Gardens In and About Twickenham* (London, 1767); and as *A Peep into the Principal Seats and Gardens In and About Twickenham (The Residence of the Muses)* . . . *To which is added, A History of a little Kingdom on the Banks of the Thames, and its Present Sovereign, his Laws, Government, etc.* (London, 1775). The 1775 edition is somewhat revised. My quotation is from the undated Brentford edition, pp. 3–4, 5–6. Horace Walpole thought the pamphlet "most inaccurate, superficial, blundering" (to Cole, 25 April 1775: I 367); but he is not perhaps an unbiased witness. He may have felt (with some justification) that the proprietor of Strawberry Hill made a more suitable successor to Pope's throne than R. O. Cambridge.

31. Thomson, *Spring*, 1161–2, 1164.

32. See L. I. Bredvold, "The Gloom of the Tory Satirists," *Pope and His Contemporaries* (1949); A. D. McKillop, "The Background of Thomson's Liberty," *Rice Institute Pamphlets*, XXXVIII (1951).

33. See, for example, Christopher Hussey, *The Picturesque* (1927), and his introductions to Margaret Jourdain's *The Work of William Kent* (1948) and Dorothy Stroud's *Capability Brown* (1950, rev. ed. 1957); B. Sprague Allen, *Tides in English Taste* (2 vols., Cambridge, 1937); I. W. U. Chase, *Horace Walpole, Gardenist* (1943); Laurence Whistler, *The Imagination of Vanbrugh and His Fellow Artists* (1954); and Hadfield (cited above, n. 25).

34. Maren-Sofie Røstvig, *The Happy Man: Studies in the Metamorphoses of a Classical Ideal* (2 vols., Oslo, 1954, 1958).

35. The phrase was used by the Duke of Shrewsbury of Vanbrugh's Blenheim, according to an undated letter of Pope's to an unnamed lady (I 431); Pope applies it to Timon's Villa in the *Epistle to Burlington*, 110.

36. To Martha Blount, 22 June [1724]: II 238. The "Large Mount" in Pope's own garden had its "Forest Seat" (*Newcastle General Magazine*, I 27).

37. *Spectator*, No. 477, 6 September 1712.

38. Thomas Whately rates these "among the principal ornaments" of The Leasowes (*Observations on Gardening*, 2d ed., 1770, p. 170).

39. Other buildings and areas at Stowe of associative and psychic intent were the "Elysian Fields," the "Gothic Building," the "Grecian Valley," the "Garden of Venus," the "Temple of Ancient Virtue," the "Temple of Concord and Victory," etc. Some of these remain today and may be seen pictured in Margaret Jourdain's *Kent* (above, n. 33). Descriptions will be found in Whately (above, n. 38), pp. 213 ff.

40. See, especially, D. C. Allen, *Image and Meaning: Metaphoric Traditions in Renaissance Poetry* (Baltimore, 1960), ch. vii.

41. See Earl Wasserman, *The Subtler Language* (Baltimore, 1959), ch. iii.

42. *Georgics,* II 473–4:

extrema per illos
Iustitia excedens terris vestigia fecit.

43. Ll. 181–8.

44. *Epistle to Burlington,* 57 ff.

45. "To the courteous and well-willing Readers."

46. *Spectator,* No. 477 (above, n. 37).

47. 28 January. See Browne's *Works* (ed. Simon Wilkin, 1836), I 375–6.

48. Pp. iii, iv.

49. *Life and Letters of Edward Young* (ed. H. C. Shelley, Boston, 1914), p. 282.

50. Some associative possibilities of the Twickenham estate are discussed in the second essay referred to in note 1. There is a fuller account in *The Garden and the City,* to be published in 1965 by the University of Toronto Press.

51. To Atterbury, 19 March 1722 (II 110).

52. To the Earl of Strafford, 5 October 1725 (II 328).

53. *Imit. Hor., Sat.* II vii 77–8.

54. 19 September 1730 (III 134).

55. *A History of the Modern Taste in Gardening* (above, n. 3), p. 28.

56. In describing to Mann the art of Pope's garden (20 June 1760: XXI 417), Walpole seems to hint that it showed something of the same love of intricacy, compression, and repetition-with-change that his poetic art shows: ". . . it was a little bit of ground of five acres, enclosed with three lanes and seeing nothing. Pope had twisted and twirled and rhymed and harmonized this, till it appeared two or three sweet little lawns opening and opening beyond one another, and the whole surrounded with thick impenetrable woods."

57. *Works* (1754), III 318.

58. The features mentioned here are indicated by Serle in his *Plan of Mr. Pope's Garden* (1745), with the exception of the quincunxes, which may, however, be the actual form of the groves he depicts. Pope refers to "my Quincunx" in *Imit. Hor., Sat.* II i 130; Spence speaks of "two quincunx groves."

59. Serle indicates urns and statues in his *Plan,* but does not distinguish them. Some of the urns were given Pope by the Prince of Wales in the spring of 1739. Lyttelton, Pope's friend and the Prince's secretary, writes that the poet is to have "six small ones for your Laurel Circus, or two large ones to terminate points, as you like best" (*c.* April: IV 170). The language Pope uses in a letter to Allen that spring (18 May: IV 181) suggests, though it does not prove, that he chose the six small urns. The inventory (below, n. 68) taken of Pope's goods after his death lists, "In the Garding," i.e., garden, four "Lead Urns"

and sixteen "Stone Urns and Pedestals." It also lists "a Venus with Stone Pedestall," possibly the one referred to by Curll; "a Mercury with a Wood Pedestall," "a Stone Statue with a Wood Pedestall," and "4 Busstos Antike with Stone Termes." An attack on Pope in 1732—*Of Good Nature: An Epistle Humbly Inscrib'd to His G[race] the D[uke] of C[handos]*—mentions "Niches" with "Deities" in his grounds, specifying a Jove and a Hercules. Some leaden urns now preserved in the gardens at Mapledurham House, seat of the Blount family, are presumed to have come from Pope's villa by way of Martha Blount, his legatee.

60. This essay prefaces his *Iliad*, II (1716).

61. Kent to Burlington, 28 November 1738 (Pope's *Correspondence*, IV 150).

62. P. 11. "Language of the heart" appealed to Pope also: it is for this he pays tribute to Cowley in the *Epistle to Augustus*, 75–8:

> Who now reads Cowley? if he pleases yet,
> His moral pleases, not his pointed wit;
> Forgot his Epic, nay Pindaric Art,
> But still I love the language of his Heart;

and to his father in the *Epistle to Dr. Arbuthnot*, 398–9:

> Un-learn'd, he knew no Schoolman's subtle Art,
> No Language, but the Language of the Heart.

63. To Hugh Bethel, 9 August 1726; to Caryll [1726]; to Fortescue, 23 August 1735 (II 387, 380; III 486).

64. Ll. 157–60.

65. October (III 138).

66. Lamb held Pope's verse compliments "the finest ever paid by the wit of man. Each of them is worth an estate for life—nay, is an immortality." After reading some of them aloud, "his voice totally failed him, and throwing down the book, he said, 'Do you think I would not wish to have been friends with such a man as this?'" (Hazlitt, "Of Persons One Would Wish To Have Seen," *Selected Essays*, ed. Geoffrey Keynes, 1930, pp. 530–31).

67. 21 September [1736]: IV 34. He does, however, write Marchmont on 10 October 1741 of the "motto . . . I am putting over my Door at Twitnam, Libertati & Amicitiae."

68. *Notes and Queries*, 6th series, V (1882), 363–5.

69. To Hugh Bethel, 20 February [1744]: IV 500.

70. *Epilogue to the Satires: Dial.* ii 78–9.

71. *Essay on Criticism*, 729.

72. That Pope was fully conscious how much a man's walls expressed their owner, we may gather from his remark to Ralph Allen (30 April [1736]: IV 13): "A Man not only shews his Taste but his Virtue, in the Choice of such

Ornaments: And whatever Example most strikes us, we may reasonably imag-ine may have an influence upon others, so that the History itself (if well chosen) upon a Rich-mans Walls, is very often a better lesson than any he could teach by his Conversation. In this sense, the Stones may be said to speak, when Men cannot, or will not."

73. To Digby, 20 July 1720 (II 50). According to the inventory cited above (n. 68), Pope's library contained busts of both "Poladio" and "Inigo Jones." It would be a plausible guess that these were copies of those made by Rysbrack for Chiswick House. See M. I. Webb, *Michael Rysbrack, Sculptor* (1954), fig-ures 36, 37.

74. *The Four Books of Andrea Palladio's Architecture* (tr. Isaac Ware, rev. by Burlington, 1738), p. 38.

75. Ibid.

76. Ibid. 81–2.

77. L. 198.

78. *Four Books,* p. 82.

79. See Rudolf Wittkower, *Architectural Principles in the Age of Humanism* (2d ed., 1952), pp. 63–6, and part iv: "The Problem of Harmonic Proportion in Architecture."

80. They had been followed to the letter by Lord Herbert and Robert Mor-ris's kinsman, Roger, in the design of rooms at Marble Hill. See Lees-Milne (above, n. 16), pp. 86–9.

81. *Lectures on Architecture* (1734), p. 74.

82. Ibid. p. 94. Morris was the theorist of the neo-Palladian movement, as Summerson notes (*Architecture in Britain,* p. 219). The subtitle of his *Essay in Defence of Ancient Architecture* (1728), an attack on the baroque principles of Hawksmoor and Vanbrugh, reveals its tendency: "a Parallel of the ancient Buildings with the modern, shewing the Beauty and Harmony of the Former, and the Irregularity of the Latter." So does the sub-title of his *Lec-tures on Architecture:* "Consisting of Rules founded upon Harmonick and Arithmetical Proportions in Building." His *Select Architecture* of 1755 had considerable influence in the American Colonies as well as at home.

83. Dryden, *Song for St. Cecilia's Day,* 11–15. This phase of the doctrine has recently been discussed in John Hollander's *The Untuning of the Sky* (Prince-ton, 1962).

84. *Characteristics* (4th ed., 1727), I 353. See Pope, *Imit. Hor., Ep.* II ii 202–5.

85. 14 August (II 192).

86. 13 January (III 341).

87. *Architectural Principles* (above, n. 74), p. 124.

88. Ibid. p. 57. See the engraved title in Ware's translation of the *Four Books.*

89. Addison, *Spectator,* No. 465, 23 August 1712.

90. Spence, p. 273 (in the forthcoming edition by J. M. Osborn, No. 620).

91. Ll. 211–12.

92. Ll. 215–19.

93. III 15 ff.

94. To Mann, 20 June 1760 (XXI 417).

"Dramatic Texture" in Pope

DONALD J. GREENE

I

"EVERY poem is 'dramatic' . . . someone is speaking to someone else": so Reuben Brower begins the first chapter of *The Fields of Light*.[1] This is true and important, and to neglect it can result in the misreading of a great deal of poetry, especially eighteenth-century poetry. The point is underlined by a remark in Eliot's essay on Yeats, where he warns against the "dangerous luxury" of the "beautiful line for its own sake," divorced from context (and, incidentally, disqualifies once for all Arnold's "touchstone" method of judging poetry):

What is necessary is a beauty which shall not be in the line or the isolable passage, but woven into the dramatic texture itself. . . . One of the most thrilling lines in *King Lear* is the simple
              Never, never, never, never, never
but, apart from a knowledge of the context, how can you say that it is poetry, or even competent verse?[2]

Exactly. Eliot here is talking specifically about "dramatic poetry" in the narrow sense, the formal stage play. But surely the observation applies equally to a very great deal of what is usually classed as "non-dramatic" poetry. "Thou wast not born for death, immortal Bird!" could easily be a line from some feeble late nineteenth-century sonneteer or some Pope-and-water late practitioner of the heroic couplet. Taken in isolation, it might well be condemned for its tautology—if the bird is immortal, it was of course not born for death: why say so twice?—or for the use of the weak generality "bird," or indeed for the somewhat clumsy, muffled texture of

31

vowel and consonant sound in the line. But in the "dramatic texture" into which Keats has "woven" it, after the poem has brilliantly created for us the *persona* of the life-loving youth condemned to death, the line, coming at the dramatically right moment in the structure of the poem, and magnificently supported by the surrounding lines, is poetically most effective and moving.

One reason for the inability of some readers—fewer than there once were, but still too many—to respond fully to the richness of Pope's mature poetry is that they wrest that poetry out of the genuinely "dramatic" context in which it subsists. The most appalling object-lesson in this kind of misreading is the second of Arnold's two "touchstones" of "an age of prose and reason," where Arnold extracts from its context Pope's couplet

> To Hounslow Heath I point, and Banstead Down;
> Thence comes your mutton, and these chicks my own.

and presents it as straight-faced factual statement, as though Pope were compiling a market-research report.[3] But nothing could be more fatuous than to read this kind of thing in Pope as "poetry of statement." It is precisely as much poetry of statement as "Never, never, never, never, never," which, if one wanted to, one could describe with perfect accuracy as statement of a very direct, emphatic, and unequivocal kind.[4] Statements in poetry are not to be read as statements *in vacuo,* as statements in, say, a physics textbook: a poetic statement is a statement *made by someone.* As Eliot points out, there could be no particular emotional response to "Never, never, never, never, never" without some picture in the reader's mind of who speaks it and in what circumstances. Who is speaking the Popean lines, and in what circumstances?

The couplet occurs, in fact, in the course of a complexly dramatic work, the *Imitation of the Second Satire of the Second Book of Horace.* The poem begins with an announcement by the first speaker in the poem, whom we may call "the narrator" or "Pope" (as long as we carefully preserve the inverted commas):

> What and how great, the virtue and the art
> To live on little with a cheerful heart . . .
> Let's talk, my friends.

The reader's heart warms to the candor and simplicity of the *naïf,* honest, uncomplicated individual who makes this hackneyed but

morally unimpeachable proposal in such straightforward, unso-
phisticated language. Yet already in the third line, he is presented
with a little puzzle—"(A doctrine sage, but truly none of mine)."
Why does "Pope" strengthen into what sounds like a disclaimer
Horace's neutral and unambiguous stage-direction, *Nec meus hic
sermo sed quem praecepit Ofellus* (117 of the 180 lines of the poem
are going to be a speech on the virtues of the simple life by the
speaker's friend Bethel, a country gentleman who is apparently
in the habit of talking along such lines)? Is "Pope" hinting to
the intelligent reader that there is a little of the tongue-in-cheek
in what follows—that Bethel is unconsciously a bit of a poseur
(not to say a bore), and although this "doctrine" may satisfy
Bethel's simple mind, the more critical "Pope" knows that the
problem of the good life is more complicated than Bethel makes
it seem?

The vast bulk of the poem is the speech assigned to Bethel, who
is termed "One not versed in schools, But strong in sense, and
wise without the rules." The speech is described as "Bethel's
sermon," which at first glance seems a most inept translation of
"sermo"—but perhaps, on second thought, isn't. The section
includes, by the way, a short but effective speech quoted from an
anonymous nobleman, revealing "His Lordship's" arrogance.
After Bethel is at last finished, the narrator continues somewhat
the same argument, but with the introduction

> Thus Bethel spoke, who always speaks his thought
> And always thinks the very thing he ought:
> His equal mind I copy what I can,
> And as I love, would imitate the man.

This is about as frank an avowal as "Pope" ever makes—the same
"Pope" who turns up as a character in most of the other poems in
the *Imitations of Horace* volume—that the mock-naïve role he is so
fond of playing *is* a role; that while he is "imitating Bethel" (and
he does so because, like many an intellectual and poet before and
after him, he genuinely "loves" the uncomplicated mind of Bethel
and his like, and wishes that his own could be like it), he knows
after all that things will never seem so simple to his own complex
sensibility. Bethel "thinks the very thing *he* ought"; in the end,
"Pope" will have to think the things *he* has to. Bethel, in short,

is cast as a kind of intellectual Fortinbras to "Pope's" Hamlet.

It is in the speech by the narrator that follows Bethel's that the notorious "age of reason" couplet occurs—

> To Hounslow Heath I point, and Banstead Down;
> Thence comes your mutton, and these chicks my own.

One editor of Arnold's essay protests, "The lines are strangely unrepresentative of Pope's verse, especially in rhythm."[5] Precisely: it is the awkward, rustic rhythm of a Squire Western or Squire Trelooby—of Squire Pope of Twickenham Hall, in fact. The careful specification of the clumsy local place names contributes to the effect ("Why, everyone knows where Banstead Down is!"). Pope is having great fun, as he so often does in his poetry, though the fact escapes Dr. Thomas Arnold's son. The speech contains such other delightful examples of the mock rustic as

> Content with little, I can piddle here
> On broccoli and mutton, round the year

("little . . . piddle . . . broccoli"—what other major poet, except possibly Pope's disciple Byron, could have made poetry out of such words?) and

> 'Tis true, no turbots dignify my board,
> But gudgeons, flounders. . . .
> The dev'l is in you if you cannot dine.

The dev'l is in the reader who misses the point of the juxtaposition "turbots, gudgeons, flounders . . . dignify": the name of the "U" fish is quite as laughable as those of the "non-U" fish.

But there are other turns of the screw. Between the clumsy naïveté of the Hounslow Heath couplet and the "honest forthrightness" of "The dev'l is in you" come three lines of beautifully composed descriptive verse almost as exquisite as any in *The Rape of the Lock*—

> From yon old walnut tree a show'r shall fall;
> And grapes, long-ling'ring on my only wall,
> And figs, from standard and espalier join.

The lovely combination of liquid sounds, the choice of the fine word "espalier" are there to remind us that the simple rustic babbling of his chicks and broccoli and mutton from Banstead

Down is only a mask loosely and temporarily worn by a sensitive and sophisticated artist. "Pope" has been trying to be "Bethel," but it is hard work to keep the real "Pope" from breaking in.

Now another speaker (labelled "Swift") is allowed to interject some "blunt common sense" into the narrator's rhapsodic "imitation" of Bethel's thinking "the very thing he ought"—which may be very well for Bethel, but sounds (and is intended to sound) strained in the narrator's mouth. "Pray heav'n it last! (cries Swift) as you go on; I wish to God this house had been your own." This has the effect of bringing the narrator down to earth from his extravagantly primitivistic flights, and the poem ends with his sober and moving plea, "What's property, dear Swift! . . . Let lands and houses have what lords they will, Let us be fix'd and our own masters still."

There was, to be sure, no need to present a detailed analysis of the complex variety of "tone" to be found in the poem: this has already been excellently done for it (as for much of Pope's other poetry) in Brower's masterly *Pope: The Poetry of Allusion*.[6] Brower comments on how "bluff and British" the opening of the poem seems. "We occasionally catch a coarse Swiftian accent. . . . There is an almost Horatian depth of melancholy in the simple question 'What's Property? dear Swift!'" Brower notes the contrast in "the latter half of the poem" (that is, presumably, in the part where the narrator, not Bethel, is speaking), and "the charm of the poetry" in the opening twenty lines of the narrator's long speech (which include the "Hounslow Heath" couplet)—"The praise of the Sabine Farm has been perfectly transposed into the idiom of Twit'nam with echoes of Ben Jonson's epistle, *Inviting a friend to supper* (Pope's amiable picture of cosy friendship seems to have been startlingly like and unlike the reality)." My object here, and in the later part of this essay, is to show how a sensitive, subtle, and accurate reading, like Brower's, of the individual parts of such a poem is enhanced when those parts are seen in the context of the dramatic structure of the poem as a whole. Briefly and crudely, then, the "drama" of the *Second Satire* consists of

1. A short prologue (ll. 1–10) in which the narrator ("Pope") states the subject straightforwardly but with some reserve, and introduces the right-thinking Bethel.
2. Bethel's "sermon" (ll. 12–128)—vivacious, positive, assured, down-

right, "strong in sense" (but not in subtlety), rising at times to a genuinely sermonizing, even crusading, note ("Oh, impudence of wealth! with all thy store, How dar'st thou let one worthy man be poor!"). Included in it are four lines (111–14) in which "His Lordship" speaks and manifests the "impudence of wealth."

3. The narrator's attempt (ll. 129–60) to "copy what he can" of Bethel's "equal mind"—a charmingly unsuccessful attempt which results in a comically exaggerated rusticity at some times, at others a dropping back into the lovely poetic texture of the speaker's naturally artistic idiom.

4. "Swift's" interjection (ll. 161–4), recalling the narrator from his rhapsodies about Homeric hospitality with the blunt reminder that he lives only in a rented house—that he is living in the days of Locke, not Homer. Surely the point is made—Bethel's primitivism is no longer enough; "Pope" is "Pope," and should not try to be Bethel.

5. The narrator, sobered, drops his rhapsodizing tone and goes to the heart of the matter, though this is not to agree with "Swift's" "realistic" view, which is as much an oversimplification as Bethel's idealistic one. True, this is the Lockean age of property—but "What's property, dear Swift?" Not extrinsic things, neither "Swift's" property nor Bethel's gudgeons and flounders, but non-material ones are the final values: "Let us be fix'd, and our own masters still."

It is a miniature drama, with two major and two minor (but not negligible) actors, and the manifold varieties of verbal technique ("tone," as Brower calls it) in the dialogue are brilliantly suited to the dramatic strategy of the work. And it *has* a strategy, it seems to me, a genuinely dramatic structure: a pattern of complication (Bethel's speech), the development of stress ("Pope's"), the unexpected introduction of a catalytic agent ("Swift's" interjection), then a sudden resolution ("What's property, dear Swift?"), followed by a kind of denouement. The reader who follows it closely finds himself going through the archetypal pattern of emotional effect of classic drama—the false calm and assurance of the beginning, the increasing strain and tension of "Pope's" speech, preparing for the catastrophe or anagnorisis ("Swift's" comment—and here, perhaps, biography for once can help us when we comprehend what "Pity! to build without a son or wife" must have meant to Pope), and then the sudden release, in which genuine emotion, pent up, inhibited by the compulsion to "think the very thing he ought" along with Bethel, comes flooding in ("What's property, dear Swift?") and sweeps away the false and factitious. To read the poem with a proper degree of "empathy" can indeed result in a kind of Aristotelian catharsis.

II

One wonders how the legend grew up that the eighteenth century was impersonal, objective, dispassionate. No age ever abounded more in self-conscious, self-dramatizing writers. If the Romantics loved to contemplate their own images, they had ample precedent for doing so: it is perhaps not too surprising after all that the inventor of "Byronism" was the fervent admirer of Pope. The works of Dryden, Swift, Pope, and Johnson are liberally sprinkled with the pronoun "I" and with highly charged scenes in which that "I" holds the center of the stage:

> Already I am worn with cares and age,
> And just abandoning th' ungrateful stage:
> Unprofitably kept at Heaven's expense,
> I live a rent-charge on his providence.

> 'Tis true—then why should I repine
> To see my life so fast decline?
> But why obscurely here alone,
> Where I am neither loved nor known?
> My state of health none care to learn;
> My life is here no soul's concern.
> And those with whom I now converse
> Without a tear will tend my hearse.

> I left no calling for this idle trade,
> No duty broke, no father disobeyed.
> The Muse but served to ease some friend, not wife,
> To help me through this long disease, my life.

I may be surely contented without the praise of perfection, which, if I could obtain, in this gloom of solitude, what would it avail me? I have protracted my work till most of those whom I wished to please have sunk into the grave, and success and miscarriage are empty sounds: I therefore dismiss it with frigid tranquility, having little to fear or hope from censure or from praise.[7]

"However feeble the written drama of the eighteenth century may
have been," one student writes, "the period was histrionic; it was
an age of great acting, with Garrick, Mrs. Siddons, and Foote."[8]
There were great actors on the literary scene too, as the quotations
above show, and the most versatile of them was Alexander Pope.
Like Dryden, Swift, and Johnson, he does the "injured innocent"
to perfection, but in addition he has a whole repertory of other
well-rehearsed roles, in which, especially in the Horatian imitations, he delights to display himself.

The *Epistle to Arbuthnot* is a virtuoso exhibition of his talents
as a quick-change artist. We begin with the busy, successful man-
of-letters, with a proper consciousness of his own importance, normally urbane but now justly irritated—

> "Shut, shut the door, good John!" fatigu'd, I said,
> "Tie up the knocker, say I'm sick, I'm dead. . . ."

Half-humorous self-pity enters—

> All fly to Twit'nam, and in humble strain
> Apply to me, to keep them mad or vain.
> Arthur, whose giddy son neglects the laws,
> Imputes to me and my damn'd works the cause.

The mask of the "busy public man" is suddenly dropped at line
27: the speaker becomes the simple, lonely, wistful, modest poet—

> Friend to my life (which did not you prolong
> The world had wanted many an idle song). . . .

If, for purposes of poetic analysis, we describe this too as a "mask,"
a pose, it need not make the lines less moving. "Pope" pities himself, it is true, but he convinces us that he has justification for pity-
ing himself. Sometimes the self-pity is consciously exaggerated,
and "Pope" dons another of his favorite masks, that of the "hurt
little boy" (we are expected to smile at it—"Pope" himself smiles
at it):

> Seiz'd and ty'd down to judge, how wretched I!
> Who can't be silent, and who will not lie. . . .
> I sit with sad civility, I read
> With honest anguish, and an aching head. . . .

("Why do people *do* these terrible things to me?")

There follows (ll. 40–68) a fine comic set-piece that might easily be staged—the rapid-fire exchange of dialogue between the harried "Pope" and the importunate poets. The poets are finally ejected, and "Pope" sits down again in his arm-chair and addresses his friend in the role of "sober, serious intellectual" ("Come, let us reason together")—"Is not mine, my friend, a sorer case . . .?" The friend, the interlocutor, as usual in these dialogues, plays the part of the prudent, worldly-wise counsellor, the culmination of whose system of values is to stay out of trouble, to avoid offending powerful people (these characters in Pope's dialogues, for all that they are described as "friends" and handled in a deceptively gentle way, really add up to a devastating portrait of the "outer-directed" individual—so often the object of attack by Swift as well). "You deal in dang'rous things," the friend complains. His short-sighted "prudence" begins to make "Pope" angry; and "Pope's" poetic anger, building up gradually from brief ejaculations of contempt to the exalted and sustained wrath of the righteously indignant crusader, is, artistically, a splendid thing to behold. It progresses from "Nothing? if they bite and kick? . . . Who shames a scribbler? . . . One flatt'rer's worse than all," through the bitter sarcasm of the parody of the flatterer,

> Go on, obliging creatures, make me see
> All that disgrac'd my betters met in me . . .
> And when I die, be sure you let me know
> Great Homer died three thousand years ago,

to the grandly rhetorical denunciation of

> He, who hurts a harmless neighbour's peace,
> Insults fall'n worth, or Beauty in distress . . .
> That fop whose pride affects a patron's name
> Yet absent wounds an author's honest name . . .

and so on, in one of those long, long sentences (ll. 286–304) which, interspersed among the generally short, even choppy, units of sense and rhythm that make up the bulk of the piece, indicate its dramatic climaxes.

The chief such climax in the Arbuthnot epistle—the point at which the intensity of emotion seems to reach its peak, after which it gradually subsides and levels off in the calm and deeply affection-

ate tributes to his parents and Arbuthnot at the end of the poem—
is probably the even longer sentence (ll. 334–59) in which "Pope"
lists the qualifications of the virtuous poet and asserts his own
claim to them. Self-praise has, of course, been a recognized privilege of the poet, from Horace's *Exegi monumentum* on; the
reader is to assume that he is entitled to it, not in his capacity
of private individual but that of *sacer vates*. In the Horatian
epistles "Pope" take full advantage of the privilege, and in such
passages as this he contrives an exaltation of tone, even an incan-
tatory effect (to borrow one of Eliot's more useful critical terms),
that can indeed make the reader feel he is listening to an inspired
poet-prophet, hurling defiance at a world populated by the enemies
of God—

> That not for fame, but virtue's better end,
> He stood the furious foe, the timid friend,
> The damning critic, half-approving wit,
> The coxcomb hit, or fearing to be hit;
> Laugh'd at the loss of friends he never had,
> The dull, the proud, the wicked, and the mad,

and so on, with the emotional power relentlessly building up, in a
miraculously long and sustained rhythmical unit that leaves the
reader exhausted by the time he reaches the end. The rapt bard,
the inspired crusader, the exalted narrator of *Gesta Dei per Alex-
andrum*—in the later poems, Pope has built up the role to perfection.

The development of what I have just tried to present, the main
dramatic and emotional "line" (as I see it) in the *Epistle to Arbuthnot,* is not at all straightforward, but is interrupted by many
seeming disgressions—the great autobiographical passage ("Why
did I write? . . . This long disease, my life"), which, though it is
full of self-pity, is more restrained and serious, therefore more
impressive, nobler, than the earlier half-whimsical complaints; the
three great "characters" of Atticus, Bufo, and Sporus. Each of these
portraits, it should be noted, is in a different vein from the others:
the first is polished, detached, urbane (like Addison himself?)—
"Who but must laugh, if such a man there be? Who would not
weep, if Atticus were he?"; the second, open, careless, almost jovial
in its contempt (Bufo is not worth a polished dart)—"Much they

extolled his pictures, much his seat, And flattered every day, and sometimes eat: Till grown more frugal in his riper days, He paid some bards with port, and some with praise" (Dryden comes into the passage, and there is a kind of Drydenian looseness and ease in its rhythms); and finally, most deadly of all, the tightly-controlled, white-lipped, frightening hatred of the Sporus portrait, with the virulent epithets spitting out—"And he himself one vile Antithesis!" But it is wrong to call these digressions or interruptions. Each contributes in its own way to the total dramatic effect. To attempt a really complete analysis of the dramatic and emotional pattern of this long and complex work would be a difficult task, though it should be done: no one who has read it and fully responded to it doubts that it has such a structure, that it is an artistic unity. Clearly the pattern on which it is constructed is that of a series of successively more intense climaxes, rather than a straightforward building up to a single climax, followed by release, as in the more simply constructed *Second Satire of the Second Book*. Although the imitation of actual Horatian poems furnished Pope with an excellent opportunity to practise "dramatic" techniques, his freedom from such restraint in the *Epistle to Arbuthnot* allows him to use a larger canvas and a more varied palette.

III

The poems in which Pope most strikingly creates drama by use of a shifting series of *personae* (and consequently of "tones," to use Brower's term) are generally his later ones. Like some other supreme poets, notably Shakespeare and Yeats, Pope's verse shows a marked development, as it matures, in the direction of greater vigor, economy, audacity, variety, ability to surprise—in short (to use conventional terms), from a "lyric" to a "dramatic" mode. The difference between the verse of, say,

> Where'er you walk, cool gales shall fan the glade;
> Trees where you sit shall crowd into a shade:
> Where'er you tread the blushing flow'rs shall rise,
> And all things flourish where you turn your eyes

and that of

> The pois'ning dame—You mean?—I don't.—You do.
> See! now I keep the secret, and not you

is comparable to the difference between the verse of *Love's Labour's Lost* and that of *King Lear,* or between that of *The Lake Isle of Innisfree* and that of *The Circus Animals' Desertion.*[9] The point is, of course, that the mature poet's greater skill and freedom in using a dramatic *structure* for his poetry is inseparable from a marked change in the *texture* of the verse; and the reader who misses what is happening in the dramatic structure of the work is probably going to fail lamentably, like Matthew Arnold, in his response to the verse texture.

Of Pope's later poems, the most obviously dramatic are those generally referred to as the *Imitations of Horace,* with which are usually included the imitations of Donne and the non-Horatian *Epistle to Arbuthnot* and the twin "Dialogues" that form the "Epilogue to the Satires" (the dramatic elements in *The Dunciad* and the various *Essays* ought certainly to be investigated too). It is of course not possible in a short exploratory article to analyze the dramatic structure of all these. It is tempting to stop and look at the versions of Donne, where the *persona* of the narrator seems to be a curious compromise between "Donne" and "Pope,"[10] or the early, tentative, but highly successful *First Satire of the Second Book,* which looks like a simplified trial run for the *Epistle to Arbuthnot*—

> Tim'rous by nature, of the rich in awe,
> I come to counsel learned in the law.
> You'll give me, like a friend, both sage and free
> Advice: and (as you use) without a fee,

the speaker begins, with a delightful mock-naïveté which would take in only a Matthew Arnold. But Pope's most compelling use of the overtly dramatic is surely in his last composition (with the exception of his masterpiece, Book Four of *The Dunciad,* which owes something of its force to the experience gained in the work that preceded it)—the two-part "Dialogue," *1738,* that was later entitled *Epilogue to the Satires.*

With experience had come freedom, boldness, sureness, power. The dramatic "line" of *1738* (it is clearly intended to be read as a single poem) is basically a simple one, rising to two major climaxes, one at the end of the first dialogue (ll. 141–70), the other

even more forceful one at the end of the second (ll. 197–253). In
their sustained power and exaltation of tone, these two perora-
tions are matched only by the conclusion of *The Dunciad*: whereas
most of the earlier Pope is Mozartean in quality (and Mozart is
capable of great depth and power), these begin to verge on Beetho-
ven. The danger of the "grand style" is, of course, the melodramatic. Taken by themselves, such lines as

> Yes, the last pen for freedom let me draw

and

> Are none, none living? Let me praise the dead

could, if not prepared for and supported by the whole structure
of the poem, be simply rant, the sort of thing nineteenth-century
post-Byronic scribblers churned out by the hundred. As it is, they
are perfectly prepared for and sustained: with his impeccable
artistic instinct, Pope, like a great singer, does not attempt heroic
tones like these until his voice, through training and practice, is
ready for them, or without providing adequate "support" for them
in the preceding part of the song. By comparison, other would-be
"powerful" versifiers—W. E. Henley, for instance—resemble the
conceited amateur who, using only will-power, strains an un-
trained organ and makes hideous cacophony. Pope never "forces
the tone off the voice."

The preparation is, of course, a "dramatic" one. The reader's
mind and feelings are prepared, by involvement with what "Pope"
is involved in, to accept as his own the intensity of feeling that
"Pope" is to express. Hence the role of the "friend," the interlocutor, is enlarged from that of the harmless stooge feeding "Pope" a
line or two, as in earlier poems, to a fully developed character, and
a very unpleasant and ominous one. Conformism, "dullness," no
longer content with interjecting an occasional demurrer, now
takes the offensive: the anonymous "friend" opens the poem with
a studied attack on "Pope," refuses to listen to "Pope's" counter-
arguments, but goes on wrangling querulously and aggressively,
very sure of his own rightness. Indeed, for much of the first dialogue the "friend" holds the center of the stage and dominates
the "action"; up to "Pope's" long peroration, the "friend" has

much more to say than "Pope." The lengths of the six speeches which make up the first dialogue are, in order,

Friend	*"Pope"*
26½ lines	9½ lines
26 lines	24 lines
18 lines	68 lines

The "friend" is versed in all the clichés of conformism and uses them relentlessly: "Pope's" verse, since he has begun writing satires, has lost its old "rapture" and grows merely "correct"; moreover, he has become "too moral for a wit"—interesting pieces of criticism, which support the thesis of this paper, that Pope's technique has matured during the period of the "Horatian imitations" (though we, his readers, should approve this development as much as the "friend" deplores it). Then—an important passage —comes the "friend's" description of how Horace would do it so as not to make anyone angry—Horace, who "could please at court, and make Augustus smile." This, I think, must be taken very seriously: Pope, having tried to imitate the compromise and "urbanity" of Horace, at last deliberately rejects him; something stronger and better than Horace is wanted. One remembers Pope's fine epitaph "On One Who Would Not Be Buried in Westminster Abbey," written at this same time:

> Heroes and kings, your distance keep:
> In peace let one poor poet sleep,
> Who never flatter'd folks like you:
> Let Horace blush, and Virgil too.

"This epitaph was obviously never meant to be taken too seriously," its latest editors comment.[11] Why not, one wonders. To Pope's readers, brought up to revere the classics, it must have seemed a startlingly arrogant declaration, and we are prepared for the "friend's" parting shot in *1738*, "You're strangely proud." But it is arrogant only in the way that "I go . . . to forge in the smithy of my soul the uncreated conscience of my race" is arrogant. And indeed it seems to me that Pope's purpose in these later poems is not unlike Joyce's, and his rejection of Horace not unlike Stephen Dedalus's rejection of his earlier masters.

After patiently listening to all this, "Pope's" voice is at last

given a chance to be heard, interrupting the friend's nagging
in the middle of a line when Walpole is mentioned. "See Sir
Robert! Hum—." He contents himself with pointing out mildly
that Walpole's private face and his public one are different, and
is silent again. The friend is going to be allowed all the time he
needs to state the case against "Pope"—or all the rope he needs to
hang himself, which he very effectively does. He continues with
the familiar loaded terms of conformism, "impartial," "balance,"
"judicious." "Pope's" next intervention is longer and more energetic and acerb: "Adieu distinction, satire, warmth, and truth."
The collocation is important: satire implies truth, discernment,
emotional warmth, the converse of the values the friend stands for.
It is also funny—"The gracious dew of pulpit eloquence, And all
the well-whipt cream of courtly sense" are delightful images; the
devastating innuendo against Queen Caroline (Pope is to be
hampered by no conventions about *nil nisi mortuis*), "All parts
performed and *all* her children blest," is succeeded by sheer gam-
boling—"So—Satire is no more—I feel it die—No gazetteer more
innocent than I!" One can almost see the speaker acting this out
with appropriate gestures and facial expressions.

The attempt to keep the discussion on a humorous plane makes
no impression on the friend, who grows more solemn, pompous,
and arrogant than ever: "Why so? If satire knows its time and
place, You still may lash the greatest—in disgrace." He continues
with the wonderful biblical parody in which "some gentle minis-
terial wing" receives the loyal party hacks into the heaven of
"place," where "all tears are wip'd for ever from all eyes." "Pope"
then takes over, and after the bitter irony of "Virtue, I grant you,
is an empty boast, But shall the dignity of Vice be lost?" builds up
to the great scenic climax of the apotheosis of Vice, reminiscent
of the conclusion of *The Dunciad* and hardly inferior to it:

> Chaste matrons praise her, and grave bishops bless:
> In golden chains the willing world she draws,
> And hers the gospel is, and hers the laws:
> Mounts the tribunal, lifts her scarlet head
> And sees pale virtue carted in her stead!
> Lo, at the wheels of her triumphal car
> Old England's genius, rough with many a scar,
> Dragg'd in the dust!

and, at the end, his own contemptuously abrupt dissenting manifesto,

> Yet may this verse (if such a verse remain)
> Show there was one who held it in disdain.

Pope published what he had written of the "Dialogue" up to
this point, for it makes a unified composition, but he saw how it
could be brilliantly continued. The second part goes on without
a break. The friend's " 'Tis all a libel, Paxton, sir, will say" refers
presumably to the peroration of the previous part. From now on
"Pope" dominates the scene, and the friend is reduced to brief,
hostile interjections, " 'Tis all a libel," "Stop, stop!", "You're
strangely proud." The passages of rapid-fire dialogue are very fine,
and something Pope has not tried before:

> P. Ye rev'rend atheists— F. Scandal, name them. Who?
> P. Why, that's the thing you bid me not to do. . . .
>   The pois'ning dame— F. You mean— P. I don't. F. You do.
> P. See! now I keep the secret, and not you.
>   The bribing statesman— F. Hold! too high you go.
> P. The brib'd elector— F. There you stoop too low.
> P. I fain would please you, if I knew with what.

The mental confusion of the friend, which was apparent enough
in the labored "arguments" of the first dialogue, is now made
unmistakable by this object lesson. The verse is a far cry from the
"neat, monotonous regularity" of the heroic couplet that one reads
about in literary histories. Pope's growing mastery of dramatic
style enables him to do surprising things: for instance, the striking
interruption (interestingly, by a phrase that Eliot makes fine dramatic use of in *The Waste Land*) and sudden shift of tone after
some lines that sound like the beginning of a fervent rhapsody, as
though to give the reader a foretaste of what is in store for him at
the end of the poem:

> No pow'r the Muse's friendship can command:
> No pow'r, when Virtue claims it, can withstand:
> To Cato, Virgil paid one honest line;
> O let my country's friends illumine mine!
> —What are you thinking?

"Pope" does well to be suspicious of the friend who replies

> Faith, the thought's no sin,
> I think your friends are out, and would be in.

The shift from the exalted tone to the colloquial tells us something of the friend's mind, which reduces everything to its own vulgarity. Pope, to be sure, gives us, his readers, a chance to smile too at the exaltation of "Pope" in these passages; but perhaps we should be cautious about taking too great advantage of the invitation.

Of the peroration, which begins with the breathtaking

> *F.* You're strangely proud.
> > *P.* So proud, I am no slave:
> So impudent, I own myself no knave.
> So odd, my country's ruin makes me grave.
> Yes, I am proud; I must be proud to see
> Men not afraid of God afraid of me

and goes on with perfectly sustained force and grandeur for fifty lines, there is nothing to say except that it is magnificent drama, and that the reader who "stays with it" all the way is exhausted at the end of it, as at the end of the storm scene in *King Lear*. And afterwards there is no other way to terminate the poem than by the friend's rueful postscript,

> Alas, alas, pray end what you began,
> And write next winter more Essays on Man.

By putting such advice in the mouth of the contemptible "friend," is Pope hinting broadly that he would rather that we remember him by the *Dialogues* than by the *Essay*? It seems plausible.

IV

It may be useful to glance briefly at some matters of general critical theory arising out of the foregoing discussion. There are probably readers to whom "All poetry is dramatic" will seem a novel and dubious assertion. True, students of prose fiction, who have long been aware how central to criticism of it the problem of "point of view" is ("Just *who* is telling the story?") and are familiar with Henry James's advice to novelists—all novelists—

"Dramatize, dramatize," will probably find nothing very alarming in the proposition. But critics of poetry too often suffer from an urge to classify and pigeon-hole. Two years after Brower published the work quoted at the beginning of this article, T. S. Eliot delivered a lecture which, it seems to me, plunges the whole matter into confusion again. This is his well-known "The Three Voices of Poetry": "The first voice is the voice of the poet talking to himself. . . . The second is the voice of the poet addressing an audience. . . . The third is the voice of the poet when he attempts to create a dramatic character."[12] The first voice gives us "meditative poetry"; the third "poetic drama"; and the second—the existence of which Eliot says he began to suspect only in the previous three years: a strange admission from one who first made his name with *The Love Song of J. Alfred Prufrock*—gives us poetry "that has a conscious social purpose," and includes the "dramatic monologue."

It is not hard to find points of weakness in Eliot's argument. In order to preserve the distinction between his "second" and "third voices," he has to give an exceedingly odd account of the "dramatic monologue":

What we normally hear, in fact, in the dramatic monologue, is the voice of the poet [not of the "character," as in "poetic drama"], who has put on the costume and make-up either of some historical character, or of one out of fiction. His personage must be identified to us—as an individual, or at least as a type—before he begins to speak.[13]

This is simply not so, even with Browning, whose dramatic monologues are the only ones Eliot cites. How many of Browning's readers, coming to the poems for the first time, identify Abt Vogler or Fra Lippo Lippi either as individuals or as types before they begin to speak? Their individuality, or typicality, is disclosed only by the development of the poem itself; their existence as "characters" *is* created by the poem: surely that was why Browning selected such obscure figures from history as his protagonists, in order that he *would* be free to "create" them in his poetry, unhampered by preconceptions the reader had picked up from his historical studies. "Dramatic monologue," Eliot continues, "cannot create a character. For character is created and made real only in action, a communication between imaginary people." But there is certainly communication with imaginary people in Browning's dramatic monologues (so that the term is really a misnomer). Bishop Blougram is addressing Gigadibs the literary man (who has a small speaking and acting part of his own), Andrea del Sarto his wife, the bishop who orders his tomb his "nephews." And does character cease to be created, does the poetry cease to be "dramatic," does the "third voice" stop and the "second voice" take over, when Hamlet and Iago, as they so frequently do, drop into soliloquy and no longer address "imaginary people"? Clearly not, since Eliot cites approvingly as an instance of "dramatic poetry" "Tomorrow and tomorrow and tomorrow," which Macbeth speaks to no one in particular.[14]

Eliot's "first voice," which produces "meditative poetry," is supposed to be merely the poet "talking to himself." Perhaps. One wonders how, in that case, it gets put on paper and circulated. But even if it were so, there is still an audience. As everyone who has done any writing knows, the speaking "self" and the hearing "self" are not identical: one's voice persists in forming words which one's ear as persistently rejects as false, inappropriate, "not what one wants to say." After a while, from fatigue, one's voice stops searching for still better words and is content to present to the world, and to one's still dissatisfied "hearing self," an "image," a *persona*, which is only a rough approximation to the inner, ultimately inexpressible "reality." In the end, then, all literary composition is dramatic, since whatever words we commit to paper or the air— *nescit vox missa reverti*—can only be those of a "dramatic character," a fictional person, a mask, never those of the "real self" (if anyone ever has a consistent "self," since the "self" of the morning after is often not the "self" of the night before).

But perhaps the most disturbing thing in Eliot's essay is his assertion "When we listen to a play by Shakespeare, we listen not to Shakespeare but to his characters; when we read a dramatic monologue by Browning, we cannot suppose that we are listening to any other voice than that of Browning himself." If this is so (and for many readers it may well be), it is deplorable. Surely this is only another manifestation of the ubiquitous "biographical fallacy": if the reader of *Bishop Blougram's Apology* is in fact engaged in listening not to Bishop Blougram but to Robert Browning (1812–89) (or to Cardinal Manning, 1808–92), one can only say that he is listening very badly indeed. He is not reading *the poem,* but is doing a small piece of biographical or historical research. If we are more in the habit of listening to Hamlet rather than to Shakespeare in Hamlet's soliloquies (though there was certainly a time when students *were* in the habit of "listening to Shakespeare" in them), it is because we fortunately have much less biographical information about Shakespeare than about Browning; and also, perhaps, because in the last few decades Shakespearean critics have made a determined effort to stop readers from perverting the text of a Shakespearean play in this way; to re-educate readers and audiences of Shakespeare, in effect. Such a campaign of re-education needs to be extended to readers of other poetry, in particular of eighteenth-century poetry.

If, of course, the important poetry in the English language were published without designation of its authorship, as has been done in a number of useful anthologies—and it is hard to see what objection the critic, *qua* critic, can have to the practice—Eliot's distinction collapses. The reader then has no means of finding out, when he is reading *Bishop Blougram's Apology,* whether he ought to be listening to Browning or Tennyson or Arnold or X; in desperation, he will be forced to listen simply to Blougram, and a good thing too. No doubt "Blougram" is an aspect, to some degree, of Browning, as Prufrock is of young Tom Eliot ("And I, Tiresias, have foresuffered all"); as Hamlet is of William Shakespeare. But how can the precise proportion of the autobiographical which the "I" of a poem contains (and therefore, apparently, which of the "poetic voices" is at work) be determined? If it can be done at all, it must be the job of the biographer, not the critic. And, although the biographer may find the question a fascinating one, what, after all, does the *reader* of the poem care? The poem remains the same: all he knows, or needs to know, or, if he is a good reader, wants to know, is that there is someone *in the poem* who is speaking.

The justification for preaching incessantly to the reader of poetry (as this article does) "Dramatize, dramatize" is that if he does not do so voluntarily, he will do so involuntarily: whether he thinks he is doing so or not, he *will* attribute the words spoken in the poem to a speaker; and if he does not, as he should do, "reconstruct" the speaker from the evidence in the poem itself (*this* may be an unconscious process), a speaker from outside the poem will rush in to fill the vacuum, and the reader will find himself listening (as Eliot confesses he does) to a bearded figure named "Robert Browning," the sage of Camberwell, or to a hunchbacked, irascible little man who lived at Twickenham and quarreled with Lord Hervey, Colley Cibber, and so on. He will "listen to" this unappealing figure with detachment, consider his pronouncements, and either, like the Reverend Whitwell Elwin, condemn them and him outright, or, at best, "explain" them, in terms of his biography or as manifestations of the spirit of the age, and so "understand" (and presumably forgive) them.

The fact is that "listening to" Hamlet is a very inadequate description of what the good reader or theatre-goer does. Rather, he "identifies with" Hamlet, "empathizes" with him, he *lives* Hamlet. F. R. Leavis goes to the heart of the matter: "Words in poetry invite us, not to 'think about' and judge, but to 'feel into' or 'become'—to realize a complex experience that is given in the words."[15] It may well be true, as Eliot's remark suggests, that readers find this easier to do, or at least are more willing to do it, when they watch costumed figures on a stage than when they are confronted with a piece of printed paper bearing the superscription "by Robert Browning" or "by Alexander Pope." Before such a piece of paper, it seems, they have difficulty responding to or "realizing" the words in front of them; instead, they conjure up from their (mis)education a stereotype labelled "Browning" or "Pope," and, no matter what the text says, see only and hear only that familiar figure. If by use of the term "dramatic"—if by pointing out that it is perfectly easy to "stage" the *Epistle to Arbuthnot* or the *1738 Dialogues* in one's mind; to watch, hear, and respond as the characters in them shout, whisper, strut, grimace, cringe, wheedle, roar, denounce, prevaricate, laugh, cry; to act all this out along with the characters themselves—readers can be persuaded to forget "Browning" and "Pope" for the moment and see and hear and react to what is actually going on in front of them (and to sense, in the poems mentioned at least, that all this adds up to a unified, organized, and valuable experience), then the amount of delight and instruction obtainable from great poetry should be significantly increased. Perhaps the exhortation "Read Pope's (and other) poetry *in dramatic context*" means essentially nothing more than "Read the poem *as* a poem"—"feel into" it, "become" it, "realize" the experience that is *in* the poem: do not, as a reader, merely "listen to" it, in the way Arnold did, as a series of straight-faced declarations by a biographical construct (and probably, by good biographical standards, a ludicrously inadequate construct) whom you have been taught to call "Alexander Pope."[16]

NOTES

1. New York, 1962, p. 19 (Galaxy Books); first published 1951. The statement is made as a comment on some remarks by Robert Frost on the problem of poetic communication. My approach to Pope's poetry in this article differs somewhat from Brower's, in that he concerns himself in the first instance with variations of "tone" in the verse itself, whereas I try to look first at the overt "dramatic structure" of the poem. The two are closely interrelated, of course.

2. "Yeats" (1940), in *On Poetry and Poets* (New York, 1957), p. 305.

3. "The Study of Poetry" (1880). Brower's demolition of the other "touch-stone" ought to be better known:
> "A milk white Hind, immortal and unchang'd,
> Fed on the lawns, and in the forest rang'd. . . .
What do we find? Prose and reason? Hardly, but something like the opening of a dream-vision: a single distinct image of a mysterious creature seen in a landscape precisely named 'the lawns' and 'the forest' but located in the time-less nowhere of Spenserian narrative. Our sensations are not only visual, but of heard and felt movement as we make our way through this couplet of finely varied balance and bell-like swing. The image of the Hind is made more distinct by the bold laying down of three successive stresses, and her stately progress is further enacted in the gratifying echo of 'fed' and 'forest,' and in the closing ample rhyme. This is most surprising 'prose,' much nearer to music and painting than to reason." *Dryden*, ed. Reuben A. Brower (New York, 1962), p. 8 (Laurel Poetry Series).

4. For some doubts that eighteenth-century poetry generally can be said to be distinguished by a concern for "logical statement," see my article " 'Logical Structure' in Eighteenth-century Poetry," *Philological Quarterly*, XXXI (July, 1952), 315–36.

5. E. K. Brown, in his edition of Matthew Arnold, *Four Essays on Life and Letters* (New York, 1947), p. 83 (Crofts Classics).

6. Oxford, 1959, pp. 291–3.

7. Dryden, "To My Dear Friend Mr. Congreve"; Swift, "In Sickness"; Pope, *Epistle to Arbuthnot;* Johnson, Preface to *A Dictionary of the English Language.*

8. Wylie Sypher, *Four Stages of Renaissance Style* (New York, 1955), p. 280 (Anchor Books). One might go further and speculate whether the dramatic impulse of the time, deprived of its natural expression in the work of the playwright, did not find its outlet in the other arts. Vanbrugh's architecture, Handel's music, Reynolds's portraiture, the portrait sculpture of Roubiliac and Nollekens, Brown's landscaping—has any other century in England produced art more frankly concerned to achieve bold dramatic effects?

9. The importance of self-dramatization in Yeats's later poetry is sufficiently indicated by the title of Richard Ellman's book, *Yeats: The Man and the Masks.*

10. Is it possible that it was from Donne that Pope learned that self-dramatization can furnish fine material for poetry (and that Byron learned it from Pope)? Pope was "adapting" Donne ("Satire II") in his early twenties.

11. Norman Ault and John Butt, eds., *The Poems of Alexander Pope* (London, 1954), VI, 376 (Twickenham ed.).

12. *"On Poetry and Poets,"* p. 96 (delivered in 1953).

13. Ibid. p. 103.

14. "Poetry and Drama" (1951), in *On Poetry and Poets,* p. 89.

15. *Scrutiny,* VI (1937–38), 60–61.

16. This article was completed before the publication of Irvin Ehrenpreis's attack on the use of the concept of the *persona* in literary criticism (*Restoration and Eighteenth-Century Literature: Essays in Honor of A. D. McKillop,* Chicago, 1963, pp. 25–37), but readers may like to consider whether Section IV above does not in some measure provide a reply to it. It would be ungracious not to acknowledge the general indebtedness of this, like much other recent work on "how to read Pope," to Maynard Mack's pioneering essay "The Muse of Satire" (*Yale Review,* XLI [1951], 80–92). Another relevant study is Pierre Legouis, "The Dramatic Element in Donne's Poetry," reprinted from *Donne the Craftsman* (1928) in Helen Gardner, ed., *John Donne: A Collection of Critical Essays* (*Twentieth Century Views*), New York 1962, pp. 36–51.

An Image of Pope

———•———

W. K. WIMSATT, JR.

T HE substance of this essay is to be found in a series of pictures.
Still some words are needed to explain them. At the beginning
I would profess myself to be aware that a certain element of fiction sustains the argument. The efforts of the literary or art his-
torian are usually directed toward recovering states of mind. He
wishes to discover the full allusion and meaning of a poem or a
picture either for the creator at the time of conception or for his
best contemporary audience. The collocation of these six pictures
of Alexander Pope is, then, in a sense unhistorical. It is not strictly
relevant to the history of the aesthetic consciousness. For not a
single person within the historic period concerned, 1742 to about
1800, was fully aware of all these pictures and their relations to one
another. Van Loo when he painted Pope was of course not concerned with either Warburton, Ireland, or Blake. Ireland came
perhaps as close as anybody to a full awareness of the history up
to the date of his own performance, and this produced a curious
result. The relative indifference of Blake, or his innocence, is part
of the interest in his contribution to the series. We may call our
brief examination of pictures, in fact, an exercise in the faculty
of vision. We are the first who ever tried to put the pictures together—almost the first, in fact, who would have been interested
in doing so.

All during his career as a man of letters Pope was a notably successful opportunist in the promotion of his own fame and the
projection of the correct public image of himself. To begin with,
he was painted two or three times by his early friend and instructor

Charles Jervas, then, as his fame increased, three times by Sir Godfrey Kneller, and once by Michael Dahl. Within a few years nearly all these paintings had been engraved, not only in large mezzotints but in smaller line cuts, as for the frontispieces of volumes of Pope's *Correspondence* issued piratically by Edmund Curll. There were numerous later and less publicly known images. During the 1730's Pope was repeatedly the subject of drawings, etchings, and oil paintings by his intimate friend the elder Jonathan Richardson, last of the old Baroque school of portraitists, who died a year after Pope, twenty years his elder. On a visit to Prior Park in the winter of 1739–40 he was painted by the Bath society artist William Hoare. He had sat during the *Dunciad Variorum* days to the Flemish sculptor Michael Rysbrack for a bust which apparently he did not like, and about 1738 to the French sculptor Roubiliac for one which it would seem both he and his friends liked exceedingly. From the austere terra cotta were multiplied marble derivations by the hand of Roubiliac himself which became a kind of inner circle and official Roman image of Pope. In 1741 the Swiss medallist J. A. Dassier did a copper profile of Pope which in its own miniature idiom was equally successful. And in 1742, the last serious portrait of Pope, and one of the most ambitious, was painted by the most recent foreign artist of note to arrive in London.

I AND II

According to George Vertue, the Boswellian chronicler of English art in this period, the French court painter Jean Baptiste Van Loo arrived in England in December 1737 and set up in Henrietta Street, Covent Garden, and then in Great Queen Street.[1] By the rapidity of his execution (he managed up to five sittings in a day) and by a technique of slickly finished yet realistic flattery, he soon won a large clientele. A major success was Sir Robert Walpole, who while sitting to Van Loo told him that "if it had not been for an Act of Parliament that prevents foreigners . . . to . . . enjoy places of salary in the government, he would have presented him with the place of King's Painter." This conversation took place shortly after the death in November 1739 of Pope's old friend Charles Jervas, who had held onto the office of court painter since the death of Kneller in 1723, and who was succeeded, somewhat

I. Oil on canvas, 44 × 35½ inches. By J. B. Van Loo, 1742.
W. S. Lewis, Farmington, Connecticut.

ALEXANDER POPE,
Poeta Anglus.
OB: Aº 1744 Ætat: 57

Hanc Imaginem ex ipso Archetypo a *Vanlo* picto 1742 exprefsam
viro *HONORABILI* GULIELMO MURRAY *SOLICITATORI GENERALI* apud quem Deponitur
Humillime D. D. D.

II. MEZZOTINT, 14 × 10 inches (with lettering). By John Faber after J. B. Van Loo, *c.* 1744. *From an impression owned by Professor F. A. Pottle, New Haven, Connecticut.*

preposterously, by another of Pope's friends, the landscape gardener and architect William Kent. A painting by Van Loo which was no doubt typical of his London success but which has most regrettably vanished was a large group portrait of Pope's (and Kent's) Palladian patrons, Lord and Lady Burlington and their two daughters, all in virtuoso poses. Pope seems not to have been overly quick to take advantage of the presence of the new celebrity. Van Loo's portrait of Pope was perhaps one of the last that he did before returning in bad health, during October 1742, to his native Aix-en-Provence, where a few years later he died.

Van Loo actually did two fine oil paintings of Pope, in the same pose and no doubt from the same sitting. One of these was the source of the excellent mezzotint by John Faber, Junior, published apparently not long after Pope's death in 1744. From the lettering of this mezzotint we learn most of what we can securely say about the episode of the painting: that it was indeed painted by Van Loo, in the year 1742, and that it belonged to Pope's friend William Murray, the Solicitor General, later the celebrated Lord Mansfield, lord chief justice of England. This portrait, along with a portrait of Betterton said to have been painted by Pope himself, after Kneller, and a mysterious bust of Pope, remained at Lord Mansfield's home Kenwood, in Hampstead, until about 1922, when it was removed to Scone Palace, the Earl of Mansfield's seat near Perth, where it still is. The second of the two oils painted by Van Loo is a larger canvas with a more elaborate background, of column, drape, and statue. Both are remarkable for their lively realism, joined with formality and firmness. In the second, a close inspection seems to reveal even a hint, at the shoulders, of Pope's deformity, something carefully screened out of all the other approved portraits. This second picture came to public notice first in 1842 at the sale of a collection that had belonged to a grandnephew of Lady Mary Wortley Montagu, the 2nd Earl of Upper Ossory; it was acquired by a nephew of the Earl, the 3rd Marquess of Lansdowne. It remained in the Lansdowne collection until 1930. In 1957 it arrived at its present home, the Museum Arbuteanum of W. S. Lewis at Farmington, Connecticut. Both paintings were well known during the nineteenth century, and both, for reasons which are obscure, were during this period attributed to Jervas.[2]

III

The publishers of Alexander Pope's authorized *Letters* in May 1737, John and Paul Knapton, sons of the lately deceased veteran publisher James Knapton, had two other brothers, George and Charles, both artists. George, a painter and engraver, had been the pupil of Jonathan Richardson in the 1720's, before travels to Italy. He was later the first painter to the Society of Dilettanti. Charles was an engraver who collaborated with the pastel artist and engraver Arthur Pond between 1732 and 1736 to produce a series[3] of 69 or 70 notable engravings after old-master drawings of landscapes in the collections of such connoisseurs as Pope's friends Jonathan Richardson and Dr. Richard Mead. Another venture, in which perhaps all four brothers were engaged, along with Pond and George Vertue, was the series of *Heads of Illustrious Persons of Great Britain,* with biographical notices by Thomas Birch, published in two folio volumes by the Knaptons in 1743 and 1751. The last plate in the collection is Alexander Pope, the third picture in our present exhibit, an oval line engraving surrounded by emblematic adjuncts, "A. Pond pinxit. In the Possession of Mr. Arthur Pond. Impensis J. & P. Knapton Londini. J. Houbraken sculps. Amst. 1747." Vertue is the author of a few engravings in this collection, but he seems to have lost out in a competition with Houbraken to which he alludes in a staccato passage or two in his *Note Books.* Fortunately for our inquiry, he tells us, too, exactly what was the role of the minor painter, capable engraver, and dealer in art supplies for virtuosi, Arthur Pond, in the making of the *Heads.* In the summer of 1737, "Mr. Pond began his circuit in the Country to Noblemens and Gentlemens houses in quest of busines. or to coppy heads in Chiaroscure.—for Knapton's Illustrions to be gravd after."

The Pond-Houbraken picture of Pope, so clearly a reduced, simplified, and reversed copy of the Van Loo type, no doubt was engraved by Houbraken in Holland from an intermediate painting (possibly a pastel) by Pond, which, no doubt too, was returned to England and remained in the "possession of Mr. Arthur Pond." Almost any one of a rather large number of oils and pastels of this type surviving today might be Pond's copy. The image, through Faber's mezzotint and Houbraken's line engraving, became rapidly one of the best known images of Pope. It appeared repeatedly in smaller derivative engravings, some of which bore the name of Van Loo, but a greater number, that of Pond. By the omission of the book under Pope's elbow, the latter group supplied a further hint of their direct debt to Houbraken rather than to Faber. The engraving by Houbraken after Pond, together with another very small and very poor medallion engraving signed by Pond and used on the title pages of editions of Pope's *Essay on Man* put out by Warburton between 1745 and 1751, gave rise apparently to a notion, which appears in the *DNB* article on Pond, that he was the painter of two original likenesses of Pope.

The fancy emblematic devices which surround the Heads of Birch's *Illustrious Persons* were designed, we are told on the title page, by a French engraver then resident in London, Hubert François Bourguignon, called Gravelot. Those for Pope include a medley of classical symbols of art and inspiration surmounting and fortifying at lower right and left the oval containing the portrait. Beneath the portrait, a sun bursting forth in splendor from behind sullen clouds, sheds its rays into a panel having a scene of the nine *Muses* grouped around Apollo, who extends a crown of bays toward an aged Homeric-looking figure as he approaches, supported on either side by youthful escorts, who point forward and spurn back the reaching arms of satyr-like and deformed creatures lying tangled in shadow.

> Still green with Bays each *ancient* Altar stands,
> Above the reach of *Sacrilegious* Hands,
> Secure from *Flames,* from *Envy's* fiercer Rage,
> Destructive *War,* and all-involving *Age.*
> . . . .
> Oh may some Spark of *your* Cœlestial Fire
> The last, the meanest of your Sons inspire.

IV

The team of Francis Hayman and Charles Grignion did their first picture of Pope in the spring of 1747 as a title-page vignette for William Mason's quarto poem *Musaeus: A Monody to the Memory of Mr. Pope.* Here Chaucer, Spenser, and Milton convene in a grotto scene where Pope, a generalized bardic figure in classical robes, falls back on a rustic stone seat and droops his head as he is received into the arms of a goddess of poetic virtue.

But what might that avail? Blind Fate before
Had op'd her shears, to slit his vital thread;
And who may hope gainsay her stern behest?
Then thrice he wav'd the hand, thrice bow'd the head,
And sigh'd his soul to rest.

—*Musaeus*, 1747, p. 20

The picture of Pope is Pope in a sense—or a token of Pope.

For Warburton's octavo edition of Pope's *Works* in nine volumes, 1751, Hayman and Grignion and other artists did a number of conversation pieces showing the speaker of Pope's poems, again a generalized bardic figure, in various transactions illustrative of the poems. In some of these pictures, however, the image of Pope inclines perhaps to resemble a specifiable portrait type, that created by Van Loo and already made so well known by the efforts of Faber, Pond, and Houbraken. In one illustration by Hayman and Grignion, that for the opening of Pope's *Epistle to Arbuthnot* (vol. IV, facing p. 9), the resemblance is unmistakable. Let 1735 be 1742.

> Shut, shut the door, good John! fatigu'd I said,
> Tye up the Knocker, say I'm sick, I'm dead.

v

From the dignity of his elegant study,[4] with *Homer*, manuscripts, pen and ink, oval table and leather-backed chair, or from a writing table set up under lofty architecture and against a noble sculptural background, Pope is transferred by Hayman and Grignion to a setting plainer and more workaday, vexed by intrusions from the outer world of the hacks and libelers. In the next version of the image which we are to notice, the elderly and anxious face of the poet moves back in time to join a friend of his youth, long dead, in the even ruder decor of a coffee house. The aquatint by the "picturesque" engraver Samuel Ireland, father of the better-known William Ireland, the Shakespeare forger, is, in my opinion, indeed a portrait of Pope, or was intended by Ireland as such, but it acquired its degree of resemblance to Pope in a very curious way. Ireland was a Hogarth collector and transformer, who in 1794 published the first volume of a collection of engravings with explanatory text which he called *Graphic Illustrations of Hogarth*.

III. LINE ENGRAVING, 13⅞ × 8½ inches (plate mark). By J. Houbraken, after a painting by Arthur Pond (after Van Loo), 1747. For *The Heads of Illustrious Persons of Great Britain . . . with Their Lives and Characters*, by Thomas Birch, vol. II, 1751.

Plate XVI   Vol. IV. facing p. 9.

F. Hayman inv. et del.   C. Grignion sculp.

Shut, shut the Door, good John! fatigu'd I said
Tye up the Knocker, say I'm sick, I'm dead.

Ep: to Arbuthnot.

IV. LINE ENGRAVING, 5½ × 3½ inches. By Charles Grignion from a drawing by
Francis Hayman. Plate XVI, facing p. 9 of vol. IV of *The Works of Alexander
Pope,* ed. William Warburton, 1751.

Pope

D.ʳ Garth

Hogarth del.ᵗ

S.Ireland fecit

Characters who frequented Button's Coffee-house about the year 1720

V. AQUATINT, 5 × 7⅜ inches. By Samuel Ireland after a drawing by William Hogarth. For Samuel Ireland's *Graphic Illustrations of Hogarth from Pictures, Drawings, and Scarce Prints*, vol. I, 1794.

VI. OIL AND TEMPERA ON CANVAS, 15 × 30½ inches. By William Blake, 1800. *Manchester City Art Gallery.*

Four wash drawings which he owned, and which have long since passed into the collection at the British Museum and are accepted by the modern authorities as genuine works of Hogarth, show a series of coffee-house scenes. "Button's Coffee House," decided Ireland, "about the year 1730," in the lettering of a first state of the engravings, dated 1786. For a second state, which appears in the *Graphic Illustrations* of 1794, he moved the date back to 1720. Ireland thought he could identify six coffee-house characters: Daniel Button himself, Martin Folkes, Addison, Dr. Arbuthnot, a mysterious Count Viviani, Dr. Garth, and Pope. Modern Hogarth scholars reject these identifications, considering the heads to be simply generic Hogarth types. They incline to the view that the roughness of the drawings, exemplified in such odd features as the absence of table legs, shows the work to be early Hogarth. My own concern is with one of the aquatints by Ireland (Plate 4 in the series in his *Graphic Illustrations*), rather than with the drawing that stands behind it. We ought to remark of this drawing, however, that two faces in it do bear at least a curious degree of resemblance to Pope and to his friend Dr. Garth. Garth died in 1719, and the image of Garth in question would be the Kit-Cat portrait by Kneller, widely known of course in the mezzotint by Faber, 1733. But the image of Pope, so far as it is Pope, can only be that of the Van Loo type, popularized by Faber and Houbraken in 1744 and 1747. Thus these two friends come together in a ghostly posthumous sort of approximate or potential resemblance, by prophecy, as it were, in an "early" work by Hogarth (*c.* 1720, the experts might say). Whatever the facts beyond these conjectures, Samuel Ireland was impressed by the juxtaposed resemblances, though not by the chronological oddity. Fortunately he gives us a good clue to the source of his interpretation. "There is a peevishness and anxiety in the lineaments of the face," he observes of the "Pope" figure, "that we find in most of his finished portraits, and which are so strongly characteristic of the man, as to leave no doubt of the identity." Then a little further on he says: "The portrait of Dr. Garth, in conversation with Pope, has some similitude to that introduced into Birch's 'Lives of Illustrious Persons.'" Pope by Houbraken after Pond, as we have seen, is the last portrait in the Knaptons' second volume of Birch's *Heads* in 1751. And Dr. Garth, by Houbraken after Kneller, is the second

from last (only Dr. Samuel Clarke intervening).[5] Ireland's interpretation was plausible enough. No doubt he felt well justified
in strengthening the lines of resemblance in the face of Pope,
bringing out the peevishness and anxiety. He inscribed on his
plate above the two figures "Dr Garth" and "Pope." The authority of the two portraits may be questioned, but scarcely the fact
of their being intended (by Ireland) as portraits, and of their being
in fact (by a blend of intentions, or by intentions superimposed on
accident) something more than merely nominal or token portraits.

VI

The prevalence of the Van Loo image of Pope, whether through
the Houbraken reduction in Birch's *Heads* or through numerous
inferior derivatives, can not be better illustrated than in the painting by William Blake with which I conclude this history. After
Blake had moved to Felpham in Sussex during the late summer of
1800 to work for his new patron, the poet and virtuoso William
Hayley, one of his first commissions was a series of eighteen or
twenty life-sized oil and tempera poets' heads, with symbolic adjuncts, for the library of Hayley's marine villa Turret House.
Within twenty years after Hayley's death in 1820, Turret House
passed out of the possession of his family, and the poets were lost
to sight. When Gilchrist was writing his *Life of Blake*, about 1860,
he knew of five which were in the hands of a London bookseller.
W. M. Rossetti, however, in his Catalogue of Blake's Pictures,
appended in 1863 to Gilchrist's *Life*, was able to report that
eighteen pictures had been reassembled. These came subsequently
to rest in the Manchester City Art Gallery. They have been edited
for the Blake Society in an illustrated volume by Thomas Wright,
1925.
The identification of the heads has been a matter of some
debate, but on the present official view the English poets are
Chaucer, Spenser, Shakespeare, Milton, Dryden, Otway, Pope,
and Cowper. Three of these images could have been derived by
Blake from the gallery in Birch's *Heads*—namely Dryden, Otway,
and Pope. There is no way of proving that he actually consulted
Birch for any one of these common types, but the derivation of
Pope ultimately from Van Loo cannot be in doubt.

Blake's symbolic embellishment of the heads is worthy of close examination. Rossetti in his Catalogue noticed that Cowper was provided with his favorite dog. He noted, too, that one of the two figures that accompany Pope is Eloisa praying in her cell. The other, he thought, would be difficult to identify. Kenneth Povey, in a communication to *Notes and Queries*[6] after Wright's 1925 edition of the *Heads,* was the first, I believe, to point out that this figure represents the subject of Pope's *Elegy to the Memory of an Unfortunate Lady.*

Blake's sympathy for Alexander Pope, we know, was limited. If he did turn to the last plate in Birch's *Heads,* Gravelot's allegory of the bard enjoying safe conduct past the misshapen figures of low-spirited envy must have seemed a contemptible instance of the general Augustan conspiracy against the imagination. Blake's "Imitation of Pope: A Compliment to the Ladies," found in the Rossetti Manuscript, is a striking revelation.

> Wondrous the Gods, more wondrous are the Men.
> More Wondrous Wondrous still the Cock & Hen,
> More Wondrous still the Table, Stool & Chair;
> But Ah! More wondrous still the Charming Fair.

How then would Blake manage to pay a compliment to Pope, on Hayley's assignment?

The smoothly rejuvenated head is framed to the left by branches which bear what are apparently bay leaves, though much elongated. To the right the flame-like curling tongues of a strange plant bear some dark tricorne leaves which are no doubt what Rossetti alludes to in the word "ivy." Thus Blake, in a highly stylized way, continues the tradition of "the poet's bays and critic's ivy" (*Essay on Criticism,* l. 706). (The two foliages had seemed to vie with each other in portraits of Pope by Kneller and Richardson—but I find it difficult to read Blake's painting as an allusion to those portraits, all but unknown in his day.) The whole panel is a soft composition in shades of chrome green and creamy whites and yellows. Even the moon is creamy. A single small point of orange light gleams in the lamp flame that lights the vigil of Eloisa. With this touch of bright paint Blake has picked out one of the most persistently repeated motifs of Pope's passionate poem.

> Ah hopeless, lasting flames! like those that burn
> To light the dead, and warm th'unfruitful urn.
> (ll. 261–2)
>
> I waste the Matin lamp in sighs for thee.
> (l. 267)
>
> In seas of flame my plunging soul is drown'd,
> While Altars blaze, and Angels tremble round.
> (ll. 275–6)
>
> Here, as I watch'd the dying lamps around,
> From yonder shrine I heard a hollow sound.
> (ll. 307–8)
>
> Thither, where sinners may have rest, I go,
> Where flames refin'd in breasts seraphic glow.
> (ll. 319–20)

On the other side of Pope's head, the Unfortunate Lady walks
in moonlight, doubly equipped, with dagger and sword, for both
the manner of speaking (the rhyme word) and the actual sense of
Pope's opening lines—in an Elegy which shares symbols with
Eloisa and like *Eloisa* vibrates in a range of feeling not very alien
to that Blake who sang the contrary states of the human soul.

> What beck'ning ghost, along the moonlight shade
> Invites my steps, and points to yonder glade?
> 'Tis she!—but why that bleeding bosom gor'd,
> Why dimly gleams the visionary sword?
> Oh ever beauteous, ever friendly tell,
> Is it, in heav'n, a crime to love too well?
> (ll. 1–6)

> Children of the future Age
> Reading this indignant page,
> Know that in a former time
> Love! sweet love! was thought a crime.

Professor R. K. Root of Princeton, in his *Poetical Career of
Alexander Pope*, 1938, used as frontispiece a reproduction of an
engraving by George Vertue (from a cavalier-looking portrait of
Pope by Charles Jervas, which today hangs in the Bodleian
Library). The engraving had been used by Pope himself as frontis-

piece to his first collected *Works* in 1717, the volume in which he first gave to the world his *Eloisa to Abelard* and his *Verses to the Memory of an Unfortunate Lady.* In a chapter on Pope's early poetry ("The Maze of Fancy") Professor Root speculated fondly on the "completely romantic" image which would have lingered in our memory and "colored our reading" of the man and the poet had Pope died ten years before he published his *Dunciad.* For William Blake, in the required moment of celebrating Pope, this premature death had scarcely been necessary.

NOTES

1. More precise documentation of all the statements made in this essay will be found in my book on the Portraits of Alexander Pope to be published by the Yale University Press.

2. The close association of the Kenwood portrait with Pope's oil of Betterton, done probably under the tutelage of Jervas, perhaps started the long-persisting mistake. On 22 June 1792 Fanny Burney visited Kenwood and came away reporting that the portrait of Pope was by himself, in the style of Jervas (*Diary & Letters,* ed. Barrett and Dobson, I, 1905, 98–9).

3. Not published as a book, but separately, or in portfolio? This remarkable collection (at the Cottonian Library, Plymouth, and at the British Museum) is described by Henry Hake, "Pond's and Knapton's Imitations of Drawings," *Print Collectors' Quarterly,* IX (1922), 325–49.

4. Or his study as re-created in Van Loo's studio, for the chair, the table, and the inkwell were apparently Van Loo props. Very similar objects appear in his portrait of the actor Owen MacSwinney, and the chair, at least, in a portrait of Lord Hervey.

5. The portraits occupy the same position in the second volume of the second edition, 1752 (copies of 1751 and 1752 at the Library of Harvard University). In a copy of the single-volume edition of 1756 (at the Library of Congress), Garth's portrait comes two places earlier. In William Baynes's edition of 1813, Garth again is second from last (Yale University Library).

6. CLI (24 July 1926), 57–8. Povey's careful observations correct several of Rossetti's identifications and relate the symbolic adjuncts of the pictures to William Hayley's *Essay on Sculpture, Essay on Epic Poetry, Life of Romney,* and *Memoirs of Thomas Alphonso Hayley.*

Johnson's Poetic Fire

FREDERICK W. HILLES

I N a letter that long lay buried among the Boswell papers John Wilkes, not a man from whom we expect praise of Dr. Johnson, declared that what made Johnson superior to his contemporaries was his humor—and his poetry. The admiration Wilkes expressed for Johnson's poetry he shared with his friend Boswell. When suffering from a severe case of melancholia in Holland, young Boswell picked up *The Vanity of Human Wishes,* read it, and in his own words "grew bold." That night he sat down and in verses of his own paid tribute to Johnson's "poetic fire." Neither Wilkes nor Boswell, we may be sure, would have been surprised to learn that Johnson himself, when reading aloud from that poem, "burst into a passion of tears."[1] To them it was a powerful and moving poem.

Johnson's reputation as poet, which has fluctuated during the past two centuries, seems to be high at the present time. Eliot's famous assertion, "I should myself regard Johnson as a major poet by the single testimony of *The Vanity of Human Wishes,*" has been echoed and developed by many a scholar, many a critic, in recent years.[2] Even so, there is still a considerable body of the unpersuaded. Johnson's verse, we are told by a reviewer, is "not that of a poet." "It is conceivable," writes a scholar, "that if Johnson had lived in a different age he might have written emotional poetry of a fairly high quality." And a critic of discrimination has characterized *The Vanity* as "a poem in which the author fails to achieve either of the two effects which Johnson himself declares are inevitably produced by the 'most engaging powers of an author.' Here are certainly no new things to be made familiar; and, to one reader at least, the 'familiar things are not made new.' "[3]

67

The persisting adverse criticisms of *The Vanity,* when assembled and clothed in Johnsonian dress, might read as follows: "In this poem there is no emotion, for there is nothing personal; there is no art, for there is nothing new. Its form is that of a satire, arid, didactic, and therefore disgusting: whatever images it can supply are long ago exhausted; and its inherent pessimism always forces dissatisfaction on the mind." To what extent are these charges true?

No part of the poem has been as severely criticized as the very opening:

> Let observation, with extensive view,
> Survey mankind, from China to Peru.

Among the many mocking paraphrases Tennyson's, an echo of Coleridge's, is the most succinct: "Let observation, with extended observation, observe extensively."[4] Admittedly the first line displays, in Boswell's words, "an inflated Rotundity and Tumified Latinity of Diction."[5] It has, nevertheless, its defenders. "Observation," wrote Saintsbury, "may be either broad and sweeping, or minute and concentrated; Johnson specifies the former kind in the last half of the first line. Observation may be directed to men, to things, &c.; it is to mankind that he wishes it directed, and he says so in the first half of the second. Further, as this is too abstract, he gives the poetic and imaginative touch by filling in the waste atlas with 'China' and 'Peru,' with the porcelain and the pigtails, the llamas and the gold associated with mankind in those countries. And in the name of Logic, and Rhetoric and Poetry into the bargain, 'What for no?' "[6] I have no quarrel with the associations Saintsbury perceived in "China" and "Peru." Johnson was writing when *chinoiserie* was the rage and when Hogarth's poor poet dreamed of gold mines in Peru. But surely the lines insist upon something more important, upon establishing at the outset a point of view. The reader, endowed by the poet with extraordinary far-sightedness, looks eastward all the way to China, where the sun rises. As his gaze follows the path of the sun, he discovers in the remote west, where the sun sets, Peru. Beyond China to the east, beyond Peru to the west, there is nothing but water. Between the two countries lies the inhabited globe. But if we are to observe men so widely separated we must be above the world, looking down.

Only so can our view be as extensive as the poet demands. And what happens when we look down on the world from high altitudes? Even the greatest of men dwindle. We have a new perspective on what we observe; and farsightedness has long been equated with good judgment.

Placing the reader on high to observe the little world of man was a device often employed by Johnson's contemporaries. Goldsmith was to adopt it for his most Johnsonian poem, *The Traveller*, in which the speaker is perched on top of the Alps, whence he examines Italy and France, Holland and England. He has, so to speak, disengaged himself for the moment from his fellow men. Fielding's method of narration, at least in *Joseph Andrews* and *Tom Jones*, is somewhat analogous. In fact this concept is closely bound up with his theory of comedy; we are able to say "what fools these mortals be" only if we hold ourselves aloof as we say it. To be sure *The Vanity* is not comedy, but its clear-eyed view of man's strength and weakness brings it close in mood to comedy. In the early part of the poem the poet invokes the laughing philosopher, but excludes Heraclitus, whom Juvenal had coupled with him. Democritus is called upon to look once more at motley life (motley the costume of the fool) and to do so with "chearful wisdom and instructive mirth." It is in such a spirit that Johnson invites us to regard mankind.

The distinctive character of the opening is at once apparent if we compare it with Dryden's version:

> Look round the Habitable World, how few
> Know their own Good; or knowing it, pursue.

In five words, it would seem, Dryden says what it takes Johnson two lines to say. But Dryden is not expressing Johnson's thought. Johnson prefers to lift us up, and in language that is properly elevated suggests the magnitude of the habitable world. "The poet," said Imlac, must "consider himself as presiding over the thoughts and manners of future generations, as a being superior to time and place." In *The Vanity* Johnson shares that superiority with his readers.

The poem begins with the suggestion of elevation; it ends on a different note. Throughout we have been looking down on the world, endowed, as I have suggested, with farsightedness. Now in the concluding paragraph we are looking up toward the *skies* (a word that appears twice), and making appeals to *heaven* (a word that appears three times). Our wishes *rise*, we *raise* our prayers, our devotion *aspires* toward the abode of One "whose eyes discern afar/The secret ambush of a specious pray'r." In the "eyes" of the poem's close the "extensive view" of its beginning shrinks to a proper humility.

If we were to map what lies between the opening and the close as a surveyor maps the earth's surface, the contour lines would be many and would be very close to each other. The careers of the various individuals introduced characteristically follow an up-and-down, high-low pattern.

> Unnumber'd suppliants croud Preferment's gate,
> Athirst for wealth, and burning to be great;
> Delusive Fortune hears th'incessant call,
> They mount, they shine, evaporate, and fall.
> On ev'ry stage the foes of peace attend,
> Hate dogs their flight, and insult mocks their end.

Johnson's misquotation of this last line, when he introduced it into his Dictionary, is illuminating:

> Hate dogs their *rise*, and insult mocks their *fall*.

The catalogue of individuals begins with Cardinal Wolsey. In a paragraph of twenty-two lines the first ten depict him "in full-blown dignity" rising from a high station to "new heights." The central couplet records the turn of his fortune:

> At length his sov'reign frowns—the train of state
> Mark the keen glance, and watch the sign to hate.

The last ten lines exactly balancing the first, describe the dramatic fall of the Great Man. In the paragraph that immediately follows, this dual pattern is repeated:

> For why did Wolsey near the steeps of fate,
> On weak foundations raise th'enormous weight?
> Why but to sink beneath misfortune's blow,
> With louder ruin to the gulphs below?

With Wolsey's life in mind we perceive the same rise and fall as we read of Swedish Charles, of Xerxes, of the bold Bavarian, and the rosy-lipped maiden. Wherever we turn we note that the ambitious, those who soar only to come crashing down, lack one important virtue—a sense of balance. This concept, though not directly stated, is implied by the way Johnson phrases his account of their careers.

The *dramatis personae* lose their balance, but we readers are not allowed to do so. The poet demands that we face the facts of life with poise, and he himself offers us such poise. This idea he supports and emphasizes throughout by a skillful use of rhetorical devices. It goes without saying that the metrical basis of the poem, the couplet form, lends itself to his purpose. The Augustan couplet naturally expresses stability. It is therefore peculiarly appropriate in this poem. Not only does couplet balance couplet, line balance line, but frequently half-line balances half-line:

> Shuns fancied ills,/ or chases airy good;
> A frame of adamant,/ a soul of fire,
> Perversely grave,/ or positively wrong.

Chiasmus is called on to make these balances more insistent—in the single line:

> The fruit autumnal, and the vernal flow'r;

in the couplet:

> Against your fame with fondness hate combines,
> The rival batters, and the lover mines;

in the passage:

> With fatal heat impetuous courage glows,
> With fatal sweetness elocution flows,
> Impeachment stops the speaker's pow'rful breath,
> And restless fire precipitates on death.

In the last example the leader in battle is equated with the leader in parliament. Their tragic ends are compared, but in the second couplet warrior and orator exchange places: the third line looks to the second, the fourth to the first. The arrangement is double chiastic, for grammatically the third and fourth lines are in opposition, *impeachment* and *death* being the key words. The couplet begins with the one, ends with the other. It is a weighty passage, but one in which the ballast has been so distributed as to enhance in us the feeling of poised acceptance.

More subliminal are the auditory effects. Here is an extreme example:

> Great Xerxes comes to seize the certain prey.

Somewhat simplified, the sounds of the first three syllables are *ray, zer, seez*. The last three accented syllables are an echo in reverse order: *seez, ser, ray*. Perhaps this could be called a chiamus in sound; certainly it harmonizes with the reversals of word-order and interchanges of words in the poem. In this connection a line already quoted is noteworthy: "With chearful wisdom and instructive mirth." One expects to hear that wisdom is instructive and mirth cheerful. The reversal of adjectives creates a diagonal arrangement. Like the diagonals used in building, this arrangement creates a feeling of stability and strength.

A poem may be soundly built, and yet fail to please. *The Vanity*, we are told, lacks freshness: it presents no new things that are made familiar, and what is familiar is not made new. Surely this criticism betrays a lack of sympathy for Augustan poetry. Johnson introduces an eager young student:

> Through all his veins the fever of renown
> Burns from the strong contagion of the gown.

Here the gown is a humble but very real part of the scholar's daily life. It is also much more than that. In its context it becomes an emblem of the academic (and clerical) environment. Love of fame is a disease, a burning fever, a fact that adds point to the important word *contagion,* which here works in a double capacity: we are reminded of its Latin origins. Furthermore, as Boswell was the first to point out, the conjunction of *burns, contagion,* and *gown* calls to mind the fatal tunic that doomed Hercules.[7]

The idea of an eager young student at the beginning of a college year is admittedly not new, but Johnson's treatment is fresh, rich, unforgettable. What oft was thought is here phrased magnificently. The poet wishes the young scholar well.

> Yet should thy soul indulge the gen'rous heat,
> Till captive Science yields her last retreat;
> Should Reason guide thee with her brightest ray,
> And pour on misty Doubt resistless day;
> Should no false Kindness lure to loose delight,
> Nor praise relax, nor Difficulty fright;
> Should tempting Novelty thy cell refrain,
> And Sloth effuse her opiate fumes in vain;
> Should Beauty blunt on fops her fatal dart,
> Nor claim the triumph of a letter'd heart;
> Should no Disease thy torpid veins invade,
> Nor Melancholy's phantoms haunt thy shade;

After this series of personifications that serve the same end as figures in a morality play, after the poet has admitted the possibility of success, in metaphorical language that tends to be polysyllabic, comes a sharp, staccato-like couplet:

> Yet hope not life from grief or danger free,
> Nor think the doom of man revers'd for thee.

The warning is set apart by the use of monosyllables. Then follows a couplet that might serve as epigraph to the poem as a whole:

> Deign on the passing world to turn thine eyes,
> And pause awhile from letters, to be wise.

These are the lines that caused Johnson to burst into tears. Presented in an impersonal manner, they are obviously based on personal experience. Miss Lascelles has reminded us that this is one of the passages that departs sharply from Juvenal.[8]

Those who consider heroic couplets monotonous, written by puling infants swaying about upon rocking horses, might take another look at this passage. Johnson's mastery of his medium is everywhere to be seen. The last line quoted is a good example, in which the weakness of the fourth foot makes us hover over the third and give added stress to the fifth. Originally the line read: "And pause awhile from Learning to be wise." The revision not only does away with an unhappy ambiguity; it forces us to read the line correctly.

Johnson's revisions are almost always improvements. The ending of the opening paragraph of the poem has been quoted above.

Here is its last line, contemplating the death of a young Hotspur, as set down in the manuscript: "And restless enterprise impells to death." The revised line links itself more closely to "fatal heat" three lines earlier; but more important are the connotations of the new verb: "And restless fire precipitates on death." To precipitate, "to throw headlong down," is cognate with precipice, and in this passage conforms to the contours of what is to follow.

"And Sloth's bland Opiates shed their fumes in vain" is not a line that can be read lazily. When he altered it, adding another internal rhyme and ridding it of a cluster of consonants, ("And Sloth effuse her opiate fumes in vain") the poet was making the sound seem an echo to the sense. "Beauties of this kind," he later asserted, "are commonly fancied; and when real are technical and nugatory."[9] No doubt he is right, and yet we cannot overlook the effectiveness of what is merely technical. Compare for example,

> *And his last sighs* reproach the faith of kings

with the marching rhythm of

> For such the steady Romans shook the world

or the desolation hinted at in "Superfluous lags the vet'ran on the stage," a line that was one of Scott's favorites.

Johnson's favorite couplet, we are told, was one which to my ear sounds mediocre. Certainly it is a pale reflection of its counterpart in Juvenal. Concerning the humiliation of Xerxes, the Roman poet asks: "in what plight did he return? Why, in a single ship; on blood-stained waves, the prow slowly forcing her way through waters thick with corpses!"[10]

> sed qualis rediit? nempe una nave, cruentis
> fluctibus ac tarda per densa cadavera prora.

Johnson's version "produces an effect which is farcical, grotesque and horrific all at once":[11]

> A single skiff to speed his flight remains;
> Th'incumber'd oar scarce leaves the dreaded coast
> Through purple billows and a floating host.

Why this should especially appeal to its author—but a Johnsonian phrase is here pat: "the reason of this preference I cannot discover."[12]

As a poet Johnson was no innovator. He was content to write in the idiom of his masters, Dryden and Pope. Nor was he above borrowing from them. "And pour on misty Doubt resistless day" clearly echoes Pope's line: "Truth breaks upon us with resistless day."[13] Other echoes are less clear, and if they are echoes Johnson may have been unconscious of them. One wonders whether when describing the young Oxford scholar ("And Bacon's mansion trembles o'er his head") he had in mind the downfall of learning in *The Dunciad*:

> Rome's gray-hair'd synods damning books unread,
> And Bacon trembling for his brazen head.

Or whether with a similar reverse twist another line from *The Dunciad*, "The mother begg'd the blessing of a rake," could lie behind

> The teeming mother, anxious for her race,
> Begs for each birth the fortune of a face.

When occasionally, to my ears, Johnson strikes a false note, he is, I believe, misled by his masters. Fatal Learning, we are told, led Laud to the block, where he was beheaded; Laud had been forced to lay his head upon the block. The poet's comment on this, "But hear his death, ye Blockheads, hear and sleep," sounds to me off-key.[14] It would have fitted in Dryden's version of Juvenal's poem, because the tone of Dryden's version is one of contempt. Dryden's style is racy; Johnson with rare exceptions, as the one just quoted, favors the stateliness, the declamatory grandeur, that he admired in Juvenal. In other words, although he is in the tradition of Dryden and Pope, he takes their language and makes of it something that is his own.

In *The Vanity* Johnson expresses his fundamental philosophy of life, what has been termed Christian stoicism. Because he strikes out against blind optimism some of his readers assert that the theme is a pessimistic one, that it represents a negative approach to life. Surely this is a misreading of the poem. In his *First Anniversary* (*An Anatomie of the World*) Donne addresses himself to the young Mirandas who are impressed with their brave new world:

> This new world may be safer, being told
> The dangers and diseases of the old:

> For with due temper men do then forgoe
> Or covet things, when they their true worth know.

Here *temper* means mental balance. If we are warned of dangers ahead, we shall be better poised to meet them. *The Vanity* is Johnson's *Anatomie of the World*. "The business of life," he was to write in Idler 72, "is to go forwards; he who sees evil in prospect meets it in his way."

Johnson, always hostile to tempting novelty, is saying nothing new; he is saying what the wisest men in and out of Christendom have said before him; but he is saying it in a Johnsonian way, is giving a new look to familiar things. His poem reflects his clear vision, betrays his strong feelings (controlled though they are), and displays brilliantly the eloquence, the powerful manner of expression for which he was to become famous. When properly read his lines "sing in the mind."[15]

NOTES

1. Wilkes to Boswell, 1 October 1785, in Yale Library; *Boswell in Holland,* ed. F. A. Pottle, McGraw-Hill, 1951, pp. 202–3; Mrs. Piozzi's *Anecdotes,* 1786, p. 50.

2. Notably by F. R. Leavis (essays reprinted in *The Common Pursuit* and *Revaluation*) and by A. R. Humphreys in the fourth volume of *Pelican Guide to English Literature.* For Eliot's comment see *Sewanee Review,* Winter 1946.

3. Raymond Mortimer in *The New Statesman and Nation,* 1 November 1941; C. H. Conley in *The Reader's Johnson,* American Book Co., 1940, p. 71; Joseph Wood Krutch, *Samuel Johnson,* Henry Holt & Co., 1944, p. 65.

4. Quoted in *Poems of Samuel Johnson,* eds. Nichol Smith & McAdam, Clarendon Press, 1941, p. 30n. Unless otherwise noted, all quotations from *The Vanity* are from this edition.

5. Journal for 21 September 1762, in Yale Library.

6. George Saintsbury, *A History of Criticism,* 1904, iii.223.

7. Johnson toyed with the idea of having the gown become in the student's imagination the costume of a bishop. At this point in the manuscript is a couplet that he deleted: "On Isis banks he wares [i.e., wears], from noise withdrawn/ In sober State th'imaginary Lawn." The manuscript is in the Hyde collection, Somerville, New Jersey. I am indebted to Mr. and Mrs. Hyde for permission to quote from it.

8. *New Light on Dr. Johnson,* ed. F. W. Hilles, Yale University Press, 1959, pp. 50–51.

9. *Lives of the Poets,* ed. Hill, Clarendon Press, 1905, iii.232.

10. Translation by G. G. Ramsay in Loeb Classical Library.

11. Donald Davie, *Purity of Diction in English Verse,* New York, 1953, p. 50.

12. *Lives of the Poets,* ed. Hill, iii.250.

13. *Essay on Criticism,* l. 212. The lines quoted from *The Dunciad* below are III 104 and IV 286.

14. In the manuscript Johnson underlined the first syllable of *Blockheads.*

15. Benét's phrase. See C. A. Fenton, *Stephen Vincent Benét,* Yale University Press, 1958, p. 304.

The Mighty Moral of *Irene*

MARSHALL WAINGROW

> Our daring Bard with Spirit unconfin'd,
> Spreads wide the mighty Moral for Mankind.
> Learn here how Heav'n supports the virtuous Mind,
> Daring, tho' calm; and vigorous, tho' resign'd.
> Learn here what Anguish racks the guilty Breast,
> In Pow'r dependent, in Success deprest.
> Learn here that Peace from Innocence must flow;
> All else is empty Sound, and idle Show.

So the Prologue to Johnson's tragedy serves up the moral—a moral affirmed in the concluding lines of the play, which are spoken by the Turkish Aga, Mustapha:

> So sure the Fall of Greatness rais'd on Crimes,
> So fix'd the Justice of all-conscious Heaven.
> > When haughty Guilt exults with impious Joy,
> > Mistake shall blast, or Accident destroy;
> > Weak Man with erring Rage may throw the Dart,
> > But Heav'n shall guide it to the guilty Heart.

The "haughty Guilt" and "impious Joy" are of course Irene's. "Mistake" and "Accident" refer to the false accusation of her treachery against Mahomet, the failure of communication of her message to Mahomet, and her consequent murder. The last two lines approve the paradox that divine justice employs human injustice: in this instance, Irene, though innocent of the crime as charged, is guilty of a greater, and the punishment intended for the one serves for the other. Mustapha may be supposed to speak with Johnson's own voice here as elsewhere in the play. This Turk is every inch a Greek, and from the beginning he has avowed the principles of virtue and religion:

79

MUSTAPHA.

Those pow'rful Tyrants of the Female Breast
Fear and Ambition, urge her to Compliance;
Dress'd in each Charm of gay Magnificence,
Alluring Grandeur courts her to his Arms,
Religion calls her from the wish'd Embrace,
Paints future Joys, and points to distant Glories.

CALI.

Soon will th' unequal Contest be decided,
Prospects obscur'd by Distance faintly strike.
Each Pleasure brightens at its near Approach,
And every Danger shocks with double Horror.

MUSTAPHA.

How shall I scorn the beautiful Apostate!
How will the bright ASPASIA shine above her!

CALI.

Should she, for Proselytes are always zealous,
With pious Warmth receive our Prophet's Law—

MUSTAPHA.

Heav'n will contemn the mercenary Fervour,
Which Love of Greatness, not of Truth, inflames.

(I, iii, 12–27)

Yet, Mustapha's declamation at the end of the play is from a dramatic standpoint curiously detached. He has just, taking his cue from Mahomet, upbraided and threatened the servant Murza for his failure to deliver Irene's self-exonerating report of the Greek plot to escape. At this point Mustapha appears more troubled by the loss of Irene than by any deficiencies in her character:

Behold the Model of consummate Beauty,
Torn from the mourning Earth by thy Neglect.

More significantly, Mustapha's moral is delivered in the presence of Mahomet, who, crushed by a sense of Irene's innocence and his own guilt ("murder'd Innocence that call'd on me"), must hearken to these words with stunned incomprehension, unless he sees their primary application to himself. And such a meaning Mustapha surely would not, and indeed dare not, intend. We may more plausibly imagine an unattending Mahomet wrapped up in his own woes and a front-and-center Mustapha addressing the audience for the purpose of sending them home with an unequivocal message.

In the scant notice that the tragedy has received since its own day, there is nothing to suggest that the moral has been apprehended differently from the viewpoint expressed in the Prologue and in Mustapha's last speech. Nichol Smith, in his introduction to the play (*The Poems of Samuel Johnson*, eds. David Nichol Smith and Edward L. McAdam, Oxford, 1941), puts the case thus:

Irene is represented not as a helpless victim of the Sultan's passion [as in Johnson's main, if not sole, source, Richard Knolles' *The Generall Historie of the Turkes*], but as the mistress of her fate. Will she sacrifice her creed to attain security and power? She has freedom to decide. . . . In order that this freedom may be emphasized, she is placed in contrast to Aspasia, a new character for whom there is no warrant in the original story. Aspasia is the voice of clear and unflinching virtue; and she is rewarded with her escape from slavery in company with the lover of her choice. But Irene yields, and pays the penalty. She hesitates, complies, and half repents, then is betrayed and ordered to die. Her death is exhibited by Johnson as the punishment of her weakness. . . .

Virtue is rewarded, vice (or weakness) punished; the cause of poetical justice has been conventionally served. Bertrand Bronson, in his comprehensive study of the play (*Johnson Agonistes & Other Essays*, Cambridge, 1946), while arguing that Johnson's high seriousness as a Christian poet raises poetical justice above any critical canon or concession to an audience, still regrets the sacrifice of dramatic complication and interest (possibilities available to Johnson in his sources) to the exigencies of a clear-cut ideology. He does not read the moral of the play any differently from his predecessors; he is simply much more astute in recognizing directions which it might have taken. The purpose of the present essay is to show that *Irene,* for all that it appears a loaded debate with a foregone conclusion, dramatically uncovers a complicated action and a complicated moral, and that it possesses the special kind of interest that arises from the flight of a free poetic imagination over a confined area of belief.

Boswell reports a saying of Johnson's: " 'Yes, Sir; there are two objects of curiosity,—the Christian world, and the Mahometan world. All the rest may be considered as barbarous' " (10 Apr.

1783). Whether we regard this as a narrow or as a broad-minded observation, we recognize in it a willingness to give a great rival religion its due—a willingness which appears on a superficial view of *Irene* to be annulled by the dramatic necessity of eliminating a real preference on the part of the heroine for one religion over the other. Though the faith of the Mahometan world of Johnson's play is nowhere decried, it is the power and the glory (and the present security) of that world which tempt Irene to apostasy. Opinion on both sides is against her, as it could hardly be if her choice were a choice of religions. All agree that Irene's motives are suspect: they are either base or falsely rationalized. Her desertion of the Greeks is an affront to their religion, but her submission to the Turks is no obeisance to theirs.

Having taken pains to eliminate a religious conflict, Johnson opposes the two national characters. But even here we can find no simple opposition. Virtue and vice are fairly evenly divided on both sides. The Greek fall is attributed by the Greek leaders themselves to pride, venality, corruption, and complacence. " 'Twas Vice that shook our Nerves, 'twas Vice, LEONTIUS,/ That froze our Veins, and wither'd all our Powers," says Demetrius (I, i, 56–7). The loss of Greece at the beginning of the play is linked with the loss of Aspasia, who plainly represents Virtue Itself. Her disappearance is both an incidental consequence and a symbolic expression of the failure of the Greek character; her recovery and eventual liberation look forward to the restoration of that character. But virtue is not the exclusive possession of the Greeks. To Mustapha's adulation of Aspasia may be added the gratitude of the Turkish captain Caraza toward Demetrius, and the acquiescence of his fellow-captain Hasan in the proposal to spare Demetrius in the general punishment of the plotters. The quality of mercy shown on this occasion by the two Turkish captains is felt again by them in the scene in which Irene is carried off to her death (V, ix), but it is constrained by their sovereign's command. Most notably, however, it is the idealism of Cali Bassa, the First Vizier, that bespeaks the Turkish virtue, though he is placed in the classically ambiguous role of practising treason against tyranny. The most (perhaps only) famous speech of the play is his—that which deplores the Turkish State and envisions an ideal body politic:

Such are the Woes when arbitrary Pow'r,
And lawless Passion, hold the Sword of Justice.
If there be any Land, as Fame reports,
Where common Laws restrain the Prince and Subject,
A happy Land, where circulating Pow'r
Flows through each Member of th' embodied State,
Sure, not unconscious of the mighty Blessing,
Her grateful Sons shine bright with ev'ry Virtue;
Untainted with the Lust of Innovation,
Sure all unite to hold her League of Rule
Unbroken as the sacred Chain of Nature,
That links the jarring Elements in Peace.

(I, ii, 53–64)

If the ideal indicts Turkish politics, it also admonishes the Greek
State (as it was meant to admonish Johnson's England). Still, Cali's
admiration for the Greek character is strong, and he answers the
threats of Abdalla, his Turkish fellow-conspirator, against Demetrius with the appeal: "O spare the gallant *Greek*, in him we lose /
The Politician's Arts, and Heroe's Flame" (IV, iv, 26–7).

A basic ideological agreement, love of liberty, makes possible the
political alliance which moves the plot. Turkish tyranny provokes
a rebellion which allies itself with the enemy, before and after that
enemy's defeat. The Greek hope depends upon an act of treason,
which is virtuous insofar as it involves resistance to slavery (I, i,
111–14). The motives of Cali Bassa are clearly mixed: he may be a
sincere champion of his country's freedom, but he is also concerned
to save his own skin from the mounting hostility of Mahomet.
But if Cali is not troubled by a moral qualm, Aspasia is. She puts
the question to Demetrius directly: "Will not the Patriot share
the Traytor's Danger? / Oh could thy Hand unaided free thy Country, / Nor mingled Guilt pollute the sacred Cause!" (IV, i, 62–4).
"Mingled guilt" can only mean guilt by association; the Greeks
are under no moral obligation to submit to the tyrant's yoke.
Aspasia would have the sacred cause of freedom served only by the
pure in heart; yet the action of the play shows this to be impossible.
Demetrius is forced to give an equivocal answer: "Permitted oft,
though not inspir'd by Heav'n, / Successful Treasons punish impious Kings."

The moral issue thus settles on the question of ends and means.

Aspasia staunchly defends the purist position in her "instruction" of Irene (III, viii):

> Be virtuous Ends pursued by virtuous Means,
> Nor think th' Intention sanctifies the Deed:
> That Maxim publish'd in an impious Age,
> Would loose the wild Enthusiast to destroy,
> And fix the fierce Usurper's bloody Title.
> Then Bigotry might send her Slaves to War,
> And bid Success become the Test of Truth;
> Unpitying Massacre might waste the World,
> And Persecution boast the Call of Heav'n.

Mustapha's final speech, quoted above, attempts in the manner of Demetrius to elucidate the relation of heavenly ends and earthly means. As Bronson has observed, the passage as it appears in Johnson's draft is more dangerously explicit: ". . . Man . . ."

> By vice or passion driv'n
> Is but the executioner of Heavn—or Instrument
> When erring Fury throws the random dart
> Heav'n turns its point upon the guilty Heart
> Behold Irene—oe'rthrown
> By crimes abhord, and treasons not her own
> Eternal justice thus her doom decreed
> And in the traytress bad th' Apostate bleed.
>
> (*Poems*, p. 345.)

But however it is put, heavenly justice is viewed as proceeding opportunistically, and can man himself do differently? One may avoid committing an evil, but how can one avoid gaining from the evil committed by another? Moral profiteering may be technically innocent ("permitted oft"), but at the least it is embarrassing to the spirit of moral condemnation. It is hardly sporting, we may say, for the winner to insult the loser who has collaborated in his victory.

Here then is the problem of Aspasia, which is to say Johnson's problem. As his moral exemplar, Aspasia carries the burden of right thinking and right acting throughout the play (shared of course by Demetrius, her moral counterpart). Her principal task, after defending her own virtue, is to confront Irene with the error of her ways. In Aspasia's view, Irene may not justify apostasy (the means) by an intention to use her new-gained power benevolently (the end). It is this doctrine that stirs Aspasia's moral uneasiness over the Greek alliance with Cali, who perhaps no more than Irene can justify treason (the means) by an intention to use his new-gained power benevolently (the end). If there is danger that the Greek cause shall be polluted by complicity in the evil means of the Turk, there is comparable danger to anyone who shall profit from Irene's vicious acts. Does anyone so profit?

Plainly Aspasia does. When Cali recounts for Demetrius Mahomet's blandishments and threats in wooing Aspasia, Demetrius asks: "Say, did a Voice from Heav'n restrain the Tyrant?/Did interposing Angels guard her from him?" (I, ii, 115–16). The question is in the same vein as the earlier speculations between Demetrius and Leontius over the fate of the lost Aspasia. Leontius imagines: "Some virgin Martyr,/Perhaps, enamour'd of resembling Virtue,/With gentle Hand restrain'd the Streams of Life,/And snatch'd her timely from her Country's Fate" (I, i, 95–8). But Cali's reply discloses no voice from heaven, no interposing angel, no virgin martyr:

> Just in the moment of impending Fate,
> Another Plund'rer brought the bright IRENE;
> Of equal Beauty, but of softer Mien,
> Fear in her Eye, Submission on her Tongue,
> Her mournful Charms attracted his Regards,
> Disarm'd his Rage, and in repeated Visits
> Gain'd all his Heart; at length his eager Love
> To her transferr'd the Offer of a Crown.
>
> (I, ii, 117–24)

If Irene is not a true virgin martyr, she is at least an effectual surrogate, and it is her submission that ultimately enables the liberation of all the Greek prisoners as well as Aspasia. In Mahomet's temptation of Irene, she is promised "the Power to bless—IRENE's Nod/Shall break the Fetters of the groaning Christian" (II, vii, 75–6). Taking Mahomet at his word, we may suppose the Greek escape unnecessary; but the action of the play precludes the fulfillment of the promise. Irene never gains the security with which to exercise her power to bless; indeed, she stoops to condemn her fellow Greeks in order to promote this security. That the attempt fails is of course no credit to her; yet this very failure brings

Irene to a recognition of her guilt and loss, and a state of mind in which she can, if not bless, at least join in the blessings of heaven upon the virtuous:

> Go, happy Bark,
> Thy sacred Freight shall still the raging Main.
> To guide thy Passage shall th' aerial Spirits
> Fill all the starry Lamps with double Blaze;
> Th' applauding Sky shall pour forth all its Beams
> To grace the Triumph of victorious Virtue;
> While I, not yet familiar to my Crimes,
> Recoil from Thought, and shudder at myself.
>
> (V, vi, 5–12)

The salvation of the Greeks and the damnation of Irene are bound up together. The chances for success in the planned escape are improved by the negligence of Mahomet, who, though warned by Mustapha of the potential danger, vacillates and finally delegates his power. First:

> Suspend his [Cali Bassa's] Sentence—Empire and IRENE
> Claim my divided Soul.   This Wretch unworthy
> To mix with nobler Cares, I'll throw aside
> For idle Hours, and crush him at my Leisure.

Then:

> The strong Emotions of my troubled Soul
> Allow no Pause for Art or for Contrivance;
> And dark Perplexity distracts my Counsels.
> Do thou resolve: For see, IRENE comes!
> At her Approach each ruder Gust of Thought
> Sinks like the sighing of a Tempest spent,
> And Gales of softer Passion fan my bosom.
>
> (II, vi, 68–71, 87–93)

The plot to murder Mahomet in Irene's chamber is both a practical and a moral stratagem, practical because there his guard is down and moral because there pleasure may be punished by virtue. The suspicion that falls on Irene rises from circumstantial evidence alone: Cali, under torture, had revealed the place appointed for the murder, and Mahomet, already persuaded that Irene had yielded to him out of ambition rather than love (IV, vii), is prepared to believe the worst. Mahomet's mind, taking a Greek turn, equates her supposed shortcomings as a mistress with her apostasy (IV, vii), and her apostasy with her supposed treason (V, vii, 21). But the Graeco-Christian point of view suppresses the facts of the case, and Irene is doomed to bear the guilt of others. The servant Murza, who carries the testimony of Irene's innocence, is intercepted by the Greeks, who by this act both save themselves and unknowingly condemn Irene.

If, according to Aspasia's teaching, evil means cannot be justified by good intentions, neither, we suppose, can evil intentions be justified by a happy outcome. In short, Irene can no more be credited with the liberation of the Greeks by an action calculated to thwart their escape than she can be credited with saving Aspasia from the clutches of Mahomet by submitting herself. Yet the fact remains that it is Irene in both instances who diverts and distracts the Turkish threat; she is the sacrificial victim, however willing in the one instance and unwilling in the other, who enables the preservation of "Freedom, Glory, Greece, and Love" (I, ii, 146).

"All political measures are in some degree right and wrong at the same time; to benefit some they very frequently bear hard upon others." So says Johnson in one of his Parliamentary Debates, written (April 1742) after he had completed his tragedy. *Irene* appears to argue a double moral standard, one for politics and one for personal virtue, but in effect the action of the play enmeshes the two moralities. The central debate, between Aspasia and Irene (III, viii), is one-sided and decisive in Aspasia's favor only if we wrench it out of the play into the realm of abstract moral thought. The key speech is Aspasia's exhortation (ll. 26–35):

> Reflect that Life and Death, affecting Sounds,
> Are only varied Modes of endless Being;
> Reflect that Life, like ev'ry other Blessing,
> Derives its Value from its Use alone;
> Not for itself but for a nobler End
> Th' Eternal gave it, and that End is Virtue.
> When inconsistent with a greater Good,
> Reason commands to cast the less away;
> Thus Life, with loss of Wealth, is well preserv'd,
> And Virtue cheaply sav'd with loss of Life.

Ironically, Irene, as the action evolves, betters Aspasia's instruction. The value of Irene's life is proved by its use; it does not, it turns out, serve herself but the nobler end of Greek virtue. Being the lesser good, it is reasonably cast away. The difference of course is that her martyrdom is that of the sinner rather than the saint; yet the "end" is the same. Mahomet had promised her the role of saviour of the Christians, as we have seen. She now asks Aspasia: "Shall I not wish to chear afflicted Kings/And plan the Happiness of mourning Millions?" (67–8). "Dream not of Pow'r thou never can'st attain" is Aspasia's reply. Yet, in an unexpected way, this power is given to Irene.

Aspasia in this passage is pleading the cause of enlightened self-interest, and is concerned only with that virtue which is personal. Irene from her position cannot plead the same cause and therefore necessarily resorts to the common weal for her justification. The two together comprise the whole Greek conception of virtue; separately they represent antagonistic forces. Aspasia is pure but passive (that is, feminine) virtue, Irene impure but active (that is, masculine) virtue—a contrast explored by the characters themselves in their debate (ll. 36–50):

IRENE.

If built on settled Thought, this Constancy
Not idly flutters on a boastful Tongue,
Why, when Destruction rag'd around our Walls,
Why fled this haughty Heroine from the Battle?
Why then did not this warlike Amazon
Mix in the War, and shine among the Heroes?

ASPASIA.

Heav'n, when its Hand pour'd Softness on our Limbs
Unfit for Toil, and polish'd into Weakness,
Made passive Fortitude the Praise of Woman:
Our only Arms are Innocence and Meekness.
Not then with raving Cries I fill'd the City,
But while DEMETRIUS, dear lamented Name!
Pour'd Storms of Fire upon our fierce Invaders,
Implor'd th' eternal Power to shield my Country,
With silent Sorrows, and with calm Devotion.

Aspasia's kind of virtue may inspire the cause of freedom, but it is helpless by itself to achieve freedom because it is that part of the Greek character that refuses to "mix."

The same opposition of virtues is stated by Mahomet in answer to Cali's request that he be permitted to go on a pilgrimage to their Prophet's tomb:

CALI.
This Pilgrimage our Lawgiver ordain'd—

MAHOMET.
For those who could not please by nobler Service.—
Our warlike Prophet loves an active Faith,
The holy Flame of enterprizing Virtue,
Mocks the dull Vows of Solitude and Penance,
And scorns the lazy Hermit's cheap Devotion;
Shine thou distinguish'd by superior Merit,
With wonted Zeal pursue the Task of War,
Till every Nation reverence the *Koran,*
And ev'ry Suppliant lift his Eyes to *Mecca.*
(I, v, 23–32)

That the argument is put in terms of Turkish goals does not alter the fact that it represents an important part of the Greek ideal as well.

If Demetrius needs Aspasia for inspiration, she in turn needs him to activate her virtue. Irene (in a significant departure from some earlier versions of the story) acts out her part without a protector. To Bronson's argument that the abandoning of a love interest for Irene keeps the lines of the religious issue clear at the expense of making the heroine uninteresting, I would reply that it is the heroine's very detachment from the temptation to love that lends her distinction, in the play's terms. All the principal characters but Cali Bassa and Irene are bound by love, or lust. In the case of Aspasia and Demetrius, though a potential conflict between love and patriotism is sketched, love is affirmed as a virtuous passion. Yet love, or lust, produces treachery in the character of Abdalla, and Aspasia acknowledges her guilt for having been the object of temptation:

> Oh curs'd ASPASIA,
> Born to compleat the Ruin of her Country;
>
> (V, iii, 10–11)

Demetrius is quick to clear her of this guilt, but Aspasia's own doubts have a claim to consideration.

Cali, like Irene, is invulnerable to personal love. He assures Mahomet that his age demands "Desires more pure, and other Cares than Love" (I, v, 7–8), and significantly it is he who is commissioned to guard Irene. Mahomet's sexual jealousy is ironically misplaced: nobody can get to Irene, not even himself. In his despondent soliloquy lamenting his empty successes (IV, vii), Mahomet yokes Cali and Irene together:

> His Fav'rite faithless, and his Mistress base.

Wherefore base?

> Ambition only gave her to my Arms,
> By Reason not convinc'd, nor won by Love.

Paradoxically, Irene's guilt, as construed by Mahomet, reveals a basic innocence: she has not capitulated to the Turk; on the contrary, he has capitulated to her:

> Ambition was her Crime, but meaner Folly
> Dooms me to loath at once, and doat on Falshood,
> And idolize th' Apostate I contemn.

In the wooing scene (II, vii) Mahomet, having failed to persuade Irene of "Love's Joys," appeals to the nobility of her nature—to the power for doing good that his throne will confer. If this is the ambition that gave her to his arms, then her innocence is enhanced. But it is plain that Irene's motives are mixed: self-preservation makes her yield, and love of humanity makes her yielding morally presentable. In the ironic outcome Irene fails in the primary motive and succeeds in the incidental one.

Johnson wrote in the preface to his translation of Lobo's *Abyssinia,* what he often expressed elsewhere: "wherever human nature is to be found, there is a mixture of vice and virtue, a contest of passion and reason." So defined, human nature in Johnson's tragedy is to be found, if anywhere, in the divided minds of Cali

Bassa and, especially, Irene. In the last act, when asked by Demetrius to make her choice once and for all, Irene hesitates:

Stay—in this dubious Twilight of Conviction,
The Gleams of Reason, and the Clouds of Passion,
Irradiate and obscure my Breast by Turns;
(V, v, 43–5)

Is her doubt genuine, or is this a delaying tactic to thwart the Greek escape? The following lines may seem so far-fetched as to support the latter reading:

Stay but a Moment, and prevailing Truth
Will spread resistless Light upon my Soul.

Yet one cannot be sure. The more thoroughly mixed the motives, the harder to separate. At various points in the action, both Cali and Irene appear open to the charge of hypocrisy, but what seems like mere duplicity to a detached outside view may more adequately reflect a genuine dubiety in the involved self. Furthermore, these individual mixtures of vice and virtue, passion and reason, which are Cali and Irene, are also paradigms of the ideological issues which make up the substance of this most ideological of dramas. The characters' vices—Cali's treason and Irene's apostasy—combine in an unholy alliance to move the plot to its holy conclusion. That this conclusion is both consistent with their own nobler aspirations and yet destructive of themselves gives the tragedy its point and interest.

This essay means to offer the suggestion that the heroine of *Irene* is Irene. Johnson the moralist, for all his devout acceptance of the absolute imperatives of the Christian religion, is constant in his study of human nature and its capacities. A characteristically tolerant view is stated in *Rambler* No. 14 (5 May 1750): "It is the condition of our present state to see more than we can attain; the exactest vigilance and caution can never maintain a single day of unmingled innocence, much less can the utmost efforts of incorporated mind reach the summits of speculative virtue." Johnson's appeal, and cogency, as a moralist depend very largely on his perception of the intimacies existing between virtue and vice, even while his practical utilitarian bent disposes him to untangle them. In any case, neither the perfection of virtue nor the perfection of vice constitutes for him a reality sufficient to command his attention for long. In *Rambler* No. 70 (17 November 1750) he sketches a three-fold division of men in "the moral world":

There are some whose principles are so firmly fixed, whose conviction is so constantly present to their minds, and who have raised in themselves such ardent wishes for the approbation of God, and the happiness with which he has promised to reward obedience and perseverance, that they rise above all other cares and considerations, and uniformly examine every action and desire, by comparing it with the divine commands. There are others in a kind of equipoise between good and ill; who are moved on the one part by riches or pleasure, by the gratifications of passion and the delights of sense; and, on the other, by laws of which they own the obligation, and rewards of which they believe the reality, and whom a very small addition of weight turns either way. The third class consists of beings immersed in pleasure, or abandoned to passion, without any desire of higher good, or any effort to extend their thoughts beyond immediate and gross satisfactions.

The second class is so much the most numerous, that it may be considered as comprising the whole body of mankind. Those of the last are not very many, and those of the first are very few; and neither the one nor the other fall much under the consideration of the moralist, whose precepts are intended chiefly for those who are endeavouring to go forward up the steeps of virtue, not for those who have already reached the summit, or those who are resolved to stay for ever in their present situation.

Aspasia is plainly a heroine of the first class, Irene of the second. If the latter's struggle up the steeps of virtue appears deficient in ardor, the former's secure position upon the summit appears deficient in human interest. Yet, though the zeal of the moralist may tend to dull the reader's sense of the reality of the moral world, the art of the dramatist moves to awaken it. The prevalence of Johnson's imagination has endangered the mighty moral, but has saved something of the tragedy.

The Poetry of Collins Reconsidered*

A. S. P. WOODHOUSE

IT is no mere metaphor, to say that Collins inhabited two literary worlds. They really existed in and after the 1740's, abutting on each other and sometimes overlapping, but also sometimes seeming far apart.

One was a palpable continuation from the earlier part of the century when Addison, Swift and Pope dominated the higher reaches of literature, and Grub Sheet struggled and starved. It is too familiar to require description. In criticism the standards of Neoclassicism still prevailed, though somewhat liberalized by the last great classical influence to become operative, that of Longinus, by Addison's quiet extending of frontiers, and by the emergence of the school of Taste. In poetry the influence of Pope was at its zenith, and it was now pre-eminently that "every warbler had his tune by heart." Satire, varied by panegyric, and (as Joseph Warton complained) the moral essay in verse, were the prevailing kinds of poetry: evidence at once of the dominance of conceptual thinking therein, and of the close adherence of the Neoclassical imagination to the actual and the immediate, to the life and interests of the age. Poetry was quite as much a social as an individual utterance: rationality and common (that is, generally accepted) sense were at a

* Over thirty years ago I published an essay ("Collins and the Creative Imagination: a Study in the Background of his *Odes*," *Studies in English by Members of University College, Toronto,* 1931) which broke some new ground, but now appears to me in several respects defective. It left out essential elements in the background of Collins's poetry; it did not penetrate sufficiently deeply into his artistry, and it failed to differentiate him decisively from his nearest relatives, the Wartons. I am glad of this opportunity to take a fresh (and, I trust, more mature) look at the poetry itself in relation to its background, and at Collins's poetic development.

premium, and restraint was a necessary virtue (except perhaps in the irregular Pindaric, where it was more to spur than curb the Muse's steed—if one could). The lyric impulse was at one of its lowest ebbs in the whole history of poetry. All this, of course, is common knowledge; but it is well to remind ourselves of the literary world into which Collins stepped when he quitted Oxford, the world of which Johnson (still in early middle age) was to be the last and greatest representative.

By its surface glamour, hiding the dark under-side of struggle and disappointment, Collins was evidently attracted. The *Epistle to Hanmer* and two or three of the recently discovered *Drafts*[1] may be read as his attempt to gain a footing there; and later projects bear some relation to it. The proposed "Friendly Examiner"[2] stands in the direct line of the periodical essay; the plan for a "History of the Revival of Learning" sorts well enough with a hope of turning his studies to something that the age would comprehend and read (had not Pope looked back to the era of Leo X as the harbinger of his own Augustan age?); and the *Poetics,* on which Collins thought to write an extended commentary, was the foundation, more honoured than understood, of Neoclassical doctrine. Nor, despite the monetary motive, should we regard them as mere concessions to necessity: there is evidence that as projects they awakened his interest. It seems quite possible also that to an optimistic spirit the publication of the *Persian Eclogues,* the *Hanmer* and even the *Odes* might seem to offer a chance of taking the town by storm with poems different, but not too different, from those to which it was accustomed: in the *Seasons* Thomson had succeeded in just such an effort. The *Hanmer* hews closest to the line: it belongs at once to the traditions of panegyric and of the critical essay in verse, and its interests, literary and dramatic, remind us of Dryden's, while its form, whether of structure (with the historical survey from ancient to modern times, like that of the concluding section of the *Essay on Criticism*)[3] or of the couplet, more resembles Pope's. The *Eclogues* might be construed as an attempt to revivify the pastoral tradition with new subjects and settings appealing to the continuing interest in the East; and of the *Odes,* several had a contemporary and patriotic reference, *Liberty* was on a current theme, the *Manners* was not altogether remote in subject and attitude from the poetry of the day, and the *Passions* takes its place in the tradition of the ode for music coming down from Dryden through Addison and Pope.

For his place in this literary world Collins had the requisite "polite learning" (his Greek was perhaps superfluous). We may even, though with reserve, associate the sense of form and of decorum, which marks all his best poems, with its standards, and refuse to write off the traditional elements in his poetry as total loss. But that is as far as we can go.

The second literary world was in many ways quite different, and of course less clearly defined because it was, so to speak, the world of tomorrow, whose values had still to be assembled and co-ordinated. We may call it the world of Pre-romanticism and admit at once that it is not very easy to describe, partly because much that was in the air came to full and concrete expression only after the close of Collins's brief career, partly because in Collins himself such expression was always controlled by his artistry, by his constant sense that he was writing a poem and not merely indulging in an effusion of sentiment or essaying a daring opinion. Since the Wartons, whose interests and enthusiasms he shared, were of coarser temper and less subject to beneficent restraints, they will let us some way into the sentiments of the Pre-romantic world.[4]

Of these Joseph Warton's early poem, *The Enthusiast* (1744), is indeed a miscellany. The title is an echo from Shaftesbury's most romantic effusion, *The Moralists,* and to the same source ultimately may be traced the sentimental naturalism of:

> O taste corrupt! that luxury and pomp,
> In specious names of polish'd manners veil'd,
> Should proudly banish Nature's simple charms!
> All beauteous Nature! . . .
>   O where shall I begin thy praise,
> Where turn th'ecstatic eye!

"Dark forests," the "ever-gushing brooks," "the distant water-fall"

> Now faintly heard, now swelling with the breeze,
> The sound of pastoral reed from hazel-bower,
> The choral birds: . . .
>   all, all conspire

> To raise, to soothe, to harmonize the mind,
> To lift on wings of praise, to the great Sire
> Of being and of beauty.

This note had already been taken up from Shaftesbury by Thomson and other Pre-romantic poets, and is not deeply characteristic of the Wartons, but thence it is an easy step to the antithesis of nature and art, which is much more so:

> Can Kent design like Nature? . . .
> Can the great artist, though with taste supreme
> Endu'd, one beauty to this Eden add?
>
> . . . .
>
> What are the lays of artful Addison,
> Coldly correct, to Shakespear's warblings wild?
> Whom on the winding Avon's willow'd banks
> Fair Fancy found. . . .[5]

Primitivism, of which this is one variety, is widespread among the Pre-romantics, and gets its record in *The Enthusiast* in yet another form. In a long passage commencing "Happy the first of men," Warton (as he tells us in a footnote) paraphrases Lucretius 5.922–1008. What he does not tell us is that he suppresses all the harsher aspects of the Roman poet's account. The result is a perfect example of what Lovejoy distinguishes as "soft primitivism"—the exalting of a life spontaneous, carefree, and voluptuous, which has nothing to do with austere virtue.[6]

By the time he has got this far the truth has dawned on the reader that what the Enthusiast seeks is the widest range of vicarious emotional experiences, and this could be confirmed by young Thomas Warton's *Pleasures of Melancholy* (where the nascent "gothic" and "graveyard" schools join forces) and will be by Joseph's *Ode to Fancy*. In *The Enthusiast* we are carried to the ancient oak, dear to "bards of old [i.e., the druids] Fair Nature's friends"; to wide prospects where "From the grove's bosom spires emerge" and the "ruin'd tops" of "Gothic battlements"; to the environs of the city, there to hear by night its mingled noises and among them "knells Full slowly tolling"; to the storm-beat coast "when wild tempests swallow up the plains":

at such solemn hours,
Demons and goblins through the dark air shriek,
While Hecat, with her black-brow'd sisters nine,
Rides o'er the earth, and scatters woes and death.
Then too, they say, in drear Egyptian wilds
The lion and the tiger prowl for prey
With roarings loud! . . .
                        while the hollow echoing vaults
Of pyramids increase the deathful sounds.

But a quieter scene is obviously required, if the Enthusiast is to
invoke "Old Midnight's sister, Contemplation" to purge his ears,
that he

                        may hear the rolling planets' song,
And tuneful turning spheres: if this be barr'd,
The little Fays that dance in neighbouring dales
Sipping the night-dew, while they laugh and love,
Shall charm [him] with aërial notes.

What he encounters, instead, is Virtue, attended by Philosophy,
Solitude, and Wisdom, who announces their imminent departure
from a land grown corrupt, which prompts the Enthusiast also to
flee to "western climes;" "the isles of Innocence,"

Where Happiness and Quiet sit enthron'd,
With simple Indian swains, that [he] may hunt
The boar and tiger through savannahs wild . . .[7]

One would apologise for dwelling at this length on such patently
bad poetry did it not, in fact, cast a strong light on the background of Collins while at the same time pointing the difference
between him and the Wartons, for the elements which appear in
them in crude and easily recognizable form are in him subdued to
the purpose of a unified artistic effect. It might indeed have served
almost as well, to go directly to that brilliant parody of the school,
the anonymous *Ode to Horror*, which plainly alludes to Collins
and brackets him securely with the Wartons, and of course implies
what was, or was imagined to be, the judgment of the Augustan
on the vagaries of the Pre-romantic:

O goddess of the gloomy scene,
Of shadowy shapes thou black-brow'd queen . . .
O thou, that lov'st at eve to seek
The pensive-pacing pilgrim meek,
And sett'st before his shudd'ring eyes
Strange forms and fiends of giant size . . .
Dark pow'r, whose magic might prevails
O'er hermit-rock and fairy-vales;
O goddess erst by Spenser view'd,
What time th' enchanter vile embru'd
His hands in Florimel's pure heart
Till loos'd by steel-clad Britomart . . .
O haste thee, mild Miltonic maid,
From yonder yew's sequester'd shade;
More bright than all the fabled Nine,
Teach me to breathe the solemn line!
O bid my well-rang'd numbers rise
Pervious to none but Attic eyes;
O give the strain that madness moves,
Till every starting sense approves! . . .
O thou whom wand'ring Warton saw,
Amaz'd with more than youthful awe,
As by the pale moon's glimm'ring gleam
He mus'd his *melancholy* theme:
O curfeu-loving goddess haste!
O waft me to some Scythian waste,
Where, in Gothic solitude,
Mid prospects most sublimely rude,
Beneath a rough rock's gloomy chasm,
Thy sister sits, Enthusiasm;
Let me with her in magic trance,
Hold most delirious dalliance,
Till, I thy pensive votary,
Horror, look madly wild like thee;
Until I gain true transport's shore . . .
At length recline the fainting head
In Druid-dream dissolv'd and dead.[8]

In addition to some common stock of imagery in their poetry,
there were in Collins critical interests shared with Joseph Warton,
to which further reference must be made, and antiquarian and

"gothic" reading shared with Thomas.[9] He had, of course, other contacts besides the Wartons: with the school of Taste through Cooper and Harris; with Scottish popular lore through John Home; above all, through James Thomson, with the whole range of romantic sentiment revealed in *The Seasons* and *The Castle of Indolence*. Nor must we forget the effects of selection and development from ideas already given currency by the Neoclassical writers themselves, such, for example, as Addison's on the imagination, or the well-worn dictum *ut pictura poesis* (which took on new life when read in relation to Spenser and Milton, and perhaps to allegorical painting). For the two worlds, as we have said, abutted and sometimes overlapped. But here "selection" and "development" are the operative words; and we should not overlook Collins's role as an initiator, or the quality of imagination on which Johnson put his finger:

He had employed his mind chiefly upon works of fiction and subjects of fancy and . . . was eminently delighted with those flights of imagination which pass the bounds of Nature, and to which the mind is reconciled only by *a passive acquiescence in popular traditions* . . . . This idea which he had formed of excellence led him to *Oriental fictions* and *allegorical imagery*, and perhaps while he was intent upon *description*, he did not sufficiently cultivate sentiment.[10]

This does not say everything one needs to know of Collins's imagination but it isolates an essential quality; and while it fails to recognize the subtler features of his work, and notably the descriptive and symbolic mode of conveying "sentiment," it finds a place for each of the main divisions of that work, including the *Ode on the Popular Superstitions* (which Johnson had never seen) and gives us a valuable clue to Collins's poetic development.

II

About the *Persian Eclogues* Johnson was probably nearer right than was Collins himself when in later years he dismissed them as his "Irish Eclogues." Though their Orientation seems to have been based on little more than a schoolboy's reading of Salmon's *Modern History*,[11] this opened up a new scene for his imagination and indirectly for the pastoral poem.[12] There is, however, a second innovation in the *Persian Eclogues* which the remote and exotic setting is made to subserve. Retaining and exploiting, in Eclogues I and III, the idyllic note characteristic of pastoral, Collins, in II and IV, sets against it in deliberate contrast the privation and horror of the desert and the ravages of war,[13] thus attempting to extend the range of emotional experience as he was later to do, with success, in his Odes. Adherence to the conventions of the eclogue sets severe limits to realism: the fleeing shepherds pause to address each other in set speeches, and Hassan soliloquizes on his situation in formal phrase; but some vividness of imagination breaks through:

> At that dead hour the silent asp shall creep,
> If aught of rest I find, upon my sleep:
> Or some swoln serpent twist his scales around,
> And wake to anguish with a burning wound.

It is plain, however, that Collins has not here found his true medium. The first phase in his development is abortive because the lines chosen offered so few possibilities,[14] as is the last because he did not live to develop whatever possibilities the new line may have offered. It is the middle phase, represented by the *Odes on Several Descriptive and Allegoric Subjects,* that deserves close attention.

III

Though the plan for joint publication with Joseph Warton was abandoned, it was through no disagreement in principle, and one may safely infer that Warton's "Advertisement" would have introduced Collins's Odes as well as his own. It deplores the current dominance of "didactic Poetry alone, and Essays on moral Subjects," declares "Imagination and Invention to be the chief Faculties of a Poet," and, significantly, links the terms "fanciful" (i.e., imaginative) and "descriptive": this in anticipation of Warton's position in his *Essay on Pope,* with its insistence that "a clear head and accurate understanding are not enough to make a Poet," who requires "a creative and glowing imagination." With these views Collins would have agreed,[15] though he prefers to state his principles in the poems themselves.

The Ode on the *Poetical Character* is allegorical in a stricter sense than the other Odes and admits of quite precise interpretation.[16]

The strophe (1–22) develops the image, derived from Spenser's *Faerie Queene*,[17] of the magic girdle which only the chaste could wear, and applies it, by way of analogy, to the "cest of amplest Pow'r" bestowed on Fancy and in her gift alone:

> Young *Fancy* thus, to me Divinest Name,
>> To whom, prepar'd and bath'd in Heav'n,
>> The Cest of amplest Pow'r is giv'n,
>> To few the God-like Gift assigns,
>> To gird their blest prophetic Loins,
> And gaze her Visions wild, and feel unmix'd her Flame.
>
> (17–22.)

The Cest, then, symbolizes the power of poetic imagination.

The mesode first narrates (23–50) the weaving of the Cest on the day of creation. Here one must be careful to understand the structure of the passage aright. Lines 25–40 tell, first directly (25–8), then figuratively (29–40), how God "call'd with Thought to Birth" the whole created world: he did so by an exercise of the Divine Imagination, personified by the poet as "the lov'd *Enthusiast*," Fancy.

> The Band, as Fairy Legends say,
> Was wove on that creating Day,
> When He, who call'd with Thought to Birth
> Yon tented Sky, this laughing Earth,
> And drest with Springs, and Forests tall,
> And pour'd the Main engirting all:
> Long by the lov'd *Enthusiast* woo'd,
> Himself in some Diviner Mood,
> Retiring, sate with her alone,
> And plac'd her on his Saphire Throne,
> The whiles, the vaulted Shrine around,
> Seraphic Wires were heard to sound,
> Now sublimest Triumph swelling,
> Now on Love and Mercy dwelling,
> And she, from out the veiling Cloud,
> Breath'd her magic Notes aloud:
> And Thou, Thou rich-hair'd Youth of Morn,
> And all thy subject Life was born!

The "rich-hair'd Youth of Morn" is the sun (the "bright-hair'd Sun" of the *Ode to Evening*); its "subject Life" is all the living things dependent on its rays: the couplet thus returns to the idea of lines 25–8, and sums up and concludes the account of how God created all things by "Thought," that is, by an exercise of the Divine Imagination.[18] Only then (41), by a sudden transition, characteristic of the Pindaric ode, do we learn that coincident with the act of creation has been the weaving of the magic girdle, "the sainted growing Woof," and are called on to transfer our attention back to it: to note the absence of the "dang'rous Passions" and the presence at once of "Ecstatic *Wonder*" and, significantly, of "*Truth*," of "the shad'wy Tribes of *Mind*" (the personified qualities of which Collins's Odes are all compact) and "the bright uncounted *Pow'rs*" whose dwelling is Heaven (perhaps such beneficent influences as the Mercy and Peace of the Odes; perhaps, rather, the angelic powers of Milton's epic, to which the antistrophe will turn) (41–50). But before the mesode concludes, it reverts to the final lines of the strophe where we are told that Fancy "To few the God-like Gift assigns" (20):

> Where is the Bard, whose Soul can now
> Its high presuming Hopes avow?
> Where He who thinks, with Rapture blind,
> This hallow'd Work for Him designed?
>
> (51–4.)

This becomes the burden, or part of the burden, of the antistrophe (55–76). It starts with a memory of Milton's Paradise, ideal but inaccessible, to which Collins adds his own romantic touches—

> Of rude Access, of Prospect wild,
> Where, tangled round the jealous Steep,
> Strange Shades o'erbrow the Valleys deep,
> And holy *Genii* guard the Rock,
> Its Gloomes embrown, its Springs unlock—

there in an "Eden, like his own" within sound of the music of the spheres, is the accustomed Oak (from *Il Penseroso*) and hanging on it "that ancient Trump" (imported from Childe Roland's or some other romance) which the great poet is to sound:

> Thither oft his Glory greeting,
> From *Waller's* Myrtle Shades retreating,
> With many a Vow from Hope's aspiring Tongue,

My trembling Feet his guiding Steps pursue;
In vain—such Bliss to One alone
Of all the Sons of Soul was known
And Heav'n, and *Fancy,* kindred Pow'rs,
Have now o'erturn'd th' inspiring Bow'rs,
Or curtain'd close such Scene from ev'ry future View.

The poem, which starts with Spenser, ends with Milton; and Collins's discipleship, like the Wartons' of Spenser and Shakespeare, entails a repudiation of the Neoclassical—in them of Addison or Pope, in him of its admired precursor, Waller. There is no escaping the note of personal frustration in Collins (unlike the robust self-assertiveness of the Wartons), but the frustration is in part laid to the credit of an unpoetic age, which he recognizes as such, in anticipation of Blake's *To the Muses* and of Gray's complaint (in his *Stanzas* to Bentley):

But not to one in this benighted age
Is that diviner inspiration giv'n,
That burns in Shakespeare's or in Milton's page,
The pomp and prodigality of Heav'n.

This is significant of course; but more significant is the ideal of poetry and its basis in a theory of "creative imagination." Whatever the state of poetry in Collins's day, "Heav'n and Fancy" are, as the mesode has boldly asserted, "kindred Pow'rs."

The ideas that meet in this phrase have a long and complicated history, and one that does not end with Collins. To avoid, or at least to limit, the danger of distortion, we may remind ourselves of two facts: (1) that antecedent to its place in poetic theory, imagination was recognized (from Aristotle's *De Anima* onward) as having its role in the formation of knowledge, while it operated in due subordination to reason; but (2) that if this subordination were not maintained, it was thought of as an errant faculty, allied with the passions, and productive of falsehood: a view fostered by both Plato and the Stoics, and widely assumed in the eighteenth century, as witnessed not only by Johnson's famous dictum, "All predominance of fancy over reason is a degree of insanity," but in the marked distrust of the imagination manifested by Shaftesbury— which establishes it as a factor in the immediate background of

Collins and a barrier to the whole-hearted commitment, which he surmounted.

Because the *Poetics* defined poetry as an imitation of nature, and Aristotle had not drawn on his own theory of imagination to explain the process, Neoclassicism developed its conception of poetry with little reference to that faculty. When a place was found for imagination, as it was by Hobbes, that place was subordinate; and despite his important study of the psychology of imagination, he could give succinct statement to the Neoclassical view, "Judgment begets the strength and structure, and Fancy begets the ornaments of a Poem," and could add (with Spenser and the romances in view), "Beyond the actual works of nature a Poet may go; but beyond the conceived possibility of nature, never."[19]

From this position, however, Bacon had already departed by assigning poetry wholly to the imagination and at the same time divesting it of its connection with nature and truth: poetry, or "feigned history," "may at pleasure join that which nature hath severed and sever that which nature hath joined," and by presenting "a more exact goodness, a more ample greatness, and a more absolute variety," give "some shadow of satisfaction to the mind of man in those points where the nature of things doth deny it." Poetry, then, is pure fiction—is, indeed, as Bacon says, "play"; and this conclusion is in no way negated by his assertion that poetry may minister to "morality" and "magnanimity" as well as to "delectation," or that "it was ever thought to have some participation of divineness" because it submits "the shows of things to the desires of the mind, whereas reason doth buckle and bow the mind to the nature of things."[20] Here, plainly is the basis of one romantic theory of poetry, which is content to divorce romance from reality.

When Addison, by his *Spectator* papers on the "Pleasures of the Imagination," brought the term into more common critical use, what he did, in effect, was to combine with Bacon's theory of poetry Hobbes's psychology of the imagination. All the data are supplied by the sense of sight. The primary process is to form ideas (i.e., images) of objects in their presence. The secondary process is to reproduce the images "called up into our Memories or formed into agreeable Visions of Things . . . either Absent or Fictitious." For imagination has the power of "altering and compounding those Images . . . into all the varieties of Picture and Vision," so that "by this Faculty a Man in a Dungeon is capable of entertaining himself with Scenes and Landskips more beautiful than any that can be found in the whole Compass of Nature." "Because the Imagination can fancy to it self Things more Great, Strange or Beautiful[21] than the Eye ever saw and is still sensible of some Defect in what it his seen . . . it is the part of Poet to humour the Imagination . . . by mending and perfecting Nature where he describes a Reality, and by adding greater beauties than are put together in Nature where he describes a Fiction." In "the Fairy Way of Writing" (Dryden's phrase), under which Addison groups fairies, demons, and departed spirits, and with which he closely associates "another sort of Imaginary Beings," the personified passions, virtues and vices, the poet, working "altogether out of his own Invention," "quite loses sight of Nature and entertains his Reader's Imagination with Characters and Actions of such Persons as have . . . no Existence but what he bestows on them." "These Descriptions raise a pleasing kind of Horror in the Mind of the Reader and amuse his Imagination with . . . Strangeness and Novelty. . . ." We are "delighted and surprised when we are led, as it were, into a new Creation." For imagination "has something in it like Creation: it bestows a kind of Existence and draws up to the Reader's View several objects which are not to be found in Being."[22]

From Addison, rather from his sources, the Pre-romantics derived their theory of poetry and the role of imagination therein. His emphasis on visual effects, fortifying the traditional association of poetry and painting, pointed on to the outpouring of descriptive verse which marks the latter two-thirds of the century. It has its importance for Collins, as has also Addison's assumption that personifications are visual forms conceived in the imagination, and his grouping of them with the creatures of popular superstition. But our present concern is with Addison's idea of creative imagination[23] and its limitations. It is evident that for the Wartons Bacon's view of poetry as imaginative fiction and Hobbes's theory of the imagination's compounding power, as these are combined by Addison, exhaust the meaning of the oft-repeated phrase *creative imagination*. If there were any doubt of this, it would be set at rest by Joseph Warton's *Ode to Fancy;* for he, like Collins, gave his view poetic expression, and it soon appears that the difference is not one of quality alone.

Calling on Fancy to preside over his "artless songs," he describes her as a "nymph with loosely-flowing hair," her waist "with myrtle-girdle bound," her "brows with Indian feathers crown'd," and bearing "An all-commanding magic wand/Of power to bid fresh gardens blow/Midst chearless Lapland's barren snow," or to reveal "the vast various landscape." She is a "lover of the desert," and he prays her to lead him "Where Nature seems to sit alone/Majestic on a craggy throne," and at last to her "unknown sequester'd cell":

> Then lay me by the haunted stream,
> Rapt in some wild, poetic dream,
> In converse while methinks I rove
> With Spenser through a fairy grove;
> Till, suddenly awoke, I hear
> Strange whisper'd music in my ear,
> And my glad soul in bliss is drown'd
> By the sweetly-soothing sound!

Next Fancy is to lead him "Where Joy and white-robed Peace resort," and Echo listens to the shepherd's song. Or (in violent contrast):

> in her fiery car,
> Transports me to the thickest war,
> There whirls me o'er the hills of slain,
> Where Tumult and Destruction reign;
> Where, mad with pain, the wounded steed
> Tramples the dying and the dead;
> Where giant Terror stalks around,
> With sullen joy surveys the ground,
> And, pointing to th' ensanguin'd field,
> Shakes his dreadful Gorgon-shield!

Thence from "this horrid scene" to others of "visionary" (and amatory) "bliss"; and finally (after a rapid glance at the four personified Seasons, and a vow to write only at the bidding of Fancy, the "warm, enthusiastic maid") to the tomb of Shakespeare, where Fancy is besought to

Animate some chosen swain,
Who, fill'd with unexhausted fire,
May boldly smite the sounding lyre,
Who with some new, unequall'd song,
May rise above the rhyming throng,
O'er all our list'ning passions reign,
O'erwhelm our souls with joy and pain:
With terror shake, with pity move,
Rouse with revenge, or melt with love . . .
Like lightning, let his mighty verse
The bosom's inmost foldings pierce;
With native beauties win applause,
Beyond cold critics' studied laws;
O let each Muse's fame increase,
O bid Britannia rival Greece.[24]

The verses are replete with echoes—some of them from or to Collins. But nowhere does Warton go beyond the Addisonian formula or require of Fancy—that is, of creative imagination—anything more than a series of fictitious scenes and, through them, an increased range of vicarious emotional experience. That this is also an element in Collins may be readily admitted. He would gaze on Fancy's "Visions wild, and feel unmix'd her Flame," as he certainly does in the *Ode to Liberty,* and in the *Ode to Fear,* where his prayer, in reference to Shakespeare, is, "Teach me but once like him to feel," while in the *Ode to Pity* there is the phrase, "In Dreams of Passion melt away." But for Collins creative imagination means more than this.

Truth is present at the weaving of the magic girdle, as well as Wonder. The poet is not only creative but "prophetic" (as Sidney said). And how, unless the creatures of the poet's imagination were in some sort true could "Heaven and Fancy" be "kindred Powers"? Or how could Collins imply, by structure and symbol, that the poet's creation was a finite counterpart of God's? One need not infer that he has thought the problem through, as Coleridge was later to do.[25] It is at most an intuition based on a steady conviction of the dignity of poetry and on scattered hints, which can, however, perhaps be collected. First, there was the assumption in Renaissance and Neoclassical criticism that poetry, as an imitation of nature, was based on truth—an assumption which no one who set

so high a value on poetry as did Collins, would willingly surrender
unless there were something to put in its place. Secondly, again
coming down from the Renaissance, and sometimes there attached
to the conception of imitation as implying idealization, there was
the image of the poet as a creator, found, for example, in Scaliger,
Sidney, Cowley, and Shaftesbury. But it was not in general referred
specifically to the imagination.[26] There is, however, at least one
exception. In an unco-ordinated catalogue of theories about poetry
Puttenham writes: "A poet is as much as to say a maker. . . .
Such as (by way of resemblance and reverently) we may say of
God; who without travell to his divine imagination made all the
world of nought. . . ."[27] This comes within measurable distance of
Collins's perception and was perhaps enough to give him the
initial hint. As to its development Mrs. Barbauld seems to have
been on the right track when she observes that his notion was
probably "that true poetry, being a representation of nature, must
have its archetype in those ideas of the Supreme Mind which originally gave birth to nature."[28] Certainly his treatment of his
favourite abstractions is entirely consonant with a conviction that
they represent archetypal ideas, laid up, like the "beauteous
Model" of the Temple of Liberty, in a sort of Platonic heaven.[29]
A further hint for this line of thought could have come to Collins
from Dryden's *Parallel of Poetry and Painting*, where he quotes
(as "not unpleasing at least to such as are conversant with the
philosophy of Plato") the Italian critic, Bellori, to the following
effect: God, contemplating "his own excellencies," drew from
thence "those first forms which are called ideas," after which he
produced "that wonderful contexture of created beings." But
everything sublunary is subject to decay; "for which reason the
artful painter and sculptor, imitating the Divine Maker, form to
themselves, as well as they are able, a model of the superior
beauties." This model becomes the object which the artist imitates,
and, "being animated by the imagination, breathes life into the
image."[30]

IV

The *Poetical Character* is not the only ode to turn on critical
ideas, on the sources of power in poetry. The *Ode to Simplicity*,

which immediately precedes it, is a sort of companion piece, as Collins subtly suggests by describing Simplicity as the parent of Fancy and the sister of Truth.

Simplicity is also an idea with a history.[31] When Addison emphasized it as a cardinal virtue, he was not introducing a new principle, but at most recalling Neoclassicism to its true allegiance. He invokes "that natural way of writing, that beautiful simplicity, which we so much admire in the compositions of the Ancients" and condemns those who depart from it as "Goths in poetry who, like those in architecture, not being able to come up to the beautiful simplicity of the Greeks and Romans, have endeavoured to supply its place with all the extravagances of an irregular fancy."[32] There is here no suggestion of the primitive: simplicity is the mark of art, not of artlessness. He would agree with Shaftesbury, who speaks of the height of Greek civilization as the time when "in all the principal works of *Ingenuity* and *Art*, Simplicity and Nature began chiefly to be sought."[33] We must not be deceived by the words *nature* and *natural*, as common a court of appeal in the Neoclassicists as in the Romantics, but with a shift of meaning in the latter, which the ambivalence of the terms invited.

In the *Ode to Simplicity*, the central reference is likewise to Athens and Sophocles (and not even to Homer, whose more primitive character was coming to be recognized),[34] but we reach them by way of the "Mountains wild," where, taught by Nature, Simplicity nursed in Fancy "the Pow'rs of Song"; and if there is no opposition of nature to art, there is to "the Wealth of Art."

> Thou, who with Hermit Heart
> Disdain'st the Wealth of Art,
> And Gauds, and pageant Weeds, and trailing Pall: [35]
> But com'st a decent Maid
> In *Attic* Robe array'd,
> O chaste unboastful Nymph, to Thee I call.
> By all the honey'd Store
> On *Hybla's* Thymy Shore,
> By all her Blooms, and mingled Murmurs dear,
> By her whose Love-lorn Woe
> In Ev'ning Musings slow
> Sooth'd, sweetly, sad *Electra's* Poet's Ear.

Though it briefly recognizes the bearing of simplicity on both theme and structure, tone in this poem is more important than ideas: it is itself an essay in simplicity. As it began with nature, so it ends, and on a pastoral note—

> Where oft my Reed might sound
> To Maids and Shepherds round,
> And all thy Sons, O *Nature,* learn my Tale.

This is the note Collins attempted in the early songs and would achieve in the *Ode on the Death of Thomson.* Neoclassicism, in its effort to mediate between two conflicting ideals, had decided that (as Pope phrased it in the *Preface to Homer*) "simplicity is a mean between rusticity and refinement"; but in fact the scale tipped heavily in favour of refinement. Collins does something to restore the balance.[36]

Considered as companion pieces, *Simplicity* and the *Poetical Character* suggest a distinction of some interest: the stanzaic odes are quieter and less assertive, more classic in their restraint; the bolder experiments in thought and feeling and the "gothic" notes are confined to the Pindarics. This is borne out by the pair with which the volume opens, the *Odes to Pity* and *to Fear.* They, likewise, have some literary reference as dealing with the passions essential to tragedy though with closer affinity, perhaps, to sentimental drama than to Aristotle.

Pity is invoked as the personified impulse to comfort and relieve distress, and in the name of Euripides (the "master of the tender passions," as Collins explains in a note).

> By *Pella's* Bard, a magic Name,
> By all the Griefs his Thought could frame,
> Receive my humble Rite:
> Long, *Pity,* let the Nations view
> Thy sky-worn Robes of tend'rest Blue,
> And Eyes of dewy Light.

Then, with the question (half wistful),

> But wherefore need I wander wide
> To old *Illisus'* distant Side,
> Deserted Stream and mute?

the poet turns to his favourite Otway, who sang "with Youth's soft Notes unspoil'd by Art," and finally to conceiving, "by Fancy's Aid," a Temple to Pity,[37] where, as in *Hanmer,* "Picture's Toils" are to illustrate "each disastrous Tale" of the tragic poets.[38] The allusion to Truth here seems somewhat perfunctory: the real object is to "raise a wild Enthusiast Heat/In all who view the Shrine," where the poet himself may "In Dreams of Passion melt away."

The Pindaric *Ode to Fear* is a dream of passion, that seems better to deserve the epithet "Enthusiast."

> Thou, to whom the World unknown
> With all its shadowy Shapes is shown;
> Who see'st appall'd th' unreal Scene,
> While Fancy lifts the Veil between:
>   Ah *Fear!* Ah frantic *Fear!*
>   I see, I see Thee near. . . .
> For Lo what *Monsters* in thy Train appear!
> *Danger,* whose Limbs of Giant-Mold
> What mortal Eye can fix'd behold?
> Who stalks his Round, an hideous Form,
> Howling amidst the Midnight Storm,
> Or throws him on the ridgy Steep
> Of some loose hanging Rock to sleep:
> And with him thousand Phantoms join'd,
> Who prompt to Deeds accurs'd the Mind:
> And those, the Fiends, who near allied,
> O'er Nature's Wounds, and Wrecks preside;[39]
> Whilst *Vengeance,* in the lurid Air,
> Lifts her red Arm, expos'd and bare. . . .

Then an allusion to Greek tragedy leads on to the Epode (so called) devoted to that subject, with only a passing allusion to the courage of Aeschylus at Marathon,[40] and all the rest given to Sophocles. (There are links with the *Ode to Simplicity* by a reference to Hybla, and with the *Ode to Pity:* "Tho' gentle *Pity* claim her mingled Part/Yet all the Thunders of the Scene are thine," i.e., *Fear's.*) The Antistrophe asks where, now that Greek tragedy is gone beyond recall, Fear will take up her stand: "Say, wilt thou shroud in haunted Cell/Where gloomy *Rape* and *Murder* dwell," or listen to the cries of drowning seamen?[41] For his part the poet will "read the Visions old" and, lest Fear meet his "blasted View,/ Hold each strange Tale devoutly true";[42] and so, surprisingly enough, on to the superstitions of St. Mark's eve, but not, be it noted, without a faint self-depreciating smile—the only one in Collins:

> Ne'er be I found by Thee o'eraw'd
> In that thrice-hallow'd Eve abroad,
> When Ghosts, as Cottage-Maids believe,
> Their pebbled Beds permitted leave,
> And *Gobblins* haunt from Fire, or Fen,
> Or Mine, or Flood, the Walks of Men![43]

Then finally to Shakespeare, and the prayer:

> By all that from thy Prophet broke,
> In thy Divine Emotions spoke:
> Hither again thy Fury deal,
> Teach me but once like Him to feel:
> His *Cypress Wreath* my Meed decree,
> And I, O *Fear,* will dwell with *Thee!*

If this conclusion, and that of the *Ode to Pity,* suggest a desire to ascend from lyric to the higher forms of poetry, the succeeding pair (*Simplicity* and the *Poetical Character*) renounce it. More likely, however, the conclusions are primarily structural, and without much significance beyond the contexts in which they occur. What is of greater interest to observe is how the *Ode to Pity* brings Collins into the current of nascent sentimentalism, and the *Ode to Fear* into that of "gothic" romance, but how, at the same time, out of materials that demonstrate his affinity with the Wartons, and leave him open to the satire of the *Ode to Horror,* he is able to produce genuine poetry, including those vivid pictorial effects which are one of his most striking characteristics.

v

It is essential to recognize that in Collins's *Odes on Several Descriptive and Allegoric Subjects,* the two terms are in apposition: the "allegoric" is the "descriptive." Or to state the relation more precisely, the personified qualities which form the subjects of his odes, or which are repeatedly involved in them, are treated descriptively, and whatever else of description the poems contain is devoted to providing the setting for these *personae* or to reinforcing their symbolic and emotional effect.[44]

Descriptive poetry in the eighteenth century divides, it will be agreed, into two main streams: that of the *ethical-descriptive poem*, stemming from *The Seasons* and pointing on to *The Prelude;* and that of the *descriptive lyric,* which again subdivides into the *allegorical ode,* stemming in part from Milton's Companion Pieces, and reaching its full articulation in Collins and its final triumph in Keats's *To Autumn,* and the *direct lyric* of nature as it is at last established by Wordsworth.[45] In their development they respond to certain common influences noticed below, but they differ radically in mode. As is natural, the long descriptive poem proceeds by amplification, with room for philosophic reflection; the lyric, by allusion and the evocation of mood. But our concern is with Collins and his background.

There was, of course, the tradition, already mentioned, of the parallel of poetry and painting, given peculiar sanction by Horace's phrase, *ut pictura poesis;* and while it tended to become one of those fossillized commonplaces to which Neoclassicism seemed prone, it had some effect on poetry and criticism even before Addison's emphasis on the visual powers of the imagination, and more thereafter. To go no further afield than Pope, striking visual effects are not wanting, and some of these include personification. But one may doubt whether the effect of personification was usually thought of as primarily visual. It was one of the recognized figures of speech and calculated to appeal directly to the emotions —a fact of almost equal importance with its visual potentialities, in considering the background of Collins; for in his effects he unites the two. Blackmore, to take a single example, writes of "the Art of touching the Soul and agitating the Passions by bold and warm Images, Interrogations, Apostrophes, Prosopopeia's, . . . and other pathetick Forms of Diction."[46] Since the emotional effect of words was currently assumed to depend on their power to call up visual images (till Burke called the assumption in question), personification naturally shared this characteristic with other figures of speech; but one rarely finds it so extensively exploited as in the following example from Savage's long poem, *The Wanderer* (1729), which combines personification and a "prospect," to produce a sort of set piece:

The Bee hums wanton in yon Jess'mine Bower,
And circling settles, and despoils the Flower.
Melodious there the plumy Songsters meet,
And call charm'd *Echo* from her arch'd retreat.
Neat polish'd Mansions rise in Prospect gay;
Time-batter'd Tow'rs frown awful in Decay;
The Sun plays glitt'ring on the Rocks and Spires,
And the Lawn lightens with reflected Fires.
   Here *Mirth,* and *Fancy's* wanton Train advance,
And to light Measures turn the swimming Dance.
Sweet slow-pac'd *Melancholy* next appears,
Pompous in Grief, and Eloquent of Tears.
Here *Meditation* shines in Azure drest,
All-starr'd with Gems: A sun adorns her Crest.
Religion, to whose lifted, raptur'd Eyes
Seraphic Hosts descend from opening Skies;
Beauty, who sways the Heart and charms the Sight;
Whose Tongue is Music, and whose Smile Delight;
Whose Brow is Majesty; whose Bosom Peace;
Who bad Creation be, and Chaos cease . . .
Here in thy likeness, fair Ophelia, seen,
She throws kind Lustre o'er th' enliven'd Green.
Next her *Description,* rob'd in various Hues,
Invites Attention from the pensive *Muse!*
The *Muse!*—she comes! refin'd the *Passions* wait,
And *Precept,* ever winning, wise and great.
The *Muse!* a thousand *Spirits* wing the Air
(Once *Men,* who made like *her* Mankind their Care).
Inamour'd round her press th' inspiring Throng,
And swell to Extacy her solemn Song.[47]

Not to minimize the distance from Collins, which is obvious, this is perhaps the most striking example of descriptive personification before his *Odes;* and it is more detailed in its visual imagery than anything of the kind to be found in the lyric (a remark which must be qualified, but not negated, below).

As is not surprising, we come a step nearer to Collins in the strictly contemporary *Odes* of Joseph Warton. His descriptions of Fancy and her dwelling, and of the "rage of war," with its attendant personifications, already quoted, illustrate his visual treatment of allegorical figures and scenic settings. The other odes addressed to personified abstractions are less striking in this respect. Nor can we assume identity of intention with Collins: while Warton couples the "descriptive" with imagination and invention, (and later declares personification to be "one of the greatest efforts of the creative power of a warm and lively imagination")[48] the term "allegoric" occurs neither in the title nor in the "advertisement" of his *Odes*.

It is safe to say then that nothing in his immediate background anticipates or parallels the effect of Collins's visions of Pity and Danger, quoted above; or of Peace—

> O Thou, who bad'st thy Turtles bear
> Swift from his Grasp thy golden Hair,
> And sought'st thy native skies:
> When *War*, by Vultures drawn from far,
> To *Britain* bent his iron Car
> And bad his Storms arise—

(where Collins evidently remembers the descent of Peace, "with Turtle wing" in Milton's *Nativity Ode*, and now presents her reascent at the approach of War, who leans from his vulture-drawn chariot to make her his prey as he drives towards Britain, visible in the distance beneath the gathering storm clouds); or of *Mercy*—

> O Thou, who sit'st a smiling Bride
> By *Valour's* arm'd and awful Side,
> Gentlest of Sky-born Forms and best ador'd!
> Who oft with Songs, divine to hear,
> Win'st from his fatal Grasp the Spear,
> And hid'st in Wreaths of Flow'rs his bloodless Sword!

which the *Monthly* reviewer thought afforded "the finest subject for a picture that imagination can form: since Horace's rule of *ut Pictura Poesis* was never better observed."[49]

Given the "rule" here adverted to, and the strong Addisonian reinforcement of it, we may recall again Addison on "the fairy way of writing." If in the "fairies, . . . demons and departed spirits" we are pointed on to matter that would engage the Wartons, and Collins in the *Ode to Fear*, we remember that Addison associated closely with them, the poet's personifications, his representing of the passions, virtues and vices "under a visible shape." And the suggestion is elaborated by John Hughes: "Allegory is indeed the

Fairy Land of Poetry, peopled by Imagination: its inhabitants are so many Apparitions; . . . and all are visionary and typical." "Allegory . . . is a kind of Picture in Poetry."[50] Collins might almost be working to this prescription!

Nor was the *Monthly* reviewer at fault when he associated the description of Mercy with allegorical painting—a form of iconographic art which flourished in and after the Renaissance, sometimes independently, sometimes as a subordinate element when allegorical figures hovered over the idealized depiction of historical events or mingled with the already allegorized figures of classic myth.[51] John Hughes prepared a prose "Design for an Historical Picture: On the King's Accession and Arrival MDCCXIV," which, however deplorable, testifies to the continuing interest in such pieces.[52] The taste for allegorical design was, further, kept alive by the engravers' art. For the first collected edition of *The Seasons* William Kent designed an elaborate frontispiece. Over an undulating landscape, with trees shading a Palladian building (on the right) and shepherds (one playing on his pipe) and sheep (on the left), there is a rainbow (left) and, in the centre, a cloud bearing the figure of the goddess, with winged attendants extending to the right.[53] Such, then, are the converging influences that may help in part to explain some of Collins's principal innovations in poetry— but innovations they remain.

VI

All the *Odes* of 1746 employ personification, but not all in the same way. In the *Ode to Liberty,* the *persona* invoked is never described at all. As, largely, in the *Ode to Evening,* her "idea"—a universal—is suggested by a series of concomitants: a device also employed, of course, in a subordinate role in odes where the *persona* is fully depicted. In the *Ode on the Death of Colonel Ross* and the exquisite "How sleep the Brave" the "idea" is suggested without resort to any central *persona.* In the former, the personifications introduced receive fairly full description; in the latter they are hardly more than named, and there is the same reticence about the supernatural beings that accompany them:

> By Fairy Hands their Knell is rung,
> By Forms unseen their Dirge is sung;

> There *Honour* comes, a Pilgrim grey,
> To bless the Turf that wraps their Clay,
> And *Freedom* shall a-while repair,
> To dwell a weeping Hermit there!

Perhaps it would not be wrong to say that the "idea" (which requires and receives no personification) is that of awed reverence, tempered by gratitude, sympathy and affection. If one wished to gauge the distance of Collins from the Wartons, one need only try to imagine either of them writing this poem.

For the *Ode to Evening* no such device is required. Joseph Warton's *Odes on Various Subjects* includes a rhymed *Ode to Evening*, an unrhymed lyric (the *Ode to Shooting*), which differs metrically from Collins's *Evening* in the addition of a foot in the third line, as well as Thomas's translation of Horace, *Odes* 3.13 (an experiment modelled on Milton's translation of 1.5). The unrhymed poems are patently mere exercises and produce no effect remotely like Collins's. In Joseph's humanitarian ode (in substance reminiscent rather of Thomson), the Nymphs of the forest are told that they might dwell secure in Britain,

> Far from grim wolves or tiger's midnight roar,
> Or crimson-crested serpent's hungry hiss,
> But that our savage swains pollute
> With murder your retreats!

The rhymed *Ode to Evening* is Warton's best poem. Evening is a "meek-ey'd maiden, clad in sober grey," who bathes the "drooping daisies . . . in honey-dews" and nurses "the nodding violet's tender stalk." At her coming the Dryads, who have hidden from the fierce heat of day

> Return to trip in wanton evening-dance
> Old Sylvan too returns, and laughing Pan.

With these flights of fancy are mingled sights and sounds of the English rural scene: "the clamorous rooks," the skimming flight of swallows, and the "hoarse humming of unnumber'd flies," together with the more robust note of the whistling woodman and "stout plowmen" met "to wrestle on the green." The passions (named, but not depicted) sleep and, says the poet, "holy calm creeps o'er my peaceful soul":

> O modest Evening, oft let me appear
> A wand'ring votary with thy pensive train,
> List'ning to every wildly-warbling throat
> That fills with farewell notes the darkling plain.

The reader will instantly recognize here elements which find their way into Collins's unrhymed ode. What is lacking is his delicate sensibility and his artistry seen in the manipulation of the open pattern which combines vividly apprehended fact and gently indulged fancy into a unity of effect, reinforced—one might almost say, controlled—by the "dying fall" of the metre. The result is not to depict, but by its concomitants[54] to evoke, the idea—the spirit—of Evening.

In the *Ode to Liberty* Collins attempts, not quite so successfully, an evocation by combining very different "romantic" elements—and here again, incidentally, Warton can be heard stumbling heavily behind, and at an even greater distance.[55] To understand the effect at which Collins aims, and which he in part achieves, it is necessary to know something of his Pindaric form.

VII

The History of the English Pindaric is familiar enough. In likening Pindar to a mountain torrent Horace had omitted to remark that it was a torrent that kept strictly to its channel; and Cowley, elaborating on his praise could write:

> Pindars unnavigable Song
> Like a swoln Flood from some steep Mountain pours along,
>   The Ocean meets with such a Voice
> From his enlarged Mouth as drowns the Oceans noice.
> So Pindar does new Words and Figures roul
> Down his impetuous Dithyrambic Tide,
>   Which in no Channel deigns t'abide,
>   Which neither Banks nor Dikes control. . . .[56]

This was the prevailing view of Pindar's effect with its bold digressions and sudden transitions—the effect which Cowley sought to reproduce by ignoring Pindar's strophic structure and resorting to free, irregular, rhyming verse. Thus the English "Pindaric" was born. Even the sober Isaac Watts could announce,

> Wild as the Lightning, various as the Moon
> Roves my Pindaric Song.

Nothing perhaps but Pindar's name and Dryden's example could have protected so radical a departure from the Neoclassical norm; and indeed a protest was voiced by Congreve in his "Discourse on the Pindarique Ode,"[57] with its double thesis: that "Nothing can be call'd Beautiful without Proportion" and "especially the Ode, whose End and Essence is Harmony," and that "nothing is more regular than the Odes of Pindar" both as to the structure (which Congreve correctly explains, acknowledging the value of the variation in the epode from the identical strophe and antistrophe) and as to "the perpetual Coherence of his thoughts. For tho' his Digressions are frequent, and his Transitions sudden, yet is there ever some secret connexion, which . . . never fails to communicate itself to the Understanding of the Reader." Protest and precept would appear to have gone unheeded till, coincident with some renewal of the lyric impulse, the regular Pindaric was revived by Akenside (1745), Collins and Joseph Warton (1746), Gray and West (in his translation of Pindar) somewhat later. Akenside and Warton, indeed, seem to have learned the lesson too well, oversimplifying the structure and losing all that effect of *élan* which Cowley had exaggerated.

Collins, on the other hand, while adopting the strophic structure, preserved this effect. He did so by a freer treatment of the Pindaric form, employing in *Liberty, Fear,* and *The Poetical Character,* longer units (and even permitting himself within them deviations so slight as to escape the reader's notice), so that the sense of prevailing pattern was preserved without impairing the countervailing sense of rapid and excited movement. He enhances the effect of contrast within the poem which Congreve had conceded, by placing the epode (which thus becomes, strictly, a mesode) between strophe and antistrophe—necessarily, perhaps, with the longer units—and by differentiating it sharply in structure from them. Thus his Pindarics become highly distinctive, and (as we have observed) different in content and effect from his stanzaic odes.[58]

There is nothing in Gray's justly admired Pindarics (of a decade later) so entirely in the spirit of Pindar's allusions, though with added pictorial detail, than the opening of the *Ode to Liberty,*

with its memories of Thermopylae and of Harmodius and
Aristogiton:

> Who shall awake the *Spartan* Fife,
> And call in solemn Sounds to Life
> The Youths, whose Locks divinely spreading
> Like vernal Hyacinths in sullen Hue,
> At once the Breath of Fear and Virtue shedding,
> Applauding *Freedom* lov'd of old to view?
> What new *Alcaeus*, Fancy-blest,
> Shall sing the Sword, in Myrtle drest,
> At *Wisdom*'s Shrine a-while its Flame concealing,
> (What Place so fit to seal a Deed renown'd?)
> Till she her brightest Lightnings round revealing,
> It leap'd in Glory forth, and dealt her prompted Wound!

Then, after the first Epode (written for contrast in simple octosyllabic couplets) has sketched the fortunes of Liberty (identifying
with them, as in *Hanmer* and *Simplicity,* those of the arts) and has
brought Liberty at last to Britain, the Antistrophe gathers renewed
force and momentum. Here we have an excellent opportunity of
watching the imagination of Collins at work; hence the analogues
and possible sources presented in our notes.

> Beyond the Measure vast of Thought,
> The Works the Wizzard *Time* has wrought![59]
> The Gaul 'tis held of antique Story[60]
> Saw *Britain* link'd to his now adverse Strand,
> No Sea between, nor Cliff sublime and hoary,[61]
> He pass'd with unwet Feet thro' all our Land.[62]
> To the blown *Baltic* then, they say,
> The wild Waves found another way,
> Where *Orcas* howls, his wolfish Mountains rounding,[63]
> Till all the banded West at once 'gan rise,
> A wide wild Storm ev'n Nature's self confounding,[64]
> With'ring her Giant Sons with strange uncouth Surprise.[65]
> This pillar'd Earth so firm and wide,
> By Winds and inward Labors torn,
> In Thunders dread was push'd aside
> And down the should'ring Billows born.[66]
> And see, like Gems, her laughing Train
> The little Isles on ev'ry side![67]
> *Mona,* once hid from those who search the Main,

Where thousand Elfin shapes abide,[68]
And *Wight* who checks the west'ring Tide,
    For Thee consenting Heav'n has each bestow'd,
A fair Attendant on her sov'reign Pride:
    To Thee this blest Divorce she ow'd,
For thou has made her Vales thy lov'd, thy last Abode.

The "Second Epode" tells of a Temple erected there to Liberty, and destroyed, whether by Roman or by Dane. But its "idea," its essential meaning, yet remains and is to the imagination of the poet real and contemporary. This is the passage about truth as the imagination perceives it, to which we referred in discussing *The Poetical Character*:[69]

Yet still if Truth those Beams infuse,
Which guide at once and charm the Muse,
Beyond yon braided Clouds that lie,
Paving the light-embroider'd Sky:
Amidst the bright pavilion'd Plains,
The beauteous *Model* still remains.
There happier than in Islands blest,
Or Bow'rs by Spring or *Hebe* drest,
The Chiefs who fill our *Albion's* Story,
In warlike Weeds, retir'd in Glory,
Hear their consorted *Druids* sing[70]
Their Triumphs to th' immortal String.
    How may the Poet now unfold,
What never Tongue or Numbers told?
How learn delighted, and amaz'd,
What Hands unknown that Fabric rais'd?
Ev'n now before his favor'd Eyes,
In *Gothic* Pride it seems to rise!
Yet *Graecia's* graceful Orders join,
Majestic thro' the mix'd Design;
The secret Builder knew to chuse,
Each sphere-found Gem of richest Hues:
Whate'er Heav'n's purer Mold contains
When nearer Suns emblaze its Veins;
There on the Walls the *Patriot's* Sight
May ever hang with fresh Delight,
And, grav'd with some Prophetic Rage,
Read *Albion's* Fame thro' ev'ry Age.

Once more we have picture called to poetry's aid, and evidence of the essentially visual quality of Collins's imagination.

The concluding lines of this epode, and of the poem, turn again to the poets, the "Laureate Band," who are to "sooth" Liberty, pacify *Anger*, and summon "Blithe *Concord*'s social Form." The ode, which commenced with the unsheathing of the sword, ends with its resheathing. There is that much of structural justification. But the lines have been severely criticized for a falling off in poetic power and, worse, an impropriety of theme and image. There is no denying the failure in energy, and with a poet like Collins, this may very well account for an impropriety of image unparalleled elsewhere in his work.[71] But by a reader who bears the contemporary situation in mind, the theme itself can hardly be accused of impropriety.[72] It is at least significant, that in this phase of Collins's development, the allegorical and descriptive mode is employed even for his comment on contemporary events and for the expression of his sentiments of patriotism—and with better success in other odes.

VIII

Ultimately all the success of the *Odes on Several Descriptive and Allegoric Subjects,* and all their originality, depend on Collins's development—one might almost say, on his discovery—of the latent potential of personification as a poetic medium. His *personae* are no mere ethical counters dignified by a capital letter, with or without a conventional epithet: they draw on the resources of a visual imagination. Another poet might have commended Pity with a statement of its divine origin and sanction and of beneficence and sympathy as its marks. Instead, Collins forms an image which speaks for itself:

> Long, *Pity,* let the Nations view
> Thy sky-worn Robes of tend'rest Blue,
>   And Eyes of dewy Light!

The effect is not merely visual, but visionary. The figure of Pity, thus realized, becomes a correlative, a symbol, of the "idea" and its attendant emotion.[73]

In this respect the *Ode to Pity* is characteristic of the poems in which the *persona* invoked is visually described (*Pity, Mercy, Peace,* and to a lesser extent, *Simplicity, Fear,* and *Evening*). But, as we have seen, the *persona* addressed can on occasion become the focus and symbol of idea and emotion *mainly* by the pictorial presentment of concomitants (*Fear* and *Evening*) or *entirely* by this means (*Liberty*).

The range of these concomitants is striking. In *Evening* the pastoral note, landscape, the "prospect," characteristic sights and sounds (as seen in the gathering twilight, or heard in the encompassing stillness), a hint of classic myth (the Nymphs, Hours and Pleasures) and of native fairy-lore (the "Elves Who slept in Flow'rs the Day"), even of the "gothic" (Vot'ress, Pilgrim, Time-hallow'd Pile)—all these conspire to support the central personifications and give a perfect symbolic rendering of the spirit of Evening. (And here, as in "How sleep the Brave," Collins has discovered that suggestion, supported by tone, can sometimes be as effective as more detailed description.) In *Fear* concomitants of a very different sort build up a cumulative impression of wonder and terror. In the antistrophe of *Liberty* wonder is also a dominant motif, but it is paired with the classic splendour of the strophe: the "gothic" and the classic are there matched together as in the "mix'd Design" of the Temple of Liberty.

Much in these concomitants comes from the new world of Preromanticism shared with the Wartons; and Collins also shares in some degree their desire for emotional experience, achieved through the imagination, and enjoyed for its own sake. Only, he instinctively recognizes the duty of the poet to subordinate, so far as he can, everything to the structure and effect of the poem as a whole. His belief in the imagination, furthermore, differs from theirs. For him its power extends beyond providing, through fiction, for vicarious emotional experience: it bears a relation to truth, and can seize on and present the "idea" of things—of pity, of fear, of liberty, of evening, what you will. The means which it uses to this end, in the *Odes* of 1746, is essentially that of symbol. This is Collins's great discovery, and it is the basis of his best achievement in poetry.

IX

It is, however, at least as Collins employs it, a mode with very definite limits; and this, if we can judge from his last extant work, he may have come to realize. The *Ode on the Popular Superstitions*

of the Highland of Scotland Considered as the Subject of Poetry is
concerned, as are so many of Collins's poems, with poetry itself—
its subjects, mode, effect, and justification. Here he abandons the
allegoric and extends the descriptive. But more than this is involved.

At first glance it looks as if Collins were taking a step toward a
more concrete reality; in fact it is a further step in the Pre-romantic
world, in which the Wartons revelled and he himself had already
made his incursions. What he finds in Highland scene and story
(" 'Tis Fancy's land") is a source of new emotional experiences—
of wonder, sometimes touched with terror, of pathos, and of admiration for primitive virtue and primitive credulity. Here in the
traditions of the country are "themes," he feels, "of simple sure
effect" and subjects for "strange lays had charm'd a Spencer's ear."
But still in the background lurks the old problem of poetry and
truth, and demands a new solution. Collins seeks it in the "sure
effect." Granted they are "false themes"; yet if they can command
belief (here surely is a faint premonition of Coleridge's "willing
suspension of disbelief"), the effect will follow, and one can only
conclude that "scenes like these," though

> daring to depart
> From sober truth, are still to nature true.[74]

Ideally, the poet himself must (as Collins had claimed to do in
Fear) "Hold each strange tale devoutly true." Such, he thinks, was
the attitude of Tasso,

> Prevailing poet whose undoubting mind
> Believ'd the magic wonders which he sung!
> Hence at each sound imagination glows;
> Hence his warm lay with softest sweetness flows:
> Melting it flows, pure, num'rous, strong and clear,
> And fills th' impassion'd heart, and wins th' harmonious ear.

The proof is in the effect. Perhaps it is most easily achieved when
audience and poet are at one and he can "paint what all believe";[75]
but of the subjects which now engage his enthusiasm Collins
claims that

> not alone they touch the village breast,
> But fill'd in elder time th'historic page.
> There Shakespeare's self, with ev'ry garland crown'd,

> In musing hour, his wayward sisters found
> And with their terrors drest the magic scene.

Whether Collins has reached a solution, or merely a rationalization, we need not too closely enquire. Two facts are indisputable: he has taken, as we have said, a long step further into the Preromantic world; and he is still concerned, as the Wartons were not, with the perennial problem of poetry and truth—with the question raised in the *Poetical Character*.

He is also concerned with the idea of simplicity treated in the companion poem:

> But, O, o'er all, forget not Kilda's race,
> On whose bleak rocks, which brave the wasting tides,
> Fair Nature's daughter, Virtue, yet abides,—

theme for "some gentle song"

> Of those whose lives are yet sincere and plain,
> Their bounded walks the rugged cliffs along,
> And all their prospect but the wintry main.
> With sparing temp'rance, at the needful time,
> They drain the sainted Spring, or, hunger-prest,
> Along th' Atlantic rocks undreading climb,
> And of its eggs despoil the Solan's nest.
> Thus blest in primal innocence they live,
> Suffic'd and happy with that frugal fare
> Which tasteful toil and hourly danger give.
> Hard is their shallow soil, and bleak and bare;
> Nor ever vernal bee was heard to murmur there.

Here (as compared with the *Ode to Simplicity*) the emphasis seems to have shifted from the aesthetic to the ethical, and from classic simplicity to natural. About the former we must be cautious in inference: after all the subject of the whole poem is poetry and the state of mind from which it springs and to which it is addressed, though here, in the interest of unity of effect in the stanza, he actually omits a reference to poetry found in his source. About the shift from classic simplicity to natural, no such second thoughts are required. This is as clear an example of "hard primitivism" as Warton's, in *The Enthusiast,* is of "soft," and achieved by the same means of selection and suppression. In the stanza Collins turns for his chief source from Martin Martin's *Description of the Western Islands* (1703) to his *Late Voyage to St. Kilda* (1698).[76] There Martin is emphatic on the happiness and virtue of the St. Kildans, but is far from denying them the more material blessings which Collins rigorously excludes. A glance at the source makes plain Collins's method.[77] One detail in particular caught his artist's eye and perhaps conditioned his reading of the whole account: ". . . there is no sort of Tree, no, nor the least shrub grows here, nor ever a Bee seen at any time." When Collins wrote,

> "Nor ever vernal bee was heard to murmur there,"

he must have remembered his earlier invocation of Simplicity:

> By all the honey'd store
> On *Hybla's* Thymy shore,
> By all her Blooms and mingled Murmurs dear.

The contrast may serve us as an epitome of the shift in emphasis from the simplicity of classic art to the simplicity of nature.

The *Superstitions Ode* suggests indeed a whole new field of romantic poetry which Collins did not live to exploit; but the *Odes on Several Descriptive and Allegoric Subjects* remain his substantial achievement and the one most characteristic of his genius.

NOTES

1. William Collins, *Drafts and Fragments of Verse,* ed. J. S. Cunningham, Oxford, 1956: #6, "Lines addressed to James Harris" (evidence also, with the letter to John Gilbert Cooper, of Collins's contact with the disciples of Shaftesbury); #7 [To one of the Tonsons, inheritors of the publishing business]; at least in their style ##8, 9 and 10, and in content #9, and (though with a retrospective glance) #8.

2. The subject of Collins's excited letter to John Gilbert Cooper, from which it would seem that the title was chosen as an alternative to the "Clarendon Review," and that the two projects are in fact one.

3. Collins adopts precisely the attitude to the middle ages and Renaissance, characteristic of Neoclassicism and the Enlightenment:

> As Arts expir'd, resistless Dulness rose;
> Goths, priests, or Vandals,—all were Learning's foes,
> Till Julius first recall'd each exil'd maid,
> And Cosmo own'd them in th' Etrurian shade.
>   (*Epistle to Hanmer* 35–8.)

4. Professor James Sutherland would distinguish between Collins, as cultivating some new interests without being in revolt against the literary culture of his day, and the Wartons, "who did wish to destroy" and were "unorthodox because consciously in revolt" (*Preface to Eighteenth-Century Poetry*, Oxford, 1948, 158–60). But one can easily be deceived by Collins's greater refinement of sensibility and artistry, and by a sort of convention of revolt in the Wartons. Actually it might be argued in Collins's *Odes* the revolt, both in critical theory and poetic practice, cut much deeper, involving an appeal both to the Hellenic and the "gothic," and implying a view of the poetic imagination that went well beyond the Wartons'. Nor were the brothers so completely divorced from the normal interests of the period as might at first appear. Thomas had a genuine gift for satiric verse; and Joseph was able to write for the *Adventurer* literary criticism of sufficient orthodoxy to win Johnson's praise (Wooll, *Biographical Memoir*, London, 1806, p. 219, Letter X), and for all his protest against didacticism in poetry, he escapes it much less completely than Collins.

5. The assignment to "nature" of Shakespeare, "Fancy's child," initiated by Milton, supported by Dryden, Addison, and Pope himself (coupling him, in *The Preface*, with Homer as a great original) had become of course a critical commonplace as Pope smilingly acknowledged: "In all debates where critics bear a part/Not one but nods and talks of Jonson's art,/Of Shakespeare's nature . . ." (*To Augustus*). Collins takes it up in *Hanmer:* "Too nicely Jonson knew the critic's part/Nature in him was almost lost in art." It is Warton's application that deserves (and has received) notice. In *The Pleasures of Melancholy,* Thomas echoes his brother, substituting for the "primitive" the "gothic" (which is indeed another form of the primitive):

> Thro' Pope's soft song tho' all the Graces breathe,
> And Happiest Art adorns his Attic page;
> Yet does my mind with sweeter rapture glow,
> As at the root of mossy trunk reclin'd,
> In magic Spenser's wildly-warbl'd song,
> I see deserted Una wander wild.

6. The literary variety of primitivism, closely connected with the antithesis of nature and art, takes its rise in the study of Homer. Pope's *Preface* recognizes the interest of his picture of a primitive age, but attributes all his power, not to it, but to his genius (his "invention," dependent finally on imagination). Blackwell (*Enquiry into the Life and Writings of Homer*, 1735), on the contrary, plays down imagination, and attributes his power to his primitive age and condition. Neither lays any stress on primitive virtue. This is the ingredient added in Hugh Blair's *Critical Dissertation on the Poems of Ossian* (1763) together with the idea of "the moral or sentimental sublime," while genius, imagination and the primitive environment are combined and reconciled in William Duff's *Essay on Original Genius* (1767). The ethical (which includes the unethical) variety turns on the noble, or the merely happy, savage, and the antithesis of "nature" and civilization. In Thomson and other Preromantics, it often subsists in uneasy juxtaposition with a belief in progress toward a far-off divine event. Logically antithetical, the two attitudes have a common psychological basis.

7. The incongruity of the moral in itself, and in its context, serves to heighten the contrast between *The Enthusiast* and William Whitehead's ode of the same title, where, after some quietly evocative stanzas on the joys of solitary contemplation, Reason appears to rebuke the Enthusiast and send him back to the social scene.

8. This effusion, worthy of Peacock at a later date, was unearthed by Professor H. O. White from the pages of *The Student* (1751). It had been reprinted by Thomas Warton in *The Oxford Sausage* (1764). If, as I suggested (*TLS.* 24 January, 1929, p. 62) and still believe, there is some reason to suppose that Thomas Warton wrote the parody himself, it loses nothing of its significance, merely emphasizing the school's delighted sense of departure from the accepted literary norm. There are echoes of Collins in the mode of invocation (and especially of the *Ode to Fear*, reinforced by the reference to fiends of giant size); in the wistful expression of poetic aspiration, the coupling of the "Attic" with the "gothic," the allusion to the *Faerie Queene* (like Collins's, in a note to the *Poetical Character,* inaccurate), the gentler elegiac and "pensive pilgrim" notes (more characteristic of Collins than of the Wartons). Further passages here omitted include a glance at Tasso's *Jerusalem Delivered,* and at a gruesome Oriental traveller's tale with a note copied from one of Collins's in the *Ode to Liberty,* to the effect that no poetic use has yet been made of it (see note 61).

9. Referred to by Warton in the *History of English Poetry* and confirmed by recently discovered documents (see *Drafts* etc., ed. Cunningham, App. IV). It is significant that commencing to study for his projected History of the Revival of Learning, Collins drifted off into this kind of reading.

10. From the "character" contributed to the collection of Collins's verse in *The Poetical Calendar* (1763) as reprinted in the *Lives of the Poets* (italics mine).

11. E. G. Ainsworth, *Poor Collins,* Ithaca, N. Y., 1937, 200–207.

12. In his valuable study of "Eclogue Types," *JEGP* 24 (1925), 33–60, R. F. Jones gives some account of exotic eclogues derived directly or indirectly from those of Collins.

13. In Vergil's *Eclogues* I and IX there is a faint hint for the kind of contrast Collins develops. It was taken up in *Five Pastoral Eclogues* (1745) attributed to Thomas Warton by Isaac Reed, but perhaps mistakenly (C. Rinaker, *Thomas Warton,* Urbana, 1916, p. 25, n. 2). Set vaguely in contemporary Germany, they claim to be, apart from the hint in Vergil, "distinguished from any productions of the kind either ancient or modern" in presenting the opposing interests of peaceful and rural life and the "tumultuous scenes of war, with the various passions arising from thence" (Preface). They retain all the other conventions of the pastoral eclogue, save only the rhymed couplet, for which they substitute blank verse.

14. The *Hanmer* contains nothing for which there is not good Neoclassical precedent. The idea of the "sister Arts" was in the air, and the notion of the collaboration of poetry and painting (congenial as it was to Collins and sig-

nificant for the *Odes*) was caught up from a hint in Spence's *Essay on Pope's Odyssey* (1737). There are, of course, suggestions of Collins, the poet of visual imagination and delicate fancy, of strong emotion and of (at least in desire) tender sentiment—the last more evident in the "Song from *Cymbeline*" added in the second edition.

15. Creative imagination (by which he meant more than did Warton) is the subject of the *Poetical Character;* the "Descriptive" finds its place in his title, as it does not in Warton's; and he is more successful in avoiding the didactic (see note 20, below).

16. The interpretation here offered is substantially that given in my earlier essay, but more carefully argued and with closer reference to the structure of the poem.

17. Here occurs the inaccurate footnote referred to in note 8, above.

18. H. W. Garrod's failure to understand the structure led him to the startling conclusion that from the union of Fancy with the Creator was born "the rich-hair'd Youth of Morn," namely, "the Poet, who has the rich or long hair of all poets . . ." (*Collins*, Oxford, 1928, p. 69), and caused him to amend the text so as to read, "And all thy Subject—life—was born," thus placing "life" in apposition to "Subject" ("Life," which the eighteenth century would surely have called "Nature," being the subject imitated by the poet). It is obvious, of course, that "born" here is used figuratively, like "birth" (25). There is really no excuse for Garrod's literalism or for Bronson's remark (*Poems*, Boston, 1898, p. 102) that Collins's treatment of God and Fancy is "disagreeably suggestive of *Jupiter Amans*." A French scholar (it seems almost too good to be true) has discoursed solemnly on "Les Amours de Dieu chez Collins et Milton" (Pierre Legouis in *Revue anglo-américaine*, VIII [1930], 136–38); but it is possible that he is right in referring Collins's figure back to Milton, who addresses the Heavenly Muse (*PL*. 7.8–12):

> Before the Hills appear'd or Fountains flow'd,
> Thou with Eternal Wisdom didst converse,
> Wisdom, thy Sister, and with her didst play,
> In presence of th' Almighty Father, pleas'd
> With thy Celestial Song.

More likely Collins is indebted to Milton's source, Prov. 8:22–31, and thus associates, if he does not actually identify, imagination with wisdom. It is worth remembering that Joseph Warton particularly admired this passage in Proverbs as an example of personification (*Adventurer* #57).

19. *Answer to Davenant* (1651) in *Critical Essays of the Seventeenth Century*, ed. J. E. Spingarn, Oxford, 1908, 2, 59, 62). By "judgment" here Hobbes clearly does not mean the logical faculty, but rather, I think, what he elsewhere calls "prudence," that is, the power which generalized from observation. His psychological study of imagination is found in the *Leviathan*, especially chapters ii and iii.

20. *Advancement of Learning* 2; *De Augmentis* 5.1; *Descriptio Globi Intellectualis: Philosophical Works*, etc. J. M. Robertson, London, 1905, 87–9, 499–500, 677–8. If we were concerned with Bacon's sources instead of with his

influence, we should have to take into account his response to the idea of imitation conceived as idealization (as evidenced for example in Sidney's *Defence*). One concession which Bacon makes must indeed be noticed, namely, the possibility of enlisting imagination in the service of reason in didactic or "parabolical" poetry. But it is precisely this idea of didacticism in poetry that Warton and, by implication, Collins reject.

21. It is significant that Addison here draws in a phrase from Longinus, who also supports the idea of visual effects: "Moved by enthusiasm and passion, you seem to see the things of which you speak and place them before the eyes of your hearers" (*Sublime* 15, trans. A. O. Prickard).

22. *Spectator* ##411–21: quotations from ##411, 418, 419, 421 (edn., London, 1744). Though an ardent disciple of Locke, Addison seems here to be chiefly dependent on Bacon and Hobbes. Locke's theory of the ideality of secondary qualities (much admired by Addison) may have helped him toward his view of imagination as essentially subjective in its creative aspect by seeming to free it from immediate dependence on material phenomena (cf. #413). As to Addison's dependence on Bacon for his underlying theory of poetry as imaginative but essentially fictitious, his suggestion that the "final cause" of the pleasures of imagination is providential (its pleasure in the great to lead to the contemplation of God; in the new or uncommon to encourage the pursuit of knowledge; in the beautiful to forward the propagation of the species, etc., #413) no more alters the immediate character assigned to the imagination and to poetry than does Bacon's concession that imagination may minister to magnanimity and morality as well as to delectation.

23. The first effect of his papers was an increased attention to imagination as an element in the poet's equipment as seen, for example, in Pope's *Preface to Homer* when compared with his *Essay on Criticism;* the second, at a later date, in the taking up of the idea of creative imagination, in which Collins and the Wartons were not alone. In *The Excursion* (1743) David Mallet invokes the

> Companion of the Muse, Creative power
> Imagination! at whose great command
> Arise unnumber'd images of things,
> Thy hourly offspring . . .
>   O come invok'd
> To waft me on thy many-tinctured wing
> O'er Earth's extended space: and thence, on high,
> Spread to superior Worlds thy bolder flight,
> Excursive, unconfin'd.

Akenside devotes his long poem to the *Pleasures of Imagination* (1744), by whose power the artist "aspires To tempt creative praise." Though Thomson can speak of Shakespeare's "creative fancy," he still regards nature as transcending anything it can produce: "But who can paint like Nature? Can imagination boast/Amid its gay creations hues like hers?" (*Summer* 1564, *Spring* 468–70).

24. *Odes on Various Subjects,* London, 1746.

25. In the *Biographia Literaria,* chap. xii, where the primary imagination is

the organ of all perception and a finite counterpart of God's creative act, and the secondary imagination of poet and artist is identical with the primary in kind and differing only in the mode of its operation. With the imagination's creativeness recognized, but at the expense of its truth, the problem for the Romantics was to establish the validity of its creations—a problem attacked, each in his own individual way by Blake, Coleridge, and Wordsworth. The *Poetical Character* was a favourite with Coleridge (*Letters*, ed. E. L. Griggs, Oxford, 1956, p. 279).

26. J. C. Scaliger, *Poetices libri septem* 1.1; Sidney, *Defence* (*Elizabethan Critical Essays*, ed. G. Gregory Smith, Oxford, 1904, 1, 157); Cowley, *To the Muse* (*Poems*, ed. A. R. Waller, Cambridge, 1905, 185) and *Davideis* (*ibid.* 253):

> As first a various unform'd *Hint* we find
> Rise in some god-like *Poets* fertile *Mind*,
> Till all the parts and words their places take,
> And with just marches *verse* and *musick* make;
> Such was *Gods Poem*, this *Worlds* new *Essay;*
> So wild and rude in its first draught it lay;
> Th'ungovern'd parts no *Correspondence* knew,
> An artless *war* from thwarting *Motions* grew;
> Till they to *Number* and fixt Rules were brought
> By the *eternal Minds Poetique Thought*.

(Cf. a somewhat similar idea in Akenside, *Pleasures of Imagination, Poetical Works*, ed. A. Dyce, Boston, 1864, pp. 179–81); Shaftesbury (*Characteristics*, London, 1732, 1, 207) describes the true poet as "a second *Maker*, a just Prometheus under Jove. Like that Sovreign Artist, or universal Plastick Nature, he forms a *Whole*, coherent and proportion'd in itself . . ." Sidney's pronouncement can perhaps be related to imagination through his use of the term *invention*. In Cowley's *To the Muse*, Wit, Fancy and Invention are the steeds of the Muse's chariot. The rest do not allude at all even thus indirectly to imagination.

27. *Arte of English Poesie, Elizabethan Critical Essays* 2,3. Puttenham (who is repeatedly cited by Thomas Warton in his *History* and his *Observations on the Faerie Queene*, and may well have been read by Collins) protests against prejudices respecting the imagination and insists that in a healthy condition it is in its "much multiformitie *uniforme*, that is well proportioned, and so passing cleare that by it, as by a glasse or mirror, are represented unto the soule all manner bewtifull visions . . ." (ibid. 19–20).

28. Preface to her edition of Collins (1797) quoted by Bronson *(Poems*, p. 102).

29. *Ode to Liberty* 101–6, quoted below, p. 121.

30. *Essays*, ed. W. P. Ker, Oxford, 1900, 2, 117–18. Collins seems to have been familiar with Dryden's criticism from early days, echoing in *Hanmer* his contrast of Shakespeare and Fletcher. He also refers (*Drafts* #9) to DuFresnoy, whose *De Arte Graphica*, in translation, is introduced by Dryden's *Parallel*.

31. See R. D. Havens, "Simplicity, a Changing Concept," *J. H. I.* 14 (1953), 3–32.

32. *Spectator* # #60, 62.

33. *Characteristics,* 3, 141.

34. See above, note 6.

35. Collins must have remembered Milton's "Some time let gorgeous Tragedy/ In scepter'd Pall comes sweeping by" *(Il Pens.* 97–8) and have deliberately reversed the emphasis.

36. It is instructive to put beside Collins's Ode some of Joseph Warton's opinions from his paper on the same subject *(World* #26, June 28, 1753): Like Collins, he starts with an appeal to nature: "Simplicity is with justice, esteemed a supreme excellence in all the performances of art, because by this quality they more nearly resemble the productions of nature." He harks back to Addison, "who . . . first . . . banished from the English, as Boileau from the French, every species of bad eloquence and false wit," a taste for which had flourished "for want of being acquainted with the models of the great antique." He is with Addison on the absolute contradiction of gothic to classical, and condemns "the multiplicity of minute ornaments . . . which distinguishes meanness of manner in build:ng from greatness," that is "the Gothic from the Grecian," and does not share Collins's dream (in the *Ode to Liberty*) of combining the beauties of the two (which, of course, in Collins is less an architectural ideal than a symbol of different contributions to the cause of freedom): he deplores finding "a Grecian plan adulterated and defiled by the unnatural and impure mixture of Gothic whimsies" (a comment on the confused taste of the day). He cannot resist the temptation of a mild primitivism: "It seems to be the fate of polished nations to degenerate from a simplicity of sentiment." And he ends by extending his view from art to ethics: ". . . if this quality was venerated as it ought to be, it would . . . banish from the earth all artifice and treachery, double-dealing and deceit. Let it therefore be established, as a maxim, that simplicity is of equal importance in morals and in taste."

37. A device to be elaborated in the *Ode to Liberty;* see below, p. 121.

38. Anticipated in *Hanmer* 107–32.

39. This is the most definite of three allusions in the *Odes* to spirits that dwell in the elements and preside over storm and earthquake and over human deeds of violence. In *Mercy* the lines, "When he whom ev'n our Joys provoke,/The *Fiend of Nature* join'd his Yoke,/And rushed in Wrath to make our Isle his Prey," the primary reference is to human violence; in *Liberty* (see below, p. 120) it is exclusively to storm and earthquake; here, in *Fear,* the two are coupled. Taken together, they are seen to be echoes of that devil-lore which finds a place in Renaissance literature—for example, in Lady Macbeth's appeal to the spirits that "tend on mortal thoughts": "you murthring ministers/ Wherever in your sightless substances/You wait on Nature's mischief" (1.5.48–50). A passage in Thomas Nashe's *Pierce Penniless his Supplication to the Devil (Works,* ed. R. B. McKerrow, London 1904, 1, 230–31) helps us to explain more precisely Collins's allusions. Nashe speaks of one "kind of devils . . . those Northern Marcii . . . the authors of massacres and seed-men of mischief; for they have commission to incense men to rapines, sacrilege, . . . murder, . . . fury, and all manner of cruelties, and they command certain of

the Southern Spirits to wait upon them as slaves, as also great Arioch that is termed the Spirit of Revenge." (Here are the spirits that "prompt to Deeds accurs'd the Mind" and Vengeance.) But Nashe proceeds immediately to another group, "counted the most pestilent . . . spirits that are; for by help of Alrynach, a spirit of the West, they raise storms, cause earthquakes. . . ." (Here, "near allied," are the spirits that cause "Nature's Wounds and Wrecks," and also provide a link with the *Ode to Liberty,* where we find that "all the banded West at once gan rise/A wide wild storm, ev'n Nature's self confound-ing," and associated with it earthquake.)

40. It would appear that Collins reads Aristotle's *katharsis* as a literal purging away of fear. This is the view taken by James Harris (*Three Treatises,* London, 1744, 86–7), who is at pains to explain that by pity Aristotle does not mean "philanthropy, natural affection, a readiness to relieve others," but "that senseless, effeminate consternation which seizes weak minds on the sudden prospect of anything disastrous," and actually deprives "of the capacity to do the least of good offices." If Collins took this view of Aristotle on fear, he plainly did not apply it to pity, or expect tragedy to purge that passion away (see above, p. 110).

41. An echo from Warton's *Enthusiast.*

42. A hint here, and in what follows, of the next phase, that of the *Ode on the Popular Superstitions.*

43. Cf. *Comus,* 432–6.

44. This view of Collins's odes and their employment of personification, first put forward in my earlier essay, has been incorporated in two valuable studies: C. F. Chapin, *Personification in Eighteenth-Century English Poetry,* New York, 1955; and J. H. Hagstrum, *The Sister Arts: the Tradition of Literary Pictorialism and English Poetry from Dryden to Gray,* Chicago, 1958. See also E. R. Wasserman, "The Inherent Values of Eighteenth-Century Personifica-tion," *PMLA* 65 (1950), 435–63. To these I am in turn indebted.

45. A striking example of the difference in ultimate outcome can be seen by comparing John Clare's two poems on *Autumn:* one an imitation of Collins's *Ode to Evening,* the other in the manner of Wordsworth. (*The Poems of John Clare,* ed. J. W. Tibble, 2, 3–6, 412.)

46. *Essays on Several Subjects,* London, 1716, quoted by E. R. Wasserman (*PMLA,* 65, 440).

47. Canto V ll. 39 ff.

48. *Adventurer* #57.

49. *Monthly Review* 30 (1764), 24.

50. "Essay on Allegorical Poetry," in Hughes's edition of *Spenser,* London, 1715, 1, pp. xl–xli, xxx.

51. The influence of landscape on Pre-romantic poetry has been fully investi-gated, but until recently allegorical painting has been largely ignored. In my

earlier essay I suggested Reubens as an influence on Collins; but Professor Hagstrum is quite right: Reubens's figures are "too fleshy and substantial," and "his colors too bright and rich," to offer a suitable parallel to Collins (*The Sister Arts*, 282). The objection would be sustained by Collins himself, who has left us his ideal in painting: "Chaste and subdu'd the modest lights decay/ Steal into shade and mildly melt away" (*Hanmer* 113–14); cf. Joseph Warton on Reubens's "luscious and gay colouring" and his failure to achieve this very effect (*Adventurer* #57). Warton suggests Julio Romano (*Essay on Pope* 1, 30); Hagstrum, Guido Reni.

52. *Poems*, London, 1735, 2, 343–5. Hughes has already aimed at something of a similar effect in verse, in "The Court of Neptune; on King William's Return from Holland, 1699" (ibid. 1, 22–3):

> Here on the Margin of the rolling Flood,
> Divinely fair, like Sea-born Venus, stood
> *Britannia's* Genius, in a Robe array'd:
> A crown of Cities charg'd her graceful Brows . . .
> Such Tow'ry Honours on her Temples rise,
> When, drawn by Lions, she proceeds in State;
> Trains of Attendant Gods around her Chariot wait.

53. This design (which I came on many years ago) is now available in Hagstrum, *Sister Arts,* Plate 23.

54. These concomitants are "depicted" (though sound also plays a part in *Evening,* greater than elsewhere in Collins, except for the rather forced effects of *The Passions*). The landscape of *Evening,* deliberately generalized, is much less a mere catalogue than that in the admired *Grongar Hill* (1726), though John Dyer was a painter and capable of occasional touches of acute observation. A. D. McKillop, in a valuable study of Collins's *Evening* (*Tennessee Studies in Literature,* 5 [1960], 73–83) suggests the influence of Thomson's *Hymn to Solitude* (1729) where, "though attention is fixed on the central personification, her qualities, haunts, attendants, and devotees, Solitude herself is not pictorially presented" (p. 75). But there the concomitants are less pictorially presented than in Collins. It has been suggested by Mr. Hagstrum and others that the visual imagination of the eighteenth-century reader was more responsive than ours, and if he got less of visual stimulus it was because he needed less. But this leaves unexplained the great increase in visual imagery in and after Collins.

55. Warton attempts an *Ode to Liberty,* in a regular Pindaric form; it altogether lacks the combined effect of *élan* and complex metrical patterning that Collins achieves; and its content is relatively commonplace.

56. *English Works,* ed. A. R. Waller, Cambridge, 1905, 1, 178. Cowley also wrote an *Ode upon Liberty* (ibid. 2, 388–91) which places her securely "In the Golden Mean" and incidentally provides some further light on his view of the Pindaric; contrasting it with the "Heroique," and noting that in it "The Matter shall be grave, the Numbers loose and free."

57. Prefixed to *A Pindarique Ode Humbly Offer'd to the Queen,* London, 1706.

58. Writing a couple of decades later, Richard Shepherd introduces his own very inferior *Odes Descriptive and Allegorical* (1769) by observing: ". . . of the descriptive and allegorical Ode the Writings of the Ancients afford no Examples. . . . This Species of Writing is in almost every Circumstance different from the Pindarick Ode, which has its Foundation in Fact and Reality, that Fact worked up by a studied Pomp and Grandeur of Expression . . . while the other [i.e., the descriptive and allegorical ode] is built intirely on Fancy, and Ease and Simplicity of Diction are its peculiar Characteristicks." This seems a reasonably accurate distinction, and one to which Collins up to a point conforms, but he introduces into his Pindarics a large element of description and on occasion of allegorical personification.

59. Speaking, in the *Britannia,* of the separation of Britain from the Continent, Camden quotes Vergil, *Tantum aevi longinqua valet mutare vetustas* (*Aeneid* 3.415), and quotes from Seneca to express his own sense of awed wonder: "You see, there is a separation made both of Countries and nations when as some part of nature is provoked of itselfe: for when the mighty wind beateth strongly upon some sea: the force whereof as in generall is wonderfull. For although it rage but in part, yet it is of the universall power that it so rageth." (Quotations are from *Britain,* translated by Philemon Holland, London, 1610, pp. 346–7.)

60. A Pindaric formula: "But the tale is told in antique story, how that Zeus," etc. (*Olympian* 7, trans. J. E. Sandys).

61. Camden observes that "the shore of either side, where the distance between is narrowest, riseth up with cliffes of the same matter, as it were, and colour, so as they may seeme to have beene riven a sunder." In a footnote, Collins comments on the correspondent "Disposition of the two opposite Coasts," and notes that the "Tradition [of the separation] is mention'd by several of our old Historians." It seems clear, however, that Camden is his principal source. He adds, "I don't remember that any Poetical Use has been hitherto made of it" (the boast parodied in the *Ode to Horror;* see note 8, above). This would mean that he had overlooked Drayton's brief reference in the *Polyolbion,* and with it Shelden's *Illustrations.*

62. Cf. Spenser's phrase (in another mythological context): "Out of his Albion did on dry-foot pas/into old Gall" (*FQ.* 4.11.16).

63. Cf. "Loud as the wolves on Orcas' stormy steep/Howl to the roarings of the northern deep" (Pope, *To Augustus* 328–9).

64. It seems probable that the reference to "all the banded West" as rising to cause havoc in nature, goes back to the passage in Nashe's *Pierce Penniless,* cited in connection with the *Ode to Fear* (see note 39, above).

65. Camden, following Geoffrey of Monmouth, speaks of the giant inhabitants of pre-historic Britain (*Britain,* p. 5): cf. Milton's "Earth's giant sons" (*PL,* 1.778), and Dryden's "wild amazement . . . withers ev'n the strong" (*Palamon and Arcite* 3.302–03).

66. Camden suggests that the separation was caused by the "rushing of the

waves or else by occasion of some earthquak." Milton refers to the popular belief that earthquakes were caused by winds under the earth's surface, and couples with them the operation of the sea: "Winds underground or waters forcing way/Sidelong, had push'd a mountain from his seat" (*PL.* 6.196–7). He may also have supplied the "pillar'd Earth" by his reference to violent storms which seem "dangerous to the pillar'd frame of Heaven/Or to the Earth's dark basis" (*PR.* 4. 455–56), as Spenser may have done "the should'ring Billows": "Eftsoons of thousand billows shouldred" (*Ruins of Rome* 213).

67. Cf. Milton's "all the Sea-girt Isles/ . . . like to rich and various gems" (*Comus* 21–22).

68. George Waldron's *History and Description of the Isle of Man* (3rd ed.), London, 1744, recorded a number of supernatural wonders, and the belief, widespread among the inhabitants, "that there is not a Creek or Cranny in the Island but what is haunted either with Fairies or Ghosts" (pp. 132–3); and also the legend that in earlier times it "was inhabited by a certain Species called Fairies, and that everything was carried on in a kind of supernatural manner; that a blue mist hanging continually over the land, prevented the ships that passed from having any suspicion there was an island" (p. 14). This covers everything in Collins's text, but his footnote refers to the story of a mermaid in love with a youth, quite different from the version in Waldron (pp. 131–2), and attributes the mist to her resentment at being repulsed.

69. Above, p. 107.

70. The term "Druid" which seems to have had a fascination for Collins and his circle, opens up a large field of enquiry (see A. L. Owen, *The Famous Druids,* Oxford, 1962). A. D. McKillop has noticed Thomson's association of the Druids with liberty and its bearing on this passage. Milton's association of the Druids with the Muses (*Lycidas* 50–53) resulted in making the term almost a synonym for inspired poet. May I add in support of this statement one reference which seems to have escaped attention, and from a sufficiently unexpected source, Swift's "To Mr. Congreve" (1693); first printed in Nichols' *Miscellaneous Pieces,* 1789:

> Here by a mountain's side, a reverent cave
> Gives murmuring passage to a lashing wave. . . .
> Here, on a better day, some druid dwelt,
> And the young Muse's early favour felt;
> Druid, a name she does with pride repeat,
> Confessing Albion once her darling seat;
> Far in this primitive cell might we pursue
> Our predecessor's footsteps still in view;
> Here would we sing—But ah! you think I dream. . . .

71. Whether or not he consciously remembers the source in *Lycidas* 68–9, it is shocking to be asked to visualize "Our Youths" playing with "the Tangles" of Freedom's "Hair."

72. In the "Forty-five" freedom has perforce to be defended by the sword, and Anger and Rage were the inevitable legacy of civil war; but as the poet in the same context had pleaded for mercy (*Ode to Mercy*) he now pleads for union and concord under the aegis of Liberty.

73. There are other potentials in personification which Collins does not so fully develop: for example, the psychological insight of a figure like Spenser's Despair or the brief dramatic force of Gray's "These shall the fury Passions tear,/The vultures of the mind," etc. Collins's *personae* are more purely visual, like Milton's in the Companion Pieces, but with an added suggestion of the visionary. In "From Action to Idea: Theories of the Lyric in the Eighteenth Century" (*Critics and Criticism*, ed. R. S. Crane, Chicago, 1952, 408–60) Norman Maclean illustrates the change by contrasting *The Passions* with Dryden's famous ode on the power of Music, *Alexander's Feast;* condemning Ruskin's contrast between symbol and personification, Bertrand Bronson ("Personification Reconsidered," *ELH.* 14 [1947], 167) declares, "A personification is but one among many kinds of symbol." Personification is a form of metaphor and only becomes an effective symbol when, as in Collins, it is central to the whole effect of the poem.

74. If this means true to the workings of the human mind, Addison had admitted as much in explaining the power of "the fairy way of writing."

75. Whether Collins remembered it or not, Blackwell in his *Enquiry* had attempted to explain Homer's power, especially the effect of wonder, by reference to the ignorance and credulity of the times.

76. Pointed out in my discussion in *TLS.,* 20 December 1928, p. 1011, and noticed about the same time by Oliver Elton, *Survey of English Literature 1730–80,* London, 1928, 2, 52–3.

77. The following passages from Martin's *Voyage to St. Kilda,* London, 1698, when compared with the quoted stanza sufficiently illustrate Collins's inclusions and omissions: "The Inhabitants of St. Kilda are much happier than the generality of Mankind. . . . What the Condition of the People in the Golden Age is feign'd by the Poets to be, theirs really is, I mean, in Innocency and simplicity. . . . They are altogether ignorant of the Vices of Foreigners, and govern'd by the Dictates of Reason and Christianity, as it was first deliver'd to them . . ." (p. 131). "They are reputed very Cunning, and there is scarce any Circumventing them in Traffick and Bartering. . . ." (p. 73.) "There are some of both Sexes who have a Genius for *Poetry,* and are great admirers of Musick" (ibid.). "In this Isle there are plenty of excellent Fountains or Springs," described in detail (p. 24). The island is of rock, and the earth thin "except on the tops of the Hills, where . . . it affords them good Turf; the Grass is very short but kindly, producing plenty of Milk . . . (pp. 26–7). "The Soil is very grateful to the Labourer, producing ordinarily Sixteen, Eighteen or Twenty Fold sometimes . . ." (p. 28); but ". . . there is no sort of Trees, no, not the least Shrub grows here, nor ever a Bee seen at any time" (p. 31).

Gray's *Elegy* Reconsidered

IAN JACK

The Province of Eloquence is to reign over minds of slow perception & little imagination, to set things in lights they never saw them in—to engage their attention by details & circumstances gradually unfolded, to adorn & heighten them with images & colours unknown to them to raise & engage their rude passions &c.

Gray's *Common Place Book*, iii, p. [1,111],
transcribed from the Pocket Book of 1755.

IF it were not for William Mason, critics of Gray's most famous poem would have less scope for disagreement. Mason tells us that Gray

originally gave it only the simple title of "Stanzas written in a Country Church-yard." I persuaded him first to call it an ELEGY, because the subject authorized him so to do; and the alternate measure, in which it was written, seemed peculiarly fit for that species of composition.[1]

Mason complicates matters further when he tells us that he is inclined to believe that the poem was "begun, if not concluded,"[2] soon after the death of Richard West. Taking their cue from Mason, subsequent critics have often associated the poem with West's death, while some have even regarded it as in a sense an elegy on Gray's early friend. As a result of this anyone who wishes to come to terms with the *Elegy* today is obliged first of all to make his own assessment of the evidence about the date of composition and the original intention of the poem.

There are two different sorts of poem: poems whose writers know from the beginning what they intend to say: and poems whose writers do not. This distinction in terms of the way in which a poem comes into existence is antecedent to distinctions of genre or "kind" in the more usual sense. In the first case a poet sits down to write a poem, and the result may be *To his Coy Mistress, Paradise Lost,* or *The Rape of the Lock.* In the second case a poem —or more probably a fragment of poetry—pushes a poet into a chair and makes him write, and the result may be *Kubla Khan, Endymion,* or *In Memoriam.* The traditional European Art of Poetry is based on the study of poems of the first sort—poems which may be regarded as artifacts produced by men with particular intentions in mind, so that their technique can be considered in terms of the skill with which they have attempted to achieve their ends. Romantic aesthetic is more helpful when we approach poems of the second sort, because it lays more emphasis on the spontaneous power of the poet's imagination than on questions of intention and rhetoric.

If this distinction is valid, then there are two misconceptions we must guard against. One is the assumption that the first sort of poem is typically "classical" or Augustan and the second typically "romantic" or modern. Although poems of the second sort have probably become more common in the last two centuries, it seems likely that poems of both sorts are written in most periods. The other misconception is to suppose that any given poem must be of one sort or the other, and cannot contain elements of both: that a planned poem can owe nothing to "inspiration," that an "inspired" poem can owe nothing to planning. In every great poem (on the contrary) there is almost certain to be an element of planning as well as an element of "inspiration." It is because there is no planning in *Kubla Khan* (or no planning of which the poet himself was conscious) that Coleridge was unwilling to publish it: it is because there is so little but careful planning in *Cato* that the tragedy lies unregarded in the pages of Addison's *Collected Works.*

Because we have always known Gray's poem as an Elegy—as *the* Elegy—and because it is so obviously the work of a learned poet who is superbly in control of his technique, we naturally assume that it is a poem of the planned sort; yet the little that we know or can guess about the process of its composition suggests a different view—as does a careful analysis of the poem itself.

The most important evidence about the date of composition is that contained in a letter from Gray to Horace Walpole which was written on the 12th of June 1750. Enclosing a copy of the completed poem, he wrote:

Having put an end to a thing, whose beginning you have seen long ago, I immediately send it you. (*Correspondence*, ed. Paget Toynbee and Leonard Whibley, 1935, i, 326–7.)

Since there is no question of the poem's having been begun before 1741, and since Gray and Walpole were estranged from that year until the end of 1745, "long ago" cannot refer to a date earlier than 1745–46. This would confirm Walpole's remark to Mason, when the latter was engaged on the Memoirs:

The *Churchyard* was, I am persuaded, posterior to West's death [1742] at least three or four years. . . . At least I am sure that I had the twelve or more first lines from himself above three years after that period, and it was long before he finished it.

(Yale Edition, Vol. 28, 117–18.)

The only reason for doubting this chronology is a statement in Mason's *Memoirs* which Walpole is usually considered to have accepted as a correction to his own view. After mentioning the poems that Gray wrote in August 1742, Mason continues:

I am inclined to believe that the Elegy in a Country Church-yard was begun, if not concluded, at this time also.

(*Memoirs*, p. 157.)

This is so important an assertion that we are bound to ask what sort of evidence Mason can have had for making it. He cannot himself have seen any part of the poem at that early date, as he did not meet Gray until 1747. He cannot have had a letter proving that the poem was written in 1742, or he would certainly have printed it. He cannot have had Gray's word for such a date, or he would not have said merely that he was "inclined to believe" it. It seems that he must have been speculating, on the basis of circumstantial evidence, and it may well be that he wished to prove that Gray had anticipated Shenstone's use of what came to be known as the "elegiac stanza" in 1743.[3] It is misleading of Mason to use the words "if not concluded." He immediately acknowledges that, "as it stands at present, the conclusion is of a later date," printing the earlier conclusion in his notes with the admission that Gray's "after-thought was unquestionably the best."[4] His meaning (there-fore) is presumably that the earlier version was probably concluded in 1742. But if that is true, then apparently Gray waited three or four years before showing any part of the (completed) poem to anyone—then showed Walpole only about twelve lines—and then waited another four or five years before writing a new conclusion and so completing a poem now eight years old. It seems most un-likely. Gray once told West that he grew "less enamour'd" of his own productions "the older they grow,"[5] and we may well conclude that if after four years he had been dissatisfied with all but a dozen lines of a poem he would have abandoned it or at least refrained from showing so brief a fragment to Horace Walpole. Unless (therefore) important new evidence makes its appearance, I doubt whether Walpole's enigmatic remark in a letter that Mason's "ac-count of the Elegy puts an end to my other criticism"[6] can be taken as proof that Walpole sincerely and rightly accepted all that Mason had said about the date of composition. It seems to me more likely that Walpole was referring to some different "criticism," or that he wrongly allowed himself to be persuaded by Mason, or that he was simply bored by that rather tedious man.

So we are driven back to the most likely hypothesis, that Gray began the poem about the year 1746; and there are two sentences in his letters which fit in very well. On the 10th of August 1746 he wrote to Thomas Wharton (later the recipient of one of the three MSS. of the poem which still survive):

The Muse, I doubt, is gone, & has left me in far worse Company: if she returns, you will hear of her.

On the 11th of September he told him that he was writing "a few autumnal Verses . . . dureing the Fall of the Leaf": an apt enough description (surely) of the opening of the *Elegy*. As Thomson had written in a poem that Gray knew very well, Autumn is the time

> For those whom wisdom and whom nature charm
> To steal themselves from the degenerate crowd,
> And soar above this little scene of things—
> To tread low-thoughted vice beneath their feet,
> To soothe the throbbing passions into peace,
> And woo lone Quiet in her silent walks.
>
> (*Autumn*, 964–9.)

Autumn was the season when "Philosophic Melancholy" might appropriately demand

> ... the sigh for suffering worth
> Lost in obscurity.
>
>   (1022–3.)

Whether or not the first lines of the poem to be written were the initial stanzas describing sunset in the churchyard, it seems likely that the poem was born of a mood. The first few lines may even have come with a misleading spontaneity. We may be reminded of a revelation of A. E. Housman's about one of his own poems:

Two of the stanzas, I do not say which, came into my head, just as they are printed, while I was crossing the corner of Hampstead Heath. . . . A third stanza came with a little coaxing after tea. One more was needed, but it did not come: I had to turn to and compose it myself, and that was a laborious business. I wrote it thirteen times, and it was more than a twelvemonth before I got it right.[7]

We know that lines and stanzas occasionally "came into [Gray's] head" too. Once when he was "walking in the spring in the neighbourhood of Cambridge" with his friend Norton Nicholls he told him of two such lines—

> There pipes the wood-lark, & the song thrush there
> Scatters his loose notes in the waste of air.

These lines (of which the second, characteristically, owes something to a passage in Thomson)[8] never found their poem, but it is quite possible that the lines which were destined to form the opening of one of the most celebrated poems in the language "came into [Gray's] head" in a similar way. If so, it is conceivable that he did not know what the poem was to be about. The opening lines merely set the scene: the only thing we can say with certainty of the poem that is to follow them is that it must be pensive and melancholy. It must be something in the vein of "Il Penseroso"—a title that Gray had already appropriated to himself in a letter to West. It is not surprising to find that he would have liked to use Virgil's famous line—

> Sunt lacrimae rerum, et mentem mortalia tangunt

—as the motto of the poem, if Young had not already used it for his *Night Thoughts*.

We do not know how long it took Gray to write the earlier version of the poem, as it has come down to us.[9] The evidence of its later history, as contained in the Eton College MS., suggests that he may almost from the first have worked slowly, with many corrections. A passage from a letter to West about Gray's unfinished tragedy, *Agrippina*, makes it clear how self-critical he was, and how willing to delete inferior lines:

Faulty expressions . . . are easily altered or omitted: and indeed if the thoughts be wrong or superfluous, there is nothing easier than to leave out the whole. The first ten or twelve lines are, I believe, the best. . . . Now, if you are of my opinion . . ., you need not fear unravelling my web. I am a sort of spider; and have little else to do but spin it over again, or creep to some other place and spin there. . . . It makes the hours pass, and is better than ἐν ἀμαθίᾳ καὶ ἀμουσίᾳ καταβιῶναι.[10]

(*Correspondence*, i, 193–4.)

In any event, the earlier version of the poem as we have it consists of the first 18 stanzas of the *Elegy* as it is usually printed (in a slightly different text), followed by four further stanzas, of which three were later omitted and the fourth rewritten to become lines 93–6.

In this form the poem begins with the familiar series of stanzas in which the poet reflects that some of the humble villagers buried in the churchyard might have become famous, if they had been given the opportunity. Instead of despising them, we should reflect that it may have been their very obscurity that preserved their innocence. This leads naturally to the conclusion:

> The thoughtless World to Majesty may bow
> Exalt the brave, & idolize Success
> But more to Innocence their Safety owe
> Than Power & Genius e'er conspired to bless
>
> And thou, who mindful of the unhonour'd Dead
> Dost in these Notes their artless Tale relate
> By Night & lonely Contemplation led
> To linger in the gloomy Walks of Fate
>
> Hark how the sacred Calm, that broods around
> Bids ev'ry fierce tumultuous Passion cease

In still small Accents whisp'ring from the Ground
A grateful Earnest of eternal Peace

No more with Reason & thyself at Strife;
Give anxious Cares & endless Wishes room
But thro' the cool sequester'd Vale of Life
Pursue the silent Tenour of thy Doom.

The conclusion which the poet applies to his own case is presumably equally valid for the reader: it is foolish to repine because one is not a leading actor on the great stage of life.

The poem at this point clearly derives from a large family of moralising poems written in the seventeenth and eighteenth centuries—a family that traced its ancestry back to the *Georgics* and to Horace, and included in its genealogical tree the Countess of Winchilsea's *Nocturnal Reverie* as well as Parnell's *Night-Piece on Death:*

Time was, like thee they Life possest,
And Time shall be, that thou shalt Rest.
  Those Graves, with bending Osier bound,
That nameless heave the crumbled Ground,
Quick to the glancing Thought disclose
Where *Toil* and *Poverty* repose.

Tovey[11] considered that the original ending of the poem was bald and abrupt, but it may be doubted whether the average reader of the 1740's would have felt this: he would have recognised that he was reading a poem of a reassuringly familiar sort, in a metre that was just beginning to be fashionable.

Yet Gray himself was dissatisfied with the original ending. When he sent the completed poem to Walpole he expressed the hope that he would "look upon it in the light of a *thing with an end to it; a merit that most of my writings have wanted.*"[12] To bring this about he had not only worked hard: he had also made a radical change in the direction and meaning of the poem.

While both versions of the poem present us with Gray's Meditations among the Tombs, there are two great differences between the earlier version and that published in 1751. While it might be an overstatement to say simply that the later version is more "personal," it certainly tells us more about the poet. In the earlier version all that we hear of the poet is that he has been "with Reason & [himself] at Strife," troubled by "anxious Cares & endless Wishes." In the later version we hear how he would wander about or lie—like Jaques[13]—

> And pore upon the brook that babbles by,

so making himself ridiculous in the eyes of the country people who saw him. The first two stanzas of the Epitaph give us further information about him:

> Here rests his head upon the lap of Earth
> A Youth to Fortune and to Fame unknown.
> Fair Science frown'd not on his humble birth,
> And Melancholy mark'd him for her own.
>
> Large was his bounty, and his soul sincere,
> Heav'n did a recompence as largely send:
> He gave to Mis'ry all he had, a tear,
> He gain'd from Heav'n ('twas all he wish'd) a friend.

Stylised as this is, the Poet himself has now become a part—and an important part—of the poem.[14] The second difference is that the original moral of the poem—that the poet (and presumably his readers) should be content to live in obscurity—is now dropped, in order to make way for a conclusion acknowledging his desire to be remembered after his death: a common human sentiment which he shares with the villagers buried in the churchyard. So a poem of Christian Stoicism is rewritten as a poem of Sensibility. The final statements made by the two versions of the poem are so different that it might be less misleading to regard the versions as two different poems.

We may conjecture that Gray's true reason for rejecting the earlier ending of the poem was not merely that it was too abrupt (Tovey's objection), but rather that it preached a Stoic attitude to life that he could not accept, at the deepest level of his mind and heart. Fortunately we can look over his shoulder and watch him arguing the point, in one of his Common Place Books. Under the heading "Affectus" [Passions] he records that "We find in A: Gellius, Lib: 19: Cap: 12: a discourse of Herodes Atticus, a Great Man of his time, where he argues against the Apathy of the Stoicks

with much Good Sense." I quote in English the passage which Gray
goes on to quote in Latin:

That no man, who felt and thought normally, could be wholly exempt
and free from those emotions of the mind, which he called πάθη,
caused by sorrow, desire, fear, anger and pleasure; and even if he could
so resist them as to be free from them altogether, he would not be
better off, since his mind would grow weak and sluggish, being deprived of the support of certain emotions, as of a highly necessary
stimulus. For he declared that those feelings and impulses of the mind,
though they become faults when excessive, are connected and involved
in certain powers and activities of the intellect; and therefore, if we
should in our ignorance eradicate them altogether, there would be
danger lest we lose also the good and useful qualities of the mind which
are connected with them. Therefore he thought that they ought to be
regulated, and pruned skilfully and carefully, so that those only should
be removed which are unsuitable and unnatural. . . . Those disciples
of insensibility, wishing to be thought calm, courageous and steadfast
because of showing neither desire nor grief, neither wrath nor joy,
root out all the more vigorous emotions of the mind, and grow old in
the torpor of a sluggish and, as it were, nerveless life.[15]

Gray comments that "The Passions, as Mr Lock has shew'd, are in
the human Mind but Modes of Pleasure & of Pain, & consequently
can never be eradicated, while it shall continue to covet Good, & to
avoid Evil, that is in other Terms, as long as it exists; but they not
only are in the Mind, it is necessary to our Wellbeing, that they
should be there. We should be in the state almost of mere
Vegetables without them, for why should we act, but to some End,
& what end can we have, but to gain the pleasure resulting from
some Good, or avoid the Pain accompanying, what we call Evil?"
A few lines later we find Gray quoting from the Second Epistle of
the *Essay on Man*. Although he does not here quote lines 101-2, it
is clear that they were often in his mind:

> In lazy Apathy let Stoics boast
> Their Virtue fix'd; 'tis fix'd as in a frost.

In the passage about Grief and Compassion which makes up part
of the entry "Affectus" we find (I think) the matrix of Gray's
famous Latin stanza on the Tears of Sensibility. "Grief inclines,
& softens us to commiserate, & redress, if we be able, the Misfor-

tunes of others in the like unhappy Circumstances; indeed we
should be insensible to their Woes,

> Non ignara mali, miseris succurrere disco,

had we not felt, what it was to be wretched; nor could we form
any Idea of them, but by comparison with our own:

> mollissima corda
> Humano generi dare se Natura fatetur,
> Quae lacrymas dedit. Haec nostri pars optima sensus:

Compassion then, the Mother of so many generous actions, arises
from this." It is an easy transition from these speculations to line
16 of the "Hymn to Adversity"—

> And from her own she learn'd to melt at others' woe

—or line 32:

> And Pity, dropping soft the sadly-pleasing tear.

The transition to the Alcaic stanza is no less clear:

> O lachrymarum Fons, tenero sacros
> Ducentium ortus ex animo; quater
> Felix! in imo qui scatentem
> Pectore te, pia Nympha, sensit!

It seems to me that this same entry also throws light on Gray's
acknowledgment of the human desire to be remembered after
death: an acknowledgment which is so central to the concluding
stanzas of the 1751 *Elegy*. Lines 85–8—

> For who to dumb Forgetfulness a prey,
> This pleasing anxious being e'er resign'd,
> Left the warm precincts of the chearful day,
> Nor cast one longing ling'ring look behind?

—might have been written as an explicit challenge to "the Apathy
of the Stoicks." By ending the poem with a recognition of our
unwillingness to be forgotten Gray is making it clear that he is not
one of the "apathiae sectatores" who refuse to acknowledge human
instincts and passions. Like the simple villagers, the poet himself
participates in that species of self-love which makes us wish to be
remembered and paid "the passing tribute of a sigh."

Such an apparent shift of sensibility as that between these two versions of Gray's poem, at the still centre of the eighteenth century, must arrest our attention. Only two years after the *Elegy* was published Rousseau was to write his *Discours Sur l'Origine et les Fondements de l'Inégalité parmi les hommes,* quoting the second of the Virgilian passages that we have just seen in Gray's Common Place Book in order to illustrate "le pur mouvement de la nature, antérieur à toute réflexion."[16] I do not wish to argue that Gray's own sensibility was transformed between the date of the earlier version of his poem and that of the later: that would be a naïve and melodramatic account of the matter. The interesting thing is that he was capable of writing both versions, at about the same point in his life, but felt that the later version was somehow truer to human nature, and therefore more satisfying. And so it came about that a poem which was already accepted as a classic soon after the middle of the eighteenth century continued to be regarded as a classic in the following century, when the Poet himself was so often to be the subject of the poem, and when topics from humble life were to call forth tears from a greater poet than Gray:

> To me the meanest flower that blows can give
> Thoughts that do often lie too deep for tears.

Yet we must not exaggerate. One has only to recall the poetry of the nineteenth century to acknowledge that the *Elegy* remains a highly formalised composition. We must bear this in mind when we consider Mason's suggestion that its composition was closely connected with the death of West.

It is true that West's friendship had meant a great deal to Gray. Walpole and West appealed to two facets of Gray's character, and it was West who appealed to the more important—the poet and the man of Sensibility. "I well remember how little you love Letters, where all the Materials are drawn out of oneself," Gray wrote to Walpole four years after West's death, while in another letter he remarks: "Of all people living I know you are the least a friend to letters spun out of one's own brains, with all the toil and constraint that accompanies sentimental productions."[17] The letters between Gray and West, on the other hand, have all the features of a sentimental correspondence. On the 5th of June 1740, for example, West wrote to Gray in the vein that we associate with the Man of Feeling thirty years later:

I know it is very seldom that people trouble themselves with the sentiments of those they converse with; so they can chat about trifles, they
never care whether your heart aches or no. Are you one of these? I
think not. But what right have I to ask you this question? Have we
known one another enough, that I should expect or demand sincerity
from you? Yes, Gray, I hope we have.

Gray replied swiftly:

You do yourself and me justice, in imagining that you merit, and that I
am capable of sincerity. I have not a thought, or even a weakness, I
desire to conceal from you.

(Correspondence, i, 165–8.)

In the same vein, West more than once expressed the hope that
Gray would remember him after his death:

> Unknown & silent will depart my breath,
> Nor nature e'er take notice of my death.
> Yet some there are (ere sunk in endless night)
> Within whose breasts my monument I'd write:
> Loved in my life, lamented in my end,
> Their praise would crown me, as their precepts mend:
> To them may these fond lines my name indear,
> Not from the Author, but the Friend sincere.[18]

On a later occasion Gray sent West a poem concluding with the
following lines:

> When then my Fates, that breath they gave, shall claim,
> When the short Marble shall preserve a Name,
> A little Verse, my All that shall remain;
> Thy passing Courser's slacken'd Speed detain,
> (Thou envied Honour of thy Poet's Days,
> Of all our Youth th'Ambition & the Praise!)
> Then to my quiet Urn awhile draw near,
> And say, (while o'er the place you drop a Tear)
> Love & the Fair were of his Life the Pride,
> He lived, while She was kind, & when she frown'd, he died.

(Correspondence, i, 199.)

The element of formality and convention in these passages is very obvious. West's poem is based on Tibullus III, v, and on a letter of Pope's to Steele, while Gray's lines are a translation of Propertius II, i. The description of West as

>   Of all our Youth th'Ambition & the Praise

no more corresponds to reality than does the statement that "Love & the Fair" were the "Pride" of Gray's life.

This perhaps makes it the less surprising that when we turn to the earlier of the extant versions of the *Elegy,* which must have been written closer to the date of West's death than the later, we find nothing that can be construed as an allusion to the death of Gray's friend. Several writers have pointed out that Gray echoes a phrase from one of West's poems in line 35, and it is conceivable that the quatrain which contains it helped to influence Gray's choice of metre—

>   Ah me! what boots us all our boasted power,
>   Our golden treasure, and our purple state?
>   They cannot ward *th' inevitable hour,*
>   Nor stay the fearful violence of fate.[19]

But apart from that there is nothing in the first version of the poem to suggest West. Even in the second version one cannot do much more than echo the traditional conjecture that Gray may have had West in mind when he wrote the Epitaph. That is not to suggest that the whole Epitaph is in fact about West: so far from being of "humble birth," he was—as Dodsley recorded in his *Collection of Poems*—"Son to the Chancellor of *Ireland,* and Grandson to Bishop BURNET." The line

>   He gave to Mis'ry all he had, a tear

may echo (as Tovey points out) a passage from Gray's tribute to the memory of West at the end of his *De Principiis Cogitandi:*

>   has lachrymas, memori quas ictus amore
>   Fundo; quod possum.

Clearly the "Youth" of the Epitaph is a highly formalised figure, and the poet might well have devised a similar conclusion even if no close friend of his had in fact died. In any age friendship is an important part of the pattern of life, and it was as important to the eighteenth-century Man of Sensibility as it had been to the καλὸς κἀγαθός of Greek antiquity. The question of the identity of the "friend" in the Epitaph is a question of little critical significance— if indeed it is a meaningful question at all.

This brings us back to the word "Elegy." When Mason remarked that "the subject authorized" Gray to call the poem an elegy, he did not necessarily mean that its subject was the death of a particular person. As Joseph Trapp had pointed out at the beginning of the century, "Elegies admit almost of any Matter, especially if it be treated of seriously. The Contempt of Riches, the Pleasures of the Country, are in great measure the Subject of them."[20] About the middle of the century the vogue for elegiac writing in this wide sense became very marked, and no one gives so helpful a description of "the *use* and *end* of elegy" as Shenstone:

There is a truly virtuous pleasure connected with many pensive contemplations, which it is the province and excellency of elegy to enforce. This, by presenting suitable ideas, has discovered sweets in *melancholy* which we could not find in *mirth;* and has led us with success to the dusty *urn,* when we could draw no pleasure from the sparkling bowl; as pastoral conveys an idea of simplicity and innocence, it is in particular the task and merit of elegy to shew the innocence and simplicity of rural life to advantage; and that, in a way distinct from *pastoral,* as much as the plain but judicious landlord may be imagined to surpass his tenant both in *dignity* and *understanding.* It should also tend to elevate the more tranquil virtues of *humility, disinterestedness, simplicity,* and *innocence:* but then there is a *degree* of elegance and refinement, no way inconsistent with these *rural* virtues; and that raises *elegy* above that *merum rus,* that *unpolished* rusticity, which has given our *pastoral* writers their highest reputation.

Wealth and splendor will never want their proper weight: the danger is, lest they should too much preponderate. A kind of poetry therefore which throws its chief influence into the other scale, that magnifies the sweets of liberty and independence, that *endears* the honest *delights* of love and friendship, that *celebrates* the *glory* of a good name after death, that ridicules the futile arrogance of birth, that recommends the innocent amusement of letters, and insensibly prepares the mind for that humanity it *inculcates, such* a kind of poetry may chance to please; and if it please, should seem to be of service.

Although Shenstone's "Prefatory Essay on Elegy" was not published until his *Works* were collected in 1764, two separate footnotes assure us that it had been written "near twenty years ago," so that his account of the matter dates from about the time when Gray was working on his *Elegy*. We know that Shenstone began writing his own *Elegies* in or about the year 1743, and it seems likely that Gray had seen at least two of them—IV and XV—before he wrote his own poem. Shenstone's *Elegy IV* contains a number of lines that remind us of Gray, while his rhetorical question—

> Why has such worth, without distinction, dy'd,
> Why, like the desert's lilly, bloom'd to fade?

—may have helped to suggest Gray's lines,

> Full many a flower is born to blush unseen,
> And waste its sweetness on the desert air.

Elegy XV also reminds us of Gray on more than one occasion, notably in lines 45–6:

> No wild ambition fir'd their tranquil breast,
> To swell with empty sounds a spotless name.

Internal evidence of this kind might, I think, be used to strengthen the case against the view that the *Elegy* was begun in 1742, but the argument would have to be extended to include other poems (such as the *Odes* of Collins and Joseph Warton) that Gray was reading in the later months of 1746. It is even conceivable that Gray saw a draft of Shenstone's "Prefatory Essay," and that this helped to define the tone of his own Elegy. But it is time to turn from conjecture to certainty, from the obscure history of its composition to the challenging fact of the poem itself.

While it seems likely that Gray's choice of stanza owed something to the example of Shenstone, he had already shown his liking for alternate rhyme in the "Sonnet on the Death of Richard West" (which has the rather unusual rhyme-scheme, abab, abab, cdcdcd), while his notes on Metre in his Common Place Books remind us that he was familiar with the cross-rhyming stanza in earlier English poetry. Under the heading, "The Measures I find principally in use among our Writers," we find the following:[21]

Verse	*Order of the Rhymes*
Stanza's, of four, as	Alternate. call'd by the French
Ld Surreys Verses, written in	Rime croisée, or entrelassée,
Windsor-Castle. Epitaph on	(whether there were two, or more
S^r T: Wyat.&c:	Rhimes that answer'd one
Dryden's Annus Mirabilis.	another, as in all that we call
Spencer . . Colin-Clout's come	Stanza's
home again, & April. Gascoyne's	
Councell on travelling. his	
Woodmanship,	

Although it is unfortunate that this entry cannot be precisely dated, it matters less than it might because none of the examples that Gray mentions is of any importance as a model for the verse of his *Elegy*. It is in an earlier poem than *Annus Mirabilis,* the *Heroique Stanza's* to the memory of Cromwell, that we find Dryden coming closest to Gray's use of the metre:

> His Ashes in a peacefull Urne shall rest,
> His Name a great example stands to show
> How strangely high endeavours may be blest,
> Where *Piety* and *valour* joyntly goe.

Gray must have been familiar with Dryden's comment on the measure:

I have chosen to write my Poem in *Quatrains* or *Stanza's* of four in alternate rhyme, because I have ever judg'd them more noble, and of greater dignity, both for the sound and number, than any other Verse in use amongst us.

He goes on to acknowledge that he is making this high claim for quatrains in spite of the fact that he himself finds it easier to write in couplets,

for there the work is sooner at an end, every two lines concluding the labour of the Poet: but in Quattrains he is to carry it farther on; and not onely so, but to bear along in his head the troublesome sense of four lines together. For those who write correctly in this kind must needs acknowledge, that the last line of the Stanza is to be consider'd in the composition of the first.

(*Poems*, ed. James Kinsley, i, 44–5)

Annus Mirabilis may be taken to prove that quatrains are not a suitable metre for a long poem, but when Gray began his *Elegy* a recent poet was considered to have used the stanza successfully in the elegiac mode. Although Hammond's *Love Elegies* make insipid reading today, Gray is almost certain to have known them, and there are one or two stanzas that may have caught his eye: the conclusion of *Elegy III,* for example—

> With flowry Garlands, each revolving Year
> Shall strow the Grave where Truth and Softness rest,
> Then Home returning drop the pious Tear,
> And bid the Turf lye easy on her Breast

—or that of *Elegy IX,* an epitaph on the poet himself of the sort that was already a convention:

> Here lyes a Youth born down with Love and Care,
> He cou'd not long his DELIA's Loss abide,
> Joy left his Bosom with the parting Fair,
> And when he durst no longer hope, he dy'd.

In a letter Shenstone refers to the quatrain as "Hammond's Metre."[22] Here is his comment on the matter in his "Prefatory Essay":

The public ear, habituated of late to a quicker measure, may perhaps consider *this* as heavy and languid; but an objection of that kind may gradually lose its force, if this measure should be allowed to suit the nature of elegy.

The "quicker measure" was of course the pentameter couplet, as used by Pope; and there is no doubt that the slower movement of the quatrain is essential to the effect of Gray's *Elegy*. The best way to demonstrate this is to see what happens if we transpose some stanzas into couplets:

> The Curfew tolls the knell of parting day,
> The plowman homeward plods his weary way,
> The lowing herd wind slowly o'er the lea,
> And leaves the world to darkness and to me.
> . . . .
> Beneath those rugged elms, that yew-tree's shade,
> Each in his narrow cell for ever laid,
> Where heaves the turf in many a mould'ring heap,
> The rude Forefathers of the hamlet sleep.

> The breezy call of incense-breathing Morn,
> The cock's shrill clarion, or the echoing horn,
> The swallow twitt'ring from the straw-built shed,
> No more shall rouse them from their lowly bed.

It remains respectable verse; yet what has gone is the source of the peculiar distinction of the *Elegy*—the great suspended chords that sound through the poem and give it its characteristic inevitability. This is due to the way in which Gray handles the quatrain, rather than to the quatrain itself, as we may verify by looking at one of Shakespeare's sonnets:

> Like as the waves make towards the pebbled shore,
> So do our minutes hasten to their end,
> Each changing place with that which goes before,
> In sequent boil all forwards do contend.

These lines express an urgency which would be out of place in Gray's poem. The struggle enacted in Shakespeare's lines is to Gray rather a subject for philosophic contemplation.

The fact that so many of the stanzas of the *Elegy* can be transposed into couplets is a reminder that the greater part of the poem consists of more or less self-sufficient lines. Although Gray insisted that it should not be printed as separate quatrains, on only three occasions is the sense carried on from one quatrain to another. As a rule the first three lines lead with an air of finality to the fourth. Some of the most memorable lines occur at the end of their quatrains: line 32, for example—

> The short and simple annals of the poor:

line 56—

> And waste its sweetness on the desert air:

and line 76—

> They kept the noiseless tenor of their way.

Gray understood as well as Dryden that "the last line of the stanza is to be considered in the composition of the first," and it was by remembering this that he was able to march so irresistibly towards the final assertion of line 36—

> The paths of glory lead but to the grave

or of line 92—

> Ev'n in our Ashes live their wonted Fires.

Such lines burst like great universal breakers on the shores of our limited personal experience.

The Common Place Books make it clear that the position of the caesura in a line of verse was one of the aspects of the Art of Poetry that interested Gray.[23] He takes Milton, "the best example of an exquisite ear, that I can produce," as his exemplar, and scans passages from "L'Allegro" to show how in octosyllabic verse the caesura may occur after the second, third, fourth or fifth syllable of the eight. "The more we attend to the composition of his harmony," he comments, "the more we shall be sensible, how much he loved to vary his pauses, his measures, & his feet, wch gives that enchanting air of freedom & wildness to his versification, unconfined by any rules,—but what his own feeling, & the nature of his subject demanded." He illustrates a similar freedom in the heptasyllabic parts of "Il Penseroso" by marking the caesurae in the following lines. I also transcribe his partial scansion:

(Ŏft ŏn ă plāt | of rising ground	Oct: [on the 4th]
I hear | the far-off Curfeu sound,)	on the 2^d.
Ōver some | wĭde-water'd shore,	on the 3^d.
Swinging slow | with sudden roar.	on the 3^d.

Turning to the structure of decasyllabic verse, he writes:

But the greatest confinement, that Puttenham would lay on our Verse, is that of making the Caesura constantly fall on the 4th syllable of the decasyllabic measure wch is now become our only heroic metre for all poems of any length. This restraint Wyat & Ld Surrey submitted to, tho' here & there you find an instance of their breaking thro' it . . . But our Poets have long since got loose from these fetters. Spencer judiciously shook them off; Milton in his Paradise lost is ever changing & mingling his pauses, & the greatest Writers after him have made it their study to avoid what Puttenham regarded, as a rule of perfect versification.

By adopting Gray's own mode of notation we may watch him "changing & mingling his pauses" in lines 29–32:

Let not Ambition mock | their useful toil,	on the 6th.
Their homely joys, | and destiny obscure;	on the 4th.

Nor Grandeur hear | with a disdainful smile,   on the 4th.
The short and simple | annals of the poor.   on the 5th.

Once or twice the caesura falls after the second syllable, as in the line—

    If chance, | by lonely contemplation led

—or after the seventh—

    Mutt'ring his wayward fancies | he would rove;

but as a rule it falls after the fourth, fifth or sixth syllable. As we watch Gray varying its position in this way we are studying a profound student of Latin verse who was also an almost daily reader of Milton.

The use of the caesura most frequently noticed by modern critics of Augustan poetry is that which subserves the purposes of antithesis, as in Pope's line

    Less wit than mimic, more a wit than wise.

In the *Elegy* Gray takes great care to avoid such antitheses. Most of the lines are without medial punctuation, and when such punctuation does occur, there is hardly ever the least hint of antithesis. On the contrary, the second half of the line is likely to amplify or parallel the first:

    The boast of heraldry, the pomp of pow'r,
    And all that beauty, all that wealth e'er gave.

Norton Nicholls tells us that the first line of the poem originally read

    The curfew tolls the knell of *dying* day,

and that Gray changed "dying" to "parting" in order "to avoid the *concetto*."[24] This is easy to believe. Although I have argued that Gray did not, as he wrote the poem, think of himself as composing an "elegy" in the specialised sense, it is as true of him as of the writer of an elegy in Trapp's account of the genre that he "aims not to be witty or facetious, acrimonious or severe." Trapp rules that "with this Kind of Poem, every Thing that is epigrammatical, satirical, or sublime, is inconsistent."[25] Once or twice Gray does in fact approach the sublime, but throughout he carefully avoids the "epigrammatical [or] satirical." Gray had a flair for epigram, but "Nunc non erat his locus"[26] and throughout one notices that he avoids the kind of wit that makes a fleeting appearance in Pope's *Elegy to the Memory of an Unfortunate Lady*. He also avoids the temptation—always strong, for a poet writing in this metre—to use the last two lines for an image amplifying or illustrating the statement made in the first two—as Dryden so often does in *Annus Mirabilis*. The rhetoric of wit would be out of keeping with the spirit of the "autumnal Verses" in which Gray set down his reflections on human destiny.

From the first stanza onward we are aware that we are reading a carefully-patterned poem:

> The *Curfew* tolls the knell | of p a r t i n g *day,*
> The l o w i n g *herd* | winds s l o w l y o'er the *lea,*
> The *plowman* h o m e w a r d plods | his w e a r y *way,*
> And leaves the *world* | to *darkness* and to me.[27]

We notice at once that the movement of the first and third lines, in which the caesura falls after the sixth syllable, differs from that of the second and fourth, in which it falls after the fourth syllable. We also notice that each line contains a substantive in each of its halves, and that five of the eight half-lines also contain an adjective or adverb. The lonely position of the words "and to me" at the end of the quatrain gives them an effect of what might be termed pathetic emphasis. When we move to the second quatrain we find Gray subtly and skilfully gaining an effect of varied continuity:

> Now fades the g l i m m e r i n g *landscape* | on the *sight,*
> And a l l the *air* | a s o l e m n *stillness* holds,
> Save w h e r e the *beetle* | wheels his d r o n i n g *flight,*
> And d r o w s y *tinklings* | lull the d i s t a n t *folds.*

Here the way in which the caesura in the first line falls after seven syllables (or, more precisely, after seven and a half) differentiates it sharply from any line in the preceding stanzas, as does the fact that the initial verbs occur in the first foot of line 1 and the last foot of line 2. Otherwise there is a general similarity of pattern. Once again each line contains two nouns, one in each half: once again the noun is usually preceded by an adjective or adverb. The last line quoted may well remind us of Latin verse. In the preface to

Sylvae Dryden remarks that Claudian has only four or five types of line in his repertoire,

perpetually closing his sence at the end of a Verse, and that Verse commonly which they call golden, or two Substantives and two Adjectives with a Verb betwixt them to keep the peace.

(Poems, i, 392.)

The term "golden verse" or "golden line" is commonly used by classical scholars to describe a line in which two adjectives are followed by a verb and then two substantives. As Latin is an inflected language, there is no doubt which adjective accompanies each substantive:

M o l l i a   l u t e o l â pingit *vaccinia calthâ*.[28]

In view of the great popularity and influence of the *Georgics*, in which such lines are relatively common, the question of the English equivalent of the "golden line" is a matter of some interest. The nearest equivalent would appear to be a line in which the principal words follow the sequence adjective-noun-verb-adjective-noun. The *Elegy* contains almost a dozen examples:

C h i l l   *Penury* repress'd their   n o b l e   *rage.*

Such analysis further reveals that the commonest line-pattern of all in the *Elegy* follows the general sequence adjective-noun-adjective-noun, as in line 17:

The b r e e z y *call* of i n c e n s e - b r e a t h i n g *Morn,*

or line 57:

Some v i l l a g e - *Hampden,* that with d a u n t l e s s *breast.*

There are fifteen or more lines of this general type, and we notice that they often occur first in their quatrains. There is a different type of line which tends to occur fourth in its quatrain, and on occasion in the third and fourth lines successively. This consists of verb-noun-adjective-noun (sometimes with an adjective before the first noun, and sometimes with another verb at the end):

To scatter *plenty* o'er a   s m i l i n g   *land,*
And read their *hist'ry* in a   n a t i o n ' s   *eyes.*

It is not suggested that the essence of the *Elegy* is to be found in any formula. Yet it is (after all) the poem *par excellence* of recur-

rent patterns and subtle variations from the established norm, and
to discern the shadow of the "golden line" and of what may be
termed the balanced adjectival line beneath the surface of the verse
may help us to appreciate the rhetorical structure of this remarkable composition.

As we study the diction of the *Elegy* we are supported by the
knowledge that Gray himself had decided views on the nature of
the language that a poet should use. His most celebrated observation occurs in a letter to West. In April 1742 Gray had sent him a
long speech from a projected tragedy, *Agrippina,* and West had
replied that he considered the style "too antiquated," recommend-
ing the example of Racine, who "no where gives you the phrases
of Ronsard: His language is the language of the times." Gray
replied:

As to matter of stile, I have this to say: The language of the age is never
the language of poetry; except among the French, whose verse, where
the thought or image does not support it, differs in nothing from prose.
Our poetry, on the contrary, has a language peculiar to itself; to which
almost every one, that has written, has added something by enriching it
with foreign idioms and derivatives: Nay sometimes words of their own
composition or invention. Shakespear and Milton have been great
creators this way; and no one more licentious than Pope or Dryden,
who perpetually borrow expressions from the former. (*Correspondence,*
i, 189–92.)

West proceeded, very sensibly, to limit the range of disagreement
by reminding Gray of the criterion of appropriateness:

Old words revived . . . [are] of excellent use in *tales.* . . . One need only
read Milton to acknowledge the dignity they give *the Epic.* . . . They
ought to be used in *Tragedy* more sparingly, than in most *kinds* of
poetry. (i, 195; my italics.)

"A Long Story" exemplifies the sort of "language" that Gray considered appropriate to light verse:

> Each hole and cupboard they explore,
> Each creek and cranny of his chamber,
> Run hurry-skurry round the floor,
> And o'er the bed and tester clamber.

What we are concerned with in the *Elegy* is the "language" proper to one sort of poetry: a species of meditative poetry written in an elegiac mood.

Once or twice the language of the poem comes close to that of "the age," as in lines 3–4:

> The plowman homeward plods his weary way,
> And leaves the world to darkness and to me,

but that is quite exceptional. It is true that when we analyse the diction we find no words of Gray's own "invention" and none even of his own "composition" (unless "ivy-mantled" or "incense-breathing" is new, which seems unlikely). Such an analysis reveals that a considerable number of the words in the poem are slightly archaic and poetical—words like jocund, oft, yonder, bower, glebe and save (= except). We also notice that most of the nouns and verbs are everyday words, usually monosyllabic; and that there is a remarkably high number of adjectives. But the most important result of the analysis is to remind us that "language" consists of *words as they are used* and not as separate and independent entities. Wordsworth's failure to understand this is one of the sources of the confusion in the Preface to the second edition of *Lyrical Ballads*. As soon as we look at the *Elegy* again with this in mind we find that its "language" is very remote from that of "the age":

> The struggling pangs of conscious truth to hide,
> To quench the blushes of ingenuous shame,
> Or heap the shrine of Luxury and Pride
> With incense kindled at the Muse's flame.

There is hardly a word there which Gray might not have used in conversation, but the way in which the words are being made to work is not the prose way. In the space that remains I wish to examine one or two aspects of the "peculiar language" of our poetry as exemplified in this poem.

Every reader notices Gray's use of abstract personifications, which is reminiscent of *The Vanity of Human Wishes*. Like Johnson, Gray uses personification in a non-pictorial way natural to a scholar conversant in Latin poetry. It is perfectly true that the presence or absence of a capital letter may be all that determines our decision whether or not a given abstraction is a personification.

There seems no particular reason why "Luxury" and "Pride" should be capitalised, in line 71, while "conscious truth" and "ingenuous shame" in lines 69–70 are not. In fact, it hardly matters. Like Johnson, Gray has no wish to "bring his personifications to life": like Johnson, he is using them to gain weight and conciseness, as in lines 49–50:

> But Knowledge to their eyes her ample page
> Rich with the spoils of time did ne'er unroll.

Gray was worried by what he regarded as the increasing flabbiness of the English language. On one occasion we find him commending West for translating a passage from Tacitus "freely," because nothing else is possible: "[Our language] is too diffuse, & daily grows more & more enervate." On another occasion he remarks that in a passage of *Agrippina* he himself has taken "fifty lines" to say what Tacitus said "in five words." His use of abstract personifications was a device to escape from the wordiness of English, and the "concise sententiousness" for which he elsewhere[29] praises Tacitus is equally characteristic of the stanza in which he himself makes the transition from his initial description of the villagers to the weighty reflections which follow:

> Let not Ambition mock their useful toil,
> Their homely joys, and destiny obscure;
> Nor Grandeur hear with a disdainful smile,
> The short and simple annals of the poor.

Such a grave sententiousness follows naturally from the highly generalised observations which have gone before:

> The breezy call of incense-breathing Morn,
> The swallow twitt'ring from the straw-built shed,
> The cock's shrill clarion, or the echoing horn,
> No more shall rouse them from their lowly bed.

Here we are in the generalised world of "L'Allegro" and "Il Penseroso," and it might be said of the Elegy as truly as it was of Milton's poems that "it is not a particular ploughman, milkmaid, and shepherd that [Gray] sees." To explain this lack of particularity Mr. Eliot invoked Milton's later blindness, his love of music, his limited sensuousness and "the peculiar education which he received."[30] Now Gray was not blind, and while the education that he received must have resembled Milton's in most respects—although it was less abnormally intense—his meticulous notes and his exquisite little drawings of birds and insects remain as evidence that his sensory perceptions were in no way impaired. If his descriptions are generalised, it is because he wishes them to be generalised: because particularity would ruin the effect that he is bent on achieving.

Another striking feature of the language of the *Elegy* is the frequency with which Gray uses verbs or verbal phrases which would not occur in prose and which strike the reader as slightly foreign even in verse. Like the abstract personifications, these are almost entirely confined to the part of the poem which is already present in the earlier version. I have in mind such phrases as "the air . . . a . . . stillness holds," "wheels his . . . flight," "ply her . . . care," "oft did the harvest to their sickle yield," "how bow'd the woods beneath their . . . stroke," "impute to These the fault," "provoke the silent dust," "hands, that the rod of empire might have sway'd," "Penury repress'd their noble rage," "they kept the . . . tenor of their way," and "implores the . . . tribute of a sigh." It is at once obvious that a number of these locutions are of Latin origin. In "repress'd their noble rage" the word "rage" is an English equivalent of the word "furor," with the favourable meaning that it bears in such a phrase as "furor poeticus"; while the verbal usage may be paralleled by such a phrase as "furorem exsultantem reprimere" in Cicero (*Pro Sestio,* 44, 95). It is unnecessary to search for particular instances of Latin parallels to "impute the fault" and "provoke the dust." "Ply her care" is obviously an instance of "cura," one of Virgil's favourite words, influencing the English idiom. Mr. J. C. Maxwell has traced one of the most famous lines—

They kept the noiseless tenor of their way

—to an unexpected origin in the *Agricola* of Tacitus, where a disputed passage reads "idem praeturae tenor et silentium," probably with the meaning "his praetorship followed the same quiet course."[31] In the earlier version of the *Elegy* Gray wrote "silent tenour": the revision to "noiseless tenor" makes the Tacitean echo harder to catch. Latin parallels for most of the other locutions mentioned above could readily be found. It is no surprise that the *Elegy* should have been translated into Latin more often and more successfully (perhaps) than any other English poem.

It is not suggested that no one had used these phrases in English before. On the contrary, analogues (at least) may be found for almost every one. A rather cursory search has revealed "bowd down in battle, sunk before the spear" and "impute Folly to mee" in Milton, "generous rage" in Dryden, "a hero's rage," "pines bow low Their heads" and "our Country's Cause provokes to Arms" in Pope, and "the . . . plover wheels Her . . . flight" and "Woods" which "bow" beneath a "burden" of snow in Thomson.[32] In Gray's own *Ode on a Distant Prospect of Eton College* the boys "their murm'ring labours ply"—perhaps a reminiscence of the way in which Adam and Eve "ply Thir growing work" in *Paradise Lost* (IX, 201–2). By making his housewife "ply her evening care" Gray is merely giving the phrase a more Virgilian turn. A further phrase not so far quoted—"froze the genial current of the soul" —probably derives from Virgil's

> Frigidus obstiterit circum praecordia sanguis,

perhaps by way of Thomson's translation,

> If the cold current freezes round my heart,

and Gray's own lines:

> Dried the soft springs of pity in my heart,
> And froze them up.[33]

A careful search through the pages of Milton, Cowley, Dryden, Pope and Thomson would no doubt produce parallels for every idiom of this sort, while many might be traced further back to Spenser, Shakespeare and the Elizabethan translators.[34]

But that is not the point. Gray liked these expressions precisely because they are Latinate. As he was in the habit of reading and writing Latin more or less daily throughout his life, he must sometimes have used a Latin idiom without caring whether it had been used by an earlier English writer or not. When he knew that it had, he no doubt regarded it as one of the "foreign idioms and derivatives" with which his predecessors had enriched the language of English poetry. He found that such phrases enabled him to achieve effects which he could not achieve in any other way. When he revised

> Forgive, ye Proud, th'involuntary Fault,
> If Memory to these no Trophies raise

to read

> Nor you, ye Proud, impute to These the fault,
> If Mem'ry o'er their Tomb no Trophies raise,

no doubt one reason was the fact that "th' involuntary" followed too closely on "th'inevitable hour" in the previous stanza; yet if he dropped one Latin word he brought in another, and "impute" is a fine example of what Dryden would have termed "significant and sounding" language.

Gray knew what to take from Latin: he also knew what to avoid. We have only to look into Thomson to find the sort of empty Latinate polysyllables which are notably absent from the *Elegy:*

> Now, by the cool declining year condensed,
> Descend the copious exhalations.   (*Autumn,* 707–8.)

In the same way, Gray avoids tired classical mythology: his owl complains to "the Moon," not to Cynthia, while the *Elegy* contains no parallel to the line

> And redning Phoebus lifts his golden Fire

in the earlier *Sonnet on the Death of Richard West.* Gray banishes "fleecy care" and "finny tribe," and with them the whole outdated charade of the pastoral convention; while in the revised text of the poem Cato, Tully and Caesar make way for Hampden, Milton and Cromwell. This does not mean that Gray wished to write directly about country people—he was no Crabbe, still less a Clare. His subject is Man, and he does not affect familiarity with the inhabitants of the village. His idiom keeps them at the distance appropriate to the sort of picture that he intends to paint.

The same generalising effect may be noticed in Gray's use of adjectives and present participles. They are so numerous that many critics have agreed with Goldsmith that the *Elegy* is "overloaded with epithet." Every other noun is accompanied by an adjective, and as most of the nouns are monosyllabic and most of the adjectives are not, it becomes apparent how important a part the adjectives play in the final texture of the verse. Goldsmith pointed out that parts of the poem may be reduced to tetrameters by the simple expedient of omitting some of the adjectives:

> The Curfew tolls the knell of day,
> The herd wind slowly o'er the lea,
> The plowman homeward plods his way . . .[35]

—an experiment which reminds us once again that the *Elegy* stands in the line of descent from "Il Penseroso." Often a noun is accompanied by a composite adjective, or by two separate adjectives—as in "dark unfathom'd caves" and "cool sequester'd vale." In lines 85–8 only one of the six nouns is without an adjective, and two of them have two adjectives each:

> For who to dumb Forgetfulness a prey,
> This pleasing anxious being e'er resign'd,
> Left the warm precincts of the chearful day,
> Nor cast one longing ling'ring look behind?

The same stanza may serve as a reminder of the importance of present participles, which is particularly marked in the opening stanzas. Throughout there is something ambivalent about their effect. On the one hand they give the lines a static, pictorial quality: on the other they draw our attention insistently to the impermanence of the scene which we are regarding—the impermanence of every human scene. Jean Hagstrum has pointed out that Gray seems to have been remembering Poussin's great painting, "The Shepherds of Arcady," as he wrote the concluding lines.[36] There is a profound nostalgia in these lines, the nostalgia of Virgil's "lacrimae rerum," the nostalgia of mankind aware of mortality. That nostalgia is the subject of the poem.

NOTES

1. *The Poems of Mr. Gray. To which are prefixed Memoirs of his Life and Writings,* 1775, p. 106.

2. *Memoirs* (separately paged), p. 157.

3. J. Fisher investigated the question of Gray's possible indebtedness to Shenstone in *Modern Philology*, 32 (1934–35). The suggestion of a motive on Mason's part is my own.

4. *Poems*, p. 106.

5. *Correspondence*, i, 196.

6. Yale Edition, vol. 28, p. 123.

7. *The Name and Nature of Poetry*, penultimate paragraph.

8. The relevant passages from Nichols's *Reminiscences* are given as Appendix Z in vol. iii of the *Correspondence*. This couplet occurs on p. 1290. Cf. Thomson's *Spring*, lines 24–5:
> The plovers when to scatter o'er the heath,
> And sing their wild notes to the listening waste.

9. It is most readily accessible in Appendix I of *The Poems of Gray and Collins*, ed. Austin Lane Poole, 4th ed., 1941. For the Eton College MS. see Publication Number 31 of the Augustan Reprint Society, Los Angeles, 1951, ed. George Sherburn, which also gives a facsimile of the first edition.

10. living out one's life without learning or the arts.

11. *Gray's English Poems*, ed. D. C. Tovey, Cambridge, 1898, p. 153.

12. *Correspondence*, i, 327.

13. Mason refers to Gray's "moralizing Muse" in his "Elegy II: Written in a Church-Yard in South Wales, 1787," adding a note: "This Epithet is used to call to the Reader's recollection a passage in Shakespear, descriptive of a Character to which in its best parts Mr. Gray's was not dissimilar." The character is Jaques.

14. It will be apparent that I disagree in many respects with Frank H. Ellis's most interesting essay, "Gray's *Elegy:* The Biographical Problem in Literary Criticism" (*PMLA* lxvi, 6: December 1951), and in particular with his view that "in his revision of the *Stanza's*, what Gray did was to depersonalize them entirely."

15. Common Place Books, I, 3. Most of the passages from the Common Place Books which I quote have appeared in print before, but I take my text direct from the MS. For the translation of Aulus Gellius I rely on the Loeb edition of *The Attic Nights*, trans. John C. Rolfe, iii, 1952, 395–7.

16. Ed. F. C. Green, Cambridge 1941, p. 54.

17. *Correspondence*, i, 231, 326.

18. I quote West's lines as they occur in Gray's Common Place Book, i, 105. As Toynbee and Whibley point out (iii, 1199), the versions published by Mason seem to have been "corrected and improved."

19. "A Monody on the Death of Queen Caroline," in Dodsley's *Collection of Poems*, 1748, ii, 273. My italics. Cf. line 35 of the *Elegy*.

20. *Lectures on Poetry . . . Translated from the Latin,* 1742, p. 165.

21. Common Place Books, ii, 765. The poems of Gascoyne which Gray refers to may be found in *The Posies,* ed. John W. Cunliffe, Cambridge 1907, pp. 344–52.

22. *The Letters,* ed. Marjorie Williams, 1939, p. 62.

23. II, 757–9.

24. *Correspondence,* iii, 1, 297.

25. *Lectures on Poetry,* p. 169.

26. Horace's phrase, quoted by Dryden near the end of the preface to *Annus Mirabilis.*

27. I have tried to emphasize the pattern by italicising nouns, underlining verbs, and double-spacing adjectives, present participles and significant adverbs. I have taken "tolls the knell" as a verbal phrase.

28. Virgil, *Eclogues,* ii, 50: "sets off the delicate hyacinth with the golden marigold."

29. *Correspondence,* i, 196, 193, 188.

30. "A Note on the Verse of John Milton," *Essays and Studies by Members of the English Association,* xxi, 1936.

31. *Notes and Queries,* 9 June 1951, p. 262: *Agricola* vi, 4.

32. *Paradise Lost* I, 436 and X, 620–1; *Palamon and Arcite* I, 117; *Iliad* XVII, 305, *Dunciad* (B) II 391–2, and *Ode on St. Cecilia's Day,* 36; *Spring* 696 and *Winter* (1726 text) 225.

33. *Georgics* ii, 484; Preface to 2nd edition of *Winter* (reprinted in *The Complete Poetical Works of James Thomson,* ed. J. Logie Robertson, 1908, p. 242); and Gray's *Agrippina,* 177–8.

34. Probable sources for two of Gray's most celebrated lines appear to have escaped the notice of his editors. In the 43rd sonnet of William of Hawthornden we find the line
    Farre from the madding Worldlings hoarse discords
(*Poetical Works,* ed. L. E. Kastnerx, i, 1913, p. 38), while the fine image in "The Bard"—
    Youth on the Prow, and Pleasure at the helm
—seems to derive from line 196 of Rochester's "A Letter from Artemisa in the Town to Cloe in the Country":
    Youth in her Looks, and Pleasure in her Bed.

35. *Boswell's Life of Johnson,* ed. G. Birkbeck Hill, rev. L. F. Powell, i, 404n. In the second line Goldsmith omitted "slowly," not "lowing."

36. *The Sister Arts,* Chicago 1958, 292–301.

On a Special Decorum in Gray's *Elegy*

BERTRAND H. BRONSON

WHEN Chesterfield expatiated to his son on the ideal of decorum, it was not an artificial or narrow code of drawing-room manners he was expounding but an ideal of conduct transcending rules and permeating the whole habit of man's moral being. It is to be sensed in every particular of a man's demeanor, whatever the circumstances. It is the noble ideal of Cicero, and Cicero is its most eloquent expositor. "The right and prudent use of reason and speech," Cicero declared, "the doing of everything considerately, the finding out of truth and the defending it, looks well in any man. . . . And so whatsoever is just is also graceful; and whatsoever is unjust or dishonest is likewise misbeseeming. . . . Wherefore the decorum I here speak of appears likewise in all other virtues. . . . There is in all virtue somewhat that is graceful, and only separable from virtue by imagination. As the gracefulness and beauty of the body cannot well be separated from health, so it is with the gracefulness here in question. It is a decorum that is in a manner so confused with virtue that it is incorporated with it. . . . But the special decorum, as dependent upon the general, is a quality so congruous to Nature that moderation and temperance appear in it with the very image of a generous soul. This we may judge to be the decorum which the poets observe" (from Cicero's *De Officiis,* in L'Estrange's translation).

In critical discussion today there is much about the Augustan proprieties of style and diction among the several genres. The rules, since they were so clearly formulated, were not likely to be ignored. But the niceties of which Cicero was here speaking are of a subtler kind, closer to instinct than to rule. In the decades of

Gray's maturity, a period of shifting values, while Chesterfield was preaching the Ciceronian decorum as the preventer of social discord, the creator, adorner, and strengthener of friendship, there were many others who were openly challenging the classical precepts, if not flouting them. In literary activity there were many others, among whom we recognize Gray himself, who were quietly undermining the established ways. In poetry, Gray was interested in more various subject-matter, and in a more individual and even personal style and diction. In asserting that "the language of the age is never the language of poetry," he is applauding the contributions of lively individual invention, not antiquarian revival. He praises Shakespeare and Milton for being "great creators" of words, and declares that none have been "more licentious" in diction than Dryden and Pope. In his own poetry, Gray went much too far in this direction to satisfy Dr. Johnson, whose conservative taste memorably balked at his innovations. "Honied spring" and "many-twinkling feet" from a scholar!

In the face of Gray's willingness to drive literary expression "beyond common apprehension," it is worth while to mark the boundaries of decorum against which he goes to extraordinary lengths not to transgress, even when the nature of his personal involvement would seem to be forcing him to the trespass. I wish to focus attention briefly on a special decorum in the *Elegy* in which "moderation and temperance" display themselves "with the very image of a generous soul." I refer to the decorum of Gray's handling of the poem's inescapable egocentricity. This aspect of the *Elegy* exhibits, I think, a grace far beyond the reach of art.

Gray has designed the structure so that the climax of the poem consists in the concluding epitaph. Assuming for the nonce that the "me" of the opening stanza and the "he" of the epitaph refer to the same person, and that person the poet, the immediate, crucial difficulty is how to devise a memorial in the form of inscriptional verses for oneself that shall be perfectly serious and emotionally sincere; that shall be neither objectionably self-abasing nor apparently self-satisfied; neither too cold and impersonal to communicate emotion nor too revealing of private emotion or self-commiseration. Gray's solution of this extremely delicate problem —supposing our reading of it to be accurate—is worth scrutiny.

But we must be very sure we understand the epitaph's literal meaning. Its felicity, objectively taken alone, is so great that its three stanzas have been memorized by countless readers; yet I doubt that even by these it has always been correctly understood. The first line is not infrequently read as a complete statement in itself:

Here rests his head upon the lap of Earth.

Tam cari capitis? The head, we would say, of a youth unknown. But, to the contrary, *rests* is of course a transitive verb here, of which *head* is the object, not the subject: It is not a mere *Hic jacet*. A more willing submission is implied: not simply *lies* but *lays to rest*. Here in Earth's lap a youth lays his head to rest. The third and fourth lines that follow indicate two favors the youth enjoyed while he lived. In spite of his humble birth, the fruits of the intellectual life were not denied him. The *And* that precedes *Melancholy* in the fourth line proves that She too was welcomed as a blessing. She was Milton's "*divinest* Melancholy, Whose saintly visage is too bright To hit the sense of human sight:" She is the coryphaea of Music, Philosophy, Melpomene, Divinity, and Wisdom.

"Large was his bounty, and his soul sincere" at first sounds rather too smug. But immediately we learn what it implies: that, having a soul capable of commiseration and mutual, responsive sympathy, he denied nothing to these appeals and therefore gave himself entirely to each genuine human claim, and received equal payment of reciprocal devotion. Could Life offer any higher good? "He gave to Mis'ry all he had, a tear,/He gain'd from Heav'n ('twas all he wish'd) a friend." It is of course not meant that he was content with a single friend, any more than that his charitable impulses were exhausted by a single object of pity; but that he had experienced true friendship, as he had shared in another's woes. As Blake would one day restate the underlying thought:

Man is Love
As God is Love: every kindness to another is a little Death
In the Divine Image, nor can Man exist but by Brotherhood.

This youth lived, the epitaph declares, in lovingkindness and in the life of the mind. Neither his faults nor his virtues require to be further enumerated here. Leave them undisturbed to await their desert in the fullness of time from the justice and mercy of the Heavenly Father.

On due consideration, we have taken the Epitaph to be auto biographical. But it is introduced by a descriptive sketch of the anonymous "youth" from the mouth of a conjectural ancient villager lacking personal acquaintance, who knew his subject only from detached observation of his outward habit. Such a one, "some hoary-headed swain," may haply recall how the young man would hurry out to meet the rising sun, would laze away the noontide, and wander about muttering to himself and moping melancholy-mad, careless of appearances and woebegone. Before any one knew he was ill, he was dead. The stone will tell you more. . . . He *was* dead? The death is only hypothetical, and the swain too is imaginary. Set in such a frame, the sketch itself seems only a fancy-piece.

But on this point we can bring to bear collateral evidence. There is another sketch written by Gray, and not much earlier, which tends to show, or to confirm, the essential psychological truth of this one. Comparison is revealing, for one has details that the other lacks, and the lights in the two pictures are different. In the *Elegy,* we read as follows:

> There at the foot of yonder nodding beech
> That wreathes its old fantastic roots so high,
> His listless length at noontide would he stretch,
> And pore upon the brook that babbles by.

The companion sketch occurs in an ode at first entitled "Noontide," later altered to "Ode on the Spring." There we find:

> Where'er the oak's thick branches stretch
> A broader browner shade;
> Where'er the rude and moss-grown beech
> O'er-canopies the glade,
> Beside some water's rushy brink
> With me the Muse shall sit, and think
> (At ease reclin'd in rustic state). . . .

The hoary-headed swain of the *Elegy* could have no idea of what the poet was thinking when "now smiling as in scorn . . . now drooping, woeful wan;" but in the other sketch we are told what it was:

> and think
> How vain the ardour of the Crowd,
> How low, how little are the Proud,
> How indigent the Great!

But that would be it, of course! The Elegist had already shared these thoughts with us. They have formed the substance of his poem: "the madding crowd's ignoble strife," "Nor you, ye Proud," and "Nor Grandeur hear with a disdainful smile." The preoccupations of each are alike: only the tone of self-mockery is closer to the surface in the *Ode*, autobiographically rounding in an ironic turning of the tables at the end, where the insects retort:

> Poor moralist! and what art thou?
> A solitary fly! . . . .
> On hasty wings thy youth is flown;
> Thy sun is set, thy spring is gone.—
> We frolick, while 'tis May.

But there is no doubt that the same sitter is observed in both sketches: the poet himself.

But the first sketch was written before Gray knew that his friend Richard West, to whom he sent it, was already dead. The second, in the *Elegy*, seems to have been begun a couple of months *after* the news reached him. In imagination, he identified West's death with his own: they were of an age, and West had died at 26.

In the whole *Elegy* there is only one occurrence of the first-personal pronoun as from the poet's own mouth. It closes the first stanza:

> And leaves the world to darkness and to *me*.

But at line 93, after the eight poignant lines on the need of every one to be sustained at death by some fond being, to bid him good-bye and to shed tears at parting—a need which Gray, absent and unknowing, was unable to fill when West lay dying,—at line 93 occurs for the first time the *second*-personal pronoun:

> For *thee*, who mindful of th'unhonour'd Dead
> Dost in these lines their artless tale relate.

For nearly ninety lines the poet had, as it were, disembodied himself, diffusing his identity in generalized, impersonal statement. What he wishes to say after that point is intensely personal, of a nature so private as to be almost incommunicable without breach of decorum. Virtually, it is an autobiographical obituary, occupying a full third of the poem's length. And we now can see how he contrives it. He has so long ceased to mention himself that we have been projecting into his lines our own identity, so that it is *our* voice which has been speaking our own train of thought all this while. It seems, therefore, perfectly natural to be addressing another as "thee." This transference is surely one of the subtlest effects in our literature. For now, we join the poet in addressing himself in the second person, continuing the identification as we imagine "some kindred spirit" inquiring about *us:*

> For *thee*, . . .
> If chance, by lonely contemplation led,
> Some kindred Spirit shall inquire *thy* fate.

The supposed answer is further insulated from the man, Gray, by being attributed to an imaginary stranger, unknown both to him and to us, so that we are not roused from our meditative imagining, nor divided from the poet. When, finally, the summary epitaph comes, it is still further removed from reach of Gray's apparent personal responsibility by being read on a headstone, unauthored, possessed of lapidary detachment and finality. Let this stand as a sufficient example of Ciceronian Decorum, that "duty, wherein bashfulness (pudor) and a certain gracefulness of life, temperance, modesty, the composure of all perturbations of the mind, and moderation" appear in so excellent a kind "that it is inseparable from virtue; for whatsoever is decent is likewise honest, and whatsoever is honest is becoming."

Structure and Meaning in Gray's *Elegy*

FRANK BRADY

F EW English poems have been so universally admired as Gray's
Elegy, and few interpreted in such widely divergent ways.
Though almost every critic has concurred in Dr. Johnson's judgment that the *Elegy* "abounds . . . with sentiments to which every
bosom returns an echo," these echoes have been disconcertingly
dissimilar; after two hundred years not merely are the poem's
structure and meaning matters of debate, but no general agreement exists about who is saying what to whom. Far from being a
simple poem composed of noble commonplaces, the *Elegy* provides
an unexpected example of T. S. Eliot's assertion that poetry can
communicate before it is understood.

Argument about the *Elegy* centers on the interrelated questions
of structure and meaning, unsurprisingly so since in this poem
structure largely determines meaning.[1] Of course, some critics deny
that the *Elegy* has any structure at all; according to a critic in the
Times Literary Supplement, Gray "seems to have found progres-
sion of thought a supreme difficulty. . . . The ideas do not always
grow out of each other, or, if they do that, are not always quite on
the right scale."[2] Even those critics who maintain that the *Elegy*
has "a firm and clearly perceptible structure"[3] are apt to be vague
about where this structure is to be found, and usually take refuge
in general paraphrase. F. H. Ellis, however, has marked out the
basic structure as an alternation of descriptive and reflective passages: stanzas 1–4 are descriptive, 5–19 reflective, 20–21 descriptive,
22–23 reflective, 24–29 descriptive, and 30–32 reflective. In this
structure, Mr. Ellis says, "The descriptive parts simply supply an
'ornamental' background for the reflections which constitute the

real 'subject' of the poem. . . . The *Elegy* is not simply a loco-descriptive poem, but a philosophical poem or, as Gray would have said, a poem of 'moral reflections.' "[4]

Whether Mr. Ellis's scheme is accurate or not in every detail—stanzas 5–7, for example, seem as much descriptive as reflective—it does point to a descriptive-reflective alternation in the poem; the real trouble with this pattern, apart from its dubious division of the poem into ornamental and non-ornamental parts, is that it does not tell us enough about the poem's structure. In particular, this pattern does not solve in itself the aspect of the poem that has most concerned critics: the relationship of stanzas 24–32 to the rest of the poem (though Mr. Ellis does deal with this problem elsewhere in his essay). Again, a number of critics have argued that the poem simply falls apart after stanza 23, that the early version preserved in the Eton MS., some 22 stanzas long, "possessed a unity of structure and of sentiment which the final version does not retain."[5] Yet clearly Gray himself thought the revised version was structurally unified when he wrote to Horace Walpole, "You will, I hope, look upon it [the *Elegy*] in the light of a *thing with an end to it;* a merit that most of my writings have wanted, and are like to want" (12 June 1750). His conscious concern with design also appears in the suppression of the famous "redbreast" stanza as well as of the stanza beginning, "Him have we seen the Green-wood Side along."[6]

The structural problem has been complicated by disagreement over the subject of the *Elegy's* closing section, the "thee" who appears in

> For thee, who mindful of th' unhonour'd Dead
> Dost in these lines their artless tale relate. . . .
> (ll. 93–4).

Traditionally, the "thee" has been identified with Gray, that is the Gray *persona*, who in modern terms may be called the Narrator. Forty years ago, however, Odell Shepard identified this "Youth" (l. 118) for biographical reasons with Richard West, and more recently H. W. Starr has argued that "the obvious person" described in the Epitath "is merely a young rustic versifier, a poetic ideal of a sort."[7] This second suggestion has been most ingeniously

elaborated by Mr. Ellis, and the present state of confusion over the
identity of the Youth is illustrated by Graham Hough's contention
that he "might be either West or Gray himself, and is, indeed, by a
process familiar to dream-analysts, a sort of fusion of the two."[8]

As Mr. Ellis reads the *Elegy*, Gray wished to depersonalize the
version preserved in the Eton MS., which unequivocally identifies
the Narrator at the beginning with the figure who comments in its
final three stanzas, and so "shifted the bearing of the poem from
the Poet to the rustics. . . . Then, in the sixteen additional stanzas
which he added in the manuscript, Gray created a dramatic situation involving four characters." These four are a Stonecutter, our
Youth, now a peasant-poet who composes "uncouth rhimes" (l. 79)
for the gravestones, and is alluded to in the phrase, "th' unletter'd
muse" (l. 81); a Spokesman, the "me" of line 4, who has been kind
enough to compose the Epitaph for the Stonecutter; an Enquirer,
the "kindred Spirit" (l. 96); and the "hoary-headed Swain" (l. 97.)[9]

Perhaps both the attractions and the difficulties of this reading
are obvious. By dividing the Narrator into Spokesman and Stonecutter, any lingering idea that Gray is describing himself vanishes;
also, it adequately accounts for the discrepancies between the
Swain's account of the Youth and the Epitaph's description of him.
Most important, it supports Mr. Ellis's interpretation of the poem
as a whole: "the imagined death of the peasant-poet supplies the
dramatic example which illustrates and makes cogent the large
generalities of the previous argument," in particular the concern
with "unrecognized potentiality" and the desire for fame. "The
unrealization of his 'noble Rage' is presented as pathetic and his
premature death as tragic."[10]

Two arguments against this reading have been effectively stated
by J. H. Sutherland. The first is that "it does violence to grammar
and logic to read 'thee' as referring to a stonecutter who is not even
mentioned in the poem—whose existence is only indirectly suggested by the abstract phrase, 'th' unlettered muse' "; the second is
that the Epitaph does not fit the Stonecutter. Mr. Ellis faced a
sticky problem when he tried to reconcile "th' unletter'd muse"
and his "uncouth rhimes" with the Epitaph's "Fair Science frown'd
not on his humble birth," which he resolved by defining "Science"
as "native wisdom."[11] But, as Mr. Sutherland points out, every

other time it appears in Gray's poetry, "Science" means "knowledge gained as the result of education."[12] Such an argument is not
conclusive, of course, but it does put the burden of proof on Mr.
Ellis.[13]

In the best-known modern analysis of the *Elegy*, Cleanth Brooks,
adopting the traditional identification of the Youth with the Narrator, confronts the structural problem raised by the last nine
stanzas directly. They provide, he says, the "resolution" of the
poem, which up to this point has been concerned with the apparent contrast between rich and poor; they become ironically
similar when faced with the inevitability of death. The resolution
hinges on the question of choice: "First, we have had the case of
those who could not choose, the 'rude Forefathers of the hamlet';
next, the Proud, who chose, but chose in vanity; lastly, there is the
present case, the man who is able to choose, and chooses the
'neglected spot' after all." This choice "is a kind of vindication of
the lot forced upon the rustics," but Mr. Brooks carefully differentiates the Narrator from them: he has refrained consciously,
through wisdom, from straying from "the cool sequester'd vale of
life," while they have been restrained by ignorance.[14]

Here Mr. Brooks's interpretation runs into difficulties. To relate
the Narrator's conscious avoidance of "the madding crowd's
ignoble strife" to the rustics' isolation through ignorance from it,
he is forced to argue that Knowledge has done the rustics a favor by
withholding "her ample page," and that Knowledge is distinct
from the Science which "frown'd not" on the Narrator.[15] But in
the stanza,

> But Knowledge to their eyes her ample page
> Rich with the spoils of time did ne'er unroll;
> Chill Penury repress'd their noble rage,
> And froze the genial current of the soul,
>
> (ll. 49–52)

the statements about Knowledge and Penury are obviously parallel
rather than antithetical, and lack of knowledge is deplored. If in
Gray's later balancing of the good and evil involved in limiting the
rustics' potentialities, lack of knowledge becomes ambivalent, it
never becomes transformed into something basically good. Also,
the argument that Science, by being associated with Melancholy

(ll. 119–20), turns into a kind of saving wisdom, and so is differentiated from Knowledge, can hardly be more than speculative; it
turns Melancholy into a quality like Prudence, a confusion which
seems unlikely in 18th-century literature. The more prosaic reading of these lines, rejected by Mr. Brooks, that the Narrator "had
the knowledge requisite for entering into the competition for
fame, but he was incapacitated by Melancholy,"[16] is thematically
closer to the truth.

But what is perhaps the central point in Mr. Brooks's argument
is also the weakest. The Narrator, he says, *chooses* to be buried in
this "neglected spot," yet the only evidence offered for this reading
is Mr. Brooks's interpretation of the Science-Melancholy association. Nowhere in the poem does the question of choice on the
Narrator's part ever arise; if the Swain's account can be trusted at
all, he does not even have full control of his thoughts and actions.

In suggesting a different reading of the *Elegy* from those of Mr.
Ellis and Mr. Brooks, it is helpful to return to the "Stanza's Wrote
in a Country Church-Yard" to see what changes Gray made in the
poem. This version corresponds fairly closely to the first 18 stanzas
of the *Elegy,* but includes 4 more stanzas. In the first of these the
Narrator indicates that the life of the rustics is preferable to that
of the great:

> But more to Innocence their Safety owe
> Than Power & Genius e'er conspired to bless.

In the next three, the Narrator preaches resignation to himself,
finding in "the sacred Calm . . . A grateful Earnest of eternal
Peace":

> No more with Reason & thyself at Strife;
> Give anxious Cares & endless Wishes room
> But thro' the cool sequester'd Vale of Life
> Pursue the silent Tenour of thy Doom.

The changes Gray made in turning the "Stanza's" into the *Elegy*
are extensive and striking. The most apparent is the addition of
the contrasting portraits of the Narrator, those presented first by
the Swain and then by the Epitaph (stanzas 24–32). This contrast,
often commented upon, does not stand by itself, however; it
recalls and reinforces the poem's opening contrast between the

Narrator and the rustics (stanzas 1–7), which impressed Roger Martin: "Le poète n'est-il pas lui même déjà mort à ces joies? . . . N'est-ce pas là la vie interdite, et dont l'ardent désir se confond en lui avec le regret de la tombe?"[17] The situation of the narrator, an observer in darkness and isolation of the living and dead around him, is juxtaposed sharply against the social, vital, and purposeful life of the rustics, somewhat as the sensuous darkness surrounding the narrator in the *Ode to a Nightingale* is contrasted to the "sunburnt mirth" of pastoral festivity.[18]

Structurally, the relationship between these contrasts is important because it shows that in revising the poem Gray did not just tack on two discordant and rather inexplicable sketches of the Narrator to a meditation on the lives of rich and poor; instead, the transformed poem involves three major contrasts, in which the opening and closing ones resemble in some ways the outside panels of a triptych. In the first of these contrasts, just described, the Narrator looks at the world of nature and society immediately around him. In the second and most extended contrast, the Narrator generalizes about the lives, both actual and potential, of the poor, and the common reaction of rich and poor when faced with death. This section of the poem has been thoroughly discussed, but perhaps one further point can be made about it. While it is quite true, as Mr. Brooks shows, that rich and poor are equalized by death, that the paths of the rustics lead to the grave as inevitably as the paths of glory,[19] it is important to see that the Narrator does not stand apart from society, balancing at an equal distance the careers of rich and poor; rather, he adopts the viewpoint of the poor, even though he sees far beyond it. And here abstractions are used brilliantly, since from the viewpoint of the poor, and even perhaps from the viewpoint of the narrator himself, it is natural that the "Proud," with their attributes of Honour, Flatt'ry, Luxury, and (tautologically) Pride, should be shadows which are close to abstractions. Even such terms as Knowledge and Penury, though the rustics certainly know what it is to be poor, are in a class with Ambition and Grandeur as concepts too remote for them to be concerned with; the rustics lived in the concrete world of nature, family, and work described in stanzas 5–7.[20]

If the virtues of the rustics and their lives are emphasized in the poem's middle section, especially by stanza 19 ("Far from the madding crowd's ignoble strife"), their limitations appear clearly in the final contrast between the Swain's view of the Narrator and that provided by the Epitaph. The Swain's view of the Narrator is concrete, visual, and external; it is also, at best, very incomplete. The reader naturally identifies with the "kindred Spirit," who can read and understand the Epitaph.[21]

While it is easy to see what changes Gray made in the poem, it is less easy to explain why he made them, or, in modern critical terms, to describe their function and effect. In particular, two difficult questions persist about the final section of the poem: (1) since the Swain's account of the Narrator is highly partial, even misleading, why is it included at all? (2) though the Epitaph complements and unifies the earlier epitaphs of rich and poor, is this its most significant function?

The first of these questions involves the problem of perspective, which interested many 18th-century writers and fascinated Gray. Fundamentally, it is a philosophical problem dealing with mind-matter and subject-object relationships, to which Locke, Berkeley, Hume, and Kant offered well-known solutions; but it also found poetic "solutions" ranging from Pope's in the first *Moral Essay* to Blake's in *Auguries of Innocence*. Yet where Pope's ruling passion and Blake's inward eye provided a firm basis for their poetry, no such formula seems to have satisfied Gray. Lord David Cecil asserts that Gray is "the first great English writer for whom the imaginative sense of history is an important source of inspiration, the first who consciously cultivates the sense of period,"[22] but it is possible to generalize further: Gray's poetry depends again and again on the perspectives of time and space; they are the coordinates of such poems as the *Eton Ode, The Progress of Poesy,* and *The Bard*. Perspective can also imply, as it often does in Gray's poetry, an alienation between the perceiver and the perceived, between the individual and nature or society. So, in the *Sonnet on the Death of Richard West,* the narrator's grief for the loss of his friend cuts him off from nature and other men. Finally, perspective implies consciousness and its consequences: civilization, knowledge, learned behavior, loss of spontaneity. This aspect of perspective is treated in varying ways in Gray's poetry. Satirically in the

Hymn to Ignorance, directly in *The Alliance of Education and Government,* knowledge is related to happiness, power, and individual fulfillment, yet in the *Eton Ode* emphasis falls on the price exacted by knowledge or insight. In the *Ode on the Spring* and the *Ode on the Pleasure Arising from Vicissitude,* the immediacy of natural life is contrasted to the long-range vision of "Contemplation's sober eye."

That all these aspects of perspective blend in the *Elegy* hardly needs demonstration, but perspective also operates as a technical device in the poem: the Narrator looks at the present scene surrounding him, evokes the past life of the Forefathers (and, by implication, the present life of the village), thinks of how their lives look to the Proud, considers the unrealized possibilities for good and evil in the rustics, and, in stanzas 20–23, generalizes on their end. Then the Narrator begins to look at himself in perspective, the "me" of the poem's opening stanza turning into "thee" (l. 93),[23] and this shift in perspective concludes in the descriptions of the Swain and the Epitaph.

Simple and obvious as this matter of technical perspective is, it serves to suggest the complementary nature of form and content in the *Elegy,* because Gray is implying, among other things, that what we are involves the question of perspective, of how we look to others and how we look to ourselves. The Narrator has the "Knowledge" to see what the rustics are and might have been, and of how they fit into the framework of society; but they see him too. Here the relevance of the Swain's description of the Narrator becomes evident: what he sees, though incomplete, is also important. Not merely does the Narrator stand apart from the shared life of the village, but his life is apparently unproductive and unfulfilled.[24]

It remains to show how the opening and closing contrasts between the Narrator and the rustics are related to the central contrast between rich and poor. This relationship cannot be reduced to one in which the death of the Narrator embodies or resolves the central contrast by identifying him with the rustics, either, as Mr. Brooks argues, to show the wisdom of remaining in obscurity, or, as Mr. Ellis argues, to show the pathos of unrealized potentiality. Rather, a complex thematic connection is established, which is complicated by the fact that the *Elegy* thematically makes a number of interrelated assertions. It is concerned first with the alienation between the Narrator and society, either of rich or poor, as well as the alienation between rich and poor, and second with the inevitability of death and the human urge to transcend it. By adding stanzas 20–21 ("Yet ev'n these bones from insult to protect") to the original "Stanza's," Gray established the ironic parallel between the "storied urn" of the rich and the "frail memorial" of the poor, which are equally external and impotent defenses against death;[25] the only way in which we can even partly transcend death is through the connection between individuals, as is indicated in stanzas 22–23 ("For who to dumb Forgetfulness a prey"). These stanzas serve as climax to the middle section, and are central to the poem's meaning. At the moment of dying, everyone needs someone else on whom to rely, who can be trusted to sympathize with him and to remember him after death:

> Ev'n from the tomb the voice of Nature cries,
> Ev'n in our Ashes live their wonted Fires.
> (ll. 91–2)[26]

And these lines lead into and make clear the significance of the Kindred Spirit's inquiries.

If this were all Gray had to say, it would be natural to wonder whether the contrast between rich and poor was necessary. But the urge to transcend death is only a focus for a larger thematic concern of the poem, the relationships among potentiality, assertion, limitation, and resignation, or to combine these relationships into one question: to what extent can man fulfill himself? The "Stanza's" suggested simple resignation to obscurity as the answer, but Gray's revisions show that in the *Elegy* he arrived at a more complex formulation. To go back over the poem once more: stanzas 5–7 present the shared fulfillment of rustic life from which the Narrator is cut off, but the limitations of this fulfillment are immediately indicated by considering it from the viewpoint of the Proud. Next, the Narrator balances the potentialities for virtue and vice denied to the rustics, against the background of the ostentatious, empty "fulfillment" of the Proud; in the end, this discussion implies that any attempt at fulfillment in society is a risky business. Yet to stop here would not do justice to the situation: man's impulse to assert himself appears even while he is dying, not in terms of achieving power, rank, glory, etc., but in terms of what is really important at the moment of death (and so, implicitly, in life), his relation to someone else. In this interpretation, the central section of the poem explores the possibilities for fulfillment in society for both rich and poor, and finds them lacking; it prepares for the final contrast.

It is now possible to return to the second question about the closing section of the *Elegy*, which asks what the most significant function of the Epitaph is. Here one characteristic of the elegy as a genre may be important. The English elegy, at least, is in one evident way the obverse of satire: where the elegy mainly praises (or, what is essentially the equivalent, laments), but often includes satiric elements, satire mainly condemns, but often includes an ideal portrait to establish a norm. In *Lycidas* Milton condemns the false pastors, as in *Adonais* Shelley condemns the "deaf and viperous murderer." In contrast, *Absalom and Achitophel* ends with the portrait of the reawakened David, the second *Moral Essay* and the *Epistle to Arbuthnot* with the portraits of the admirable "Friend" and "Pope" respectively, *The Vanity of Human Wishes* with the description of right behavior and attitude, and so forth. It is important that such portraits often occur at the end of a satire, since it seems possible that Gray has adapted what is something of a satiric convention to his own use, and that the Epitaph presents an ideal of fulfillment. Such an hypothesis naturally cannot be demonstrated in isolation, but it can be considered in a reading of the *Elegy* as a whole.

One clue to the "truth" of the Epitaph is the Swain's preceding account of the Narrator, which, if informative, obviously does not provide the whole truth, and prepares for the rectification of the Epitaph. Here the matter of perspective also resolves itself. We are, to some extent, what we seem to others: the rustics are almost beneath the notice of the Proud, but the Narrator sees that the Proud themselves end in monumental emptiness; similarly, the Narrator and the Swain, representing the rustics, perceive an aspect of the truth about each other. But, in the end, only the individual can know to what extent he has fulfilled himself, which is what the Epitaph reveals about the Narrator. Though favored by "Science," the Narrator has been "a Youth to Fortune and to Fame unknown"; Society has limited him in these respects, and Nature has marked him with melancholy. Yet within these limitations the Narrator has realized his potential; if the final accounting of his merits and frailties rests with God, at least on earth by acting and feeling properly "he gain'd from Heav'n ('twas all he wish'd) a friend." The Epitaph in this way develops and makes specific the general conclusion of the rich-poor contrast in stanzas 22–3: "On some fond breast the parting soul relies."

If considering the revisions of the poem has helped to clarify its structure and meaning, the transformation of the "Stanza's" into the *Elegy* at the same time offers an unusual glimpse of F. A. Pottle's "shifts of sensibility" in process. In spite of its quatrain form, the "Stanza's" is a poem predominantly in the Augustan mode: it focuses on the general state of society, and the Narrator, by choosing a kind of identification with the rustics and by refusing active participation in the social struggle, does little more than make explicit the "moral reflection" which the rich-poor contrast entails. This moral reflection is itself characteristically Augustan; submission to one's condition or fate is an important theme in the *Essay on Man*.

In the *Elegy*, Gray makes a far different point. It is now the Narrator's elegy—"it is Margaret you mourn for," so to speak—not a general threnody, and resignation is balanced by self-realization.[27] Instead of being thematically central, the rich-poor contrast becomes subordinate to the total development of the poem, serving as a basis for the closing focus on the Narrator and his limited fulfillment. Yet this shift in interest from society to the individual does not make Gray a member of that non-existent group, the pre-romantics. Instead, the *Elegy* falls within the mode of the "sublime" if, following Josephine Miles, sublime is used "as a descriptive term for the whole realm of interest including the pathetic, for the whole ethos-pathos range of discernment."[28]

NOTES

1. Structure is used here to mean the relation of parts to parts or parts to whole.

2. 27 July 1933, p. 502. One of Gray's earliest commentators, John Scott of

Amwell, remarked that "the principal respect in which it [the *Elegy*] has been supposed defective, is a want of plan" (*Critical Essays*, 1785, p. 185).

3. Gilbert Highet, *The Powers of Poetry*, 1960, p. 281.

4. "Gray's *Elegy:* The Biographical Problem in Literary Criticism," *PMLA*, LXVI (1951), 998–9. A slightly different arrangement of alternating descriptive and reflective passages appears in J. H. Hagstrum, *The Sister Arts*, 1958, p. 292. Mr. Hagstrum asks, "What is this poem if not a succession of visually rendered scenes, each leading to a relevant verbalized reflection? . . . The poem is not basically dramatic or narrative; its progress is not that of logical step-by-step argument or even of emotional effusion guided by the law of free association. A series of pictorially static moments to which reflections have been added, the poem suggests the art of painting and is therefore an example of the neo-classical picturesque" (p. 301).

5. R. W. Ketton-Cremer, *Thomas Gray*, 1955, p. 98. This version is headed "Stanza's Wrote in a Country Church-Yard."

6. For Gray's comments on weakness in design, see H. W. Starr, *Gray as a Literary Critic*, 1941, pp. 95–6.

7. Odell Shepard, "A Youth to Fortune and to Fame Unknown," *Modern Philology*, XX (1923); H. W. Starr, " 'A Youth to Fortune and to Fame Unknown': A Reestimation," *JEGP*, XLVIII (1949), p. 106.

8. *The Romantic Poets*, 1953, p. 15. Mr. Hough's assertion might seem more convincing if the *Elegy* were a dream rather than a poem. Mr. Shepard had also considered the possibility that the personalities of Gray and West were fused in the Youth ("A Youth to Fortune," p. 361).

9. Ellis, pp. 983–6.

10. Ellis, pp. 1002–4. His *dramatis personae* have been enthusiastically, if perhaps obscurely, refined upon by Morse Peckham, who discovered that the Stonecutter-Poet and other figures were projections of the Spokesman's imagination, and that the Friend (l. 124) wrote the Epitaph ("Gray's 'Epitaph' Revisited," *Modern Language Notes*, LXXI, 1956, 409–11).

11. Ellis, p. 1000.

12. Or, as the OED defines it, "knowledge acquired by study" (s.v. Science, 2). J. H. Sutherland, "The Stonecutter in Gray's 'Elegy,' " *Modern Philology*, LV (1957), 11–13. Mr. Sutherland points to the lack of evidence that Gray wished, in the *Elegy*, to change the pronoun references of "thee" and "these lines," but lack of evidence proves nothing.

13. Apart from the unproved and unprovable assertion that the Spokesman wrote the Epitaph, Mr. Ellis's argument follows closely from his assumptions. He makes a curious lapse, however, when he identifies the Enquirer with the Friend of the Epitaph (p. 986). Surely the lines,
> If chance, by lonely contemplation led,
> Some kindred Spirit shall inquire thy fate,
suggest that any connection between the Enquirer and the Youth was tenuous.

14. *The Well Wrought Urn,* 1947, pp. 107–8. Though I am unable to agree with either Mr. Ellis's or Mr. Brooks's reading of the *Elegy,* I have learned a great deal from both their essays.

15. Brooks, p. 105.

16. Brooks, pp. 109–10.

17. *Essai sur Thomas Gray,* 1934, p. 419.

18. A. E. Dyson, who also compares the *Elegy* to the *Ode to a Nightingale,* sees in both poems complementary pulls towards life and death ("The Ambivalence of Gray's Elegy," *Essays in Criticism,* VII, 1957, 257–61).

19. Brooks, pp. 104–5.

20. This interpretation of Gray's use of abstractions is intended to extend rather than to contradict Mr. Brooks's fine discussion of it (pp. 99–101).

21. Brooks, pp. 111–12. Mr. Brooks convincingly demonstrates the connection between the Epitaph and the earlier "storied urn" and "shapeless sculpture."

22. "The Poetry of Thomas Gray," *Proceedings of the British Academy,* XXXI (1945), 48.

23. Brooks, p. 107.

24. A number of critics have remarked on the role of alienation in the *Elegy:* in particular, Mr. Brooks on the differences between the Narrator and the rustics (see n. 14), and Mr. Ellis similarly on the differences between his Stonecutter and the rustics (p. 1003). Mr. Dyson, who maintains that the Narrator identifies himself with the rustics in the Epitaph, argues that Nature as well as Society is an "enemy to man's fulfilment": the wood is "smiling as in scorn" (l. 105) as well as the Narrator (p. 259). But stanzas 5–7 make it plain that the rustics exist in pastoral rapport with Nature, while the Narrator, who portrays Nature neutrally in the first four stanzas, appears to the Swain as an accustomed part of the natural setting.

25. Brooks, p. 106.

26. In the Eton MS., the point is made even more clearly in an earlier version of the second line: "And buried Ashes glow with Social Fires."

27. The *Elegy,* as Mr. Ellis (pp. 999–1003) and others have justly remarked, is not concerned with protest against or acquiescence in contemporary social conditions. Gray simply sets down the social facts, which are subsumed under the more important question of individual fulfillment.

28. *Eras & Modes in English Poetry,* 1957, pp. 48–9. It is inappropriate here to pursue Miss Miles's perceptive discussion of the "sublime" as the dominant poetic mode between 1700 and 1770, except to add that her characterization of the work of Thomson, her central example, as "the poetry of sensuous sensibility, the poetry of politics and universal survey, the poetry of massive personification, the poetry of patiently detailed description" (p. 63) fits the *Elegy* equally well.

Local Attachment and Cosmopolitanism—
The Eighteenth-Century Pattern

ALAN D. MC KILLOP

THE purpose of this paper is to note with brief illustration the forms in which the English eighteenth century received and used the ideas suggested by such terms as "local attachment," "citizen of the world," and "exile." For convenience I have borrowed the term "local attachment" from late eighteenth-century sources. The ideas themselves are of great antiquity, but the ways in which emphasis was shifted and alternative views presented serve to throw some light on changing attitudes and sentiments within the period.

The coexistence of local attachment and philosophic cosmopolitanism is clearly presented in ancient times and need be indicated here only in the most summary fashion. War uproots the Homeric hero, but in life or death his thoughts turn to his sweet native place, and the yearning of Odysseus "to see were it but the smoke leaping up from his own land"[1] becomes proverbial. Later reflection yielded what we may call an anthropological generalization about this mysterious attachment. "Ulysses hastens back to the rocks of his Ithaca as eagerly as Agamemnon speeds to the kingly walls of Mycenae. For no man loves his native land because it is great; he loves it because it is his own."[2] The exiled Ovid sets forth the whole theme in a few lines:

None doubt the Ithacan's wisdom, but yet he prays that he may see the smoke from his native hearth. By what sweet charm I know not the native land [nescioqua natale solum dulcedine] draws all men nor allows them to forget her. What is better than Rome? What worse than the cold of Scythia? Yet hither the barbarian flees from that city.[3]

Ovid goes on to argue that if Ulysses could be so attached to his rough little island, a Roman should be much more attached to his glorious city. And Seneca could write in the same way about his exile in Corsica. But it was also Seneca who furnished one of the most familiar statements of the Stoic-Cynic consolation for exile, calling for complete philosophical detachment. His official position, so to speak, was given in the *Consolatio ad Helviam,* addressed to his mother from Corsica. Wherever fortune places a man he must rely upon nature and virtue; he confronts the same universe and looks on the same heavens, governed by inexorable law. Plutarch and Cicero had already treated the theme and made use of the familiar instances: Heracles said, "There is no fort in Greece but is my country"; Socrates said he was not an Athenian or a Greek, but a citizen of the world (*mundanus* or *civis totius mundi* in Cicero).[4] But Plutarch's collection of commonplaces on the subject shows that the philosopher in exile could stop short of absolute indifference; what is often commended is a free choice of residence or perfect flexibility. The wise man will make the best of what is offered. "Every city," says Plutarch, "at once becomes a native city to the man who has learned to make use of it."[5]

To illustrate the recurrence of this theme in the Renaissance we may use a familiar passage in *Richard II,* John of Gaunt's address to the exiled Bolingbroke:

> All places that the eye of heaven visits
> Are to a wise man ports and happy havens.
> Teach thy necessity to reason thus:
> There is no virtue like necessity.[6]

But in his answer Bolingbroke declines the consolation:

> Where'er I wander, boast of this I can,
> Though banish'd, yet a trueborn English man.

And we remember that soon afterward John of Gaunt, despite the consolation for exile which he has offered, utters on his deathbed the most famous patriotic speech in Shakespeare. Ovid continued to be the model for assertions of local attachment, and in particular for poets expressing their own feelings in exile. Thus Clément Marot in Venice echoes the *nescioqua natale solum dulcedine* of Ovid, and for Ovid's Scythians gives us the Germans and Greeks who prefer their own rough land to the delights of France.[7] Joachim du Bellay in Rome imitates and inverts Ovid; for the French poet residence in glorious Rome is exile; his humble ancestral dwelling means more to him than Roman palaces; the Loire surpasses the Tiber; the very air of Anjou has a unique charm.[8] The opposite extreme appears in Robert Burton, who makes large use of the traditional Renaissance consolations for exile and gathers the familiar classical texts under the topic: "Banishment is no grievance at all." In advancing once more the Stoic view he cites with disapproval cases parallel to Ovid's Scythians and the Ithacan Odysseus:

'Tis a childish humour to hone after home, to be discontent at that which others seek; to prefer, as base *Icelanders* and *Norwegians* do, their own ragged Island before *Italy* or *Greece,* the Gardens of the world. There is a base Nation in the North, saith *Pliny,* called *Chauci,* that live amongst rocks and sands by the sea side, feed on fish, drink water: and yet these base people account themselves slaves in respect when they come to *Rome.*[9]

The time was soon to come when the claims of such "base people" were to be strongly urged on natural or anthropological grounds, apart from the tradition of patriotism or civic pride.

The seventeenth century saw the infiltration of a special folk-theme by way of medical literature into the traditional discussions of cosmopolitanism, patriotism, and local attachment. The early history of the word *Heimweh,* originally from a Swiss-German dialect, has been elaborately studied by continental scholars and will be considered here only in connection with related themes in England.[10] The word first appears in Swiss documents in 1569, but its international currency to mark the homesickness of the exile, considered particularly as a characteristic of the Swiss, belongs to the seventeenth century. The term *nostalgia* first appears in Johannes Hofer, *Dissertatio Medica de Nostalgia oder Heimweh* (Basel, 1688), and the course of the term in scientific and popular literature thereafter has been elaborately charted.[11] But the question would immediately arise: Is the *Heimweh* of the Swiss a mere disease, or an example of the natural effect of the environment upon man, or an expression of an inexplicable and mysterious

attachment? After all, wrote Cardinal Bentivoglio, there is a
natural affinity between the Swiss and the Alps.[12] Pierre Costar's
Lettres (1658–59) put a favorable treatment of the idea into a
literary context, and will be convenient for our purpose since his
discussion appeared in English translation early in the eighteenth
century. Costar offers "critical Reflections upon C. Bentivoglio's
Letters."

What he says of the *Swiss,* seems to me happily imagin'd; that the *Alps*
are made for them, and they for the *Alps. L'Alpi son per gli Suizzeri,
e gli Suizzeri per l'Alpi.* Indeed, so savage a Nation little deserv'd a
more kind Climate. . . .

Delightful Countries produce Men of the same Temperament, and
little fitted to the Fatigues and Perils of War. So that it may be said,
if Men cultivate Countries, Countries cultivate Men; they soften their
Manners, and polish their Minds. Yet do the *Swiss* grow uneasy and
tir'd, sometimes, with their Abode in *France* or *Italy.* They pine after
their Snows and Ice, they are impatient, and eager to return to their
Lawns [landes] and Mountains, to such a Degree, that if they are
refus'd this Liberty, they will fall into a mortal langishing [sic]
Malady, which they call their *Country Sickness [la maladie du logis].*
This confirms the Saying, *That the Smoak of our own Country, seems
more clear and bright than the best Fires of Foreign Nations.*[13] And
altho' it be a Maxim, that honest Men find their homes in all Places
that furnish the Conveniencies of Living:

> Per tutto e buona Stanza, ove altri goda
> Et ogn' Stanza al valent huomo e patria.[14]

Yet it is certain, that Nature inspires us with an inexpressible secret
Passion for our own Country, which admits of no Decay, and which
never dies.

> Che dio Natura al Nascimento humano,
> Verso il caro paese, ov'altri e nato,
> Un no so che di non inteso affetto,
> Che sempre vive, e non invecchia mai.[15]

Though local attachment could be tolerated, accepted, or
praised as natural or inevitable, it could at the same time, even by
the same critic, be deprecated as irrational. Thus François de La
Mothe Le Vayer writes with full cognizance of the classical attitudes and the special case of the Swiss:

L'amour de la Patrie . . . n'est pas tout ce que le Bourgeois grossier &
sedentaire se fait parfois accroire; & cette passion qu'Ovide exilé mettoit
au dessus de toute raison,

> Rursus amor patriae ratione valentior omni
> [*Ex ponto* i.iii.29]

est peut-estre celle de toutes qui a le moins de fondement, & qui se doit
le plus facilement surmonter par le moindre usage de nostre chère
Philosophie. En effet si vous la prenez pour un certain charme physique
qui nous lie d'affection à cette piece de terre que nous avons la première
foulée aux pieds, & que les Latins ont sur cela nommée *Natale solum,*
y a-t-il rien de plus ridicule? . . .

Quoiqu'il en soit, nous voions les Suisses, que nous prenons pour les
hommes d'Europe de la plus grosse paste, quoiqu'il s'en trouve de
trés-excellens en toute sorte de professions, estre sujets à une foiblesse
pour ce regard, que les autres Nations n'éprouvent point si extréme
qu'ils la ressentent. La plûpart de ceux qui quittent leurs Cantons in-
cultes & sauvages pour venir en France ou ailleurs, tombent dans une
maladie qu'eux mesmes nomment *Heimuei,* c'est à dire, *de chez luy,*
parce que le seul désir de revoir leur païs les rend si hectiques, & si
imbecilles, qu'ils courent fortune de la vie s'ils ne retournent visiter
leurs foiers & leurs montagnes aussi affreuses qu'infertiles. J'avoüe que
cela prouve assez manifestement combien cette passion est naturelle, &
que les Grecs ont eu sujet de nommer νόστιμον ce qui est doux &
agreable, par une metaphore prise de νόστος, qui signifie la retour en
sa patrie, parce qu'il est presque toûjours accompagné de beaucoup de
contentement. Mais toutes les passions que la raison doit maistriser,
n'ont-elles pas le mesme fondement dans nostre humanité; & n'est-ce
pas estre brutal de se laisser transporter comme le reste des animaux
à des mouvemens, qui pour estre avoüez par la Nature ne le sont pas
souvent par la superieure partie de nostre âme?[16]

The more direct the influence from classical moral philosophy
the more reluctance there was to grant validity to inexplicable special attachments. Shaftesbury was keenly aware of the emphasis on
such special claims, and was eager to counter it by asserting universal principles which could lead the free citizen from an enlightened patriotism to a rational devotion to mankind at large.
He does not make special mention of the Swiss, but after recognizing the universality of *"natural Affection to a Country [Natale
Solum]"* he emphatically rejects the attempt "to resolve the very
Essence and Foundation of this generous Passion into a Relation to

mere Clay and Dust."[17] The patriot is attached to a civil state, and true liberty has nothing to do with soil or climate.

Bolingbroke, taking essentially the same position as Shaftesbury on this subject, has left us some "Reflections on Exile," written about 1716 but first published 1752, virtually a translation of Seneca's consolation, which have particular interest because they use the example of the Swiss:

Among numberless extravagancies which have passed through the minds of men, we may justly reckon for one that notion of a secret affection, independent of our reason, and superior to our reason, which we are supposed to have for our country; as if there were some physical virtue in every spot of ground, which necessarily produced this effect in every one born upon it—"Amor patriae ratione valentior omni" [*Ex ponto* i.iii.29]. As if the heimvei was an universal distemper, inseparable from the constitution of an human body, and not peculiar to the Swiss, who seem to have been made for their mountains, as their mountains seem to have been made for them.[18]

In the *Letters on the Study and Use of History,* to which these "Reflections" were appended, Bolingbroke belittles national vanity, and gives an unfavorable turn to the evidence brought in by the travelers; national and local preferences are illustrated by the absurd prejudices of the Chinese, the Samoyedes, and the Hottentots.[19]

Thus both Shaftesbury and Bolingbroke advocate an exclusive and rigorous cosmopolitanism, in line with the Stoic origin of their views. They admit love of country if there is sound reason for it, but, to quote Bolingbroke again, "a wise man looks on himself as a citizen of the world: and, when you ask him where his country lies, points, like ANAXAGORAS, with his finger to the heavens."[20] We note the operative phrase, "citizen of the world," but should remind ourselves that it may have various meanings: it may imply that the world-citizen accepts national and regional differences instead of holding himself aloof by applying a rigorous standard. Thus Addison calls himself "a Citizen of the World" as he observes the various nationalities in the Royal Exchange.[21] The philosopher could take an inclusively cosmopolitan position, with love of home or country as a necessary part of an infinitely varied scheme.

Attention was likely to be centered, however, on extreme cases of attachment to a harsh environment, duly noted by the physico-theologists.[22] These providential arrangements were often described in terms of what we should call adaptation; the nature of the environment was a primary cause of the character of the inhabitant.[23] In 1705 Johann Jakob Scheuchzer, to quote an English reviewer, "ascribed the *Nostalgia* of the Swiss to the lightness and purity of the air which they breathe."[24] The idea was in line with medical theory inherited from antiquity, and was restated by the Abbé Du Bos: "Cette maladie qu'on appelle le *Hemvé* en quelques païs & qui donne au malade un violent desir de retourner chez lui, *Cum notos tristis desiderat Haedos* [Juvenal xi.153], est un instinct qui nous avertit que l'air où nous nous trouvons n'est pas aussi convenable à notre constitution que celui pour lequel un secret instinct nous fait soûpirer."[25] On a comparative view of different peoples this adaptation appears as part of a general design:

Nature, without any partial View, adjusts the Wits of Men, so as to render them the fittest for the Places where they inhabit.

The *Samoyedes*, who dwell in the cold marshy Provinces of *Muscovite Tartary*, are Objects of Compassion to us, and we pity them as the most unfortunate of Men. But are they really so? Quite the contrary; they look on their chilly, frozen Coasts, as the Paradise of the World: Instead of envying other Regions, they contemn them; and in case they are by Accident remov'd from their native Land, they discover the same earnest Longings for these inhospitable Dwellings, as if they had been borne away from *Italy*, or the pleasant Plains of *Hungary*.[26]

Until well into the eighteenth century the force of the idea of an instinctive local attachment deeply rooted in human nature was checked both by a satirical and critical view of human nature itself and by the enduring tradition of classical cosmopolitanism, the latter often connected with devotion to the ideal of liberty. Thus a French compilation, following and quoting La Mothe Le Vayer, recognizes homesickness as characteristic of many peoples besides the Swiss, and gives two examples: the homesick Greenlanders at the court of Denmark, and the Hottentot who pined away in England and returned joyously to the Cape of Good Hope. But this discussion continues to treat homesickness as a disease, and is at pains to distinguish it from true patriotism.[27] Writers were not always consistent. Thus the *Weekly Miscellany*, March

18, 1736–37, describes the case of another Hottentot who, after seeing the Dutch settlements in India and the amenities of Holland, "returned with inexpressible Pleasure to the Grease and brutal Manners of his Native Soil." This, we are told, is a beneficent arrangement of Providence. But the writer goes on to reduce the instinct to self-love, and the widening of human attachments to "Genuine Disinterestedness" and "Publick Spirit" is held up as the ideal.

John Campbell praises the Lapps for their complete adaptation to hard natural conditions and adds a familiar political motif: "For how, my Friend, can a Nation be called *Base,* who are so remarkably fond of *Liberty*[?]"[28] It should be noted that in descriptions of northern peoples local attachment and what Lovejoy calls "hard primitivism" do not always persist; important northern nations ("Scythians" or "Goths") moved from one region to another, and, according to current history, brought liberty to southern Europe, promoting what we might call progressive and cosmopolitan ideas. Or, if they stayed at home, they were likely to develop soft pastoral virtues by their very contentment and innocence, like the Lapps in an important addition to Thomson's *Winter* (1744) or the Swiss in Albrecht von Haller's *Die Alpen* (1732). Thomson's long passage on the Swiss in *Liberty* IV (1736) combines the hard and the soft veins in primitivism, and also the primitive and the progressive: the mountains are the natural setting for a hardy free people, but they do not altogether block a progressive culture; they enclose fertile vales where "unguilty Cities rise," and the Swiss "give the dreadful *Alps* to smile, / And press their Culture on retiring Snows" (IV, 337–8). In characterizing the Swiss and their country Thomson makes the first important use of the specific idea of *Heimweh* by a British poet:

> Even, chear'd by ME, their shaggy Mountains charm,
> More than or *Gallic* or *Italian* Plains;
> And sickening Fancy oft, when absent long,
> Pines to behold their *Alpine* Views again.
>
> (IV, 344–7)

The poet adds a note: "It is reported of the *Swiss*, that, after having been long absent from their Native Country, they are seized with such a violent Desire of seeing it again, as affects them with a kind

of languishing Indisposition, called the *Swiss Sickness.*" Here the
"Swiss Sickness" is interpreted as a natural devotion to mountain
liberty and to "Alpine Views," and the topic inspires a magnificent
passage on mountain landscape, combining the picturesque and
the sublime. An important link with descriptive poetry is thus
established, but it may be remarked that Thomson does not read
nostalgia into other descriptions which are based on his own early
experiences on the Border. At this stage the theme is likely to have
a distancing effect, to deal with simple people in remote regions.

The further development of local attachment as a literary motif
was largely to depend, as we shall see, on the confluence of descriptive poetry and the association psychology. Meanwhile the themes
we have already noted in such writers as Shaftesbury and Bolingbroke continued to dominate, and were in fact congruous with
much in Thomson himself. Aaron Hill, shortly after he had read
Thomson's *Liberty,* addressed some lines "To the Editor of Al-
bania," that is, to the man who had just published an anonymous
piece in praise of Scotland. Though Hill's verses are mediocre, his
lengthy statement is convenient for our purpose. He praises the
unknown poet and then continues:

> But, where *domestick dearness* warp'd his lays,
> And partial *birth* mis-led the patriot praise,
> Wilt thou not join, to *blame* the *bounded zeal,*
> That bids us, *only* for our *country, feel?*
> Yes—thou wilt censure the *too scanty* care,
> That shuts out *pity,* and appropriates *pray'r:*
> Thou wilt *enlarge* affection, till it *sees*
> Beyond *itself,* and pants for *publick* ease.
> Stretch *liberty,*—to disengage *mankind;*
> And, ev'n from *nature's byass,* free the *mind.*
> What, tho' (we know not why) soft, inbred, *Pride*
> Makes *home* seem *sweetest,* and can choice *misguide;*
> Till native darkness erring taste constrains;
> And *Lapland deserts* rival *China plains?*
> Let the *soul's reach* the heart's restraint *reprove,*
> And widen, to the *world,* our *country's* love.
> Base are these *local* limits to mens hearts,
> That canton out *humanity,* in parts.
> *Truth* has *no districts,* to divide her toil;
> And *virtue* is *at home,* in ev'ry soil.[29]

Similarly Christopher Smart belittles national differences and exhorts us to be "patriots of mankind."[30] Extreme positions might lead to what Dr. Johnson called "cant." An intermediate position is possible, and the independent mind of Tobias Smollett sought to find it; he would reject the mystery of local attachment and base love of country on grounds both rational and natural.

I am at last in a situation to indulge my view with a sight of Britain, after an absence of two years; and indeed you cannot imagine what pleasure I feel while I survey the white cliffs of Dover, at this distance. Not that I am at all affected by the *nescia* [sic] *qua dulcedine natalis soli,* of Horace [that is, Ovid]. That seems to be a kind of fanaticism founded on the prejudices of education, which induce a Laplander to place the terrestrial paradise among the snows of Norway, and a Swiss to prefer the barren mountains of Solleure [Soleure] to the fruitful plains of Lombardy. I am attached to my country, because it is the land of liberty, cleanliness, and convenience: but I love it still more tenderly, as the scene of all my interesting connexions; as the habitation of my friends, for whose conversation, correspondence, and esteem, I wish alone to live.[31]

II

The interplay of cosmopolitanism and local attachment is basic for the plan of Goldsmith's *Traveller* and is helpful for some parts of *The Deserted Village*. Parallel alternatives appear in Churchill's *Farewell,* published in June 1764, six months before *The Traveller*. In Churchill's verse-dialogue the cosmopolitanism of one speaker, the Friend, is contrasted with the patriotism of the Poet himself; yet while the Friend commends a "grand view" which includes and loves all mankind, the Poet, starting with love of self, admits the possibility of extending this love beyond narrow limits to country and mankind, so that the contrast may be resolved on a philosophic level. Some such solution is sought by the central figure in *The Traveller,* a detached figure engaged in a philosophic quest or pursuit of happiness, with a touch of personal color characteristic of Goldsmith.[32] The biographical background is too familiar for repetition, but an early personal comment of Goldsmith's, a playful recognition and humorous depreciation of local attachment, will be helpful here:

Unaccountable [fond]ness for country, this maladie du Pays, as the french [call] it. Unaccountable, that he should still have an affec[tion for] a place, who never received when in it above civil [contem]pt, who never brought [anything] out of it, except his brogue [an]d his blunders; surely my affection is equally ridiculous with the Scotchman's, who refused to be cured of the itch, because it made him unco'thoughtful of his wife and bonny Inverary.[33]

It is hardly necessary to show in detail that the cosmopolitanism of *The Citizen of the World* and *The Traveller* involves an ultimate rejection of local attachment by the philosophic mind, even though local attachment is recognized in both works. Goldsmith's Chinese philosopher can say:

There is something so seducing in that spot in which we first had existence, that nothing but it can please; whatever vicissitudes we experience in life, however we toil, or wheresoever we wander, our fatigued wishes still recur to home for tranquillity; we long to die in that spot which gave us birth, and in that pleasing expectation opiate every calamity.

(Letter 103)

He begins his letters home by asserting that "those ties that bind me to my native country, and you, are still unbroken, while by every remove, I only drag a greater length of chain" (Letter 3). The "lengthening chain" of the man who sentences himself to exile, a figure perhaps taken from Racine's *Andromaque* (I.i.44), appears also at the opening of *The Traveller:*

> Where'er I roam, whatever realms to see,
> My heart, untravelled fondly turns to thee,
> Still to my brother turns, with ceaseless pain,
> And drags at each remove a lengthening chain.

But as the exact opposite of local attachment the literature of exile had always recognized the sheer impulse to wander. Goldsmith's Chinese observer, Lien Chi Altangi, corresponds with a friend at home who more than once accuses him of sacrificing happiness by traveling out of idle curiosity (Letters 6, 42). In reply Lien Chi Altangi claims a philosophic purpose: "A man who leaves home to mend himself and others is a philosopher; but he who goes from country to country, guided by the blind impulse of curiosity, is only a vagabond" (Letter 7).

The particular form which the philosophic quest takes in *The Citizen of the World* and *The Traveller* was determined by what we may call altruistic cosmopolitanism. "The philosopher, who extends his regard to all mankind, must have still a smaller concern for what has already affected, or may hereafter affect himself: the concerns of others make his whole study, and that study is his pleasure" (Letter 44). At the same time, this concern with the happiness of others leads Goldsmith's observer to reject the Stoic pride (Letter 47). The detached philosopher must be at the same time a sympathetic observer.

Similarly *The Traveller* weighs the possibility of an ardent, sympathetic, and inclusive as against a severe, rigorous, and detached cosmopolitanism.

> When thus Creation's charms around combine,
> Amidst the store, should thankless pride repine?
> Say, should the philosophic mind disdain
> That good, which makes each humbler bosom vain?
> Let school-taught pride dissemble all it can,
> These little things are great to little man;
> And wiser he, whose sympathetic mind
> Exults in all the good of all mankind.
> Ye glitt'ring towns, with wealth and splendour crown'd,
> Ye fields, where summer spreads profusion round,
> Ye lakes, whose vessels catch the busy gale,
> Ye bending swains, that dress the flow'ry vale,
> For me your tributary stores combine;
> Creation's heir, the world, the world is mine.
>
> (ll. 37–50)

This passage expresses a wish to reject the strict Stoic position, and to make a comprehensive survey which should accept sympathetically all local attachments and patriotisms. But an underlying difficulty here is the fact that the philosophic observer is both inside and outside these local attachments. What is he to do with his own local attachment? In the lines immediately following those just quoted (ll.51–62) Goldsmith seems in his own way to be stating this difficulty. The traveler as a human being must find his satisfaction in a particular spot, but as a philosopher he knows that he cannot do so. Moreover, this philosophic conclusion can be reached on two levels: as a detached observer he knows that other places may yield other satisfactions just as eligible, and ultimately, as a follower on occasion of Johnson's Christian Stoicism, he must conclude that locality is indifferent, for after all no place yields ultimate satisfaction.

But for the present his personal needs and the conclusions of Christian Stoicism drop into the background, and in the survey of nations a law of compensation gives ground for cosmopolitan sympathy. The poet who sighs "to see the hoard of human bliss so small" can also describe Nature as "a mother kind alike to all." Elsewhere he thinks of the hard primitivism of the North as a signal example of adaptation and local attachment, and uses the instance of the Greenlander at the Danish court.[34] The principle is generalized in *The Traveller* (ll.81–98), with striking illustration in so many words of the softening of hard primitivism: "These rocks, by custom, turn to beds of down" (l.86). The Swiss are the supreme example, with a full statement of the principle that the limitations and privations of the native region actually increase local attachment (ll.199–208). But any impulse to primitivism is firmly checked; the Swiss are denied decisive advantages, let alone superiority. And there is a final reversion to Stoic doctrine in the concluding lines supplied by Dr. Johnson. Strictly speaking, Johnson's conclusion changes the direction of the poem, for it dwells on the self-sufficiency of the philosophic mind regardless of public life or the international prospect, and would thus belittle or ignore the diverse goods discovered by the traveler's survey.

Both *The Traveller* and *The Deserted Village* are concerned in large part with the relation of local attachment to a general scheme of human history or human destiny, but local attachment is presented in a more subjective and intimate way in the later poem. A vein of impersonal generalization persists; the downfall of the village is connected with the change from simple virtue to corrupt luxury which had played such a prominent part in the characterization of the English in *The Traveller*. On the other hand *The Traveller* itself had dwelt on the poet's sympathy with the exiled English country folk in the American wilderness (ll.419–22). The later poem fills in the picture of the English home with specific though not sharply localized detail, but the formal conclusion substitutes for the local attachment which might seem to be getting dominance a cosmopolitan view of the power of poetry. The implications of this somewhat neglected passage cannot be fully considered here; the compensatory power of poetry seems to be intended as a reconciliation of the regional and the cosmopolitan, somewhat in the manner of *The Traveller* and with a remarkable resemblance to the central doctrine of a poem which Goldsmith belittled, Gray's *Progress of Poesy*.

III

The later eighteenth century saw the identification of local attachment with an archetype of simple virtue which was widely accepted and richly elaborated. This falls in with general tendencies which we may call primitivistic and sentimental, and with the growing popularity of loco-descriptive poetry and in general the poetry of natural description. Themes of locality were treated with heightened subjectivity. A familiar example is the fragment of an intended Book IV of *The Pleasures of Imagination* which Akenside composed about 1770. In planning to trace "the secret paths / Of early genius" Akenside reverts to the scenes of his childhood:

> O ye Northumbrian shades, which overlook
> The rocky pavement and the mossy falls
> Of solitary Wensbeck's limpid stream,
> How gladly I recall your well-known seats
> Belov'd of old, and that delightful time
> When all alone, for many a summer's day,
> I wander'd through your calm recesses, led
> In silence by some powerful hand unseen.[35]

It has been remarked more than once that this is closer to Wordsworth than to Thomson's treatment of his early days on the Border. An important force at work here was the wide influence of the doctrine of the association of ideas. Although the tradition of Locke had minimized casual association of ideas as promoting irrationality and obscurity, the growing acceptance of the associationist psychology and approval of associationist diversity gave more and more scope for local attachment. Addison's recognition of the association of ideas among the pleasures of imagination is particularly important.[36] The general importance of this theme from

Sterne to Proust cannot be touched on here—the evocative power of a single image or object in the intricate emotional and imaginative life of man. A subtler analysis of the response to familiar places was thus promoted; as Boswell put it in 1775, "There are ideas attached to particular places which it is almost impossible to express."[37]

Here we may point out, without exaggerating its importance, the representative quality of the specific Swiss theme. The central figure came to be the Swiss soldier sent abroad to fight and moved to intolerable nostalgia by the notes of a certain tune, the *Kuhreihen* or *ranz des vaches*. Recorded in Switzerland early in the eighteenth century,[38] this report appears in England in *Common Sense*, 14 October 1738, and also in Johann Georg Keyssler's *Travels* (English translation 1756),[39] and was given further currency by Rousseau in his *Dictionnaire de Musique*, written in 1764 and published in 1768.[40] John Brown has the story in his *Dissertation on the Rise, Union, and Power . . . of Poetry and Music* (1763) and so does James Beattie in his *Essays on Poetry and Music* (1776). Beattie's adaptation of Rousseau's article may stand as representative of many restatements of the theme:

There is a dance in Switzerland, which the young shepherds perform to a tune played on a sort of bagpipe. The tune is called *Rance des vaches;* it is wild and irregular, but has nothing in its composition that could recommend it to our notice. But the Swiss are so intoxicated with this tune, that if at any time they hear it, when abroad in foreign service, they burst into tears; and often fall sick, and even die, of a passionate desire to revisit their native country; for which reason, in some armies where they serve, the playing of this tune is prohibited. This tune, having been the attendant of their childhood and early youth, recals [sic] to their memory those regions of wild beauty and rude magnificence, those days of liberty and peace, those nights of festivity, those happy assemblies, those tender passions, which formerly endeared to them their country, their homes, and their employments; and which, when compared with the scenes of uproar they are now engaged in, and the servitude they now undergo, awaken such regret as entirely overpowers them.[41]

It may be added that general interest in the Swiss setting and in the national struggles of Switzerland after the French invasion of Switzerland kept this special theme alive in minor English verse well into the nineteenth century.[42] Though the most famous of nostalgic lyrics, "Home, Sweet Home," was said to be based on a Sicilian air, John Howard Payne also had in mind "something approaching the measure of the 'Ranz des Vaches.' "[43] The most familiar instance in European literature is the reworking of the German folksong of the deserter so that the central figure becomes a Swiss mercenary at Strassburg moved by the notes of the Alphorn.[44]

It is impossible to trace fully the persistent idea that homesickness is particularly characteristic of inhabitants of remote and primitive places; instances mount up beyond our reckoning. In Jacques Delille's *Les Jardins* (1782) we read of a native of Tahiti moved to an intense vision of home and an agony of tears by the sight of a tropical tree from his own island. The Portuguese *saudade* has been traditional from the time of the voyages of discovery to the present day.[45] Parallels to the Ranz des Vaches appear among other peoples, the Moors in Spain or the Gascon soldiers in *Cyrano de Bergerac*.[46] The mountaineer and the soldier remained typical nostalgic figures. Universally known French lyrics continued the theme in the nineteenth century—Chateaubriand's "Souvenir du pays de France," also called "Le Montagnard exilé," Béranger's "Les Hirondelles" and "La Nostalgie." Among the special nostalgias of the British world, the Highland clearances helped to make the Swiss-Scottish parallel a familiar theme.[47] Mrs. Anne Grant describes a Highland air, played as the emigrants depart, which is the equivalent of the Ranz des Vaches,[48] and Scott also refers to this theme in the Introduction to *A Legend of Montrose* (1819). Byron, with special reference to nostalgic Highland airs, speaks of the "calentures of music."[49] In *Quentin Durward*, innocently anachronistic, Scott has the Lady Hameline say of the young hero: "The poor youth is like a Swiss mountaineer, mad with partiality to his native land; he will next tell us of the vines and olives of Scotland" (chap. xviii). We can easily understand why the "Canadian Boat-Song" (*Blackwood's Magazine*, September 1829) became known throughout the English-speaking world as the great nostalgic lyric of the Highland settlements in Canada.

In the late eighteenth century two historically interesting treat-

ments of the general theme try to connect it more or less systematically with the association psychology. Samuel Rogers' *Pleasures of Memory* (1792) combines the subject of early recollections,
in the manner of Goldsmith, with some exposition of the laws of
association. As the Analysis of the First Part says: "The Poem
begins with the description of an obscure village, and of the pleasing melancholy which it excites on being revisited after a long
time." The Swiss is one of Rogers' examples, with the familiar
reference to Rousseau. In 1790 a minor Cornish poet Richard
Polwhele undertook a comprehensive treatment of the subject, and
published his poem in 1796 under the title, *The Influence of Local
Attachment with Respect to Home*.[50] Among his numerous examples he includes the Laplander, a Welshman in his poor hereditary shed, an old Devonshire peasant in a picturesque spot near
Buckfast Abbey, a Highland chief in an Ossianic landscape, Ulysses
longing for Ithaca and Catullus for Sirmio, and of course the Swiss.
Polwhele's interesting and even erudite collection of examples attracted the attention of Samuel Jackson Pratt, who in later editions
of his poem *Sympathy* (first published 1781, revised edition 1807),
incorporated some of Polwhele's notes.

Scott's reception and use of the current doctrine of local attachment can be briefly illustrated by the address to Erskine in the
Introduction to Canto III of *Marmion*. The ideas are familiar:
whether this "secret power" is innate or formed by early habit it
rules with "despotic sway," and "drags us on by viewless chain"
(Goldsmith's figure again); it leads the Belgian to prefer his own
flat country to any mountainous region, and the Scot to prefer his
rugged country to the verdant landscapes of England. One thinks
of Jeanie Deans on Richmond Hill.[51] Local attachment becomes
intensely autobiographical in both Scott and Wordsworth; in Scott
it finds rich and varied documentation; in Wordsworth it is explored more deeply for its place in life, its ultimate meaning, its
implications and limitations.

Without entering fully into the subtleties of Wordsworth's inner
life and the intricate chronology of his literary development, we
may consider his reception and transformation of the eighteenth
century tradition. The indebtedness of his *Descriptive Sketches* to
Goldsmith's *Traveller* in its presentation of the traveler's quest

and the connection between landscape and national character need only be mentioned.[52] The theme of the homesick Swiss, evidently taken from the French version of Coxe's *Travels in Switzerland*, by Ramond de Carbonnières, is included (ll.627–31 of the original version). Various relations to place continue to play a major role in Wordsworth's work. They hardly lend themselves to chronological arrangement, but it is natural to begin with simple attachment to the unique place. "The Reverie of Poor Susan" turns on the point that a slight stimulus, a note of music, is enough to evoke the nostalgic vision. And in "The Brothers" the shepherd boy at sea recalls his native Patterdale with the vividness of the calenture, the sailor's feverish vision of green fields in the ocean depths.[53]

But the most important expressions of local attachment in Wordsworth are of course autobiographical. In 1787 he wrote a long poem known as "The Vale of Esthwaite," a few lines of which were revised and published in 1815 as "Extract from the conclusion of a poem composed in Anticipation of Leaving School."

> Dear native regions, I foretell,
> From what I feel at this farewell,
> That, wheresoe'er my steps may tend,
> And whensoe'er my course shall end,
> If in that hour a single tie
> Survive of local sympathy,
> My soul will cast the backward view,
> The longing look alone on you.
>
> Thus, while the Sun sinks down to rest
> Far in the regions of the west,
> Though to the vale no parting beam
> Be given, not one memorial gleam,
> A lingering light he fondly throws
> On the dear hills where first he rose.

In *The Prelude*, VIII, 462–75, Wordsworth gives the history of the composition of these lines in a memorable sunset hour by Thurston Mere (Coniston). Raymond Havens remarks, "This incident must have had for Wordsworth a significance that none of his four versified descriptions of it communicates to the reader."[54] Its meaning for Wordsworth can perhaps best be understood in terms of relating localized experience to wider tracts of space and time. The following familiar lines, no doubt directly related to the experience underlying "Dear native regions," give a richer and fuller restatement of the theme:

> Thus were my sympathies enlarged, and thus
> Daily the common range of visible things
> Grew dear to me: already I began
> To love the sun; a boy I loved the sun,
> Not as I since have loved him, as a pledge
> And surety of our earthly life, a light
> Which we behold and feel we are alive;
> Nor for his bounty to so many worlds—
> But for this cause, that I had seen him lay
> His beauty to the morning hills, had seen
> The western mountain touch his setting orb,
> In many a thoughtless hour, when, from excess
> Of happiness, my blood appeared to flow
> For its own pleasure, and I breathed with joy.
> And, from like feelings, humble though intense,
> To patriotic and domestic love
> Analogous, the moon to me was dear;
> For I could dream away my purposes,
> Standing to gaze upon her while she hung
> Midway between the hills, as if she knew
> No other region, but belonged to thee,
> Yea, appertained by a peculiar right
> To thee and thy grey huts, thou one dear Vale![55]

The relationship to the native place is developed and varied both intensively and extensively; from simple attachment it becomes a basis for the poet's most profound understanding of nature and humanity. And as life goes on, the poet remembers, returns to, and chooses one place or another. *Tintern Abbey* is the classic of recollection and return; a given place, native or not, becomes unique as the basis of the poet's deepest intuitions. And *Michael* may be considered a dramatically fused presentation of the shepherd's life and external nature in a precisely localized and revisited setting. "Michael is Wordsworthian Man," writes Professor Bloom, with a cross-reference to the magnified figure of the shepherd in Book VIII of *The Prelude*.[56]

Characteristically Wordsworthian is the persistence of the place as the central part of the experience. A classic statement is found in the draft of Book I of *The Recluse,* called "Home at Grasmere," written in 1800. As a boy he had thought of the all-sufficiency of a life lived completely "within the bound of this high Concave,"[57] and now he deliberately returns to the "dear Vale." "A thousand nooks of earth" may have similar natural beauties,

> but no where else is found,
> No where (or is it fancy?) can be found
> The one sensation that is here; 'tis here,
> Here as it found its way into my heart
> In childhood, here as it abides by day,
> By night, here only; or in chosen minds
> That take it with them hence, where'er they go.
> 'Tis, but I cannot name it, 'tis the sense
> Of majesty, and beauty, and repose,
> A blended holiness of earth and sky,
> Something that makes this individual Spot,
> This small Abiding-place of many Men,
> A termination, and a last retreat,
> A Centre, come from wheresoe'er you will,
> A Whole without dependence or defect,
> Made for itself; and happy in itself,
> Perfect Contentment, Unity entire.
>
> (ll. 135–51)

The chosen place is both *terminus a quo* and *terminus ad quem;* the place keeps its unique status as the poet realizes simultaneously both the particular and the universal quality of his experience. A lyrical expression of the same theme appears in the familiar lines "To a Skylark":

> Type of the wise who soar, but never roam;
> True to the kindred points of Heaven and Home![58]

Though we are not undertaking a chronological report of Wordsworth's attitudes, we should remind ourselves that this reassertion and deepening of local attachment came after a period of relative detachment in Cambridge and France, which brought with it an adoption in part of traditional cosmopolitan patterns. He is detached from Cambridge and to a certain extent from his native regions; his mind, thrown back on itself, can make a world out of "universal things," "the common countenance of earth and sky" (*Prelude*, III, 106–7). Locality as a starting point for the generalization drops into the background. We have more to do with universal truth on a rational or intellectual level. Proceeding to France, he became, he reports, "a patriot of the world" (*Prelude*, X,242); he believed

> that there was,
> Transcendent to all local patrimony,
> One nature, as there is one sun in heaven—
> *(Prelude,* X,156–8)

and that

> Not favored spots alone, but the whole Earth,
> The beauty wore of promise—
> *(Prelude,* XI,117–18).

At no time did this mean complete rejection of the local, but rather its submergence or suppression. Thus he describes himself in France as

> In brief, a child of Nature, as at first,
> Diffusing only those affections wider
> That from the cradle had grown up with me,
> And losing, in no other way than light
> Is lost in light, the weak in the more strong.
> *(Prelude,* XI,168–72).

This is very close to what has been called above inclusive cosmopolitanism, differing alike from nostalgic attachment to a place and from the preservation of the unique locality in the universal. Nostalgia is rare in Wordsworth, though it appears in the German winter of 1798–99, and finds expression in the Lucy poems.

If it is argued that the poet uses locality in so many different ways that we cannot attach much significance to any of them, we may perhaps answer that a consciousness of locality, whether it be acceptance, change, or rejection, may be so clearly present and so strongly emphasized as fairly to be called characteristic of his work. Of course the free spirit may consciously and deliberately move here or there. At the very beginning of *The Prelude* we have the suggestion of a free choice:

What dwelling shall receive me? in what vale
Shall be my harbour?[59]

Though Wordsworth's feeling and vision in his best work depend largely on the concept of the unique locality, other forces lead him away from the intensely or exclusively local—his additional travel experiences, his inclination to philosophic generalization under low imaginative pressure, his conception of English patriotism as embodying a universally valid idea of liberty. As he later puts it, the active principle in the universe is

Spirit that knows no insulated spot,
No chasm, no solitude.
(*Excursion*, IX,13–14).

Or the independent spirit nurtured in the Vale may simply delight in variety: "Departure from the Vale of Grasmere" (composed 1811), opening *Memorials of a Tour in Scotland 1803,* supplements "Home at Grasmere" thus:

O pleasant transit, Grasmere! to resign
Such happy fields, abodes so calm as thine;
Not like an outcast with himself at strife;
The slave of business, time, or care for life,
But moved by choice; or, if constrained in part,
Yet still with Nature's freedom at the heart;—
To cull contentment upon wildest shores,
And luxuries extract from bleakest moors;
With prompt embrace all beauty to enfold,
And having rights in all that we behold.

Here we have a recreative and imaginative mood which dwells on enjoyment of various places in a tolerant and receptive way. To clarify Wordsworth's position we may indulge in some special terminology and say that in his work we can find the uniquely local, the multi-local, and the cosmopolitan. His fondness for the figure of the wanderer is too well known for full illustration. "I, too, have been a wanderer."[60] The attraction of the open road can be an "invitation into space" or "guide into eternity" (*Prelude*, XIII, 150–51). In his description of the Pedlar in *The Excursion* he shows that he is conscious of the coexistence of the traditional local attachment of the mountaineer with a simple instinct to wander:

> That stern yet kindly Spirit, who constrains
> The Savoyard to quit his naked rocks,
> The freeborn Swiss to leave his narrow vales,
> (Spirit attached to regions mountainous
> Like their own stedfast clouds) did now impel
> His restless mind to look abroad with hope.
>
> (*Excursion,* I,316–21).

In this poem precise locality is still important as an appropriate setting for meditation and discussion, but is not treated as unique or essential. The valley in which the Solitary dwells (II, 329–69), for example, is comparable as a delightful retreat with the Vale of Grasmere, but the Poet's farewell to the place is much in the spirit of Goldsmith:

> Lingering behind my comrades, thus I breathed
> A parting tribute to a spot that seemed
> Like the fixed centre of a troubled world.
> Again I halted with reverted eyes;
> The chain that would not slacken, was at length
> Snapt,—and, pursuing leisurely my way,
> How vain, thought I, is it by change of place
> To seek that comfort which the mind denies
>
> (*Excursion,* V,14–21).

The *Poems on the Naming of Places* are largely on the level of genial and varied association.

Meanwhile the patriotic poems of the 1800's included in *Poems Dedicated to National Independence and Liberty,* though they make use of the traditional association of mountains with liberty, maintain a national rather than a regional tone. On occasion they assert the independence of the mind, and even man's ultimate freedom from milieu:

> And is it among rude untutored Dales,
> There, and there only, that the heart is true?
> And, rising to repel or to subdue,
> Is it by rocks and woods that man prevails?
> Ah no! though Nature's dread protection fails,
> There is a bulwark in the soul.
>
> (Part II, Sonnet xiii)

Local attachment of a pure and direct kind continued, however, as in the lines with the self-explanatory title, "Composed when a probability existed of our being obliged to quit Rydal Mount as a residence" (1826). And in conclusion we may note that Wordsworth could still think of the extension and deepening of the special Swiss theme in the sonnet "On Hearing the Ranz des Vaches on the Top of the Pass of St. Gothard" (1820 or 1821):

> I listen—but no faculty of mine
> Avails those modulations to detect,
> Which, heard in foreign lands, the Swiss affect
> With tenderest passion; leaving him to pine
> (So fame reports) and die,—his sweet-breath'd kine
> Remembering, and green Alpine pastures decked
> With vernal flowers. Yet may we not reject
> The tale as fabulous.—Here while I recline,
> Mindful how others by this simple Strain
> Are moved, for me—upon this Mountain named
> Of God himself from dread pre-eminence—
> Aspiring thoughts, by memory reclaimed,
> Yield to the Muse's touching influence;
> And joys of distant home my heart enchain.

NOTES

1. *Odyssey* i.58. Loeb Library translation.

2. Seneca *Epistulae morales* 66.26.

3. *Ex ponto* i.iii.34–8. Loeb Library translation. Cf. also *Tristia* i.v.57–70; Cicero *De oratore* i.196.

4. Cicero *Tusculan disputations* v.108. For a useful record of occurrences of the phrase "citizen of the world" see Hamilton Jewett Smith, *Oliver Goldsmith's "The Citizen of the World"* (New Haven, 1926), pp. 29–30.

5. Plutarch *Moralia* 601 F.

6. *Richard II*, I.iii. See John L. Tison, Jr., "Shakespeare's 'Consolatio' for Exile," *MLQ*, XXI (1960), 142–59.

7. Clément Marot, *Epîtres*.

8. Sonnet xxxi in *Les Regrets* (1558). *Oeuvres Poétiques*, ed. Chamard (repr. 1927), II, 76–7.

9. *Anatomy of Melancholy*, Part II, Sect. III, Mem. IV, ed. A. R. Shilleto (London, 1893), II, 201–2. The reference in the quotation is to Pliny, *Natural History*, xvi.1.

10. Recent publications which give the essential bibliographical information are Fritz Ernst, *Vom Heimweh* (Zürich, 1949); Wolf-Dieter Stempel, "Das Heimweh und seine Bezeichnung im Romanischen," *Archiv fur das Studium der neueren Sprachen und Literaturen*, CXCIX (1963), 353–74.

11. Hofer's dissertation has been translated by Carolyn Kiser Anspach, *Bulletin of the Institute of the History of Medicine*, II (1934), 376–91.

12. *Raccolta di Lettere* (Rome, 1654), p. 4.

13. Cf. M. P. Tilley, *A Dictionary of the Proverbs in English*, etc. (Ann Arbor, 1950), S572; Erasmus, *Adagia*, "Patriae fumus, igni alieno luculentior." Cf. note 1 above.

14. Ultimately from Ovid, *Fasti* i.493: "Omne solum forti patria est."

15. Tamworth Reresby, *A Miscellany of Ingenious Thoughts and Reflections* (London, 1721), pp. 102–3. Cf. Costar, I, 397 ff.

16. François de La Mothe Le Vayer, *Oeuvres* (Paris, 1684), XI, 142–3, 146–7. This letter "De l'Eloignement de son Pays" originally appeared in *Petits Traités en forme de lettres* (1659–60). See also his letter "De la Patrie et des Etrangers," *Oeuvres*, VIII, 43–54.

17. *Characteristicks* (London, 1737), III, 144.

18. *Works* (London, 1770), IX, 440–41. For the last sentence see references to Bentivoglio and Costar above, notes 12 and 15.

19. *Works*, IX, 25–6.

20. Ibid. pp. 442–3.

21. *Spectator*, No. 69.

22. See Bernard Nieuwentydt, *The Religious Philosopher*, trans. John Chamberlayne (London, 1724), I, 165–6.

23. See Alan D. McKillop, *The Background of Thompson's "Seasons,"* (Minneapolis, 1942), p. 119; John Arthos, *The Language of Natural Description in Eighteenth-Century Poetry* (Ann Arbor, 1949), under "Element (native)," especially p. 156.

24. *New Memoirs of Literature*, III (1726), 149–50.

25. Jean Baptiste Du Bos, *Réflexions critiques sur la poésie et sur la peinture* (Paris, 1733), II, 249. Originally published 1719. The quotation from Juvenal refers to the countryman away from home who "thinks wistfully of the kids he knows so well." Du Bos goes on to quote Lucretius *De rerum natura* vi. 1103–6.

26. *Applebee's Journal*, May 26, 1733, repr. *London Magazine*, II (1733), 250.

27. *The Ceremonies and Religious Customs of the Various Nations of the Known World* [translated from the French of Jean Fréderic Bernard and others] (6 vols.; London, 1731), III, 63–5. The story of the Greenlanders is here

said to be taken from *"Collection of Voyages to the North,* Vol. I." The reference is presumably to Bernard's *Recueil de voiages au Nord* (Amsterdam, 1720). The same story of the Greenlanders brought to the Danish court, their mortal homesickness, and their attempt to escape in their own boats is told in Churchill's *Collection of Voyages and Travels* (1704), I, 554 (account of John Monck's voyage), and John Harris, *A Compleat Collection of Voyages and Travels* (1705), I, 634 (from Tancred Robinson's collection of 1694). For Goldsmith's use of this story, see below, note 34.

28. [John Campbell], *The Polite Correspondence: or, Rational Amusement* (London, 1741), p. 164.

29. *Gentleman's Magazine,* VII (1737), 249. Reprinted in Hill, *Works* (1753), IV, 98–103. Cf. also Hill's poem on Peter the Great, "The Northern Star," *Works,* III, 191.

30. "The English Bull Dog, Dutch Mastiff, and Quail," *Poems,* ed. Norman Callan (London, 1949), I, 60.

31. *Travels through France and Italy* (London, 1766), Letter xli.

32. See Morris Golden, "The Family-Wanderer Theme in Goldsmith," *ELH,* XXV (1958), 181–93.

33. *Collected Letters,* ed. Katharine C. Balderston (Cambridge, 1928), p. 28.

34. *New Essays by Oliver Goldsmith,* ed. R. S. Crane (Chicago, 1927), p. 20. For Goldsmith's source see above, note 27.

35. *The Pleasures of Imagination,* IV, 38–45. Cf. Abbie Findlay Potts, *Wordsworth's Prelude* (Ithaca, 1953), pp. 257–8; Jeffrey Hart, "Akenside's Revision of *The Pleasures of Imagination,"* *PMLA,* LXXIV (1959), 74.

36. Cf. *Spectator,* No. 417. For a valuable survey of the subject, see Martin Kallich's articles, *ELH,* XII (1945), 290–315; *SP,* XLIII (1946), 644–67; *MLN,* LXII (1947), 166–73; *MLQ,* XV (1954), 125–36.

37. Boswell: *The Ominous Years 1774–1776,* ed. Ryskamp and Pottle (New York, 1963), p. 161.

38. In Theodor Zwinger's treatise *De Pothopatridalgia* (his name for nostalgia), included in a collection of medical dissertations published at Basel in 1710. Cf. Fritz Ernst, *Vom Heimweh* (Zürich, 1949).

39. I, 141. This passage gives the first example of the word *home-sickness* recorded in the *OED.*

40. Articles, "Musique" and "Ranz des Vaches." Cf. also Rousseau's letter to the Maréchal de Luxembourg, 20 January 1763 (*Correspondance générale,* ed. Dufour, IX [Paris, 1928], 11).

41. James Beattie, *Essays on Poetry and Music* (3rd ed.; London, 1779), p. 163.

42. Some representative references may be given: Edward Hamley, *Sonnets* (London, 1789), Sonnet IX, p. 13, "On the Melancholy of the Swiss Soldiers

on hearing a certain Song"; J. W. Spencer, "Observations and Opinions," in the *Bee*, XII (1793), 325; William Lisle Bowles, *The Sorrows of Switzerland* (1801); James Grahame, *The Sabbath* (3rd ed.; Edinburgh, 1805), p. 53; [David Cary], *The Reign of Fancy* (1804), pp. 87–8; James Montgomery, *The Wanderer of Switzerland* (1806); "The Swiss Emigrant," *American Poetical Miscellany* (Philadelphia, 1809), pp. 115–18; "Reflections of a Swiss Soldier," *Belfast Monthly Magazine*, IV (1810), 371–2; Henry Thomas Hitchcock, "The Swiss Soldier's Soliloquy," in *Original Poems* (Lewes, 1812), p. 75; Thomas Moore, *A Melologue upon National Music* (1820); Ralph Waldo Emerson, *Journals* (Boston, 1909), I, 350–51, entry of February 1824: C. A. Somerset, *Home, Sweet Home, or the Ranz des Vaches* (1829); Emily Jane Brontë, *Complete Poems*, ed. Clement Shorter and C. W. Hatfield [1924], p. 41.

43. Gabriel Harrison, *John Howard Payne* (Philadelphia, 1885), p. 109.

44. Cf. L. Achim von Arnim and Clemens Brentano, *Des Knaben Wunderhorn*, ed. Karl Bode (Berlin, n.d.), I, 94; II, 489.

45. Emily Hahn, "The Azores," *New Yorker*, November 14, 1959, pp. 148–9.

46. Charles Bucke, *The Philosophy of Nature* (1813), II, 151; Edmond Rostand, *Cyrano de Bergerac*, IV, iii.

47. William Coxe, *Travels in Switzerland*, repr. in John Pinkerton, *General Collection of Voyages and Travels* (1809), V, 814; L. A. Necker de Saussure, *Travels in Scotland* (1821), p. 23; Mrs. Anne Grant, *Letters from the Mountains* (5th ed.; London, 1813), II, 80–81.

48. Mrs. Anne Grant, *Poems on Various Subjects* (Edinburgh, 1803), p. 112, n. 5.

49. *Don Juan*, XVI, xlvi. For the use of the calenture as a symbol for homesickness, see below, note 52.

50. Polwhele said that the first version of *Local Attachment* was independent of Rogers, but admitted that he wrote his extensive notes with Rogers before him (P. W. Clayden, *The Early Life of Samuel Rogers* [1887], pp. 314–15).

51. Cf. also Minna's speech to Cleveland in *The Pirate*, chap. xxii.

52. On this relationship see Abbie Findlay Potts, *Wordsworth's Prelude* (Ithaca, 1953), pp. 132–40.

53. Byron also associated the calenture and the effect of the *ranz des vaches* with the patriotism of the exile (*The Two Foscari*, III, i). For examples of the earlier use of the calenture in poetic imagery see James Sutherland, *A Preface to Eighteenth Century Poetry* (Oxford, 1948), pp. 135–6. The association of the calenture with nostalgia seems to be the work of the romantic poets.

54. R. D. Havens, *The Mind of a Poet* (Baltimore, 1941), p. 467.

55. *Prelude*, II, 175–97. Wordsworth's use of sun, moon, and stars to represent the universalizing of his feelings for nature and man appears also in *Prelude*, IV, 231–47.

56. Harold Bloom, *The Visionary Company* (New York, 1961), p. 178.

57. Ll. 43–45. *Poetical Works,* V (Oxford, 1949), 313 ff.

58. Cf. also "A Morning Exercise," ll. 31–48.

59. *Prelude,* I, 10–11; cf. I, 70–74. For our purpose it is not necessary to in-quire where the chosen vale is.

60. *Prelude,* VI, 252. See Havens's note on this line, *The Mind of a Poet,* pp. 416–17.

The Revival of Vernacular Scottish Poetry in the Eighteenth Century

JOHN BUTT

I

THE revival of Scottish literature, which began after the Union of the Kingdoms in 1707, was complex in character. It was manifest partly in the rediscovery of the vernacular for the purposes of poetry, and partly in the mastery over a closely related, yet still an alien, language. Though a man should speak Scots, it seemed good sense to learn how to write English, for English had become the language of parliament as well as of the court, and was as useful in a united kingdom as Latin had been in medieval Europe. Furthermore it seemed to some Scotsmen that in the previous century, a century so crucial to the development of the arts and sciences in other lands, their country had been inhibited from growth by the unhappy political situation. The point is well made by William Robertson at the end of his *History of Scotland* (1759):

> Thus, during the whole seventeenth century, the English were gradually refining their language and their taste: in Scotland the former was much debased, and the latter almost entirely lost. In the beginning of that period, both nations were emerging out of barbarity; but the distance between them, which was then inconsiderable, became, before the end of it, immense. . . . At length, the union having incorporated the two nations, and rendered them one people, the distinctions which had subsisted for many ages gradually wear away; peculiarities disappear; the same manners prevail in both parts of the island; the same authors are read and admired; the same entertainments are frequented by the elegant and polite; and the same standard of taste, and of purity in language, is established. The Scots, after being placed, during a

whole century, in a situation no less fatal to the liberty than to the taste and genius of the nation, were at once put in possession of privileges more valuable than those which their ancestors had formerly enjoyed; and every obstruction that had retarded their pursuit, or prevented their acquisition of literary fame, was totally removed.[1]

Cogent as the argument may seem, not every Scot would have agreed with it; not every Scot will agree with it today. Thus it is at once clear that if the political premises of Robertson's argument had been generally acceptable, there would have been no Jacobite rebellions. But even granted the desirability of catching up with the English and showing them that the Scots were a match for them in their own language, Robertson makes the task look altogether too easy. Fine indeed as his own achievement was, it was something of a *tour de force*. "He writes," said Burke, "like a man who composes in a dead language, which he understands but cannot speak."[2] The same point was made by Alexander Carlyle when trying to explain to Lord Mansfield how it was that Mansfield, in reading Robertson and Hume, felt he was not reading English:

to every man bred in Scotland [said Carlyle] the English language was in some respects a foreign tongue, the precise value and force of whose words and phrases he did not understand, and therefore was continually endeavouring to word his expressions by additional epithets or circumlocutions, which made his writings appear both stiff and redundant.[3]

James Beattie writes to much the same effect: "We are slaves to the language we write," he complains sadly to Sylvester Douglas in 1778, "and are continually afraid of committing *gross* blunders; and, when an easy, familiar, idiomatical phrase occurs, dare not adopt it, if we recollect no authority, for fear of Scotticisms," a glossary of which he published in 1787 in order to "correct Improprieties of Speech and Writing."[4]

The number of Scotsmen ready to run these risks is remarkable —historians, philosophers, critics, novelists, essayists. They invade the English literary scene; and, as always happens after successful invasions, the scene is not the same as before. Perhaps it might be said that in the later eighteenth century, English prose became British, that the invaders contributed their influence to a shift of manner in prose writing, which many contemporaries noticed and several deplored. "Our tongue was brought to perfection in the days of Addison and Swift," Beattie declared in the preface to his *Scoticisms*, "but has now lost not a little of its elegance, particularly in the articles of simplicity, vivacity, and ease." Another Scot, Hugh Blair, attributed the difference to a change in vocabulary. He detected a departure from Swift's standard of "the strictest Purity and Propriety in the choice of words."

At present, [he continued], we seem to be departing from this standard. A multitude of Latin words have, of late, been poured in upon us. On some occasions, they give an appearance of elevation and dignity to Style. But often also, they render it stiff and forced.[5]

Blair had Dr. Johnson in mind. Though neither Blair nor we can adequately characterise Johnson's prose so shortly, it is broadly true that Johnson, Burke, and Gibbon represent the stately periods of the latter part of the century which contrast so markedly with the colloquial ease of Dryden, Addison, and Swift; and it is because this prose is no longer based upon colloquial idiom that the Scottish writers found it relatively easy to adopt.

II

If writing prose in a foreign language is difficult, writing poetry in that language is surely more difficult still. Yet here too the Scots were determined to excel. What Burke said of Robertson may also be said of Thomson, in *The Seasons* at any rate, that "he writes like a man who composes in a dead language, which he understands but cannot speak." Yet Thomson was readily absorbed into the English tradition. He contributed to it something that was not there before, and the subsequent history of purely English poetry was affected by what he wrote. We fail to understand him as well as we might if we forget that he was a Scot, but we do him no essential injustice if we discuss him in the context of his English contemporaries. The same is true, by and large of Mallet, Armstrong, Falconer, Robert Blair, Beattie, and other poets of even smaller stature. They are mentioned here to emphasize that there is an Anglo-Scottish tradition in eighteenth-century verse as well as in eighteenth-century prose. That they would have written better if they had always written in Scots is not susceptible of proof, even though

Hamilton of Bangour's only memorable poem, and Beattie's best poem in the judgment of some critics, was the only poem either poet wrote in Scots. That they did not choose to write in Scots except on rare occasions will become clearer when the state of the vernacular is taken into account.

The range of opportunities in poetry that the vernacular offered could best be appreciated by looking back to the poetry of earlier days. This was what James Watson, the King's Printer, provided when he published in three parts his *Choice Collection of Comic and Serious Scots Poems* (1706, 1709, 1711), "the first of its Nature," he proudly claimed, "which has been publish'd in our own Native *Scots* Dialect." Not all the poems were in Scots; for Watson included Drummond's "Polemo-Middinia" besides lyrics by Ayton and Montrose. But here was "Christ's Kirk on the Green," the prototype of many a later poem of rustic revelry; here was Montgomerie's "The Cherry and the Slae," whose stanza was to appeal to many an imitator, including Burns himself; here was "Lady Anne Bothwel's Balo" and an early version of "Old-Long-syne," to represent Scottish lyrics; here was Sempill's "Life and Death of the Piper of Kilbarchan," better known as "Habbie Simson," which was to prompt so many later comic elegies; and as if to show that the ancient spirit was not dead, here was a modern poet, little more than thirty years old, William Hamilton of Gilbertfield, putting Sempill's stanza to use in the first of many sentimental elegies on a dead animal, "The Last Dying Words of Bonny Heck, a Famous Grey-Hound in the Shire of Fife."

Watson's commendable attempt to display the resources of the vernacular was supported by Allan Ramsay, who in 1724 published both *The Ever Green, Being a Collection of Scots Poems, Wrote by the Ingenious before 1600* and *The Tea Table Miscellany*, described in a later reprint as *A New Miscellany of Scots Sangs*. The success of *The Ever Green* was modest at best, for only one more edition of it was issued; but Ramsay can at least claim from it the credit for being the first to restore the work of the makars. He had access to the Bannatyne MS. in the Advocates' Library and printed a generous selection of Dunbar's poetry, Henryson's "Robin and Makyn," and, among much that was less worthy of survival, one ballad at least, the ballad of Johnny Armstrong. In commending these poems to his readers he applauds their native imagery, and contrasts their "natural strength of thought and simplicity of stile" with the "affected Delicacies and studied Refinements" of modern writings. But though he felt assured in appealing to readers of "the best and most exquisite discernment," he adopted a more defiant apology in the face of some who were evidently not prepared to countenance a revival of interest in the vernacular:

There is nothing can be heard more silly than one's expressing his *Ignorance* of his *native Language;* yet such there are, who can vaunt of acquiring a tolerable Perfection in the *French* or *Italian* Tongues, if they have been a Forthnight in *Paris* or a Month in *Rome*: But shew them the most elegant Thoughts in a *Scots* Dress, they as disdainfully as stupidly condemn it as barbarous. . . . But this affected Class of Fops give no Uneasiness, not being numerous; for the most part of our Gentlemen, who are generally Masters of the most useful and politest *Languages,* can take Pleasure (for a Change) to speak and read their own.[6]

Ramsay does not directly urge the modern Scot to model himself upon his forebears; but he offers encouragement to him who will, so long as he is prepared to risk the charge of vulgarity. The glossary of old Scots words provided in *The Ever Green* for the modern reader and poet was more convenient than accurate; Ramsay had not even consulted the glossary compiled by Thomas Ruddiman for his edition of Douglas's *Aeneis* (1710); and his own skill, as Lord Hailes was soon to remark, "scarcely extended beyond the vulgar language spoken in the Lothians at this day."[7]

The verse in *The Ever Green* is for the most part non-lyrical; *The Tea Table Miscellany* is a collection of lyrics meant for singing. The quality of the poetry is with a few exceptions much inferior; it places a much lighter tax upon the understanding; and it was a much more popular success. Ramsay's aim in this collection was the same that was to prompt Burns sixty years later, an enthusiasm for Scottish song. He prints no music; it was enough to provide new words to known tunes, for which he himself supplied more than sixty and secured about thirty more from "some ingenious young gentlemen, who were so well pleased with my undertaking," says Ramsay, "that they generously lent me their assistance." As for the rest, they were "such old verses as have been done time out of mind, and only wanted to be cleared from the dross of blundering transcribers and printers."[8] Many of the poems are uncompromisingly English and liable to censure, one might suppose, for their "affected delicacies and studied refinements"; others reveal their northern origin by the irruption of an "ilk" or a "bonny" in an otherwise southern setting; but in a few others, notably "Jocky said to Jeany, Jeany, wilt thou do't" and Hamilton of Bangour's "Busk ye, busk ye, my bonny bonny bride," we can see the beginnings of a revival—or perhaps the reappearance at the surface—of Scottish folk-song-writing which was to culminate in the work of Burns.

But the judicious reader did not need to rely for long either on Ramsay's texts or on Ramsay's selections. The makars were restored to their proper shape by Lord Hailes in his selection of *Ancient Scottish Poems. Published from the MS. of George Bannatyne* (1770), a work to which he said he had been prompted by "the many and obvious inaccuracies of *the Evergreen.*" There seemed to be no longer any need to apologise for the older poetry. In Hailes's view its merits were self-evident; but he commended it in terms likely to appeal more to the antiquary than to the general public, for the volume was designed to offer "such a selection as might illustrate the manners and history, as well as the state of the language and poetry of Scotland during the sixteenth century."[9]

The reader of songs and ballads was even better supplied. That famous collection, *The Reliques of Ancient Poetry,* published though it was south of the border, contained several Scottish ballads hitherto unprinted that Percy had obtained from Hailes and other Scottish correspondents; and its success stimulated David Herd, a learned and self-effacing antiquary, to publish the best of the collections he had made in a volume which he called *The Ancient and Modern Scots Songs, Heroic Ballads, &c. Now first Collected in one Body* (1769). The preface promised a further volume. This was delayed for seven years, partly because Percy had been asked for his advice and was dilatory in returning the collection.[10] But the revised version of *Ancient and Modern Scottish Songs* (2 vols., 1776) is much superior to the original volume. This was by far the best collection of ballads and songs that had appeared so far. Much that an amateur could reasonably require was now supplied, except for the tunes themselves, and they were soon to appear in ample measure, so far at least as folk song was concerned, thanks to the work of Robert Burns and James Johnson.

While the modern student of ballad and folk-song is immeasurably grateful to these early collectors, he is exasperated from time to time by their attitude to their sources. The origin of their texts is rarely stated with precision, even when such ballads as "Sir Patrick Spens" and "Edward" are concerned that gave them so much delight in the discovery. Furthermore the best scholars relied heavily upon the authority of printed and manuscript sources. How much recourse was had to the living work is difficult to establish. There were collectors before the end of the century. The famous Mrs. Anne Brown, the daughter of an Aberdeen professor, was amassing her collection about 1760, and was dictating them to her nephew, Professor Robert Scott, about 1783.[11] But Herd himself seems never to have collected from the living word. He mentions in a letter to George Paton, a fellow antiquary, "an old Ballad, which I got upwards of two years ago from one William Bell, who had picked it up in Annandale; it was all in detached scraps of paper, wrote down by himself at different times, as he met with those who remembered anything of it—part of these he had lost, and some of the remainder were illegible, being chaff'd in his pocket."[12] Is this an unusually forlorn instance of a normal process of transcription? It is difficult to say; and it is impossible to guess how many William Bells in the eighteenth century anticipated Sir Walter Scott's "raids" into Liddesdale. Yet even Scott himself, though he heard the ballads in Liddesdale, relied for the texts he published in the *Minstrelsy of the Scottish Border* upon manuscript and printed sources.

In his two miscellanies Ramsay may be said to have displayed some of the resources of the vernacular for poetry, and in his own verse he showed that the tradition was not broken. He saw that the life of the Edinburgh streets still offered opportunities for the comic or satiric elegy, and he showed that the stanza used by Sempill for his elegy on Habbie Simson—"Standart Habby," as Ramsay called it—was still good for the purpose. Standart Habby —The Burns stanza as we now call it—was also found suitable for the familiar verse epistle, and Ramsay exchanged a series with a brother-poet, Hamilton of Gilbertfield. These Doric Horaces send invitations to pass the day in each other's company, and exchange compliments on each other's verse in terms which are lacking neither in warmth nor in vigour:

> Thy raffan rural Rhyme sae rare,
> Sick wordy, wanton, hand-wail'd Ware,
> Sae gash and gay, gars Fowk gae gare*
>   To ha'e them by them;
> Tho gaffin they wi' Sides sae sair,
>   Cry,—"Wae gae by him."**

Merry-making in the countryside prompts another canto of "Christ's Kirk on the Green" in the same stanza; the "Cherry and the Slae" stanza is used for an Horatian poet's wish on the theme of *Quid dedicatum poscit Apollinem Vates;* Horace's Soracte ode is translated into an Edinburgh scene, with "Pentland's tow'ring Tap Buried beneath great Wreaths of Snaw" and gowfers prevented from "driving their baws frae Whins or Tee"; and the poet takes leave of his book *"After the Manner of* Horace, *ad librum suum"* hoping he will never

>   see thee lye
> Beneath the Bottom of a Pye,
> Or cow'd out Page by Page to wrap
> Up Snuff, or Sweeties in a Shap.

But if Ramsay showed that the vernacular was no obstacle to exhibiting a genial poetic personality, he made the limitations of the vernacular seem no less clear. The implied comparison with Horace only served to underline how far from the centre such poetry was; and the language itself, though Ramsay had been at pains to choose a common denominator of Scottish dialects and lace it with English poetic diction, was seen to be no longer one of the literary languages of Europe that Dunbar's Scots had been.

---

* Make People very earnest. *Ramsay's note.*
** Tis usual for many, after a full Laugh, to complain of sore Sides, and to bestow a kindly Curse on the Author of the Jest. But the Folks of more tender Consciences have turned their Expletives to friendly Wishes, such as this. . . . *Ramsay's note.*

To southern ears especially, this pretty bastard Scots must have enhanced the freshness of Ramsay's pastorals; here southern readers
must have felt was the modern equivalent of the Doric appropriately used for a true representation of rural manners. But it is not
altogether surprising that at Ramsay's death there should be few
signs of wider interest in the opportunities of the vernacular for
modern poetry. Those Scots who, like Robertson, felt strongly the
need of catching up with the English in taste and elegance, could
be expected to disdain it. "Those who now write Scotch," Beattie
told Pinkerton in 1778, "use an affected, mixed, barbarous dialect,
which is neither Scotch nor English, but a strange jumble of
both."[13] Perhaps it is not surprising that the songs published in
Scotland before the time of Burns are overwhelmingly English in
number; and, to take a single instance, there is not one Scots poem
to be found in Ruddiman's *Edinburgh Magazine* for 1759 amongst
its monthly "poetical essays." The same is true of *A Collection of
Original Poems,* published in 1760 by "The Rev. Mr. Blacklock,
and other Scotch Gentlemen." The volume contains pastoral ballads, elegies, and odes indistinguishable in effeteness from any that
might have been published the same year in London; and there is
not so much as a word of native Scots in the conversation of two
Edinburgh [sedan-] chairmen in a "town eclogue," modelled upon
Gay. Even Hamilton of Bangour, in spite of his association with
Ramsay and his lofty Jacobite patriotism, could apparently see no
opportunity in Scots either for the elegant compliments or the
vigorously expressed reflections he wished to write. It is only for
such a folk-song as his ancestors and their retainers had been composing for centuries that he turned, naturally, to dialect.

A few writers followed Ramsay's lead. There was Alexander
Nicoll, for example, a schoolmaster, and Alexander Ross, another
schoolmaster, of Lochlee, Angus, who was encouraged by Beattie,
when he called on the professor at Aberdeen, in 1768, to publish
the best of the poems he had written long ago to amuse his solitude. The most substantial of these is *The Fortunate Shepherdess,
a Pastoral Tale in Three Cantos,* a somewhat tedious poem of the
manners of rustic life, redeemed from time to time by descriptions
of mountainous scenery. Ross tells his readers what instructions
his muse had given him:

> Speak my ain leed, 'tis gueed auld Scots I mean,
> Your Southron gnaps, I count not worth a preen.
> We've words a fouth, that we can ca' our ain,
> Tho' frae them now my childer sair refrain.

The capture of Havana in 1762 could, perhaps appropriately, inspire him to a brisk song in plain English, and elsewhere he will use Ramsay's recipe of Anglo-Scots; but in other songs, such as "The Rock and the wee pickle Tow," which are no less brisk, he attempted to follow the tradition of *The Tea Table Miscellany* by writing new words in the Buchan dialect to old tunes.

"The dialect is so licentious," wrote Beattie to Blacklock, of Ross's volume, "(I mean it is so different from that of the south country, which is acknowledged the standard of broad Scotch), that I am afraid you will be at a loss to understand it."[14] This ever-nagging problem did not prevent Beattie from trying his hand in the same dialect for the limited purpose of commendatory verses addressed to Ross. It is interesting to note that he instinctively chose "Standart Habby" for his stanza, and was surprised to find, as he admitted to Blacklock, that he could write it with ease—and, let it be added, with unusual elegance.

A younger contemporary of Alexander Ross was John Skinner, schoolmaster of Monymusk and Episcopalian minister of Longside, Aberdeenshire. In the late 1750's he had followed Ramsay's lead in using the stanza of "Christ's Kirk on the Green" to describe "the Monymusk Christmas Ba'ing," and the tradition of Hamilton of Gilbertfield's "Bonny Heck" is revived in Skinner's sentimental elegy on "The Ewie wi' the Crookit Horn." Skinner was to live long enough to correspond with Burns both in prose and in "Standart Habby," for he had written what Burns considered "the best Scotch song ever Scotland saw,—'Tullochgorum's my delight!' "[15] Acknowledging the compliment paid to that uproarious song, Skinner explained in a letter to Burns how his daughters "being all tolerably good singers, plagued me for words to some of their favourite tunes."[16]

If Ramsay could be credited with inspiring all the work of the Scottish poets who were setting new words to old tunes, he would have had a numerous progeny. But a movement so widespread could not spring from a single book, however popular *The Tea Table Miscellany* had proved to be. The very fact that Ramsay could so easily enlist ingenious young Gentlemen to help him in his task suggests that the practice was already current; and indeed Lord Yester's reputed setting of words to "Tweedside" and Lady Grizel Baillie's "Werena my Heart Licht" are examples earlier in time than Ramsay. The practice, of which the publication of *The Tea Table Miscellany* merely took advantage, persisted throughout the century. Thus Herd mentions in the preface to *Ancient and Modern Scottish Songs* (1776) that there were "many of these adopted words to ancient tunes . . . being composed by eminent modern Scots poets." More or less romantic stories were circulated about the origin of Jean Elliot's "The Flowers of the Forest," of Mrs. Cockburn's inferior English version, and of Lady Anne Lindsay's "Auld Robin Gray"; but all stories agree that the poet was stimulated by the haunting melody of a Scottish tune.

Most of the writers mentioned in the last paragraph came from families of noble blood. It seems that in several of these families the tradition of singing old Scots songs and ballads was still surviving. Whether it was the servants who sang them or their masters we cannot be certain; but it is worth noticing that when Percy first printed the ballad of "Edward" in the *Reliques* he had been sent that incomparable version by Sir David Dalrymple (Lord Hailes), who had already printed "Edom of Gordon" (1755) "as it was preserved in the memory of a lady"; and the excellent "Sir Patrick Spens," which was also printed for the first time in the *Reliques,* seems ultimately to have been derived from "an old Lady Dowager of Blantyre."[17] Did these noble singers do nothing to improve the versions that they inherited? Did they never invent new verses? Did they never pass upon the auditors more skillful imitations of the old traditional poems than Lady Wardlaw perpetrated in *Hardiknute?* Had Sir Walter Scott no predecessors in this art of innocent deception? Perhaps we shall never be able to answer these questions; but the evidence suggests that there existed a well-established affection for the folk-poetry and folk-song of Scotland and that it was being kept alive by imaginative reconstruction. This was the tradition that Burns inherited.

III

But great as Burns's achievements were in lyrical poetry, they do not represent the full capacity of his genius, and this he might never have reached had it not been for Fergusson. Burns was always willing to acknowledge his debt: "Rhyme . . . I had given up," he wrote to Dr. John Moore, on 2 August 1787; "but meeting with Fergusson's Scotch Poems, I strung anew my wildly-sounding, rustic lyre with emulating vigour."[18] This acquaintance seems to date from 1784; and we can judge the excitement of the experience of reading Fergusson when we reflect that before 1784 Burns had written nothing in Scots, apart from songs, except verse epistles modelled upon Ramsay, and "The Death and Dying Words of Poor Mailie" suggested by Hamilton of Gilbertfield's "Bonny Heck"; it was in the three years following his discovery of Fergusson in 1784 that he wrote all but one of his great non-lyrical poems.

Fergusson showed opportunities for the poet in Scots that lay well beyond Ramsay's reach. If a man may be called slow who achieved so much in a bare twenty-four years of life, Fergusson was slow in using the vernacular for verse, and he never used it exclusively. As a schoolboy he had written an irreverent elegy on one of his professors at St. Andrews; but his first appearances in Ruddiman's *Weekly Magazine* (1771) suggest his admiration of such modern masters as Shenstone, Gray, Cunningham, and John Philips. Fergusson was prepared to exercise his skill in English pastoral, ode, epigram, and mock-heroic till the end of his short career; but his poetry would have been forgotten (even his clever satire on Henry Mackenzie, "The Sow of Feeling") if he had not been prompted to exercise in Scots the skill he had already learned in English.

"The Daft Days" was the beginning. It appeared on 2 January 1772, and must have surprised the discerning reader of the *Weekly Magazine*. It was not merely the first poem Ruddiman had published in Scots, but it plainly announced a new poet. Here was one who had mastered the rhythmical opportunities of Standart Habby and had found a new use for that well-worn stave. Instead of the customary verse epistle and mock elegy, the stanza was now being used as an invitation to merry-making, and the appeal is strengthened by that unfailing traditional Scottish contrast between foul weather and warm hearths. But what might well promise most for the future was the range of diction displayed in that poem, the sheer skill in handling words. The poet seemed determined to widen the range of the vernacular. Allowing that it could be used with obvious propriety to convey the cosy and familiar ("Sma are our cares, our stamacks fou O' gusty gear") or a canny reflection ("When fou we're sometimes capernoity") or a bout of flyting, it needed strengthening to deal with a wider variety of expression, and Fergusson can be seen blending his native Lothian speech with words from other regions, with written Scots, obsolete words picked from the makars, and for certain limited purposes with thieves' argot. He even finds a place for those Latinate words which are still spoken by Scottish lips with evident relish; and so "the bleer-ey'd sun" runs his race in December days "thro' his *minimum* of space," and "a canty Highland reel . . . even *vivifies* the heel To skip and dance." Nor, if the vernacular was to hold its head in a wider context of modern British poetry, could it avoid those admirable conventions that all allow, such as the vivid personification; and so,

> Tho' Discord gie a canker'd snarl
> To spoil our glee,
> As lang's there's pith into the barrel
> We'll drink and gree.

Fergusson shows that he had already learned a lesson that Pope and Gray could have taught him. While they delight us with a well-placed vulgarism in a passage of otherwise elegantly familiar verse, Fergusson delights us by his skill in placing words from a wider British usage into a Lothian setting.

This scarcely amounted to the reconstitution of Scots as a literary language suited to all the purposes of poetry; so much could not be expected from one man in a bare two years' work, which was all that was allowed to Fergusson after writing "The Daft Days." For certain themes and kinds of verse, such as the serious elegy, the ode, the burlesque, he continued to rely largely on English. This is not at all surprising. Twelve years after Fergusson's death, Henry Mackenzie could write in *The Lounger* (No. 97) reviewing Burns's poems, that "even in Scotland, the provincial dialect which Ramsay and [Burns] have used, is now read with a difficulty which greatly damps the pleasure of the reader," and a writer in *The Mirror* (No. 83) in 1780 assumed that "grave dignified composition," in poetry as much as in prose, must necessarily be written in a manner different from that in which the writer speaks; only if he "descend to common and ludicrous pictures of life" will his language approach that of common life. Scots was still felt to have a "hamely" tang: its "auld-warld wordies clack In hame-spun rhime"; and though, good patriot as Fergusson was, he saw plenty to engage his attention in the life of Scotland, and more nearly in the manners of the Edinburgh streets, he seems to have found himself restricted when writing Scots to certain attitudes. It is to his credit that these attitudes were not exclusively "common and ludicrous." Some were obviously appropriate to the Doric. Thus Ramsay had already shown how favourable the vernacular was to a naturalistic pastoral, and Fergusson in following him extended his range. Thus in one poem Willie advises his brother ploughman Sandie on his household troubles, and in another Geordie joins Davie in lamenting the death of a fellow shepherd, no less a man than Dr. William Wilkie, poet and natural philosophy professor at St. Andrews, but more especially interesting to his mourners in Fergusson's poem for his agricultural experiments. These poems are skillfully devised mutations upon the Virgilian pastoral, and they justify Fergusson in his unfulfilled ambition of completing Gavin Douglas's work with a version of Virgil's Eclogues and Georgics. But even more original and ambitious than his two dialogues, is the lovingly-detailed genre-painting of "The Farmer's Ingle." It is a townsman's poem written for townsmen; unlike his English contemporary Crabbe, Fergusson recalls none of the ills and inconveniences of country life; but without trace of sentimentality, and with no more than a touch of patronage, the poem generates a warm admiration for the countryman's best qualities. It is just such a reinstatement of the pastoral as Dr. Johnson would have approved, and it is presented in a dignified elaborate stanza quite foreign to those that Ramsay had retrieved from the past. Fergusson might have discovered a suitable verse form amidst the manifold richness of Dunbar; but in choosing to adapt the Spenserian stanza, he showed his readiness to learn from English poetry. Shenstone before him had employed the Spenserian stanza to describe rustic manners; but perhaps the recent success of Beattie's *Minstrel* (1771) was needed to persuade Fergusson that the stanza admitted dignity as well as simplicity of style, and that obsolete expressions, the bane of earlier poets who had used it, were not a necessary adjunct.

This dignity had already been apparent in the "Elegy, on the Death of Scots Music," and in much of "Auld Reekie," Fergusson's longest and perhaps his most successful poem. It demonstrates most obviously Fergusson's capacity to rise above the vulgarity with which Ramsay had associated the vernacular and its principal verse forms. Nevertheless it is the "low" humours of Edinburgh life that provide the staple of Fergusson's poetry. Restrictive as this topic is, it is remarkable what range of voice lay within his control. Standart Habby is used, for more varied purposes than ever before, to convey the good cheer of "Caller Oysters," the contemptuous merriment of "The King's Birth-Day in Edinburgh," and the ironical exposure of citizens who judge a man's merits by the "Braid Claith" he wears. It is equally serviceable for perhaps the first revival of "flyting" since the makars in "To the Tron-kirk Bell," and for the compliments proffered to the bonny lasses of Edinburgh in "Caller Water." There is more flyting in the two dialogues "Mutual Complaint of Plainstanes and Causey, in their Mother-tongue" and "A Drink Eclogue: Landlady, Brandy and Whisky," two poems which recall Swift's verse not only in the metrical skill and Hudibrastic rhymes of their octosyllabics, but in the adaptation of a rural "kind" to city life that Swift had been the first to invent in his two "georgics," "A Description of the Morning" and "A Description of a City Shower." And closely related to these is Fergusson's sturdy admonishment addressed "To the Principal and Professors of the University of St. Andrews, on their superb treat to Dr. Johnson," where the vigour and vulgarity of the vernacular enhance the abuse.

To these poems we may add the gay descriptions of "Hallow-Fair" and "Leith Races," both written in the tradition of "Christ's Kirk on the Green," whose stanza is intelligently adapted for the purpose. All of them reveal a strong poetic personality, self-confident, irreverent, outspoken, yet pithy of speech, observant, and eminently sociable, one admirably suited to stand up for Scottish rights, and to represent those qualities which were felt to distinguish the Scotsman from the Englishman. If he had been able to cultivate his lyric vein—for in spite of his close friendship with David Herd, Fergusson was not stimulated to write more than one song in Scots—he would have qualified as the laureate poet of a small nation (with the restriction in scope that that title implies); for even though his work is based on city life, he could suit his lines, as an admirer told him, "to fock that's out about 'Mang hills and braes." In an exceptionally short career he had shown what could be done in the vernacular to any who might follow him; and those who were ready to look beyond the personality to the craftsman could see the opportunities that Scots offered an educated poet, one who was prepared to learn his trade from classical and modern masters, who could see where the local dialects needed strengthening, who would not be content with the limited resources of a few traditional staves, and who might rise from the local and temporal (as Fergusson scarcely succeeds in doing) to the universal.

IV

In the years immediately succeeding Fergusson's death it is possible to find a little more Scots verse. Whereas Ruddiman had published nothing in Scots before Fergusson's arrival, in 1780 there are five poems in "Standart Habby" in *The Weekly Magazine*. And it is even possible to claim that the quality is a little higher, insofar as Charles Keith's *The Farmer's Ha'* (1776), though obviously prompted by "The Farmer's Ingle," is a vivid and cheerful reconstruction of a familiar scene. But in surveying this minor verse, it is impossible not to sympathise with Alexander Geddes in the "Dissertation on the Scoto-Saxon Dialect" which he contributed to the *Transactions of the Society of the Antiquaries of Scotland* in 1792; he complains that the poets "have not duly discriminated the genuine Scotish idiom from its vulgarisms." Their attitude to vocabulary was, he thought, all too like the English Spenserians': "nothing more was deemed necessary than to interlard the composition with a number of low words and trite proverbial phrases, in common use among the illiterate; and the more anomalous and farther removed from polite usage those words and phrases were, so much the more apposite and eligible they were accounted." Geddes's dissertation deserves the attention of the modern Scots poet. It came too late for Burns to consider, even if it would have appealed to him.

To consider Burns in this context is to marvel at the coincidence of the man and the moment. Could he possibly have chosen a better time, when the vernacular had been familiarized as a medium of verse, and yet was still regarded in large measure as the language of "fock that's out about 'Mang hills and braes"? He had no need, in short, to appear other than he was, to receive a welcome. Furthermore, the verse forms and the literary kinds appropriate to the vernacular had been defined; and yet the life had not yet been worked out of them. Perhaps he does not show the same keenness of interest and capacity for experiment with verse, with language, and with literary kind that Fergusson had shown in his short career, for he was content by and large with the forms bequeathed him; he was not much attracted by literary experiment.

And what a happy coincidence that a man with such a genius for song should arrive at such a moment, when the efforts of Ramsay and others had encouraged an interest in the national inheritance, and when James Johnson—and even George Thomson, with all his shortcomings—were there to provide the means of publication.

Burns was generous in acknowledging his literary debts. He writes, in the preface to the Kilmarnock edition, of Ramsay and Fergusson, "those two justly admired Scotch poets," as he calls them, "whom he has often had in his eye in the following pieces, but rather with a view to kindle at their flame, than for servile imitation." It was well said. Of course we cannot fail to recall them as we read him, just as we cannot fail to recall the classics of further south in whom he was equally well read, Pope, Gray, Shenstone, Goldsmith, and others. In one sense, there is nothing he has to say that had not been said before; but if we leave it at that, we overlook the most important thing of all, the effect of kindling at their flame. Though what he said had oft been thought, it was "ne'er so well-express'd," and expressed with that astonishing force of personality that sets him apart from his predecessors and makes us all warm toward him irrespective of creed or nationality. To come upon his work at the end of the eighteenth century is to see him unmistakably as a man of his time, a man who could not have said those things or said them in that way at any other time; but how profoundly thankful we must be that these circumstances of time and place and verse and language gave him just the opportunity he needed of releasing the full force of his personality.

NOTES

1. *Works* (London, 1825), ii. 245–6.

2. Reported in *James Beattie's London Diary 1773*, ed. Ralph S. Walker (Aberdeen, 1946), p. 54.

3. *Autobiography,* ed. J. H. Burton (London, 1910), p. 543.

4. W. Forbes, *An Account of the Life and Writings of James Beattie, LL.D.* (London, 1824), i.417.

5. *Lectures on Rhetoric and Belles Lettres* (London, 1783), i.188. The evidence for the application of this passage to Johnson is contained in a student's notes on Blair's lectures in the Edinburgh University library.

6. *The Ever Green,* i., pp. x, xi.

7. *Ancient Scottish Poems, Published from the MS. of George Bannatyne* (Edinburgh, 1770), p. viii.

8. *The Tea Table Miscellany* (11th edition, London, 1750), i., p. viii.

9. Hailes, p. vii.

10. *The Correspondence of Thomas Percy and George Paton,* Ed. A. F. Falconer (New Haven, 1961), pp. 171–2.

11. Paton mentioned taking down the words of a song and recalled a friend taking down the words of a ballad in Norn (*Correspondence,* op.cit., pp. 26, 130).

12. *Letters from Thomas Percy . . . and others, to George Paton* (Edinburgh, 1830), pp. 80–81.

13. Dawson Turner, *The Literary Correspondence of John Pinkerton* (London, 1830), i.7.

14. Forbes, op.cit., i. 108.

15. Burns to Skinner, 25 October 1787; *Letters,* ed. J. DeL. Ferguson (Oxford, 1931), i.133.

16. *Amusements of Leisure Hours: or Poetical Pieces, chiefly in the Scottish Dialect. By the late Reverend John Skinner* (Edinburgh, 1809), pp. 30–31.

17. *The Correspondence of Thomas Percy & David Dalrymple, Lord Hailes,* ed. A. F. Falconer (Baton Rouge, 1954), p. 155.

18. *Letters,* op.cit., i.19.

Robert Burns's Use of Scottish Diction

RAYMOND BENTMAN

S COTTISH and English are so closely related that they are little more than different dialects of the same language. It is often difficult to distinguish between them. But in Burns's poetry the distinction between "Scottish" and "English" is inaccurate and misleading. Burns wrote some poems in pure English, most of them in neoclassic style, but he wrote no poems in pure vernacular Scottish. The "Scottish" poems are written in a literary language, which was mostly, although not entirely English, in grammar and syntax, and, in varying proportions, both Scottish and English in vocabulary. "Scots wha hae," as Sir James A. H. Murray points out, "is fancy Scotch." Spoken vernacular Scottish would be "Scots at haes."[1]

These mixed poems, which I call the "vernacular" poems, vary from poems like "Halloween," parts of which are difficult to understand without a glossary, to songs like "Sweet Afton" or "A Red, Red Rose," which differ from English in only a few words. Throughout the vernacular poems Burns interchanges, arbitrarily, the grammatical suffixes "an," "in," "in'," and "ing." Franklyn Bliss Snyder points out that even in the 1786 Kilmarnock Edition, where the Scottish endings are most frequent, they are concentrated in a few poems and are neither uniform nor predominant in those.[2] Burns denotes the past indicative and past participle at times by the Scottish suffix "it" and at times by the English "ed." He interchanges the Scottish forms "keepit" and "foughten" with the English "kept" and "fought." He employs the relative pronouns "wha," "whase," and "wham" and the interrogative "wham," none of which exist in spoken Scottish. He even changes some of the sources to make them closer to English grammar. He changes "Green grows the rashes" to "Green grow the rashes" which is grammatical English but ungrammatical Scottish—in the present tense of the verb the Scottish uses an "s" suffix for the plural unless the proper personal pronoun immediately precedes: "they grow" but "the rashes grows" and "green grows the rashes."

In spite of the evidence of Sir James Murray and of all other philologists who have written on the subject, the belief persists that Burns wrote as he spoke. I have heard this belief expressed by many literary scholars; and it has been written, since Murray's monograph, by Robert Louis Stevenson,[3] Matthew Arnold,[4] William Ernest Henley,[5] and recently by John Speirs—to mention only a few. Speirs's beliefs are typical: "Poetry made, as are these poems, out of a spoken language . . . is almost necessarily counter to pretension and affectation both literary and moral."[6] While the advocates of this belief seem to rely mostly on their feelings to establish linguistic details, they do present some evidence from Burns's prose statements, usually one comment: "I have not that command of the language [English] that I have of my native tongue.—In fact, I think my ideas are more barren in English than in Scotish" (II, 268).[7]

Other prose comments of Burns's, if looked at with sufficient haste, may also be made to say that he claimed to be writing in Scottish. In the Preface to the Kilmarnock Edition he says of himself: "Unacquainted with the necessary requisites for commencing Poet by rule, he sings the sentiments and manners he felt and saw in himself and his rustic compeers around him, in his and their native language." But other prose comments are in direct contradiction. In his correspondence with the song editors James Johnson and George Thomson he constantly makes such remarks as:

The sprinkling of Scotch in it, while it is but a sprinkling, gives it an air of rustic naïveté, which time will rather increase than diminish (II, 205).
I will vamp up the old Song, & make it English enough to be understood (II, 268).
I could easily throw this into an English mould; but to my taste, in the simple & tender of the Pastoral song, a sprinkling of the old Scotish, has an inimitable effect (II, 273).

I have sprinkled it with the Scots dialect (II, 204).
If you are for *English* verses, there is, on my part, an end of the matter.
—Whether in the simplicity of the *Ballad,* or the pathos of *the Song,* I can only hope to please myself in being allowed at least a sprinkling of our native tongue (II, 122).

A "sprinkling" accurately describes his changes. In "Wha Is That at My Bower Door," based on an older Scottish song in English, "Who But I, Quoth Finlay,"[8] he changes "come no further" to "gae your gate," "who" to "wha," and "quoth" to "quo'." Often he simply drops the final "g" of an "ing" ending, or makes minor spelling changes like "summer" to "simmer," "good" to "guid," or "oft" to "aft." At other times he interchanges a few words which do not alter the meaning in context, as "then" to "syne" and "one" to "ae."

Why Burns referred to his "native language" when he meant a "sprinkling" can be speculated upon: an attempt, also in the epistles, to create an elaborate *persona* for the Kilmarnock volume, much as Housman did later in *A Shropshire Lad;* a cynical attempt to attract attention from the sentimental admirer of the heaven-taught plowman; a self-delusion; too great a reliance on Ramsay's confused theories, which were in turn part of certain confusions in other British Augustan theories; or an ambiguity in terms, similar to the ambiguity which often causes a misreading of Wordsworth's theories of poetic diction.

Many modern biographers and critics agree that Burns did not write in vernacular Scottish[9] but offer little concrete explanation of his contradictory statements or his artificial language. Burns was most probably following, for personal and nationalistic reasons, the tradition established partly by Ramsay and Fergusson and partly by older Scottish writers. But great poets use traditions; they are not enslaved by them. Any evaluation of Burns's ability as a poet and of his place in the trends of British poetry must take into large account his use or misuse of the tradition he follows.

*   *   *

Burns shows little compunction about interchanging Scottish and English words to fit his needs. He uses "sword" in both neo-classic and vernacular poems, but "glaive" once when it rhymes with "save" ("When Guilford Good"). He uses "Gizz" once ("Address to the Deil" XVII) and "wig" twice ("To John Goldie" and "The Kirk's Alarm" XIII) always in vernacular poems and always to facilitate the rhyme. "Hawk" is the usual word in both neoclassic and vernacular poems, except where "gled" rhymes ("Killie-crankie" and "Ballad Fourth: The Trogger").

The distinction between Scottish and English words is not always so easy to make as in the examples above. Since Scottish of the eighteenth century had no standard spelling, Scottish dialect poets often used the English spelling when a Scottish word had a near-English equivalent. Intermixing such words as "fae" and "foe" or "gi'e" and "give" may only indicate that Burns is, like most writers who have attempted dialect, an inconsistent speller. But Burns takes care to spell "have" when the rhyme demands the English pronunciation, even in such vernacular poems as "Kellyburn Braes," where "have" rhymes with "crave," or as "When First I Saw," where "have her" is supposed to rhyme with "favour." "Foe" is frequently substituted for "fae" to help the rhyme, as in "Scots Wha Hae," where it rhymes with "low" and "blow," words which could never be brought to rhyme with "fae." "Fight" replaces the more common "fecht" to rhyme with "wight," "sight," and "tight" in "The Author's Earnest Cry and Prayer" (X).

Burns is equally free in interchanging words to facilitate alliteration. "Chapman" is the standard word used in vernacular poems except for "Kellyburn Braes": "And like a poor pedlar he's carried his pack." He uses "Callet" in all vernacular poems except in "Tam O'Shanter": "There was ae winsome wench and wawlie" (line 166) and in the "Soldier's Song" of "The Jolly Beggars" for rhyme, even though in the same song there is the line: "I'm as happy with my wallet, my bottle and my callet." Again, he uses an English word consistently except when the Scottish helps alliterate: "Corbies and Clergy are a shot right kittle" ("The Brigs of Ayr," l. 178) but "Your locks were like the raven" ("John Anderson, My Jo"); in "Willie Wastle": "The cat has twa [eyes] the very colour" but "Auld Baudrons by the ingle sits." One function of using both Scottish and English, then, is expediency; to facilitate rhyme and alliteration.

But sometimes Burns, for no apparent reason, interchanges Scottish and English words of almost identical meaning where

neither rhyme nor alliteration nor meter is aided: "ragged"—
"duddie" ("Second Epistle to John Lapraik" XVI, and "The Twa
Dogs" line 76); "coft"—"bought" ("Tam O'Shanter" line 178, and
"The Weary Pund o' Tow"). Interestingly, he more often uses an
English word mistakenly for a Scottish word than the other way
around. For example, "daisy" is used in "Lament of Mary Queen
of Scots": "And spreads her sheets o' daisies white," but never is
"gowan" used in a passage which is clearly neoclassic. The only
error of this type that I have found is "lug" used for "ear" in a
neoclassic passage in "The Brigs of Ayr" (line 208).

Apparently Burns did not even attempt to write a pure Scottish.
Words like "gowan," "gled," "chapman," "baudron," and
"corbies" had no magical power for him. He discarded them when
it fit his convenience to do so and did not, at other times, watch
them closely.

*   *   *

Many Scottish words which Burns uses have specific, unambiguous meanings and point to concrete objects. The great majority of
these words refer to farming, peasant home life, or Scottish institutions. For example, farming: "braik," "cairn," "calf-ward,"
"calker," "crap," "fell," "graip," "thraive," "icker," "ripp," "rip-
ple"; peasant home life: "but and ben," "cake," "cootie," "cotter,"
"cran," "creel," "fecket," "girdle," "tacket"; Scottish institutions:
"bowkail," "philibeg," "creepie-chair," "ell," "ferintosh," "groat."
These words offer an advantage which other Scottish words offer
less obviously. They help define the speaker and place of the poem.
The words may not always be those which an eighteenth-century
Scottish peasant would have used, but they suggest that the speaker
is a person who has an easy familiarity with the minute details of
farm implements or kitchenware.

Such a concretely defined speaker helps avoid the sentimentality
which always hovers near in poetry about rustic life. The farmer in
"The Auld Farmer's New-Year Morning Salutation to His Auld
Mare, Maggie" remains probable and realistic when he draws his
doggedly optimistic conclusion, "Here to crazy age we're brought, /
Wi' something yet" because he so clearly speaks out of concrete
experience; because he shows the frank materialism of a farmer
when he recalls the exact details of his dowry and lists, as one of

his fondest recollections of Maggie, that her colts "drew me thret-teen pund and twa,/The vera warst"; and because he knows and talks about the hardships they both went through in an obviously "weary warl'."

The syntax of the poems written before 1790 often sounds like conversation but proves rather formal on close examination. The sentences are long and well-constructed, the rhetoric is often balanced ("Come to my bowl, come to my arms,/My friends, my brothers!"), the adjective often follows the noun ("prospects drear"), lines almost invariably end with a comma or period. Burns achieves the sound of conversational syntax through the use of the short line in the Standard Habbie stanza for emphatic after-thoughts ("They gang in stirks, and come out asses,/Plain truth to speak") or asides ("So dinna ye affront your trade,/But rhyme it right"), through the use of words of familiarity or endearment, and through simple, direct diction. Burns can re-create the rhythms of conversation ("Ha! whare ye gaun") even when he retains, often ironically, Augustan parallelism ("He's stampin, an' he's jumpin!").

Burns often uses provincial words, picturesque spelling, and conversational-sounding diction in his satiric poems to create an ironically oafish speaker, one who looks at the world with wide-eyed astonishment and little apparent understanding. In "To a Louse," the speaker finds an ostensibly trivial object worthy of discussion. But he misses the point, in fact he turns the argument upside down by blaming the louse for the disorder in the scheme of things ("in some beggar's hauffet squattle"), rather than by blaming Jenny and those other humans who pretend to an order that does not exist. In the last stanza the irony disappears, as do the provincial words and Scottish idioms. The picturesque spelling and Scottish diminutive, however, enforce the theme stated here sa-tirically, and in other poems lyrically, that there is a wisdom to be found in homely experience ("What airs in dress an' gait wad lea'e us,/An' ev'n devotion!"). The oafish diction allows Burns to have it both ways, for the speaker's mock-awe denies the sentimental inference that wisdom is necessarily and only found in the simplest men; but the truth behind his wonder, his realization that some-thing is wrong, confirms in essence what the poem pretends to deny in tone. There is, Burns says, a native, uneducated wisdom which derives from one's feelings and which is neither better nor worse than other kinds of wisdom.

About half the Scottish words of specifics which Burns uses were used by either Ramsay or Fergusson. But Ramsay never mentions a detail of Scottish peasant life without making a sermon, most of it in rather Augustan English:

> Be that time Bannocks, and a Shave of Cheese,
> Will make a Breakfast that a Laird might please;
> Might please the daintiest Gabs, were they sae wise,
> To season Meat with Health instead of Spice
> ("The Gentle Shepherd," I, i, 165–8)

Burns uses the same bannocks with both greater humor and greater affection and suggests, without overt statement, that bannocks, however they may compare to other foods, are still deserving of attention:

> Tell yon guid bluid of auld Boconnock's,
> I'll be his debt twa mashlum bonnocks,
> An' drink his health in auld Nanse Tinnock's,
>   Nine times a-week.
> ("The Author's Earnest Cry and Prayer," Stanza XXI)

Fergusson has a lighter touch than Ramsay and appears to have a more genuine affection for the homely details. But he does little with them. For example:

> The readied *kail* stand by the chimley cheeks,
> And had the riggin het wi' welcome steams,
> Whilk than the daintiest kitchen nicer seems.
> ("The Farmer's Ingle," Stanza III)

Such comparisons inevitably entail a note of self-righteousness and insincerity even when the diction gives the sense that a peasant is speaking. Fergusson and Burns knew that the only advantage of peasant cooking is its economy. When Burns follows Fergusson too closely, as he does in "The Cotter's Saturday Night," which is modeled after and distinctly inferior to Fergusson's "Farmer's Ingle," he is as patronizing as Fergusson and as sanctimonious as Ramsay. In his best poetry, like "Epistle to James Smith," he cares much less about lowering and raising kitchen items according to their social class:

> "While ye are pleased to keep me hale,
> I'll sit down o'er my scanty meal,
> Be't water-brose or muslin-kail,
> 　　Wi' cheerfu' face,
> As lang's the Muses dinna fail
> 　　To say the grace"
>
> 　　　　　　　　(Stanza XXIV)

Burns only says that when we accompany kail with health, with cheer, with poetry, and with grace (in both senses), the meal may not become less scanty but it does gain something. Even the most humble parts of life can become symbols of a joyous scheme which includes art, emotions, and perhaps God.

　　　　　　*　　*　　*

Among the hundred and sixty-odd words which Burns uses more than fifty times, a considerable majority are English and most of the others differ from English in spelling but not in meaning, as "amang," "gae," "guid," "hae," "lang," "mair," "mony," "sae," "sair," "twa," and "wha." I have found only six words whose meanings differ from English which are used frequently, "ay," "bonie," "brae," "braw," "fou," and "ken." The indication, however, is not that Burns found few Scottish words useful but that he found so many useful that he did not have to depend on them repeatedly, as he seems to have with such English words as "sweet," "fair," "heart," "soul," "nature," and "love." Burns apparently found Scottish words to have a suggestiveness, a poetic ambiguity, a fluidity, which he seems to have found in late eighteenth-century English in only self-consciously "poetic" and rather tired words.

The "Epistle to J. Lapraik" offers many examples of his facility with diction. Stanzas XIII and XIV are among the best known of the poem:

> Gie me ae spark o' Nature's fire,
> That's a' the learning I desire;
> Then, tho' I drudge thro' dub an' mire
> 　　At pleugh or cart,
> My Muse, tho' hamely in attire,
> 　　May touch the heart.
>
> O for a spunk o' Allen's glee,
> Or Fergusson's, the bauld an' slee,

Or bright Lapraik's, my friend to be,
       If I can hit it!
That would be lear eneugh for me,
       If I could get it.

The metaphor of fire runs through the two stanzas. "Spunk" can mean "spark" or "small fire" but it extends to mean "life," "spirit," and "mettle," in the sense it still has in colloquial English. The metaphor is sustained by "glee," which in both English and Scottish implies "brightness" as well as "mirth" and "joy"; by "bauld," which in Scottish retains some of the implications of "fiery" and some of the older meaning of "to kindle"; and by "bright." The bright and fiery suggestion of Stanza XIV contrasts, on one hand, to the "spark" of the previous stanza to suggest, with characteristic modesty, that Burns hopes only for the beginnings of what the older poets have all excelled in, and contrasts further with the drudgery and "dub an' mire" in which Burns, both in livelihood and in poetry-writing, finds himself. The English "bold" and "sly" had settled in the eighteenth century into discretely separable words. "Bold" meant "vigorous" or "courageous"; but in Scottish it retained some pejorative sense of "fierce." "Sly" meant "cunning"; in Scottish it retained some of the more favorable sense of "skillful" and "dextrous." In English the two separable words would have indicated only two kinds of behavior. In Scottish the two flow into one another to create a scope which allows no clear distinction between "courageous" and "cunning" but suggests that the whole of man, good and bad, contributes to poetry.

The setting, described in the early stanzas, is rich in connotations of simple life warmly expressed: "rockin," "ca' the crack," "weave our stockin," and "hearty yokin." "Rockin" means "social gathering" but retains implications of its origin, the "rock" which is the distaff of a spinning wheel. "Hearty yokin" employs both the English advantages of "hearty" and the dialect "yokin," which means "bout" or "contest." Together, they sustain the ideas of "weaving," "being together," and "simplicity" and carry them further to the instinctive, passionate qualities of a peasant contest. The following three stanzas express the concept of the unity of the whole being by using words that describe both emotional and physical reactions to poetry and marital love. The line "thirl'd the heart-strings thro' the breast" uses the Scottish "thirl'd," which goes beyond the English "thrilled" (the word Burns had originally used) to mean "cause to vibrate," and exploits the English "heart-strings" and "breast." "Fidgin-fain" combines the meaning of a physical restlessness (the English "fidgit") with emotional excitement. Stanza VI indicates that poetry is by no means limited to the simplicity of a peasant "rockin"; it can be "douce," "merry," or "witty." The three adjectives, standing out in the relatively unconnotative stanza in which they appear, flow into one another: "merry" to mean "pleasant" and "friendly" as well as "joyous" (hence picking up the setting); "douce" to mean "pleasant" and "kind" as well as "sedate" and "sober"; and "witty" to mean "amusing" and "clever" as well as "intelligent."

The effect of the poem, a brilliant one, is to suggest the universal range of poetry, which can grow out of the simple life and be written by humble men, but which extends to works of great masters. That the whole of man reacts to poetry serves both to exalt man and exalt poetry. Burns concludes the poem amusingly, gaily, humbly, profoundly, by rhyming "epistle" to recall poetry; "grissle" which emphasizes that the pen originated in something alive; "fissle" which combines physical and emotional "tingling"; and "sing or whistle" which recalls his own humility.

In "To a Mouse" much of the diction conveys physical details which are in close approximation to the actuality of a farmer's life rather than to an idealized portrait. The speaker uses many homely words, "daimen icker," "thrave," "foggage," and "coulter," all of which suggest that a farmer is speaking, someone well acquainted with the details of peasant work. But highly suggestive words are intermixed. "Cowrin" conveys, in both Scottish and English, the state of fear and the physical position assumed in fear, but in Scottish it can refer to the normal squatting position of an animal. Hence the word both conveys the continuity of physical state and emotional sensation, and allows the farmer to attribute a human reaction to the animal without becoming unconvincingly imaginative. "Bickering" in Scottish means "hastening" but also carries the English "fighting," "squabbling," "brawling," and thus conveys antagonism as well as fear in the mouse. "Breastie," by its diminutive form, conveys some of the affection of the farmer but also gives the mouse human implications, both physical and emotional, by virtue of the breadth of meaning of the word, while its rhyme with "beastie" recalls that the mouse's human qualities do not make it human. "Ill" goes further in Scottish than in English, suggesting "annoyed," "vexed," "hostile," (still in the English "ill-tempered") thus picking up the sense of antagonism in the first stanza and, with "dominion," contrasting "social union" and "companion." "Nature's social union" is a rare example of Burns's ironic use of English; perhaps it is inappropriate diction for a farmer, but it expresses, through its irony, Burns's contempt for abstract theodicies, for well-laid schemes. "Silly," in Stanza IV, carries the Scottish meaning of "deserving of pity," "frail," "meager," while retaining the English and Scottish "plain," "simple," "homely." Hence the word conveys both the physical state of the shelter and the farmer's compassion for it, while demonstrating the continuity of the two.

The farmer states explicitly what the two have in common; they are both "earth born" and "mortal." Burns enriches the relationship of the two by the farmer's tender language, through words which suggest that there is something human about the mouse, and through words which convey the emotional contact between the two living and dying beings. But in the undertone of hostility and fear he says that something is "agley," that is, "off the straight," "irregular," "wrong." The two "poor" companions, "impoverished," "pathetic," "ill-fortuned," are united in a scheme which makes prospects "drear" or frightening, in which living and dying is the only certain pattern, in which life justifies "ill opinion," not "social union." Yet life can offer some consolation, although few accept it, through sympathetic contact between living beings and through recognition that "dreary winter" and the "cruel coulter" are far more serious problems than "a daimen icker in a thrave."

Burns is not saying the farmer is a philosopher any more than he is saying the mouse is a human. His point is that such distinctions are unimportant. The philosophic understanding of the farmer may be limited, but it is the best understanding we are likely to have.

A diction of discrete, unambiguous words would express a degree of clarity or organization which Burns considers outside actuality. The fluid, suggestive diction conveys poetically that rigid distinctions have little to do with the world as it is, that we must be satisfied with the consolation which comes from the sympathy of all living beings, that schemes to organize nature, either philosophically or practically, will only delude us with "promis'd joy."

In these, as in other vernacular poems, Burns does not rely entirely on Scottish words. He readily employs any English words which help convey his poetic intent. But Scottish words provide a higher proportion of the poetically effective words. Further, the Scottish words lend something else, not so easily defined, but which calls for more investigation.

I have found no evidence that Burns learned his use of Scottish from Ramsay and Fergusson. They probably gave him the idea of using the mixed language,[10] but taught him few of its specific advantages. The use of highly concrete diction to convey a poetry which comes out of everyday experience occurs rarely in their poetry and then in such a stylized and unconvincing way, especially in Ramsay's poetry, as to make it more like Ambrose Philips than Burns. Nor do either of them use the poetic suggestiveness of Scottish in the way Burns does. The Scottish words and meanings which Burns uses with great facility, as "bauld," "thirl'd," "douce," "fissle," "bicker," "silly," "cowrin," and "ill," Ramsay uses either not at all or rarely and uninterestingly. Fergusson uses less than half of the words and never the techniques of Burns. For example, "spunk," which Burns uses to help create a rich suggestive metaphor in "Epistle to J. Lapraik," Fergusson uses once:

> Then what is Man? why a' this Phraze?
> Life's Spunk decay'd, nae mair can blaze.
> Let sober Grief alone declare
> Our fond Anxiety and Care:
> Nor let the Undertakers be
> The only waefu' Friends we see.
> ("Auld Reikie," ll. 171–6)

Fergusson picks up figures and uses them as befits his point, so that the fire metaphor is only a passing convenience for the sake of articulation, to be discarded when another point must be made. There is nothing to suggest that fire and life are joined in a poetic or philosophic scheme. "Slee," which Burns uses in "Epistle to J. Lapraik," Fergusson uses in "Elegy on the Death of Scots Music" combined with "pawky":

Macgibbon's gane: Ah! waes my heart!
The man in music maist expert,
Wha cou'd sweet melody impart,
    And tune the reed,
Wi' sic a slee and pawky art;
    But now he's dead.

(ll. 37–42)

Burns also combines the two words in "Epistle to James Smith":

Dear Smith, the slee'st, pawkie thief,
That e'er attempted stealth or rief!
Ye surely hae some warlock-breef
    Owre human hearts;
For ne'er a bosom yet was prief
    Against your arts.

(stanza I)

Burns follows Fergusson in using the words to describe a reaction of affection mingled with a sense of magic, but Burns also uses their favorable and unfavorable connotations to describe the happy reluctance with which one gives up his heart. Fergusson showed considerable promise as a poet but he did not express, in either themes or diction, the idea, which Burns developed so successfully, that distinction must be subordinated to connection. Whatever he gained through the use of Scottish, he did not use the dialect in the same way as Burns.

*   *   *

The most obvious change in Burns's diction from his earlier to his later career is, as everyone notes, toward more English and less exclusively Scottish words. The most apparent reason, as everyone also notes, is that after 1790 he wrote mostly songs. The one important poem written after 1790, "Tam O'Shanter," uses a great many Scottish words. The few songs written before 1790 use fewer Scottish words than the poems written during those years.

One unfortunately inescapable reason for more English words in the songs is that songs are made to be sung. The listener cannot consult a glossary such as Ramsay, Fergusson, and Burns put at the back of their collected poems. Notably, Burns continues in the songs to use Scottish words which are easily understandable to an English-speaking listener, as "auld," "fa," "fit," "aft," "fause," "rin," "saft." When he alters the source from English to Scottish the change is usually to an easily understood word. In "O, Let Me in This Ae Night," based on a song in Herd,[10] he changes "would" to "wad," "waking" to "waukin" and "foot" to "fit."

But another reason emerges from the subject matter. Most of the songs express a simple feeling—love, friendship, loneliness, regret, contentment, yearning. They less often need a provincial speaker, whether for purposes of self-ridicule, or to express the wisdom found in concrete experience, or to create any of the shadings of irony Burns often employs. The few songs which have this irony, like "The Deuk's Dang O'er My Daddy," "Willie Wastle," or "Landlady, Count the Lawin," have more Scottish. Likewise, the songs whose subject matter calls for a provincial setting, such as patriotic songs, use more Scottish words. But generally, Burns uses the simplicity of the song to express what the provincialism of the poems expresses. He need not, in an expression of love, remind us that this feeling is available to all classes.

Franklyn Bliss Snyder hypothesizes that the larger proportion of English words in the songs was in part the result of Burns's greater assurance with the language as a result of his Edinburgh visit and the favorable reception of his poetry.[11] Yet an examination of the diction of the songs fails to uphold this speculation.

Burns bases the first stanza of "I Do Confess Thou Art Sae Fair" on a seventeenth-century English metaphysical poem, "To His Forsaken Mistress."[12] He changes English words to Scottish but leaves the grammar and syntax intact, a practice which is typical of his method. The source is:

> I do confess thou'rt smooth and fair,
>   And I might have gone near to love thee,
> Had I not found the slightest prayer
>   That lip could move, had power to move thee;
> But I can let thee now alone
>   As worthy to be loved by none.
>
> I do confess thou'rt sweet, but find
>   Thee such an unthrift of thy sweets:
> Thy favours are but like the wind
>   Which kisseth ev'rything it meets;
> And since thou canst with more than one
>   Thou'rt worthy to be kiss'd by none.

Burns's first stanza is:

> I do confess thou art sae fair,
>   I wad been o'er the lugs in luve,
> Had I na found the slightest prayer
>   That lips could speak thy heart could muve.
> I do confess thee sweet, but find
>   Thou art so thriftless o' thy sweets,
> Thy favours are the silly wind
>   That kisses ilka thing it meets.

Some of the changes are simply the improvements of a better poet but some are improvements that the latitude of using both Scottish and English allows. The change of "every-" to "ilka" (10, 8) smooths out the sound of the line with the repeating "i" sound, emphasizes the word with the hard stop on "k," and connects the word, amusingly, contemptuously, with the sound of "kisseth." The advantage depends entirely on the sound, since the two words have no difference in meaning and Burns uses them interchangeably, often using "every" in vernacular poems and songs. "Lugs" allows Burns to alliterate with "love," creating an amusing comparison which helps the speaker satirize both himself and passionate, misplaced love. Some changes achieve greater simplicity and avoid self-conscious poeticisms. "Kisseth" to "kisses" (10, 8) is one example. "But like" to "silly" (9, 7) smooths out the syntax and further clarifies the speaker's feeling for the woman, since "silly" means both "frail" or "weak," "dear" or "innocent," as well as "foolish" (cf. "Its silly wa's the winds are strewin") and thus refers to both the woman and the wind. The removal of the appurtenance of the simile (9, 7) is a typical simplification, in spite of "O, my luve is like a red, red rose." Burns has added a few easy Scotticisms, like "na," "o," "muve," which give some informality, but he has retained the poetic second-person singular pronoun. The rhetoric is obviously controlled. Burns removes the source's pun on "move," substituting an Augustan parallelism (line 4), satiric and sardonic in emphasis rather than metaphysical in implication.

The tendency, then, is toward a simplified, easy-flowing, and unself-conscious diction, but one of restrained gentle familiarity rather than one that is vernacular. Yet again, as in the poems,

Burns seems able to use an almost Augustan rhetoric and still attain
the rhythms of common speech which give the sense that the poet is
writing as the thoughts and phrases first occur to him ("As fair art
thou, my bonnie lass,/So deep in luve am I").

The changes Burns makes over his songs tend to be largely, although not invariably, away from concreteness. I had expected to
find a general pattern of changes toward racy, sensuous detail. This
kind of change does occur, as in "The White Cockade," based on
"Ranting Roving Lad" in Herd (II, 179). But more often he lessens
the specificity and adds more suggestive diction.

In "How Lang and Dreary Is the Night," based on "The Day
Begins to Peep" in the Herd manuscript,[13] he changes:

> I ne'er can sleep a wink,
> Tho' ne'er so wet and weary,
> But ly and cry and think

to:

> I restless lie frae e'en to morn
> Tho' I were ne'er sae weary.

Burns shortens the poem from nine stanzas to three stanzas and a
chorus, mostly by eliminating the concrete and sensuous details of
the source. This decrease allows the highly suggestive rhyme-words,
"dearie," "weary," "dreary," and especially "eerie" to attain much
greater importance; for in the source all are obscured by the quan-
tity of details. "Eerie" in eighteenth-century English was limited to
the current sense of "weird," but in Scottish retained its older
senses of "superstitiously fearful," "lonely from fear," "fearful of
something unknown," "uneasy," "melancholy." This word is reflected by "lanely nights," "dreams," "absent," "restless," "heavy
hours," and "joyless" as well as the rhyme words, so that the girl's
many fears and sorrows spread out over the poem, indicating the
terror of both loneliness and the unknown.

In "The Lea-Rig" he removes the specific, indecent "rowe"
from the source (Herd MS. pages 100–101), substituting "meet,"
and changes the poem from a proposition to a statement of love.[14]
He changes "dark" to "mirkest," which combines the English
"dark" and the English "murky." He adds "eerie" and "wild,"
which combine with the original "weary," to contrast with "scented

birks," "dew . . . hangin clear," "morning sun," and "heart sae cheery"; and he changes the social comment of:

> While others herd their ewes and lambs
> And toil for warldly gear, my jo

to:

> When . . .
> . . . owsen frae the furrow'd field
> Return sae dowf and weary, O.

"Dowf" includes "weary" but puts the emphasis on "dullness" and "listlessness" rather than on the physical part of tiredness, and adds "melancholy," "numbness," and "dreariness." The result is that the two moods run through the poem; the mood of darkness, weariness, melancholy, fear, superstition, the unknown, the wild; and the mood of light, clearness, joy, and love. Within a life where fear, weariness, and gloom are the commonplace, the lovers find brightness and joy, even, or especially, at "gloamin grey." The emphasis is entirely on the mood and feelings of the lovers; the obvious comment on life is left unspoken and only slightly implied.

There is not much evidence, then, that Burns turns toward more English words in the songs because of his greater facility or assurance. He uses both English and Scottish words with facility in both poems and songs. It is more likely that he turned away from Scottish because of the change in form which needed less concreteness in subject and in definition of the speaker, and, perhaps, required more clarity for an English-speaking person.[15]

*   *   *

Since Burns's use of Scottish does not come from Ramsay, Fergusson, or the Scottish folk song and since he shows facility with English as well as Scottish, he may have learned the techniques from his favorite English poets, Pope, Thomson, Goldsmith, or Cowper. A separate study is needed of Burns's English diction and its relation to that of other eighteenth-century writers. Yet, even if a similarity does appear, it will raise as many questions as it answers. If Burns learned techniques of diction from English writers and then applied them to Scottish, the pattern of his diction would probably be reversed. We would expect Burns to employ more English words in the earlier poems, then turn to more Scottish words as he acquired facility with the techniques. While we cannot exclude, without further exploration, the possibility of English influence on his diction, we must at least allow for considerable originality in his way of handling diction. His prose comments suggest that he was indeed trying something new. In his *First Commonplace Book* Burns says:

It may be some entertainment to a curious observer of human-nature to see how a plough-man thinks, and feels, under the pressure of Love, Ambition, Anxiety, Grief with the like cares and passions, which, however diversified by the Modes, and Manners of life, operate pretty much alike I believe, in all the Species.[16]

Burns is a poet of common ideas and common emotions, "which, however diversified by the Modes and Manners of life, operate pretty much alike . . . in all the Species." We need accept in his poetry no philosophic or religious schemes; no tradition of love, courtly or otherwise; outside of "Is There for Honest Poverty," no political or economic system; not even, the diction reminds us, a tradition of literature ("But I shall scribble down some blether/ Just clean aff-loof"). Burns's argument is that man can find ethical and aesthetic direction in life without elaborate schemes. What better symbol of the freedom from political, aesthetic, or religious systems than a poor independent farmer, an uneducated poet, or a love-sick peasant girl? But it is vastly minimizing his accomplishment to say that he simply creates, through Scottish words and picturesque spellings, the sense of a provincial speaker.

Since Burns admits that he does not write as he speaks, surely we can give his statement that he writes in his "native language" some metaphoric interpretation. A statement which Burns made in a letter to Margaret Chalmers and considered worth recording in his *Second Commonplace Book* helps explain his theory of poetry: "The whining cant of love, except in real passion, and by a masterly hand, is to me as insufferable as the preaching cant of old Father Smeaton. . . . Darts, flames, Cupids, loves, graces, and all that farrago, are just a Mauchline [sacrament], a senseless rabble."[17] He speaks elsewhere against both poetry written without passion (II, 5) and emblematic poetry. (II, 167) Neither denunciation is surprising in Burns. But the sequence in the quotation, which equates overly-stylized poetry with love poetry written without passion, has particular significance. His denunciation is directed not only against stylized imagery but against highly stylized poetry generally. A large part of contemporary British poetry had become over-intellectualized, abstract, lifeless. Poets frequently described love, misery, poverty, and the simple life as if their only experiences with them were literary, and wrote in a language which had gone sterile with inbreeding. Burns advocates poetry which describes "incidents and situations from common life" and which expresses "the spontaneous overflow of powerful feelings" in a "language really used by men."

His attempt to write poetry which has suggestive, fluid diction and which expresses feelings at once passionate and commonplace leads him to theorize about and to attempt the same renewal of the language of poetry which Wordsworth and Coleridge demand. The many poets and critics, Stevenson, Arnold, Henley, Speirs, who insist, in spite of contrary evidence, that Burns writes as he speaks, are eloquent attestations to Burns's success in creating "a plainer and more emphatic language" which keeps "the reader in the company of flesh and blood" and which has the power "to give the charm of novelty to things of every day, and to excite a feeling analogous to the supernatural, by awakening the mind's attention from the lethargy of custom, and directing it to the loveliness and the wonders of the world before us."

NOTES

1. "Historical Introduction," *The Dialect of the Southern Counties of Scotland* (London, 1873), p. 71, n. 1, and *passim*. Other philologists agree about the linguistic situation: Karl Luick, *Historische Grammatik der Englischensprache* (Leipzig, 1921) and *Untersuchungen zur Englischen Lautgeschichte* (Strassburg, 1896), Richard Jordan, *Handbuch der Mittelenglischen Grammatik* (Heidelberg, 1925); and about Burns's use of Scottish: Sir James Wilson, *The Dialect of Robert Burns as Spoken in Central Ayrshire* (Oxford, 1923) and Sir James Colville, *"The Literary Art of Robert Burns,"* delivered in 1897, printed in the Burns Chronicle, III, 7 (1958), 3–28, and *Studies in Lowland Scots* (Edinburgh and London, 1909).

2. "Notes on Burns's First Volume," *MP* 16 (1919) 480.

3. "Some Aspects of Poetry," *The Cornhill Magazine*, 40 (1879) 426.

4. "General Introduction," *The English Poets*, ed. Humphrey Ward (New York, 1880), I, xl–xli.

5. "Life: Genius: Achievement," *The Poetry of Robert Burns*, ed. W. E. Henley and T. F. Henderson (Edinburgh, 1896–97), IV, 264–5 and 268–9.

6. "Burns and English Literature," *From Blake to Byron: The Pelican Guide to English Literature*, ed. Boris Ford, V (London, 1957), pp. 102–3. See also "Revaluation (III): Burns," *Scrutiny*, 2 (1934) 334–6.

7. All references to the letters are from *The Letters of Robert Burns*, ed. J. DeLancey Ferguson (Oxford, 1931).

8. *The Poetry of Robert Burns*, ed. W. E. Henley and T. F. Henderson (Edinburgh, 1896–97), III, 376–7.

9. David Daiches, *Robert Burns*, (New York, 1950), pp. 32 and 337. Franklyn Bliss Snyder, "A Note on Burns's Language," MLN, 43 (1928) 514; *Robert Burns—His Personality, His Reputation, and His Art* (Toronto, 1936), p. 95; Kurt Wittig, *The Scottish Tradition in Literature* (Edinburgh and London, 1958), pp. 202–6; Thomas Crawford, *Burns: A Study of the Poems and Songs* (Edinburgh and London, 1960), p. 90.

10. David Herd, *Ancient and Modern Scottish Songs* (Edinburgh, 1776), II, 167.

11. *MP* 16 (1919) 482.

12. Henley-Henderson, III, 372.

13. *David Herd's Manuscript*, ed. Hans Hecht (Edinburgh, 1904), p. 238.

14. In spite of *The Merry Muses of Caledonia* Burns's usual pattern is to clean up the songs; never through prudery, but simply because he realized the greater effectiveness of understatement. For example, in "When She Came Ben She Bobbed," based on a song in Herd (II, 206), he removes a detailed discussion of the girl's pregnancy but changes "And he kist the collier lassie" to "And kissin a collier lassie an' a'."

15. A. N. Buchan, in "Word and Word Tune in Burns," *SP* 48 (1951) 40–48, discusses Scottish words and musical rhythms.

16. *Robert Burns's Commonplace Book*, ed. James Cameron Ewing and Davidson Cook (Glasgow, 1938), p. 1.

17. *Letters*, I, 129–30 and *Second Commonplace Book, The Works of Robert Burns, With Life by Professor Wilson*, (Glasgow, Edinburgh and London, 1859), II, 395.

The Picturesque Moment

———•———

MARTIN PRICE

THE picturesque, like so much aesthetic theory, was an attempt to win traditional sanctions for new experience. This required a reordering of the field of aesthetic experience, and any such process shifts attention to new elements within the field. William Gilpin drew together tendencies that had become strong in eighteenth-century poetry—in Thomson, Dyer, Collins, for example—by seeking in nature the aesthetic interest of great landscape paintings. He took this interest beyond the limits of the cultivated garden or park into the wild natural scene, and he demanded for the wild the attentiveness and refinement of observation that painting had traditionally won.

Uvedale Price took over the values Gilpin had established but applied them to a new area of aesthetic interest. More than Gilpin he stressed the complexity of pictorial composition, and particularly the landscape painter's use of irregular outlines and broken areas of light and color. Price was not equally interested in all kinds of painting. He drew especially upon the Venetian colorists of the High Renaissance and various forms of baroque. His initial object was to attack an excessive simplicity in landscape design (in his strictures on Capability Brown he was joined by Richard Payne Knight), and his chief concern was with the kind of complexity that could be created or fostered by art. He therefore divorced the picturesque from the sublime, as Gilpin had not, and distinguished it from that sublime art (to be found in painting or poetry) which conveyed the sense of the unlimited or infinite as much as he did the formal and regular.

Richard Payne Knight, in turn, saw how uncontrolled and ill-

defined were the categories that Price wished to dignify as picturesque. He insisted that their aesthetic effect depended for the
most part on the association of ideas one brought to the various
forms of irregularity, and he limited the term "picturesque" either
to the experience that drew specifically on direct associations with
landscape paintings or to the kind of experience that abstracted the
purely visual features (such as could be directly represented in a
painting). Knight gave primary emphasis to the energies of mind
expressed in the work of art, and he tried to account for all artistic
forms as stimulants and modifications of this energy.

Each of these uses of the key term can be shown to have its
grounds in a distinctive aesthetic system, and each can be shown to
serve a different immediate aim in redirecting our attention.[1] I shall
be concerned, however, with the common elements of sensibility
the term picturesque serves to promote. It seems proper to talk of
the picturesque rather than of picturesques so long as we are more
interested in the sensibility than in the means by which it was
accommodated to various structures of thought. One may, however, distinguish aspects of picturesque theory:

(1) The recognition of the value of roughness and complexity as
"interesting"; the adjective is cool and noncommittal, an
assertion of aesthetic appeal without any attempt to characterize it.

(2) The appeal to the principles of composition to be found in
landscape painting as a justification of and model for
roughness and variety. The breadth of the appeal, which
extends to Dutch genre painting in some cases, includes a
picturesqueness of architecture and of human figures.

(3) The applications of principles of perception to the creation
of landscape and architectural design, to the planning of
towns and villages. At its most conspicuous and fashionable,
this takes the form of the passion for improving estates; at its
highest, it guides the designs of John Nash for a pictorially
rich and varied townscape.

(4) The dissociation of visual, pictorial, or generally aesthetic
elements from other values in contemplating a scene. This
is, in effect, a restriction placed late upon the picturesque,
and its full import depends upon the values that are ob-

served to be excluded by the picturesque point of view. Since the picturesque defines itself from the outset, as in (1), by aesthetic categories (which are meant in turn to attract new sentiments and feelings) it lays itself open to the misunderstanding that it neglects other values.

In writing of the picturesque moment, I wish to explore more fully Christopher Hussey's statement that "the picturesque interregnum between classic and romantic art was necessary in order to enable the imagination to form the habit of feeling through the eyes." Hussey's terms seem by now somewhat inadequate.[2] We have come in recent years to hear more and more of the picturesque as a dominant theme in romantic architecture and painting. More striking still is the revival of picturesque doctrine in the last two decades by English town planners.[3] The *Architectural Review* has devoted a great deal of study to the picturesque, and applied its teachings to the problems of townscape. The interest in texture may find its application in the study of paving materials as means of giving variety of surface and of defining areas. The concern with visual composition may apply on a large scale to land-use, the creation of meaningful and agreeable urban spaces, the relationship of buildings to landscape or to each other; or it may apply on a small scale to the lettering of business signs; the distinctive furniture and decoration of the pub; or the design of street lamps.

The picturesque remains a living concern so long as we are interested in planning variety, fostering the lucky accident, preserving the significant ruin (such as the tower of a bombed-out church) or the local character of a town. The contemporary interest in the picturesque is in part a response to the severity and uniformity of an established architectural style. But it may also be, on an American college campus as in the greater world of European town planning, the adjustment of a new architecture to old styles: additions to a complex of Gothic or Georgian buildings. To the extent that the picturesque explored with impartiality a variety of historical and exotic styles, deriving from them the features a new sensibility required, it provides a counterpart to the architect's role in many instances today. He may turn away from the forms of the International Style in search of greater plasticity and movement, and he may draw upon—and allude to—styles of the past without following them in the manner of nineteenth-century eclecticism. The new colleges at Yale University built by Eero Saarinen evoked the spatial feeling and the texture of an Italian hill town for the architect, and the towers were likened by him to those at San Gimignano. Again, the new fine arts building by Paul Rudolph creates fantasies of space and a constant succession of surprise and abrupt transitions, as calculated as those that William Shenstone created in his gardens in eighteenth-century England.[4]

When the architect declines to make use of traditional forms, his interest in surface variation and in calculated surprise becomes all the more conspicuous. The formal effects that were given sanction by tradition—the detail of a capital, the rhythmic breaking of a wall with giant pilasters, the divisions of space created by chapels and ambulatory—are now more frankly sought in new forms by an independent architect. The buildings are no longer evocation of the solemnities of the past but inventions of the present, and they acquire thereby a degree of arbitrariness and playfulness. It need not be levity; the old sanctions of tradition are replaced in part by the new sanctions of functional rigor. But one may, in the more audacious of these buildings, find oneself almost trapped within the surprises and manipulations of an artist's invention, as one might be imaginatively trapped in a dazzling play of perspective in Piranesi, haunted by the difficulties of "reading" the structure and identifying the interpenetrating spaces, perhaps happily surrendering to the puzzle and enjoying the release from familiar coordinates.

This brings us to the meaning of the "picturesque moment." Picturesque theory emerges from Edmund Burke's discussion of the sublime and the beautiful. By reducing the beautiful from a comprehensive aesthetic term to the name of a limited and lesser experience, Burke opened the way for others to identify new aesthetic categories. The picturesque was established by Uvedale Price as a third term to be set beside the others, but it proved to be an unstable term. The picturesque moment is that phase of speculation —a recurrent one, as I have tried to indicate—where the aesthetic categories are self-sufficient. Once the appeal of the picturesque is given moral or religious grounds, the picturesque moves toward the sublime. The picturesque, then, as an unstable term, looks back to the earlier discussions of wit and forward to later conceptions of imagination. Its very instability is important, for the aesthetic detachment it represents allowed a new sensibility to reclaim for artistic attention what had previously been neglected. Once the reclamation had been performed, the new objects were given a new basis of interest.

We can see the movement toward a new basis of interest in Ruskin's distinction between the nobler picturesque and the surface-picturesque. The latter, for Ruskin, is the pursuit of aesthetic patterns at the expense of moral sympathy. Ruskin seizes upon the problem that enters picturesque thought from the outset in William Gilpin: that the aesthetic and the moral may conflict; the idle man or the bandit is pictorially more interesting than the industrious citizen, and the ruined church or the terrible castle may appeal to the picturesque eye more than the busy center of parish life or the peaceful homestead. Ruskin compares the windmills represented by Turner and by Clarkson Stanfield. Stanfield is not in the least moved by the ruin of his mill:

On the contrary, he is delighted, and evidently thinks it the most fortunate thing possible. The owner is ruined, doubtless, or dead; but his mill forms an admirable object in our view of Britanny. So far from being grieved about it, we will make it our principal light;—if it were a fruit-tree in spring blossom, instead of a desolate mill, we could not make it whiter or brighter; we illumine our whole picture with it, and exult over its every rent as a special treasure and possession.

Turner, on the other hand, sees "a dim type of all melancholy human labour" in his, "catching the free winds, and setting them to turn grindstones." This is "poor work for the winds . . . not their proper work of marshalling the clouds," bearing rain and cool air to the plants. "So, also," Ruskin goes on, "of all low labour to which one sets human souls"; that "grinding in the darkness, for mere food's sake, must be melancholy work enough for many a living creature." And Turner, therefore, "has no joy of his mill." It is seen "dark against the sky," "not ashamed of its labour, and brightened from beyond, the golden clouds stooping over it, and the calm summer sun going down behind, far away, to his rest."[5]

One need hardly emphasize the difference between the two windmills: one a merely aesthetic object; the other a symbol of the moral state of dark suffering, whose sun provides the ironic contrast of natural rest but also the hopeful promise of ultimate benediction. The nobler picturesque has become symbolic, almost emblematic, and instinct with a moral awareness. The surface-picturesque is a "heartless" ideal:

the lover of it seems to go forth into the world in a temper as merciless as its rocks. All other men feel some regret at the sight of disorder and ruin. He alone delights in both . . . . Fallen cottage—deserted village—blasted heath—mouldering castle—to him, so that they do not show jagged angles of stone and timber, all are sights equally joyful . . . . What is it to him that the old man has passed his seventy years in helpless darkness and untaught waste of soul? The old man has at last accomplished his destiny, and filled the corner of a sketch, where something of an unshapely nature was wanting.

But Ruskin qualifies this scorn, for he finds in the aesthetic pursuit a small measure of unconscious sympathy:

a sad excitement, such as other people feel at a tragedy, only less in degree, just enough, indeed, to give a deeper tone to his pleasure, and to make him choose for his subject the broken stones of a cottage wall rather than of a roadside rank . . . [and] a vague desire, in his own mind, to live in cottages rather than in palaces; . . . a secret persuasion (in many respects a true one) that there is in these ruined cottages a happiness often quite as great as in kings' palaces, and a virtue and nearness to God infinitely greater and holier than can commonly be found in any other kind of place; so that the misery in which he exults is not, as he sees it, misery, but nobleness. . . .[6]

So even the lower, surface-picturesque finds, for Ruskin, its grounds in moral and religious feeling, and the seeming conflict of the aesthetic and the moral is avoided.

These observations of Ruskin tell us more about his need to give moral sanction to aesthetic experience than they do about the picturesque. They clearly mark, at any rate, the absorption of the aesthetic into the moral, and Ruskin gives us as well an account of the absorption of the picturesque into the sublime. He speaks of the picturesque as "a sublimity not inherent in the nature of the thing, but caused by something external to it; as the ruggedness of a cottage roof possesses something of a mountain aspect, not belonging to the cottage as such." This fanciful association of ideas may appear strained, but he moves on to a more telling association:

And this sublimity may be either in mere external ruggedness, and other visible character, or it may lie deeper, in an expression of sorrow and old age, attitudes which are both sublime; not a dominant expression, but one mingled with such familiar and common characters as prevent the object from becoming perfectly pathetic in its sorrow, or perfectly venerable in its age.

Here Ruskin treats the picturesque as the external form of the sublime, made visible by its mixture with the familiar. Later, he returns to the familiar cottage or mill acquiring sublimity by associations with noble natural objects. "This sublimity," he goes on, "belonging in the parasitical manner to the building, renders it, in the usual sense of the word, 'picturesque.' " In one case the sublime is tempered by the familiar; in the other, the familiar acquires associations of the sublime. In both, the outward appearance created by this fusion is the picturesque. Here we can see another indication of the instability of the picturesque and its readiness to be absorbed into the sublime.[7]

Ruskin's is the most intense and most fundamental criticism of the picturesque except for that in the twelfth book of Wordsworth's *Prelude,* with which I shall deal later. But we can see both the distrust of the picturesque and its prevalence, even its persistence, as a point of view in other writers. Perhaps the most interesting testimony is Jane Austen's, since she is so little a proponent of romantic imagination. When Elizabeth Bennet is forced out of Darcy's company by the rudeness of the ladies who share a narrow walk with him, she gaily refuses to let Darcy intervene: "No, no; stay where you are. You are charmingly grouped, and appear to uncommon advantage. The picturesque would be spoilt by admitting a fourth. Good-bye." Elizabeth is invoking the principle that only an odd number of objects will compose pictorially; Price's instance is three cows in a pasture. But Elizabeth has neatly connected the self-regard of the ladies with the self-conscious posing of picturesque objects; their unfeeling behavior is easily related to the "heartlessness" of the picturesque.

Jane Austen's most extensive account of the picturesque is given in *Northanger Abbey,* where Catherine Morland is schooled in the fashionable doctrine by Henry Tilney and his sister.

They were viewing the country with the eyes of persons accustomed to drawing, and decided on its capability of being formed into pictures, with all the eagerness of real taste. . . . It seemed as if a good view were no longer to be taken from the top of a high hill, and that a clear blue sky was no longer proof of a fine day.

One may admire Jane Austen's delicate use of "capability," the watchword of Lancelot Brown, who was the very *bête noir* of the picturesque theorists. The picturesque is here taken in its most fundamental sense; its standard is that of pictorial composition rather than the features of ruggedness and abrupt transitions that were to be abstracted from it. There is the typical picturesque preference for the composed view from a low point to a spectacular but sprawling vista, and there is the picturesque celebration of clouds.

He talked of foregrounds, distances, and second distances; side-screens and perspectives; lights and shades; and Catherine was so hopeful a scholar, that when they gained the top of Beechen Cliff, she voluntarily rejected the whole city of Bath, as unworthy to make part of a landscape.

What is most telling in this is that the tutor in the picturesque is the delightfully ironic Henry Tilney, who seems to bring to the subject the lightness and playfulness that are inherent in it as a mere aesthetic exercise. He may be contrasted with such a militant improver (in the manner of Capability Brown) as John Dashwood in *Sense and Sensibility:* "The walnut trees are all to come down to make room for [Fanny's greenhouse]. It will be a very fine object from many parts of the park, and the flower garden will slope down just before it. . . . We have cleared away all the thorns that grew in patches over the brow." This ostentatious impoverishment of nature accords with Dashwood's unutterable selfishness. He is, like the improvers in Pope's epistle *To Burlington,* too self-centered to consult the genius of the place.

Another of Jane Austen's improvers is the volatile and selfish Henry Crawford of *Mansfield Park.* His vision of Edmund

Bertram's parsonage at Thornton Lacey is a magnificent account of industrious alteration: "You are a lucky fellow," he exclaims to Edmund. "There will be work for five summers at least before the place is livable." Henry would turn all of Thornton Lacey around, reverse the approach and shift the garden, and purchase nearby meadows that are "finely sprinkled with timber." And as for the stream—"something must be done with the stream, but I could not determine what. I had two or three ideas."

Edmund Bertram is contented with comfort, but Henry's plans are more expansive. "The place deserves it, and you will find yourself not satisfied with much less than it is capable of." And, between bids at cards, he elaborates:

You may give it a higher character. You may raise it into a *place*. From being the mere gentleman's residence, it becomes, by judicious improvement, the residence of a man of education, taste, modern manners, good connections. All this may be stamped upon it; and that house receive such an air as to make its owner be set down as the great landholder of the parish. . . .

There is some point in the fact that Henry is creating the kind of estate his sister would consider appropriate if she were to occupy it as Edmund's wife, but most of all one is struck by the calculations of social prestige that govern Henry Crawford's landscape improvements. It is not that we feel a meanness in Henry or Mary Crawford, but they betray for the most part an essential shallowness, a reluctance to surrender their pleasures, even as here the pleasure in a kind of meretricious knowingness.

One may note in passing the two houses that Jane Austen seems to celebrate most: Donwell Abbey and Pemberley. In *Emma,* we see Donwell Abbey as the center of Knightley virtues; Emma views

the respectable size and style of the building, its suitable, becoming, characteristic situation, low and sheltered—its ample gardens stretching down to meadows washed by a stream, of which the Abbey, with all the old neglect of prospect, had scarcely a sight—and its abundance of timber in rows and avenues, which neither fashion nor extravagance had rooted up.—The house was larger than Hartfield, and totally unlike it, covering a good deal of ground, rambling and irregular, with many comfortable and one or two handsome rooms.—It was just what it ought to be, and it looked what it was—and Emma felt an increasing respect for it, as the residence of a family of such true gentility, untainted in blood and understanding.

Pemberley, where Elizabeth Bennet finds an unprejudiced image of Darcy's virtues, is

a large, handsome stone building, standing well on rising ground, and backed by a ridge of high woody hills; and in front, a stream of some natural importance was swelled into greater, but without any artificial appearance. Its banks were neither formal nor falsely adorned. Elizabeth was delighted. She had never seen a place for which nature had done more, or where natural beauty had been so little counteracted by an awkward taste.

When she enters the house, it is to admire the prospect: "from every window there were beauties to be seen." Donwell Abbey stolidly neglects prospects, but Pemberley realizes them to the fullest; each is an example of an honest sensibility, although Pemberley, its furniture "neither gaudy nor uselessly fine," is a work of higher taste. It is, however, the moral qualities revealed in the control of taste that Jane Austen stresses.[8]

I have cited these cases of the picturesque viewer and the improver because they catch most of the criticisms that are brought against the picturesque. Henry Tilney gives us the jargon and Catherine Morland the automatic response that are so often mocked; only here we can feel that Henry Tilney knows what he is about and can mock himself with as much grace and point as can anyone else. John Dashwood is not a picturesque improver, but Henry Crawford may well be; to different degrees, they connect zealous improvement with the readiness to impose self upon the world about one. The criticism does not rise to the high generality of Ruskin's, but the failure of moral sympathy is still part of it.

Yet the picturesque persists as a pattern of thought where one least expects it. One recalls Wordsworth's lines about his youthful response to landscape:

> I felt, observed, and pondered; did not judge,
> Yea, never thought of judging; with the gift
> Of all this glory filled and satisfied.[9]

Beside this we can set these words so typical of the picturesque improver, from Wordsworth's *Guide through the District of the Lakes:*

The islands . . . are neither fortunately placed nor of pleasing shape; but if the wood upon them were managed with more taste, they might become interesting features in the landscape.

Worse was to come in 1844:

a vivid perception of natural scenery is neither inherent in mankind, nor a necessary consequence of even a comprehensive education. It is benignly ordained that . . . all the ordinary varieties of rural Nature should find an easy way to the affections of all men, and more or less so from early childhood till [old age]. But a taste beyond this . . . is not to be implanted at once; it must be gradually developed both in nations and individuals. Rocks and mountains, torrents and widespread waters . . . cannot, in their finer relations to the human mind, be comprehended, or even very imperfectly perceived, without processes of culture or opportunities of observation in some degree habitual.[10]

True, this is part of Wordsworth's desperate and futile effort to forestall "the molestation of cheap trains pouring out their hundreds at a time along the margin of Windermere." The distinction that Wordsworth draws between the "easy way to the affections" and the "finer relations in the human mind" serves once more to exclude the picturesque from the realm of elementary passions and moral sympathies, but the passage reveals at the same time an acceptance of the picturesque as a serious point of view.

II

For Price and Knight the framing of picturesque theory begins as a reaction to a specific instance of impoverished beauty, the landscape gardening of Capability Brown. Brown's designs may be seen as a counterpart of Palladian architecture. They sacrifice the interest of texture for bold effects of structure. They emphasize the plasticity of the landscape and trim its surfaces or mass its trees (in clumps or belts) so as to create curves and volumes of space that correspond to the strong plasticity of the neo-Palladian buildings. These buildings have been shown to depart from true Palladian design in their tendency to spread out and isolate the elements that interpenetrate each other in Palladio. The Palladian or Venetian window ceases to be an essential interweaving of structural units and becomes an isolated decorative effect—breaking the large smooth mass with its elaborate kind of opening. The wings of the neo-Palladian building tend to spread apart and become distinct masses, only loosely linked with the central mass and therefore all the more assertive in their own right. This can be seen as a rationalizing of baroque forms, a pulling apart of elements so that each may be seen in isolation as well as combination. It has also been seen, from another point of view, as the anticipation of that plasticity of elementary geometrical forms we can find in Boullée and Ledoux later in the century.[11]

Brown's landscape gardening seems to draw upon something of the same geometrical spirit. The shaven lawns that Knight ridicules reveal the massive swell of the landscape or its gentle descent into pasture and field. Knight printed with his satirical comments on Brown in *The Landscape* (1794) two engravings. One of them shows a severely geometrical house standing boldly on a prominence amid bare lawns, with a few clumps of trees breaking the "uniform, eternal green," and a conspicuously artificial stream demonstrating between smooth banks Hogarth's serpentine line of beauty. Of Brown's clumps of trees, Price observes that they are an unhappy union of two "opposite extremes of being too crouded or too scattered. . . . It is scattered in respect to the general composition and lumpish when considered by itself." And "it would be difficult to invent any-thing more wretchedly insipid, than one uniform green surface dotted with clumps, and surrounded by a belt." For the extended lawn loses "that happy union of warm and cool, of smooth and rough, and picturesque and beautiful" that marks the best compositions of landscape painting. Even more, as Price points out, Brown's desire for smoothness could deprive trees of their characteristic display of roots, "which seemed to fasten to the earth with their dragon claws." When "the spurs of a large oak, which give its base such a look of firmness and stability" are covered up, the trunk loses its character and "looks like an enormous post stuck into the ground."[12] As Christopher Hussey puts it, Brown's landscape was "fundamentally physical and intellectual in its appeal. . . . The visual qualities—of texture, colour, contrast, scarcely entered into it." A more recent critic speaks of his "linear compositions in three dimensions."[13]

The picturesque critics make frequent use of the idea of play. Brown's landscape, Price writes, has "a want of that playful variety

of outline, by which beautiful scenes in nature are eminently distinguished." On the other hand, there is, Price points out, "a wide
difference between an avowed and characteristic formality, and a
formality not less real, but which assumes the airs of ease and
playfulness." In creating a lake shore, the art consists "in preserving
a general play and connection of outline, yet varied by breaks and
inlets of different heights and characters." Or again, Raphael drew
the naked figure he meant to drape, "knowing how much the
grace and play of that drapery must depend on what was beneath. . . ."[14] Clearly, play has the sense of elasticity in some of these
instances, of lightness in others; it keeps before us the sense of a
flexible resourcefulness, not too deeply engaged to become rigid,
alert to novel possibilities and constantly alive.

This sense of play is a conspicuous feature of later eighteenth-
century sensibility. It takes the form of play-acting, of the pleasures
in ruins and follies, of subtly contrived garden views designed to
be seen in telling succession, of revivals of styles in literature and
architecture, of exoticism, of that peculiar assertiveness that comes
out of skepticism. Some part of this sense of play derives from the
growing interest in the way the mind creates its world. An empirical philosophy had created a model of the mind constructing its
universals out of sense experience, and the model lent itself to the
kind of speculative physiological psychology one finds in David
Hartley or in Edmund Burke. The exploration of associative processes moves from the model-building of Locke, which shows a
passing concern with pathological associative processes, to the
recognition of the constructive force of emotions in the associative
process, their fusion or coalescence of images, to build a structure
of problematic epistemological value but great strength and appeal.
The skeptical mind, aware of the need for reasonable common
truths but aware as well of the imaginative power of arbitrary
structures and accidental associations, finds itself torn between external nature and the mind's art, between knowledge and power.

This skeptical double awareness encourages the sense of play one
finds in so much of the art of an age of sensibility. Where the
imagination is most peremptory, in the sublime of the visionary
poet, it has an assertiveness that is often defensive or defiant. It
creates new world pictures and mythologies that oppose tradition

in two ways: they desert the imagery and personalities of classical
or Christian myth, and they invert the orthodoxy of the classical
Olympus or of institutional Christianity.[15] Where the commitment
is less thoroughgoing, we find a trying-on of exotic roles and idioms
—of oriental or medieval costume and manners—and an allusive-
ness that evokes Spenserian or Miltonic resonances. The more detached and free of willfulness or self-hypnotism the artist, the more
obviously playful his work.

Nikolaus Pevsner has written of this element of play in Reynolds's *Master Crewe as Henry VIII*—"a sturdy pink-cheeked little
boy of four dressed up as Henry VIII and standing, legs wide apart,
in the famous pose of Holbein's portrait of the King." It is, he
writes, "not simply parody of Holbein, it is an easy and superior
play on several levels, never taken too seriously, a play with Holbein, the King, the boy and also the grand portrait and those
advocating it, including Reynolds himself." Pevsner goes on to
describe this "ambiguity" as "not only English but also Rococo in
a European sense," and he cites Tiepolo's use of Veronese costume
as a counterpart of Reynolds's use of Van Dyck's. "Only that in
Italy the acting seems real whole-hearted acting, whereas in England the reticence of deportment half-defeats the costume. It makes
it impossible to take the sitter or the picture too deadly seriously."[16]
Such an art is intensely self-conscious, an instance of the "exertion"
or "irritation" of mind that becomes so common an appeal in the
aesthetic writings of the day. For, as Sir William Chambers writes,
although the human mind "doth not delight in intricacies, yet
without a certain, even a considerable, degree of complication, no
grateful sensations can ever be excited."[17]

The sense of play finds exercise both in fancifulness and in those
acts of abstraction which call attention to the arbitrariness of all the
mind's creations. Reynolds's portrait makes us aware of the artifice
of heroic portraiture by applying it to an incongruous subject, and
this helps us to see in turn the artifice of each role in which we cast
the human animal. Sterne exploits this theme more than any other
writer of the age, but he reminds us also of the fact that this artifice
is often unconscious, rooted in obsession or physical temperament,
and—most of all—the source of much that is best in us. One can
speak of artifice, but, in an age which senses the artistry of nature

and the natural basis of art as few had done before, it is more appropriate to speak of arbitrariness.

This element of playfulness, in its double awareness, looks back to that most distinctive of Augustan literary forms, the mock poem, whether mock-heroic, mock-pastoral, or mock-georgic. William Gilpin formed his views on the picturesque as early as the 1740's, and there is a telling instance of witty contrast in one of his letters from college. The prospect from his window at Queen's College, Oxford, gives on two gardens:

In one of them which belongs to New-College you have whatever Art can furnish you with; in the other, pure Nature. The former offers you a fine Variety of Vistas, Shady Walks, and Arbours, and in the open Parts deals mostly in Parterres, in one of which you may discover his Majesty's Arms cut out of Box. . . . All this makes a fine Contrast when oppos'd to Beds of Turnips and Carrots, or Rows of Pease and Beans which present themselves in the other Garden. . . . There is as much Variety too in the Inhabitants of these two Gardens. The one daily presents me with pretty Ladies or Gentlemen walking about for their Pleasure; the other as frequently offers me carefull Mothers, or busy-fac'd Matrons hanging out their Linnen, or weeding their Parsnips.[18]

This play between high and low, between artifice and commonplaceness, separates out the elements that are fused in the mock poem. Here the wit extends to symmetry but not all the way to the fusion of high forms with low subjects.

The mock poem demands a particularity we find in no other Augustan form, unless it be the debasing details of satirical description; and even these, such as the elaborate physical description of the Yahoos, represent an ugly displacement of the human into the animal. The more benign movement of the mock poem is to award aesthetic curiosity where moral admiration might originally have been appropriate. The resultant images are scarcely ugly. They fall short of the heroic in their primarily sensuous appeal, and they embody an implicit distinction between the sublime and the beautiful—or if one prefers between the sublimely beautiful and the charming or amusing. (It may be, of course, that the very charm of the aesthetic may empty the sublime of its vitality and suggest its hollowness; or, as in the case of Gilpin's gardens, the conventional decorum of the high may be emphasized in contrast to the novel charm of the low. One can, in fact, see the beautiful drawn between the "grand" and the "novel," between what commands awe and admiration and what stirs curiosity. Such a division cannot help but force the grand toward lifeless convention.)

One can see the aesthetic sense of texture—of surface and color —appearing in such famous passages as the coffee service in *The Rape of the Lock*. One can cite as well the passage on the fish stalls in Gay's *Trivia* (which may allude to Pope's description of the fish in *Windsor Forest*):

> The golden-bellied carp, the broad-finn'd maid,
> Red-speckled trouts, the salmon's silver jowl,
> The jointed lobster, and unscaly sole,
> And luscious 'scallops. . . .[19]

And beside this, one may set these remarks of Gilpin:

A parcel of char, just caught and thrown together into the luggage-pool of a boat, make a pleasant harmony of colouring. The green-olive tint prevails; to which a spirit is here and there given by a light blush of vermilion; and by a strong touch of red, if a fin happen to appear. These pleasing colours are assisted by the bright silvery lights, which play over the whole; for nothing reflects light more beautifully than the scales of a fish.[20]

We may be struck not merely by the closeness of observation but by the dissociation which can see the fish as a problem in pure color and reflecting surface, a dissociation that comes to its startling superlative: "nothing reflects light more beautifully." Such dissociation is one of the essential properties of wit. It is a play of mind that can free a term or a quality of its customary associations and exploit it in a startling singleness of meaning. The wit of Donne often involves the entry through analogy into a term or image whose ambiguous fullness allows the poet to depart with a new meaning and the basis for a shockingly new analogy. It is this power of dissociation that relates the picturesque to the tradition of wit.

We can see the relationship drawn most clearly by Price in an analogy he makes between the picturesque in visible objects and "what in some measure answers to it—the quick, lively, and sudden turns of fancy in conversation":

Few persons have been so lucky as never to have seen or heard the true *proser;* smiling, and distinctly uttering his flowing commonplace nothings, with the same placid countenance, the same even-toned voice: he is the very emblem of serpentine walks, belts, and rivers, and all Mr. Brown's works; like him they are smooth, flowing, even, and distinct; and like him they wear one's soul out.

There is a very different being of a much rarer kind, who hardly appears to be of the same species; full of unexpected turns, of flashes of light: objects the most familiar, are placed by him in such singular, yet natural points of view; he strikes out such unthought-of agreements and contrasts; such combinations, so little obvious, yet never forced nor affected, that the attention cannot flag; but from the delight of what is passed, we eagerly listen for what is to come. This is the true picturesque, and the propriety of that term will be more felt, if we attend to what corresponds to the *beautiful* in conversation. How different is the effect of that soft insinuating style, of those gentle transitions, which, without dazzling or surprising, keep up an increasing interest, and insensibly wind round the heart.[21]

This is a somewhat cruel attempt to deny Brown claims even to the beautiful, for it makes clear that wit (or the picturesque) and beauty have a common complexity. The beautiful in conversation is "insinuating" and accomplishes more than its appearance suggests, for its "gentle transitions"—although they neither dazzle nor surprise—still "keep up an increasing interest." Both are opposed to the prosing that is all on the surface, merely what it seems, and in fact no art at all. For, Price goes on, art conveys "an idea of some degree of invention; of contrivance that is not obvious; of something that raises expectation, and which differs with success from what we recollect having seen before."

III

The picturesque offers its witty complexity and playfulness as an appeal to the energy of man's mind. "Men grow weary of uniform perfection; nor will anything compensate the absence of every obstacle to curiosity, and every hope of novelty." At this level of psychological and moral generality Price sounds very much like Johnson. The principle is amplified by Richard Payne Knight:

Man, as he now is, is formed for the world, as it now is, in which
He never is, but always to be blest—
that is, his real happiness consists in the *means* and not in the *end*:—
in *acquisition,* and not in possession. The source and principle of it is,

therefore, *novelty*. . . . If everything were known, there would be nothing to be learned, if every good were possessed, there would be none to be acquired; and if none were wanting, or there were no evil, there would be none to be done; and consequently all would be dead inaction, or action without motive or effect.

This theme goes back, in aesthetics, at least to Addison's papers on the pleasures of the imagination, where "the new or uncommon . . . fills the soul with an agreeable surprise, gratifies its curiosity, and gives it an idea of which it was not before possessed. . . . We are quickly tired with looking upon hills and valleys, where everything continues fixed and settled in the same place and posture, but find our thoughts a little agitated and relieved at the sight of such objects as are ever in motion and sliding away from beneath the eye of the beholder."[22]
When we move from the natural scene to the human subject, the theme of energies is still present. For Knight, the "glowing energy of language" is "the very essence of poetry, and that which gives it all its power over the soul." Knight attacks the Burkian stress on obscurity and formlessness as qualities of the sublime. He defends instead a union of vigor and sensibility of mind: "What is it, that makes the impassioned language of Achilles, Macbeth, and Othello so interesting, but the strong sense and energy of mind that beams through it?" Man is likened to landscape as Knight contrasts the tameness of Addison's Cato with the vigor of Homer's Achilles:

The one is like a yew in a garden, which has been pruned and shorn into a determinate and regular shape, that it may fit its place, and not overshadow or injure the more tender plants, that grow near it: but the other is like an oak in the forest, which spreads its branches widely and irregularly, in every direction, over the smaller trees that surround it; and while it protects some, blights others.[23]

The energies of mind of the spectator are engaged—even infected with contagion—by the energies expressed in the visible object. We move away from the stress upon pictorial composition to the experience of complexity in particular objects. The recourse to the criterion of the painter's composition becomes, in the end, an appeal to art against art—or, more precisely, an appeal to unlimited complexity against limited canons of beauty. Once the standard of complex composition has done its work and fades away, the standard becomes affective or expressive. This is the tendency in all criticism of existing formal categories; in order to break out of them, one must reassert and free the energies that they contain. "The cistern contains; the fountain overflows," as Blake puts it. At its most extreme such criticism replaces categories of form by a measure of intensity. The picturesque scene promotes a certain intensity of awareness, and that intensity finally is given new grounds that are primarily moral. We can see this process at work in each of the central categories of the picturesque: texture and color, character as opposed to beauty, the artistry of time and accident.

The picturesque in general recommends the rough or rugged, the crumbling form, the complex or difficult harmony. It seeks a tension between the disorderly or irrelevant and the perfected form. Its favorite scenes are those in which form emerges only with study or is at the point of dissolution. It turns to the sketch, which precedes formal perfection, and the ruin, which succeeds it. Where it concentrates upon a particular object, the aesthetic interest lies in the emergence of formal interest from an unlikely source (the hovel, the gypsy, the ass) or in the internal conflict between the centrifugal forces of dissolution and the centripetal pull of form (ruined temples, aged men). Clearly this is a dramatic emphasis. The center of attention is displaced from the work of art as we traditionally conceive it to the larger sphere in which it plays its role, and the drama is readily cast into the form of the energies of art wrestling with resistant materials or the alternative form of the genius of nature or time overcoming the upstart achievements of a fragile but self-assertive art. The drama of the picturesque achieves neither the full tragedy of the sublime nor the serene comedy of the beautiful. Price likens its effect to that of the mixed genre, such as tragicomedy: "by its variety, its intricacy, its partial concealments, it excites that active curiosity which gives play to the mind, loosening those iron bonds, with which astonishment chains up its faculties." So, when Reynolds rejects the tyranny of the "rigid forms" of tragedy in his defense of tragicomedy, he argues: "Man is both a consistent and an inconsistent being, a lover of art when it imitates nature and of nature when it imitates art, of uniformity and of variety, a creature of habit that loves novelty. The principles of art must conform to this capricious being."[24]

When Uvedale Price compares Michelangelo and Vanbrugh, he makes a related point about the artist: "Where an artist of genius has any point strongly in view, and pursues it with enthusiasm, he will generally go beyond the mark: what he does produce, however, will not have that worst of faults, insipidity." He goes on to recognize that Michelangelo's excesses are corrected by Raphael, but "even then, though the style would be purer, and altogether more excellent, it might lose something of original character; and of that, perhaps, inseparable mixture of excellencies and blemishes, which sometimes appear to belong to each other, and to strengthen the general effect."[25] Here Price is praising for their expressive or dramatic power what a formal language can only call blemishes, and in fact the very statement of their power is defined by their violation of categories of beauty. For the work becomes a drama more than a composition, and our response is to the presentation of character rather than to the internal coherence of the object.

We can see the same problems raised in a recent discussion of Michelangelo's Rondanini Pietà by Henry Moore:

Why should I . . . find this work one of the most moving and greatest works we know of when it's a work which has such disunity in it? There's a fragment—the arm—of the sculpture in a previous stage still left there; here are the legs finished as they were perhaps 10 years previously, but the top recarved so that the hand of the Madonna on the chest of Christ is only a paper-thin ribbon.

But that's so moving, so touching; the position of the heads, the whole tenderness of the top part of the sculpture, is in my opinion more what it is by being in contrast with the rather finished, tough, leathery, typical Michelangelo legs. The top part is Gothic and the lower part is sort of Renaissance. So it's a work of art that for me means more because it doesn't fit in with all the theories of critics and estheticians who say that one of the great things about a work of art must be its unity of style. . . . I think [Michelangelo] came to know that, in a work of art, the expression of the spirit of the person—the expression of the artist's outlook on life—is what matters more than a finished or a beautiful or a perfect work of art.

I'm sure that had he taken away the nearly detached arm we should find it less moving because that part is near the new part. And undoubtedly, in my opinion, had he recarved the legs to have the same quality as the top, the whole work would have lost its point. This contrast, this disunity of style, brings together two of the Ages of Man, as it were.[26]

It is not hard to see here what we can see in the picturesque: a conception of structure based upon the overthrow of limited ideas of unity. When the picturesque theorist finds in a ruin the interplay of natural forces and human art, the softening and variegating work of time upon the rigid form, he is conceiving a new kind of unity, like Moore's emphasis on the two Ages of Man as the embracing conception of Michelangelo's statue. We can see this new kind of unity most clearly in the typical picturesque preference for a house designed to be seen amid trees and in a given landscape, to the house rising from a landscape artificially carved away to present its architecture boldly.

Geoffrey Scott argues eloquently against the picturesque view. "In Piranesi, the greatest master of the picturesque in art, Nature holds architecture in its clasp, and, like the 'marble-rooted fig tree,' shatters and tortures it in its embrace." For Scott, the baroque style "intellectualised the picturesque" by subduing its movement to the logicality of architectural law; it imposed a "broad serenity" upon the excitement of the picturesque and gave to its vitality a "massive finality of thought." He speaks of what I have called the picturesque moment at the close of the eighteenth century: "For a single moment, while the past still imposed the habit upon thought, disaster was arrested. The cult of Nature was a convention like the rest, and sought a place within the scheme. But the next step was the suicide of taste. Taken in isolation, made hostile to the formal instincts of the mind, Nature led, and can only lead, to chaos. . . ." Scott sees this chaos as man's abdication of his own law for Nature's, a rejection of "the typical law and specific character of humanity, to impose order and rhythm on our loose, instinctive movements and proportion on our works. . . ."[27]

One may compare Scott with Knight, both seeking a balance of mind and vitality, Knight haunted by a topiary Cato, Scott by a chaotic Nature. Scott celebrates the need for control and order, Price and Knight the need to give oneself over to a process that eludes our conceptions of order, or to imitate its very elusiveness

in our own designs. Clearly, Price and Knight espouse a humanism
that finds order and rhythm inherent in our loose, instinctive
movements. In the same way, Sterne finds an artistry in the spontaneous gestures of his characters—an artistry he can define only by
likening their stance to Raphael's figures or their gestures to
Hogarth's line of beauty. One might say that Scott favors nature-
in-art, the picturesque art-in-nature. There arises the question of
primacy. Is the ordering power of mind the only source of serenity
and dignity, or is this power to be seen as a temporary and limited
adaptation of a larger order of which it is at most a part? And one
can hardly help seeing the relation of mind to nature as comparable
to the relation of mind to the whole sentient human organism. If
we see the full capacities of the human reflected in the range of
nature, the claims of humanism may well demand a more intimate
union of art and nature—not caught within the structures of art
but subsisting around them, embracing the house rather than embraced within it.

If one sees the picturesque unity as a counterpart of those curious
and playful fusions of mind and body in Sterne's expressive
gestures, one is kept aware of the somewhat detached curiosity that
explores this interpenetration of art and nature. As one moves
progressively into seeing these loose, instinctive movements as the
dramatic expression of deep and invisible energies within the
character, the way is open to the sublime and to a religious regard
for the sanctity of these depths and secret places or a moral regard,
like Ruskin's, for the piety with which they are apprehended. Because the depths are secret and invisible, the sublime tends toward
the dissolution of limits and the evocation of the infinite. The
picturesque remains firmly within the sphere of the visible, but its
very concentration upon it and dissociation of it from conventional
associations prepares the way for seeing it as an element of a new
dramatic unity, a moment in a process of change. Coleridge's
definitions are of some value here:

> Where the parts by their harmony produce an effect of a whole, but
> where there is no seen form of a whole producing or explaining the
> parts of it, where the parts only are seen and distinguished, but the
> whole is felt—the picturesque.
> Where neither whole nor parts, but unity as boundless or endless
> allness—the sublime.[28]

The movement from texture—the shaggy coats of asses, the varied outlines of Gothic architecture, the mellow tints of time-worn stone—to the physiognomy of people is a clear one. We can see an intermediate stage in Gilpin's observations on the eyebrow of a lion:

It is true, the eye-brow of the lion has not that precision, which we find in the human countenance. It consists of a great muscular fullness, assisted by a small annular turn of the hair. In this grand muscle resides that power of contraction, which we shall see, when we speak of *expression,* greatly contributes to cloath his head with terrour. Here, in a *quiescent state,* is placed that thoughtful severity, which is so characteristic in him. This may arise in part from his brows being horizontal; which is perhaps peculiar to the human race, and that tribe, of which the lion is the principal.[29]

Here again one can see the close study of physical processes moving toward their possibilities as expressive instruments.

In treating the human face, Gilpin finds the picturesque in its "force of expression," in "that energetic meaning, so far beyond the rosy hue, or even the bewitching smile of youth." In Rubens' *Jesus at the House of Simon the Pharisee* (now in Leningrad) he describes the passion of the Magdalen: "A penitential sorrow, beyond the sense of anything but it's own unworthyness, has taken possession of her. Her eyes are finely coloured with high-swoln grief." As Gilpin explains, the history painter has not access to the play of scale that landscape uses to achieve the sublime; he has "only the same dimensions for his hero, & his clown. A man will not admit of plus & minus, like a mountain." The chief source of the sublime in history painting, therefore, is "energy of character & expression," which contributes in intensity what is lost in scale.[30]

Gilpin is not much interested in the treatment of commonplace humans. His wild landscapes require banditti; neither people of elegance nor "peasants *engaged in their several professions.*" These scenes require men doing "for what in real life they are despised—loitering idly about, without employment." Even more than this, however, Gilpin dislikes "all *vulgarity* of form—modern dresses—modern utensils—any thing, that occurs commonly to the eye. I consider painting as a kind of poetry, which excludes all vulgarisms." Nothing, he writes to his friend, Mary Hartley, can reconcile him to a cottage in a painting: "Some people have a taste prepared either for the grandeur of Homer, or the elegance of a sonnet. I am enraptured only with the Homerian style of painting."[31]

After considering the pure picturesque in a scene of gypsies in a hovel, Price goes on to the admixture of the beautiful and the picturesque in the view of a clergyman's daughter in a parsonage. A naïve speaker records his impressions:

There is a sort of resemblance between the good old parson's daughter and his house; her features have a little of the same irregularity, and her eyes are somewhat inclined to look across each other, like the roofs of the old parsonage: yet a clear skin, clean white teeth, though not very even, and a look of neatness and chearfulness, in spite of these irregularities, made me look at her with pleasure. . . .

To this Price's spokesman adds: "Here is a house, and a woman, without any pretensions to beauty; and yet many might prefer them both, to such as had infinitely more of what they, and the world, would acknowledge to be regularly beautiful. . . ."[32]

The mixture of the picturesque with either the beautiful or the sublime gives the human figure its appeal—without some elements of beauty the parson's daughter would not attract—but it gives that appeal to figures who might, in a language that did not admit the term "picturesque," be dismissed as ugly. Price reserves the term "ugly" for mere deprivation of form and tries to give proper credit to irregularity. The "merely picturesque" gypsies and beggars make little direct appeal to sympathy; as picturesque objects they "bear a close analogy to the wild forester and the worn out cart-horse, and again to old mills, hovels, and other inanimate objects of the same kind." But characters of dignity—that is, with moral import—"such as a Belisarius, or a Marius in age and exile, have the same mixture of picturesqueness and of decayed grandeur, as the venerable remains of the magnificence of past ages." From Price's celebration of character at the expense of beauty, it is no long step to Knight's assertion that in poetry "there can be nothing pathetic, unless it be, at the same time, in some degree, sublime."[33]

With the full growth of romanticism, this sublimity need not be made explicit in the individual, for it inheres in humanity and in each individual as a child in that large family. George Eliot, in her famous seventeenth chapter of *Adam Bede* turns, as she says, "without shrinking, from cloud-borne angels, from prophets, sibyls, and heroic warriors, to an old woman bending over her flower-pot" or to a village wedding "where an awkward bridegroom opens the dance with a high-shouldered, broad-faced bride, while elderly and middle-aged friends look on, with very irregular noses and lips . . . but with an expression of unmistakeable contentment and goodwill." Most people are, in fact, ugly. "Yet there is a great deal of family love among us. . . . Yes! thank God; human feeling is like the mighty rivers that bless the earth; it does not wait for beauty— it flows with resistless force and brings beauty with it." The sublimity emerges in the account of human feeling, and in its capacity to create beauty through love.

The tenor of the passage, with its reference to Dutch painting, is an attack upon the traditional canons of both the beautiful and the picturesque. "In this world there are so many of these common coarse people, who have no picturesque sentimental wretchedness! . . . Neither are picturesque lazzaroni or romantic criminals half so frequent as your common labourer, who gets his own bread, and eats it vulgarly but creditably with his own pocket-knife." In fact, the picturesque George Eliot attacks is the surface-picturesque that Ruskin derides; her delight in Dutch painting is anticipated by Price. "The pleasure which we receive from beauty and grandeur of character, is more refined and exalted," he writes; "still however there is a peculiar relish, which arises from many rude, and even mean but strongly marked picturesque circumstances." Terms like "relish" and qualifications like "strongly marked" represent the tone of the picturesque moment. George Eliot effects a dramatic transference of sublimity to the low and ugly:

Paint us an angel, if you can, with a floating violet robe, and a face paled by the celestial light; paint us yet oftener a Madonna, turning her mild face upward and opening her arms to welcome the divine glory; but do not impose on us any aesthetic rules which shall banish from the region of Art those old women scraping carrots with their work-worn hands, those heavy clowns taking holiday in a dingy pot-house, those rounded backs and stupid weather-beaten faces that have bent over the spade and done the rough work of the world. . . .

Because the sentiment of humanity is so deep and expansive, the need for the "strongly marked" gives way to the emphatic insistence on the commonplace. We move from the picturesque stress upon character as the alternative to formal beauty, and here George Eliot places her stress upon all surfaces that can show "how kindly the light of heaven falls on them."

George Eliot's example of the village wedding recalls the picturesque interest in the complex harmony of groups: villages, crowds, markets and fairs, women washing their clothes at a stream. For Price the design and improvement of villages can exercise at once the taste and humanity of the wealthy landlord. "Whoever has looked with delight at Gainsborough's representations of cottages and their inhabitants; at Greuze's interesting pictures; at the various groups and effects in those of the Dutch masters, will certainly feel from that recollection, an additional delight in viewing similar objects and characters in nature. . . ." Price's discussion of villages is minute and interesting: he dwells on the shapes of chimneys, climbing plants and their supports, the treatment of wall surfaces, the alignment of houses. But one can see the feeling for a shared life, a family of people, that runs through so many genre pictures of the age. Here is Price on the village church and churchyard:

to the old and serious, as a spot consecrated to the purposes of religion, where the living Christian performs his devotions, and where, after death his body is deposited near those of his ancestors, and departed friends and relations: to the young and thoughtless, as a place, where, on the day of rest from labour, they meet each other in their holyday clothes; and also (what forms a singular contrast with tombs and gravestones) as the place which at their wakes, is the chief scene of their gayety and rural sports.[34]

The village wedding and the village church are both compositions of variegated details—they move toward the anecdotal as details pull apart and become occasions for inference. "I can imagine," writes Diderot of a Greuze scene, "from the book lying on the table before the eldest daughter that it was her sad task to read the prayers of the dying, while the phial by the book probably contained a cordial." Or details function like Sterne's gestures: "Look at your two comrades quarrelling, see how it is the very quarrel that establishes the position of their limbs, all unknown to them."[35] But the pulling apart need not preclude a governing structure. Greuze, we are told by Walter Friedländer, "constructed his large compositions . . . in a classicistic, Poussinist way, with additive planes and a curtain closing off the background; only the virile conviction is lacking."[36] We are close again to the claim of moral weight and possible sublimity, conveyed through the high structural forms that these humble and varied details are used to fill.

The typical picturesque object or scene—the aged man, the old house, the road with cart-wheel tracks, the irregular village—carries within it the principle of change. All of them imply the passage of time and the slow working of its change upon them. A face in which one reads experience of suffering and endurance is seen in a moment that is earned by the long processes that have gone into its creation; it is a moment of dramatic resolution, in which we see some counterpoise of the enduring substance and the accidents of time.

The playfulness of the picturesque served to bring to the fore its concern with the arbitrary and accidental; the art of the picturesque becomes a readiness to learn from and exploit accident. Ancient castles, Price observes, probably owe their picturesqueness "to their having been built at different times, just as occasion required; for by those means . . . a number of common houses become picturesque, the separate parts of which have nothing of that character. Why are they so? Because they are built of various heights, in various directions, and because those variations are sudden and irregular." The task of the architect is to achieve by means of his art effects that are comparable. It is "hardly possible to imitate those circumstances of long established habitation" in new design, and Price does not lend himself to the faking of age. His interest is in achieving the aesthetic complexity that comes of that half-accidental, half-deliberate collocation of parts we see in the castle or the village. He is not surrendering to mere chance, or inviting mere decay; he is simply pointing to their instructiveness. The free play of natural processes will not make a building "beautiful as a building," but it will produce "an object of a mixed character with many qualities of beauty." Where classical buildings have become picturesque through ruin, "the character of beauty still lingers about their forms and their ornaments, however disfigured." As time and decay remove the polish of columns, the fine detail of capitals and mouldings, they produce "the embellishments of ruins . . . incrustations and weather stains, and . . . various plants that spring from, or climb over the walls."[37]

The point to be noticed is that Price does not luxuriate in sentimental associations; he is well aware of associated ideas, but he is primarily concerned with the art of perceiving and creating visual effects. These inevitably will evoke associations, but they may be associations of high generality—the security achieved by a peculiar kind of massiveness; the freedom of a sudden expansion of space and heightened illumination; the sense of power in the bold decorative use of the constructive process, in exposed supports or the scars of concrete moulds. In a remarkable essay, Sir John Summerson has treated the need for ugliness in the work of William Butterfield. "How can we see what Butterfield saw in a brand-new, stubbily moulded Early English shaft and capital? To us its hardness and coarseness are dull. To him its hardness and coarseness were a deeply sincere protest against whatever was wiry, soft, and genteel."[38] So, too, with the picturesque. To Geoffrey Scott it represented an abdication of humanistic assertion and the denial of architecture, as well it might in 1914. To us, fifty years later, there seems renewed value in the surprise and variety that the picturesque sought to abstract from the ruinous work of time, the accidents of weather and patchwork repair, or from the clasp of Nature that Scott deplores.

But this recovery of formal values yields to the inrush of other meanings as well. Ruskin's noble passage on Calais church stresses the "large neglect, the noble unsightliness of it; the record of its years written so visibly, yet without sign of weakness or decay." Like George Eliot, Ruskin confers upon it a compelling moral significance:

its carelessness of what any one thinks or feels about it, putting forth no claim, having no beauty nor desirableness, pride, nor grace; yet neither asking for pity; not, as ruins are, useless and piteous, feebly or fondly garrulous of better days; but useful still, going through its own daily work,—as some old fisherman beaten grey by storm, yet drawing his daily nets. . . .[39]

Ruskin's emphasis upon endurance becomes a sublime conquest of time, and we can see this movement through vistas of time and change to a sense of timelessness in a passage by Ruskin's admirer and translator, Marcel Proust. Proust has beautifully rendered the Ruskinian "golden stain of time" as a transcendence of time. Memorials dissolve and reform into organic growth, and the church itself becomes a receptacle of the changes of time and still—by its very transmutations—a work of art that conquers time:

The angles of the ancient porch, pitted like a skimmer, were smoothed away and hollowed . . . as though the gentle brushing of generations of countrywomen entering and dipping their fingers had, through the centuries, acquired a power of destruction and had carved in the long-suffering flint furrows like those made by wagons on a milestone against which they daily bump. The very tombstones that covered the dust of learned abbots buried there made a sort of spiritual pavement for the choir. But they had long since lost the quality of hard and inert matter, for time had softened them in such a way that they had run like honey, overflowing with their golden sweetness the limits of their squared and proper forms, here drawing out at random a flowered Gothic capital letter, there compressing an abbreviated Latin inscription, introducing an additional caprice into the arrangement of the shortened wording, crowding the letters of a sentence of which the rest were stretched immoderately. . . .

All these ancient things combined to make the church, for me, into something that was entirely different from the rest of the village, a building, if I may so put it, occupying a four-dimensional space—the fourth dimension being that of time; into a great ship sailing across the centuries and seeming, from span to span, from chapel to chapel, to have conquered and overleaped not only a few yards of ground, but successive epochs above which it towered victorious. . . .[40]

IV

The movement I have tried to chart from the picturesque to the sublime, from the aesthetic to the moral or metaphysical, has its pivot in Wordsworth. One can see in the Leech Gatherer of "Resolution and Independence" an instance of a picturesque old man turned into Ruskin's Calais church—even the image of a cloud turned into a stability that is the very negation of its conventional meaning: "That heareth not the loud winds when they call;/And moveth all together, if it move at all." The poem plays the rock-like immobility of the old man against the remoteness and seem-

ing insubstantiality of a transcendent order: "Like one whom I
had met with in a dream:/Or like a man from some far region
sent. . . ." The particularity remains stubborn and clumsy—"gathering leeches, far and wide"—and yet the poem has stripped all picturesqueness away. "Sublimity," Wordsworth wrote in his *Guide,*
"is the result of Nature's first great dealings with the superficies of
the earth"; and, while he calls her subsequent operations works of
beauty, he describes them in highly picturesque terms: "masses of
rock . . . lie in some places like stranded ships, or have acquired the
compact structure of jutting piers; or project in little peninsulas
created in native wood."[41] In the Leech Gatherer we feel the "first
great dealings" and no elaborations that tease our fancy or induce
play of mind.

The twelfth book of the *Prelude* is Wordsworth's principal discussion of the picturesque. The condition Wordsworth describes
in himself is a loss of "natural graciousness of mind" (50), a distrust
of heroism and human dignity, a divorce from any sense of the
continuity of past and present, a rejection of all "mysteries of
being" that are the source of communion among men. Wordsworth
commits himself to reason and to the senses, judging with detachment by "rules of mimic art transferred/To things above all art"
(111–12). Wordsworth's aestheticism is an aspect of his rationalism;
both are instinct with pride, and we feel that this is nothing less
than Wordsworth's hell. It is interesting to compare his words on
a visit to Uvedale Price from a letter of 1811:

A man by little and little becomes so delicate and fastidious with respect to forms in scenery, where he has a power to exercise a controul
over them, that if they do not exactly please him in all moods, and
every point of view, his power becomes his law; he banishes one, and
then rids himself of another, impoverishing and *monotonizing* Landscapes, which, if not originally distinguished by the bounty of Nature,
must be ill able to spare the inspiriting varieties which Art, and the
occupations and wants of life in a country left more to itself never
fail to produce. This relish of humanity Foxley wants, and is therefore
to me, in spite of all its recommendations, a melancholy spot—I mean
that part of it which the owner keeps to himself, and has taken so
much pains with. . . .[42]

It seems to be the leveling of resistances and otherness that Wordsworth resents in Price's estate; all has become too tediously the

image of the planner's mind. It is a comparable imposition of a conscious, judging mind that Wordsworth contemplates in himself. He neglects the Soul of Nature in both its order of law and its plenitude of "impassioned life." And from this descent he returns through the example of his sister: "She welcomed what was given, and craved no more" (158).

It is from this concern with the surface-picturesque that Wordsworth moves to the great passage on "spots of time," those moments of transcendence when the outward senses give way to the Powers which lie in the depths of man's spirit, when the visual beauties dissolve into sublime mystery. This movement beyond the visual is a movement downward into the "depth of things" and the depth of self; in fact, into that depth where they seem to have become one. This movement is of such enormous importance in Wordsworth because of the very intensity of visual experience. We know that Wordsworth owned and read some of Gilpin and later read both Price and Knight, and it is clear that he could fall back into picturesque idiom in his later years. Yet from the very first he is a poet of the sublime, and from the very early years he is at work on the conversion of what might have been picturesque to sublime. "I had once given to these sketches the title of Picturesque," he wrote in a note to *Descriptive Sketches,* "but the Alps are insulted in applying to them that term." It is impossible, he goes on to say, "to describe their sublime features" according to "the cold rules of painting." Ironically, this was written just as Price and Knight were preparing to publish their first works on the picturesque. For Wordsworth the picturesque moment had already passed.

NOTES

1. The individual systems of thought are carefully distinguished in Walter J. Hipple, Jr., *The Beautiful, the Sublime, and the Picturesque in Eighteenth-Century British Aesthetic Theory,* Carbondale, Illinois, 1957. The best treatment of the sensibility is Christopher Hussey, *The Picturesque: Studies in a Point of View,* London and New York, 1927. Important discussions appear in Elizabeth Wheeler Manwaring, *Italian Landscape in Eighteenth Century England,* New York, 1925, and in Samuel H. Monk, *The Sublime: A Study of Critical Theories in XVIII-Century England,* New York, 1935; Ann Arbor, Michigan, 1960. This essay builds upon my earlier discussion in *To the Palace of Wisdom: Studies in Order and Energy from Dryden to Blake,* Garden City, N. Y., 1964.

2. Hussey, p. 4.

3. Nikolaus Pevsner, *The Englishness of English Art,* London, 1956, pp. 163–80; Gordon Cullen, *Townscape,* London, 1961. On the picturesque in architecture see Henry-Russell Hitchcock, *Architecture: Nineteenth and Twentieth Centuries* (Pelican History of Art), Baltimore, Md., 1958, pp. 93–114, and C. L. V. Meeks, "Picturesque Eclecticism," *Art Bulletin* 32 (1950) 226–35. For a more general discussion, whose emphasis I cannot accept, see Wylie Sypher, *Rococo to Cubism in Art and Literature,* New York, 1960, pp. 48–109.

4. On architectural allusions in Yale buildings, see Jonathan Barnett, "Yale: A Continuous Stream of Architecture," *Yale Alumni Magazine* 27 (1963–64) 16–32.

5. *Modern Painters* IV, Part V, Chapter I ("Of the Turnerian Picturesque"), para. 11.

6. *Modern Painters* IV, Part V, Chapter I, para. 12. One may compare the absorption of Mrs. Ramsay, in Virginia Woolf's *To the Lighthouse,* into a patch of color which fills a corner of Lily Briscoe's painting. One might see a parallel between the aestheticism of the surface-picturesque and that of Roger Fry's and Clive Bell's doctrine of significant form. Fry is said to have referred to a figure of God the Father in some painting as "this very important mass" (F. E. Sparshott, *The Structure of Aesthetics,* Toronto and London, 1963, p. 328).

7. *Modern Painters* IV, Part V, Chapter I, para. 13, 1, 8.

8. *Pride and Prejudice,* Chapter 10; *Northanger Abbey,* Chapter 14; *Sense and Sensibility,* Chapter 33; *Mansfield Park,* Chapter 22. For Donwell Abbey, *Emma,* Chapter 42; for Pemberley, *Pride and Prejudice,* Chapter 43. The picturesque cottage receives Jane Austen's attention, also. In *Sense and Sensibility* (Chapter 6) Barton Cottage tellingly lacks the irregularities of the picturesque ("as a cottage it was defective"), but in *Persuasion* (Chapter 5) we find "a farmhouse, elevated into a cottage" at Uppercross. I have passed over the familiar and frequently cited defense of the picturesque by Marianne Dashwood, and the reply of Edward Ferrars, in *Sense and Sensibility.*

9. *The Prelude* (1850), XII, 188–90.

10. *A Guide through the District of the Lakes* (Fifth Edition, 1835), reprinted with introduction by W. M. Merchant, London, 1951, p. 72; this passage first appeared in the fourth edition of 1823. Cf. *Wordsworth's Guide to the Lakes,* ed. Ernest de Selincourt, London, 1926, p. 38 and note. De Selincourt reprints the two letters on the Kendal and Windermere Railway; this passage appears on pp. 150–51.

11. Emil Kaufmann, *Architecture in the Age of Reason,* Cambridge, Mass., 1955, pp. 3–15.

12. Uvedale Price, *Essays on the Picturesque,* London, 1810 (this reprints in three volumes the original work of 1794 and subsequent additions); I, 288, 291, 375.

13. Dorothy Stroud, *Capability Brown*, London, 1950, with introduction by Christopher Hussey, p. 17. Derek Clifford, *A History of Garden Design*, London, 1962, p. 159.

14. Price, *Essays*, II, 159, 133, 22, 25–6.

15. See Northrop Frye, "New Directions from Old," in *Fables of Identity: Studies in Poetic Mythology*, New York, 1963, pp. 52–66.

16. Pevsner, *Englishness of English Art*, p. 56.

17. *Dissertation on Oriental Gardening*, London, 1772; cited and discussed by Arthur O. Lovejoy in "The Chinese Origin of a Romanticism," *Essays in the History of Ideas*, Baltimore, 1948, p. 128.

18. Carl Paul Barbier, *William Gilpin: His Drawings, Teaching, and Theory of the Picturesque*, Oxford, 1963, p. 110 (27 March 1742).

19. *Trivia; or, The Art of Walking the Streets of London*, 1716, II, 414–17.

20. *Observations, Relative Chiefly to Picturesque Beauty, Made in the Year 1772, on Several Parts of England; Particularly the Mountains, and Lakes of Cumberland, and Westmoreland*, London, 1786, I, 152.

21. Price, *Essays*, I, 341–2. The following quotation is from I, 344–5.

22. Price, *Essays*, II, 194. Richard Payne Knight, *An Analytical Inquiry into the Principles of Taste*, London, 1805, Part III, Chapter III, para. 40. Joseph Addison, *The Spectator*, No. 412, 23 June 1712.

23. Knight, *Analytical Inquiry*, Part III, Chapter I, para. 84, 85, 25.

24. Price, *Essays*, I, 89. For Reynolds, see *Portraits by Sir Joshua Reynolds*, ed. F. W. Hilles, New York, 1952, Appendix I.

25. Price, *Essays*, II, 223.

26. "The Genius of Michelangelo as Seen by Moore," an interview with David Sylvester, *New York Times Magazine*, 8 March 1964, pp. 17, 43. On the problems raised by Geoffrey Scott below, see another interview, "Henry Moore Talking," in *The Listener*, 29 August 1963, p. 307: "A painting has its frame . . . but a piece of sculpture is with the weather and with its surroundings. . . . The ideal setting for my sculpture is . . . in Scotland, near Dumfries, in a landscape which is, I should say, exactly as it was 30,000,000 years ago."

27. *The Architecture of Humanism: A Study in the History of Taste*, Garden City, N. Y., 1954, pp. 75, 74, 78, 69.

28. Cited by J. Shawcross, in his edition of *Biographia Literaria*, Oxford, 1907, II, 309.

29. Barbier, *William Gilpin*, pp. 36–7 (from a manuscript "On the character, & Expression of Animals," written late in Gilpin's life).

30. Gilpin, *Three Essays*, London, 1792, p. 12. On Rubens, see citation from *Eastern Tour* in Barbier, *William Gilpin*, p. 47. On the history painter, see letter of 4 December 1782, cited by Barbier, pp. 129–30, n. 5.

31. Barbier, *William Gilpin*, pp. 144 (cf. *Lake Tour*, II, 44), 145 (20 December 1791), 113 (13 October 1789).

32. Price, *Essays*, III, 291–2.

33. Price, *Essays*, I, 63. Knight, *Analytical Inquiry*, Part III, Chapter I, para. 41.

34. Price, *Essays*, II, 367, 359.

35. These passages from Diderot are given in Elizabeth G. Holt, *A Documentary History of Art*, Garden City, N. Y., 1958, II, 320 (*Salon* of 1765), 314 (*Essay on Painting*).

36. *David to Delacroix*, Cambridge, Mass., 1952, p. 10.

37. Price, *Essays*, II, 265–6, 345–6, 249–50, 259–60.

38. "William Butterfield; or, The Glory of Ugliness," in *Heavenly Mansions and Other Essays on Architecture*, London, 1949, p. 175.

39. *Modern Painters* IV, Part V, Chapter I, para. 2.

40. This passage was first published in *Le Figaro* on 3 September 1913 and reprinted in *Chroniques*, Paris, 1927. It appears in Gerard Hopkins's translation in Marcel Proust, *Pleasures and Days and Other Writings*, ed. F. W. Dupee, Garden City, N. Y., 1957, pp. 286–8.

41. *Guide*, p. 69 (cf. Merchant's introduction, p. 28) or De Selincourt's edition, p. 35.

42. *Letters of William and Dorothy Wordsworth: The Middle Years*, ed. E. de Selincourt, Oxford, 1937, II, 466 (To Sir George Beaumont, 28 August 1811). Cf. John R. Nabholtz, "Dorothy Wordsworth and the Picturesque," *Studies in Romanticism* 3 (1963–64) 118–28, where further studies on William Wordsworth and the picturesque are announced.

Blake and the Metrical Contract

JOHN HOLLANDER

IN recent years, the most illuminating studies of prosody have
been devoted to showing the relation of patterned sound and
semantic sense in particular poems. This concern with the music
of poetry, with the expressive function of rhythm, has centered
primarily on the analysis of how the poem's sound structure,
formed within the limits of a particular metrical scheme, amplifies
from moment to moment what is being said. This is an important
matter, of course, and for lyric poetry in particular; since the
fundamental separation between the lyric poem and the actual
text for music early in the seventeenth century, the expressive
rhythms of language have come to permit the lyric poem to sing
its own song.

But by and large, prosodists since Saintsbury have been less
concerned with another dimension along which the problems of
poetic meter may be viewed. This dimension I should call purely
conventional, or formal, rather than expressive, and its function
is rather like a definitive or axiomatic one for the whole literary
work. It involves the elements of convention which link a metrical
style or type to a whole poetic genre and, hence, a poet's choice of
meter to a larger intention. In an age of canonical metrical styles
like the Augustan period, the relation between meter and intention is very clear. In the nineteenth century it is less so, and in our
own day the *sine qua non* of originality has led to an almost obsessive concern, in American poetry in particular, with metrical
format.

As Northrop Frye has suggested,[1] the Age of Sensibility represents an interesting period of transition in the history of English

meter as well as in the history of the literary imagination. In very different ways and for very different reasons, Smart, Ossian, Chatterton and, finally Blake, all seem to threaten the very basis of English literary meter—the accentual-syllabic system that is normal from Chaucer through Tennyson—in outbursts of self-made song. This threat may be brought about as the result of the influence of the English Bible, as in the case of Ossian; or it may result from the completely graphic reality of Chatterton's fake dialect, a speech that his heart may have heard but his ears, never. In any event, the major Romantic poets' extremely sophisticated sense of literary history and of their own various relationships to the past gave them to understand that iambic verse, official though it may have been, was by no means necessarily the strained, cruel voice of an enemy. But this *rapprochement* had to be accomplished, I think, only after an expense of some awkwardness, and I think that the whole problem of metrical choice may be usefully reconsidered for a moment.

The stylistic choices (which I am calling *metrical,* rather than *rhythmic*)[2] occur at a different level of decision-making from those of the mysterious choices which must occur in actual composition. (This remains true, I think, even though the poet himself could not or would not differentiate between the types of choice.) The metrical choice provides a basic schematic fabric of contingencies governing the range of expressive effect. But it also establishes a kind of frame around the work as a whole. Like a title, it indicates how it is to be taken, what sort of thing the poem is supposed to be, and, perhaps, taken in historical context, what the poet thought he was doing by calling his curious bit of language a poem at all.

But there are some cases in English literary history where a poet does seem to acknowledge the importance of metrical choice. One with which we are probably all familiar is that of the prose apology prefaced to *Paradise Lost.* In it, Milton defends his choice of blank verse as a measure for the poem, and seems to allow his choice of meter to stand emblematically for the entire mode of language of his epic. He never touches upon his Latinate syntax, reinterpretation of the use and structure of epic simile and so forth, and only in the poem itself does he deal with his choice of subject or his myth of the poem's origins. The metrical mode is there, we are told, both a fabric and a frame for what will be worked within it.

Now we know that Milton, even more than most learned writers of the seventeenth century, was acutely aware of the classical notion of musical modality. Although unable to understand its empirical bases, Renaissance and later neoclassicism often took as a model notion of style this canonical correspondence in Greek music between each type of musical scale and its particular *ethos* or persuasive quality. One knew from Plato alone, who admitted to or excluded from his Just City certain scales because of their necessary effects upon a listener, that the Dorian scale was considered vigorous and manly, the Lydian, relaxing, the Phrygian, wild, etc.

The relation of a mode or scale to its particular *ethos* was held to be as fixed as that of a word to its meaning. Thinkers since the Renaissance have looked in vain for some necessary, unwavering connection between melodic contours and feelings generated by their perception; the association between musical mode and human mood remained one that was maintained by convention alone. The words of the poetic text to which the melody was sung, we must remember, gave to the melody's succession of intervals its duration and accent: the meter gave to the pitches half of what we would call its melodic quality. The meaning of the text, its form and poetic occasion seem to have been the decisive factors in maintaining the convention of *ethos*.[3]

There are good grounds for suspecting that Greek thinkers themselves believed that modality had its affective consequences for human behavior because of connections established by nature rather than by convention. In any event, successive ages would conclude, from their experience of classical theoretic and mythological writings only, that music and poetry in Antiquity had been mysteriously wed, and that subsequent literary history was a record of their divorce. Moreover, it was easy to move from the close connection of mode and mood in music to an analogical correspondence, longingly pursued by the Renaissance, of meter, diction, image, subject, presentation or performance style, and occasion. Certainly Alexandrian literature contained the modern notion of the literary occasion *per se* (rather than the public ones of theatre, ritual ceremony, games, formal inscription, etc.). And in any event, what had been for classical Greek poets canonical metrical uses became for Roman ones a matter of choice, a choice personal and in its own way expressive.

The very idea of literature is in some senses based upon an extension of this notion of modality. Even in Latin poetry, where we see the beginning of the dislocation of stylistic genre from its original context in Greek life, there emerges the phenomenon of metrical forms beginning to take on a life of their own, and something very like a kind of *ethos* developing for them. As early as Longinus, we see hexameters being praised as the proper meter for epic because of their stirring manly qualities, rather than the other way around.[4] A Roman poet will imitate a Greek metrical form, sometimes for an analogous type of poem and sometimes not; but in any case the form constitutes a kind of badge of literary authenticity. We are faced, quite early in the history of Western literature, with the problem of metrical genre and its relation to individual intention and the history of style in general.

Of the genres of Greek poetry, all clearly differentiated by form, occasion, musical accompaniment, and presentation style, as well as by content, only comedy, tragedy, epic and lyric have in any way been transmitted to successive cultural epochs. Distinctions among various types of solo and choral lyric, dithyrambic, iambic and elegiac poetry became blurred even in Latin poetry, and traditional forms began to be used for different purposes. The modern theories of genre propounded by literary historians tend, as René Wellek has observed, to treat literary types as something very like political or social institutions, preserving either form or content, but not both, throughout changing historical contexts.[5] Studies of genre may concentrate upon form or underlying strand of content; their classification may be modeled either on taxonomy or on embryology, or, as we might say, on either a synchronic or diachronic linguistic approach. Hobbes's famous tripartite distinction in his letter to Davenant divided the world of human affairs into three realms, court, city and country, and suggested that to each of these there corresponded tragedy and epic (courtly), comedy and satire (urban), and pastoral (rural);[6] this association is full of historical mistakes (about pastoral, for example) if taken as a genetic approach. But it seems to anticipate certain strains in modern criticism both by taking very seriously the concept of literary occasion and by establishing a kind of central mythic pattern within which genres may be said to have a kind of analogically general significance (as in the critical theory of Northrop Frye).

Meter has always remained a curiously strong indication or emblem of genre. Whether or not a seventeenth-century writer like Milton might choose to use the names of the Greek musical modes metaphorically to describe a general shift of poetic style (or even use the word "monody" in such an extended sense in the subtitle of "Lycidas"), he would certainly tend to think of the meter of a particular poem in a frame of previous ancient and modern use. And although the stylistic connotations of certain metrical schemes from the early sixteenth through the late eighteenth centuries in England may be seen, from a historical point of view, to have been rather grotesquely acquired, it nevertheless remains true that during that period, English poetry is written in a framework of canonical metrical style; innovation and individual invention tend usually to consist of a unique rhythmic style, using and interpreting the underlying formal fabric of the meter.

Milton's defense of his blank verse, against the expectation, for example, that he might, like Sylvester in his translation of Du Bartas, use couplets, is addressed then to those who might feel he was inventing the *use of* a meter, a subject and genre and occasion for a particular formal pattern so wrenched away from previous traditions of use that it might be said to be actually a new meter. But let us look for a moment at some particularly perceptive remarks on meter, also produced in the course of stylistic polemic, nearly 150 years after Milton. They represent at the same time an unusually clear understanding about just this question of genre being entailed by meter, and an eventual refusal to consider meter as being too important in itself.

"It is supposed that by the act of writing in verse an author makes a formal engagement that he will gratify certain known habits of association; that he not only thus apprises the reader that certain classes of ideas and expressions will be found in his book, but that others will be carefully excluded. This exponent or symbol held forth by metrical language must in different eras of literature have excited very different expectations: for example in the age of Catullus, Terence and Lucretius, and that of Statius or Claudian; and in our own country, in the Age of Shakespeare and Beaumont and Fletcher, and that of Donne and Cowley, or Dryden, or Pope. I will not take upon me to determine the exact import of the promise which, by the act of writing in verse, an author in the present day makes to his reader; but it will undoubtedly appear to many persons that I have not fulfilled the terms of an engagement thus voluntarily contracted."

This is Wordsworth, writing in the 1800 preface to *Lyrical Ballads*. In the 1802 appendix to the preface, he again says of the "unusual" language of poetry: "In process of time metre became a symbol or promise of this unusual language." Wordsworth's concern here, of course, is not with type or style of meter, just as he gives no indication of even a trivial neoclassical interest in poetic genre. His problem was to defend an attitude about poetic diction, and his discussion of poetic language comes down to that matter almost immediately. Still, the sense that a meter as distinguished from a prose format does represent a kind of contract, involving "certain known habits of association," is a keen and sure one. It is interesting to find a poet dealing with the question of meter from the point of view of a choice conditioned by variables of expectation on the part of an audience—a modern literary-historical concept, in short, of convention.

Insofar as the early Romantics considered the question of the effect of rhythm at all, it was a matter eliciting feeling or giving pleasure; here is Wordsworth again, from the 1800 preface: "Now the music of harmonious metrical language, the sense of difficulty overcome, and the blind association of pleasure which has been previously received from works of rhyme or meter of the same or similar construction, an indistinct perception perpetually renewed of language closely resembling that of real life, and yet, in the circumstance of meter, differing from it so widely—all these imperceptibles make up a complex feeling of delight, which is of the most important use in tempering the painful feeling always found intermingled with powerful descriptions of the deeper passions." "The sense of difficulty overcome," of course, is more that of the poet than of the reader, who in a sense shares the poet's feeling through sympathy if he has it at all. This is a theme which becomes more and more important in the informal metrical remarks of twentieth-century poets; we can see it in Frost's casual "Free verse is like playing tennis without a net," or in Valéry's famous prescription: "The exigencies of a strict prosody constitute the artifice which bestows upon natural speech the qualities of an unyielding material, foreign to our spirit, and almost deaf to our desires. If they were not a bit mad, and if they did not encourage our rebellion, they would be basically absurd."[7] Again, we can see a touch of this notion in Coleridge's remark on the origin of meter (although "origin" is used in an extremely peculiar sense): "This I would trace to the balance in the mind effected by that spontaneous effort which strives to hold in check the workings of passion. It might be easily explained likewise in what manner this salutary antagonism is assisted by the very state, which it counteracts; and how this balance of antagonists became organized into *metre* (in the usual acceptation of that term) by a supervening act of the will and judgement, consciously and for the foreseen purpose of pleasure."[8] But Coleridge, like Wordsworth, goes on to talk about poetic diction, which is far more important to his concerns at the moment.

Here, then, is the notion of the metrical contract. For Wordsworth it covers only the commitment engendered by writing verse rather than prose; but what I have been pointing out as the framing or defining function of a particular metrical choice extends the idea of the contract to cover the choice among various metrical possibilities. Wordsworth and Coleridge would dismiss meter as a criterion for the poetic character of an utterance. But unless we are judging or being polemical, I think we must take the fact of verse form as an indication that the writer feels he has written a poem—whatever he may mean by that—and expects it to be recognized as such.

This aspect of the metrical contract, the choice of a particular style, did not interest the Romantics very much. They attended to it at the pragmatic level, and their actual choices and inventions had far-reaching effects. Even so, Wordsworth, in the first of his remarks quoted, realizes that different historical epochs embody various accepted styles of meter, with various modal significances which serve as the unstated terms against which the contract is drawn. (I am ignoring for the moment Blake's marginalia on Wordsworth's remarks: "I do not know who wrote these Prefaces, they are very mischievous & direct contrary to Wordsworth's own practise.") The real difficulty here comes from the fact that every canonical style has evolved from some earlier one, and that the metrical forms take on new modal significances with each new use, and with different sorts of awareness of past ones. Perhaps the test of the canonical status of a metrical mode is the inability of anyone working within its range and age of power to see that it rules not by divine right but, as Milton's Satan said of God, by convention.

Metrical traditions in English have evolved, however. Aside from the metrical crises—Whitman, Hopkins, twentieth-century free verse—that underline dramatically the drawing up of a new contract, there remains the long history of the so-called iambic tradition itself. As opposed to these crises, the milder variations of metrical evolution occur within the boundaries of a particular system. Even the briefest sketch of the normative pattern of accentual-syllabic verse in English shows that, time and again, certain formal patterns within the system have become displaced from previous sorts of usage and adapted to new ones. In the centuries before Chaucer, English had replaced the pure accentualism of Germanic verse with the fairly regular tendency, in octosyllabic lines borrowed from the French romance, to alternate stressed and unstressed syllables; it was Chaucer's stroke of invention to see this system as capable of embracing an adaptation of the Italian *endecasillabo,* which, because of the invariable placement of a final /e/ at the end of the line, regularized itself into the pentameter line of English verse. Chaucer's adaptation, it must be remembered, was made not to preserve a form for its own, or for some symbolic sake, but in order to write in a genre that had previously existed only in other languages—Italian and French. The *Canterbury Tales* contain examples of many genres and types of medieval storytelling; most of them usually appeared in English in completely different metrical clothing from Chaucer's pentameter couplets (octosyllabics, for the most part). But his triumph of accomplishment depends in some part on his having seized upon one style for his overall voice in the poem: such a choice is always basic to the conception of literary, or, as C. S. Lewis calls it, *secondary* epic.

In the century after Chaucer, however, we begin to see instances of metrical evolution through utter formal dislocation, occasioned by an interest in practicing a particular form without regard to any of its significance as an emblem of literary type. The extremely complicated stanza-forms of the medieval drama in England, of the Wakefield cycle in particular, are derived from lyric poetry, where we expect in the later middle ages to see more complication and flexibility in stanza form than in narrative verse. Through the early Tudor morality play we see this use of a lyrical verse form for dramatic poetry continuing, and it is only odd when humanist drama, written with the eye glued to the Senecan and Plautine model, begins to enmesh actual popular theatrical conventions that the modern use of a unilinear form for poetic drama develops. Perhaps the modern sense of the peculiar rightness of such an association of unilinear forms with narrative and dramatic verse is the result of unavowed latent neoclassicism: it was only Greek lyric poetry, it will be remembered, which was strophic, while narrative and iambic dramatic verses were always arranged *kata kôlon,* or unilinearly.

There are many other examples of metrical evolution or transfer in the sixteenth through the eighteenth centuries in England. They vary in the degree to which the new or adapted use of the metrical pattern wishes to engage prior associations—and which associations in particular—generated by other uses. The history of blank verse in English is obviously a case in point: it moves from the early dramatists, through the later ones, to Milton, through the eighteenth-century speculative poem consciously connected with Milton's spirit, through *The Prelude* and eventually toward the later Romantic lyric. The crisis here occurs with Milton; and yet it is during the eighteenth century that all poetry save for the sung lyric begins to have to confront the growth of prose as an authentic vehicle of imaginative expression. For Milton, blank verse had the virtues of a canonical poetic cadence, but by the middle of the eighteenth century, it was important that it be more like prose in some ways than rhymed verse could ever be.

Then again, there is the case of the preservation of lyric stanza forms over the categorical change in genre from the Elizabethan to the Metaphysical lyric. The Elizabethan lyric poem is a song text *per se;* it may merely extend a popular or courtly convention, or it may, like the songs in Shakespeare's plays, play itself off against those conventions in order to perform the far more intense and exacting work of a kind of summarizing symbolist lyric, catching up and embodying the themes and movements of the whole play. But the Metaphysical lyric, starting with Donne, is not in any

essential way modeled on the song, but rather on the written text
for study. Emblem verses, patristic writings and other theological
disputation, natural philosophy, all lie behind Donne's *Songs
and Sonnets*, with the additional complication that each poem
generates its own immediate dramatic context. There is always a
particular erotic situation behind the rhetorical one of every poem,
and the relation behind the lyric ego and the "you" is quite complex. It is as if the stylized Petrarchan lover, the "I" of the sonnet
tradition, had suddenly acquired real knowledge instead of lore,
and real feelings in place of gesture. But Donne and his followers
invariably employ the variety of line and strophe forms used by the
Elizabethan lyric, wherein a density of formal texture is compensated for by an attenuation of semantic and iconographic complexity—they can be comprehended upon hearing, or rapid
reading, for the most part. The Metaphysical lyric is to be read and
studied and considered, and the overall formal shape of the poem is
often at ironic odds with the cognitive density of the thought and
language. But the effect of the maintenance of the song forms, of
the name "song" for poem, is the literary justification for the new
departure, and the justification is based, as it is so often, upon the
authority supplied by continuity itself.

The concept of "elegy" in English, insofar as it involves purely
metrical matters, is an interesting one too. The genre is metrically
defined by neoclassical poetry, and entails a longish poem in
couplets, often indistinguishable from the sort of poem called a
"satire" in the seventeenth century, as well as from the verse epistle
imitated also from the Latin poets. It is only toward the end of the
eighteenth century, when Gray's tranquilly recollected quatrains,
or Cowper's hippity-hop anapests in "The Poplar-Field" define for
romanticism and ever after the elegiac tone as a mood, rather than
as a formal mode:

> Twelve years have elaps'd since I first took a view
> Of my favorite field and the bank where they grew;
> And now in the grass behold they are laid,
> And the tree is my seat that once lent me a shade.

would have served, in the seventeenth century, as the proper meter
in which to frame a coyly erotic lyric; in the earlier eighteenth

century, they would have violated the voice of seriousness. But for Cowper, the form of these lines stands for the emotional authenticity of the personal. It is the meter alone which is significant here, by the way, for the parallelism of syntactic and rhetorical structure is firmly in the eighteenth-century tradition.

All of these instances, however, represent what I have called metrical evolution within the limits of a metrical system. The emblematic character of particular forms is employed to cover the shifts in literary milieu, in a kind of eternal struggle to maintain the condition of a poem as a Platonic entity: as if a poem were a poem always, by virtue of some quintessential character which different ages may merely call by different names. Metrical form (and we have, of course, been considering the larger variations in form, line lengths, stanza forms, rhyme patterns, etc.), then, acts to define a type of poem, even a poem itself, as well as to set up formal contingencies within which some linguistic event will become a poetic one, and something literary may be said to have happened.

What, then, of the metrical crisis, where the very conditions of the metrical system seem to be questioned? What looks to be a pathological form emerges, and it appears that the contract of meter has been broken. For example, there is an interesting aspect of Christopher Smart's *Jubilate Agno:* it ought properly never to have been an eighteenth-century poem at all. Written while its author, in his late thirties, was confined in a madhouse with the degenerative psychosis from which he never fully recovered, the poem consists of 32 foolscap sheets covered with 1735 long, unmeasured lines. Lost in Smart's lifetime, it seems to have ceased to exist in its own age and come to life only in the literary Bedlam of the twentieth century when the MS. was discovered and first edited in 1939. *Jubilate Agno* could really only be considered a poem in our time, for its methodical madness, prophetic bursts of energy, obsessive learning and almost symbolist associative coherence could only be read as a realized poem by an audience with the Romantics, Whitman, and Pound's *Cantos* behind it.

Smart's meter in the poem is aggressively Hebraic. Not only is it conditioned by the language of the English Bible, but by the cadences of the actual Hebrew which Smart knew. The verses are all self-contained and end-stopped, and a recent edition suggests that many of them may have been written antiphonally, in pairs. They all exhibit intralinear or line-to-line parallelism. The actual rhythm of these lines is exceedingly complicated and various, and to describe it would entail an involved analysis of syntax, classical and biblical references, interlingual puns and the like, as well as some consideration of the rhythmic effects of lists and catalogues, acrostic sections, balancing of symbolic allusion and autobiographical detail and other rhetorical devices. Representing a complete break with accentual-syllabism in English, Smart's meter had no immediate results. Had the poem been made public in its time, it would have been dismissed as lunatic ravings; by the time it was discovered, it could begin to be read with recognition.

Jubilate Agno, historically speaking, is an encapsulated event. For the modern notion of a personal meter that flows, like rhetoric, like personality, from the source of the self, we must turn to the specialized consequences of Romanticism in Whitman and Hopkins. In both cases, a new type of metrical contract is being drawn, in which the commitment is made not to convention, but to the poetic self. For both poets, the terms of the metrical contract become the bases of a whole aesthetic, but in radically different ways. Hopkins's constant allegorization of metrical terms like "stress" and his very clear historical commitment to what he feels are "inner" or underlying prosodic traditions—Old English, Celtic— are in one sense a far cry from the myth of organic form in Whitman. When Whitman says: "I and mine do not convince by arguments, similes, rhymes,/We convince by our presence," he is insisting that readers recognize his attempt to finesse all the framing, formal implications of meter which I have been discussing. In a prose passage,[9] he is even more explicit about his verse: "Its analogy is *the Ocean* . . . the liquid, billowy waves, ever rising and falling, perhaps wild with storm, always moving, always alike in their nature as rolling waves, but hardly any two exactly alike in size or measure, never having the sense of something finished and fixed, always suggesting something beyond." In our terms, it might be said that Whitman is claiming to have made a metrical principle out of the unique shapes of rhythm. The actual constituents of his metrical style are syntactic; his invariably end-stopped lines are connected by parallelisms, expansions of sentence matrices, types of catalogue and so forth, and the interactions of recognizable stress-pattern with these syntactic formulae are frequently reminiscent of the prophetic and lyric sections of the English Bible. But his claim nevertheless remains that expression takes on natural form from the self that releases it.

The study of metrical choice in the eclectic twentieth century must start from these two crucial breaks with tradition. But much of their avowed intention to allow an idiosyncratic meter almost to stand for an aesthetic manifesto is foreshadowed earlier, not by Smart's aesthetically unavowed poem, not by Milton's thundering choice of what had been a dramatic meter for his epic one, but by the very problematic metrical invention of William Blake.

Blake's metrical contract has deceived some of his most sympathetic readers. Swinburne, for example, spoke of "an exquisite and lyrical excellence of form, when the subject is well in keeping with the poet's tone of spirit" as characterizing the verse of both Blake and Whitman, and he is constantly treating Blake's long lines as if they were the undulant outpourings of the other poet. In short, he was able to take the meter of, for example, *Jerusalem* and consider it as an example of what I have been calling a crisis. But it surely represents within Blake's own development a carefully and even systematically evolved style. Even the barest outlines of this development reveal an astonishingly consistent attempt to evolve a whole metrical system to serve as an alternative to the normal one, emblematic of the profoundly systematic undertaking of the engraved canon of Blake's works.

In the *Poetical Sketches,* the move toward freer accentualism than one would find in, say, Collins, is perhaps even less significant than the atmosphere of real experimentation that prevails. There seems to be a conscious formal perversity to the Spenserian imitation, for example, in which every stanza is "defective" if taken from one point of view, or "adapted" if from another. There are startling enjambments that quite exceed some of Donne's in his *Satyrs.* In the closing strophe of "To Summer," he writes blank verse as perfectly end-stopped as that of the Elizabethan "drab" style, and in the conclusion of "To Winter," he will appear to employ not merely a different mode, but a different system. In any event, the two poems represent considerably different versions of

what iambic pentameter is to be. What emerges from this experimentation is, of course, a commitment to a traditional-sounding
accentualism. There are overtones of balladry in the freely accentual stanzas of the short poems from the manuscripts and from
the *Songs of Innocence and of Experience,* but this is inevitable in
such cases. Just as "free verse" in English so often turns out to be a
version of the English Bible (or, in the twentieth century, to be
modeled on line-for-line prose translations of the classics), loosely
handled rhymed quatrains will smack of popular poetry, particularly when there is a dactyllic flavor to them.

The pure fourteeners of "Holy Thursday" are rhymed and are
among the most syllabically regular of all the verses in *Songs of
Innocence.* These are probably Blake's first production[10] in a
meter which is to become profoundly important for him later on.
The unrhymed fourteeners of *The Book of Thel* and *Tiriel,* still
quite regular in their alternations of stressed and unstressed syllables, present no problems to the prosodist or to the critic. It is
only what Blake was to make of his inherited line that became
problematic.

The fourteener in English verse had been the meter of Chapman, Phaer, Golding, and Warner's *Albion's England.* Moreover,
fourteeners in couplets are merely an alternate way of notating
ballad-stanzas, and their use in broadsides, Leveller verses and
other popular and even sub-literary verse continued through
Blake's own day. For Blake to use the strict, unrhymed fourteener
as the basis for further expansion and modulation of a metrical
style is more than merely an unfettering of poetry by enlarging its
cell to the size of a long line. It seems to result from a positive attempt to create an anti-meter, as opposed to the norm of blank
verse. Just as the iambic pentameter had crowded out the late
Elizabethan experiments in seven-stressed lines, consigning them
to the sub-literary dungeon of doggerel, so Blake may have thought
to resurrect them and some of what they stood for. His attempts
to undermine metrical conventions are present everywhere in his
shorter poems. The last two lines of *The Garden of Love,* for example, break the expected conclusion of what begins like a sentimental song in quatrains, and thunder out in a little sub-quatrain
of their own, with the epigrammatic tension of the kind of inscrip-

tion or motto Blake uses elsewhere. "The Question Answered" is
an anti-epigram:

> What is it men in women do require?
> The lineaments of gratified desire.
> What is it women do in men require?
> The lineaments of gratified desire.

The whole Augustan tradition of the two-couplet epigram is under-
mined by the unyielding hammered insistence of the repeated line
and the ironic absence of wit. The reader is implicitly rebuked for
expecting a logical movement toward the discovery of a conclusion
—as if all epigrams were merely circular, just as logical proofs
produce only new tautologies—and the form plunges us into the
identity without remorse. It is not surprising, then, to find one of
Blake's most explicit anti-epigrams couched in a couplet of fourteeners: "Her whole Life is an Epigram, smart smooth & neatly
pen'd,/Platted quite neat to catch applause with a sliding noose at
the end." Epigrammatic tautology, for Blake, seems to be a kind of
death.

Blake's subversion of English meter proceeds through his modulation of the strict fourteener in the later long poems. In the
puzzling, longer, still early lines of "The French Revolution" an
accentual, seven-stressed core remains, the number of syllables
varying from fifteen to more than twenty-one or twenty-two within
a group of five or six lines. After this rather peculiar poem, Blake
evidently decided that his modulation of the septenarius lay not in
the direction of free-accentual expansion, and in the subsequent
longer poems we see him adapting the basic line in forms analogous
to those of normative meter. His stanza-forms in *Europe*, in Nights
2 and 5 of *Vala* and various staves of three, four, and five lines in
other poems, even the enigmatic short lines in *Ahania, Los* and
Urizen (where it has been suggested that the engraving called for
longer, thinner columns)[11] involve combinations and units of four
and three stresses—the relation of Blake's meters to traditional
iambic lines of varying length are like that of a duodecimal modulo
number system to a decimal one.

The rhythmic possibilities established by the fourteener are
interesting, for the tendency of the familiar ballad-rhythm to in-

trude on the ears of the reader allows for frequent syntactic juncture after the fourth stress. Blake's rhythmic derivations from
Ossian and from the English Bible, which have been so frequently
commented upon, often involve structural parallelism hung across
such a juncture—again, an underground substitute for the balance
and antithesis of Augustan verse. But Blake never completely sur-
renders to the Whitmanesque program of claiming that rhythm is
its own meter. At first glance, the metrical apology prefaced to
Jerusalem suggests this, in terms clearly implying an alternative to
the apology to *Paradise Lost:*

> Of the measure in which
> the following poem is written.

... When this Verse was first dictated to me, I consider'd a Monotonous
Cadence, like that used by Milton & Shakespeare & all writers of English Blank Verse, derived from the modern bondage of Rhyming, to be
a necessary and indispensible part of Verse. But I soon found that in
the mouth of a true Orator such monotony was not only awkward, but
as much a bondage as rhyme itself. I therefore have produced a variety
in every line, both of cadences & of number of syllables. Every word and
every letter is studied and put into its fit place; the terrific numbers
are reserved for the terrific parts, the mild & gentle for the mild &
gentle parts, and the prosaic for inferior parts; all are necessary to each
other. Poetry Fetter'd Fetters the Human Race. Nations are Destroy'd
or Flourish in proportion as Their Poetry, Painting and Music are
Destroy'd or Flourish! The Primeval State of Man was Wisdom, Art
and Science.

Blake is suggesting here a kind of traditional modality of meter,
albeit in the guise of a declaration of rhythmic independence. It
would be the expressive rhythms that would be fettered for him in
a "Monotonous Cadence." What he in fact does in *Jerusalem* is to
extend the loosening of the fourteener in several directions, from
regular to loose, from syllabic fourteeners with only five or six
major stresses to cluttered ones of eight. He frequently enjambs
lines in ways that he had only done previously in the blank verse
of the *Poetical Sketches,* allowing a mono- or disyllabic word at the
line-break to count for a strong stress, even though the principle
of his free accentualism throughout his work has been to let
speech stress, in its syntactic and rhetorical context, govern the
metrical role of syllables.

As for his rhythmic modes of mild, terrific and prosaic, it is obvious from the text that the key is provided not by the measure of syllable or stress, nor by some referential rhythmic pattern alone, but by the diction. In some ways, Blake's sense of meter here is closer to the concerns of Wordsworth than one might think. But throughout the poem, the fourteener is never far away, and the poem's meter is most like a transformed equivalent of the freest kind of blank verse. Were the norm to have been five stresses rather than seven, there would never have been as much puzzling about Blake's meter as there has been.

Blake's meter, then, results not from a nihilistic smashing of metrical conventions in order to free an oppressed rhythm (he is not Whitman), but rather to use metrical choices in the way that certain twentieth-century poets, historically self-conscious, have used them: to engage certain prior conventions and, rejecting others, to form a new tradition, discontinuous in some ways as it might be. His contract was, in a sense, with the Devil's party which, he felt, Milton finally betrayed, and his task to "bring out number, weight & measure in a year of dearth." Elusive as his intentions are, his metrical program avows the emblematic, framing, defining role of metrical format as consistently as does that of Whitman, Hopkins or some poets of our own day. And I think that it is this emblematic metrical function that must become increasingly important even in prosodic studies oriented toward the strictest formalism. Without it, any discussion of the prosody of twentieth-century verse will be severely impeded.

NOTES

1. Northrop Frye, "Toward Defining an Age of Sensibility," in *Fables of Identity* (New York, 1963), pp. 132–4.

2. I have discussed this at greater length in "The Metrical Emblem," *Kenyon Review* XXI (1959), pp. 279–96.

3. Also see my *The Untuning of the Sky* (Princeton, 1961), pp. 206–20.

4. Pseudo-Longinus, *On the Sublime*, xxxix, 4.

5. See Rene Wellek and Austin Warren, *Theory of Literature* (New York, 1949), pp. 235–47.

6. In *Critical Essays of the XVIIth Century,* ed. J. E. Spingarn (New York, 1908), I, 54–5.

7. Paul Valéry, "Au Sujet d'Adonis," in *Varieté* (Paris, 1924), p. 70 (my translation).

8. S. T. Coleridge, *Biographia Literaria,* Everyman Edition, p. 179.

9. See Horace Traubel, *With Walt Whitman in Camden* (Boston, 1906), I, 414.

10. It predates the version in *Songs of Innocence,* first appearing in *An Island in the Moon.*

11. George Saintsbury, *A History of English Prosody* (London, 1910), III, 26.

"The Wrath of the Lamb"
A Study of William Blake's Conversions

JEAN H. HAGSTRUM

BLAKE, who was not much given to symbolic diagrams, did create two that together express one of the deepest conflicts of his intellectual and artistic life. One [Plate I A], an imperfect circle flanked by two weeping angels in flames, bears the inscription: "Continually Building. Continually Destroying because of Love & Jealousy."[1] The pessimistic tone of this design is explained by a closely similar one [Plate I B]: the same imperfect circle, which is here surrounded by nude female bodies that rise upward, is labeled "This world."[2] Two of its four corners (the North and South) are designated "Reason" and "Desire"—a tragic division of human faculties that has been sufficiently commented on. But the Western and Eastern polarities, Pity and Wrath, constitute a division that is equally tragic and infinitely more personal. Of the divorce of Pity and Wrath, Blake said, "The separation was terrible"; he makes the Father of Lies himself the villain responsible for the disaster:

> And Satan not having the Science of Wrath, but only of Pity,
> Rent them asunder, and wrath was left to wrath, & pity to pity.[3]

That "terrible" division led to the perversion of each quality in Experience and produced the "Tyger of Wrath." Experience was preceded by the rule of the Lamb of Mercy in Innocence, and will be followed by the triumph of that Jesus who is both "the God *of Fire* and Lord *of Love*" and who will make humanity "wholly One."[4]

I

THE LAMB OF INNOCENCE

Blake created Innocence in "the Interest of True Religion and Science . . . as a Soldier of Christ."[5] For that magnificent achievement is not primarily an embodiment of a pre-lapsarian Eden available only as a far-off racial memory. Blake's Innocence is in every Western man's own personal history—in childhood, in nature, in the innumerable relations of simple faith—as child to parent, man to woman, teacher to pupil, nurse to ward, human being to angel. Innocence breathes through all of life the spirit of suspended wrath and rescuing mercy.

> When wolves and tygers howl for prey,
> They [angels] pitying stand and weep;
> Seeking to drive their thirst away,
> And keeping them from the sheep;
> But if they rush dreadful,
> The angels, most heedful,
> Receive each mild spirit,
> New worlds to inherit.[6]

"Heedful" angels preside over Innocence. They appear on the branches of borders, in the hearts of the flowers, and as the lovely wanderers of the night-time scene. They inspire the child on a cloud and the good firefly, who as the watchman of the night leads the wandering emmet home and who in the design is a man emerging from a tree-trunk carrying a staff and a lantern. Both word and design illustrate Blake's own dictum: "God is in the lowest effects as well as in the highest causes; . . . every thing on earth is the word of God & in its essence is God."[7]

The vital immanence of Innocence is neither romantic naturalism nor theological pantheism. It is incarnation, however simply or undogmatically conceived. Although God is everywhere, he is not identified with nature: "He became a little child"; ". . . creation is God descending"; "God becomes as we are. . . ."[8]

The God who is present in nature but separate from it is a man —or, more precisely, an individual being, sometimes a man, sometimes a woman, sometimes a child. In "The Little Black Boy" he appears specifically as Christ. On the flame-flower of "The Divine

I A.

I B.

II.

Image" he appears as Christ in the lower right, lifting a fallen man, and on the upper left he appears as a female deity descending from the sky. In the frontispiece the divine image is a child on a cloud. Individual, indestructible, identifiable human form is Blake's most fundamental postulate of both man and God, who were united in the "human form divine."[9] Back of the *Songs of Innocence* lay this belief: "Think of a white cloud as being holy, you cannot love it; but think of a holy man within the cloud, love springs up in your thoughts, for to think of holiness distinct from man is impossible to the affections. Thought alone can make monsters, but the affections cannot."[10]

Artistically embodied, the idea is subtle and beautiful. In "The Little Boy lost" a child weeps in the dark night as a vapor—a triangle of abstract light—leads him astray. In "The Little Boy found" the rescuing God of Innocence, who restores the child to his mother, appears in the text "like his father in white" but in the design like a haloed woman dressed in a flowing gown.[11]

Where may parallels in thought and art be found to illuminate Blake's unsentimental sensorium that vibrates with the individual and embodied life of the Divine Image, "Mercy, Pity, Peace, and Love"? Certainly not in Sterne and the sentimentalists, whose world is perfumed with either the heavy indoor scent of erotic play or the odor of dissenting sanctity. Certainly neither in the pre-Romantic poetry that Blake professed to admire—with its Art-obsessed imagery—nor in the Nature-obsessed visions of Romantic poetry, which deadened and obliterated Blake's imagination.

The seeds that flowered in Blake's Innocence were, with one possible exception,[12] not planted in English, eighteenth-century soil. They lay deep in the Bible, for Blake in one sense does exactly what the Gospel does; he bids us "Consider the lilies how they grow: they toil not, they spin not; and yet . . . Solomon in all his glory was not arrayed like one of these."[13]

But the Bible, that mighty Anthology, can seldom teach without a teacher, and Blake seems to have been led into it by three acknowledged masters of his mind and art, Paracelsus (1493–1541), Böhme (1575–1624), and Swedenborg (1688–1772).[14] Because it was one of the central preoccupations of each of these to read "the bright and lively signatures of a divine mind"[15] in creation, their message has a peculiar relevance to Blake's Innocence. Of these three, Paracelsus, as the remotest in time and idea, provides the fewest parallels. But those few are striking, for this complex personality of the sixteenth century, who touched alchemy, medicine, magic, philosophy, and religion, also touched William Blake. As a doctor he believed that "le principe de la medicine est l'amour";[16] and no principle is more fundamental to Blake's *Innocence* than that of love as a personal magnetism in nature, to which all creation turns as the flower to the sun. Paracelsus, like Blake, believed in the transforming power of the imagination, and few thinkers have so movingly described what the human fancy can do in changing the material life of man in society. Paracelsus's world of sexual metals, tinctured with the spirit of the sun (that divine fire pervading nature), anticipates Blake's world of attracting and coalescing impulses.

Paracelsus deciphered the divine signatures in nature; but Blake's other mentor, Böhme, whom William Law had introduced to the English eighteenth century in translation and paraphrase, is a more immediate and cogent example of the same faith. Böhme's conversion led to the writing of that most Blakean book, *De Signatura Rerum:* the poor herder of cattle went to the fields one day "and viewing the Herbs and Grass of the Field, in his inward Light, he saw into their Essences, Use and Properties, which were discovered to him by their Lineaments, Figures, and Signatures."[17] The tree that stands so central in Blake's *Innocence* and *Experience* is the most fundamental of Böhme's images, and the spirit of love, which for Böhme as for Paracelsus and Blake is a moving force in nature, is the very "ground and original" of all life, "an eternal will to all goodness," possessing "the meekness of the light and air and water of the world." This sweet quality, lovely, pleasant, mild, and meek, that mitigates "fierceness and wrath"—the gracious, amiable, blessed, friendly, and joyful love—is surely one of the clearest anticipations of the Mercy, Pity, Peace, and Love of Blake's animated nature.

But the auguries of Innocence in Swedenborg are even more unmistakable. As the closest to Blake in time, as one to whom Blake may have made a commitment of his spirit, the Swedish seer must take his place with Milton and Michelangelo as one of the poet-painter's chief begetters. The very grammar and vocabulary of Swedenborg's vision are also Blake's. Jesus is the sun, from whom streams a continual *emanation,* a divine efflux that fills all nature, even its *minute particulars.* The universal heavens are constituted by one formative human body, and the whole creation is *"a grand and divine man."* Life is cyclic, and moves by *contraries;* the right and the left sides of bodies are peculiarly significant; Innocence is a uniquely beautiful but also an especially threatened condition; black men have more vision than others—and their souls are white; man's good is challenged by his *proprium* or selfhood; there is "a certain image in every created thing"; and the divine essence is divisible into four-fold virtues of delight—essential love, essential wisdom, essential good, essential truth. Swedenborg's lyrical "History of Worms" glows with Blakean color and life: "Under the Impulse of Pleasure, arising from some innate Affection," these creatures aspire to a heavenly State .They hide themselves in the ground, they infold themselves in a covering, they return to the womb from whence they look for a new birth, and they become "Chrysalises, Aureliae, Nymphs and, at length, Butterflies":

and when they have . . . put on their beautiful wings . . . , they fly abroad into the open Air, as into their proper Heaven, where they indulge in all festive Sports, solemnize their Marriage Rites, and lay their Eggs with a view of continuing their kind . . . ; and they feed upon a sweet and pleasant food, extracted from the Flowers of the Field.[18]

II

THE TIGER OF EXPERIENCE

There are two aspects to Experience. The first is the condition itself, which, as primarily a social and political condition and only derivatively a cosmic one, is almost wholly bad—"acquired folly," to apply to it a Blakean phrase.[19] The second aspect of Experience is the response appropriate to that social and political condition— and it is here that an ethical dilemma arises. How shall moral man behave in an immoral society? If Experience is a congregation of pestilential social and political vapors, will it not pollute the Mercy, Pity, Peace, and Love of Innocence? And what does man do then? Blake had said that "acquired folly" is reproached by the innocence of a child. But is that a sufficient reproach? If not, what moral choices does a more vigorous and even violent response to evil entail?

Paradoxically, the author of "The Lamb" had always been temperamentally impatient under the yoke of Christian meekness and under the ethic of the Sermon on the Mount. William Law had written, "The sincere love of our Enemies is perhaps of all other Tempers the hardest to be acquired. . . ."[20] Blake found its acquisition not only hard but impossible and seems soon to have given up the struggle. In 1788, on the threshold of his career, Blake called severity in judging another "a great virtue," and confessed he could not love an enemy.[21] As an older man, who after his revolutionary wrath had returned to Christianity, Blake is in the same mood:

> Anger & Wrath my bosom rends . . .
>
> I profess not Generosity to a Foe . . .
>
> He has observed the Golden Rule
> Till he's become the Golden Fool.[22]

Blake was a man to whom prophetic wrath came rather more easily than Christian humility.

Nevertheless, when Blake stooped to wrath and immoralized his song, he did vastly more than indulge his temper. He responded as an artist-prophet to social and political evil, and became one of the most unrelenting satirists of Pity and Love that England ever produced. The "Bard's Song" that introduces *Milton* tells the story of Satan-Hayley, who had the Science of Pity alone but not of Wrath. When the story is done, the Eternals murmur that "Pity and Love are too venerable for the imputation of guilt."[23]

What guilt did Blake impute to these virtues, which are not only venerable, but stand at the very heart of his own *Innocence?* The indictment, made during the revolutionary period in the Lambeth prophecies, is (1) that society has polluted the fresh waters of divine mercy to produce the thick ooze of established pity and piety and (2) that society has transformed the natural and unashamed love of Innocence to a hideous parody of that lively and instinctual virtue. Love under the Western establishment has become the coy, sacrificial, female-dominated, passive, jealous love-fear that characterizes Anglo-Saxon courtship and marriage.

Both these tragic results are the work of Urizen, the god of the Establishment, a figure of the greatest complexity. With Greek and Roman blood in his veins, he is nonetheless the Hebrew god of repressive Sinaitic law. An intellectual and philosophical tyrant, he is also a political and social dictator, a warlike conserver of established "values." He is an amalgam of George III, Dr. Johnson, Jupiter, Newton, and Locke. And yet, for all his diverse relevance to many men and many movements, he is an unforgettably individual and palpable figure whose presence in Blake's words and designs haunts the imagination.

Just as Blake's Innocence and its presiding deity were clearly adumbrated in the religious tradition from which he sprang, so the antithetical God of Experience, Urizen, also comes directly from the poet's intellectual milieu. Urizen and his minions often inhabit caves under the ground or the roots of trees, inhuman or at the most sub-human beings; they resemble the gnomes, or halfmen, of Paracelsus, who live under the earth, possessing flesh and blood but no spirit, incapable of living in the wind and the air.[24] Just as Urizen rose from the one single man of Eternity, separating himself from primal unity and creating a shuddering void or negation in nature, so Böhme's deity has within himself the potentiality of evil. That anti-God, who nevertheless arises from the very heart of universal being, is a wintry force, "a very tart, terrible sharpness," "a hard, dark, and cold attraction or growing together, like winter when there is a fierce bitter cold frost, when water is frozen into ice." Take away the sun, says Böhme, and you get some idea of what the "pith" of God is like. That "pith" is the wrath of God, and in this quality stands Hell. Blake's Urizen, in the book that bears his name, is closely related to Böhme's wintry anti-God. Urizen has a frosty beard on which his tears freeze. He creates bones of solidness, fetters of ice, and other cold horrors; and he is the hoary spirit that haunts the chilling and empty distances of Newtonian space.[25]

But it is Swedenborg who is once again the closest to Blake, not imagistically (for it would be difficult to get closer to the image of Urizen than the negative side of Böhme's deity) but in basic idea. Swedenborg looked upon evil as institutional—and Urizen is primarily an institutional and social personification. Swedenborg's Last Judgment is executed not on those who have no relation to the

FROM SENSIBILITY TO ROMANTICISM

Gospel but on those who are "in civil and moral good"[26] but who lack charity—who believe in a cruel atonement, who affront a benevolent Deity by supposing he required blood-sacrifice, and who insult his integrity by believing in three persons. In other words, Swedenborg's sharpest attack, like Blake's and that of most dissenters, was upon the established church of his day and upon the intellectual formulations and the political alliances of orthodoxy.

Although Blake is thus anticipated by his predecessors, he is always bolder and more powerful than any of them; and in his conception of Urizen as the God of Pity, he makes one of his most radical and telling adaptations. For Urizen is more than a cold negation; he is also a "merciful" god, who writes the laws of "pity, compassion, and forgiveness."[27] He sometimes stares in frozen horror, but he also sheds tears of pity. He presides, almost literally, over the *Songs of Experience*. In the poem called "The Human Abstract," which is an almost exact parody or reversal of "The Divine Image" of *Innocence,* Urizen is palpably present in the design at the bottom of the page, where he rises from the ground and weaves the web of religion [Plate II and III A]. At the top of "The Little Vagabond" the deity is not a loving father welcoming an erring prodigal but Urizen, who patronizingly forgives the sinner and forces his body to bend in abject worship [Plate III B].

Urizen as the God of Pity is a direct perversion of the good—a reduction to evil of a noble virtue. With arms extended, he recalls Christ on the cross and the man who stands before it; and Old Nobodadday's eyes often look like a sad-eyed parody of mercy [Plate V].[28] He is that worst of all evils, the corruption of the best —a Simonist, a trafficker in holy things, to whom the only dignified human response is flat and uncompromising disobedience.

> . . . who commanded this? what God? what Angel?
> To keep the gen'rous from experience till the ungenerous
> Are unrestrain'd performers of the energies of nature;
> Till pity is become a trade, and generosity a science
> That men get rich by; & the sandy desart is giv'n to the strong?
> What God is he writes laws of peace & clothes him in a tempest?
> What pitying Angel lusts for tears and fans himself with sighs?
> What crawling villain preaches abstinence & wraps himself
> In fat of lambs? no more I follow, no more obedience pay![29]

III A.

III B.

The terror answerd: I am Orc. wreath'd round the accursed tree:
The times are ended; shadows pass the morning gins to break;
The fiery joy, that Urzen perverted to ten commands,
What night he led the starry hosts thro' the wide wilderness:
That stony law I stamp to dust: and scatter religion abroad
To the four winds as a torn book, & none shall gather the leaves;
But they shall rot on desart sands, & consume in bottomless deeps;
To make the desarts blossom, & the deeps shrink to their fountains,
And to renew the fiery joy, and burst the stony roof.
That pale religious letchery, seeking Virginity,
May find it in a harlot, and in coarse-clad honesty
The undefil'd tho' ravish'd in her cradle night and morn:
For every thing that lives is holy, life delights in life;
Because the soul of sweet delight can never be defil'd.
Fires inwrap the earthly globe, yet man is not consumd;
Amidst the lustful fires he walks: his feet become like brass,
His knees and thighs like silver, & his breast and head like gold

IV.

V.

Even after Blake returned to Christian love, he continued to hate Urizenic mercy. In his Christian prophecies Satan takes Urizen's place as a god of pity, and, in the *Everlasting Gospel*, written in 1818, almost a full generation after his revolutionary period, Blake attacks with lacerating irony that anti-Christ, the "Yea Nay Creeping Jesus" of the Establishment—the Jesus who is the friend of all mankind, obedient, gentle, humble; who loves his enemies but who hates and betrays his friends, who is humble as a lamb or an ass, who gives with charity a stone. Such a humble Christ blots out nature, buries the soul, distorts the heavens, poisons perception, leads to secret love and secret adultery; he is the Jesus who must be destroyed in the Last Judgment.

The humility of this Jesus and of the Urizen who created and established him leads directly to secret love and to secret adulteries and is somehow responsible for the evils that attend the domestic life. The God of Pity has tamed the vigorous, natural affections of Innocence and made them perverse, passive, jealous, and destructive.

It is not only Urizen who is called Pity in Blake's myth, but also Enitharmon, who sprang from the prophet Los, as Venus had sprung from the head of Zeus and as Eve had been created out of Adam's side. No other episode in Blake's long and involved myth so obsessed its creator as her birth, her motherhood, her relations with her husband, Los. Blake repeated her history again and again for almost a decade, with and without variations, in poems and paintings [See Plate IV], published and private.[30] Who would venture to say dogmatically what this obsessive story meant in all its personal, artistic, political, and social ramifications? But one thing is certain: in the Enitharmon myth Blake viewed love, courtship, and marriage as victims of Urizenic domination. The married state of Enitharmon and Los is often one of cruelty, of perverse coyness, of shame, of jealous torment, as well as love—of male strength separated from female beauty, of tears, of desires that are frustrated in fear, aggression, and withdrawal. In the lyrics of *Experience* and in the notebooks the same indictment is made. A young lady drives away love and arms her fears with shields and spears. Thus protected from aggressive love and from herself, she becomes old and gray. A nurse turns green and pale as she hears the whisperings of the dale and remembers her youth. Love, alarmed by the fire of

desire, yields only to the bribery of soft deceit. A virgin wishes that
she had been a prostitute, for only the prostitutes, not the English
wives, bear the lineaments of gratified desire.[31] The fresh, natural,
instinctual emotions of *Innocence* have been poisoned. Love now
subsists only by denials, sighs, tears, procrastinations, jealousies,
hypocrisies, and the commerce of the night. Such is the "pity" of
Enitharmon.

Innocence has been lost—

> Infancy! fearless, lustful, happy, nestling for delight
> In laps of pleasure: Innocence! honest, open, seeking
> The vigorous joys of morning light; open to virgin bliss.[32]

Innocence will be regained when the fiery Orc of revolution
tramples the Urizenic prohibitions to dust:

> I'll lie beside thee on a bank & view their wanton play
> In lovely copulation, bliss on bliss, with Theotormon:
> Red as the rosy morning, lustful as the first born beam,
> Oothoon shall view his dear delight, nor e'er with jealous cloud
> Come in the heaven of generous love, nor selfish blightings bring.[33]

But in the present, young lovers are separated, as in the famous
Tate painting "Hecate," by the dark and brooding goddess of
jealousy and old night [Plate VI].[34]

In Innocence, "Wrath was followed up and down / By a little ewe
lamb."[35] But in Experience the Tiger of Wrath has swallowed up
the little ewe-lamb. And when the virtue of humility has been appropriated by the sneaking serpent, what can the just man do but
"rage in the wilds"?[36]

What is the wrath of Experience, separated, as it was, from the
conventional safeguards of innocence and humility? It was, of
course, associated with the hellish energy, the impulse, the excess,
the bodily lust, and the fiery liberty that Blake praised with such
pungent originality in the *Marriage of Heaven and Hell* and with
such hysterical stridency in *A Song of Liberty*. But did the wrath of
Experience also embrace violence, warfare, revolutionary action?

One of the antitheses of the *Marriage of Heaven and Hell* is
love-hate, and the rhetoric is the same for this pair as for the
others: hate is absolutely necessary. The dominion of Edom that
Blake and Isaiah believed must precede the final apocalypse is the

day of the angry God. The Lord has a sword in the thirty-fourth chapter of Isaiah, to which Blake refers us, and the stench of corpses will rise and the mountains melt with blood. In this period, says Blake, we must plow over the bones of the dead, roar like the lion, wear his fell, and, like Jesus, take up the sword. In *America* all obedience ceases, and Orc's fierce flames "burn around the abodes of men." In the *Song of Los* kings and priests are *driven* from their lairs. And in *Europe* Los calls his sons "to the strife of blood."[37]

It must be impossible to limit with any exactitude a commitment to revolution. But the implications are clear: revolution means action, and action envisages violence, direct or indirect. Wrath, standing alone, as it does in Blake's myth, is a violent and destructive emotion, and the poet makes no attempt to moderate its fury.

Blake's "Tyger" burns bright with the fires of revolutionary wrath, and its fearful symmetry has much more to do with the red destructiveness of Orc than with the sublime of Burke or the savage place of Coleridge. The "Tyger" stands in the forests of Urizen's night and is about to spring in violent action. But its creator has not forgotten that he had also created Innocence.

> Did he who made the Lamb make thee?

This is the cry of a man nurtured in Christian mercy, who nevertheless does not flinch at the affirmative answer. The deadly terror must be clasped. Wrath must be met with wrath.

III

"THE WRATH OF THE LAMB"

On 12 September 1800, Blake casts a retrospective eye on the period of revolutionary wrath and implies that he is now emerging from "nervous fear." That fear, he makes clear, was related to the political upheavals in America and France and to his own intense and terrible visions. Of these inner and outer events, Blake uses the strongest language: "terrors" in heaven and hell boded "a mighty and awful change" that "threatened the earth." "The dark horrors" of "the American War," and "the thick clouds" of the French Revolution brought him to the door of either death or despair.

And My Angels have told me that seeing such visions I could
     not subsist on the Earth,
But by my conjunction with Flaxman, who knows to forgive
     Nervous Fear.[38]

Blake thought he was rescued *de profundis* by his decision to live
in Felpham by the sea. But in fact the experience he describes in a
letter to Thomas Butts of 2 October 1800,[39] just after he arrived at
his rural cottage, is, for all its beauty of expression and for all its
sincere recollections of Innocence, no more than a pseudo-conversion. Blake promises his friend, whom he addresses as the
"Friend of Religion and Order," that he will in the future be "a
determined advocate of Religion and Humanity, the two bands of
Society"—a pledge that is followed by a lovely hymn to Innocence.
The poet himself remains a child by the side of the sea; he, his
sister, and his wife descend like infants to their new abode, and all
he had ever known before now shines bright in the lovely light of
Felpham. Had Blake in fact become a humble, pliant Christian
living in the after-glow of recollected Innocence, we should of
course have to come to terms with that fact. But he did not. The
poem expressed no more than a temporary relief; and as for becoming an advocate of humility to please the friends of religion and
order, Blake, if he ever referred again to the obedient promise of
this letter, could only have regarded it as a capitulation.[40]

Blake's pseudo-conversion did not last, and the Felpham breezes
soon turned cold and blew such torment as he had known in the
revolutionary nineties. But this too was to change and lead directly
into an experience, or series of experiences, that must be called a
genuine conversion. This experience is described in another letter
to Butts, dated 22 November 1802,[41] which contains another autobiographical poem vastly different from the Song of Innocence
written in 1800. The most important difference is that, although
the present poem begins in lovely Innocence (". . . happiness
stretched across hills / In a cloud that dewy sweetness distills"), the
poet is no longer meekly submissive but angrily triumphant over
the specter that had tormented him. His mind now arrayed with
light, he recommits himself to battle, taking up his spear, his bow,
and his arrows, which glow in their golden sheaves as the heavens
drop gore. Anger, energy, action now impel him, and he has become once again the dedicated artist-prophet.

It is to this experience and to its subsequent deepening that Blake refers in many later letters and also in the mythic story that concludes Night VIIa of *The Four Zoas*. That conversion follows a condition in the world of Blake's myth that must have been a mighty projection of the poet's own spiritual and intellectual suffering during the period of revolutionary wrath. Orc has been born as a serpent from the womb of Enitharmon and has now become, by the wiles of Urizen, a worm of deceit. Other mythic persons have fallen from a primal virtue into an opposite and related vice: Luvah, once love, is now hate; Urizen, once faith, is now doubt; Enitharmon, once the beautiful queen of heaven, is now a pale and jealous wife; Los, the poet-prophet, Blake's surrogate, has become what he has beheld in Urizenic society and is now fierce, frustrated, envious, and loudly blasphemous. Urizenic pity and the pity of Enitharmon have produced in Los a consuming wrath that extends through all of nature.

> The Eternal Mind, bounded, began to roll eddies of wrath ceaseless
> Round & round. . . .[42]

That wrath affects the relation of Los and Enitharmon, who love and flee, caught in the sexual wars of jealousy and domestic strife.

Such is the night of nature that precedes Los's conversion. But then the change begins. Enitharmon beholds the Lamb of God descending and fears that his return will lead to her and her husband's eternal death, "fit punishment for such / Hideous offenders." But Los feels his fires being kindled afresh and the delight of ancient times returning. Enitharmon responds to these quickened powers with a hymn to "lovely, terrible Los, wonder of Eternity" and hopes that he will proceed in "sweet moderated fury" so that their souls will be able to live. Los, though inspired, does in fact "modulate his fires," and the co-operation of Los and Enitharmon is immediately restored: he draws "a line upon the walls of shining heaven" and she "tinctures it with the beams of blushing love." Finally, Los and Enitharmon "assimilate" all their sons in "forms, Embodied & Lovely," restoring them to Innocence but enlisting them in battle. The wonder of wonders is that even Urizen is now in the hands of Los, who loves his ancient enemy with his whole soul and sees him as a lovely infant, "breathed from Enitharmon."[43]

Blake's mythic account of Los's conversion, coupled with the letters written during and after the stay at Felpham, tells the story of a man saved from harrowing fear of his enemies, from doubt in his own ability, from domestic jealousy, and restored to personal and artistic integrity, domestic harmony, and faith in his own past and future. Los's victory is also a victory over destructive wrath and a re-dedication to Christian love. For the Lamb of God returns to Blake's pages—not to consume the "Tyger" of wrath as that beast had consumed the Lamb of Innocence, but to lie down with it in the new Jerusalem. For Blake, though he moderates his fury, does not reject his prophetic past. He assimilates it, and views himself during the period of trial and tribulation as the prophet who kept the fires burning. He had undoubtedly become too wrathful, stooped to violence, tortured his wife, destroyed their co-operative art. But in creating forms, he had kept the imaginative life from destruction and prepared the way for "the Great Harvest & Vintage of the Nations."[44]

Although Blake came to terms with his past and did not, like Tolstoi, disown his children, two unmistakably new elements entered into the poet's thought and art as a result of this conversion: (1) the rejection of violence and a dedication to what Blake will obsessively call *intellectual* battle; (2) a return to unorthodox Christianity, conceived of chiefly as the mutual and continuing forgiveness of sin.

When it becomes clear in Blake's great epic[45] that Milton will return to the created universe and prepare the ground for the last great vintage, Rintrah and Palamabron worry that the poet's return will unchain Orc and let loose Satan and many other evils upon England. These sons of Los, who were very close to Blake's own emotions during the revolutionary period, are finally reassured and partake in the battle because Los makes it clear to them that he himself has embraced Milton's course, has purged him of his war-like and Calvinistic fury, and has re-created him in the image of universal brotherhood and mercy.

Los, his sons, and the new Milton go to war, but the war is now unmistakably and solely "mental fight." Los now calls for his bow, his arrows, his spear, but these are now "intellectual" things, like the tear and the sigh of a martyr's woe. Blake wrestles "not against flesh and blood, but against . . . spiritual wickedness in high places." The noise of battle is the "clangor of the arrows of intellect." Urthona (Los, after his return to primal unity and strength, and Blake, after his conversion) rises from the "ruinous walls" that stand for the evils of a bad society:

> In all his ancient strength to form the golden armour of science
> For intellectual War.[46]

As the "war of swords" is supplanted by "intellectual War," the "Dark Religions" also depart and "sweet Science reigns." Such fundamental change is the work of Christian mercy, which led Blake through the gates of Wrath to what he called "a fresher morning."

> To find the Western Path
> Right thro' the Gates of Wrath
> I urge my way;
> Sweet Mercy leads me on:
> With soft repentant moan
>
> I see the break of day.
> The war of swords & spears
> Melted by dewy tears
> Exhales on high;
> The Sun is freed from fears
> And with soft grateful tears
> Ascends the sky.[47]

What does the return of Christ to Blake's poetry and art imply? Certainly not orthodox or dogmatic Christianity, for that kind of Christianity Blake continued to fight in the full panoply of intellectual battle. Nor is Blake's new or restored faith an acceptance of the conventional meekness and piety that Blake had once seen as Urizenic, for his attack on the mild Hayley and the meek Stothard continues with unabated fury. Nor does Blake's rededication to a radically simplified Christian faith imply the death of organic or sexual nature. The mild, female-dominated sexuality of Enitharmon's reign is over, and the excrementitious husk that covered and smothered love in the dispensation of Urizen has been removed. But that "evaporation"[48]—to use Blake's word—reveals the true lineaments of man as never before. It does not destroy but humanizes nature: for all creatures—the lion, the tiger, the horse, the elephant, the eagle, the dove, the fly, and the worm, and even the wondrous serpents in all their glory—live the intense life of their own being. They are not burned up in religious conflagration but made more truly "human" and beautiful than they had ever been before.

Blake's Christianity is the practice of art and the restoration of Innocence to man and nature. But it is also ethical action. It involves what Blake describes as the "Mutual Forgiveness of each Vice,"[49] and the death of the talonic law of revenge. The practice of such religion, in which "every kindness to another is a little Death,"[50] a man of Blake's stubborn selfhood could not have found easy. But he did find it challenging, and to its realization in himself and society he gave all the energies of his unflagging spirit.

> And O thou Lamb of God, whom I
> Slew in my dark self-righteous pride,
>   Art thou return'd to Albion's Land?
> And is Jerusalem thy Bride?
>
>   Come to my arms & never more
> Depart, but dwell for ever here:
>   Create my Spirit to thy Love:
> Subdue my Spectre to thy Fear.[51]

It would be a profound mistake if the music of Blake's simple lyric should be allowed to suggest quietistic piety. For his new faith combined the forgiveness of sins with "mental fight" and united the prophetic anger and the Innocent meekness that a corrupt society had put asunder. The Jesus who returns to Blake's art is "The God *of Fire* and the Lord *of Love*"[52] and the mild virtues are made fiery by the "wrath of the Lamb."[53]

NOTES

1. *Jerusalem*, Plate 72.

2. *Jerusalem*, Plate 54.

3. *Milton*, I, ix, 46–7 in Geoffrey Keynes, ed., *The Complete Writings of William Blake*, (London and New York, 1957), p. 490. This edition will hereafter be referred to as *CW*.

4. *Jerusalem,* "To the Public," Plate 3 (*CW*, p. 621).

5. Letter to Thomas Butts, 10 January 1802 (*CW*, p. 812). Since I regard Blake's Innocence as an essentially Christian vision, I feel justified in applying to it language Blake used of himself after his conversion, following the dark trials of his revolutionary period. Blake conceived of this conversion as in part a return to what he once had been.

6. "Night," *Songs of Innocence* (*CW*, p. 119).

7. Annotation to Lavater, *Aphorisms on Man* (No. 630), written about 1788 (*CW*, p. 87).

8. "The Lamb" (*CW*, p. 115); Annotation to Lavater, *Aphorism* No. 630 (*CW*, p. 87); *There is no Natural Religion,* second series, 1788 (*CW*, p. 98).

9. "The Divine Image," *Songs of Innocence* (*CW*, p. 117).

10. Annotation to Swedenborg, *Wisdom of Angels concerning Divine Love and Divine Wisdom,* p. 12; written about 1788 (*CW*, p. 90).

11. These related *Songs of Innocence* together illustrate later lines of Blake, which also enforce the idea of divine-human individuality:

> God Appears & God is Light
> To those poor Souls who dwell in Night,
> But does a Human Form Display
> To those who Dwell in Realms of day.

"Auguries of Innocence," ll. 129–32 (*CW*, p. 434).

12. Berkeley's philosophy. There is no convincing evidence that Blake knew it before about 1820, when he annotated *Siris;* but Berkeley does provide many parallels, which, though not as close as others discussed in this essay, do anticipate Blake's vision. Berkeley believed that the language of the universe testifies to a constant creation in visual signs that dissolve, combine, are transposed, and diversified in an "ever shifting scene." Such language proves the existence, not of a clock-maker but of spirit or thinking being "actually and intimately present." *Alciphron,* IV, xiv.

13. Luke xxi, 27.

14. J. G. Davies says correctly: "The writers with whom Blake has most mental affinity were Swedenborg, Paracelsus, and Böhme" (*The Theology of William Blake* [Oxford, 1948], p. 31). Davies discusses Swedenborg at length but not the other two. Blake avowed that "Paracelsus & Behmen appear'd to me" (Letter to Flaxman, 12 September 1800 [*CW*, p. 799]). Blake read and studied Swedenborg early in life, later disagreed with him and even parodied him in the *Marriage of Heaven and Hell,* but still later took the subject of a painting from him and recommended "the works of this visionary" as "well worth the attention of Painters and Poets; they are foundations for grand things" (*Descriptive Catalogue,* 1809, No. VIII [*CW*, p. 581]).

15. Berkeley, *Siris,* sec. 173.

16. Robert-Henri Blaser, *Paracelse et sa Conception de la Nature* (Geneva and Lille, 1950), p. 4. See also the following works of Paracelsus: *Of the Supreme*

Mysteries of Nature, tr. R. Turner (London, 1656), sig. B 2 r and v and pp. 1, 23–4, 61–3 (on the power of the imagination in time of war); *Archidoxes,* tr. by "J. H. Oxon." (London, 1661), p. 62; *Aurora* (same translator; London, 1659), *passim.*

17. William Law, ed., *The Works of Jacob Behmen* (London, 1764), I, xiii. See also pp. 9–10 (and Fig. 2), 23–4, 25, 40–42, 62 ff.; II, 54; and *The Works of the Reverend William Law,* VIII (London, 1766), p. 5.

18. Emanuel Swedenborg, *True Christian Religion* (London, 1781), I, 15. See also pp. 3, 64, II, 77; and *A Treatise concerning Heaven and Hell* (London, 1778), pp. 3, 8, 36, 39, 167; *A Treatise on the Nature of Influx* (Chester, 1798), pp. 18 ff.; *Wisdom of Angels concerning Divine Love* (London, 1788 [annotated by Blake; cf. *CW,* pp. 89–96]), pp. 10–11, 103–4; *The Wisdom of Angels* (London, 1790 [annotated by Blake; cf. *CW,* pp. 131–3]), pp. 11, 278; *A Continuation concerning the Last Judgment and the Spiritual World* (London, 1791), pp. 66–8. See also Martin Lamm, *Swedenborg En Studie öfver hans Utveckling* (Stockholm, 1915), pp. 329–30. Italics added to emphasize words used by both Blake and Swedenborg's translators.

19. Annotation to Lavater, *Aphorism* No. 633 (*CW,* p. 87).

20. "A Practical Treatise upon Christian Perfection," in *Works of . . . Law* (London, 1762), III, 131.

21. Annotations to Lavater, *Aphorisms,* Nos. 36, 248 (*CW,* pp. 67, 72).

22. MS. Note-Book, 1808–11 (*CW,* pp. 538, 541, 540).

23. *Milton* I, xiii, 48–9 (*CW,* p. 495); ibid. I, x, 46 (*CW,* p. 490).

24. *Of the Supreme Mysteries of Nature,* tr. R. Turner (London, 1656), p. 51. Cf. design on Plate 2 of *America.*

25. *Works,* ed. Law (London, 1764), I, 124–6; *Book of Urizen,* i, 6; iv [b], 4, 6; viii, 6–7 (*CW,* pp. 223, 228, 235).

26. *The Apocalypse Revealed* (Manchester, 1791), II, 508–9. See also *A Brief Exposition of the Doctrine of the New Church* (London, 1769), pp. 27–8, 53, 91.

27. *Book of Urizen,* ii, 8 (*CW,* p. 224). "And he wept & he called it Pity,/And his tears flowed down on the winds" (*Urizen,* viii, 5 [*CW,* p. 235]).

28. *America,* Plate 8 ("The Terror answer'd"); *Jerusalem,* Plate 76.

29. *America,* Plate 11, lines 7–15 (*CW,* p. 200).

30. *Book of Urizen,* v, 7–10 (*CW,* pp. 230–31); in the *Four Zoas* (Night the Fourth, between lines 287 and 288) Blake writes: "Bring in here the Globe of Blood as in the B. of Urizen" (*CW,* p. 305); *Jerusalem,* I, xvii, 48–58 (*CW,* p. 639). For visual renditions of the same story, see *Urizen,* Plate 15; *Song of Los,* Plate 8 [see my Plate IV]. The myth of Enitharmon and Los is complex and should be made the subject of a special study that would consider not only the plates in the engraved poems but separate drawings and paintings in

the British Museum and the Tate Gallery. In the series of color prints of 1795, most of which are at the Tate, at least three seem to be concerned with this myth: "Pity," "Lamech," and "Hecate."

31. See "Nurse's Song," "The Angel," "I laid me down," "Silent, Silent Night," "The Question Answer'd," "Several Questions Answered," "O I cannot find, cannot find" (*CW*, pp. 212–13, 213–14, 162, 168, 180, 184).

32. *Visions of the Daughters of Albion,* vi, 4–6 (*CW*, p. 193).

33. Ibid. vii, 25–9 (*CW*, p. 195).

34. I do not know that this interpretation has ever before been proposed. Blake is thought to have illustrated *Macbeth* III, v, or IV, i, or *Midsummer Night's Dream* V, i, 391. But he usually illustrates, not his source, but his own myth. The landscape of this color-print is Urizenic—like that of all the others in the series done for Butts in 1795. The figure on the right is a male (Los?) and on the left a female (Enitharmon?), separated by the goddess of jealousy. The print is an allegory of love and marriage under Urizen.

35. *Book of Los,* I, v, 4–5 (*CW*, p. 256).

36. *Marriage of Heaven and Hell,* Plate 2, line 19 (*CW*, p. 149).

37. Ibid. Plates 3, 7, 8; *America,* Plate 16, line 23; *Song of Los,* Plate 6; *Europe,* Plate 15, line 11 (*CW*, pp. 149, 150, 151, 203, 247, 245).

38. Letter to Flaxman (*CW*, p. 799).

39. *CW*, pp. 804–6.

40. I suggest he may refer to his humble and temporary submission to religion and order in *Milton* I, vii, 6–17 (*CW*, 486), when Los, yielding to the blandishments of Satan's "incomparable mildness" and "most endearing love," turns over to him the harrow of the Almighty. Los, who should have known that "pity divides the soul/And man unmans" (ibid. I, viii, 19–20 [*CW*, p. 488]), very quickly realizes his mistake and calls his action "blamable."

41. *CW*, pp. 816–19. Blake dates the poem and therefore the experience out of which it grew "above a twelve-month ago," that is, before November 1801.

42. *Four Zoas,* IV, 208–9 (*CW*, p. 303).

43. Ibid. VII *b*, 424–99. This passage G. E. Bentley, Jr., regards as a "very late addition to the poem," made after Night VIII had been completed. See *William Blake, Vala or the Four Zoas* (Oxford, 1963), pp. 195–6. I regret that I have not yet had the time to study fully the implications for my argument of this impressive piece of scholarship.

44. *Milton,* II, xliii (*CW*, p. 535).

45. Ibid. I, xxii, 27-I, xxiv, 43 (*CW*, pp. 505–9).

46. *Four Zoas* XIX, 853–4. For other references in this paragraph, see "I saw a Monk," last stanza, *Jerusalem,* Plate 52 (*CW*, p. 683); ibid. Plate 98, line 7 (*CW*, p. 745); *Milton,* Plate I, last two stanzas; Ephesians vi. 12 (Blake's epigraph for the *Four Zoas*).

47. "Morning," from Note-Book of 1800–1803 (*CW*, p. 421). See *Four Zoas*, IX, 825 (*CW*, p. 379).

48. *Jerusalem* Plate 98, lines 18–19, 42–5 (*CW*, pp. 745–6).

49. Prologue to *For the Sexes: the Gates of Paradise*, line 1 (*CW*, p. 761).

50. Words of Jesus in *Jerusalem*, Plate 96, line 27 (*CW*, p. 743).

51. *Jerusalem*, Plate 27, lines 65–72 (*CW*, p. 651).

52. Ibid. Plate 3 (*CW*, p. 621).

53. Revelation vi. 16.

"Terrible Blake in His Pride"
An Essay on *The Everlasting Gospel*

DAVID V. ERDMAN

THE *Everlasting Gospel*, begun by Blake in his sixties and probably never completed—though we cannot rule out the possibility of a lost final draft—is a somewhat baffling but extremely powerful and attractive-repulsive poem which has never been given and perhaps can never be given wholly satisfactory editorial treatment. Dante Gabriel Rossetti put it first in his severely selective transcription of "All that is of any value" in Blake's manuscript volume now sometimes called the Rossetti Notebook. The reader of Blake in a chronological edition comes upon *The Everlasting Gospel* as a fresh outburst of "The Voice of the Devil" almost thirty years after *The Marriage of Heaven and Hell*. Here is a new and more intricate exercise in irony by the "Cynic" of 1784 (*An Island in the Moon*), or the "Devil" of 1790, or the poet who could write of this "Spectre" self: "Uprose terrible Blake in his Pride" (for such is a true reading of the second line of the Klopstock verses of about 1798).[1] In Geoffrey Keynes's first and latest editions it comes immediately after *Jerusalem,* and the reader whose brow has been widened by that prophetic epic with its message of Forgiveness and Brotherhood dictated to the poet by heavenly Spirits is well advised to go on to read this fiery *Gospel* in the vulgar tongue dictated by the poet's terrible Spectre. Its Jesus who "will not do/ Either for Englishman or Jew" is calculated to remove in the nick of time the temptation to accommodate the Blakean message to an orthodox creed. It is not an easy and certainly not a soothing poem.

Some of its difficulty lies in its density of allusion, both to other writings of Blake and to the Bible. Michael J. Tolley in a recent article dealing with the "Chastity" section of the poem[2] has demonstrated how its exegesis line by line can be assisted by analysis of Biblical references—which then must be given a turn of the Blakean screw to come right: the Biblical references "cannot take the reader the whole of the way" into Blake's meaning, but they "are essential in taking him part of the way." And its most rewarding difficulties arise perhaps from the intellectual double-somersaults required, not simply to read the Bible white for black, but to keep up—even Blake himself could not—with the violent dynamics of its irony and its mockery, forces that sometimes support each other but sometimes pull apart. The feet that stamp the stony law to dust are not shod in limp leather; to fight sneaking or tyrannic or Satanic pride requires "honest triumphant Pride"—which is sometimes more terrible than manageable. Blake himself as his own reader, the day after (or months after), felt that the couplet, "To be Good only is to be/A God or else a Pharisee," required either a gloss or a correction: he wrote "Devil" in pencil, half above and half on top of "God" in a way that leaves an editor puzzled whether to treat it as one or the other. Another passage might be drawn upon to resolve this difficulty with the inference that "God" and "Devil" are practically identical deviations from honest humanity: "Thou art a man God is no more." But then we must note that these words are spoken not by Blake to the reader but by God to Christ on the cross. Pursuit of this intrinsic puzzle in Blake's equation of Divinity and Humanity and Poetic Genius would lead us to what many consider the doctrinal crux of the poem, with its central pivot the ambiguous pronoun "his":

> But when Jesus was Crucified
> Then was perfected his glittring pride (.)[3]

Mr. Tolley, who (I believe correctly) takes the antecedent of "his" to be the "shadowy Man" twelve lines earlier who rolls away like a serpent "From the Limbs of Jesus," suggests that "the full meaning" may have to be sought in "esoteric traditions." (The Antinomianism of the Ranters, perhaps, or the three ages of Joachim of Flora?)[4] But one need not search elsewhere for the simple Blakean historical point: that the moment of Jesus' death on the Cross is also the moment of the birth of "this False Christ" of the churches. Just as Christ enters completely into "The Real Man The Imagination which Liveth for Ever" (to quote Blake's words at the approach of his own death),[5] his "Foolish Body" is perfected as the image of Corporeal Pride, the "Simulative Phantom" of Natural Religion.[6]

Some of the difficulties encountered by the serious student of *The Everlasting Gospel,* however, are extrinsic or editorial, and it is the purpose of the present essay to reduce or isolate these by a careful examination of the manuscript fragments which constitute the received text of this work.

The text as printed in Keynes's 1957 edition, with modernized punctuation, pages 748–59, and his account of the manuscript sources, pages 920–22, represent a great advance over previous presentations and afford a gratifyingly firm basis for discussing the problem posed by Sir Geoffrey in his assertion that "No attempt to weld [the fragments] into a consecutive poem could be successful." Following the previous editor, John Sampson, Keynes treats nine "widely separated" entries in the Rossetti Notebook as fragments of a single poem, lettering them from *a* to *i,* even though *i* strictly speaking is on a scrap of paper sewed into the Notebook (sewed in by Blake presumably but not certainly). He then presents as "Supplementary Passages" three other fragments, which he does not letter (let us call them *j, k,* and *l),* even though these are written on a still different scrap of paper, *never* sewed into the Notebook.

Here is a table of all the sections, with their locations and with catch-phrases of identification, for convenient reference:

Sections in Blake's Notebook (abbreviated *N*)

a (opposing Visions of Christ) *N* 33 (Keynes p. 748)

b (Was Jesus gentle) *N* 100–01 (Keynes 748–9)

c (Was Jesus Humble) *N* 98 (Keynes 750–51)

d (Was Jesus Humble, revised) *N* 52–4 (headed "The Everlasting Gospel" and concluded with the tally "78 lines" and a catch-line to cue in section *e*) (Keynes 751–3)

e (Was Jesus Chaste) *N* 48–52 (concluded with the tally "94 lines") (Keynes 753–5)

f (This Jesus will not do) *N* 54 (a couplet written marginally near the end of section *d*) (Keynes 756) g (Seeing this False Christ) *N* 52 (a couplet written below section *e* and followed by a catch-phrase "What are those &ᶜ" to cue in another section which does not correspond exactly with any of those extant) (Keynes 756)

h (Did Jesus teach doubt) *N* 48 (two couplets written sideways in pencil in the margin of section *e*, probably but not necessarily related to a pencil note along the top of the page: "This was spoke by My Spectre to Voltaire Bacon &ᶜ"—the note being obviously not a part of the poem but a comment on all or part of it, by location the beginning of *e*) (Keynes 756)

i (Virgin Pure) *N* 120 (the fourth page of a small fold of paper sewed in at the end of the Notebook—a scrap salvaged from the inner margins of a sheet printed for the fourth Hayley Ballad of 1802)[7]

Sections not attached to the Notebook

j (Covenant of Jehovah) Prose paragraph (in pencil on page 1 of a folded leaf of 1818 note paper now in the Rosenbach Foundation library)[8] (Keynes 757)

k (If Moral Virtue) 14 lines (in ink, on page 4 of the same leaf, but marked "This to come first" and numbered "1") (Keynes 758)

l (What can this Gospel) 43 lines (in ink, on pages 2, 3, and the top of 4 of the same leaf, with inserted section number "2") (Keynes 758–9)

m (What are those) ? (section alluded to in *g* and presumably now lost, though just possibly, as Keynes suggests, an intended revision of lines 11 ff. of section *k*)

We may observe that when Sir Geoffrey speaks of having retained "the division . . . into fragments determined by their position in the MS.," he does not mean to imply that his text represents simply the sequence of manuscript entries, which would be *a, e, h, g, d, f, c, b* for those in the Notebook proper. Putting *j, k, l* to the rear as Supplementary, he has attempted if not to "weld" at least to arrange the other fragments into a meaningful sequence, following clues other than those merely of position. I suggest now that the process be pushed further, with the consideration of still other clues.

It would seem desirable to discover the poet's latest intention, as to arrangement and perhaps selection—though no passages were physically deleted (except by non-inclusion in the Notebook). But we must first discover if possible the sequence of original composition. In the following pages I argue that the order of writing of the twelve surviving and one lost fragments was: *j, l, k, i, (m), a* (with some doubt), *e, g, h*(?), *b, c, d, f* (except that the lost *m,* if a variant of *k,* may have preceded *i*). I then consider which of the earlier sections may be thought to have been eliminated by the writing of later ones, concluding hypothetically that the poet's intention may have been to reduce the poem to the sequence *d e b.* But then, somewhat withdrawing from the rigor of that hypothesis, I attempt to discover whether more inclusive arrangements are possible.

The most drastic revision of our ideas about *The Everlasting Gospel* that this reconstruction calls for is the recognition that passages *j, l, k,* the first prose, the second little more than rhymed prose, and the third spirited verse moving unsteadily toward dramatic vision, cannot be "Supplementary" to poetic strophes which exhibit such formal sureness and such confident fusion of rhetoric and vision as those which ring changes on the tune,

> Was Jesus Humble or did he
> Give any Proofs of Humility(.)

They are rather preliminary gropings, rendered obsolete and redundant by the strophes built on this pattern in Notebook sections *b, d, e, h.* By the same reasoning section *i* must represent an intermediate stage, previous to the discovery of the triumphant final form (or formula). We have also to confront the probability that section *a* ("The Vision of Christ that thou dost see"), whether thought of as an introduction or a postscript, has been considered a part of the poem only by a kind of editorial divination and without any evidence that Blake himself considered it to be such. Suspending that question for the moment, however, let us pursue the indications that the composition of the main body of the poem did not end but begin with the 1818 sections.[9]

Blake's other writings in the period extending roughly from 1818–20 to 1822 consist of a number of brief, aphoristic primers of advice: the "Keys" to emblematic Gates of Paradise, with ironic advice to Satan, the Laocoön inscriptions, the paragraphs "On Homers Poetry" and "On Virgil," and the "Revelation" addressed

"To Lord Byron in the Wilderness" (*The Ghost of Abel*). Two forces, in a combination we lack enough information to plot with any precision, may well have stimulated Blake's writing of these tracts. With the etching and printing of *Jerusalem* (two copies over the years 1818–20 and then two more perhaps more rapidly) his long task of concentration on "voluminous" poems was completed; there was creative relief and delight in turning to briefer, lighter forms. And with the acquisition of a new audience, some of them readers of *Jerusalem* and, best of all, young disciples in Art (beginning with John Linnell in 1818 who subscribed for a *Jerusalem*), there must have arisen, in Blake's mind at least, a direct demand for glosses on the larger work and some forthright and authentic yet vernacular explications of his gospel. The happy condition had returned, it must have seemed, which he had depicted in *The Marriage of Heaven and Hell:* honoring God's gifts in other men, Blake conversed with angelic devils, often reading the Bible together with them—counterclockwise. Even in *Milton* his exhortations to "Young Men of the New Age" had been addressed especially to "Painters," "Sculptors," and "Architects," the practicing artists who must set their foreheads against the ignorant hirelings of "the Camp the Court & the University." And in *Jerusalem* his studied appeals to Jews, Deists, and Christians, while broadly exhorting these large categories of professors of religion to join Christ in striving against "the Wheel of Religion," defined a true response as engaging in "the exercise of the Divine Arts of Imagination." But now in the briefer writings he seems to speak more immediately in the language of an artist, so that even when he concentrates upon the resistance to Moral rules we feel that the God of his abomination is as much Joshua Reynolds as Jehovah of the Churches. His plate on Homer and Virgil dwells on the importance of "Living Form," his first words "To Lord Byron" concern Outline, and his engraved aphorisms encircling his living version of the Laocoön statue spell out the implications of the axiom that "Christianity is Art"—in all directions. Flatly, "Jesus & his Apostles & Disciples were all Artists," though "Their Works were destroyd by the Seven Angels of the Seven Churches in Asia, Antichrist Science."[10] Indeed, "What can be Created Can be Destroyed," so that "Without Unceasing Practice . . . you are lost." But Practice requires "Naked Beauty displayed," and Spiritual War against accusers of Sin, and the leaving of "Fathers & Mothers & Houses & Lands if they stand in the way of Art." In the orientation of these gnomic addenda to *Jerusalem*, one would say that it was because of failure to exercise the Arts of Imagination that "The Bishop never saw the Everlasting Gospel any more than Tom Paine" (as Blake had observed in his "Notes on the B. of L's. Apology for the Bible" in 1798—the date of which reminds us that neither theme nor title was new, that *The Everlasting Gospel* is a reaffirmation).

The Everlasting Gospel seems to spring from the same soil as these, yet to turn the antagonism of Moral Virtue and Practice in Art into a visionary definition of life and death. Here Blake returns to the bracing diabolic sophistry about Jesus and the Ten Commandments which had been so successful in making converts in *The Marriage*. But the argument begins—or at least Blake's pencil notes for an argument—with a development of one of the Laocoön gnomes, "If Morality was Christianity, Socrates was the Saviour." This prose paragraph (*j*) is the seedbed of the poem:

> There is not one Moral Virtue that
> Jesus Inculcated but Plato & Cicero
> did Inculcate before him what then
> did Christ Inculcate. Forgiveness of
> Sins This alone is the Gospel & this
> is the Life & Immortality brought to
> light by Jesus. Even the Covenant of
> Jehovah which is this If you forgive
> one another your Trespasses so shall
> Jehovah forgive you That he himself
> may dwell among you but if you
> Avenge you Murder the Divine Image
> & he cannot dwell among you [by his]
> because you Murder him he arises
> Again & you deny that he is Arisen(.)

Having written this paragraph on a small folded sheet of note paper (part of a notebook, perhaps, but not the Rossetti Notebook), Blake opened the sheet (or turned the page), changed to pen and ink, and put the same points into rhyme:

(l)

> What can this Gospel of Jesus be
> What Life & Immortality
> What was [It] it that he brought to Light
> That Plato & Cicero did not write[11]
> The Moral Virtues in their Pride
> Did [ove(r)] oer the World triumphant ride (.)

More than into rhyme, he put them into a narrative vision of history, a scene in a folk drama: the Virtues rode; the "Souls to hell ran trooping"; and (in and out of historical present, at the exegencies of rhyme) at once comes the climactic confrontation of "The Accuser Holy God of All," who "Beams," and Jesus, who "rose & said to men. . . ."

At this point (but whether he saw it coming we cannot tell) Blake changed "men" to "Me," putting himself into the center of the scene:

> Then Jesus rose & said to Me
> Thy Sins are all forgiven thee
> Loud Pilate Howld loud Caiphas yelld
> When they the Gospel Light beheld
> Jerusalem he said to me. . . .

Blake quickly resisted the temptation to put a resumé of *Jerusalem* into Jesus' mouth, deleted that line, and went on to the next page. Here he started again, redundantly:

> It was when Jesus said to Me
> Thy Sins are all forgiven thee
> The Christian trumpets loud proclaim
> Thro all the World in Jesus name
> Mutual forgiveness of each Vice (.)

The promised scene now gets complicated by its simultaneity: *when* Jesus spoke, the trumpets proclaimed and "oped the Gates of Paradise," but at the same moment the Moral Virtues formed cross and nails and spear,

> And the Accuser standing by
> Cried out Crucify Crucify.

Nothing happens, it is a painting not an action, but not a painting either, for the Accuser now simply argues, and exhorts himself and his "daughters" (the Virtues, belatedly personified).

Having reached the last page of his small folio, Blake turned back to versified definition:

(k)

If Moral Virtue was Christianity
Christs Pretensions were all Vanity (.)

He must have at once intended "This to come first" (as he marked it), for he left a space and inserted the numeral "1" above this aphoristic section, going back to number the more dramatic unit "2."[12] Here was a complete poem of sorts. But it led nowhere; if it were to be expanded it would need to be recast; and after Blake had patched it with a few marginal additions (lines 5–8 and 36–7 of 2 and 9–10 of 1) he made no further extant attempts to build on this beginning.

The next fragment, begun in ink and in verse, represents a significant advance, especially in particularity of argument and personification. An advance also, alas, in ambiguity; Blake seems now to be thinking in much larger potential sweeps than the few lines he writes down. Fragment k need not have led to anything larger. This second one (i) is obviously going somewhere—and is too busy with the future to explain itself.

But there can hardly be any question about the sequence of composition. From the prose of j ("This . . . is the Gospel . . . brought to light by Jesus") to the still general question of l ("What can this Gospel of Jesus be") to the more particular and less merely rhetorical question of i ("Was Jesus Born of a Virgin Pure"), the direction of development is evident enough. And the speech of the Accuser to the Moral Virtues (during which the idea of calling them his daughters emerges as an afterthought) can be seen to have suggested the speech of Caiaphas in i. The reverse seems impossible.

In i, furthermore, Blake is still uncertain about rhetorical form and tone (the ironies criss-cross each other), and he makes only a rough beginning on the biography of Jesus as Vagrant Artist breaking all the rods of Earthly Parents. It is hardly conceivable that the poet should have first written the elaborate, harmonious biographies of b, c, d, e and then written the more simply enumerative sketch of *i*. Indeed much of the latter is only the last "Memorable Fancy" of *The Marriage* put into rhyme.

> He mockd the Sabbath, & he mockd
> The Sabbaths God . . .
>
> . . . . .
>
> And thus he others labours stole
>
> . . . . . .
>
> And from the Adulteress turnd away
> Gods righteous Law that lost its Prey(.)

Compare:

> . . . did he not mock at the sabbath, and so mock the sabbaths God?
> . . . turn away the law from the woman taken in adultery? steal the labor of others to support him?

(Marriage 23)

Then compare the high finish of section *e,* the whole of which is a dramatic presentation of the trial of Mary, with Jesus in Moses' Chair reversing the course of Heavenly judgment. The sequence is clearly from *The Marriage* (via *Jerusalem* 61 and 77 possibly) to section *i,* and on to *e* and its variants. It might be argued that, having written the more sophisticated passages, Blake *could* have relaxed later into the cruder sarcasm of *i,* just as the whole poem is a colloquialization of themes in *Jerusalem.* If that were the case we might well expect to hear echoes in *i* of the loftier passages. But the echoes we do hear are from the prose of *The Marriage*—and from the preliminary couplets of section *l.*

The most transitional aspect of *i,* however, is its patched and ambiguous irony. The earlier fragments began and remained essentially argument, and when drama entered it was still of simple logical pattern: Christ and Lucifer argue their opposite views; "I" stand by and am addressed by Christ; the "Moral Virtues" are inspired and exhorted by the Accuser. The Socratic answers to Blake's original Socratic questions remain asserted and simple: What distinguishes Christ's Gospel from Plato's and Caiaphas' is mutual forgiveness; what Moral Virtues rest upon is Satanic Accusations of Sin. In *i* the sarcastic wit of "terrible Blake" (still far removed from the Enthusiasm in section *e,* for only in the latest passages will the poet's mood rise to one of high seriousness) seizes every blunt weapon in the armory of satire to drive this question or non-question into the ground. Was Jesus born of a Virgin? By the logic of Sin & Deliverance "The Mother should an Harlot been." By the same logic, if one answers, Yes, a Virgin Pure, then accusation must find out some Secret Sin. Magdalen hid "seven devils"; "were Jew Virgins still more Curst/And more sucking devils nurst"? (This couplet was an afterthought, added in the margin, to sharpen the attack.) It is of course, in the Blakean gospel, the Pretence to Purity that needs forgiving. But in the opening questions and answer of *i*, it is not clear who is speaking. If the poet, it is only as a retailer of gossip (with tongue in cheek). After the couplet,

> Yes but they say he never fell
> Ask Caiaphas for he can tell(,)

the Keynes editions supply quotation marks to the end of the fragment. But this would make Caiaphas speak with the voice of the Devil of Blake's "Memorable Fancy." In other words, if the intention was, as is probable, to quote Caiaphas on Jesus, the poet forgets to keep his speech in character—especially in the inserted marginal lines 21–6, which first read:

> End the Tent of Secret Sins & its Golden cords & Pins
> Tis the Bloody Shrine of War Pinnd around from Star to Star
> Halls of Justice hating Vice
> Where the Devil Combs his Lice (.)

Perhaps "End" is a slip for "Ended": Christ ended the tent of sins. It was revised to "Oerturnd," perhaps at once. Even so, there is more Blake than Caiaphas in the lines on the "Bloody Shrine of War" and the "Halls of Justice." Throughout, the speaker is primarily not the Accuser (with whom one would identify Caiaphas) but the casuist Blakean "Devil" proving that Jesus was all virtue and acted from impulse, never from rules. Think of a sin, or of a law against it, and he'll show you how Jesus overturned it.

Such entangled cross-purposes are not uncharacteristic for Blake. When his wit is leaping ahead of his invention, he often ignores the persona established in one line while he is composing the next. I do not argue that inferiority in a passage signifies priority of composition—nor indeed that *i* is altogether inferior: it is laden with effective and memorable couplets. I do argue that it shows Blake still groping for the pattern which gives unity and strength to the necessarily later sections climaxing in *e*. It is partly his not having yet attained the sure form of the later sections that opens *i* to such intrusions as the lice-combing and the subsequent passage on the swine and the Jews. Shock tactics offensive to Christians are here complemented by shocks to Jews: Jesus turned devils into swine to make manifest the hell of corporeal desire: broke the ritual law and tempted Jews to become non-Jews, their pretence to Cleanliness being a variant of the Christian pretence to Purity. What may get across to puzzled readers is that the doctrine of "Mutual Forgiveness of each Vice" will need to be called into play in relation to the poet himself—whose own proud confession in *Jerusalem* comes to mind: "I am perhaps the most sinful of men I pretend not to holiness. . . ."

The work of section *i* is to recollect the argument of *The Marriage of Heaven and Hell* and put it into rhyme. Next, or simultaneously, Blake wrote another section, now lost, beginning "What are those" (*m*)—possibly a variant of the last four lines of *k*. At least presumably he wrote this before turning to his Notebook.[13]

By 1818 this book was crammed with the drawings and essays and epigrams and songs of thirty years; indeed any time after 1811 it held only a scattering of open pages left for use. Leafing forward from the front, Blake was not skipping any blanks of great size when he inscribed section *a* on page 33, though there were slightly larger spaces on 27, 28, and 30. Perhaps his first intention was a 6-line stanza; the next 8 lines are amplification, somewhat crowded in. After page 33 he might have used pages 44–5, but the next opening was discernibly more useful, beginning with two open pages (48–9) with only faint, expendable drawings in the centers and continuing with large blanks on 50 and 51, smaller on 52–4.[14] On 48–52 he wrote section *e*, and he was not skipping any considerable blanks when he turned on to 98 for *c* and 100–101 for *b* (though page 64 may only now have been inscribed with the prose remark about Jesus' nose which is thematically related to *a*). Finally Blake rewrote *c* as *d*, squeezing it in after *e* on pages 52–4, with *f* as a sort of marginal note on 54, and inserting a title, "The Everlasting Gospel," at the head of *d*.[15]

The first of these Notebook strophes, *a*, may just possibly be an independent poem which was there before Blake began *The Everlasting Gospel* at all. The only links are thematic and rhythmic, and our attaching *a* to the larger poem is essentially no more than an editorial leap of faith. Since, however, it must belong to this stage in the *Gospel's* composition if it belongs to any, we may treat it here for its function (intended or not) as a useful and timely explanation of what is going on:[16]

(a)
The Vision of Christ that thou dost see
Is my Visions Greatest Enemy
. . . .
Socrates taught what Melitus
Loathd as a Nations bitterest Curse
And Caiphas was in his own Mind
A benefactor to Mankind
Both read the Bible day & night
But thou readst black where I read white(.)

Melitus, Caiphas, and "thou" (including "Voltaire Bacon &c" if we consult *h*) are the accusers; Christ, Socrates, and "I" are speakers "in parables to the Blind." But here, to shake us from any smugness, the reprobate pride of the author bursts forth in a confession of physiognomic identification:

Thine has a great hook nose like thine
Mine has a snub nose like to mine
Thine is the friend of All Mankind
. . . .
Thine loves the same world that mine hates (.)

The prose note on page 64 explains: "I always thought that Jesus Christ was a Snubby or I should not have worshiped him if I had thought he had been one of those long spindle nosed rascals." We learn from Lavater's *Essays in Physiognomy,* for which Blake had engraved a few illustrations, that Socrates had a nose like Blake's, expressive of independent genius; inevitably Blake's subsequent Visionary Head of that worthy shows this. We do not, however, find any snub-nosed Christ—either in Lavater or in Blake's own numerous drawings and paintings; in these Jesus' nose is straight and usually long. Blake kept his proud Spectre out of his paintings and abided by the vision of his admired Raphael (whose allegedly idealized noses are presented in Lavater as the ultimate perfection). We do well to remember, both from the assertion in fragment *h* and from the more "terrible" passages in the preliminary sections, that Blake's Spectral Selfhood is never far offstage in this poem, if not always the presiding spirit. When he scribbled in pencil across the top of page 48, "This was spoke [or *spoken,* if the trailing off of the stroke intends an *n*] by My Spectre to Voltaire Bacon &ᶜ," he had already almost filled that page with the first 26 lines of section *e* (presumably the "This" of the pencil note), the section in which the poet at last has found his poem's voice, the Socratic rhetorical pattern it needed, and attacks directly the subject of Secret Sin and Divine Forgiveness:

(*e*)
Was Jesus Chaste or did he
Give any Lessons of Chastity
The morning blushd fiery red
Mary was found in Adulterous bed
Earth groand beneath & Heaven above
Trembled at discovery of Love(.)

That this woman taken in Adultery is Mary Magdalen, and not the Virgin, the satiric poet only gradually discloses. But now the thread of the Harlot-Saviour theme in *i* and the clues there for a confrontation of Jesus and the Law in the vicious "Halls of Justice" are elaborated and given dramatic structure in a tremendously momentous vision of Jesus "sitting in Moses Chair" with his transmuting hand laid "on Moses Law." The "trembling Woman" (line 8) and "The Earth trembling" (line 15)—compare Blake's echoing of Milton's Nativity Ode in *Europe*—recognize not simply "the breath of God" in Jesus' dismissal of "God" but also what I think we have to call the unity of his Second Coming with his First: a unity which the crucifixion, dealt with adverbially at the end of the passage, can only postpone but not obscure. At the crucifixion Satan's "glittring pride" was "perfected" (line 92); in the fiery morning of Mary's judgment it had already been outlawed and replaced by the "breath Divine" of "Love."[17]

Minor details of the composition of *e* show steadiness of conception and rapid pace. Lines 1–26 went swiftly onto page 48, with little mending. Page 49 began with the exhortation to "Thou Angel . . . That didst create this Body . . ." (now lines 29–30), but in the margin an explanation of that Angel/Devil was soon added (perhaps, if *e* is fair copy, this was accidentally omitted at the beginning of a new page):

> To be Good only is to be
> A God or else a Pharisee (.)

This couplet, marked to go in as 27–8, assists the modulation of "God" to "Good" to "Angel" to (11 lines further) "Serpent"; but at some later time, perhaps with the pencil that attributed all "This" to the Spectre, a more drastic attempt was made to signify the abrupt movement of contraries within "God" by inserting the word "Devil"—perhaps a tentative return to the ironic inversions of *The Marriage*.

On page 50 the writing is rapid, with shifts from "crime" to "shame" and "where" to "that" (reported in Keynes, lines 62–4) and from "Let me see't" to "Let me see it" (in which accuracy of rhyme—with "Deceit"—yields to decorum of Divine speech). And the four lines, "And hide in secret . . . Expands its wing," are a current expansion, written in the same pen and ink, in small space in the corner and marked to come in as 65–8. On page 51, lines 85–6 and 87–90 are insertions brought in from the top of the page; they fit, but the rearrangement obscures the continuity of reference from "the Shadowy Man" (line 81), all that remains of the "Angel of the Presence" of line 29, to "his" (line 82), to "Glittering with festering Venoms" (84), to "his glittring pride" (at first 86 but now 92).

Section *e* concluded at first with lines 93–4, on page 52,

> In three Nights he devourd his prey
> And still he devours the Body of Clay

and the poet counted up and inscribed his total as "94 lines." Later he added 95–6 in an adjacent column.

Immediately below the total he wrote two and a half lines, with an etcetera, meaning to bring in a passage from somewhere else:

(g)

Seeing this False Christ In fury & Passion
I made my Voice heard all over the Nation
What are those &ᶜ (.)

This is designated fragment g in Keynes's arrangement, but the intention may have been to continue directly on the "shadowy Man"/"False Christ" theme. Indeed the lost passage *may* be, as Keynes suggests, a variant of lines 11–14 of k. These would simply round out the passage, though anticlimactically unless the lines were somewhat transformed, with some curtain lines by the poet himself (I remove, as the cue-line suggests, an obtrusive "For" in the first line):

what is Antichrist but those
Who against Sinners Heaven close
With Iron bars in Virtuous State
And Rhadamanthus at the Gate (.)

We cannot, however, reconstruct the "&ᶜ" with any confidence. Nor can we be quite sure whether Blake next wrote h, c, or b. In each of these what he did with evidently triumphant speed was to work out the successful formula of e in application to other Moral Virtues: Humility (c), Gentility (b), and the philosophical "doubt" of Voltaire and company who "are constantly talking of the Virtues of the Human Heart" (*Jerusalem* 52):

(h)

Did Jesus teach doubt or did he
Give any lessons of Philosophy
Charge Visionaries with decieving
Or call Men wise for not Believing(?)

These four lines comprise the whole of h, written sideways in the margin of the first page of e, in pencil. It would be a neat, but fanciful, explanation to suppose that this side thrust was penciled when Blake had run out of his brownish ink and had not yet purchased or prepared the new supply, of a blacker color, with which he wrote the rest of the poem.[18] But he can have made the entry at any time after e; it remains an unpursued charge, a potential but arrested variant of the central formula.

As for the next fully developed variants, it is my impression, from rather meager evidence, that Blake first wrote the Gentility section (*b*, on pages 100–101, the first large open space after *e*) and then the Humility (*c*, in a narrow column on page 98). The spacing of the manuscript lines of sections *a, e, b* (and also *i*) is about 4 to 4½ to an inch, regardless of crowding, while *c* and its revision *d* (on pages 52–4) are spaced about 5½ to 6 lines an inch. Whether this change is the effect of the use of a finer pen or is a symptom of increased concentration and momentum, it does seem to confirm the sequence *b c*. If, then, Blake moved directly from *e* to *b*, he was resuming his bold opening challenge with the moral pointer turned sharply about to a "Virtue" which might have seemed implied by the loving protection Jesus extends to his "trembling Dove" in *e:*

(*b*)
Was Jesus gentle or did he
Give any marks of Gentility
When twelve years old he ran away
And left his Parents in dismay(.)

Now Jesus is "angry" and as loud-voiced as "Sinais trumpet," a man of "furious ire" and violent action, trampling Hipocrisy, dragging Satan at his chariot wheels, scourging the Merchant (from his mind), binding the Hellish Crew, and subduing Nature's dross "with wrath." In a number of small ways *b* is close to *e* in conception if not in texture—in tone, in drama, in its culminating with the crucifixion as a double event. The text is indeed rough hewn, as Blake may have felt a denial of "marks of Gentility" should be (compare lines 7–8 with the more articulate and graceful version in *c* and *d* or, for that matter, *i*). But there are few hesitations in the writing—only a quick change of construction in line 33 ("with" revised to "his") and a mending of "wheel" to "wheels" in 45— until the very end, where the final couplet

He took on Sin in the Virgins Womb
And on the Cross he Seald its doom

was crossed out and replaced by a triplet qualifying the finality of the "doom":

> He took on Sin in the Virgins Womb
> And put it off on the Cross & Tomb
> To be Worshipd by the Church of Rome(.)

Again both Christ and Antichrist triumph.

Perhaps Blake felt that "Seald its doom" would conclude the whole poem, while "To be Worshipd" would keep it open; or perhaps his triplet was intended to conclude it. What he did was to go on and apply the formula to still another "Virtue":[19]

> (c)
> Was Jesus Humble or did he
> Give any proofs of Humility
> When but a Child he ran away
> And left his Parents in dismay
> When they had wanderd three days long
> These were the words upon his Tongue (.)

The use of similar opening lines may for a moment suggest that *c* was meant to replace *b*, but the two sections are quite different in theme, matter, and structure; the Humility-Pride opposition cannot take the place of the Gentility-Wrath; each draws definition from the other. But we are now brought closer to the poet at work; with *c* and its immediate second draft, *d*, the handwriting shrinks and the mending, revision, and rearrangement of lines increase— not necessarily from increase of speed or purpose. Blake may now be wavering as he comes to grips with this polyp of a poem which will ultimately defy and escape his effort to nail it to the Cross. He will reach the point of writing in a title; in his manuscripts this usually signifies a satisfied "imprimatur." But he will not leave clear directions for editor or printer; we must remain uncertain whether the finished poem he *saw* was some arrangement of what we see in the Notebook or still only a vision in "the Temple of his Mind." Yet it is instructive to observe these final but uncompleted stages of the poem's growth in the manuscript.

Section *c* has many indications of being a first draft—for perhaps the relatively untroubled appearance of *a, e, b* is due to their being in part transcriptions from earlier drafts made elsewhere. Immediately after the opening "Earthly Parents" lines, taken over from *b*, the couplets jump about and the poet finds he must rearrange lines 10–15 (by numbering them 1 4 5 2 3 6). Lines 19–22 and

29–33 were moved to their present position after composition on other parts of the page. There is some stumbling, such as "he" for "that Jesus" in 34, "the Sinner to Judment bring" mended to "the Sinner to Judment to bring," line 46, and "made upo" mended to "made up of" in 51. The incomplete mending and the failure to correct "they" for "thy" in line 43 suggest that Blake went on quickly to his second draft of the whole section. (It should be remarked, however, that the modulation that appears in Keynes from "wonder'd" in 5c to "wander'd" in 7d is a mistake of transcription; the reading should be "wanderd" in each case.) In line 25 the word "Antichrist" is an afterthought. The line first read "If he had been the Creeping Jesus"; the revision strengthens the hypothesis that the "&ᶜ" intended for g was something deriving from the "Antichrist" lines in k but also might indicate the abandonment of that idea (which would free "Antichrist" for use here). (Oddly enough, when the line is repeated in d the whole process is copied—first reading, deletion of "the," and insertion of "Antichrist" above the line—probably from haste; possibly the revision was made at some later time, but then why in both drafts?)

The marginal additions in c sound like intrusions of the poet: "This is surely not what Jesus intends/He must mean . . . so he must mean . . ." (20–2); "This is the Trick . . ." (29–32). In revision (d) Blake curtails these passages. Yet at the same time he accepts this impulse to step directly into the poem, taking care to make dramatic use of it:

> What can be done with such desperate Fools
> . . . .
> I was standing by when Jesus died
> What I calld Humility they calld Pride(.)
>
> (21–4 d)

With this stroke he recovers the inspiration of section l ("Jesus . . . said to men" revised to "Me") and thus locates the debate raging through the poem not in the poet's room or the intellectual marketplace but at the foot of the Cross. The "desperate Fools" are the "Scribes & Pharisees" of all eras, however, and much of the enlargment of the Humility section comes from the conversational inclusion of Doctor Priestly and Bacon and Sir Isaac Newton as well as Caiphas and Caesar. Yet as the discussion expands, in d, so also does the narrative of Jesus' doings and sayings. Even so the whole section is much less dramatic than the "Chastity" and "Gentility" sections. It is discursive and much more susceptible to gnomic and epigrammatic development, and Blake finally recognizes its potential service as an *introduction* to the more dramatic sections, as we shall see.[20] On the other hand it could be argued that the long addition at the end of the section, expanding one couplet on Life-as-Contradiction into an 18-line essay which increasingly threatens to depart altogether from metrical control (91–108), represents a triumph of the didactic impulse over the dramatic which leaves the work in ruins.

It will be noticed that Blake added up *d* to "78 lines" *before* most of this expansion had taken place, and it is well to take stock of the manuscript as it then stood. When Blake chose to crowd his revised "Humility" section, *d,* into the rather limited space left on pages 52–4 immediately following *e* and *g,* he must have done so primarily to obtain the sequence *e g d,* or at least *e d* (dropping *g* when he made the "Antichrist" insertion). He made a halt to count up "78 lines" in *d,* as he had counted "94 lines" in *e,* yet he continued adding to *d.* (He had added 51–8, 69–70, 91–108 to his first draft, before counting 78; he went on to add 3–4, 21–4, 31–50, 87–90 [two couplets replacing one].) The long addition of 87–108 could best justify itself as a concluding epilogue: the poet, present at the dramatic moments of Christ's defiance toward Caiphas and of the crucifixion, now moves gently down from the theatrical to the meditative. If *e d* is to be the sequence, or *b e d* (Gentility, Chastity, Humility), the gnomic quality of *d* will mean inevitably a structure of lessening tension.

Blake's next step was to decide that his quietest section ought to be his first, and he inserted his title, "The Everlasting Gospel," at the head of *d;* at the end of it he appended the cue line "Was Jesus Chaste or did he &ᶜ" to achieve the sequence *d e.* (Late insertion of title may not signify that the title was an afterthought; it was Blake's usual practice—almost without exception throughout the Notebook—to write his titles last, when he was sure where they belonged, i.e., when he felt that he was largely through adding or subtracting or rearranging lines.) Some of the marginal additions in *d* and *e* may have been made after this time, but the only certain subsequent addition was the couplet

(f)

I am sure This Jesus will not do
Either for Englishman or Jew(.)

These words were written just alongside the last line of *d,* "When
the Soul slept in the beams of Light." I take them to be not a
further passage in *The Everlasting Gospel*—for if Blake had meant
to cue them in after "Was Jesus Chaste . . . &ᶜ" there was room
enough—but an aside upon its subject. Though ironic, may they
not mark a decision to give up the poem? Or do they mark, with
the titling, a decision that the poem is complete? It was given, so far
as we know, no further delineation, and no deletion lines were
drawn through discarded segments, as Blake's practice had been
with earlier poems written and perfected in the Notebook.

The idea that any one arrangement of parts must be the only
perfect arrangement of the whole, the search for the poet's final
intentions, might have seemed to Blake ridiculous or what "the
Ancients calld . . . eating of the tree of good & evil" (*On Homers
Poetry*). He himself kept rearranging his *Songs* and the plates of
Urizen and *Milton* and *Jerusalem,* to the last. He enjoyed writing a
circular poem, *The Mental Traveller,* and a scrambled one,
Auguries of Innocence, and arranging the Laocoön inscriptions
to be read starting from any point. "Every Poem must necessarily
be a perfect Unity," he continued in the Homer note, but "its
Goodness or Badness is another consideration. . . . Unity &
Morality. are secondary considerations & belong to Philosophy &
not to Poetry."

We ought to be content that we have the title and as many parts
as we do have of this poem—and that we may try all arrangements.
Yet ought we to attempt to include all the extant sections as
legitimate parts? Section *a* does well as Prologue, where Keynes
places it; yet neither inclusion nor placing is clearly authenticated.
The first "Humble" section, *c,* is of course a discarded draft; so
surely are *i, j, k, l,* unless we choose to rescue *i* for a summary—
but where? Blake's placing the title above *d* hardly leaves room for
a Prologue, whether *i* or *a;* can *i* really serve as Epilogue? Blake
seems to have been discarding *g* (with the lost *m*); *h* ("Did Jesus
teach doubt") may be but a start and *f* ("This Jesus will not do") a

note. Perhaps Blake's "final" sequence was *d e b* (Humble, Chaste, Gentle); we are sure of *d e;* and *b* could easily follow *e,* as it did in composition. The extension of the concluding couplet of *b* into a triplet looks as if it were current, but it may have been a later change signifying a decision to end the poem here. (And this would leave *i* and *a* quite out of the picture.) The "pure" editorial reduction of the text must be to *d e b,* I suspect.

Good structural arguments could be made for the crescendo sequence *d b e* (Humble, Gentle, Chaste), however, and even for *e d b* (Chaste, Humble, Gentle) or *b e d* (Gentle, Chaste, Humble). And if we are to admit insertions between the title and *d,* we may have the two couplets of *h* as an opening refrain. Of possible arrangements assigning auxiliary functions to *h, i,* and even *a,* an attractive sequence might be: *h i d e b a.*[21] Yet it is perhaps even more important to recognize the shape of the poem that was emerging as Blake modeled each new section in more markedly parodistic relation to the last. Vision against Vision: Was Jesus Chaste? Was Jesus Gentle? Was Jesus Humble? Each set of Contradictions explodes or "rolls away" into another—taken in either direction. To plagiarize lines 50–51 of *c,* do what we will this Poem's a Fiction and is made up of Contradiction.[22]

NOTES

1. "When Klopstock England defied," Notebook p. 5. The nature of the German poet's challenge to English poets throws light on this vein in Blake. In English and German magazines, 1796–99, the weakness of "English hexameter" was debated. One German prophesied "that the English poets will soon be able to forge hexameters on the anvil of the Muses, with as much skill as Klopstock and Voss"; Klopstock himself, in correspondence and conversation, challenged Englishmen, blaming Swift's influence for the coarseness of English diction. To "my German Herder" he wrote (21 March 1797) that "we Germans owe the English some literary revenge ever since Swift sounded a coarse or vulgar note against us [seitdem ihnen Swift einen gewissen und beinah plumpen Ton wider uns angegeben hat]. I know very well . . . because I talk to many Englishmen, that for some time they have modified their attitude; but that for me doesn't burn the Moor Swift and his followers white." When this challenge reached Blake, in some letter or magazine he took to his outhouse, he read it as a direct cry from "old Nobodaddy . . . to English Blake"—and took on the mantle of Swift, in the matter of coarse diction; what he could do when he "sat down to write" was exhibited in the more-than-hexameters, the "long resounding strong heroic Verse," of *Vala.*

2. *Notes and Queries,* May 1962, pp. 171–6.

3. The text quoted is derived from a fresh transcription of the manuscripts. Square brackets are used to signify deleted words or letters, parentheses to enclose my editorial insertions.

During the course of the essay I have managed to quote all the lines that happen to contain substantive variations from the readings in *The Complete Writings of William Blake,* ed. Geoffrey Keynes, 1957.

4. A. L. Morton's comparisons along this line, in *The Everlasting Gospel: A study in the sources of William Blake,* 1958, are helpful as background for the Antinomianism in Blake's milieu, but somewhat misleading for the precise meanings in Blake's poem. For Joachim, however, see Morton, p. 35, and Désirée Hirst, *Hidden Riches,* 1964, p. 102.

5. Letter to George Cumberland, 12 April 1827.

6. The half-deleted phrase "[Simulative] Phantom" is in *Jerusalem* 4:23–4. For the strife of the true and phantom Jesus, see *Jerusalem* 77.

7. I called the remnant edges of printed words on this leaf to the attention of G. E. Bentley, Jr., who recognized it as belonging to the *Ballads;* he has given "minutely careful" measurement and description of it on p. 161 of his facsimile edition of *Vala or The Four Zoas,* 1963; these confirm his identification.

8. Laid note paper watermarked "1818"; not the heavy Whatman paper of the same date used in *Jerusalem.* That this "small folded leaf . . . may have been at one time inserted with the other small leaf at the end of the *Notebook*" (Keynes p. 921) is a plausible conjecture, not born out by the evidence. Stitch marks show that the sheet was once bound into some book (probably a notebook of its size) but they do not match the marks in the Rossetti Notebook. The Notebook "small leaf" is 13.6 x 13.5 cm.; the "1818" leaves are 9.6 x 16.3 cm. (very close in size to the 9.7 x 16.6 of the leaf forming pp. 141–2 of *The Four Zoas,* presumably another "small notebook" scrap).

9. Reading Keynes's note about the dating of the poem, p. 920, we can see that the unhappy term "Supplementary" was given to these passages without definitive intent but as a plausible and tentative conclusion from three evident points: that the Notebook entries (including *a*) because of their location require a date not earlier than 1810, that the paper of the Rosenbach fragment (*j, k, l*) bears the date "1818," and that all one's impressions derived from the style, the handwriting, and the nature of most of the drafts as a series of improvisations under a single inspiration suggest no great passage of time for the whole composition. Sir Geoffrey sees that it would be possible to date the poem "1820 or even later," more judicious to assign it "to *about . . .* 1818"—and then, as a concession to the tug of 1810 as a *terminus ab quo,* to label the 1818 sections "Supplementary."

10. A convenient reproduction of the Laocoön engraving is the frontispiece to the second volume of *The Prophetic Writings of William Blake,* ed. D. J. Sloss and J. P. R. Wallis, 1926; another is plate 37 in G. Keynes, *Separate Plates* (Dublin, 1956).

11. Lines 5–8 were added later in the margin.

12. The "2" is crowded onto the G of "Gospel."

13. I deduce that *i* was written before the small sheet containing it was sewed into the Notebook, and if the deduction is sound then the sewing was done to preserve *i*. The first three pages of the sheet are taken up with a draft for the Prospectus of Blake's engraving of Chaucer's Pilgrims (Keynes pp. 587–9) which was printed about 1810. Since the draft was largely copied out of the *Descriptive Catalogue* of 1809 and in turn not much changed when printed, there was no reason for Blake's treating the sheet as other than a scrap with a remaining blank page; he had apparently given a revised draft to the printer. The failure to sew in the other preliminary scrap, containing *j k l*, signifies a more definite rejection of those sections. (We do not *know* that the sewing in was done by Blake, but the probability is extremely slight that any such pains would have been taken by William Palmer, who received the Notebook from Mrs. Blake and sold it to Rossetti in 1849 for ten shillings, or by Rossetti, who did not include *i* in his copying of the poem.)

If this deduction is erroneous, then the page on which *i* was written would have been the blank end page of the Notebook, and the only modification of my reconstruction of the sequence would be to describe *i* as the first section entered in the Notebook (always possibly excepting *a*) rather than the last written before use of the Notebook. This possibility does influence the question of the relative position of *b*, we shall see.

Perhaps my judgment that Blake wrote the brief summary of his themes in *i* before their extensive development in *e b c* is too impressionistic. But there are difficulties in the way of assigning the summary last. Would a recapitulation written *after* the Chaste, Gentle, Humble, and doubting sections have been so *uninfluenced* by or disconnected from these? Blake, I believe, kept this early section because he had not used it up as the poem progressed. He had, however, borrowed the "Fathers Business" couplet from it. When he repeats that couplet in his Gentle, Humble, Chaste sections it functions as a refrain put each time to a different use. But in both *b* and *i* the use is identical, for the theme of Obedience; so if we accept *b* into the poem we cannot have *i* also. Here too, I admit, one could argue that the reverse is possible: Blake *is* rejecting *b* when he writes, for summary, *i*. The Obedience passage in *b* is indeed cruder than that in *i*. But does not this come from the extension and expansion attempted in *b*, as Blake moves to enlarge the compact elements of *i*? I think so.

14. Whether a Notebook page or area containing a pencil drawing seemed available for other use evidently depended upon Blake's feeling about the drawing and his urgency as the Notebook filled. Thus we cannot always be certain where he would or would not have seen space for writing.

15. As the poem took shape, Blake clustered the sections as close together as the spaces in the Notebook permitted. Note that *if* one argues for a late date for *j k l* as truly "Supplementary," he must account for their being written outside the Notebook when there was ample room for them on pages 44–5 and elsewhere.

The same point applies to *i*, unless one insists on the least likely case, that the leaf was sewed into the Notebook before *i* was written on it. One can understand the salvaging of an early scrap by sewing it in, but if the poem had already begun in the Notebook, why should one strophe be added on a separate scrap (*i* is not particularly rough copy)?

16. If *a* had been in the Notebook and Blake had thought now to incorporate it into his developing poem, he would surely have cued it in or entered his next section close to it. But if he were now simply composing *a* and then *e*, the link between them might be strong enough in his own mind to obviate such signposts for the time being. He did not finally make any thorough linking up or crossing out of sections, to guide us.

The ink of *a* and the snub-nose passage on page 64 is brownish, and so is the ink of *e* and *g*. That of all the other ink sections is the more usual black. But all I can determine about Blake's ink is that his supply varied, with both brown and black at early and late periods. The similarity of ink in *a* and *e* permits their having been written at the same sitting. The change to black ink in *b* and *c* requires at least time out for the purchase or preparation of a new supply.

17. Mr. Tolley, in correspondence, has pointed out a further congruence, which I have asked his permission to cite here. In lines 29–30, 39–42 Jesus is saying that the Creator ("Angel of the Presence Divine") who made Adam's body (Genesis 1.27;2.7) also made Jesus' own body. "A sequence of accusing lines beginning 'Tho . . .' culminates in 'Tho thou didst all to Chaos roll'—and we are suddenly back to Genesis 1.2, when the 'earth was without form, and void' (or before Milton's 'Heavens and Earth/Rose out of Chaos'). But we don't realize this until the next couplet, when we are told that in spite of the fact that the Creator has reduced all to its original chaos, 'Still the breath Divine does move', still does the Spirit of God move 'upon the face of the waters'—and now we learn that this Spirit is Love. It is a wonderful climax (though somewhat inconsistent with the former threats), and holds together contradictory suggestions (it is implied that the 'breath Divine' is the same now as at the Creation, and yet the 'Angel' clearly lacks Love). This sort of effect is very difficult to describe, but it certainly fits what Coleridge described as 'The grandest efforts of poetry' in its 'substitution of a sublime feeling of the unimaginable for a mere image.' "

18. The pencil note "This was spoke . . . to Voltaire . . ." seems to apply directly to these four lines on doubt; yet from the arrangement of the writing on the page we see that the note is inscribed above the first line of *e*. Blake must have written it there and then turned the book sideways to write the "doubt" lines, as a more direct fling at the philosophers. (Postscript when reading proof: I fear I have overlooked the "&ᶜ" in "Bacon &ᶜ" as a cue to another lost passage, probably but not necessarily prose. This suggests something other than an impulsive aside.)

19. Unless, of course, *b* with its concluding triplet was written last. But the triplet may be an afterthought.

20. Passages new in *d* are lines 3–4, 21–4, 27–8 (over erased lines that may

have been 21–2 of *c*), 31–58, 69–70, and 87–108—105–8 being adapted from *Auguries of Innocence*.

21. John E. Grant suggests that "an honest if imperfect poem" could be constructed from all the materials (except replaced *c*) somewhat as follows:

h	(with motto)	4 lines	Teachings
k	(1)	14	Moral Virtue
l	(2)	43	Gospel
i		48	Birth
a		14	Vision
b		59	Gentle?
d		108	Humble?
e		95	Chaste?
g		2	False Christ
j	(very tricky)	Prose	Plato and Cicero
f		2	Coda

22. I wish to thank T. C. Skeat and Désirée Hirst and Martha W. England for help in supplying gaps of information, and J. E. Grant and M. J. Tolley for critical suggestions.

Wordsworth's *Lyrical Ballads* in Their Time

CHARLES RYSKAMP

THE date 1798 is probably the one first stamped on the mind of the student of English literature, and if he goes very far in his studies he almost surely learns that few moments of literary history have been so frequently described or so thoroughly worried as the year which gave birth to *Lyrical Ballads*. From the early discussions of Wordsworth and Coleridge themselves to the recent (and excellent) investigations of men like Robert Mayo and Stephen Maxfield Parrish, the question of the originality of *Lyrical Ballads* has been debated endlessly. The comments here are not meant to be a rephrasing of the well-known judgments, such as those of Wordsworth's Preface of 1800, concerning that which "distinguishes these Poems from the popular Poetry of the day." But some other ways of looking at both Wordsworth's revolutionary and traditional achievements in 1798 will be attempted—a criticism aimed at discovering remarkable qualities in Wordsworth's poetry published in that year (though some of it was written as early as 1795) in comparison with the finest and the most popular poetry of his time.

It is particularly valuable to place beside a few of Wordsworth's poems from *Lyrical Ballads* some of Cowper's verse during the last two decades of the eighteenth century. Cowper was important in showing Wordsworth the way, not only toward a direct and simple response to nature, but also to an honest delineation of humble and rustic people. Wordsworth felt that Cowper and Burns were the two "great" authors who helped him to counteract the "mischievous" and extravagant manner of contemporary English and German writers; Cowper was for Coleridge, according to Hazlitt, "the best modern poet."

We might well begin by looking once more at the title of the volume: *Lyrical Ballads, with a Few Other Poems.* To some readers at the end of the eighteenth century the words "Lyrical Ballads" may have sounded tautological. "Lyrical" might suggest anything of the nature of song. "Ballads" might well have called up the traditional or folk ballads (the poems, for example, from Bishop Percy's famous *Reliques*), but the most common meaning of the word was just "song," a simple song. Under "Ballad" in the *Encyclopaedia Britannica* of 1797 we read only of "a kind of song, adapted to the capacity of the lower class of people; who, being mightily taken with this species of poetry, are thereby not a little influenced in the conduct of their lives. Hence we find, that seditious and designing men never fail to spread ballads among the people, with a view to gain them over to their side." Thus the title, *Lyrical Ballads,* may have been read by many in 1798 as men in the seventeenth century probably read the title of another celebrated collection of English poems, Donne's *Songs and Sonets.* A "sonet" meant a song or short poem; there are no "sonnets" in the strict sense of the word in Donne's volume.

Lyrics and lyrical qualities, however, were often associated with the direct expression of a poet's sentiments, and his personal involvement in the thoughts of the poem; in the true ballad, on the contrary, the teller of the story—his individual style—should not be present. Kittredge has described the ballad as "a song that tells a story, or—to take the other point of view—a story told in song. More formally, it may be defined as a short narrative poem, adapted for singing, simple in plot and metrical structure, divided into stanzas, and characterized by complete impersonality so far as the author or singer is concerned." If then there were a new mode in *Lyrical Ballads* which was the lyrical, subjective interposition of the author into the traditionally impersonal narrative of the ballads, one could understand the special relevance of the title. But this mode was certainly not new. "Objective" and "subjective" ballads are "found in profusion"—as Professor Mayo has thoroughly illustrated—in the magazines of the late eighteenth century, in Percy's *Reliques,* as well as in *Lyrical Ballads.* He showed that if we consider the popular poetry of Wordsworth's time, "the title of the *Lyrical Ballads* is ambiguous and confusing. Significantly, in the final classification of his poems, Wordsworth abandoned the category 'lyrical ballad.' " Whether or not the title was chosen casually (and, it might seem, clumsily), or purposely to be nondescript, it is not especially appropriate to the volume; yet as a title it was so similar to many of the time that it "was likely to surprise nobody."[1]

The contents, however, might well have amazed readers if they were looking for the *lyrical,* musical qualities which were characteristic of the best ballads of the eighteenth century. In all likelihood the ballads would have surprised William Cowper, though he was regarded by Coleridge as "the founder of the modern school" of poetry. In a letter of 4 August 1783, Cowper wrote that "the ballad is a species of poetry, I believe, peculiar to this country, equally adapted to the drollest and the most tragical subjects. Simplicity and ease are its proper characteristics. Our forefathers excelled in it; but we moderns have lost the art. It is observed, that we have few good English odes. But to make amends, we have many excellent ballads, not inferior perhaps in true poetical merit to some of the very best odes that the Greek or Latin languages have to boast of."

"Simplicity" in verse was demanded by Cowper, and of him and his contemporary poets by the critics. It was most frequently mentioned as the quality necessary to correct the faddish Della Cruscan strain in the late eighteenth century. Simplicity of form and subject was immediately recognized in *Lyrical Ballads* by most of the critics, and also parodied almost at once. By "simplicity" the critics of the 1790's meant nothing more than the language natural to men, lines which were unforced, artless, vigorous. They wanted at the same time the language of "true taste"—really the sane, poised language common to the best prose of the century, and most of its best verse. In the first extensive criticism of Cowper (it appeared in the Dublin periodical, *The Flapper,* in May-June 1796, and remains very good), Alexander Knox wrote that "the discerning reader will easily perceive that simplicity is a prevailing character in the poetry of *Cowper";* in the poet's descriptions of nature, the simple mode has "a kind of mysterious power of captivating the human mind. The degree of the pleasure they [nature and simplicity] afford is greater than can be rationally accounted

for." They "are the means, as well as the preservatives of innocence
and tranquillity." The criticism could as well have been written
about the finest verse of Wordsworth. Simplicity of language, "the
language of conversation in the middle and lower classes of society
. . . adapted to the purposes of poetic pleasure," was what Wordsworth believed constituted the experiment which he described in
the Advertisement of 1798. It was made manifest particularly in
the ballads among the poems of that volume, which were closer to
the halfpenny ballads being hawked about the streets, than to the
lyrical adaptations of Percy. In the rest of Wordsworth's verse the
language is not so severe, bare, matter-of-fact. The others more
fairly reflect the repeated emphasis on song in the title. Among
Wordsworth's poems in *Lyrical Ballads, with a Few Other Poems,*
the ballads themselves are the least lyrical.

What they lack is the "ease" required by Cowper as the second
characteristic of a ballad. In his letter quoted above, he went on to
name his touchstone of balladry, the *Ballad* from Gay's "Tragi-
Comi-Pastoral Farce," *The What D'Ye Call It* (1715). It is well
worth rescuing from its near oblivion.

I.

'Twas when the seas were roaring
    With hollow blasts of wind;
A damsel lay deploring,
    All on a rock reclin'd.
Wide o'er the rolling billows
    She cast a wistful look;
Her head was crown'd with willows
    That tremble o'er the brook.

II.

Twelve months are gone and over,
    And nine long tedious days.
Why didst thou, vent'rous lover,
    Why didst thou trust the seas?
Cease, cease, thou cruel ocean,
    And let my lover rest:
Ah! what's thy troubled motion
    To that within my breast?

III.

The merchant, rob'd of pleasure,

Sees tempests in despair;
But what's the loss of treasure
    To losing of my dear?
Should you some coast be laid on
    Where gold and di'monds grow,
You'd find a richer maiden,
    But none that loves you so.
                IV.
How can they say that nature
    Has nothing made in vain;
Why then beneath the water
    Should hideous rocks remain?
No eyes the rocks discover,
    That lurk beneath the deep,
To wreck the wand'ring lover,
    And leave the maid to weep.
                V.
All melancholy lying,
    Thus wail'd she for her dear;
Repay'd each blast with sighing,
    Each billow with a tear;
When, o'er the white wave stooping,
    His floating corpse she spy'd
Then like a lily drooping,
    She bow'd her head, and dy'd.

If we compare with Gay's ballad some lines from *We Are Seven,* we may be able to evaluate more precisely Wordsworth's contribution to the ballad form:

So in the church-yard she was laid,
And all the summer dry,
Together round her grave we played,
My brother John and I.

And when the ground was white with snow,
And I could run and slide,
My brother John was forced to go,
And he lies by her side.

The implicative style (a significance or pleasure greater than "can be rationally accounted for") which Knox perceived as an achievement of Cowper is even more remarkable in ballad stanzas like these of Wordsworth. Just so is simplicity as a means toward and a preservative of innocence and tranquillity. The lack of variation or complication in the central narrative by Wordsworth's "simple child," unlike the diverse rich images of the damsel's story, creates immediate, sharply focused recognition. Wordsworth's emphasis is on emotional states resulting from the narrative instead of on mood. Mystery—or wonder—grows out of the implications of the narrative or the ideas, rather than from image or verbal coloring. Concrete pictures or statements with symbolic overtones have replaced metaphor and simile. In some ways a truer ballad is realized ("a *story* told in song"), and a more realistic and primal experience; one might say also, despite its more constant gentleness, that *We Are Seven* achieves a more dramatic (though mental) action in the child's unadorned response; but these qualities which push one to quick recognition and then reflection, inhibit the lingering ease which brings forth music and song. In Wordsworth's avoidance of soft endings and of adjectival modification, with stress only on basic, active parts of speech, we find a directness of subject matter and a simple, crisp movement which detract from the flow and dying fall of song. Delicacy has not been denied, but grace and ease have been to a great extent replaced by the "seemly plainness" which Wordsworth later discussed in *The Prelude*.

In the years immediately preceding *Lyrical Ballads* few verses became so readily established in the minds of the people and in critical commentary as the "Crazy Kate" passage from *The Task* (1786). If Cowper's portrait of Kate is compared with poems like *The Thorn* and *The Mad Mother*, we may see how Wordsworth leaped free from the establishment of *The Task*, though as yet not at all with the assured poise and nobility of *Michael*. In *The Thorn* and *The Mad Mother* there are still many crudities in the excessively flat, particular description of person and scene, in repetition which deadens instead of gathering power, in the attempts at verisimilitude and a vernacular mode which are often clumsy, even banal. Such fumblings are not found in the description of "Crazy Kate," but Cowper, without Wordsworth's dialogue, whether suggested or dramatically presented, does not achieve a cumulative movement toward recognition; there is no action— rather blunt revelation and obtrusive moral commentary. The

reader is not led in "Crazy Kate" to the discovery of significance;
the values are not grounded in gradually illuminating perceptions
but are simply given to us. We do not see any psychological prob-
ing. There is instead a balanced description which creates external
portraiture only.

In *The Thorn* and *The Mad Mother* we are brought, through
internal or external dialogue and through sharp contrasts between
conflicting emotions and observations, to dramatic perception.
There is a movement of mind which makes the portrait come alive.
Through the self-revelation—usually unconscious—of the central
figure we discover a pathos largely free of sentimentality. In Wordsworth's mad mother we watch a deranged mind in which (as
Coleridge wrote in *Biographia Literaria*) "from the increased
sensibility the sufferer's attention is abruptly drawn off by every
trifle, and in the same instant plucked back again by the one
despotic thought." It is, above all, this conflict and evolving dramatic dimension which one misses in Cowper's poems before *The
Castaway* (1799). Here is his "Crazy Kate," easily separated from
the body of *The Task*, as it frequently was for magazines of that
time.

> There often wanders one, whom better days
> Saw better clad, in cloak of satin trimm'd
> With lace, and hat with splendid ribband bound.
> A serving maid was she, and fell in love
> With one who left her, went to sea, and died.
> Her fancy follow'd him through foaming waves
> To distant shores; and she would sit and weep
> At what a sailor suffers; fancy, too,
> Delusive most where warmest wishes are,
> Would oft anticipate his glad return,
> And dream of transports she was not to know.
> She heard the doleful tidings of his death—
> And never smil'd again! And now she roams
> The dreary waste; there spends the livelong day,
> And there, unless when charity forbids,
> The livelong night. A tatter'd apron hides,
> Worn as a cloak, and hardly hides, a gown
> More tatter'd still; and both but ill conceal
> A bosom heav'd with never-ceasing sighs.

She begs an idle pin of all she meets,
And hoards them in her sleeve; but needful food,
Though press'd with hunger oft, or comelier clothes,
Though pinch'd with cold, asks never.—Kate is craz'd!
(*The Task*, I, 534–56).

The dramatic implications of psychological discovery are nullified also because of Cowper's pictorial emphasis. This is not at all surprising. Throughout the eighteenth century painting and poetry were associated intimately. Artistic comparisons and painterly effects were repeated motifs in poetry. "You remember, dear Dick," wrote the schoolboy, Joseph Warton, about 1739, "that our Discourse last Evening turn'd upon the usual Subjects of Poetry & Painting." Warton and his school friends, like William Collins, hour by hour paired poets and painters, selecting "characters in either of these Sister Sciences, that would exactly match, & tally with each other."[2] Chaucer—Heemskerck; Spenser—Rubens; Shakespeare—Van Dyck; Dryden—Titian; Thomson—Claude or Salvator Rosa; etc. One might hope that for Cowper and Wordsworth they would select neither portrait painter nor landscape artist, but one who rendered a landscape animated by human life or people involved in the natural world. This inter-relationship is much more characteristic of Wordsworth than Cowper; in fact, in Wordsworth's best descriptive poetry the involvement of the two is so subtle that pictorial details, though not forgotten nor submerged, seem by the end of a poem to be of secondary interest. Yet critics in the 1790's and in the first years of the nineteenth century continued to stress the resemblances of the poems of Cowper or Wordsworth to the works of painters. The vignettes of *The Task*, one said, are like "the sketches of a *Raphael*" (*The Flapper*, 1796); *The Idiot Boy* "resembles a Flemish picture in the worthlessness of its design and the excellence of its execution" (*Critical Review*, 1798); *The Mad Mother* is "in Michael Angelo's bold and masterly manner" (*Monthly Review*, 1799). But whatever meanings these comparisons held for readers through the century, by the end of the period most analogies appear to be hollow and worn-out conventions. Fuseli, Stothard, Greig, Westall, and others made sketches for engravings of "Crazy Kate" (she seems to have been the favorite subject among the illustrators of Cowper's poems); few artists or artistic comparisons, however, could re-create the psychological and moral implications of Wordsworth's descriptions.

The ballads among Wordsworth's poems in the volume of 1798 most notably present the revolution in language which he himself drew attention to in the Advertisement. For the most part, Coleridge and Hazlitt in their accounts of the writing of the poems emphasized the same characteristic. Hazlitt wrote in *My First Acquaintance with Poets,* that when Coleridge in 1798 read aloud *The Thorn, The Mad Mother,* and *The Complaint of a Forsaken Indian Woman,* he "felt that deeper power and pathos which have been since acknowledged . . . as the characteristics of this author; and the sense of a new style and a new spirit in poetry came over me. It had to me something of the effect that arises from the turning up of the fresh soil, or of the first welcome breath of Spring. . . ." Wordsworth's ballads, as we have seen, were unlike the best eighteenth-century ballads in tone and ease, and unlike ballads of the 1790's because of a new vocabulary and because of psychological subtlety. Yet they were closest of all the poems in the volume to the popular verse in the magazines and miscellanies of the time, and were, in turn, most immediately approved by the people. They established as fashionable what was already found everywhere. Of all of them, "Goody Blake and Harry Gill" was "unquestionably the most popular."[3] It was also among the first to be parodied (though there are echoes of other poems from *Lyrical Ballads* in the parody), in *Barham-Downs; or, Goody Grizzle and her Ass. A Lyrical Ballad, in the Present Fashionable Stile.* The nearly scatological—"fundamental"—parody was published in the *European Magazine* for September 1801, just three years after the publication of *Lyrical Ballads.* Within a few years Coleridge would be writing of Wordsworth as "the Head & founder of a *Sect* in Poetry," and Jeffrey, in the *Edinburgh Review,* would strike at "the gentlemen of the new school . . . Mr Wordsworth and his associates."

The ballads may have held for Hazlitt the freshness of newly-turned soil, a new depth of power and pathos, but for most readers today this strength of originality can best be seen—as it was, in fact, seen by a few critics when *Lyrical Ballads* was first published —in *Expostulation and Reply, Lines Written in Early Spring,*

Lines Left upon a Seat in a Yew-Tree, Old Man Travelling, and *Lines Written a Few Miles above Tintern Abbey.* The forms of these poems are not in themselves extraordinary for that time, and several are clearly indebted to Milton, yet they reveal more profoundly a new voice in poetry; not novelty, but an authentic and lasting contribution to English verse. Southey in the *Critical Review* wrote that "in the whole range of English poetry, we scarcely recollect any thing superior" to part of *Tintern Abbey.* Dr. Burney in the *Monthly Review* lamented the tincture of "gloomy, narrow, and unsociable ideas" in *Tintern Abbey,* but discovered "reflections of no common mind; poetical, beautiful, and philosophical." The *Monthly Mirror* quoted in its entirety, "as a specimen of the author's talents," *Lines Left upon a Seat.* This periodical, though largely unknown today, was keen in its observations on the decline of the old forms during the latter part of the century and the rise of a new poetry. "Since the time of Pope, our vernacular poetry has been verging to mere sound, and . . . in labouring to polish the verse, the strength and vigour of the thought is lost, and the boldness and animation of genius is overlooked in the fondness for meretricious ornaments" (from a memorial piece on Cowper, May 1800).

The originality and full achievement of Wordsworth in *Lyrical Ballads,* 1798, is most impressive in *Tintern Abbey.* Here we can see a great change from the other poems in his masterful control of the rhythms and the developing patterns of ideas. *Tintern Abbey,* the last poem of the volume, was written and slipped into the collection as it was being printed. It was the most distinguished of Wordsworth's poems to that time, and a notable rise above the high-water mark of descriptive and reflective verse in the two decades preceding, such as a section like this from the fourth book of *The Task.*

> I saw the woods and fields, at close of day,
> A variegated show; the meadows green,
> Though faded; and the lands, where lately wav'd
> The golden harvest, of a mellow brown,
> Upturn'd so lately by the forceful share.
> I saw far off the weedy fallows smile
> With verdure not unprofitable, graz'd

> By flocks, fast feeding, and selecting each
> His fav'rite herb; while all the leafless groves,
> That skirt th' horizon, wore a sable hue,
> Scarce notic'd in the kindred dusk of eve.
> To-morrow brings a change, a total change!
> Which even now, though silently perform'd,
> And slowly, and by most unfelt, the face
> Of universal nature undergoes.
> Fast falls a fleecy show'r: the downy flakes,
> Descending, and with never-ceasing lapse,
> Softly alighting upon all below,
> Assimilate all objects. Earth receives
> Gladly the thick'ning mantle; and the green
> And tender blade, that fear'd the chilling blast,
> Escapes unhurt beneath so warm a veil.

Cowper's lines are radically different from seventeenth-century descriptive verse. It is perfectly clear that there are none of the naked, concrete images of a poem, say, like Marvell's *Garden* or *Upon Appleton House.* There is no hard, sharp sting of metaphysical epigram. We do not find the ambiguous implications, nor the sudden, surprising weight on particular words. In Marvell we should expect more mysterious strangeness and much more intimate intensity. We should have always been more aloof and yet— and this is also possible—more boldly familiar at the same time. Or, if one thinks of the pastoral poetry of Pope, as in *Windsor Forest,* one may see how the social terms of reference so strong in Pope have been diminished by Cowper. The personified garden of Pope was described with almost completely ornamental sketching, to give the general quality of the landscape, as opposed to any effect of looking at a real place. There are hints of personification in the passage quoted from Cowper: "the meadows green,/Though *faded;* and the lands, where lately *wav'd*/The golden harvest . . . ," "the weedy fallows *smile*/With verdure not *unprofitable* . . . ," "the leafless groves,/That *skirt* th' horizon, *wore* a sable hue. . . ." There is, we can see, even a trace of a pun, though in no way does it have the force of Pope's "chequered scene" in *Windsor Forest.* The moral fiber of Cowper's passage develops gradually, then is revealed with solemn strength. There is no ambivalence or paradox about Cowper's statements: "To-morrow brings a change, a total change!" And afterwards we gather the bits of poetic diction, the "fleecy show'r" and the "downy flakes," into the increasingly prosaic verse. There is a marked absence of concentration in the structure and rhythm. The tightness of Pope's couplet gives a tension to his observations which is lacking for the most part in *The Task.* Nevertheless, though quiet and muted, the lines move inevitably until the particularities of the landscape—more intimate and individual than in Pope—become universal evening and winter. Then also the personification is complete, and the total realization is traditional and familiar, not heterogeneous, nor abstract, nor wittily sophisticated.

Look then at the opening of *Tintern Abbey:*

> Five years have passed; five summers, with the length
> Of five long winters! and again I hear
> These waters, rolling from their mountain-springs
> With a sweet inland murmur.—Once again
> Do I behold these steep and lofty cliffs,
> Which on a wild secluded scene impress
> Thoughts of more deep seclusion; and connect
> The landscape with the quiet of the sky.

In Wordsworth's lines the passing years of his life and the scene before him are linked to the spiritual world. The relationships seen by the poet give significance to the superficially literal picture of nature. Concrete natural objects, as a result, create emotions which transfigure man until the spirit prevails. Passiveness and "thoughts of more deep seclusion" bring repose to the mind. If we read on a little further in this poem, we shall discover that the pictures of nature, which have been becoming more gently familiar and benign—from Marvell to Pope to Cowper—are now much more so in Wordsworth. Moral implications and personifications are less explicit, and the physical descriptions themselves much more individual and realistic. In temperament and kind of natural perception, in structure of line and stanza, Cowper is far closer to Wordsworth than to Pope. Yet in his overt emphasis on moral and general ends he remains with the Augustan poets.

Another poem, often forgotten, deserves our careful attention in measuring Wordsworth's accomplishment in the volume of 1798: *Old Man Travelling; Animal Tranquillity and Decay, A Sketch*. (The first part of the title, *Old Man Travelling*, was omitted after 1798.) It was neglected in its own day, and not quoted or reprinted in magazines or miscellanies. Dr. Burney (in his criticism in the *Monthly Review*, June 1799) was one of the few who mentioned it. He wrote that it was "finely drawn: but the termination seems pointed against the war; from which, however, we are now no more able to separate ourselves, than Hercules was to free himself from the shirt of Nessus. The old traveller's son might have died by disease."

The last six lines of the poem, about which Dr. Burney particularly wrote, troubled Wordsworth also. In 1800 the old man's reply was given in indirect discourse and in the past tense. In 1815 Wordsworth dropped the concluding lines altogether. The text given here is from the first edition of *Lyrical Ballads*.

> The little hedge-row birds,
> That peck along the road, regard him not.
> He travels on, and in his face, his step,
> His gait, is one expression; every limb,
> His look and bending figure, all bespeak
> A man who does not move with pain, but moves
> With thought—He is insensibly subdued
> To settled quiet: he is one by whom
> All effort seems forgotten, one to whom
> Long patience has such mild composure given,
> That patience now doth seem a thing, of which
> He hath no need. He is by nature led
> To peace so perfect, that the young behold
> With envy, what the old man hardly feels.
> —I asked him whither he was bound, and what
> The object of his journey; he replied
> "Sir! I am going many miles to take
> A last leave of my son, a mariner,
> Who from a sea-flight has been brought to Falmouth,
> And there is dying in an hospital."

The success of the dialogue which concludes the poem may be doubtful. But the shift in tone here is characteristic of several of

Wordsworth's poems from his first decade of publishing verse. We find a movement between monolithic portraiture and matter-of-fact observation, between visionary thought and plain views of people or nature, between "settled quiet" and troubling dialogue. Wordsworth invests his rustic figures with a dignity that makes them more magnificent than mere light of verisimilitude would allow. They also have a depth which the sentimental portraitists of the time could not imagine. Wordsworth's old man travelling is not like one of the beggars or cottagers which Gainsborough painted in the 1780's—portraits which quickly became fashionable and were widely imitated. Wordsworth's noble and simple studies proceed from a realistic reporting of facts like those which drive the old man to go on his journey, and the subjective evaluation of those facts does not cloud the honest observations as it does in the portraits of rustics (by writers or painters) in the age of sensibility, even when the portraits have originated in real life. Wordsworth's beggars and other solitary figures were the common and "well-authenticated facts" of every day in Alfoxden or Grasmere.

We can find similar facts in Dorothy Wordsworth's journals. Her journals from 1798–1802 record meetings with razor-grinders wearing soldiers' jackets, a "broken soldier" who came to beg, old rag-men, old scissors-men, leech-gathers, women and children begging. She writes, "Yesterday an old man called, a grey-headed man, above 70 years of age. He said he had been a soldier, that his wife and children had died in Jamaica. He had a beggar's wallet over his shoulders; a coat of shreds and patches, altogether of a drab colour; he was tall, and though his body was bent, he had the look of one used to have been upright" (2 June 1802). "As we came up the White Moss, we met an old man, who I saw was a beggar by his two bags hanging over his shoulder; but, from a half laziness, half indifference, and a wanting to *try* him, if he would speak, I let him pass. He said nothing, and my heart smote me. I turned back, and said, 'You are begging?' 'Ay,' says he. I gave him a halfpenny. William, judging from his appearance, joined in, 'I suppose you were a sailor?' 'Ay,' he replied, 'I have been 57 years at sea, 12 of them on board a man-of-war under Sir Hugh Palmer.' 'Why have you not a pension?' 'I have no pension, but I could have got into Greenwich hospital, but all my officers are dead' " (22 December 1801).

In the first draft of the lines *On Man, on Nature, and on Human Life* (probably written in March 1798) Wordsworth announced that

> ... by words
> Which speak of nothing more than what we are,
> Would I arouse the sensual from their sleep
> Of Death, and win the vacant and the vain
> To noble raptures;

and that he would reveal "how exquisitely the individual Mind" is fitted to the external World, and the external World to the Mind. This fitting requires at times a trumpet blast of Miltonic echoes to arouse the sleeping to noble raptures. The fitting may also demand a plainness that leaves one with an authentic moment of mortality locating the solitary figure in time and space. The final lines of *Old Man Travelling* do not appear to be pointed against the war. But they may be seen as an urgent, direct observation giving force and immediacy to the quiet wisdom which precedes. As in the scene which stands alone and which concludes *There Was a Boy*, we are given the poignant details without touches of coloring. The "last leave," and the mute standing at the boy's grave, and the wild eyes at the end of *Tintern Abbey* bind the reader to the wise man's personal involvement in nature. They are not unlike the wisp of hay in Mrs. Wilcox's entrance in *Howard's End*. By knowing honestly the plain facts or the concrete images of animal tranquillity and decay one is led by nature to a "peace so perfect." The transcendental world develops from and returns to the light of common day. The generalized sense of a thing and the sense of the infinite come from the steady observation of things as they really are. Thus Wordsworth's old beggar is like a thousand old beggars from journals or sketchbooks or newspapers of the time, and yet is also—if we may turn once more to art—like one of the many beggars which Rembrandt has drawn or etched. In his study of Wordsworth in *The Spirit of the Age*, Hazlitt wrote that Wordsworth's eye "does justice to Rembrandt's fine and masterly effects. In the way in which that artist works something out of nothing, and transforms the stump of a tree, a common figure into an *ideal* object, by the gorgeous light and shade thrown upon it, he perceives an analogy to his own mode of investing the minute details of nature with an atmosphere of sentiment . . ."; that is to say, sentiment which is honest, personal emotion, not the attitudes of refined and tender sensibility of the preceding decades. The action of the poem is a transformation which follows the motion of the sensations and the movement of the mind, and, at the same time, the spirit within and outside the mind and the heart. When this happens in one of the *Lyrical Ballads* we see Wordsworth's unique contribution to poetry in 1798 and for all time. It may be found also in a poem like *There Was a Boy,* which Wordsworth wrote and sent to Coleridge at the end of this marvelous year. When he received these verses, Coleridge said he would have recognized them anywhere. "Had I met these lines running wild in the deserts of Arabia, I should have instantly screamed out 'Wordsworth!' " (10 December 1798). They are truly words "which speak of nothing more than what we are," but win "the vain/To noble raptures." And in some instances we shall find (to quote Coleridge once more —this time out of context—from the letter like Ecclesiastes, to his brother George, 2 October 1803) that ". . . all is vanity that does not lead to Quietness & Unity of Heart, and to the silent aweful idealess Watching of that living Spirit, & of that Life within us, which is the motion of that Spirit—that Life, which passeth all understanding."

NOTES

1. Robert Mayo, "The Contemporaneity of the *Lyrical Ballads,*" *PMLA,* LXIX (June 1954), 508–11.

2. Essay or letter contained in the "Winchester Gathering Book, 1739," Warton MSS., Trinity College, Oxford.

3. Mayo, pp. 520–21.

Wordsworth and Human Suffering: Notes on Two Early Poems

CLEANTH BROOKS

I N the Fenwick note on "The Old Cumberland Beggar," Words-worth tells us that the poem was written in his twenty-eighth year at a time when the "political economists were . . . beginning their war upon mendicity in all its forms, and by implication if not directly, on Almsgiving also." This war upon mendicity Words-worth calls a "heartless process" and there is, of course, no reason to doubt Wordsworth's fervor in terming it such. Yet to modern ears Wordsworth's own attitude toward the beggar may seem some-what heartless: he does not want the old beggar shut up within doors; he wants him to be unconfined, able to pursue his usual rounds. He wants him to have the advantages of solitude and, as the last two lines of the poem indicate, to be able to die in the eye of nature "as in the eye of nature he has lived."

These are not modern sentiments. That the old man should be allowed to wander on the roads and in various weathers is some-thing that the modern humanitarian feels to be cruel treatment. And indeed, a superficial reading of this poem might very well convey the impression that Wordsworth primarily wanted the beggar to remain, even though to his own discomfort, a kind of picturesque adornment to the countryside or a means for prompt-ing in the people of the countryside moral feelings which other-wise they might not experience.

Wordsworth thus may seem to contemplate the beggar as he might a noble stag or any other fine wild animal that ought not be penned up but allowed to live out its own life at large in nature. Wordsworth, to be sure, regards man as nobler than any mere animal, but the argument does take something of this form: like an old stag, the beggar deserves to live out his days unconfined, and to be allowed to die in his native habitat.

Later in the poem, Wordsworth is to admonish his reader: "deem not this man useless." Yet throughout the first part Wordsworth has presented him as completely useless. The beggar has placed his staff upon the pile of stones and we see him looking over his profits for the day, "the dole of village dames." He is examining one scrap and fragment after another,

> with a fixed and serious look
> Of idle computation.

As described here, the beggar becomes a kind of parody of the business man, casting up his accounts, or of the miser fingering his treasures. One notices that Wordsworth passes over an opportunity to have the beggar consciously share his meal with the little birds, he, having received charity, passing on his own bit of charity to lesser creatures. He only *seems* to be dispensing his largess to the birds as the crumbs shower from his hands, for Wordsworth makes it plain that his palsied hands cannot hold the crumbs, and that the feast for the birds is being spread quite involuntarily. The stress on the birds' caution points up this fact: they are attracted, but they dare not approach closer than half the length of his staff.

After this picture, so very vividly done, and honestly done, the speaker, telling us that since his childhood he has known the beggar, describes the beggar's relation to other people on the road —the sauntering horseman, the woman who minds the toll gate, the postboy. All know the beggar and all in some sense show that they pity him. With line 44 we return to the beggar as solitary, and to the world that he experiences as he moves along the high road. In terms of the thesis that Wordsworth is to present a little later in the poem, one would expect him to make much of the old man's friendly intercourse with nature and the compensations which, in spite of his age and infirmities, his life with nature gives him. Instead, Wordsworth honestly records the fact that the stooped old man sees very little of the world except that which lies just before his feet:

> One little span of earth
> Is all his prospect.

As he goes along, he sees no more than some scattered leaf or wheel marks on the road, and even here "seldom knowing that he sees. . . ." Such is his little constricted world, and he creeps through it so quietly and so slowly that everybody passes him by, even the "slow-paced waggon."

The songs of the birds are there for him to hear, but Wordsworth concedes that the beggar does not necessarily attend to them. Wordsworth will maintain that the beggar is better off because these influences of nature can play about him even if no longer upon him. But the concessions he makes to realism are important, for it behooved Wordsworth to avoid the trap of turning the old beggar into a person as sensitive as himself, simply another Wordsworth. (We have already mentioned another trap into which the poet risked falling: that of making the old beggar a picturesque object affording the well-fed and well-housed poet aesthetic delight. We shall consider later whether the poet succeeded in avoiding this trap.)

It is only after his detailed and realistic presentation of the beggar's "useless life" that Wordsworth utters his challenge: deem not this man useless. The poet's argument will be: they also serve who only creep and beg. But before he comes to a specific justification of the usefulness of the beggar, Wordsworth makes a bold generalization:

> 'Tis Nature's law
> That none, the meanest of created things,
> Of forms created the most vile and brute,
> The dullest or most noxious, should exist
> Divorced from good. . . .

This proposition is stated absolutely: presumably it will have to include the viper, the flea, and the mosquito. Life is one, and the pulse of good is "inseparably linked" to "every mode of being."

If this is true of the meanest of creatures, then it has to be true of someone who once

> owned
> The heaven-regarding eye and front sublime
> Which man is born to.

Even this comment has its precision. Wordsworth is careful to put the verb in the past tense, for he has made it perfectly plain that the

beggar's eye is not now heaven-regarding, for, as we have seen, the
beggar keeps his look fixed on the ground. Still, the beggar is more
than a "dry remnant of a garden-flower" or an "implement/Worn
out and worthless." He affects the world and exercises a function
that is important and unique.

> The villagers in him
> Behold a record which together binds
> Past deeds and offices of charity
> Else unremembered, and so keeps alive
> The kindly mood in hearts which lapse of years,
> And that half-wisdom half-experience gives,
> Make slow to feel, and by sure steps resign
> To selfishness and cold oblivious cares.

The beggar is like a kind of inverse scapegoat: instead of bearing
away the sins of the community into the wilderness, he bears back
and forth *through* the community a memory of its good offices and
charities.

Here again Wordsworth is very honest. He tells us that

> Where'er the aged Beggar takes his rounds,
> The mild necessity of use compels
> To acts of love; and habit does the work
> Of reason. . . .

This is indeed to put it bluntly and even paradoxically. Can acts of
love be compelled? Can habit really do the work of reason? Strictly
speaking, no, though perhaps the influence of Hartley made the
notion seem more plausible to the young Wordsworth than it now
seems to some of us. Yet as presented in the poem, Wordsworth's
account of the matter has a fine common sense. What Wordsworth
is really talking about is education, and it is true that men can be
coaxed and even compelled into uses which are tinged with goodness. The villager who falls into the habit of giving charity may
finally become disposed to "true goodness."

One remembers in what high repute sympathy was held by men
of the eighteenth century. Sympathy worked its miracles and in
some late eighteenth-century thought becomes the effectual mother
of all the virtues. So the beggar, by prompting that "first mild
touch of sympathy," may indeed engender what will later flower

into genuine philanthropy. The beggar reminds the prosperous and unthinking of the existence of another world, a world of want and sorrow. Thus, he prompts such people to remember their blessings, and he makes—what Wordsworth calls "no vulgar service"—these blessings "felt." So much for the prosperous. But for the very poor the beggar performs a service that is unique. He confers upon the poorest of the poor the opportunity to be a benefactor. They too

> Long for some moments in a weary life
> When they can know and feel that they have been,
> Themselves, the fathers and the dealers-out
> Of some small blessings. . . .

The beggar, as the lowest rung on the social ladder, provides a footing for the happiness of the very poor: they at least are better off than he.

The cynic may make such remarks as these bitterly. Wordsworth apparently feels that he can make them simply with cheerful honesty. At any rate, this is his case for the usefulness of the old beggar. Yet carrying out this function costs the old man something. The beggar serves, but he suffers in the process. How justify, for example, letting an old man walk the roads in all weathers? Here Wordsworth has been shockingly candid. In the very act of breathing a blessing on the beggar's head, the poet rather goes out of his way to express a wish that the beggar's blood should "Struggle with frosty air and winter snows," and adds:

> let the chartered wind that sweeps the heath
> Beat his gray locks against his withered face.

Does Wordsworth succeed with his rather audacious procedure? And if he does, can one suggest why? Well, for one thing, the implication is that the beggar has been brought to his present state by natural processes. It is the "tide of things" that "has borne him" to "that vast solitude" in which he now finds himself. But the tide of things has not merely drifted a bit of random flotsam to shore. The "vast solitude" is referred to as if it were a goal that one would long to reach, and in bearing the beggar to it the tide has evidently carried out "the law of Heaven." Though the beggar

appears "to breathe and live for himself alone" in this solitude, he
does not in fact bear only himself on his journeys but carries with
him

> The good which the benignant law of Heaven
> Has hung around him. . . .

Moreover, the beggar does not merely remind people of the uses
of charity. He makes them think—"pensive thoughts"—and deepens their knowledge of themselves and of reality.

The argument that is advanced here is really very cunningly put.
It is as if the poet were forbidding officious men to disorder what
nature itself has ordered by daring to disannul services so important as those of the Cumberland beggar.

It is only after having made this point that Wordsworth boldly
insists upon the hardships to which the beggar will be exposed as he
makes his rounds, the "Struggle with frosty air and winter snows."
Even in this recital, hardships are mingled with joys: for example,

> let him breathe
> The freshness of the valleys. . . .

Finally, Wordsworth plays his trump card. After the reference to
the chartered wind beating the old man's gray locks, Wordsworth
goes on to exhort us to

> Reverence the hope whose vital anxiousness
> Gives the last human interest to his heart.
> May never HOUSE, misnamed of INDUSTRY,
> Make him a captive!

The essence of the beggar's hope is a vital anxiousness, and it is
this anxiousness that provides for his heart a human interest. I am
not sure that the grammar here can be confidently unravelled, but
even so—and perhaps because the phrasing is ambiguous—the passage constitutes a very brilliant and effective piece of special pleading. For these cloudy lines suggest that one's interest in living
depends upon a hope whose other face is necessarily anxiety, and
that the beggar, in losing his vocation with its attendant incitements and apprehensions, would lose his very reason for being.
His freedom depends upon a "vital anxiousness." Remove the
anxiousness, and the beggar, though certain of food in the workhouse, is merely a captive.

Moreover, the workhouse will deprive the beggar of "that vast solitude" which the phrasing of the poem has suggested is the crown of a lifetime. The workhouse is noisy, a place of "pent-up din," no place for the old man who has won his right to "the natural silence of old age!" Silence and solitude are cunningly associated with freedom: for the beggar, freedom means freedom from all "life-consuming sounds." The poet thus argues: "Let him be free of mountain solitudes" and a little later the poet will pray that the light too may find "a free entrance" to his "languid orbs."

The general tone of the argument, I repeat, is that of a plea that some noble animal may enjoy its right to continue its natural freedom and to live out its life in its own accustomed way. The beggar ought, for example, to have around him the pleasant song of the birds, whether he can hear it or whether he cares to hear it. He ought to be allowed to behold "The countenance of the horizontal sun," even if his eyes have now "Been doomed so long to settle upon earth." Finally, he has earned his right to die "in the eye of Nature" even as he has always lived in the eye of Nature. The beggar has not been shut out from nature. He has always been able to view it. But, more importantly, nature has been able to view *him* so that he has lived out his life in "the eye of Nature" —whatever this may mean—and whatever it may mean, it certainly possesses powerful emotive force. A lesser poet would have emphasized the need for the old beggar to look upon nature in death as he has in life, and thus would have contradicted the fact that the old man now keeps his eyes on the ground. By reversing the pattern, Wordsworth has strengthened his case, and has at least implied that nature takes a special cognizance of the old man.

The poem, even if considered as a piece of special pleading, is very clever indeed. It may well be judged too clever to represent actually a matter of Wordsworth's *conscious* manipulation of language. Yet I would not want Wordsworth to act as attorney against me in a law suit. In this poem, all the tricks of rhetoric are skillfully employed to enforce very successfully a point which a modern reader is disposed to resist and resent. (F. R. Leavis, writing in another connection, in *Revaluation,* makes something like this point about Wordsworth's "innocently insidious" tricks.)

Lest it be thought that I have overemphasized the risks that Wordsworth has taken and the complications of tone that he has dared to develop, one might compare "The Old Cumberland Beggar" with his poem beginning "I know an aged Man constrained to dwell." In this late poem—composed in 1846—Wordsworth tells the story of an aged man who had been forced to leave his cottage and remove to "a large house of public charity" where he lived "as in a Prisoner's cell." Before this time, when he could "creep about, at will" like the Cumberland beggar, he had fed a red-breast at his cottage door. The bird had learned to peck crumbs "upon his knee." Between the bird and the man there sprang up a "dear intercourse":

> Months passed in love that failed not to fulfill,
> In spite of season's change, its own demand,
> By fluttering pinions here and busy bill;
> There by caresses from a tremulous hand.

But now the aged man, as captive, is separated from his one friend and, though surrounded by many men, has "alas! no company," unfriended, truly alone, and with only the memory of the bird to comfort him.

In this poem everything is spelled out. The man shares his food with his fellow creatures, here reduced to one companionable robin, and the memory of this friendship is apparently all that warms the old man's life while he pines within the house of "charity." But the later poem is much too explicit, and comes perilously close to descending into sentimental bathos in the last stanza. "The Old Cumberland Beggar" is, in its honesty and realism, more ambitious and, perhaps not in spite of, but because of, the risks that the poet takes, much more successful.

In this general connection, one ought to notice the little poem entitled "Animal Tranquillity and Decay." Wordsworth's note, as delivered to Miss Fenwick, indicates that these verses were an overflowing from "The Old Cumberland Beggar." "Animal Tranquillity" shows this relation unmistakably in the way in which it too transposes natural infirmity into awesome strength and defeat into virtue. For example, every limb of the old man, his look and his bending figure, the poet says, bespeak

> A man who does not move with pain, but moves
> With thought.

Is the old man in fact simply painfully arthritic? Are his deliberate movements really deliberate in that they are instinct with thought? Or is the poet saying that the old man's motions, slowed though they may be by the pain in his limbs, do not appear painful but impress an observer as those made by a man of thought?

The poet goes on to observe that the old man has been "insensibly subdued" to "subtle quiet." He has been so habituated to long patience that

> patience now doth seem a thing of which
> He hath no need.

Finally, the poet describes him as a person led by nature

> To peace so perfect that the young behold
> With envy, what the Old Man hardly feels.

(This is again an instance of brilliant double-talk—though the reader may prefer to say, as I do, that in this instance duplicity has been transmuted into the richness and subtlety of great poetry.) The old man hardly feels the perfect peace to which he has been led by nature and which the young behold with envy. This is indeed to put the best possible face on decay and the slowing down of age. There is, of course, a peace that is deeper still: the peace of death, and the recipient of that peace is so thoroughly pacified that he is not aware of it at all: he is simply not aware. I do not, by the way, mean to imply that Wordsworth had excluded the possibility of this last interpretation. The child of the "Intimations" Ode does not know it is going to die, and the little maid of "We Are Seven" cannot comprehend what death is. The old man of "Animal Tranquillity" has almost re-entered the peace that the child abandons on growing up.

Rather early in his career, Wordsworth touched upon the problem of man's self-consciousness and his alienation from nature. Consciousness becomes the very barrier which separates man from nature. The theme is to become explicit in Keats's "Ode to a Nightingale," where the bird's immortality derives from the fact that the bird, completely submerged in nature, having no memory of the past and no prevision of the future, lives in an eternal present with no sense that it can ever die; whereas man, knowing what the bird "amongst the leaves" has never known, is indeed, as the bird is not, "born for death." Man's consciousness, through which he is able to savor so fully the bird's special kind of happiness, is the very barrier which keeps him from slipping into nature and joining the bird in its state of timeless being.

Some of the problems that pertain to "The Old Cumberland Beggar" are at least implicit in other Wordsworth poems. The young poet who appears in "Resolution and Independence" presumably hopes that the old leech-gatherer will never have to be shut away from nature, and that, *faute de mieux*, he will be allowed to die in his boots beside one of the lonely pools on the moor. But the poem is focused upon something else: what haunts the "mind's eye" (of the young man and of the reader of the poem) as the poem ends is a vision of the leech-gatherer, now become almost a natural presence endowed with nature's immortality, pacing

> About the weary moors continually,
> Wandering about alone and silently.

The story of Margaret in "The Ruined Cottage" raises much more specifically the problem of loneliness, loss, and death—more sharply indeed than does "The Old Cumberland Beggar." Why is the younger man calmed and strengthened by the Wanderer's recital of Margaret's sufferings? Why does the Wanderer feel that the "purposes of wisdom" are served by attendance on her story? What consolation was there for Margaret herself?

The answer to these questions is not easy, and the difficulties are not merely those raised by a modern reader. Wordsworth's contemporaries registered some uneasiness in this area. DeQuincey thought that the Wanderer would have done better to give Margaret some cash rather than mere sympathy. John Wilson ("Christopher North") admired the poem but he remarks that the poet has "described, or rather dissected, with an almost cruel anatomy —not one quivering fibre being left unexposed—all the fluctuating, and finally all the constant agitations laid bare and naked that carried [Margaret] at last lingeringly to the grave." Wilson is not convinced of the truth of Margaret's psychology as depicted, and he rejects the Wanderer's conclusion that

> sorrow and despair
> From ruin and from change, and all the grief

"that we can suffer here below, appear an idle dream among plumes, and weeds, and speargrass, and mists, and rain-drops." It is interesting to observe that David Perkins, in his recently published *Wordsworth and the Poetry of Sincerity,* makes a related point: ". . . even poor Margaret," he notes, "seems a mere shade when compared to the final vivid image of 'spear-grass . . . By mist and Silent rain-drops silvered o'er.' " Perkins's general point is that Wordsworth loved nature "as a reality, man as an idea."

The story of Margaret is beautifully and movingly told. To the younger man, the ruined cottage seems a "cheerless spot." But for the Wanderer, the spot is suffused with the sense of human pathos and loss. To him the hills, streams, and senseless rocks can speak

> with a voice
> Obedient to the strong creative power
> Of human passion. Sympathies there are
> More tranquil yet perhaps of kindred earth,
> That steal upon the meditative mind,
> And grow with thought. Beyond yon spring I stood,
> And eyed its waters till we seemed to feel
> One sadness, they and I.

Thus, for the Wanderer, the spring shares his own sadness for the woman who once lived near here. The Wanderer goes on to tell the younger man about Margaret, but after some talk about her the Wanderer is willing to let the subject drop. Why, he asks, should one

> feeding on disquiet, thus disturb
> The calm of nature with our restless thoughts?

This last remark is curious. It may even seem subversive of the Wanderer's real feelings about nature. For a little later on the Wanderer is going to extract nourishment from these same sad and restless thoughts and, by feeding on disquiet, promises to achieve a deeper quiet. The Wanderer is more subtle than he seems. Perhaps he has meant to plant a disquieting thought to which the younger man will be forced to return. At any rate, after some talk on more trivial things, the younger man begs the Wanderer to resume the story of Margaret, and this time the Wanderer speaks something that is apparently nearer to his own notion in saying

> But we have known that there is often found
> In mournful thoughts, and always might be found,
> A power to virtue friendly. . . .

The Wanderer tells Margaret's story very effectively indeed. His is an art that conceals art. He uses restraint and is careful not to make any overt bid for sympathy. He also has an eye for the exact detail. And it is interesting to see how much he makes the details tell the story of Margaret's grief. For example, the untrimmed honeysuckle beginning to hang down in heavier tufts, the garden of the cottage, losing its pride of neatness, bits of sheep's wool hanging to the corner stones on either side of the porch of the cottage

> as if the sheep
> That feed upon the commons thither came
> As to a couching-place and rubbed their sides
> Even at her threshold.

Margaret knows what is happening to her. She parts with her elder child in order to apprentice him to a "kind master on a distant farm"—presumably for the child's own good. Presumably too she would do so with her other child if this were not impossible, for she tells the Wanderer that she knows that she has done much wrong to the helpless infant. She is so careworn and abstracted that she cannot give it a proper rearing. Her effect upon the child comes out poignantly in the Wanderer's statement that

> Her infant babe
> Had from its mother caught the trick of grief,
> And sighed among its playthings.

Margaret's grief is like that of Wordsworth's character Michael in that it does not break her heart and quickly end her life. For nine tedious years she lives on—long after the death of her baby. Her own sad decay is reflected in the gradual decay of her poor hut. Margaret is identified very cunningly with her cottage, and what is happening to the building reflects what is happening to its occupant.

When the Wanderer's tale has been completed, the younger man is overcome with the sense of pathos, and his outpouring of

grief has to be checked finally by the Wanderer himself who tells
him that

> enough to sorrow have you given,
> The purposes of Wisdom ask no more. . . .

Margaret herself found her own consolation, so the Wanderer tells
his younger friend. But what precisely is the meaning of Margaret's
story? How does it promote wisdom? And why does this story of
helpless suffering console us about the human predicament? I have
already said that I am not at all sure of the answer here.

In the long speech of the Wanderer, which begins with line 932
and goes through line 956, the references to Christianity provide
something like an orthodox answer. The way of the Cross is suffering; the problem of evil and suffering have always been finally a
mystery; yet it is clear that human beings may be asked to express
their deepest love and loyalty by being willing to suffer. Through
suffering, they come to a deeper sense of themselves and of God,
and in discovering the divine, they may find the way to a transcendent joy which makes present earthly suffering finally irrelevant. But the earlier Wordsworth's view of this matter was surely
not quite so orthodox as this, and even in the text of *The Excursion* in 1850 the earlier, more pantheistic notions are still present.
For example, the Wanderer tells us that Margaret "sleeps in the
calm earth, and peace is here." The ruined cottage and the ruined
garden have conveyed to the heart of the Wanderer an image of
tranquillity that is so calm and still and beautiful that the sorrow
and despair that one feels in experiencing a world of mortal change
simply becomes an idle dream, a dream that can

> maintain
> Nowhere, dominion o'er the enlightened spirit.

Is Wordsworth saying here that, seen in the full perspective of
nature, seen as a portion of nature's beautiful and unwearied immortality, Margaret with her sorrows is simply one detail of an
all-encompassing and harmonious pattern? One can, for example,
look at the rabbit torn by the owl in something like this fashion,
and the rabbit's agony, no longer isolated and dwelt upon in itself,
may cease to trouble us when understood as a necessary part of a

total pattern, rich and various and finally harmonious, in which even the rabbit's pain becomes not a meaningless horror since it partakes of the beauty of the whole.

One shrinks from concluding that such an interpretation as this is Wordsworth's own; and I do not mean to do so. But it may be useful to state it as a limiting term of Wordsworth's position. Behind Wordsworth there lies the eighteenth-century view of human suffering which was not wholly different from that just described. The universe was an orderly universe, and a poet like Alexander Pope had been able to argue plausibly that much that appeared to be evil was simply partial good, or good only partially understood. A great many eighteenth-century modes of thought linger in Wordsworth's poetry, but it is obvious that "The Ruined Cottage" has a different quality of feeling and a different tone from that of the quasi-deistic poetry of the Age of Reason. So much for a backward look.

If we look forward to the poetry that comes after Wordsworth, for example, to the later poetry of Yeats, we find what might be called the reconciliation of suffering in the aesthetic vision. I should describe this latter in something like this fashion: man is so various, so wonderful, capable of so much triumph and agony, suffering and joy, malice and goodness, that if one can take his stance far enough away from the individual case to allow him to see life in its wholeness, with all its rich variety—if one can do that, he can accept not only suffering but active wickedness as an inevitable and necessary part of the human drama, and can even rejoice in it as a testimony to the depths of man's feeling and his power to experience and endure.

I give this summary not necessarily to cast scorn upon it. There is a sense in which we do enjoy the suffering of a Lear or of an Oedipus. Their power to suffer and to endure is a testimony to their own greatness, and a testimony to the dimensions of the human spirit. The deepest knowledge of ourselves, that given by the greatest art, always seems to require the experience of tragic suffering. But an aesthetic attitude toward the human spectacle, so valuable and necessary and indeed even so clearly enjoined upon us if we intend to get all that we can from *literature,* is not necessarily the same thing as an ethics or a metaphysics by which one can live. Literature has its own function, a very important one, though I question whether it can become an altogether satisfactory substitute for a philosophy or a religion. There is a good deal of evidence to indicate that Wordsworth himself found in later life that there could be no substitute for a religion. Did he ever feel, even at the beginning of his career, that an imaginative vision was enough? I am not sure that he did, though the notion has been recently urged.

In any case, the view of human suffering taken by the Wanderer is much more than what I have called the aesthetic vision. It is deeply tinged with religion: the point is that it is not the Christian religion. On this matter, John Wilson's remarks can be helpful. As he put it, more than a century ago: "the religion of this great Poet—in all his poetry published previous to the 'Excursion'—is but the 'Religion of the Woods.' In the 'Excursion,' his religion is brought forward—prominently and conspicuously. . . . And a very high religion it often is; but is it Christianity? No—it is not. There are glimpses given of some of the Christian doctrines," but Wilson's point is that the various interlocutors in *The Excursion* may, "for anything that appears to the contrary, be deists."

I dare say that Wilson is probably right in remarking that the Wanderer's attitude is not Christian, and certainly right in calling it religious. Yet it would not be easy to give a systematic account of the "theology" that underlies the Wanderer's religious experience. I am not sure that Wordsworth could have done so himself. But what is important is that Wordsworth has been able to dramatize this religion for us and to do it so winningly that we are convinced of the integrity of the Wanderer's emotions and share in the catharsis that he and his young friend experience.

In short, the poet has enabled us to know what it "feels like" to hold the Wanderer's faith. This he has done through his art— through what reveals itself as a most skillful and delicate management of the resources of language. The accomplishment is of the highest importance and it must not be misunderstood: the art is not cosmetic but structural—not a rhetorical presentation of plausible arguments but a poetic creation. But to try to show this in detail would involve a commentary that would far exceed the limits of this paper.

Wordsworth, Inscriptions, and Romantic Nature Poetry

GEOFFREY H. HARTMAN

I

THE earliest genuinely lyrical poem of Wordsworth bears an elaborate title: "Lines left upon a Seat in a Yew-Tree, which stands near the Lake of Esthwaite, on a desolate part of the shore, yet commanding a beautiful prospect." The poem reached its final form between 1795 and 1797, and appears as the first of Wordsworth's productions in the *Lyrical Ballads* of 1798. Its structure is simple: an apostrophe to the passing traveller commends a solitary spot in nature; this is followed by a moral and biographical epitome of the recluse who so loved this spot and its view that he built the seat ("his only monument") mentioned in the title; the conclusion admonishes once more the passer-by, asking him to heed the story just told and the moral now drawn from it. The poem is in the mature blank verse of Wordsworth's meditative poetry, and reflects his strong eye for nature and his general moral sensitivity.

It may seem irrelevant to ask what *kind* of lyric this is. Coleridge, in the verses that follow it in *Lyrical Ballads,* invents a genre of his own, calling "The Nightingale" a "conversational poem"; and Wordsworth's lyric challenges the same apparent freedom of designation. Its value, to us at least, does not seem to depend in any way on the recognition of the species to which it may belong. This is true, of course, of many of the best Romantic lyrics: consider "Tintern Abbey" or "Old Man Travelling," to stay only with *Lyrical Ballads.* There is a pleasure in not knowing, or not being able to discern, the traditional form; the lack becomes a positive virtue; and we begin to seek, not quite earnestly, for the proper formal description. Are the "Lines left upon a seat in a Yew-Tree" a fragment of meditative-didactic verse, a chunk freed from some longer topographical poem, a disguised anecdote, an extended epitaph? To the naïve yet careful reader the form may appear, above all, as an effective way to sweeten a moral by human interest and immediacy of situation.

It is certain, however, that Wordsworth's first characteristic lyric belongs to a special genre. Charles Lamb recognized it instinctively. He heard the poem while visiting Coleridge at Nether Stowey in July 1797—the famous visit during which "dear Sara" accidentally emptied a skillet of boiling milk on her poet-husband's foot and set the stage for another of his great conversational poems: "This Lime-Tree Bower my Prison." Also during this visit, Wordsworth read the "Lines left upon a seat in a Yew-Tree," and Lamb could not get them out of his mind. Shortly after returning home he writes Coleridge about the poem. "You would make me very happy," he says, "if you think W. has no objection, by transcribing for me that inscription of his." And later in the same letter, "But above all, *that Inscription!*"[1]

The term Lamb uses twice, and the second time in a generic sense, identifies a lyrical kind that has not attracted attention, perhaps because it is such a normal, accepted, even archaic feature of the eighteenth-century literary scene. The inscription, as Lamb calls it, was more genus than species, being the primitive form of the epigram, and connected therefore with most of the briefer forms of lyric in the eighteenth century. It was in theory, and often in fact, a dependent form of poetry, in the same sense in which the statues of churches are dependent on their architectural setting or partly conceived in function of it. The inscription was anything conscious of the place on which it was written, and this could be tree, rock, statue, gravestone, sand, window, album, sundial, dog's collar, back of fan, back of painting. It ranged in scope and seriousness from Pope's inscription on the collar of the Prince of Wales' dog: "I am his Highness' dog at Kew/Pray tell me sir, whose dog are you?" to Thomas Warton's "Verses on Sir Joshua's Painted Window at New College."[2] This general form of the inscription was accompanied by a special form which we shall call

the *nature-inscription,* whose popularity seems to have been pro-
portional to that of eighteenth-century gardens. In Shenstone's
ferme ornée, The Leasowes, one of the famous show-gardens of the
time, beautiful prospects were discreetly marked for the tourist by
benches with inscriptions from Virgil or specially contrived
poems.[3] It was this kind of inscription that provided a pattern for
Wordsworth's "Lines left upon a seat"; though pattern is, perhaps,
too strong a term. Wordsworth was able to liberate the genre from
its dependent status of tourist guide and antiquarian sign-post: he
made the nature-inscription into a free-standing poem, able to
commemorate any feeling for nature or the spot that had aroused
this feeling.

A direct glance at the "Lines left upon a seat" yields many of
the characteristics both of the inscription in general and of nature-
inscriptions in particular. The swollen title, besides telling us
where the poem is supposedly found, reflects the link between
inscription and epigram. Since the epigram, especially in the later
Renaissance, tended to be as brief and pointed as possible, the
particular circumstances which had given rise to it were often
placed in the title. There are epigrams with titles longer than the
epigrams. The relation between title (lemma)[4] and epigram was
quite complex and varied, like the cognate relation between motto
and picture in the emblem; and I need hardly add that none of
this complexity is found in Wordsworth. But his elaborated title
does reflect the tradition of the epigram, and may even reproduce,
typographically, the effect of an inscription.[5] Most of the concrete
detail, however, is included in the poem itself, which is far too
lengthy to have been inscribed, and resembles the "Greek" rather
than "Greco-Roman" form of the epigram.[6]

The second feature to be noted is still common to both general
and special forms of inscription. I can best suggest it by quoting
from Lessing's treatise on the Epigram—systematic theorizing
about genre was his forte, and in England we find little or no
sustained consideration of the epigram-inscription as such. Noting
that the modern form of the epigram was derived, primitively, from
actual inscriptions, Lessing comments: "The true inscription is not
to be thought of apart from that whereon it stands, or might stand.
Both together make the whole from which arises the impression

which, speaking generally, we ascribe to the inscription alone. First, some object of sense which arouses our curiosity; and then the account of this same object, which satisfies that curiosity."[7]

The relevance of this structure to Wordsworth's poem is obvious. By the title, the admonition "Nay, Traveller! rest," and indeed by the whole opening (to line 12), it presents an object that should arouse curiosity. It then goes on to satisfy that curiosity by its story of the recluse, except that our attention, far from being dissolved, is steadily deepened. The Yew with its ingrown seat is explained, but not explained away. Our eyes are opened to a truth latent in the simplest feature of the landscape. Wordsworth moves psychology closer to archeology by resuscitating the story of the recluse from a trace strongly merged with nature.

The third feature of the inscription, and perhaps the most intriguing, is related to this sense for a life (in nature) so hidden, retired or anonymous that it is perceived only with difficulty. This sense of hidden life is peculiar to the nature-inscription and betrays itself also in formalistic ways. There is first the context of anonymity which the poem partially dispels. The lines are "left" upon the seat, and they describe a person who has (1) lived unknown, in retirement, and (2) lived an unknown life. He resembles one of the "unhonour'd Dead" whose "artless tale" Gray begins to reveal in his *Elegy*. The anonymity of nature and the anonymity of the common man join to produce an elegiac tenor of feeling.

There is, moreover, a general convergence of elegiac and nature poetry in the eighteenth century. Poems about place ("locodescriptive") merge with meditations on death, so that landscape becomes dramatic in a quietly startling way. From it there emanate "admonitions and heart-stirring remembrances, like a refreshing breeze that comes without warning, or the taste of waters from an unexpected fountain."[8] Not only is the graveyard a major locus for the expression of nature sentiment, but Nature is herself a larger graveyard inscribed deeply with evidences of past life. This convergence of graveyard and nature, or of epitaph and loco-descriptive poetry, is consecrated by the success of Gray's *Elegy* (1751) in which the division between country-side and cemetery is hardly felt. We move with insidiously gradual steps from the one to the other; and Gray enters so strongly into the spirit of his poem that he imagines himself as one of the unhonoured dead rescued from anonymity only by his epitaph graved under a thorn. His poem ends, therefore, with an archaic image of itself—an actual inscription for which the whole elegy provides the setting, and this is nature in its most regular, ancient and oblivious form.

Perhaps the clearest sign of the merging of epitaphic and nature poetry is the Address to the Traveller with which the Yew-tree poem begins. The "Nay, Traveller! rest" is the traditional *Siste Viator* of the epitaph. We are made to hear the admonitory voice of the deceased or of the living who speak for the deceased. Yet Wordsworth commemorates a strange spot in nature rather than a grave, since the seat in the Yew-Tree is not literally a tombstone. It is solely the poet's imagination which sees that pile of stones as a funeral pile.[9] The rudely constructed seat was merely the haunt of the recluse, yet because he used it as an escape, burying himself in "visionary views," and not allowing nature to take him out of his gloomy self, Wordsworth rightly treats it as his tomb. The "Lines in a Yew-Tree" exorcize the spot, and rededicate the seat to its proper purpose of marking a beautiful view.

The call from a monument in the landscape, or from the landscape itself, which deepens the consciousness of the poet and makes him feel he is on significant ground, is also encouraged by a sister-tradition to the epitaph. Most nature-inscriptions are related to the votive or commemorative epigram which plays an important role in the Greek Anthology and comes into vernacular literature chiefly from that source.[10] The votive epigram took many forms: it was a simple statement identifying the donor, giving a brief yet lucid picture of the place and object dedicated, and saying to whom they are offered; it was, as in inscriptions of this kind which survive from Theocritus, a poem celebrating a votive painting (statue), or rather animating it; and it could be a short prosopopeia, the voice of the god or genius of the place (genius loci) who warns us that we are near sacred ground. The first kind is strangely and uncertainly naïve; and only Marvell uses it in an original way in his Mower Poems, where he sharpens its naïveté deliciously:

> I am the Mower *Damon*, known
> Through all the Meadows I have mown. . . .

It does not play an important role, after Marvell, in the writing of nature poetry.[11]

The second kind does, for it is part of the tradition of iconic verse, and some of the most interesting descriptive poetry of the eighteenth century enters through such iconic and animating gestures as Behold, See, Mark; or through a rather special and limited genre, the Lines on (first) seeing a picture (artifact), which Anna Seward sometimes converts into "Inscription on the back of a Picture."[12] Since the pictures, at least in Anna Seward's case, are landscapes, a good amount of vigorous and "picturesque" description enters English poetry in this form.

I want to emphasize the third kind in which the inscription calls to the passer-by in the voice of the genius loci or spirit of the place. Like the epitaph it seems to derive from ritual formulae which admonished strangers not to disturb the remains of the dead. In the eighteenth century we find an extraordinary number of Inscriptions for Bower, Grotto, Fountain, Seat, or similar Places of Retreat and Refreshment, which both invite and exhort the world-weary traveler. Pope's verses on his grotto at Twickenham are a familiar example. Such verses were directly encouraged by the interest in gardens and participated in the antiquarian fervor of the century. A disgruntled observer, looking in 1819 through Dodsley's Collection, complains among other things about its "inscriptions in grottoes, and lines on fans innumerable."[13] But not many years before this complaint (so persistent is the fashion) we find in *Gentleman's Magazine* a competition for the best English rendering of Latin verses supposedly found on a supposed hermitage.[14]

Despite all misuses the votive inscription is important for nature poetry in that it allows landscape to speak directly: without the intervention of allegorical devices. The voice of nature that calls us does not have to be formalized or pompously accoutered, although sometimes it is. The simplification in the form responds to a rural simplicity of feeling. We begin to hear and see a nature unobstructed by magnifying artifice. A waterfall may purge, momentarily, our selfish cares:

> Come, and where these runnels fall
> Listen to my madrigal!
> Far from all sounds of all the strife,

That murmur through the walks of life;
From grief, inquietude, and fears,
From scenes of riot, or of tears;
From passions, cankering day by day,
That wear the inmost heart away;
. . . .
Come, and where these runnels fall,
Listen to my madrigal![15]

Or the nymph of the grotto, still somewhat portentous, invites us:

Come, Traveller, this hollow Rock beneath,
While in the Leaves refreshing Breezes breath;
Retire, to calm the Rage of burning Thirst,
In these cool Streams that from the Caverns burst.[16]

Such moments are rarely deepened and even more rarely sustained.[17] Southey's Inscriptions, of which eight were published in the first edition of his *Poems* (1797), often assume the bardic and officious voice of the interpreter instead of letting the genius loci speak directly to us. In this respect they do not differ from the odic or iconic modes of nature poetry in which the poet addresses the landscape in his own person, asking woods and valleys to mourn or rejoice or show their splendors or perform in one way or another. Yet the Hellenic originals, or intermediate models, chasten Southey's verse into pictures of nature almost completely free of penseroso chimaeras and allegorical personifications:

Enter this cavern, Stranger! the ascent
Is long and steep and toilsome; here a while
Thou may'st repose thee, from the noontide heat
O'ercanopied by this arch'd rock that strikes
A grateful coolness: clasping its rough arms
Round the rude portal, the old ivy hangs
Its dark green branches down, and the wild Bees,
O'er its grey blossoms murmuring ceaseless, make
Most pleasant melody. No common spot
Receives thee, for the Power who prompts the song,
Loves this secluded haunt. The tide below
Scarce sends the sound of waters to thine ear;
And this high-hanging forest to the wind
Varies its many hues. Gaze, stranger, here!
And let thy soften'd heart intensely feel

How good, how lovely, Nature! When from hence
Departing to the City's crowded streets,
Thy sickening eye at every step revolts
From scenes of vice and wretchedness; reflect
That Man creates the evil he endures.[18]

To give one more instance of this increased directness: Coleridge
has an "Inscription for a Fountain on a Heath" first published in
1802 under the title of "Epigram." It is nothing more than a detailed and affectionate picture of a sycamore, musical with bees, to
which a small spring adds its own melody. What differentiates his
poem from Southey's is that he not only mutes that sententious
moralizing which is quite foreign to most Greek models, and a
relic of medieval Christian debates concerning the active and the
contemplative life, but also, though still speaking in his own
person, lulls the reader into thinking that the place itself invites
him, so calm and murmuring is his voice:

Here Twilight is and Coolness: here is moss,
A soft seat, and a deep and ample shade.
Thou may'st toil far and find no second tree.
Drink, Pilgrim, here; Here rest! and if thy heart
Be innocent, here too shalt thou refresh
Thy spirit, listening to some gentle sound,
Or passing gale or hum of murmuring bees![19]

We do not know with certainty how many of the poets were
directly familiar with the Greek Anthology, or through what inter-
mediaries its spirit came to them. Professor Hutton, who set out to
write a history of the Greek Anthology in England, found himself
obliged to write it first for Continental literature, since the Anthology came to England via the Continent. But the temptations of the
way were so great that he did not end where he began, and we still
have no report on England.[20] From my limited perspective, therefore, I can only say two things. The general change from Neoclassical to Romantic style parallels curiously the difference between
the brief, witty, pointed epigram of the Latin tradition, influential
on the development of the heroic couplet, and the simpler, more
descriptive, anecdotal epigram which is a staple of the Greek
Anthology.[21] A conscious attempt to recall the virtues of the
simpler model is made as early as Thomas Warton the Elder who

translates three epigrams from the Greek with the advertisement that they can serve as "a Pattern of the Simplicity so much admir'd in the *Grecian* Writings, so foreign to the present prevailing Taste, to the Love of Modern Witticism, and *Italian* Conceit."[22] His first example is an inscription on a cave (see above, p. 395), his second a votive epigram from Theocritus, and the third, also from Theocritus, a little picture or anecdote. Warton's versions are not particularly felicitous—the Grecian simplicity is exaggerated into a muscular coyness and the couplet form still thrusts that simplicity into a Procrustean bed—but the very attempt is important. It is something of a shock to realize that the Grecian simplicity admired by Warton may have been achieved by Wordsworth in a poem like "Old Man Travelling." This piece could easily be taken as an epigram à la grecque—as an anecdote in plain language and with a muted point. The speech of the Old Man, its strangely quiet character, replaces here the ingenious final turn of the witty epigram.

My second remark concerning the possible influence of the Greek Anthology on nature-inscriptions and the Romantic style is that there seems to have been at least one important intermediary: Mark Akenside. As far as I know Akenside was the first, except for Shenstone, to formally print a group of poems under the collective title "Inscriptions": six poems appear under that head in Dodsley's Collection of 1758, and two are added in the 1772 posthumous edition of his poetry.[23] Southey acknowledges that his own earliest inscriptions were inspired by Akenside, and it is also interesting that one of Coleridge's first publications is an "Elegy imitated from one of Akenside's Blank-verse inscriptions."[24]

This title, in fact, gives us one clue to Akenside's importance. His inscriptions created a new short-form of poetry for blank verse. Prior to Akenside, blank verse was almost purely a dramatic, epic or didactic measure;[25] lyric, indeed, was invariably in rimed form, and rime tended to emphasize point. But Akenside, by his Inscriptions, suggested the possibility of a short-form free of the obligation of "closing" the "sense" with couplet or quatrain, though maintaining some epigrammatic firmness by a subtly latinate syntax. The inscriptions previously cited from Wordsworth, Southey and Coleridge also break the mold of the *Sinngedicht* (as Lessing called it) in which point is all and the sense is closed at short intervals. From a historical perspective, therefore, the lyrical lyric of the Romantics is a liberated epigram; and H. H. Hudson has said astutely that "the moment an epigram becomes very good—if it is not too funny or too obviously ingenious—it is now in danger of being classed as a lyric."[26]

When, to this relative freedom from point, we add a freedom from obtrusive personification, the way is cleared for a direct and sustained nature poetry. There are no persons in Akenside's inscriptions except the spirit of the place (or its interpreter) and the off-stage traveler. If this traveler, moreover, is significantly identified as the poet himself, a still closer relation is established between nature and the poet. This is what happens in Akenside's first and last inscriptions, which take the genre a good step toward the Romantic blank-verse meditation. Akenside, in the last inscription, also reverses the pattern in which the genius loci calls to the stranger, for now it is he, the poet, who in his lonely anxiety for inspiration invokes the absent Muses of the bards of Greece:

> From what loved haunt
> Shall I expect you? Let me once more feel
> Your influence, O ye kind inspiring powers:
> And I will guard it well; nor shall a thought
> Rise in my mind, nor shall a passion move
> Across my bosom unobserved, unstored
> By faithful memory. And then at some
> More active moment, will I call them forth
> Anew; and join them in majestic forms,
> And give them utterance in harmonious strains;
> That all mankind shall wonder at your sway.

Yet Akenside's sense of alienation is nothing as sharp as that of the Romantics. I suspect, in fact, that his inscriptions exerted a twofold charm: that of mixing naïve feelings for nature with melancholy and self-conscious ones, and that of clearly subordinating the latter to the former. We may recall that Wordsworth's Yew-Tree poem (like Coleridge's "Nightingale" which follows it) is intended to combat the melancholy use of nature and that for Wordsworth this melancholy is symptomatic of a morbidly self-centered mind. Nature should aid us to go out of ourselves, to broaden our feelings by meditation, and to recover original joy.

Akenside's inscriptions, like the best Greek epigrams, subdue sentiment—and sentimentality—to votive calmness of mind.

Through a reuniting, therefore, of elegiac and loco-descriptive poetry, and through the strengthening influence of the radically Greek element in the Greek Anthology,[27] a new lyrical kind emerges: the nature-inscription. It is nearest in spirit, form and potential to the Romantic lyric. I would not go so far as to call it the missing link, but it certainly is a vital intermediary between the conventional lyrical forms of the eighteenth century and the Romantic poem. The reason why it is rarely singled out as a distinctive literary kind is that as a special form of the inscription it was naturally classed among inscriptions in general, and that inscriptions themselves were not always distinguished from epigrams. Wordsworth, in 1815, lumps together epitaph, inscription, sonnet, the personal verse epistle, and all loco-descriptive poetry under the general category of idyllium.[28] This is not sheer muddleheadedness but a practical grouping that reflected the state of poetry in his time. The nature-inscription was an unstable genre, almost a chance product of the multiplication of inscriptions of all kinds in the seventeenth and eighteenth centuries. Anyone who has worked his way through anthologies of that time knows the inordinate variety of mediocre inscriptions they offer in the form of social verse, iconic verse, elegiac and commemorative verse, jeux d'esprits and emblems. From these, in their combinations, and by a process at least as mysterious as natural selection, the prototype of the Romantic nature poem arose, and was partially stabilized by Akenside's inscriptions in blank verse.

II

It was demonstrated some years ago that Wordsworth's *Lyrical Ballads* were not original in subject or sentiment, or even in many elements of form. Robert Mayo's article on their contemporaneity destroyed the clichés of literary historians who had held that this poetry was too bold for its time.[29] But the question of Wordsworth's greatness, or in what his poems really differed from their contemporary analogues, was left unanswered. To this question I would now like to address myself by using Wordsworth's relation to inscriptions as the point of departure.

What Wordsworth did is clear: he transformed the inscription into an independent nature-poem, and in so doing created a principal form of the Romantic and modern lyric. One step in this transformation has already been described. When fugitive feelings are taken seriously, when every sight and sound calls to the passing poet: "Nay, Traveller! rest," "Stay, Passenger, why goest thou by soe fast?", then the Romantic nature lyric is born.

A second step in the transformation bears directly on the form of the poem. The inscription, before Wordsworth, is strangely void of natural detail though full of nature feeling, for the reason that the genre still depends on the site it supposedly inscribes. Rather than evoking, it points to the landscape. If it has an expressive function vis-a-vis the feelings of the poet, it has a merely indicative function vis-a-vis its setting. To develop as a free-standing form the nature-lyric had to draw the landscape evocatively into the poetry itself. The poetry, as in Shakespeare, becomes full-bodied when it incorporates or even creates the setting.[30]

Yet much depends on the way the setting is incorporated. The criterion of concreteness has only a limited relevance for the nature-lyric. There is more descriptive vigor—more observations and pictures from nature—in an ordinary topographical poem like Wordsworth's own *Evening Walk* or *Descriptive Sketches* than in all of *Lyrical Ballads* together. In "Lines left upon a seat in a Yew-Tree" the natural setting is drawn into the poetry not so much as a thing of beauty that should startle the traveler but because it mingled with a human life and still mingles presently with the poet's imagination. We are made to see the vital, if perverse relationship of the solitary to his favorite spot, and to hear the poet's *viva voce* meditation on this: he writes the epitaph before our eyes.

What is truly distinctive, therefore, is Wordsworth's enlarged understanding of the setting to be incorporated. This is never landscape alone. He frees the inscription from its dependence, he gives it weight and power of its own, by incorporating in addition to a particular scene the very process of inscribing or interpreting it. The setting is understood to contain the writer in the act of writing: the poet in the grip of what he feels and sees, and primitively inspired to carve it in the living rock.[31]

But the very intensity of the desire for perpetuation produces (or reacts to) a kind of death-feeling which Shelley described directly. The writer, in composition, is but a fading coal, and his poem dead leaves. A secondary consciousness of death and change associates itself with the very act of writing. Thus, in Wordsworth, the lapidary inscription, though replaced by the meditative mind, returns as part of the landscape being meditated. The poet *reads* landscape as if it were a monument or grave: this position is common to "Lines left upon a seat in a Yew-Tree," "The Thorn" 's letter-like distinctness of pond, hill of moss and stunted tree, "Hart Leap Well" 's three pillars set, like cairn or cromlech, in a desolate place, and "Michael" 's straggling heap of stones.[32]

The setting Wordsworth recovers is therefore of the most elemental kind. Yet he recovers it neither as pseudo-primitive nor as antiquarian: always as a man dealing with what is permanent in man. Inscribing, naming, writing, are types of a commemorative and inherently elegiac act. Despite this, his poems move from past to present, from death to life, from stone to the spontaneity of living speech. The "Lines left upon a seat" attempt to be an inscription written in the language of nature: a monument that comes to life and makes nature come alive. His verse, says Wordsworth, using one of the oldest *topoi*, is a "speaking monument."[33] This is also true of such greater poems as "Michael" and "Tintern Abbey."

"Michael" bears an obvious structural resemblance to the Yew-Tree poem. Its two basic parts are again a presentation of the curious object, and the story or epitomized biography[34] which that object entails. The object, moreover, is a monument almost merged with nature: to interpret the stones of the unfinished sheepfold is to interpret nature itself. We are made to see the naked mind confronting an anonymous landscape, yet drawing from it, or interpolating, the humane story of "Michael." The poem begins in an act of the living mind bent over a riddling inscription, perhaps an inscription of death.

But "Michael" also reveals a historical connection between primitive inscriptions and nature poetry. One of the earliest forms of that poetry actually arose as a modification of the epitaph. The opening paragraph of "Michael" which carefully guides the reader to his strange destination, should be compared to Theocritus' love poem in the form of a wayside inscription, and to the wayside inscription in general. This type of epigram, stemming from the practice of wayside interments, was also used to guide the stranger to suitable watering or resting places, and branched finally into an ideal species that allowed elaborate directions in the form of pictures of nature. The Greek Anthology records many examples of the ideal type. I quote one from Leonidas of Tarentum:

> Not here, O thirsty traveller, stoop to drink,
> The Sun has warm'd, and flocks disturb the brink;
> But climb yon upland where the heifers play,
> Where that tall pine excludes the sultry day;
> There will you see a bubbling rill that flows
> Down the smooth rock more cold than Thracian snows.[35]

Wordsworth gives us stones instead of water; but as he tells his story it is clear what refreshment can flow from them. Robert Frost's "Directive" is a latter-day echo of the genre.

"Michael" leads us unexpectedly to a Greek prototype. To recognize this is to become more aware of Wordsworth's greatness in recovering elemental situations. Yet it is no part of that greatness to oblige us to recognize the specific prototype or genre. On the contrary, because Wordsworth recovers the generic factor we no longer need to recognize the genre which specialized it. Wordsworth's form appears to be self-generated rather than prompted by tradition, and the greater the poem the clearer this effect.

This is strikingly illustrated by the "Lines written a few miles above Tintern Abbey, On revisiting the Banks of the Wye during a Tour, July 13, 1798." Of the nature-inscription in which they originate, only the subtlest vestiges remain. The prospect with its monument or ruin is still nearby; the long specific title still indicates the epitaphic origin of the mode, as does the elegiac tenor; and the poem still claims to mark the very place in which it was inspired. But there is no actual corpse in the vicinity, and the historical significance of the spot is hardly felt. Wordsworth again restores the universal and deeply ordinary context: the corpse is in the poet himself, his consciousness of inner decay, and the history he meditates is of nature's relation to his mind. We recognize the archaic setting purified of hortative tombstone. The power to make him remember his end or his beginning springs simply and directly from a consciousness involved with nature.

Yet though it is Wordsworth's supreme gift to purge the factitious and restore the elemental situation—in his poetry every convention, figure or device is either eliminated, simplified, or
grounded in humanity—a distinction should be made between two
types of the elemental, on the one hand archaic, on the other
archetypal or generic. Without this distinction we can still dis-
criminate between Wordsworth's poems and their contemporary
analogues but we cannot properly separate greater and lesser in his
own corpus. It is important to recognize that the Yew-Tree poem
is more archaic in its use of particular conventions than "Tintern
Abbey," even if the Romantics were occasionally forced to return
to the archaic in order to reach a truly universal conception.[36]

The proposed distinction can center on Wordsworth's refinement of the belief in spirit of place—the archaic belief recovered
in the Yew-Tree poem. The real sin of the recluse is against the
genius loci: that beautiful prospect should have renewed his heart
and attuned him to find pleasure in nature. But Wordsworth's
belief in spirit of place determines more than the poem's doctrine.
It determines, in addition, the form of the poem, and perhaps the
very possibility of Wordsworth's kind of poetry. Formally, it is the
genius loci who exhorts reader or passer-by; and the same spirit
moves the poet to be its interpreter—which can only happen, if,
"nurs'd by genius," he respects nature's impulses and gives them
voice in a reciprocating and basically poetic act.

Even a song as bare as "Tintern Abbey" is based on the superstition of spirit of place. The poet reads nature or his own feelings as
if there were an ominous, admonitory relationship between this
spot and himself. At the end of the poem, moreover, when Wordsworth foresees his death, and urges Dorothy to perpetuate his trust
in nature, he speaks as if he were one of the dead who exhort the
living in the guise of the genius loci. But the archaic formulae are
now generated out of the natural soil of the meditation. We feel
that a superstition of the tribe has been genuinely recovered and
purified. There is nothing patently archaic or poetically archaizing
in Wordsworth's use of a belief which he grounds so deeply in the
human passion for continuity, for binding together the wisdom
of the dead and the energy of the living.

It is in the Lucy Poems that the notion of spirit of place, and
particularly *English* spirit of place, reaches its purest form. (I am

not sure that all of the lyrics originated in the same impulse and
the cycle may have a life of its own which took over from Wordsworth's intentions.) Lucy, living, is clearly a guardian spirit, not of
one place but of all English places—you might meet her ("a Spirit,
yet a Woman too"[37]) by any English fireside or any cherished grove
—while Lucy, dead, has all nature for her monument. The series is
a deeply humanized version of the death of Pan, a lament on the
decay of English nature-feeling. Wordsworth fears that the very
spirit presiding over his poetry is ephemeral, and I think he refuses
to distinguish between its death in him and its historical decline.
The Lucy Poems, brief elegies[38] that purify both gothic ballad and
mannered epigram, consecrate English spirit of place in suitable
English. One could apply to Wordsworth a famous comment in
praise of Theocritus: His muse is the muse of his native land.

The Matthew Poems, which honor a village schoolmaster, can
be our last example. Some of them try to restore the literal integrity of nature-inscription and pastoral elegy, but others almost
completely abandon the archaizing mode. In the earlier and sometimes unpublished versions, the notion of spirit of place is used in
a primitivistic manner: Wordsworth pretends, for example, that he
is moved to write his inscriptions in the very places that had known
Matthew best and where his spirit presumably lingers. One elegy
is therefore "left in the schoolroom," another is "written on a
[commemorative] tablet" in Matthew's school; and in the most
pagan and beautiful of the unpublished elegies he deplores that
Matthew is not buried near his favorite tree, on which he proceeds
to inscribe an epitaph:

> Could I the priest's consent have gained
> Or his who toll'd thy passing bell,
> Then, Matthew, had thy bones remain'd
> Beneath this tree we loved so well.
>
> Yet in our thorn will I suspend
> Thy gift this twisted oaken staff,
> And here where trunk and branches blend
> Will I engrave thy epitaph.[39]

But in "The Two April Mornings" this sense of a continuity between the noble dead and the noble living is conveyed in a natural

rather than artificially naïve way by describing a picture (a true ex-voto) that rises in the poet's mind after his anecdote about Matthew:

> Matthew is in his grave, yet now,
> Methinks, I see him stand,
> As at that moment, with a bough
> Of wilding in his hand.

The living substance on which the memorial is graved is now the poet's mind itself, which moves, as in *The Prelude,* from past to present under the continuing influence of the past.

III

The modern lyric attempts the impossible: a monument to spontaneity, a poem that coincides with the act and passion of its utterance. It tries to overcome the secondary or elegiac aspect of language by making language coterminous with life. However paradoxical this project may be, it has redeemed the short poem from the bondage of the pointed or witty style. After the Romantics, of course, and partly in reaction to their fluidities, new restraints are imposed to concentrate the lyric's fire and to recover epigrammatic terseness. The neolapidary style of the Parnassians, the mystical essentialism of the *symbolistes,* the Imagists with a doctrine that helped trim Eliot's *The Waste Land* to fragments not unlike epigrams, and the still prevalent emphasis on verbal wit and metaphor—these are restrictive and reactionary rather than liberative and revolutionary measures. The real iconoclasts are found in the period of 1750 to 1830 which saw the diverse and sometimes volcanic change of epigram into free-standing lyric.[40]

The means by which this change was effected differed from country to country, from writer to writer, and often from poem to poem. Blake, for example, could transform epigrams into proverbs in his Auguries of Innocence; he could also (going back to native or pseudoepigraphic sources) make primitive inscriptions of his own as in his pictured emblems and children's poetry; he was not above converting to his faith a Wesley-type hymn in "And did those feet in ancient times"; he recovered the mad songs of Shakespeare; he wrote his own Greek-style epitaph in "O Rose, thou art sick"; and,

in the blank-verse lyrics of *Poetical Sketches*, he paralleled Akenside's attempt to develop an unrhymed form for lyric poetry.
Herder, in Germany, by expanding Bishop Percy's idea and recovering ballads and reliques from all nations (including epigrams
from the Greek Anthology), helped to break the tyranny of the
Frenchified song, a tyranny that cooperated with the pointed style.
But for Herder, Heine's *Buch der Lieder*, which created a new
blend of song and witty style, and such collections as *Des Knaben
Wunderhorn*, would not have been possible. About Hölderlin,
Schiller and Goethe it is hard to speak in a comprehensive and
generalizing way; but the spirit of their effort—a radical classicism
opposed to that of the French tradition—is indicated by the fact
that Coleridge insists on teaching Wordsworth (when both are in
Germany) the prosody of the German classical hexameter, and
sends him an illustrative sample of verses:

> William, my head and my heart! dear Poet that
>   feelest and thinkest!
> Dorothy, eager of soul, my most affectionate sister!
> Many a mile, O! many a wearisome mile are ye
>   distant,
> Long, long, comfortless roads, with no one eye
>   that doth know us.

Wordsworth, understandably, is not at all moved by their meter,
only by their sentiment. He has already found a style: his letter of
reply contains two of the Lucy Poems as well as blank-verse episodes
later incorporated in *The Prelude*.[41]

Though Romantic poetry transcends its formal origin in epigram and inscription, and creates the modern lyric, it still falls
short of the latter in one respect. The Romantic poets do not purge
themselves of a certain moralizing strain. This is especially true, in
England, of the first generation of Romantics. The urbane didacticism of the school of Pope is replaced by an oracular didacticism
which the inscription, with its palpable design on the passer-by,
allowed. The overt interpreter is rarely absent from Wordsworth's
poems: a purely lyrical or descriptive moment is invariably followed by self-conscious explication. In "The Old Cumberland
Beggar," after passages of description subtly colored by his feelings,

Wordsworth turns to the statesmen of the world in a sudden moralizing apostrophe longer than these passages. The poem, as a result, falls strangely into two parts, each having its own life, the first part descriptive and quiet, the second oracular.[42]

Byron deplored the lack of urbanity in the Lake Poets, while Shelley and Keats tried to purify the Wordsworthian mode of didactic intrusions. "A poem should not mean but be" is a modern dictum which reflects the fact that, after Wordsworth, the only obstacle to the autonomous lyric was its self-justifying dependence on preachment. The cold, lapidary finger of the original inscriptions had turned into the oracular apostrophe pointing to humble truth. The attempt to absorb "truth" into the texture of the lyric has its own history. It tells of poets in search of a modern equivalent to that fusion of reality and idea which haunted artists and theoreticians from Winckelmann on, and which seemed to them the very secret of Greek art. It tells of Parnassians and Pre-Raphaelites endowing poetry with something of the mute eloquence or unravishable meaning of the other arts, of Mallarmé wishing to overcome even this dependence and to specialize the qualities distinguishing poetic speech from pictorial and musical, and of Yeats generating his lyrics by means of an invisible didactic framework which is the grinning skeleton behind their casual beauties. A critique of these developments is still needed: I can mention as a symbol of their limited success Keats's one mature inscription, the "Ode on a Grecian Urn," which turns from "being" to "meaning" in the final exhortation spoken by the art object itself: "Beauty is Truth, Truth Beauty. . . ." This brief oracle has caused an extended debate that ignored until recently[43] a genre essential to the rise of the modern lyric. But Keats uses the genre once more to teach what art can teach.

NOTES

1. *The Letters of Charles Lamb*, ed. E. V. Lucas (London, 1935), 2 vols., I, 112. It is pleasing to speculate that Wordsworth's verses (together with the boiling milk) may have been partially responsible for "This Lime-Tree Bower." The central emblem in both poems is a retreat, a tree-prison, and Coleridge's mind, though meditating in solitude, follows a path contrary to that of the recluse by attaching love of nature to the development of the social sense.

2. Though the "on" in Warton's title is only vestigially locative, and the poem could be placed among such different genres of the eighteenth century as effusion, impromptu, even ode, the poet's situation (his sense of locality and spirit of place, and the fact that he responds to a work of art) relates his poem genuinely to the inscription. The term "inscription," of course, simply translates "epigram." Warton wrote an explicitly titled "Inscription in a Hermitage at Ansley-Hall, in Warwickshire" (composed 1758, published 1777), and published in 1753 an inscription for a Grotto translated from the Greek Anthology. For other inscriptions see the section of that title in Richard Mant's edition of *The Poetical Works of Thomas Warton* (Oxford, 1802). Also under "Epigrammata."

3. See R. Dodsley, "A Description of The Leasowes" (1764), affixed to the second volume of Shenstone's *Works in Verse and Prose*.

4. The *lemma* seems to have been an explanatory comment added to the epigram during the process of editing but which Renaissance fashion elaborated into a title. For the fashion, see H. H. Hudson, *The Epigram in the English Renaissance* (Princeton, N. J., 1947), pp. 11–13.

5. The "left on" in Wordsworth's title, though generally equivalent to "written on," links his poem also to the votive epigram (discussed below) which might be "left" under a picture, on a hearse, etc.—I have found no study of the titling of poems. Lengthiness of title as well as the emerging significance of place and date might also have been influenced by the journalistic broadside ballad which tended toward concrete and elaborate titles. One of them is parodied in Sir Walter Scott's *The Antiquary*: "Strange and Wonderful News from Chipping-Norton, in the County of Oxon, of certain dreadful apparitions which were seen in the air on the 26th of July, 1610, at half an hour after nine o'clock at noon . . . " etc. etc. Cf. "Verses found under a Yew-Tree at Penshurst, July 18, 1791. By a Country Blacksmith" (from *Gentleman's Magazine*) or "Written Sept. 1791, during a remarkable thunder storm, in which the moon was perfectly clear, while the tempest gathered in various directions near the earth" (Charlotte Smith, *Elegiac Sonnets*, no. LIX).

6. On this distinction, see note 21 below.

7. *Zerstreute Anmerkungen über das Epigramm,* first published in *Vermischte Schriften* (Berlin, 1771). I use the translation in Hudson, op. cit. pp. 9–10.

8. Wordsworth, "Upon Epitaphs" (First Essay). See A. B. Grosart, ed., *The Prose Works of William Wordsworth* (London, 1876), 3 vols., II, 32. Professor E. Bernhardt-Kabisch of Indiana University, in "The Monumental Poet: Wordsworth and Epitaphs" (a paper delivered at the 1963 Modern Language Association), has discerned how profoundly epitaphs influenced Wordsworth's sensibility and poetry.

9. This is not altered by the fact that a fashion for funeral urns and commemorative benches prevailed in the second half of the century: see Dodsley, "A Description of The Leasowes," and J. Delille's *Les Jardins* (1780), chant IV.

10. For general information about the Greek Anthology, I am mainly indebted to J. W. Mackail, *Select Epigrams from the Greek Anthology* (rev. ed., 1906),

and the two invaluable books of James Hutton, *The Greek Anthology in Italy to the Year 1800* (Ithaca, N. Y., 1935) and *The Greek Anthology in France . . . to the Year 1800* (Ithaca, N. Y., 1946). Though the Anthology has individual parts devoted respectively to epitaphs and dedications, it will become clear that, as Mackail observes in his introduction, "the earlier epigram [i.e., the Greek as distinguished from the Greco-Roman] falls almost entirely under these two heads."

11. In English literature the naïvely paganizing strain is displaced by the Hermit poem with its Christian simplicities, but Wordsworth's lyrics on Matthew here and there touch on the spirit of the older tradition. The sonnet, which was strongly related to the votive epigram, and which allowed simple personal (and first-person) sentiment, is too large a subject to be broached here. See, however, a significant remark in Coleridge's introduction to his sonnets in the 2nd (1797) edition of *Poems on Various Subjects:* "Perhaps, if the Sonnet were comprized in less than fourteen lines, it would become a serious epigram. . . . The greater part of Warton's Sonnets are severe and masterly likenesses of the style of the Greek *epigrammata*."

12. Jean Hagstrum in *The Sister Arts* (Chicago, 1958) covers—and recovers—this tradition as it extends from Dryden to Gray, and clarifies its sources in earlier literature. I adopt his use of the term "iconic." For Anna Seward's inscriptions, see *The Poetical Register and Repository of Fugitive Poetry for 1801*, pp. 177–80, 180–81.

13. Quoted by Victor Lange, *Die Lyrik und ihr Publikum im England des 18. Jahrhunderts* (Weimar, 1935), p. 60.

14. *Gentleman's Magazine*, LXXVIII (1808), 728, 924, 1020. T. Warton's "Inscription in a Hermitage" has been mentioned. Two more examples of interest: Mrs. West's "Inscription," *Gentleman's Magazine*, LXI (1791), 68, and an anonymous "Ballad" in the *Poetical Register for 1802*, pp. 254–5. To the Hermit poems, a devotional poetry in disguise, Wordsworth adds his "Inscriptions supposed to be found in and near a Hermit's Cell" (1818). They revert to the eighteenth-century quatrain style, though this is chastened, as the persona of the Hermit required, to hymn-like simplicity. Wordsworth practised the conventional kind of inscription throughout his career: among his juvenilia are two versions of an inscription for a wayside bench which were never printed under his name, though one was published pseudonymously. His interest in Sir G. Beaumont's garden at Coleorton produces several further instances; and when he thinks he may have to leave Rydal Mount he composes an inscription to be placed in its grounds. The 1815 edition of his collected poems contains a section explicitly titled "Inscriptions." As late as 1830, remembering the old exhortation, "Woodman, spare that tree," he writes some unusually playful verses on a *stone* saved from the builder's hand.

15. W. L. Bowles, "Inscription." The poem signs off: "Bremhill Garden, Sept. 1808." *The Poetical Works of William Lisle Bowles*, ed. Rev. G. Gilfillan (Edinburgh, 1855), 2 vols., I, 155–6.

16. "On a Cave. From the Greek of Anyta, a Lesbian Poetess," in Thomas Warton the Elder, *Poems on Several Occasions* (1748).

17. The middle of Bowles's poem, quoted above, reverts to the allegorizing which vitiates so many songs and descriptive pieces of the eighteenth and early nineteenth century. For a non-didactic allegorical song, see Shelley's "The Two Spirits: An Allegory" (written 1820). But the song, as a *genre*, has its own development, and is not the subject of this essay.

18. "For a Cavern that overlooks the River Avon." Written at Bristol, 1796. I have quoted the version in the *Poems* of 1797.

19. *The Complete Poetical Works of S. T. Coleridge*, ed. E. H. Coleridge (Oxford, 1912), 2 vols., I, 381–2. The capitalization of Twilight and Coolness shows how close the allegorical habit is, and how finely subdued.

20. Hudson's *The Epigram in the English Renaissance* was left unfinished and covers but a small chronological area. Mr. Hutton was kind enough to communicate a list of authors indebted to the Greek Anthology, but the range, quality and epoch of its possible influence would need a study as thorough as his own previous works. Much knowledge of Greek can be taken for granted (see the two books of M. L. Clarke, *Classical Education in Britain*, and *Greek Studies in England 1700–1830*); the Greek influence, moreover, was mediated by the best Latin writers in such poems as Horace's *Odes*, iii.13 (to the Blandusian fountain), and iii.18 (address to Faunus), both of which spring from the votive epigram, and in Virgil's *Eclogues*, through which the blend of elegiac and pastoral poetry first reached England. It is interesting that one book of English versions of the Anthology (only three small volumes of translation have come to my hand in the period under discussion, but this might be explained by the custom of rendering the Greek into Latin rather than English) was published in 1791 for the use of Winchester School of which Joseph Warton was headmaster, and that his brother Thomas was the first to publish in England an edition of selections from the Palatine MS. (*Anthologiæ Graecæ a C. Cephala Conditæ*, 1766).

21. On the difference between the Alexandrian (and earlier) epigram and the Augustan type, see Hudson, op. cit. pp. 6–9; Mackail, op. cit. pp. 4–5; Hutton, *Greek Anthology in Italy*, pp. 55–6; and [R. Bland and J. H. Merivale,] *Translations chiefly from the Greek Anthology* (London, 1806), p. vii. Hutton states that "We preferably think of the Greek epigram as . . . the brief elegy, written before and during the Alexandrian age"; and Bland and Merivale say that "the small poems which claim the greatest attention, are those which are written as memorials of the dead, as tokens of regard for living beauty or virtue, or as passing observations and brief sketches of human life." Charles Batteux, interestingly enough, thinks the distinction between the two types of epigrams is one between the (earlier) *inscription* and the (later) *epigram:* "Plus on remonte vers l'antiquité, plus on trouve de simplicité dans les Epigrammes. . . . dans les commencemens . . . l'Epigramme se confondait avec l'Inscription qui est simple par essence. Il suffisoit alors que l'Epigramme fût courte, d'un sens clair & juste. Peu-à-peu on y a mis plus d'art & de finesse, & on a songé à en aiguiser la pointe." "Traité de l'Epigramme et de l'Inscription," *Principes de la littérature* (Paris, 1774). T. Warton's *Inscriptionum Romanorum Metricarum Delectus* (1758) tried to single out the "simplest" Roman inscriptions—so much so, in fact, that Shenstone writes they are too

simple even for his taste. See *The Letters of William Shenstone,* ed. M. Williams (Oxford, 1939), p. 496.

22. *Poems on Several Occasions* (1748). The exact date of the translations is unknown: the *Poems* are published posthumously by Joseph Warton.

23. Three Shenstone poems under the title "Rural Inscriptions" were included in Dodsley's Collection of 1755. They are "antique" and "simple" only vis-à-vis the French-Italian tradition and cannot compare with Akenside's which are genuine distillations of the mood and various types of the Greek votive epigram. Akenside seems almost to have written them against or in rivalry with Shenstone. All of the latter's inscriptions are given by Dodsley in his "A Description of The Leasowes."

24. Southey acknowledges Akenside as follows in a prefatory note to *Poems* (1797): "The Inscriptions will be found to differ from the Greek simplicity of Akenside's in the point that generally concludes them." (But what Southey calls "point" Chaucer would have called "sentence.") In the 1837 edition of his poems Southey also mentions the later influence of Chiabrera whose epitaphs had made a vivid impression on Wordsworth and Coleridge (see Wordsworth's "Essays upon Epitaphs" and his translations from Chiabrera). The Italian poet may himself be strongly indebted to the Greek Anthology. Coleridge's early imitation of Akenside was published, according to his editor, in the *Morning Chronicle* for September 3, 1794 (*Poetical Works,* I, 69–70), and has nothing Akensidean about it. The theme is treated in rime and with the sentimentality of the contemporary pastoral ballad.

25. I assert this with more conviction than I feel. There are, however, very few blank-verse lyrics which are not (1) translations or close imitations of the Classics, (2) paraphrases of the Scriptures, (3) borderline cases in which didactic and lyrical blend as in Thomson's influential didactic-descriptive *Seasons.* (Though not a short poem, it can easily be divided into short episodes.) Cf. the relevant chapters in the second volume of G. Saintsbury's *History of English Prosody* (New York, 1961); H. A. Beers, *A History of English Romanticism in the Eighteenth Century* (New York, 1899), ch. iv; and H. G. de Maar, *A History of Modern English Romanticism,* vol. I (Oxford, 1924), ch. viii.

26. Hudson, op. cit. p. 9.

27. The two factors are probably related, since the Greek epitaph was the primitive form through which nature poetry developed (see section 2, below), but I keep them distinct to suggest the peculiar English interest in "local" poetry. Topographical antiquarian articles in, for example, *Gentleman's Magazine,* as well as numerous guide-books, blend the interest in locality with interest in inscriptions, and make the "traveler" a familiar figure of English landscape.

28. *Poetical Works of William Wordsworth,* ed. E. de Selincourt (Oxford, 1940–49), 5 vols., II (2nd ed., 1952), 433. "Idyllium" was a conventional term for the kind of poetry represented by the "idylls" of Theocritus. Wordsworth esteemed Theocritus as a poet faithful to spirit of place and the simple, permanent "manners" (ethos) of his time. See his letter of 7 February 1799 to

Coleridge, *Early Letters of William and Dorothy Wordsworth*, ed. E. de Selincourt (Oxford, 1935), pp. 221–2.

29. "The Contemporaneity of the *Lyrical Ballads*," *PMLA*, LXIX (1954), 486–522.

30. One sign of the change from indication to evocation in nature poetry is that consciousness of place and of the moment of composition are stronger than before, but this shows itself, before Wordsworth, mainly in the titles, which remain, as they must, an indicative device. It is significant that a late commentator claims of Warton's "Inscription in a Hermitage at Ansley-Hall, in Warwickshire" that it was composed "upon the spot, with all the objects around him, and on the spur of the moment." See *Gentleman's Magazine*, LXXXV (1815), 387–8.

31. Cf. Northrop Frye, "Toward Defining an Age of Sensibility," in *Fables of Identity* (Harbinger Paperback, 1963). Frye overstates the degree to which, with the 1800 *Lyrical Ballads*, recollection in tranquillity took over from the Age of Sensibility's "concentration on the primitive process of writing" and "oracular process of composition." But his thesis is basically very sound and exciting. The 1800 *Lyrical Ballads* contain overtly identifiable inscriptions and also the "Poems on the Naming of Places" in which naming is a joyfully spontaneous act that almost escapes elegiac implications. About Wordsworth's "primitivism" compared to that of the poets of the Age of Sensibility, see below, especially note 36.

32. This fundamental attitude of reading the (epitaphic) characters of nature joins "The Ruined Cottage" (1797–98) to Bks. V ff. of *The Excursion*, composed more than ten years later, in which the village Pastor resuscitates his parishioners in a series of "living epitaphs."

33. From the third sonnet of Wordsworth's *The River Duddon* (1820).

34. "Epitomized biography" is Wordsworth's own phrase: Grosart, op. cit. II, 69. "The excellence belonging to the Greek inscriptions in honor of the dead," we read in the preface to *Translations chiefly from the Greek Anthology*, "consists in the happy introduction of their names and peculiar characters or occupations."

35. *Translations chiefly from the Greek Anthology*, p. 30. I have slightly modified this still frigid version: cf. Mackail, *Select Epigrams*, p. 203. For Theocritus' wayside inscription, see *The Greek Bucolic Poets*, tr. J. M. Edmonds (London and New York, 1928), p. 367.

36. The return to the archaic is found in most poets of the Age of Sensibility, and in Wordsworth's own "Vale of Esthwaite." We may have to decide that there are two, interrelated kinds of greatness; one represented primarily by Wordsworth (the directest "poet of the human heart"), the other by the tradition going from Collins to Blake and which Coleridge *elected* for his "Ancient Mariner."

37. I adapt this to the Lucy Poems from "She was a Phantom of delight." Lucy is a laric figure, if we admit that the fire she tends can burn in nature

as well as in the home—that, in fact, nature and home are one to her. Compare Lucy as she appears in "I travelled among unknown men" with Louisa who "loves her fire, her cottage-home;/Yet o'er the moorland will she roam" ("Louisa" was also composed *c.* 1801).

38. One can think of "A slumber did my spirit seal" (called "a sublime epitaph" by Coleridge) as an epigram or brief elegy (see Hutton, op. cit. p. 55). The sense of early and sudden death, the balance between personal lament and subdued hope in the living earth, and the casting of lament in the form of an epitomized action, are as if perfected from the Greek.

39. *Poetical Works of William Wordsworth,* IV, 451–4. See also the 1800 *Lyrical Ballads,* and *Poetical Works,* IV, 68–73.

40. Rimbaud is probably the greatest exception to this general statement. French developments are especially complex: they begin with Chénier, whose favorite book was Brunck's edition of the Greek Anthology, and begin a second time with Lamartine and Hugo. But the older classicism was still so strong that a third insurrection, that of Rimbaud, was needed.

41. See *Collected Letters of Samuel Taylor Coleridge,* ed. E. L. Griggs (Oxford, 1956), 2 vols., I, 450–53, and *The Early Letters of William and Dorothy Wordsworth,* pp. 203–11.

42. Wordsworth's "split structure" is curiously akin to the inscription's *ecphrasis,* in which the mute object, or its interpreter, addresses us. (The Beggar is such a mute object.)

43. The proper literary context was first pointed out by Leo Spitzer in *Comparative Literature,* VII (1955), 203–25, and was also noted by Hagstrum, op. cit. pp. 22–3. Both Spitzer and Hagstrum refer to a wealth of secondary literature showing the prevalence of art epigrams and their closeness to sepulchral epigrams.

Reflections in a Coleridge Mirror:
Some Images in His Poems

———•—•———

KATHLEEN COBURN

Iᴛ is a fairly general, if often a vague and casual opinion, that
Coleridge, although all his life reputed to be a poet, wrote but
"a handful of golden poems,"[1] and these within a short period
under the stimulus of the *Lyrical Ballads* in 1797–98. Then after a
few months of unsuccessful struggle to complete *Christabel* he proclaimed his sense of failure in *Dejection: an Ode,* published in the
Morning Post in 1802. After this he is the poet dwindled into
philosopher or theologian, or side-tracked by journalism, or the
poet who but for weaknesses of character might have become an
even greater literary critic than he was. He is the poet whose appalling fate it was to become the Oracle of Highgate, Lamb's inspired charity boy translated into Carlyle's mumbling monologist,
the soporific table-talker of Beerbohm's cartoon.

Certainly the larger constructive poetic drives disappeared.
Lamb in the touching letter dedicating his works to Coleridge in
1818 complained wistfully: "You yourself write no Christabels and
Ancient Mariners now." Lamb asks if with the years "life itself
loses much of its poetry for us," and seems, for himself, to admit
the possibility. "Yet," he says, "my old friend is the same, his hair
a little confessing the hand of time . . . but still shrouding that
same capacious brain." Many a Highgate visitor and many a notebook entry bear witness to the enduring vitality of his mind. Short
pieces continued to come to the surface sporadically, some of them
too much neglected now, for the fact is Coleridge continued to the
end to think and feel like a poet.

Little has been written of his poetical works as a whole, to illuminate either the particular case or the general picture, if such it was, of the life and death of the imagination. Yet the sense of failure of creativity is frequently recognized to have been a theme close to the bone of many of his great poems. The ways in which he dealt with his own sensibilities, consciously in *Dejection,* perhaps less consciously in *Kubla Khan,* at several levels in *The Ancient Mariner,* have, it is true, been variously examined. But a close look at some prose passages and some of the late verses with certain images particularly in mind may be fruitful.

I. A. Richards has suggested[2] that Coleridge's central failure was the failure to follow the Socratic injunction he advocated, "Know thyself." In a sense this is true. But with what reservations, and in what respect not true for other men, is worth examining, for Coleridge pursued self-analysis in a psycho-analytic sense perhaps farther than anyone of his time, and with an uncanny half-prescience of Freudian concepts. The "method" of imagination as he sees it and practises it, is a process of self-ordering, of resolution of conflict in the self, of the reconciliation of personal and impersonal, of attachment and detachment, of sameness with difference, in fact of uniting polar opposites as he said. Is he not forging to the end of his life the subjective-objective conjunction or fusion of the forms of space and time in images which articulate experience in that thought-feeling enterprise which is poetry?

In *The Ancient Mariner,* the young mariner who set forth a simple member of a ship's crew, an extrovert with a crossbow, is shaken by the horrors of guilt, and discovers himself in the desolation of forsaken southern seas (in contrast with the steady stars and the revolving moon and the beautiful creatures of the great deep) with no natural home, no abiding place, no silent joy anywhere at his arrival, always a lonely wanderer, and periodically, for all time, a compulsive talker.

Christabel, also a solitary, cut off from natural ties, goes out to search her solitude for its meaning, to pray, to look for something both natural and supernatural with which to support herself; she finds only horror and fear and unnatural malice. Her search for happiness and self-realization not only fails, but leaves her more solitary, more frightened, more estranged than before, with an intensified sense of the mysterious forces antagonistic to her life.

The speaker, one could say almost the psalmist, of *Kubla Khan,* is in similar plight. The search for the source of power that built or would build the stately pleasure dome leads from the sunny gardens bright with sinuous rills to the measureless caverns, the violent chasm, and the sunless sea. The rhythms of symphony and song that might have ordered the chaos are replaced by ancestral voices prophesying war, the self is unable to maintain its diet of honey dew, its glimpses of paradise, and the song instead of rounding to a full dome-like diapason at the close, ends in hysterical isolation and nostalgia for worlds prophesied but unborn. The rhapsodist is defeated by a too realistic sense that his own power is of the past, now without strength, and publicly exposed to the circle of spectators woven around him.

Coleridge's sense of the tragedy of human life, intensely personal and magnificently supra-personal, appears in many poems other than the greatest ones, and is present in some of the latest: *Youth and Age, Work Without Hope, The Garden of Boccaccio, Love, Hope, and Patience in Education.* Awareness of this reconciliation is sharpened by an examination of the certain images recurrent not as decoration but as the dynamic by which the poems live and move and form themselves. Some of these are often interlinked: the cone shape and the spring of water, the mirror and the babe at the mother's breast, the spider and the bee, the giant tree with deep root and the solitary or blown leaf or loose blossom— one could compile a long list.

The mirror, the looking-glass of Narcissus, is in obvious and also in less obvious ways connected with the search for the self.

There is an amusing comment from Coleridge's Göttingen days of 1799 by a fellow student who observed him "fixing his prominent eyes upon himself (as he was wont to do whenever there was a mirror in the room)."[3] In a list of projected works as early as 1795–96, he had considered an "Ode to a Looking Glass."[4] This was not from any great liking for what he saw when he looked in it, "a mere carcase of a face: fat, flabby, expressive chiefly of inexpression," he wrote at about the same time.[5] In one manuscript of a schoolboy poem in what is clearly an autobiographical reference he uses the phrase "that fat vacuity of face," and suggests that "Happiness" (the subject of the poem) would be complete

> If chance some lovely maid thou find
> To read thy visage in thy mind.[6]

He obviously did not wish anyone to reverse the process and read his mind in his face. This was perfectly evident much later when Matilda Betham wished to paint a miniature of him in 1808. With one excuse and another, genuine enough to himself, he kept putting her off. "My poor face is a miserable subject for a painter (for in honest truth I am what the world calls, and with more truth than usual, an *ugly* fellow)."[7] In 1811 there were other pretexts—he lost her address, he fell and hurt his head at Somerset House quayside, and he is full of gracious apologies for being "a truant from my promise"[8]—the very language of a school boy caught out at last.

In a letter of 16 August 1814 to John Morgan he shows again a frank realism about what his mirror told him:

Of my own portrait I am no judge. Allston is highly gratified with it, & promises himself that it will be even better than Mr. King's—which in its present state is the most looking-glassish, ipsissimous, living flesh & blood thing, I ever beheld. I cannot believe, that mine will be equal; because King's is so very far finer a face. I am not *mortified,* tho' I own I should better like it to be otherwise, that my face is not a manly or representable Face—whatever is impressive, is part fugitive, part existent only in the imaginations of persons impressed strongly by my conversation. The face *itself* is a *feeble,* unmanly face. . . . The exceeding *weakness,* strengthlessness, in my face, was ever painful to me—not as my own face, but as *a* face.[9]

In another early poem, the first version of *To a Young Ass,* the young Pantisocrat, Toil will "use his sleek cows for a looking-glass."[10] One doubts if the image came out of any dairyman experience of Coleridge's own; but such references, and the couplet, *To a Certain Modern Narcissus,*[11] suggest his awareness of the phenomenon. In *Osorio* Albert describes himself to Osorio as

> one that at his mother's looking-glass,
> Would force his features to a frowning sternness.[12]

Albert[13] in this scene in particular (Act III is full of Esteecean reminiscence, even of the runaway night on the banks of the Otter),[14] probably saw reflected in the maternal looking-glass the frowning sternness of a frightened and rejected child.

A few pages apart in Notebook 17 we find two characteristically disparate glances at mirrorment, one mocking, very possibly self-mocking, the other more solemnly contemplative.

Lavater fixed on the simplest physiognomy in his whole congregation— & pitched his sermon to his comprehension.—Narcissus either looks at or thinks of the Looking-Glass—for the same wise purpose, I presume —15

> The body
> Eternal Shadow of the finite Soul /
> The Soul's self-symbol / its image of itself,
> Its own yet not itself—16

But a few pages further on in the same notebook an entry serves as a caution against "dead letter" interpretations of living meanings by "fixing" the images too rigidly. Images must fuse, melt, dim, and unfix themselves, fused by an energy that has more than the cerebral at stake, that is concerned with knowledge not merely as percepts and concepts but knowledge as emotive, as animating, as power.

The image-forming or rather re-forming power, the imagination in its passive sense, which I would rather call Fancy-Phantasy, a φαίνειν— this, the Fetisch & Talisman of all modern Philosophers (the Germans excepted) may not inaptly be compared to the Gorgon Head, which *looked* death into every thing—and this not by accident, but from the nature of the faculty itself, the province of which is to give consciousness to the Subject by presenting to it its conceptions *objectively* but the Soul differences itself from any other Soul for the purposes of symbolical knowledge by *form* or body only—but all form as body, i.e. as shape, & not as forma efformans, is dead—Life may be *inferred,* even as intelligence is from black marks on white paper—but the black marks themselves are truly 'the *dead* letter'. Here then is the error—not in the faculty itself, without which there would be no *fixation,* consequently, no distinct perception or conception, but in the gross idolatry of those who abuse it, & make that the goal & end which should be only a means of arriving at it. Is it any excuse to him who treats a living being as inanimate Body, that we cannot arrive at the knowledge of the living Being but thro' the Body which is its Symbol, & outward & visible Sign?—*

* From the above deduce the worth & dignity of poetic Imagination, of the fusing power, that fixing unfixes & while it melts & bedims the Image, still leaves in the Soul its living meaning—17

With this caution in mind we may look at a cluster of images, selecting only some of the sharpest examples arising from that search for the self referred to above, and the co-related compulsive attempts of a creative imagination to order the egocentric chaos.

The Preface to the *Poems on Various Subjects* (1796) is largely a defence of Egotism in poetry, a statement retained in the 1797 volume, and again in the reprint of 1803; that is to say, the youthful remarks on the subject were made before the great poems of the *annus mirabilis,* and they were retained afterwards.

"Poetry without egotism," he says, is "comparatively uninteresting."[18] (The significance of the remainder of the entry—"Mem. Write an Ode to *Meat & Drink"* may become clearer presently.)

To censure it [egotism] in a Monody or Sonnet is almost as absurd as to dislike a circle for being round. . . . The communicativeness of our nature leads us to describe our own sorrows; in the endeavor to describe them intellectual activity is exerted; and by a benevolent law of our nature from intellectual activity a pleasure results which is gradually associated and mingles as a corrective with the painful subject of the description.

There is one species of egotism which is truly disgusting; not that which leads us to communicate our feelings to others, but that which would reduce the feelings of others to an identity with our own.

With what anxiety every fashionable author avoids the word *I*!—now he transforms himself into a third person,—"the present writer"—now multiplies himself and swells into "we"—and all this is the watchfulness of guilt. Conscious that this said *I* is perpetually intruding on his mind and that it monopolizes his heart, he is prudishly solicitous that it may not escape from his lips.

This disinterestedness of phrase is in general commensurate with selfishness of feeling: men old and hackneyed in the ways of the world are scrupulous avoiders of Egotism.[19]

Concealed or silent egotism (i.e., egoism) is apt to turn into contempt, "the concentrated vinegar of egotism";[20] the implication clearly must be that originally egoism is the wine of life, the proper vitality of the self—

Empirics are boastful ⟨& Egotists⟩ often because they introduce ⟨real or⟩ apparent novelty—which excites great opposition—⟨personal⟩ opposition creates re-action (which is of course, a consciousness of power) associated with the *person* reacting. Paracelsus was a boaster, it is true —so were the French Jacobins—& Wolff, tho' not a boaster, was persecuted into a habit of Egotism in his philosophical writings.—So Dr. John Brown—Milton in his prose works—&c—and those in similar circumstances who from prudence ~~have~~ abstain from Egotism in their writings, are still Egotists among their friends— / It would be unnatural effort not to be so / & Egotism in such cases is by no means offensive to a kind & discerning man.[21]

The need for a consciousness of one's power, or in our now almost hackneyed terms, a sense of identity, is recognized here, a proper possession of the full man who would articulate his sensibilities with discernment and a clear sense of values.

The element of personal experience is close to the surface. Coleridge was all his life accused of egotism, tolerated and accepted and charming in some of its youthful forms, condoned, and pardoned later, often irritating, especially in its form of self-abasement, and in some quarters never forgiven.

About 1809 he wrote in Notebook 24:

We understand Nature just as if at a distance we looked at the Image of a Person in a Looking-glass, plainly and fervently discoursing—yet what he uttered, we could decypher only by the motion of the Lips, and the mien, and the expression of the muscles of his Countenance—[22]

He had in fact put the notion into practice years earlier.

March 17, 1801. Tuesday—Hartley looking out of my study window fixed his eyes steadily & for some time on the opposite prospect, & then said—Will yon Mountains *always* be?—I shewed him the whole magnificent Prospect in a Looking Glass, and held it up, so that the whole was like a Canopy or Ceiling over his head, & he struggled to express himself concerning the Difference between the Thing & the Image almost with convulsive Effort.—I ~~think~~ never before saw such an Abstract of *Thinking* as a pure act & energy, of *Thinking* as distinguished from *Thoughts*.[23]

On the previous page he had just recently written:

> —and the deep power of Joy
> We see into the *Life* of Things—

i.e.—By deep feeling we make our *Ideas dim*—& this is what we mean

by our Life—ourselves. I think of the Wall—it is before me, a distinct
Image—here. I necessarily think of the *Idea* & the Thinking I as two
distinct & opposite Things. Now let me think of *myself*—of the thinking
Being—the Idea becomes dim whatever it be—so dim that I know not
what it is—but the Feeling is deep & steady—and this I call *I* the identifying the Percipient & the Perceived—.[24]

The identification of the percipient and the perceived is pursued
in some most interesting lines of verse in the notebooks, so extraordinary in their precision of detail as to seem to belong rather
to distant recollection than to *ab extra* observation. The babe is at
the breast and the very pulsations of its breathing and sucking are
suggested by the gentle, regular, liquid rhythms:

> Fire, That slept in its Intensity, Life
> Wakeful over all knew no gradations,
> And Bliss in its excess became a Dream,
> And my visual powers involved such Sense,
> all Thought, Sense, Thought, & Feeling,
> and Time drew out his subtle
> Threads so quick, That the long
> Summer's Eve was long one whole web,
> A Space on which I lay commensurate—
> For Memory & all undoubting Hope
> Sang the same note & in the selfsame
> Voice, with each sweet *now* of
> My Felicity, and blended momently,
> Like Milk that coming comes of its steady & in its
> easy stream Flows ever in, upon the
> mingling milk, in the Babe's murmuring
> Mouth / or mirrors each reflecting each / —[25]

It will be noticed that here is the dreamlike web of Time and
Space, blissfully supporting the sensory body, the moment of oral
felicity of the sucking Babe; here at the breast are the mirrors in
which the associating memory of times past and dreaming hope of
an unending future reflect each other in the "sweet *now*."[26]

A week after the entry about fixing the landscape for Hartley in
the looking-glass he went on to a discussion of oral-tactual
association:

Babies touch *by taste* at first—then about 5 months old they go from
the Palate to the hand—& are fond of feeling what they have taste[d]—

/ Association of the Hand with the Taste—till the latter by itself recalls the former—& of course, with volition. March 24, 1801.[27]

Twenty-four years later the blended images have coalesced in a notebook entry that culminates in the lines entitled, *Work Without Hope:*

21 Feby. 1825.—My dear Friend

I have often amused my ~~fancy~~ self with the thought of a Self-conscious Looking-glass, and the various metaphorical applications of such a fancy —and this morning, ~~I~~ it struck across ~~my~~ the Eolian Harp of my Brain that there was something pleasing and emblematic (of what I did not distinctly make out) in two such Looking-glasses fronting, each seeing the other in itself, and itself in the other.—Have you ever noticed the Vault or snug little Apartment which the Spider spins and weaves for itself, by spiral threads round and round, and sometimes with strait lines, in so that its Lurking-parlour or Withdrawing-room is an oblong square? This too connected itself in my mind with the melancholy truth, that as we grow older, the World (alas! how often it happens, that the less we love it, the more we care for it; the less reason we have to value its Shews, the more anxious are we about them!—~~and~~ alas! how often do we become more and more loveless, ~~the more this~~ as Love, which can outlive all change save a change with regard to itself, and all loss save the loss of its *Reflex,* is more needed to sooth us & alone is able so to do!)

What was I saying:—O—I was adverting to the fact, that as we advance in years, the World, that *spidery* Witch, spins its threads narrower and narrower, still closing in on us, till at last it shuts us up within four walls, walls of flues and films, ~~and~~ windowless—and well if there be sky-lights, and a small opening left for the Light from above. I do not know that I have anything to add, except perhaps to remind you, that *pheer* or *phere* for *Mate, Companion, Counterpart,* is a word frequently used by Spencer, G. Herbert, and the Poets generally, who wrote before the Restoration (1660)—before I say, that this premature warm and sunny day, ante-dating Spring, called forth the following Strain in the manner of G. HERBERT*—. : which might be entitled, THE ALONE MOST DEAR: a Complaint of Jacob to Rachel† as in the tenth year of his Service he saw in her, ~~and~~ or *fancied* that he saw Symptoms of Alienation.—~~N.B. The Thought and Images being modernized and turned into English.—~~

* Cf. G. Herbert, *Employment* I, stanza 5: "All things are busie; only I/ Neither bring Honey with the Bees,/Nor flowers to make that. . . ."

† *Jacob to Rachel:* Evidently Coleridge to Mrs. Gillman, who has inserted, "It *was* fancy."

All nature seems at work. ~~Snails~~slugs leave their lair;
The Bees are stirring; Birds are on the wing;
and W I N T E R slumb'ring in the open air
Wears on his smiling face a dream of Spring,
~~But~~ And I, the while, the sole unbusy Thing,
Nor honey make, nor pair, nor build, nor sing.
Yet well I ken the banks, where *Amaranths blow,
Have traced the fount whence streams of Nectar flow.
Bloom, O ye Amaranths! bloom for whom ye may—
For Me ye bloom not! Glide, rich Streams! away!
    ⟨? *Lips unbrighten'd, wreathless?*—⟩
With unmoist Lip and wreathless Brow I stroll:
And would you learn the Spells, that drowse my Soul?
WORK without Hope draws nectar in a sieve
And HOPE without an Object cannot live."

Below the poem as we know it are various experimental re-visions, the first partly obscured by the second which was pasted over it on a separate sheet so as to obliterate ten lines. The second version reads:

Where daily nearer me, with Magic Ties,
What home, and where (wove close with
Line over line & thickning as they rise)
The World her spidery threads on all sides spun,
Side answ'ring Side with narrow interspace;
My Faith (say, I: I and my Faith are one)
Hung, as a Mirror there! And face to face
(For nothing else there was, between or near)
One Sister Mirror hid the dreary Wall.
But *That* is broke! And with that bright Compeer / pheer†
I lost my Object and my inmost All—
Faith *in* the Faith of THE ALONE MOST DEAR:

                                      Jacob Hodiernus.

On the page opposite he tried further revisions:

Call the World Spider, and at fancy's touch
Thought becomes image and I see it such.
~~Skilled in light~~ With viscous masonry of films and threads

---

* *Literally* rendered as Flower Fadeless, or never-fading—from the Greek a
NOT and maraino, to wither. [STC]
† Mate, Counterpart. [STC]

It joins the Waller's and the Weaver's trades,
And see a twilight tent enclose me round
A dusky cell!—but hush! for all too long
I linger in the [? preamble].
With viscous masonry of films and threads
Tough as the nets in Indian Forests found
It blends the Waller's & the Weaver's trade
And soon the tent-like Hangings touch the ground
[*two lines obliterated*]
A dusky Chamber that excludes the Day—
But cease the prelude & resume the lay.[28]

In the prose preamble we have the mirror, the mutual mirrors, related to past and future "as we grow older," to winter and spring, memory and hope, relationship made and relationship broken, the open air freedom of love and life, the dark walls of the enclosing grave, self-realization in the "*Reflex*," death of the self in isolation. Scarcely below the surface is the reflexive love of mother and child: the unmoist lips (by negation suggesting the opposite), home, the sister-mirror, even the slumberer with the smile on his face.

In the revisions, there is again, in association with all the rest, the spidery web, of *CN* II 3107 above, now claustrophobic, and, in the Indian forests of the last stanza, possibly poisonous.[29]

In *Work Without Hope*, as Coleridge later entitled the poem, we have the breeding, brooding activities of spring, in contrast to the unproductive self, the fount whence streams of nectar flow but the honey dew is not drunk, where the rich stream produces no growth, no wreath of amaranths. These images are related not only to others in this entry, but inescapably to Quarles's twelfth emblem in his Book I and its accompanying illustration. The clue is another notebook memorandum:

> Quarles's Emblems—Even in the present Rage for our
> old poets, how much under-rated?

Coleridge continues by distinguishing those "of inferior merit yet meriting praise," and among those more strongly commended is No. XII in Book I, the fifth stanza particularly.[30]

Quarles's poem must be quoted in full:

XII

(Isaiah 66.11.)

Ye may suck, but not be satisfied with the breast of her consolation.[31]

1.

What, never fill'd? Be thy lips skrew'd so fast
  To th' earth's fullbreast? for shame, for shame unseize thee;
Thou tak'st a surfeit where thou shou'd but taste,
    And mak'st too much not half enough to please thee.
      Ah, fool, forbear; thou swallowest at one breath
Both food and poison down? thou draw'st both milk and death.

2.

The ub'rous breasts, when fairly drawn, repast
  The thriving infant with their milky flood,
But being overstrain'd, return at last
    Unwholsom gulps compos'd of wind and blood.
      A mod'rate use does both repast and please;
Who strains beyond a mean, draws in and gulps disease.

3.

But, O that mean, whose good the least abuse
  Makes bad, is too too hard to be directed:
Can thorns bring grapes, or crabs a pleasing juice?
    There's nothing wholsom, where the whole's infected.
      Unseize thy lips: earth's milk's a ripened core,
That drops from her disease, that matters from her fore.

4.

Think'st thou that paunch, that burlies out thy coat,
  Is thriving fat; or flesh, that seems so brawny?
Thy paunch is dropsied and thy cheeks are bloat?
    Thy lips are white, and thy complexion tawny;
      Thy skin's a bladder blown with watry tumours;
Thy flesh a trembling bog, a quagmire full of humours.

5.

And thou, whose thriveless hands are ever straining
  Earth's fluent breasts into an empty sieve,
That always hast, yet always art complaining,
    And whin'st for more than earth has pow'r to give;
      Whose treasure flows and flees away as fast;
That ever hast, and hast, yet hast not what thou hast.

6.

Go chuse a substance, fool, that will remain
  Within the limits of thy leaking measure;
Or else go seek an urn that will retain

The liquid body of thy slipp'ry treasure;
   Alas! how poorly are thy labours crown'd?
Thy liquor's never sweet, nor yet thy vessel sound.

7.

What less than fool is man to prog and plot,
   And lavish out the cream of all his care,
To gain poor seeming goods; which being got,
   Make firm possession but a thorow-fare;
     Or, if they stay, they furrow thoughts the deeper;
And being kept with care, they lose their careful keeper.[32]

The caption on the engraving overleaf, *Inopem me copia fecit*, is a tag Coleridge frequently used[33] in various contexts. It will be seen that the pictured globe with four smaller circles within it, two on each side, is so engraved or cut as to seem to portray two large breasts each like a mirror and each with a mirror above it. At each of the earth-mother's breasts is a child in fool's cap and bells, one sucking with hands conspicuously grasping the full round "milky flood," the other child-fool opposite "straining" the "treasure" "into an empty sieve." The stream incidentally, seems to pass through the sieve into the bowl of a (tobacco ? or opium) pipe. Not only are the breasts so engraved as to look also like reflecting mirrors, each of which has its double above; the centre of the earth itself is bare and mirror-like.

In other words, the looking-glass, the deep feelings and dim ideas, the need to fix an image, the babe feeling by taste and touch and learning from the small focus of mouth and breast the larger world of the hand at the arm's reach, the breast-mirror by which the babe by reflexion of touch as well as sight finds the otherness through itself as well as itself through the other, all are present in the picture if not all in the poem.

The nourishing fountain, more than its opposite, the wasting sieve, was a persistent image for Coleridge. There was the fountain or spring at Stowey, and again near Keswick

> the spring with the little tiny cone of loose sand
> ever rising & sinking at the bottom, but its surface without
> a wrinkle.—W.W. M.H. D.W. S.H.[34]

This, a notebook entry of September 1801, is followed by something closely related, perhaps really a part of the same entry:

Item—Murmur of a stream—Item—*well** *with*
Shadows. Item—Why aren't you here?—
*images & realities in the eye & memory—fantastically,
soul going into the heart of the survivor, & abiding there
with its Image.[35]

The sweet, smooth, up-welling spring observed at Keswick was an experience recorded as an image of the Grasmere companionship in contrast to the angry, uneven, destructive tempers of the Greta Hall household. The same image was used in the *Inscription for a Fountain on a Heath* published about a year later:

This Sycamore, oft musical with bees,—
Such tents the Patriarchs loved! O long unharmed
May all its aged boughs o'er-canopy
The small round basin, which this jutting stone
Keeps pure from falling leaves! Long may the Spring,
Quietly as a sleeping infant's breath,
Send up cold waters to the traveller
With soft and even pulse! Nor ever cease
Yon tiny cone of sand its soundless dance,
Which at the bottom, like a Fairy's Page,
As merry and no taller, dances still,
Nor wrinkles the smooth surface of the Fount.
Here twilight is and coolness: here is moss,
A soft seat, and a deep and ample shade.
Thou may'st toil far and find no second tree.
Drink, Pilgrim, here! Here rest! and if thy heart
Be innocent, here too shalt thou refresh
Thy spirit, listening to some gentle sound.
Or passing gale or hum of murmuring bees![36]

Here again is not only the fountain, the sleeping infant, the soft and even pulse of the waters, the hum of the productive bees of *Work without Hope*, but also a sheltering tree, a mossy seat in its deep and ample shade—solitary protector in a wide treeless world.

It will be noticed that the Quarles engraving also shows a tree-like umbrella, as prominent in the picture as it is conspicuous in an important area of Coleridge's sense of failure. A twisty and root-like shape burgeons above the globe of earth into a cornucopia full of fruit-bearing greenery and blossoms. Its tapered base reaches

XII.

Inopem me copia fecit.

48.

Francis Quarles, *Emblems, Divine and Moral; Together with Hieroglyphics of the Life of Man* (1736) Book I No. XII.

down into the centre of the world, close to the nurturing breasts. With Coleridge the root is a frequent metaphor for fertility or the lack of it, depending on whether he is referring to his more productive friends or himself. Wordsworth is a strong prolific tree with his root in a rich nutritive soil:

The soil is a deep, rich, dark Mould on a deep Stratum of tenacious Clay, and that on a foundation of Rocks, which often break through both Strata, lifting their back above the Surface. The Trees, which chiefly grow here, are the gigantic Black Oak, Magnolia, Fraxinus excelsior, Platane, & a few stately Tulip Trees.—Bart. p. 36. I applied this by a fantastic analogue & similitude to Wordsworth's Mind. March 26 1801. Fagus exaltata sylvatica.[37]

Of himself about seven years later he writes:

O there are some natures which under the most cheerless, all-threatening, nothing-promising circumstances can draw Hope from the Invisible, as the tropical Trees that in the sandy desolation produce their own lidded vessels, full of the waters from Air & Dew! Alas! to my root not a drop trickles down but from the watering-pots of immediate Friends. —And even so it seems much more a sympathy with *their* feeling rather than Hope of my own.[38]

And much later, in April 1819 he writes to a friend using the tree– root image in self-extenuation.

The Tree is not indeed dead; but the Sap is all sunk down to the root —and I think it better to wait for its reascension into the Head and Branches than to anticipate its product by artificial Buds and Blossoms, however faithful Copies or Fac Similes they might be of the natural growth.—My spirits have been so low and stagnant. . . .[39]

The tree, any plant in fact, draws its nourishment through air, or dew or through its tendrils the milk of mother earth, as in the Quarles illustration. Or in N 21½ (a metaphor for marriage):

a Flower that must fix its roots in the rich genial Soil, thence suck up nutriment to bloom strong and healthy—not to droop & fade mid sunshine or zephyrs on a soilless rock.[40]

With the Quarles emblem at least one more personal link is to be seen: the babies at breast, whether at fountain or sieve, are fools. There is no doubt that Coleridge felt himself the fool of the family, and he had considerable brotherly help toward such a view. The feeling did not diminish with the years, perhaps on either side. The subject is apt for ample illustration, but one public pronouncement is sufficiently telling. It comes in a report of a lecture on education in 1808 in which Coleridge was defending Dr. Bell's system, based on co-operation rather than authority:

On disgraceful punishments such as fool's caps he spoke with great indignation and declared that even now his life is embittered by the recollection of ignominious punishments he suffered when a child. It comes to him in disease and when his mind is dejected.[41]

An emblem could scarcely be more cogently personal. But as the protected helpless baby is the exposed fool, so have all the other images their opposites, not only their antagonist opposites, not only their mirror-opposites, but their opposition in themselves. The centre of the opposition is the self, participating positively or negatively in each, augmented or torn both ways, or twisted and complicated by the meeting of extremes. Coleridge's theory of the reconciliation of opposites may have been "overworked" *as a theory*, as Elisabeth Schneider has suggested. And sometimes the reconciliation is incomplete, tangential, momentary, a meeting of extremes that at once fly off; and we have, adapting Coleridge's magnificent words for *Lycidas* quoted to such good purpose by Miss Schneider in a memorable chapter, "the floating or oscillation of assonance and consonance."[42] Here, to use a mixture of metaphors of which Coleridge might himself have disapproved, is an assonance and consonance of images. In the *Biographia Literaria* he condemned Cowley for making Pindar's hills reflect the image of a voice.[43] Yet what we are looking at here is not a mechanical "juxtaposition," not the cerebrations of wit for purposes of surprise, but what he describes in the same passage of the *Biographia* as "the presentation of impressive or delightful forms to the inward vision."

The forms may be delightful in themselves, and impressive in respect of their opposites. They may also contain within themselves their own antithesis. And more than one of them may merge and in kaleidoscopic fashion change or fuse one into another.

The bee and the spider, to take simple opposites, make honey and a net. Both industrious, and both producers, the one ranges abroad drawing its sweetness from the blossoms of the natural world, and casts it forth transformed into a golden gift; the other spins threads from its own belly to trap other creatures to their doom. Here the bee suggests freedom, and affirmation, the spider confinement and negation, the hum of the bee a sleep-inducing sound, the spider the silent threat of a predatory web. Yet the bee is also used by Coleridge, negatively on several occasions, e.g., in the phrase "the Queen Bee in the hive of error,"[44] theological error usually; and the spider's black web of venom is a net not only for an enemy but for itself, as when Wallenstein, analysing himself as traitor, feels "caught in my own net," a "web of treason."[45]

Similarly, the tree and its life-drawing root have their ambivalences. The tree is "an emblem of Hope" like the palm in George Sandys's description of Arabia, where "their seas are deserts" and the palms "will not forsake those forsaken places";[46] it can also be a "blasted tree,"[47] or leafless,[48] or its "Leaves already on the walk scattered."[49] "Friendship is a sheltering tree," he said in *Youth and Age*,[50] another late poem in which some of the familiar images again appear. But the sheltering tree can become the "false and fair-foliaged" Manchineel,[51] the detached leaf can become the symbol of the homeless wanderer; the "unfortunate woman" is a "myrtle leaf . . . ill-besped," cut off from her "mother-stalk."[52] Hope lost, and vanished esteem, are "like a loose blossom on a gusty night."[53] Examples could easily be multiplied. Most telling is the motto of *Remorse* taken from the first scene of the play.

> Remorse is as the heart, in which it grows:
> If that be gentle, it drops balmy dews
> Of true repentance; but if proud and gloomy
> It is a poison-tree, that pierced to the inmost
> Weeps only tears of poison![54]

The frequent conjunction of the ideas of shelter and threat is conspicuous, and appears in a variety of metaphors in addition to those chiefly under discussion here, bird-images for instance. The mother-dove brooding on the nest as the spirit broods over the waters of life, has its opposite in the ostrich that lays its eggs in the sands,[55] and in the pelagic birds of which he asked on the Malta voyage, "where do they rest at night?"[56] And at the start of that voyage he had pictured "A Mother dying of a contagious Disease, unable to give or receive the last Embrace to her Orphan Child,"[57] a poignant farewell vision in which he is both the diseased parent depriving his children, and himself the orphan, deprived of maternal embraces from any quarter. Or again, and close to the ostrich eggs in the sand, the "Mother listening for the *sound* of her still-born child [finds a parallel in the] blind Arab list'ning in the wilderness,"[58] an idea used as late as 1833, in *Love's Apparition and Evanishment*.[59]

The mother-breast mirror concatenation is naturally a primary one, and like all the others is met by its opposites without and within. As the serene cone of sand has its opposite in the vortex, the deep well, so has the upward-surging fountain its downward-dragging vortex of the whirlpool of temptation.[60] The maternal breast is a large comforting pillow, the infant's pleasure-dome, but as he falls asleep it floats him on the waves and then there is the sinking "down the waters thro' Seas & Seas, yet warm, yet a Spirit"[61] to the sunless sea, the measureless caverns. Coleridge records once in Malta stretching out his arms to the blue cope of heaven[62] but, also in Malta, "I have found myself in a Bason always, sometimes on one side, sometimes in the Bottom."[63]

The great dome of heaven comforts, also shrinks mankind in his own estimation. The warm mother-milk nourishes, but may also be frozen, or polluted with blood, and may, as in the Quarles emblem, poison helpless innocence.[64] A tactual mirror in which the infant first senses himself, the breast also is the first means by which he senses himself as other than something else bigger and more powerful, which he, however, learns to use. In a quite remarkable entry Coleridge describes

the first act of the Infant—feels / exerts its individuality in announcing its helplessness ⟨and its wants⟩ & the sensation of being acted upon —is *placed* at the Mother's breast—is rendered a *cupping* machine—and *then* is entrusted with it, and from *being* it rises into *having* and using it.[65]

At a later stage the child "exerts the power excited in her as passive or negative subject by the Mother. . . ." But the entry

should be quoted entire, beginning as it does with some familiar
lines:

> And there was young Philosophy
> Unconscious of her self-pardie,
> And now she hight: Poesy—
> And like a child, in life-ful glee,
> Had newly left her Mother's knee,
> Prattles and plays with flower and Stone,
> As if with faery play-fellows
> Revealed to Innocence alone—

Exerts the power excited in her as ~~the~~ passive or negative subject by the
Mother & becoming in her turn positive acts upon her Toys, like Light,
that meeting eyeless things falls back & so reflects the image of her
inward self.

Yet what she now attributes in her play, She shall hereafter, armed
with stedfast stronger will, *awake* and *find*— ~~The~~ For Metaphor and
Simile are notes of lisping prophecy—"[66]

The mirror reflects the image of the inward self. It also distances
the self from itself. The intervention of a reflecting surface,
whether warm, animate, or cold and inanimate, asserts the essential
severance of the self from the other, from the image even, and
inspires, with whatever of fear and awe it is capable, the need to
bridge the gap, whether by philosophy or by poetry, between the
percipient and the perceived. Bridge it Coleridge occasionally did,
not by any consistent system of thought, but by brilliant aperçus
touching both the knower and the world to be known, or at least
the questioner and the questions to be asked. And some of the
successful forays into self-knowledge may be seen in some of the
short late poems where we find still (to borrow a phrase from
Wordsworth)

> . . . a mind beset
> With images and haunted by itself.[67]

The pathos of Coleridge's problems is that he is haunted by not
being able to fix an image of himself; the image in the natural glass
is always restless, changing, bedimmed, misted over by qualifications and reservations. The glimpses caught through this or that
image are far from "the egotistical sublime," though his search is

unrelenting, and the incompleteness of the satisfaction and the answers is faced and admitted.

One lifts up one's eyes to Heaven as if to see there what one had lost on Earth / Eyes—Whose Half-beholdings thro' unsteady tears Gave shape, hue, distance, to the inward Dream / .[68]

Perhaps it is not the least evidence of his genius that subsequent generations needs must ask, "What was the inward dream?"

NOTES

Abbreviations in these notes:

CL   *The Letters of Samuel Taylor Coleridge* ed. E. L. Griggs (Oxford 1956–59) Vols. I–IV.

CN   *The Notebooks of Samuel Taylor Coleridge* ed. Kathleen Coburn (New York and London 1957–61) Vols. I–II.

CPW   *The Poetical Works of Samuel Taylor Coleridge* ed. E. H. Coleridge (Oxford 1912) in two volumes.

N   Notebook still in MS.

1. E. K. Chambers, *Samuel Taylor Coleridge* (Oxford 1938) 331.

2. I. A. Richards, "Coleridge the Vulnerable Poet," *Yale Review* XLVIII (1959) 491–504.

3. Clement Carlyon, *Early Years and Late Reflections* (London 1836–54) I 29 quoted in *CN* I 174(6)n.

4. *CN* I 174(6).

5. *CL* I 259.

6. *CPW* I 32, note to lines 90–93.

7. *CL* III 83.

8. *CL* III 100; 308–9.

9. Recently acquired by the British Museum and largely published by T. C. Skeat in the *British Museum Quarterly* XXVI (1963) 17–21; also by W. Braekman and A. Devolder in "*Three Hitherto Unpublished Letters* of S. T. Coleridge to John Morgan" in *Studia Germanica Gandensia* IV (1962) 203–23.

10. *CPW* I 75, note to lines 28 ff.

11. *CPW* II 962.

12. *CPW* II 553.

13. Coleridge signed his first *Morning Post* poem "Albert": *To An Unfortunate Woman at the Theatre* (*CPW* I 171–2) and there is reason to think that Osorio was (at least in part) Southey (*CN* II 2928n).

14. *CL* I 352–3.

15. N 17 *f86ᵛ*; where notebook entries have not yet been published in the edition of the *Notebooks* now in progress, reference will be made to notebook and folio number.

16. N 17 *f97ᵛ*.

17. N 17 *ff119–119ᵛ*.

18. *CN* I 62.

19. *CPW* II 1136.

20. *CN* I 904.

21. *Ibid.*

22. N24 *f24*.

23. *CN* I 923.

24. *CN* I 921.

25. *CN* II 3107, in part.

26. A similar mother-mirror catalyst, as Professor Elizabeth M. Wilkinson has pointed out to me, activates Goethe's short lyric *Auf dem See*.

> Und frische Nahrung, neues Blut
> Saug' ich aus freier Welt;
> Wie ist Natur so hold und gut,
> Die mich am Busen hält!
> Die Welle wieget unsern Kahn
> Im Rudertakt hinauf,
> Und Berge, wolkig himmelan,
> Begegnen unserm Lauf.
>
> Aug', mein Aug', was sinkst du neider?
> Goldne Träume, kommt ihr wieder?
> Weg, du Traum, so gold du bist:
> Hier auch Lieb' und Leben ist.
>
> Auf der Welle blinken
> Tausend schwebende Sterne,
> Weiche Nebel trinken
> Rings die türmende Ferne;
> Morgenwind umflügelt
> Die beschattete Bucht,
> Und im See bespiegelt,
> Sich die reifende Frucht.

27. *CN* I 924.

28. N 29 *ff82ᵛ–84*. This notebook, in the Berg Collection in the New York Public Library, is known as the "Vellum Clasp Book"; the label has disappeared although the mark where it was at one time pasted on is clearly visible. E. H. Coleridge quotes this entry in *CPW* II 1110 as from N 29, one of the conclusive identifications of the notebook as belonging in the numbered series. But the tracing of the wanderings of this MS. would be a task suited to the powers of a Boswell editor. The entry is here printed as it appears in the notebook for the variety of its interest and not least for the question raised by the last revision: Did Coleridge regard this as still another unfinished poem? And what bearing has this question on our view of the completeness of *Kubla Khan?*

29. The spider-web image, though intensely interesting, cannot receive much attention in this context. But see its use in the *Piccolomini* Act IV, referred to in n 45, below.

30. N 25 *f85*.

31. A verse that would itself strike home, in view of his disrupted and unsatisfying maternal relationship; cf. note 57, below.

32. Coleridge noticed other emblems, and there are various interesting links with other passages in the notebooks and other poems. His edition of Quarles's *Emblems* was a reprint of 1736.

33. From Ovid: see *CN* I 1383.

34. *CN* I 980.

35. *CN* I 981.

36. *CPW* I 381–2; the date 1802 links the poem with Sara Hutchinson; for another association of this image with her see also the deeply personal sonnet of the previous year, *To Asra: CPW* I 361–2.

37. *CN* I 926.

38. N 25 *f2*.

39. *CL* IV 935.

40. N 21½ *f25*.

41. *Coleridge's Shakespearean Criticism,* ed. T. M. Raysor (London 1930) II 12.

42. Elisabeth Schneider, *Coleridge, Opium and Kubla Khan* (Chicago 1953) 286.

43. *Biographia Literaria* Ch. XVIII.

44. See *CN* II 2434 and n, especially the reference to *The Friend* (1818) III 240–41.

45. *CPW* II 690–91.

46. *CN* I 1245(1)n.

47. *CN* II 2914, clearly a self-image.

48. Even the single red leaf of Christabel's oak, the last of its clan and dancing, is surely a sign by sameness and difference, of her relation and lack of it to the parent tree.

49. *CN* I 60.

50. Line 19: *CPW* I 440.

51. *To the Rev. George Coleridge*, line 26: *CPW* I 174.

52. *CPW* I 173.

53. *The Pang More Sharp than All*, line 21: *CPW* I 458.

54. *CPW* II 820.

55. *CN* I 1248 and n.

56. *CN* II 2054 and 2556 *f75*ᵛ; these in turn have their antithesis in the caged bird. Coleridge himself is both. "I am a Starling self-incaged" he wrote Godwin in 1802. *CL* II 782.

57. *CN* II 1991 and n.

58. *CN* I 1244.

59. *CPW* I 488–9.

60. *CN* I 1706n.

61. *CN* I 1718 and n.

62. *CN* II 2453.

63. *CN* II 2105.

64. Another opposite is seen in the tightened chest of the sick man, the asthmatic. N 21½ *f47:*

There is a ~~praise, a hope, a sympathy~~ species of applause scarcely less ~~necessary~~ genial to a ~~man of genius~~ Poet, whether Bard, Musician or artist, than the vernal warmth to the feathered Songsters during their Nest-building or Incubation—a sympathy, an expressed Hope, that is the ~~May~~ open air in which the Poet breathes, and without which the Sense of Power sinks back ⟨on itself⟩ like a Sickness-sigh heaved up from the tightened Chest of a Sick Man.

65. N 21½ *f46*ᵛ.

66. N 29 *f19*ᵛ.

67. *The Prelude* (1850) Book VI 159–60.

68. N 18 *f6*.

Christian Skepticism
In *The Rime of the Ancient Mariner*

JAMES D. BOULGER

F OR many years the essay of Robert Penn Warren on "The Rime of the Ancient Mariner" held wide acceptance.[1] Warren pointed out that the two major functions of the poem were the creation of a sacramental universe by means of creative imagination and the operation within this universe of the Christian pattern of Fall and Redemption. The nature of both functions was inferred partially from outside sources, *Biographia Literaria, The Friend,* and *Aids to Reflection,* but also in the action of the poem itself there existed evidence for a certain kind of Imagination and for a Will which falls in a spontaneous uninitiated act. Some few inconsistencies in detail were pointed out in later criticism of Warren's analysis, but hardly enough to remove the impression that the reading was consistent, convincing and meaningful. Reopening the case seemed hardly justified. The appearance of Elliot B. Gose's essay "Coleridge and the Luminous Gloom,"[2] which, by inversion of Warren's view of the Sun:Moon symbolism, reads like a parody of Warren's essay while doing violent injustice to the poem, seemed to suggest that the case had been well enough left alone.

Edward Bostetter has recently presented a view of "The Rime of the Ancient Mariner" entirely at odds with Warren's,[3] and not on the trivial grounds and outside sources of Gose's essay. Disregarding the evidence in outside sources pertaining to Coleridge's characteristic feelings and values attached to the moon or sun, which all critics now must allow cuts both ways, Bostetter asserts that the Fall-Redemption pattern does not hold in the poem, and with its dismissal also disappears any notion of an active vision of creative imagination sustaining a sacramental view of the Universe. Instead Bostetter sees a nightmare world of inconsequence, illogic, terror, and meaningless suffering. "The Rime of the Ancient Mariner" is a voyage into the irrational, flinging terror at the real world, and not an imaginative order confirming the values of the real world.

I should like to say something in favor of Warren's overall position against that of Bostetter. It will not be a defense of the moral or symbolic minutiae of Warren's thought, which time has proven wrong, but only of the view that the Mariner's world is ultimately a religious one, as against the nightmare world insisted upon by Bostetter. It is a far different religious world than that suggested by the idea of a sacramental universe. Warren arrived at this latter view by using the process of the understanding (critical analysis) to explain the process of imagination and vision. The notion that the Mariner's world is a dream world, a world of the active imagination, is not taken seriously enough by Warren or Bostetter: one supplies us with a Christian gloss provided mainly by Coleridge's prose, the other with a gloss made up of notions taken from extreme Calvinism (as Bostetter understands it) and from Freudian doctrine. In order to take Coleridge's idea of the primary imagination seriously as the ground of the action and process of the poem, one must consider the mode of action that occurs in dreams, since "The Rime of the Ancient Mariner" is a dream vision. The soundest starting point for this view is in the now somewhat neglected seminal source for study of the poem, the final chapter of Lowes's *Road to Xanadu,* entitled "Imagination Creatrix." If Lowes's final position seems too scientifically detached today, a case history free of dogma and content, it at least is free of specific error. His hint was simply that the world of the primary imagination in the poem can be seen by analogy as having a good deal in common with what we know of dreams.

But a dream world as poem must have specific shape and source and inspiration, for which Lowes has supplied the most abundant evidence. From this evidence only a small amount will be drawn upon, by no means new; but not, thus far, considered of major importance in defining the dream quality of the poem. This is the relationship of certain passages in the sea world of the "Mariner" to ones of similar scope in various early books of the *Aeneid*. The similarities, but not the importance, were recognized by accomplished scholars like Lowes, who no doubt considered such schoolboy reminiscences in this connection inevitable. Source discussion has centered on more obscure yet more specific analogues, Purchas for instance. Two literary connections of "The Rime of the Ancient Mariner" with the *Aeneid* make the *Aeneid* important as a source.

The first is the biographical one, revealed in the *Notebooks*, that Coleridge was reading the *Aeneid* afresh in 1795, '96, '97.[4] This reading helped shape the nature of Imagination in "The Rime of the Ancient Mariner," and its echoes in the poem are not meaningless reminiscence. More important are the qualities Coleridge would find in the *Aeneid*, not noticed by the scholars of the early twentieth century. Coleridge's age, or at least the persons like Coleridge in it, could read epic poetry at a level hardly reached again until recent times. Witness this quotation from *Notebooks* on Milton, which surely would have startled F. R. Leavis or the early Eliot:[5]

A Reader of Milton must be always on his Duty: he is surrounded with sense; it rises in every line; every word is to the purpose. There are no lazy intervals: all has been considered and demands & merits observation.
If this be called obscurity, let it be remembered tis such a one as is complacent to the Reader: not that vicious obscurity, which proceeds from a muddled head &&.

One may assume, *datis dandis,* that he would notice the qualities in the *Aeneid*, especially in the books depicting the sea, which contemporary critics are again pointing out: the dreamlike quality of Virgil's vision of action, as opposed to Homer's dramatic sense, the pictorial quality of his scenes, the way in which elegy overtakes epic in places, along with a sense of detachment in the character of the main narrator, Aeneas himself, making his listeners attentive, as in the line (II, 1) *Conticuere omnes intentique ora tenebant.*[6] The command, respect, and spellbinding quality of the respective narrators is the most obvious case in point. But there are also more subtle borrowings.

The few direct borrowings of Coleridge from the *Aeneid* were pointed out by Lowes. *Aeneid* (III, 193) *caelum undique et undique pontus,* became

"For the sky and the sea, and the sea and the sky" (250).

Aeneid (V 140-41, 150)   *ferit aethera clamor*
                           nauticus
                           pulsati colles clamore resultant

appears in Coleridge as

> And all was still, save that the hill
> Was telling of the sound (558–9).

It is not these exact analogies that are of primary importance for our purposes, although they prove a necessary point, the fact of an exact connection between the two poems. It is the dreamlike, elegaic, detached quality of Virgil's sea world which influences in an all-pervasive spirit the Mariner's voyage of the mind, which is constructed in dream-logic sequences. This vividly alive, though detached world, allows for the active presence of winds and spirits, although Coleridge also had other sources for an animated world. In Virgil, as opposed to some of these later sources, there is no strain on credulity in accepting an active, animated universe. Amid the terrors and malignancy of the elements and the sea in Books I and III of *Aeneid,* as a part of the misfortune and seeming illogicality of certain events as seen by the participants, there remains a deeply religious sense of destiny in the hero, and an almost divine sense of benignity in the elements themselves. This sense carries over into "The Rime of the Ancient Mariner," although Coleridge's method of achieving it must be different from Virgil's. The Mariner's world is religious for the reader, who is given the role of omniscient outsider played in the *Aeneid* by Virgil himself. The moral and intellectual confusions of the Mariner, the seeming incongruity and irrationality of his world, correspond to the view of the sea and circumstance taken by Aeneas and his tribe as they act out the destined sea scenes. But Aeneas' destiny is clear to the narrator and to the reader, while the Mariner's never becomes clear to him, and is clear in the overall structure only in a peculiar way intended by Coleridge. Both narrators of the events that have happened to them have a keen sense that the sea world is a dream world of illusion, as in the lines "a painted ship upon a painted ocean" (117–18), or *Aeneid* (III, 72) *provehimur portu terraeque urbesque recedunt.* There is an arbitrary givenness and sense of illusion about both sea worlds and about the predicaments of the narrators expressed in many ways in both poems. Coleridge's "It is an Ancient Mariner," "There was a ship," relate to Virgil's (I, 12) *Urbs antiqua fuit* and (I, 31–2) *multosque per annos errabant acti fatis maria omnia circum.* Although the ultimate benignity of Fate is asserted by both poets, the sense of fate and the acts of terror common to both poems may well seem malign to the modern reader as they pass before his eyes in a series of inscrutable acts. In both poems the narrator-subject is brought finally to an act of vision which allows him to see the ultimate positive vision of the author's world, but this final turn is arbitrary in both poems in the sense that no amount of reading in Coleridge's prose for meanings attached to Sun:Moon symbolism, or in the background of Virgil's Roman religion, is going to provide logical or theological proof of the vision. Virgil's vision is more assured than is Coleridge's, but in each case the validity of the vision is finally sanctioned only by the power of the poems themselves. This essay will not presume to analyze the methods of the Latin poet, but in Coleridge's poem it seems that the motion of the dream world itself, the special logic of the state of primary imagination, is what carries the poem along to its successful conclusion, and at the same time suggests the content of that conclusion, which in Virgil is given more directly as a fiat of fate working in the service of Roman destiny.

Dream is not nightmare, nor is it sacramental vision. Each is too easy and doctrinaire a solution to the meaning of the poem. At bottom there is mystery about "The Rime of the Ancient Mariner," not found in *Aeneid,* or for that matter in any previous English poem. It is the mystery of dealing with a series of effects having intelligible and satisfactory shape whose causes remain unknown. Virgil could provide in a frame the pseudo-rational formulae within which occur arbitrary, illusory, and terrifying events, the causes of which remain unknown to the narrator. Aeneas' piety and belief carry him through to vision. "The Rime of the Ancient Mariner" plunges into an arbitrary framework which is incomprehensible to the narrator-Mariner and to us. He acts out an ultimately successful pattern of action which exacts a toll in experience and suffering. In *Aeneid,* and *Paradise Lost* for that matter, there is religious mystery aplenty, but not ultimate religious mystery. The authors have their reasons and explanations for what has occurred, which the reader may or may not accept. Coleridge's poem is the first modern religious poem in the sense that it asserts a mysterious religious universe but cannot give us even partial explanations of its nature. Like Blake, he had seen through the Age of Reason, but his response was of a different order.

Earlier commentators on the poem, especially Gingerich,[7] noting Coleridge's obsession with Necessitarianism in his 1795–98 letters, tried to work out a scheme for "The Rime of the Ancient Mariner" on a necessitarian rationale. This provided an easy but erroneous explanation, ignoring both the intensity of Coleridge's religious mentality, and the subtlety of his mind as a philosopher. Coleridge's insight into the conclusions of Necessitarianism, whether of the religious or the scientific variety, was essentially that of Isaac Newton and Jonathan Edwards, namely, that necessitarianism explained nothing in the ultimate sense. It presents us with a series of related effects, ordered within themselves, the causes of which remain unknown, and the ultimate cause unknowable, in other words Kantianism by a different route (one Coleridge was also traveling at that time). As Perry Miller puts it, the Universe, whether or not God is postulated as Ultimate, is inscrutable:

When we get behind the brilliant façade of Newtonianism, the apparently rational system, of which poets sang and which Cotton Mather embraced, we are brought more terribly face to face with the dark forces of nature than any Puritan has been while staring into the dazzling glare of pre-destination. . . . Behind the mathematical analysis . . . concealed so carefully that only the most astute might catch a glimpse of it, moved a power that could not be seen by reason's light or dispelled by science, that hid itself in matter to hold the atoms in cohesion. . . . Edwards took it [Newton's theory] to mean that cause in the realm of mechanism is merely a sequence of phenomena, with the inner connection of cause and effect still mysterious and terrifying. . . . for him the secret of nature was no longer that an efficient cause of itself works such and such an effect, but is to be defined as "that after or upon the existence of which, or the existence of it after such manner, the existence of another thing follows." All effects, therefore, have their causes, but no effect is a "result of what has gone before it."[8]

We may take it that Coleridge was as astute in these matters as Edwards, and that his greatest response to the situation was the dream world of "The Rime of the Ancient Mariner." His *Opus Maximum* and late Notebooks give us other responses, those of the systematic philosopher working out of the language of Kant.

Let us see how the above assumptions work out in a rough analysis of the structure of the poem. We now assume that the cluster of moon symbols does not consistently represent the workings of imagination, nor the sun symbols the discursive reason (Coleridge's prose understanding) together with a form of alienation, but that Imagination and understanding are present in the poem in more arbitrary ways. The epistemology of the act of cognition in the poem is quite different from our everyday mode of perceiving the world, or of our usual way of reading poems, which is to give them balance and rationality. Coleridge's conceptions of the Imagination as a participation in the great I Am (and of the Understanding used alone as the faculty which partakes of death) are to be taken quite seriously as the shaping force of the poem. Its nearest contemporary prose analogue is the philosophical system of symbolic form developed by Ernst Cassirer, which holds that philosophy can only describe phenomena and must give up the attempt to understand causality of things, but neither this system nor Coleridge's own descriptions of primary imagination in early nineteenth-century philosophical terms can be our primary guide. It is better to notice how things work out in the poem itself. For instance, understanding and syllogistic logic will be inferior categories to the higher level of imaginative perception in the action of the poem, without either being explained fully. The sailors use syllogistic logic and cause and effect in the ordinary way to calculate the morality of shooting the albatross, and of course the calculations fail, because the poem deals with effects whose causes are spiritual but unknown. Ordinary reason and dualistic cosmology are clearly inoperative in the poem, intuition has higher place than discursive reason, and a sense of the world as continuum or

flux is clearly stronger than our ordinary view of a dualistic world
of sense perception. But to know that the intuition in the poem
corresponds to the mystical "eye of reason" of Coleridge's prose
does not in any way lessen the mystery of the great imaginative intuitive act, the blessing of the water snakes by the Mariner. We see
the hierarchy of categories, but have no easy prose definition to
explain the nature of the categories. Perhaps as Lowes said, our
memories of dreams, that state in which the senses and the conscious space-time restrictions inculcated by the reasoning process
weakens, allowing (if Cassirer's view has any validity) the pre-
conscious state of pure imagination in us all to reassert itself, are
the only sound analogy to the pre-rational sense of the world of
"The Rime of the Ancient Mariner."

"The Rime of the Ancient Mariner," then, as a world of pure
imagination, will have the logic of a dream, in so far as we can
understand such logic. It is not an irrational world, as Bostetter
claims, nor a sacramental vision which implies some orderly rational way of looking at reality religiously. Nor do we have to
assume any specific content or archetypal patterns *a priori* in the
Mariner's world, as did Maud Bodkin in her study of the poem. It
is only the form, logic, and movement of the dream that is important, for that is what Coleridge saw as giving the nearest sense
of immediacy to the religious and philosophical concerns much on
his mind at the time of writing the poem. By postulating the
imaginative process itself as the mode of analysis here, we may
perhaps understand, but not rationalize away, the general meaning
of the poem. The poet wants us to play the part of the wedding
guest, to be drawn into the poem unwillingly, to resist with the
understanding, and finally to share his epistemological and perhaps
also, for the readers who still can do so, his religious anxieties.

The difference between the outside logical world and that of the
poem is brought out sharply in the first stanza, where there is a
conflict between the actual order and the dream world. The wedding, its festivities, and the anxiety of the Wedding Guest all fall
within the ordinary world of sense and logic. The Wedding Guest
is a reasonable man, so he thinks, he wants reasons for things, but
the Mariner has none to give. He also wants to participate in a
function of the actual order, while the Mariner has only his dream
to offer, "There was a ship." The arbitrary *givenness* of both the

Mariner and his adventure has been noted above in connection with Virgil. For a short while the two worlds compete, with the orderly rational world of conventional bride and wedding gaiety gradually giving way to the phantom ship, its sudden voyage, and the living sun and moon. The Mariner's glittering eye, which might be called the eye of the higher reason which surpasses understanding, transforms the Guest until the noise and conviviality of the actual world with its logic and causality are replaced by the living world of primary imagination, by the silent white seas of the pre-rational pure imagination, in which the Mariner's voyage took place. The Wedding Guest was agonized, "I fear thee Ancient Mariner," as his world slipped out from under him.

In this world of Imagination two things are immediately noticeable: the participation of all reality, living and non-living, real and spiritual, in one organic whole assumed by the author but not necessarily perceived by the participants; and the unending series of shifts between subject and object in the phenomena of the imaginative world. The Storm Blast, the mist and snow, and the Albatross are accepted without explanation by victims and readers. Normally real objects, like the sea, are not presented in descriptions which impart the qualities of actual things as we have experienced them. Everything is alive, there are no fixities and definites in this universe. At one point the Mariner is not entirely certain of his own identity (305–8). The ordinary ideas of causality and reason in this process are not operating, for whatever happens can be immediately accepted as a part of the unified whole perceived in a phenomenological way. Hence the killing of the bird as a gratuitous act of the will without causality is a very proper act to show the unexplainable failure in the Mariner's imaginative process to hold together all experience, and is the only proper way on this level to indicate the tension of pure imagination and rationalism. His Fall, and his Redemption, are basically psychological acts, whose ultimate cause, like that of the Universe itself, is inscrutable. For instance, before his Fall and after his Redemption the movement of winds, appearances of the sun and moon, the Polar Spirit, and the unifications between spirit and matter are accepted by the Mariner as modes of the imaginative whole which do not need explaining and cannot be explained rationally. When he does not rely upon logic to find out relationships and occurrences the answers are given to him according to the imaginative mode, that is, by spontaneous completion of related images as in dreams. He uses the ordinary modes of knowing during the time of his Fall only, to make mistakes in calculation, and to distinguish the "slimy" things of nature from himself. The alien world around him was of his own making. With the spontaneous act of blessing, as an uncaused and non-logical act, his imaginative power was restored. He simply accepted the water-snakes as a fact of experience, a mode of reality identified in some way with himself. At that point the Polar Spirit and other Spirits which had seemed malevolent were again viewed as they really were, and the continuum of all things existed again. The Sun and the Moon are important, but not overridingly so, as elements in this continuum. Everything again becomes a series of related effects, benign in appearance, whose causes remain unknown and now are wisely unsought.

After the imaginative synthesis has taken place, the Mariner no longer asks the wrong questions, but rather acts out his assigned role. Twentieth-century critics ask these wrong questions, reading the poem in the spirit of logicians. It does not really matter on the return voyage whether the Polar Spirit or the wind moved the ship, or whether the Sun-Moon patterns re-occur with systematic consistency. Critical preoccupation with such problems misses the point of the process itself. Such readings of the poem are not so far in spirit from the older moralistic ones, which made the poem appear as mere pother over a bird, in the sense that it applies too literal a significance to the phenomena, just as the early readers applied it to the moral action. Our view of the poem holds the Mariner's narration to be a vast dream-parable, understood partially by author and reader but not by Mariner or Wedding Guest. The Mariner's transgression, by gratuitous act of his Will, of the unity of the cosmos is a necessary failing common to us all, which is why he can speak to us; but the author speaks also of a world we can envision (and he as poet can create) but not return to or live in. The poetic logic of the world of ice and Albatross should not be entirely conformable to rationalistic analysis *a posteriori*. The analogy to our dream state where the primary imagination is again partially in control of our minds is the only entrance to the world of sudden, unmotivated succession of images which appear in the action of "The Rime of the Ancient Mariner." The dream-state acts as an existential parable for the proposition that our "real" world is appearance, and the world of imagination and process "reality." This is naturally disturbing to rationalistic critics, as it was to Coleridge himself, no mean rationalist in certain moods.

Essentially then, one man, from the world of his dreams and poetic experiences, tells another, of ordinary understanding and pursuits, about his vision of the world and how it came upon him. The entire narration takes place in a dimension quite removed from the sensory and logically perceivable world of the listener, the reader, or of much poetry, for that matter. Space permits the mention of only a few details in the poem to prove this point. The world is like a painted ship upon a painted ocean. The ideal world of memory, dream and imagination has a correspondence in Virgil's verbal pictures, and in the art of painting itself. The voyages to and from the Pole take place with dreamworld vagueness and speed. All the normal distinctions in the real order, between living and non-living, natural, preternatural and supernatural, subject and object, are dissolved in this fusion and unity of the imaginative whole whose inner cause of unity is unknown. The dissolving and fusing processes in the poem are truly dreamlike, for the colors of objects, such as the red in the ocean and the shining white of the water snakes, are clearer to the percipients than the forms of the objects themselves. The objects as things are shimmery, dim, and unsubstantial. It is a world of effects interrelated in an acceptable way, but without "cause" and "substance" in the rationalistic sense, a world with antecedents in the science of Newton, the theology of Edwards, and the poetry of Virgil. The Mariner's trance, the merging of the Albatross and the Cross, and the identification of the Spirits with the sailors' bodies are a few more examples of the breakdown of ordinary reality, which reveals itself to us as contiguity and disparity of objects in the world. In the full realization of this imaginative vision, which is not without its terrors, and with the unexplainable breeze of the One Life upon him, the Mariner shouted,

> O let me be awake, my God!
> Or let me sleep alway (470-71).

In this reading of the poem the return to harbor and to land at the end is perhaps the most shocking and difficult part to accept. Yet Coleridge manages to bring it off successfully. It is no surprise that the ship, the bodies, and all the spirits disappear on the approach of the normal order again. The Mariner's desire for ordinary Christian absolution can be understood as a re-assertion of the laws of logical thinking and causality in his mind. His redemption *has* taken place in the world of symbolic action, but does not have status on land. The basic problem in this part of the poem is the possibility of successful confrontation of the Dream world with actuality. In a ghost story of the usual variety, where things are not to be taken too seriously, such as Burns's "Tam O'Shanter," one object is usually brought back to the ordinary world as a sign of "proof" that the spirit-world existed. In this poem it is the Mariner himself who is the living proof of a more serious and deeper moral order than ours, and this fact is outrageous to the normal rationalistic sensibility. The ending is supposed to leave the author, reader and Wedding Guest believing that the Mariner's voyage was a real one into the seas of the Imagination and that his haunting vision and intuitive knowledge are more valid and powerful than our everyday world. Because the world of vision does not adjust to the world of sense and understanding, either overwhelming it or frightening it away, critical rationalism must ignore this poem as an opium dream or tidy it up into being something other than it is. The life of the imagination extracts its toll, not only upon the Mariner and Wedding Guest, but upon the reader who learns that his own life, even in its most convivial and substantial forms, is a kind of alienation from deepest reality, and that the rational order of cause-effect and substance is merely a humanistic drop in an ocean of the unknown forces and causes that Newton, Edwards and Coleridge had come to intuit. The Mariner's revelations, taken seriously, are a poison cup from which one never fully recovers again into normal perception. He assaults the sensibilities of the outside world, while at the same time suffering the penance of being forced again to live in the life-in-death world of the understanding and sense realism. He is a parable of the creative poet, of course, working in the modern rationalistic world, but he is not *maudit,* but rather a necessarily suffering being, unless one is willing to grant that all creativity is an aberration.

Coleridge as poet was one of the first, with Blake, to envision this world of interrelated effects and of moral action unsupported by causes or a clear Divine cosmology. Like Blake, he did not like what he saw, but unlike him, he did not regard it as liberating the Imagination for a new humanism. As I said earlier, you might look upon the structure of "The Rime of the Ancient Mariner" as an *Aeneid* without the author's voice and epic framework to make the unknown and terrible orderly and rational. Coleridge plunges himself, his Mariner, and his readers into a seemingly arbitrary world of effects without causes, and of accidents (appearances) without substances, presented dramatically as Storms, hidden malignancy, human evils; yet finally he manages to suggest some arational, incredibly deep faith in the nature of things, analogous to that of the stumbling yet pious Aeneas. Later in life Coleridge was to find another analogy to this condition in the post-Kantian phase of Christian philosophy and theology, which confronts a rational pious Will against a skeptical, unknowable universe. He could never bring himself to publish his speculations on this subject, and, indeed, leaves the most daring of them in Greek or Latin.[9] Yet these speculations would provide a better gloss to the poem's meaning than the archly pious and disingenuous one he gave, which has misled commentators in various ways. Coleridge's excuse, also holding for Newton's speculations, which remain unpublished to this day, was that he was afraid of his own vision, or at least of a part of it. The world of "The Rime of the Ancient Mariner" is neither a sacramental universe nor a nightmare vision, but a parable of the uneasy Christian skepticism that has been with us since Newton and Kant.

NOTES

1. Robert Penn Warren, *"The Rime of the Ancient Mariner" a poem of pure imagination* (New York, 1946).

2. Elliot B. Gose, "Coleridge and the Luminous Gloom," *PMLA*, LXXV (June 1960), 238–44.

3. Edward Bostetter, "The Nightmare World of the Ancient Mariner," *Studies in Romanticism* 1 (Summer, 1962), 241–54.

4. *The Notebooks of Samuel Taylor Coleridge* I, ed. Kathleen Coburn (New York, 1957), entry nos. 174, 311 and notes to these numbers.

5. *Notebooks* I, entry number 276.

6. All quotations from the *Aeneid* are from the Oxford Edition. *P. Vergili Maronis Opera,* ed. F. A. Hirtzel. Translations from L. R. Lind's *The Aeneid* (Bloomington, 1962). II, 1: "They were silent, and held their gaze upon him." III, 193: "No land/Remained in sight but only sky and sea." V, 140–41, 150: "Their roar rose high in the sky. . . . The hills around sent echo bounding back." III, 72: "We sailed from harbor, land and cities vanished." I, 12: "There was an ancient city." I, 31–2: "They had wandered for many years/ Pursued by the Fates across every sea."

7. Solomon Gingerich, *Essays in the Romantic Poets,* (N.Y., 1922), chap. II.

8. Perry Miller, *Jonathan Edwards* (N.Y., 1959), pp. 79, 83, 89.

9. *Critical Annotations by S. T. Coleridge,* ed. William F. Taylor, (Harrow, 1889). Marginalia to *Church of England Homilies,* 1815. In a passage on the nature of prayer Coleridge makes the discovery, which he leaves in a mixed sentence of Greek, Latin and English, that as a function of creative imagination prayer is a form of self-deification, as he had found the writing of poetry to be earlier in his career. Startled, he appends the following plea to his speculation:

I believe, Lord, help my unbelief I pray: O enable me to pray! O Word, O Spirit of the Lord, be he unto me, as Aaron and Hur, unto Moses on the Mountain. O stay up my hands until the going down of the Sun, the day-star of my mortal Life, lest Amelek and his people, even they that are within me, prevail against me!—I would fain hold up my hands—I faint, I let my hands down—O stay up my hands—O gracious Word and O unbreathed Wisdom! O Light! O Life of God—O Light of Man! Ye stayed up my hands even when they were sinking, and in my utter Fainting ye did live in me, yea, for me and instead of me—otherwise I had been utterly discomfited! Lo, I pray! O that I had the power of supplication! I believe! O Lord— help my unbeliefs.

Byron in 1816: Four Poems from Diodati

GEORGE M. RIDENOUR

IT is only lately that we have learned to trace an unbroken movement from the thought of the eighteenth century to that of
what used to be called the romantic revolt. We have learned that
insofar as a revolt in fact took place its program and its weapons
were in large part gifts of the period under attack. And certainly
some of the problems faced by the English romantic poets and some
of their ways of handling them have developed from contradictions
implicit in attitudes characteristic of the eighteenth century.

We have noticed first of all the role played by the eighteenth
century in the development of modern individualism, and that
both problems and solutions that we think of as "romantic" are
developments of this new attitude toward the individual person.
Both the social tendencies of the period and its understanding of
human nature and the human mind were beginning to focus an
attention on the individual as a separate and unique being that had
not been common in other ages, though this was countered by a
belief in the uniformity in operation of the separate human ma-
chines. With respect to the human mind, we could say that the
eighteenth century tended both to imprison each man in an individual consciousness and to reduce everything to experience within
that consciousness. Each condition can in itself induce anxiety, and
the relation between them is trying. Without insisting that this is a
fair statement of the case, it may still be fair to argue that poets of
the early nineteenth century tried to handle problems implicit in
the fundamental assumptions of the previous age without surrendering the achievements of that age. This meant especially
directing the powers of the emancipated intellect toward the solution of problems involved in that emancipation.

This description applies in any case to Byron's situation in 1816, as it appears in the third canto of *Childe Harold's Pilgrimage*. The poet speaks as a compulsory exile who is trying to take advantage of his state of deprivation—to turn exile to pilgrimage. As he recognizes, the state of affairs he finds himself in is a complex product of European history, personal temperament, and circumstance, and the poem tries to maneuver the terms into a tolerable arrangement. In his other major work of the period, the drama *Manfred,* he contends more directly with his own experience of paradoxes in the mind of the previous age. Freedom is experienced as both personal necessity and intolerable burden, determination as a necessary guarantee of the value and meaning of the individual life and as a force to be resisted in the name of the freedom which is equally indispensable.[1] The dilemma is handled by pushing both terms as far as they can go, so that the play is an enactment of a will to radical freedom and to radical determination.

But if there is some point in suggesting a connection which cannot by its nature be proved between Byron's poems and the individualism and subjectivism initiated by the preceding century, it is more obviously useful to point out a relationship that is demonstrable historically. Ian Watt, describing the close connection between the growth of individualism and the rise of the novel in the eighteenth century, has pointed out that the novel, more than any other literary form, raises the issue of its own truth.[2] This is strikingly the case with works in the tradition of Cervantes' *Don Quixote,* that build the question of their truth into themselves as part of their meaning. Byron has used the motif in this way in the third canto of *Childe Harold,* and it will play an important role in *Don Juan* and *The Vision of Judgment,* where a more than Humean skepticism is dealt with in ways made available by aspects of eighteenth-century thought that led to that skepticism in the first place. It was during the summer of 1816, while he was living in Switzerland at the Villa Diodati, that these forces took on much of what was to be their definitive form in Byron's poems.

These few months made up a crucial period in the development of Byron's imagination. Talk with Shelley and study of Rousseau had led him to take poetry more seriously than he had been used to do, and for all his joking on the subject, this may be the most important consequence of the period. In addition to work at the larger pieces already touched on, the summer was particularly rich in shorter experimental poems in which Byron examined aspects of his developing vision, trying out ways of stating it. I shall consider four of these poems, each something of a sport in Byron's work as a whole, but each revealing with special clarity the pressures he was working under and the ways he was learning to deal with them—which draw us then into the center of his imagining. The tendency of the readings, by helping us see Byron in relation to the preceding age, may teach us something of why he was so important to his own time.

I

"EPISTLE TO AUGUSTA"

Byron's imagination was "antithetical." Out of honesty, wit, and perversity, he liked to set up oppositions, in the antithetical heroes of *Childe Harold* and the early tales, in the ironies of *Don Juan*, in the oppositions of ways of living in *Beppo* and of ways of being in *The Vision of Judgment*. In the "Stanzas to the Po" an opposition is studied between the poet and the woman he loves, with the river expressing what unites and divides them.[3] The "Epistle to Augusta" is especially interesting from this point of view because of the occasion it offers for refined connection and opposition between the poet in Switzerland and his half-sister at home in England.

The poem begins with an assertion of relationship: "My Sister! my sweet Sister!" She is valuable to him for the ways in which she is close to him and far away from him, though the emphasis is on the first:

> My Sister! my sweet Sister! if a name
> Dearer and purer were, it should be thine.
> Mountains and seas divide us, but I claim
> No tears, but tenderness to answer mine:
> Go where I will, to me thou art the same—
> A loved regret which I would not resign.
> There yet are two things in my destiny,—
> A world to roam through, and a home with thee.[4]

For all the differences in tone, both the "Stanzas to the Po" and the "Epistle to Augusta" may be in the tradition of the "heroic epistle," a verse letter to an absent lover, offering passionate comment on the relationship from a distance. The letter is most often written by a woman whose lover has abandoned her. An example in English would be Pope's rendering of Ovid's "Sappho to Phaon" (Donna Julia's letter in the first canto of *Don Juan* is a variety of this), but Byron was more struck by Pope's own development of the tradition in his "Eloisa," where the Ovidian play with antithetical value and attitude is developed with especial boldness.[5] Byron's antitheses are less radical than Pope's, but they are equally pervasive. If Augusta, for example, were not the kind of woman who would be faithful to commitments that separate her from him, he would not desire her to be with him, or to return his "tenderness." (The paradox recalls Donne's "Twick'nam Garden," or one of Thomas Little's [Moore's] poems "To Rosa.") So the natural barriers are not in any case the only ones, nor are they merely barriers, as we shall see.

Augusta is a fixed point to him in his wanderings, but it is in large part negatively, as a "regret," that she fills this office. His regret for her absence and for what he has done to cause it is painful, but it is the one thing he can count on. Put positively, she is the "home" that is the antithesis to his "roam"-ing. (Byron uses sound-links a good deal in the early lines.) In the same way, his "inheritance of storms" (sts. 3 and 4) is seen as both fate and will: fated because a will such as his was given him without his asking, willed because the fate is so closely shaped to the qualities of the will. The doctrine is Greek, but not the emphasis, which falls on willful error, as in the Shakespearean couplet:

> I have been cunning in mine overthrow,
> The careful pilot of my proper woe.

The first four stanzas establish the situation, antithetically, and the remaining twelve stanzas circle around on themselves twice, defining antitheses. The first (sts. 5–9) is a movement from patience to active grief, the second (10–end) from a feeling of loss to a faith in unbroken connection. Part of the meaning here and elsewhere in Byron is that this is characteristic of him, that he is drawn irresistibly, it seems, from one point to its opposite. In *Don Juan* the effect is apt to be witty; here, as in *Childe Harold,* our feeling is one of sadness that it should be so. But we may want to notice that this movement is itself both disjunctive and connecting, alienating and reconciling.

In the course of each circling movement the poet's mind moves into the past, as he recalls his childhood. In the first instance, it is the "spirit of slight patience," the "strange quiet" brought on by his defiance and despair (and the Alpine landscape) that reminds him of his "happy childhood." But childhood reminds him of home and home of Augusta, and by the end of the ninth stanza his "philosophy" has begun to break down. The second sequence is less simple. It is now the "scenes" that remind him of a childhood spent in a similar landscape, the natural forms suggesting the natural innocence he has lost by indulging the social passions. Though it is impossible to accept Byron's analysis of his difficulty, the main point is the movement of the thought. The oppositions are passion and apathy, experience and innocence, and the poem is concerned with establishing relations among them. Out of the natural innocence suggested by the Alpine scenery he moves towards an earlier innocence associated with his sister, whose name is dear and "pure."[6] Passion has destroyed the calm of innocence and has led to apathy. The poet's problem now is to feel without feeling too much, and to be calm without falling into apathy, thus approximating the innocence he has lost. This demands both stimulation and control. The power of the poem is its achievement from a position (that purports to be) beyond despair of a state of being that precedes despair.[7] The circling movements, then, compose one circle that moves from loss to recovery of value. The poet's most agonized sufferings have been caused by separation from Augusta and by the thought of what he has done to her. But this concern for her testifies to their closeness to each other, as the Alps are both barriers and links. The poem circles round in this way to its beginning, enacting both will and fate:

> For thee, my own sweet sister, in thy heart
> I know myself secure, as thou in mine;
> We were and are—I am, even as thou art—
> Beings who ne'er each other can resign;

It is the same, together or apart,
From Life's commencement to its slow decline
We are entwined—let Death come slow or fast,
  The tie which bound the first endures the last!

It is will since it is what he wants and is the consequence of voluntary acts; it is fate because it was built into the structure of that will, and forms a pattern out of the disasters brought about by the exercise of will. In Byron's way, the antitheses are not reconciled, but they are brought into tolerable relation.

II

"DARKNESS"

The most immediately striking thing about "Darkness," considered as an apocalypse, is that it is scrupulously naturalistic. There is no feeling of divine purpose being worked out, or of any power beyond the natural energies that are running down. It was pointed out in 1825 that the poem borrows heavily on an early example of what we would now call science fiction, and there is an important element of detached scientific description in Byron's poem. Byron is in fact much more secular in his approach than the anonymous author of *The Last Man, or Omegarus and Syderia, a Romance in Futurity* (1806), who is apparently trying to be orthodox. Only apparently, because it is hard to believe that many readers would distribute their sympathies according to the author's instructions. The main impression is of an irresponsible God and a victimized humanity. This may have been one thing that attracted Byron to the work.

The poem begins with the poet's dreaming of a dying earth:

I had a dream, which was not all a dream.
The bright sun was extinguished, and the stars
Did wander darkling in the eternal space,
Rayless, and pathless, and the icy Earth
Swung blind and blackening in the moonless air;
Morn came and went—and came, and brought no day....

The force of the poem is in its depiction of enervation, powerlessness. Exhaustion of the sun is exhaustion of all man's world, and of man himself, and exhaustion for man means loss of humanity. Parts of "Darkness" suggest Shelley, but both the radical pessimism and the unindignant way it is expressed are characteristically Byronic. This vision of human weakness in the face of unmanageable forces lies behind all of Byron's work. No power of imagination can change this, no vision can make much difference. It is the outside limiting factor, like the "fate" of the Greeks, that nothing can be done about.

III

"THE DREAM"

Our life is twofold: Sleep hath its own world,
A boundary between the things misnamed
Death and existence: Sleep hath its own world,
And a wide realm of wild reality,
And dreams in their development have breath,
And tears, and tortures, and the touch of Joy;
They leave a weight upon our waking thoughts,
They take a weight from off our waking toils,
They do divide our being; they become
A portion of ourselves as of our time,
And look like heralds of Eternity;
They pass like spirits of the past,—they speak
Like Sibyls of the future; they have power—
The tyranny of pleasure and of pain;
They make us what we were not—what they will,
And shake us with the vision that's gone by,
The dread of vanished shadows—Are they so?
Is not the past all shadow?—What are they?
Creations of the mind?—The mind can make
Substance, and people planets of its own
With beings brighter than have been, and give
A breath to forms which can outlive all flesh.

(ll. 1–22)

Even among the experimental poems of the summer of 1816 "The Dream" is remarkably original. "Rousseauist" speculation on the nature of imaginative creation is combined with speculation about dreams that is perhaps closest to the German romantics.

The form is that of a series of related visions, derived largely from Old Testament prophecy, with influence perhaps from "autobiographical" poems of Ossian. But for good or ill it is really like nothing else.

"The Dream" is in fact something of a stunt; but it is an interesting stunt, one that allows Byron to exercise his imagination in valuable ways. He is playing with relations between mind and reality, and the notion of dream is helpful to him because of its equivocal middle status, between the imagined and the experienced, past and future. Here he looks at the past as if it were future, the experienced as if it were imagined, while insisting in each case on the reality of the second, "mental," term. The point of this strange maneuver, or part of it, seems to be found in the question (l. 18): "Is not the past all shadow?" I take this to mean that while it is only the past, in a sense, that is wholly real, the guarantee of this reality, its pastness, is by the same token the source of its ideality. The past, being past, is as unreal, mental, ideal as the future or the imagined. This suggests an area in which mental and real, imagined and experienced, future and past are not easily separable—an area of "real" imaginings. We can see now the relation between "The Dream" and Byron's "true epics," *Childe Harold* and *Don Juan,* both of which work to transform Byron's own experience into public dream.[8]

But the opening speculation on dream (ll. 1–22) does more than provide a general focus for the sequence of visions based on Byron's relationship with Mary Chaworth. It establishes vision as a term which will be developed in the rest of the poem. Within the enclosing vision we have a series of visionary moments, each individually characterized, and each a crux in the development of the action of the poem.

The first comes after some lines of weak Wordsworthian imitation ("Tintern Abbey") showing the young pair on a hilltop. He looks at her lovingly and sees everything through her eyes:

> ... she was his sight,
> For his eye followed hers, and saw with hers,
> Which coloured all his objects. . . .
>
> (ll. 53–5)

But she was looking in another direction for her lover. The gaze is not returned, and the rest of the poem grows out of this failure.[9] The next climax of vision comes at the wedding of the dreamer to the woman he makes caddishly clear was his second choice (ll. 158–65). "He could see/Not that which was, nor that which should have been," but the scene of his last interview with the woman he really loved.

The last two visions present the consequences to both persons of the original failure of vision:

> . . . she was become
> The Queen of a fantastic realm; her thoughts
> Were combinations of disjointed things;
> And forms, impalpable and unperceived
> Of others' sight, familiar were to hers.
> And this the world calls frenzy; but the wise
> Have a far deeper madness—and the glance
> Of melancholy is a fearful gift;
> What is it but the telescope of truth?
> Which strips the distance of its fantasies,
> And brings life near in utter nakedness,
> Making the cold reality too real!
>
> (ll. 172–83)

The vision of melancholy is a vision of reality, painfully clear and unillusioned. It is in several ways like the "philosophic mind" of Wordsworth's Imitations Ode, and one of these ways is that it is the state out of which the poem that defines it claims to be written. The cold intensity of perception formed by suffering gives access to a vision of the secrets of the nature of things (sect. viii) and makes it possible to trace the pattern of fate ("doom") acted out in two lives, a dream "Almost like a reality" (sect. ix). But of course it *is* a reality, as we are assumed to know, and what happened is visionary in its intensity, coherence, and completeness. It would be a true dream, then, in at least these ways, attempting to perceive and understand a series of events that form a period in the lives of two persons, taking account and advantage of the elements that condition all attempts at perception and understanding—a program to be carried out less pretentiously and to more effect in *Don Juan*.

IV

"A FRAGMENT"

The poem published by Moore in 1830 as "A Fragment" ("Could I remount the river of my years") combines elements of all three poems discussed so far. It has something of the brooding tone of "Darkness," and a good deal of its unindignant pessimism. And while the point of the fragment is not wholly clear, it seems to be moving towards a statement similar to that of "The Dream" and the "Epistle."

The poet tells us that if he could return through his past life to its sources, he would not do so. He would not, at least, if that were the only way; it would be a gloomy trip. (He is not saying, "If I could live my life over again. . . .") While the passing of time and the movement of life to death are disturbing, and he would like to "get to the bottom" of them, the thought of his own past is so painful that he would let his life flow quietly into the ocean of death, where personal identity is lost, rather than explore its sources in that manner. The "nameless tides" of death, then, have at least negative value. And more kinds of value are discovered. The ocean suggests peace (l. 7) and, more important, totality; it suggests "The whole of that of which we are a part" (l. 8). This second notion has special plausibility, since

> . . . Life is but a vision—what I see
> Of all which lives alone is Life to me,
> And being so—the absent are the dead,
> Who haunt us from tranquillity, and spread
> A dreary shroud around us, and invest
> With sad remembrancers our hours of rest.
>
> (ll. 9–14)

If it is true that only what is directly experienced is alive to us, those absent from us are dead to us, though for this very reason they are so intensely and painfully present—a formula which recalls especially the "Epistle." And if this is true, it does not matter whether we are separated by oceans or by the earth of the grave. The grave is in any case the final barrier.

But then the grave is finally more unifying than separating, a "dark union of insensate dust" (l. 22); the final reduction is a return of all of us to the earth from which everything has developed. And separate outgrowths, such as human lives, must be less than the original rich unity, which is found again in death. We are punningly told that the grave holds the key to earth's "profundity," its depth and value. It is there "Our elements [are] resolved to things untold" (l. 38). So the symbol of loss, or of only relative gain, is seen to offer possibilities. In answer to the problems posed at the beginning of the poem, life's sources are explored through death, the beginning through the end, and a new unity is attained through what has seemed to be separation. The implied "logical" formulation—that if the absent are the dead the dead are the absent, and therefore somehow accessible—makes clear the relation between the imagining here and in "The Dream," while the achievement of values of origin through the manipulation of consequence is common to both "Dream" and "Epistle." All three are maneuvers for making the most of the circumstances developed, in one form, in "Darkness."

*　　*　　*

The influence on Byron and Shelley of Rousseau, whom they read together in this summer of 1816, is unclear and should be worked out. The only study at any length on Rousseau and Byron is that by Otto Schmidt (Leipzig, 1890), and Schmidt's bad judgment has added to the confusion. Even on the basis of his spotty and indiscriminate quotation, it can be seen that Rousseau is a main influence on Byron's comments (in his poetry) on poetic creation and the ambiguity of the imagination (mostly the *Confessions*) and on his attempts at nature mysticism (presumably the *Rêveries*). There may be some influence on his development of the ambiguities of love, but this is less obvious. More detailed statement is difficult, since one is likely to prove only that Rousseau had developed basic forms of romantic imagining. With regard to the poems examined in this essay, the presence of Rousseau is most apparent in "The Dream."

> ... The mind can make
> Substance, and people planets of its own
> With beings brighter than have been, and give
> A breath to forms which can outlive all flesh.
>
> (ll. 19–22)

In my continued ecstasies, I intoxicated myself with full draughts of the most delightful sensations that have ever entered the heart of man. I entirely forgot the human race, and created for myself societies of perfect beings, heavenly alike in their beauties and virtues; trusty, tender, and loyal friends such as I never found in this world below. I found such pleasure in soaring into the empyrean. . . .

(*Confessions,*[10] bk. ix)

The emphasis on permanence in the passage from "The Dream" may be less Rousseauist, to be sure, than generally neoclassic, but it is at least likely that the main source is Rousseau. In the Byron, however, the creations of the mind are recollections of actual events in the past, as in the *Confessions* themselves. Such self-conscious feelings of loneliness and inadequacy, such *use* of one's own experience, deliberately setting up patterns of associations calculated to produce the greatest possible satisfaction—these to some extent "grow out of" eighteenth-century psychology, with its tendency both to enslave the individual mind and to reduce everything to it, and manifest themselves in Byron's alternate cries of helplessness and mastery, solitude and union. It is a strong element in Rousseau, and his influence may be present directly in Byron's work at this time, in addition to the affect he had on others who influenced Byron. At the very least, he was a striking representative of the sensibility expressed by that brooding over circumstances and states of mind and that interplay of loss and gain apparent in the poems examined in this essay.

NOTES

1. Cf. Paul West: "We are trapped anyway, even when we choose our own trap. So, belonging to everything, we belong to nothing except the cosmic principle which binds us: yearning for identity, we lose it in pursuing freedom." Introduction to *Byron: a Collection of Critical Essays,* in "Twentieth Century Views" (Englewood Cliffs, N. J., 1963), p. 8.

2. Ian Watt, *The Rise of the Novel* (Berkeley and Los Angeles, 1957), p. 11.

3. See the reading of "Beppo" by Andrew Rutherford, *Byron: A Critical Study* (Stanford, 1961), pp. 103–22, and that of the "Stanzas to the Po" by Harold Bloom, *The Visionary Company* (New York, 1961), pp. 269–71.

4. Byron's poems are cited from the edition of E. H. Coleridge (London, 1898–1905).

5. That Byron thought of Pope's "Eloisa" in connection with his own tortured relations with Augusta is supported by the well-known reference to his trying not to think of a nameless someone: "Dear sacred name, rest ever unreveal'd," a misquotation of the ninth line of Pope's poem. *Letters and Journals,* ed. Rowland E. Prothero (London, 1898–1901), II, 314. The passage seems most likely to refer to Augusta.

6. See the comments on the poem by G. Wilson Knight, *Lord Byron's Marriage* (London, 1957), p. 120.

7. The year offers examples of a grim, irreducible bitterness whose invincibility is a substitute for innocence. It is present in the closing lines of "Prometheus" (of July 1816), which celebrate the

> . . . firm will, and [the] deep sense,
> Which even in torture can descry
> Its own concentered recompense,
> Triumphant where it dares defy,
> And making Death a Victory.

Or in Manfred's proud claim to the spirits of Arimanes:

> I sunk before my vain despair, and knelt
> To my own desolation.
> (II. iv. 41–2)

Or in the third canto of *Childe Harold:*

> Self-exiled Harold wanders forth again,
> With naught of Hope left—but with less of gloom;
> The very knowledge that he lived in vain,
> That all was over on this side the tomb,
> Had made Despair a smilingness assume.
> (st. 16)

8. The case is rather different with *The Vision of Judgment,* which is a "true dream" (last stanza) because it sees truly and judges accurately.

9. There is a brilliant use of "staring" sight in *Parisina,* suggesting the irresistible, instinctive nature of the passions that work themselves out in the poem. Compare the preoccupation with eyes in Pope's "Eloisa."

10. Anon. trans., Modern Library ed., pp. 441–2. This aspect of Rousseau's thought is still more clearly present in the third canto of *Childe Harold's Pilgrimage.*

Byron and the Terrestrial Paradise

---·•·---

E. D. HIRSCH, JR.

ADAH: Why wilt thou always mourn for Paradise?
      Can we not make another?
CAIN: Where?

Lord Byron, Cain, III, i.

The Padre ... assured me "that the terrestrial
Paradise had been certainly in *Armenia.*" I went
seeking it—God knows where.—Did I find it? Umph!
Now and then, for a minute or two.

Lord Byron, Detached Thoughts, #55.

Like many others, she [Lady Blessington] could not believe that he was
sincere in both his sentimental and his cynical expressions, that his
longings and his ironic recognition of the unideal nature of the world
and himself were but two sides of the same coin.

L. A. Marchand, Byron, vol. 3, p. 1065.

WHEN Swinburne and Arnold praised Byron for his excellence
of sincerity and strength they were alluding to *Childe
Harold* as well as *Don Juan;* today most critics find Byron's sincerity and strength in the ottava rima poems alone—in *Beppo,
The Vision of Judgment,* and *Don Juan.* When we consider that
the generality of this opinion is an entirely modern phenomenon
(E. H. Coleridge lists forty-six editions of *Childe Harold* before
1900 as against fourteen of *Don Juan*)[1] we may conclude that behind it lies one of those reversals in taste that F. A. Pottle has
named "shifts of sensibility." It is a shift that tells us, probably,

467

more about ourselves than about Byron, and has blinded us on occasion to essential qualities in the very poems we like best.

Certainly, the current preference for Byron's satirical over his romantic poetry has sometimes accompanied a notion of his poetic development that does not correspond to the facts. "Only as Don Juan," declared Mr. T. S. Eliot, does Byron "get nearer the truth about himself." "His steady growth to adult sanity . . . can be followed in the ottava rima poems," says Mr. Ronald Bottrall: "In them he exchanged his falsetto for a speaking voice."[2] I think we should understand such remarks as reflections of the critic's preference for one of Byron's two principal styles, rather than as descriptions of his spiritual history. For we are all aware that the two styles existed side by side throughout Byron's career; that the "falsetto" and the "speaking voice" alternated in the juvenilia; that *Beppo* was finished before *Childe Harold* IV; that *Cain* was composed in the midst of *Don Juan;* and that *The Island* (in Grierson's view the best of the romantic tales) was the last major poem that Byron completed.[3] Professor Marchand rightly observed that "Byron did not, as has sometimes been said, abandon Childe Harold entirely when he took up Don Juan. Just as the facetious and satiric vein had continued to flow in his letters when the world knew him only as Childe Harold, so now he carried with him into the new poem many of the moods that belonged to that gloomy egoist."[4] Although it is valid and convenient to distinguish between Byron's early, middle, and late poetry, or to classify individual poems as "romantic" or "satiric," it is not true that the divisions into periods mark off significant changes in Byron's outlook or that the classifications, "romantic" and "satiric" reflect "a sharply contradictory spirit, divided against itself."[5] Byron is the single major romantic poet who in his poetry preserved his early outlook for more than a decade, and, as far as can be judged, he preserved it to his death. Behind Byron's contradictions, there is, I think, a unity and consistency that embraces all his moods and styles. In this essay, which, for convenience, deals largely with *Don Juan,* I shall focus my comments on a few aspects of Byron's work that are fundamental to all his poetry. I shall emphasize the "romantic" elements in *Don Juan* not simply to attack its reputation for up-to-date toughmindedness, but primarily to uncover what seems to me its inner form.

I begin by pointing to the undertone of melancholy that *Don Juan* shares with the rest of Byron's work. Take, as the nearest example, the fragment that introduces the modern editions of *Don Juan:*

> I would to Heaven that I were so much clay,
>   As I am blood, bone, marrow, passion, feeling—
> Because at least the past were passed away,
>   And for the future—(but I write this reeling,
> Having got drunk exceedingly to-day,
>   So that I seem to stand upon the ceiling)
> I say—the future is a serious matter—
> And so—for God's sake—hock and soda-water!

The tone is that of a man on the point of moving from drunkenness to sobriety. He has not yet relinquished the insouciance of drunkenness, yet recognizes that all the gaiety is about to pass. It is a middle point between inebriation and sobriety—musing on both. This kind of structure is central in Byron's poetry: the present moment, if happy, is clouded by the knowledge of an inevitable collapse; if unhappy, it is clouded by the knowledge of some glorious possibility which has been denied to us.[6] In this instance, the moment of drunkenness is a bright instant between a past that Byron wants to forget and a future that *is* a serious matter.[7] (Hock and soda-water is Byron's standard antidote to hangovers.) Presumably the speaker had got drunk to forget the past, because the past was a series of baffled hopes and lapses from momentary perfections. Not being clay, but passion and feeling, he cannot forget these failures, and, as a man of feeling, he cannot be reconciled to them; their pang persists. The undertone of melancholy expresses a constant recognition of the central Byronic experience:

> I yet might be most happy. I will clasp thee,
>   And we *again* will be—
>
>   [the figure vanishes]
>   My heart is crushed!
>   (*Manfred,* I, i, 190 f. My italics.)

If one universalizes this experience, one suffers what the Germans call Weltschmerz, a condition which Professor Rose has defined as "the psychic state that ensues when there is a sharp contrast between a man's ideals and his material environment, and his temperament is such as to eliminate the possibility of any sort of reconciliation between the two."⁸ This is a definition that sounds remarkably like Byron's explanation of Cain's state of mind, his "rage and fury against the inadequacy of his state to his conceptions."⁹ Cain himself expressed his feelings in Byron's favorite symbol for man's bafflement: the conflict between "clay" and "spirit":

> But if that high thought were
> Link'd to a servile mass of matter—and,
> Knowing such things, aspiring to such things,
> And science still beyond them, were chained down
> To the most gross and petty paltry wants,
> All foul and fulsome. . . .
>
> (*Cain*, II, i. 50 ff.)

This Byronic refusal to accept complacently the inadequacy of man's state to his conceptions is an element in *Don Juan* that tends to distinguish the satire in that poem from the satire of Pope. For Pope, man's bafflement is far less serious and far more easily resolved. Here is his version of Cain's dilemma:

> He hangs between; in doubt to act or rest;
> In doubt to deem himself a God or Beast;
> In doubt his mind or body to prefer;
> Born but to die and reas'ning but to err.
>
> (*An Essay on Man*, II, ll. 7–10.)

The contradictions are acknowledged, but implicitly resolved by the idea of a compromise. "Created half to rise and half to fall," man "hangs between." When Pope leaves man in ignorance "whether he thinks too little or too much" his phrasing implies that man should do neither, that the proper course for a creature in a "middle state" is a middle course—the one course that is not open to Manfred:

> Half dust, half deity, alike unfit
> To sink or soar, with our mixed essence make
> A conflict of its elements and breathe
> The breath of degradation and of pride
> Contending with low wants and lofty will
> Till our mortality predominates.
>
> (*Manfred*, I, ii, ll. 40–45.)

The emphasis is not on man's middle state, but on his double state, on his inevitable inner conflict. There is no middle way, no compromise and no solution except death.

This tendency to reject compromise gives Byron's satires on "the human biped" their special, "melancholy merriment":[10]

> Love's a capricious power: I've know it hold
>   Out through a fever caused by its own heat,
> But be much puzzled by a cough and cold,
>   And find a quinsy very hard to treat;
> Against all noble maladies he's bold,
>   But vulgar illnesses don't like to meet,
> Nor that a sneeze should interrupt his sigh,
> Nor inflammations redden his blind eye.
>
> But worst of all is nausea, or a pain
>   About the lower region of the bowels.
>
> (Don Juan II, 22–3.)

This commentary on Juan's seasickness may be supposed to puncture Juan's cant about his not being able to forget Julia, and thus to satirize his hyperboles. But are the hyperboles wrong? Does Byron implicitly admonish us, "love neither too little nor too much"? That is not suggested at the height of the Haidee episode.[11] The tone of these lines is good-humored, but laughter can be a mode of accommodating life when one is not completely reconciled to life. I find that Byron's laughter in *Don Juan* frequently has this melancholy undertone—particularly when the comic disproportion involves, as in this case, that conflict between clay and spirit which preoccupied Manfred and Cain:

> And the sad truth that hovers o'er my desk
>   Turns what was once romantic to burlesque.
>
> And if I laugh at any mortal thing
>   'Tis that I may not weep; and if I weep,
> 'Tis that our nature cannot always bring
>   Itself to apathy.[12]
>
> (Don Juan, IV, 3–4.)

To describe the acceptance of life-as-it-is by the pejorative word "apathy" discloses a deeply rooted unwillingness to accept life-as-it-is. But what can such unwillingness consist of? It can, in mo-

ments of pride, imply a shaking of the fist at Providence, as in
"Prometheus," or *Cain*, but that is primarily the expression of a
Weltschmerz that has lost its patience, and is not Byron's most
frequent tone—which is melancholic and ironic rather than titanic.
I think that Byron's recurrent unwillingness to accept the mixed
character of experience is rooted in his special sort of religious
faith, the most accurate (if not the most sympathetic) description
of which was written by T. E. Hulme in his attack on romantic
poetry:

> You don't believe in Heaven, so you begin to believe in a heaven on
> earth, . . . and as there is always the bitter contrast between what you
> think you ought to be able to do and what man actually can, [romanti-
> cism] always tends, in its later stages at any rate, to be gloomy.
>   (*Speculations,* London, 1924, pp. 118–19.)

To believe in a heaven on earth is to believe in the *possibility* of
an earthly perfection, and this was a faith that Byron never relinquished.

Byron's hopes and values were entirely terrestrial. He shocked
some of his contemporaries not only by rejecting the consoling idea
of Heaven, but also by rejecting with disdain the trepidations of
Hell.[13] When Cain shakes his fist at Providence he does so because
he disbelieves that his ills will be compensated for in some other
world; he knows that what is wrong *ici bas* is totally and ultimately
wrong:

> There woos no home, nor hope, nor life,
>   save what is here.
>   (*Childe Harold,* IV, 105.)[14]

One reason Byron could so vigorously resist posthumous consolations was that he never gave up his hope of the terrestrial paradise. It is true that he often denied such a possibility in *Childe
Harold* and *Don Juan,* but his very preoccupation with the dis-
crepancy between life as it is and as it should be, discloses how
uncertain such denials were. To the question, "What is poetry?"
Byron gave an answer that is valid certainly for his own poetry:
"The feeling of a Former world and a Future." The phrase partakes of the Byronic melancholy—the feeling of a past golden age
that contrasts bitterly with the present. On the other hand, the

melancholy does not lapse into apathy because it is sustained by the
hope of future perfection: "In all human affairs," Byron added in
the journal entry from which I have just quoted, "it is Hope-Hope-
Hope."[15]

This positive side of Byron's melancholy needs to be emphasized.
Professor Ridenour has brilliantly shown that the metaphors of
Don Juan persistently refer to a collapse from a former world, a
Fall from Eden.[16] While this is the most helpful observation on
Don Juan that I have encountered in recent criticism it is one that
requires a corrective footnote: in all Byron's poetry the periodic
recurrence of a Fall is predicated on the periodic recurrence of a
Redemption. Byron, for all his protective irony, hated the idea of
permanent unregeneracy as much as he hated the idea of a permanent Hell. The notion of a Future Eden is implicit, for example,
in the political faith for which he died, and for which, at times, he
wrote:

> For I will teach, if possible, the stones
> To rise against Earth's tyrants. Never let it
>   Be said that we still truckle unto thrones;—
> But ye—our children's children! think how we
> Showed *what things were* before the World was free!
>
> That hour is not for us, but't is for you:
>   And as, in the great joy of your Millennium,
> You hardly will believe such things were true
>   As now occur, I thought that I would pen you'em;
> But may their very memory perish too!—
>
>   (*Don Juan*, VIII, 135–6.)

Although words like "Eden" and "Paradise" are scattered
throughout *Don Juan,* they do not usually refer to a future state of
society, but rather to a state of nature or to a perfect love relationship, or, as in the Haidee episode, to both at once. It is generally
an Eden from which all trace of guilt or taint has been removed—
the guilt of "clay" or the taint of "civilization." Here is the way
Byron imagines the life of "General Boone, backwoodsman of
Kentucky:"

> He was not all alone: around him grew
>   A sylvan tribe of children of the chase,

> Whose young, unwakened world was ever new,
>   Nor sword nor sorrow yet had left a trace
> On her unwrinkled brow, nor could you view
>   A frown on Nature's or on human face;
> The free-born forest found and kept them free,
> And fresh as is a torrent or a tree.
>
> (*Don Juan*, VIII, 65)

Among all these recurrent visions of Edenic purity and perfection in Byron's poetry, the most important is the vision of a totally selfless and totally fulfilling love relationship. That is the principal earthly paradise in the earliest as well as the latest poetry, from the lines:

> Some portion of paradise still is on earth,
>   And Eden revives in the first kiss of love.
>
> (1807, "The First Kiss of Love")

to the lines:

> Paradise was breathing in the sigh
> Of nature's child in nature's ecstasy.
>
> (1823, *The Island*, III, 195 ff.)

Of this ideal, Byron once remarked in his journal, "My earliest dreams (as most boys dreams are) were martial, but a little later they were all for love and retirement."[17] The association of "love" with "retirement" again suggests the idea of an untainted love: it is a retirement from the world and the world's taint, and from the taint of mere lust or "clay" as well. This impulse shows itself (*pace* Mr. Wilson Knight) in Byron's lifelong male friendships and his fondness for young boys. The attraction was, I believe, less homosexual than trans-sexual. Here was a relationship that was not (at least not consciously) tainted by lust, and therefore could be perfectly selfless and spiritual: "a violent though *pure* love and passion"—that is Byron's phrase for "the then romance of the most romantic period of my life."[18] The same purity distinguishes the love of Juan and Haidee:

> When two pure hearts are pour'd in one another
>   And love too much, and yet cannot love less;
> But almost sanctify the sweet excess
> By the immortal wish and power to bless. . . .[19]
>
> (*Don Juan*, IV, 26.)

Byron's concern to preserve the possibility of genuinely pure love manifests itself in his description of the relationship between Juan and Leila, the orphan girl Juan took to Russia. Indeed, this concern is the most probable reason for her being brought into the story:

> Don Juan loved her, and she loved him, as
> Nor brother, father, sister, daughter love.—[20]
> I cannot tell exactly what it was;
> He was not yet quite old enough to prove
> Parental feelings and the other class,
> Called brotherly affection, could not move
> His bosom,—for he never had a sister:
> Ah! if he had—how much he would have missed her!
> And still less was it sensual;

And here Byron performs one of those brilliant maneuvers by which he manages to salvage his ideal without in the least denying its precariousness:

> for besides
> That he was not an ancient debauchee,
> (Who like sour fruit, to stir their veins' salt tides,
> As acids rouse a dormant alkali,)
> Although ('t will happen as our planet guides)
> His youth was not the chastest that might be,
> There was the purest Platonism at bottom
> Of all his feelings—only he forgot 'em.
>
> (Don Juan, X, 53–54.)

But in this case (as the planet does now and then guide), Juan had not forgot 'em:

> Just now there was no peril of temptation;
> He loved the infant orphan he had saved,
> As patriots (now and then) may love a nation;
>
> (Don Juan, X, 55.)

It is true that in Don Juan, as in all Byron's poems, such ideal relationships fail. That is the "sad truth" which sustains both the undercurrent of melancholy in the poem and its explicit ironies. On the other hand, it is remarkable that Don Juan is more protective of such ideals than Childe Harold or the early verse romances.

For the central figure in those poems had been a melancholy, taciturn figure whose

> early dreams of good outstripped the truth
> And troubled manhood followed baffled youth.
>
> (*Lara*, ll. 323–4.)

In *Don Juan* on the other hand, the central figure never experiences a genuine betrayal of the heart. Juan's relationship with Haidee is not betrayed from within, and his dream of good does not outstrip the truth:

> For them to be
> Thus was another Eden; they were never
> Weary, unless when separate.
>
> (*Don Juan*, IV, 10.)

The betrayal comes only from the outside, and that in itself is not a disillusioning experience. There is no disloyalty and no failure of love for Juan; all these melancholy disillusionments are allotted to the narrator of the poem, whose irony and cynicism relieve Juan of any outright cynicism of his own. It seems significant to me that Byron's announced intent to make Juan gradually *"blasé"* and *"gaté"* never comes close to being realized.[21] The closest Juan got to this was in his dalliance with Catherine the Great, and there he preserved the ideal of pure love by becoming literally sick of degraded love, and by remaining loyal to the orphan girl, Leila. Juan never relinquishes his "purest Platonism at bottom."

Finally, in the last episode of the poem, Juan encounters another pure soul whose very name, Aurora, calls up, in the midst of an English houseparty, "the former world":

> In figure, she had something of Sublime
> In eyes which sadly shone, as Seraphs' shine.
>   All Youth—but with an aspect beyond Time;
> Radiant and grave—as pitying Man's decline;
>   Mournful—but mournful of another's crime,
> She looked as if she sat by Eden's door,
> And grieved for those who could return no more.
>
> (*Don Juan*, XV, 45.)

Why is Aurora introduced into the story? I strongly suspect that she is there for the same reason Leila is there, and Leila serves no

important function in the plot. She is there to preserve the possibility of the ideal and to renew the imagination of the hero and
the narrator as well:

> And, certainly, Aurora had renewed
>   In him some feelings he had lately lost,
> Or hardened; feelings which, perhaps ideal,
> Are so divine, that I must deem them real:—
>
> The love of higher things and better days;
>   The unbounded hope, and heavenly ignorance
> Of what is called the World, and the World's ways;
>   The moments when we gather from a glance
> More joy than from all future pride or praise,
>   Which kindle manhood, but can ne'er entrance
> The Heart in an existence of its own,
> Of which another's bosom is the zone.
>
> (*Don Juan*, XVI, 107–8.)

These recurrent visions of an earthly perfection bear witness to
the power of Byron's persistent faith in the possibilities of life. It
was a faith that suffered from attacks launched continually by his
own invincible honesty, but it also prevailed to the end. Byron's
chips were all on this world: the great distinction of his epic was
that it was "true" and his most approving footnote was "Fact!" But
the world on which he staked everything was always one in which
spirit could (now and then) conquer clay, where selfless love and
genuine heroism were not only possible but were, as his true epic
showed, sometimes actually to be found.

II

Of all Byron's poems *Don Juan* is the most Byronic not because
it is more honest or less posing than the others (Byron never poses)
but because it contains more of his astonishingly varied moods
than any other: gloom, ecstasy, flippancy, indignation, pride, self-
immersion, self-assertion, guilt, insouciance, sentimentality, nostalgia, optimism, pessimism. In the preceding section I attempted
to show that beneath many of these moods resides a melancholy
refusal to accept the truth that perfection is impossible in life, and
a recurrent impulse to depict momentary fulfillments which confirm and sanction this precarious secular faith. Now my purpose

will be to qualify and amplify this general point in order to bring it closer to the incredible variousness of the poetry that Byron actually wrote. The danger in generalizing about the whole corpus of a poet's work is, of course, that the work can become merely a source of data to illustrate the generalization. I hope to convince the reader that my intent is to free Byron's poetry, and particularly *Don Juan*, from generalizations that make it seem more narrow and uniform than it is. Generalizations are necessary tools of criticism: the task is to discover the ones that most nearly fit.

One generalization that emphatically does not fit *Don Juan* is that it preserves a unity of tone. Mr. Andrew Rutherford is surely right (as he so often is) when he observes that Byron frequently evokes both a serious and a frivolous response "to the same event without having any apparent satiric purpose in so doing."[22] The following juxtaposition of tones is not untypical:

> Even Conscience too, has a tough job
> To make us understand each good old maxim,
> So good I wonder Castlereigh don't tax 'em.

> And now 'twas done—on the lone shore were plighted
> Their hearts; the stars their nuptial torches shed
> Beauty upon the beautiful they lighted.
>
> (*Don Juan*, II, 203–4.)

Hazlitt, among Byron's contemporaries, was the most memorable, though not the only, critic who found himself unable to admire these swift changes of tone:

A classical intoxication is followed by the splashing of soda-water, by frothy effusions of ordinary bile. After the lightning and the hurricane, we are introduced to the interior of the cabin and the contents of wash-hand basins. The solemn hero of tragedy plays *Scrub* in the farce. This is 'very tolerable and not to be endured.' The Noble Lord is almost the only writer who has prostituted his talents in this way. He hallows in order to desecrate; takes a pleasure in defacing the images of beauty his hands have wrought; and raises our hopes and our belief in goodness only to dash them to the earth again, and break them in pieces the more effectively from the height they have fallen.

> (*The Spirit of the Age*, "Lord Byron.")

In a footnote added after Byron's death Hazlitt admitted that these criticisms were perhaps too strong and were applicable only to the early parts of *Don Juan*. But despite Hazlitt's exaggerations, his statement does memorably point to the tonal inconsistencies of *Don Juan*. (Yet one does want to reply to Hazlitt that if *Don Juan* moved only towards deflation, paradox, and satire, and never towards elevation, hope, and sentimentality, then one could not complain that one's hopes are always being tricked—and *Don Juan* would be a far duller poem than it is. The passage from Byron quoted above illustrates this contrary kind of tonal shift.)

Let it be stated bluntly, then, that *Don Juan*, though in its own way a unified poem, has no unity of tone. It has no unity of outlook. It has not even unity of theme. I strongly suspect that some discussions of *Don Juan* "as a poem" have tried to demonstrate its conformity to standards of unity that are too narrowly formalistic or conventional. Mr. Lovell, for example, finds a thematic consistency: "That unifying principle, I suggest, is the principle of thematic unity—here the basically ironic theme of appearance versus reality."[23] So also finds Mr. Ridenour: "The poet's seemingly most irrelevant aside or digression is likely to turn out on examination to be another way of dramatizing his central paradox," i.e., that the means of grace is an occasion of sin.[24] Mr. Ridenour's comment is closer to the poem than Mr. Lovell's; indeed, it is valid for the greater part of *Don Juan*, and reflects Byron's preoccupation with the conflict of clay and spirit in man. But there are other times (as I showed in the preceding section) when Byron expressly rejects this paradox. There can be no unity of theme in *Don Juan* because there is no stability of attitude. Thematically, doctrinally, tonally, it is a poem that is founded on contradictions.

If we take the most important theme in Byron's poetry—the theme of love—the nature of these contradictions comes into sharp relief. At one moment love may be "the immortal wish and power to bless"; at another, it may be something quite different:

> And that's enough, for love is vanity
> Selfish in its beginning as its end.
>
> (*Don Juan*, IX, 73.)

And, most frequently, it is the ironic, tragi-comic conflict of selfishness with unselfishness, clay with spirit:

> The Sovereign was smitten;
> Juan much flattered by her love or lust;—
> I cannot stop to alter words once written,
> And the *two* are so mixed with human dust
> That he who *names one,* both perchance may hit on.
>
> (*Don Juan,* IX, 77.)

These are, of course, not merely logical contradictions; they are emotional contradictions—radically different responses to the same event. They reflect Byron's own mobility—his swift changes and contradictions of mood.

That such mobility was one of the most striking characteristics of Byron's temperament is a fact that he commented on more than once, and it was also a characteristic of his imagination both in poetry and prose. In his personal journal one finds precisely the same pattern of conflicting moods as in *Don Juan.* The following two passages from one day's journal entry are found on a single page in the Prothero edition.[25] The first is a typically Juanesque commentary on the mixed character of experience:

The infinity of wishes lead but to disappointment. All the discoveries which have yet been made have multiplied little but existence. An extirpated disease is succeeded by some new pestilence, and a discovered world has brought little to the old one, except the p[ox] first and freedom afterwards—the latter a fine thing, particularly as they gave it to Europe in exchange for slavery.

At this point Byron paused to receive visitors and listen to some music. He returned to write the following:

But onward!—it is now the time to act, and what signifies *self,* if a single spark of that which would be worthy of the past can be bequeathed unquenchably to the future! It is not one man, nor a million, but the *spirit* of liberty which must be spread. The waves which dash upon the shore are, one by one, broken, but yet the ocean conquers nevertheless.

In the future it will be not freedom *and* the pox, not freedom *and* slavery, but the final defeat of all vitiations of freedom. These same shifts of mood determine Byron's alternating acceptance and rejection of original sin; his waverings on the doctrine of immortality, his use of the same kind of argument to prove and to disprove that the soul is immortal.[26]

The literary question that arises from the tonal contradictions of *Don Juan* is the obvious one: Wherein lies its unity? I believe that its felt unity resides neither in its theme nor its tone but in the *pattern* of its moods. The more precise question would be: How do the divergent moods of *Don Juan* fit together to form an understandable pattern? The unity of *Don Juan* is not logical but psychological; its logic is what the Germans call *Seelenlogik*.

Mr. Rutherford makes the point very concisely when he says of *Don Juan:* "More fundamental is the unity (if one can call it that), the consistency even in inconsistencies that comes from its being unmistakably the product of a single although complex mind."[27] That, as I understand it, is another way of saying that the variety of moods and the inconsistency of ideas in *Don Juan* are exemplifications of Byron's moods and Byron's ideas, that the unity of the poem resides in the unifying idea: Byron.[28] But even when we understand that self-expression is a primary impulse in all of Byron's poetry, and that his own personality constitutes a great deal of its substance, we are still puzzled by the question: "What connects all these moods in Byron himself?"

I ask this question somewhat hesitantly in the face of Professor Ridenour's incisive comments on the importance of the author's "persona" in *Don Juan*.[29] But I think it fair to argue that in most of *Don Juan* the persona and the man himself are so mixed and fused, the "real" Byron and the projected Byron so deliberately identified that it is quite impossible to disentangle them. What are we to make of recurrent asides such as "I have a passion for the name of Mary"? Is not the distinction between that "I" and the person who enunciates it simply the distinction between any real person and the personality he projects in speech?[30] It seems to me that the Byron projected in *Don Juan* is the Byron projected in his conversations, his letters, and his journals; it is, in fact, the only Byron we really know.

How then, do all these clashing moods cohere in Byron's personality? I suggest that they are all sponsored by the two central experiences discussed in the first part of this essay: the experience of a fulfillment and the disillusioning experience of its collapse. These are not, of course, peculiarly Byronic experiences, but they are peculiarly romantic ones. Before Byron was born, Goethe had described the archetypal experience in *Werther:*

Oh, when we rush up to it, when the distant *there* becomes *here,* everything is as it was before and we stand hemmed in by our poverty.

(21 June)

And Byron echoes it in "The Dream:"

> What is it but the telescope of truth
> Which strips the distance of its fantasies
> And brings life near in utter nakedness,
> Making the cold reality too real?

(ll. 181–4)

But this experience of disillusionment would not constantly recur
were it not for a recurrence of faith in the distant "there," and this
faith, in turn, could not be preserved if one did not (now and
then) experience earnests of possible perfection. These ideal visions
of the past or the future, and even sometimes of the present, preserve the possibility of disillusionment.

It follows that all the moods of Byron's poetry are so many
versions of the three principal moods that arise from these experiences. The three moods are: (1) the ecstatic, corresponding to the
vision or experience of perfect fulfillment; (2) the ironic (which
may be humorous, melancholic, or both at once) corresponding to
the experience of a less than ideal reality; and (3) the cynical, corresponding to the complete failure of the ideal. In the last, relatively infrequent mood, Byron is capable of comments like *"What
are *all* things but a *show?"*[31] But, of course, it is the ironic mood
that is central in all his poetry, from beginning to end.

This triadic notion is not so arbitrary as it may at first seem. It
reflects, for example, Byron's preoccupation with the conflict of
clay and spirit in man, his feeling that at times we are all spirit—
and even at times all clay, but that most of the time we are an
ironic mixture of both. The triad corresponds to the fluctuations
in his attitude to women, whom he regarded in different moments
as seraphs, as inscrutable paradoxes, and as "fine animals." This
may be seen directly in the character delineations of the women in
Don Juan. First, we encounter Julia, that mixture of animality and
delicacy, loyalty and hypocrisy. The ironic-comic mode in which
her love affair is described exemplifies the ironic mood to which
she herself corresponds. The same association of ironic style with a
mixed personality is found in the treatment of Lady Adeline at the
other end of the story. Then, there is the ecstatic style in which

Byron describes the two pure spirits, Haidee and Aurora. Finally, at the lowest ebb of the poem, there is the ironic-sardonic treatment of Catherine the Great, plain clay if it ever existed.

The pattern of *Don Juan* is, then, the pattern of Byron's "mobility"—his unceasing movement from one attitude to a different one. The logic of that pattern is found in the unresolved conflict between the demands of the ideal and the demands of the real, that is, in Byron's refusal to compromise between his honesty and his faith in the terrestrial paradise. Had he been willing to give in entirely to the experience of disillusionment, his attitude and his style would have remained stable and uniform. Thus, Byron's inconsistency is the mark and measure of his faith, and his mobility preserves his loyalty to that faith. For his melancholy, his irony, his sardonic laughter are capable at any moment of giving way to an ecstasy that sustains and nourishes. But when that occurs the ideal is never for a long period of time defended against actual experience. Byron avoids a decisive battle by surrendering quickly to nostalgia or irony, and the pattern is then repeated. His own defense of this protective agility in *Don Juan* was an artistic one: it prevented dullness, sponsored honesty, and lent variety.[32] But this conscious defense simply reinforced a deeper impulse in the poem.

Probably the best metaphor for the unity of *Don Juan* is that of a journey. Travel is the structural principle of his two major poems, and the appropriate symbol of his poetry as a whole. It symbolizes the restless movement of the spirit from object to object, as well as the writing of a poem that has no fixed plan. The very unfixedness of the goal permits the pilgrimage to continue: if politics fails there is nature; if love fails there is travel itself; some beckoning Eden always remains intact. Disappointment is never permanent, scorn never completely fatal, and the pilgrimage never comes to an appointed end. *Don Juan* is, in this symbolic sense, a travel poem. Even in its satiric moods it preserves an intensity which Hazlitt called "the great and prominent distinction of Lord Byron's writings." Even in its laughter one detects the melancholy intensity of Byron's "romantic" style:

> unfound the boon—unslaked the thirst,
> Though to the last in verge of our decay,
> Some phantom lures such as we sought at first.
>
> (*Childe Harold*, IV, 124.)

But the laughter itself has a separate power. Just as Byron's melancholy is a reflex of his faith in the possibilities of the actual world, his laughter is an expression of his allegiance to the actual world in spite of its imperfections: "This unriddled wonder,/ The world, which at the worst's a *glorious* blunder."[33] That is a typical remark and the italics are Byron's. This gusto of *Don Juan* is the victory of faith over experience, and if I have emphasized the romantic flavor of Byron's faith, that is in part because I find it behind the gusto of all his poetry, including the poetry of *Don Juan*. His laughter is, no doubt, a finer thing than his gloom, but it is the laughter of a man so attached to this life as to be capable of gloom. Out of this immovable commitment to life came his melancholy and his laughter as well as his excellence of sincerity and strength.

NOTES

1. *The Works of Lord Byron. Poetry,* ed. E. H. Coleridge, 7 vols. (London, 1898–1905) VII, pp. 89–310.

2. T. S. Eliot, "Byron," p. 198; Ronald Bottrall, "Byron and the Colloquial Tradition in English Poetry," pp. 212, 216; both in M. H. Abrams, ed., *English Romantic Poets. Modern Essays in Criticism* (New York, 1960).

3. In a letter that requested Murray's opinion of "the new Juans and the translations and the Vision [of Judgment]" Byron called his romantic poem, *The Prophecy of Dante,* "the best thing I ever wrote, if it be not *unintelligible."* See *The Works of Lord Byron. Letters and Journals,* ed. R. E. Prothero, 6 vols. (London, 1898–1905), IV, p. 422.

4. L. A. Marchand, ed., *Don Juan,* Riverside Edition (Cambridge, Mass., 1958), p. xii.

5. W. J. Calvert, *Byron. Romantic Paradox* (Chapel Hill, N.C., 1935), p. 54.

6. Byron defined his "mobility" as "an excessive susceptibility of immediate impressions—at the same time without *losing* the past: and is . . . a most painful and unhappy attribute." See Byron's note to *Don Juan,* XVI, 97.

7. Compare:

> The best of Life is but intoxication:
> Glory, the Grape, Love, Gold, in these are sunk
> The hopes of all men, and of every nation.
> *Don Juan*, II, 179

8. William Rose, *From Goethe to Byron. The Development of Weltschmerz in German Literature* (London, 1924), p. 5.

9. *Letters and Journals,* V, p. 470.

10. See *Letters and Journals,* V, p. 187, and *Don Juan,* VII, 89.

11. Compare *Don Juan,* IV, 26.

12. Compare: "People have wondered at the Melancholy which runs through my writings. Others have wondered at my personal gaiety; but I recollect once, after an hour in which I had been sincerely and particularly gay, and rather brilliant in company, my wife replying to me when I said (upon her remarking my high spirits) "and yet, Bell, I have been called and mis-called Melancholy—you must have seen how falsely, frequently." "No B.," (she answered) "it is not so: at *heart* you are the most melancholy of mankind, and often when apparently gayest." *Letters and Journals,* V, p. 446.

13. As in *Childe Harold* I:

> It is the settled, ceaseless gloom
> The fabled Hebrew Wanderer bore;
> That will not look beyond the tomb,
> But cannot hope for rest before.

14. About the ending of his drama *Heaven and Earth* Byron once remarked: "I once thought of conveying the lovers to the moon or one of the planets; but it is not easy for the imagination to make any unknown world more beautiful than this." Quoted from Medwin, *Journal of the Conversations of Lord Byron* (London, 1824) by E. H. Coleridge in *Poetry,* V, p. 321.

15. *Letters and Journals,* V, 189–90.

16. G. M. Ridenour, *The Style of* Don Juan (New Haven, 1960), pp. 19–89.

17. *Letters and Journals,* V, p. 426.

18. *Letters and Journals,* V, p. 168.

19. A particularly striking example of Byron's idealization of love is found in *The Island,* II, ll. 370–97. There as elsewhere Byron uses religious words like "sanctify," "bless," and "heaven," to express the ultimacy of the experience. The lover is compared to a religious devotee:

> Is love less potent? No—his path is trod
> Alike uplifted gloriously to God;
> Or linked to all we know of heaven below.
> (ll. 374–6)

The third line is more typical than the second. Despite T. E. Hulme's bias against the romantic poets his expression, "spilt religion," seems to me an accurate description of romantic faith. See *Speculations* (London, 1924), p. 118.

20. Compare:

> Juan and Haidée gazed upon each other
> With swimming looks of speechless tenderness,
> Which mixed all feelings—friend, child, lover, brother.
> (*Don Juan,* IV, 26)

21. See *Letters and Journals*, V, p. 242.

22. Andrew Rutherford, *Byron. A Critical Study* (Edinburgh, 1961), p. 161.

23. E. J. Lovell, Jr., "Irony and Image in *Don Juan*," in Abrams, op. cit. p. 231.

24. *The Style of* Don Juan, p. ix.

25. *Letters and Journals*, V, p. 163.

26. See, for instance, *Letters and Journals*, V, p. 211, 456–7.

27. *Byron, A Critical Study*, p. 142.

28. The idea is not simply a biographical one; it is also a formal, literary idea, because *Don Juan* belongs to a poetic genre whose chief *formal* intention is self-expression, and whose formal unity resides in its noble author's projected personality. This is an important, Byronic element in all Byron's poetry, and we do well to add the adjective "Byronic" to genre classifications of *Don Juan* such as "epic satire."

29. *The Style of* Don Juan, pp. 89–124.

30. See the discussion of the linguistic "dédoublement de la personalité" in Charles Bally, *Linguistique générale et linguistique française*, 2nd ed. (Bern, 1944), p. 39.

31. *Don Juan*, VII, 2.

32. See, for instance, *Don Juan*, VIII, 65, 85.

33. *Don Juan*, XI, 3.

Shelley's Last Poetics: A Reconsideration

EARL R. WASSERMAN

To recent analysts and historians of critical theory Shelley's *Defence of Poetry* has been something of an embarrassment, if not an annoyance. The praise it has received has too often flowed from reckless rhapsodists; and the sober, while moved by its sincerity, customarily find its argument grievously flawed. The essay is valuable, we are usually told, primarily for its breathless rhetoric: disconcertingly eclectic, it does not (or could not possibly) reconcile its Platonism with its psychological empiricism; by attributing creation to inspiration it becomes a defense of automatic writing; by depending upon a single norm it collapses all arts and all poems into one and destroys the distinction between the making of poems and other superior mental pursuits; it offers unreconciled definitions of the imagination; it provides no viable poetics for the practical critic. Running through most of the commentaries is the sense not only that the essay is unusable but also that it repeatedly shifts its grounds and that its appeal, as one critic has put it, is often "more transcendental than rational." Granting provisionally the possible validity of these complaints and recognizing that Shelley's language is sometimes exuberant and unguarded, my purpose, perversely, is to consider what soundness and coherence the essay may yield to a deliberately sympathetic hearing.

I

Although fragments of the Platonic dialogues manifestly appear in the essay, together with particles of Sidney and Bacon among others, it should be axiomatic (but has not been) that they do not necessarily draw along with them, comet-like, the metaphysics and aesthetics of their original contexts, but derive their significance from their function in the ideological structure of the *Defence*. It would be well, therefore, to determine the sense in which the essay is "Platonistic," lest we impose an extraneous Platonism on it. Throughout most of his career Shelley maintained faith in the One, the ultimate reality and absolute perfection, understood in partial contexts as the True, or the Good, or the Beautiful; and, especially in 1816–17, he repeatedly wrote of it as a transcendent "Power," not inert like Plato's realm of Ideas, but dynamic, like a Platonic Demiurge acting *ab extra* on both nature and the human mind, and imparting form to the formless, but able to exert itself only inconstantly within the sphere of mutability. As Shelley was later to write, although it cannot be contained, delayed, or hidden by earthly forms, it makes everything "divine" when "for a moment" it is not "forbidden" by the mutability of its media "to live within the life" it bestows.[1] Like Plato's inspired poet, man is only a "passive instrument" of this power, transiently touched by it as an ephemeral cloud is momentarily suffused with sunlight.[2] These visitations "lend" man his knowledge, joy, hope, love, power, and life,[3] but do not constitute him; and it is his nature to be only the passive and passing medium of these lent attributes, which are retrieved by the Power when it "has need of thine,/Abandoning thee" to annihilation.[4] From time to time Shelley returned to this conception of the relation of the Power to man and nature, which is also the theme of his "Hymn to Intellectual Beauty." But in his later years, while retaining belief in a transcendent Power that imparts form to nature, he tended to conceive of man's being as constituted by and identical with the continuous presence of a particle of this perfect power *within* the individual mind, where, like the transcendent Power from which it derives, it acts only intermittently and independently of consciousness and the will. Doubtless the reorganization of these assumptions was due to Shelley's later desire to assert the immortality of man, and consequently he made the particle of eternal Power the essence of man's nature: it and its workings are "thee," not merely for a time "thine." From the transcendent One this individuated power, or soul, or mind, is derived, and to the One it eventually returns: "the pure spirit shall flow/Back to the burning fountain whence it came,/A portion of the Eternal" (*Adonais*, 338–40).

The difference between defining man as recipient of irregular visitations by the Power and assigning him a derivative portion of it does not fundamentally alter the structure of Shelley's metaphysics; but the second position permits him not only to argue the immortality of man (the "angel soul" is but an "earthly guest," *Adonais*, 153), however unindividuated, but also to construct a coherent poetics. For although the transcendent One is postulated in the structure of Shelley's reality, it is not, the commentators notwithstanding, an operative factor in the poetics of the *Defence*. The inconsistency charged against Shelley for constructing a poetics of creative self-expression out of a faculty psychology and yet maintaining faith in a transcendent Plotinian One that is the model for all imitations is in fact nonexistent, since he has located the form-revealing power within the individual human spirit and at the core of its concentric faculties, the senses, appetites, affections, intellect, and imagination (124).[5] Each mind is essentially an equivalent particle of the One Power, and since, Shelley holds, all minds perform according to the same laws, the mind of the "creator"— that is, the poet[6]—"is itself the image of all other minds" (115). And the poet "participates in the eternal, the infinite, and the one" (112), not because he is transported to or inspired by the transcendent, but because his spirit is a portion of it. Consequently, although the *Defence* speaks of inspiration, it is to be understood as a metaphor for "instinct and intuition," as Shelley calls it on one occasion (136), rather than as the inspiration from without of which the *Ion* speaks. Even in his translation of the *Ion* Shelley attempted intermittently to transform the Platonic doctrine into the more manageable idea of intuition: "by divine influence" (θείᾳ δυνάμει), for example, becomes "from the impulse of the divinity within them [poets]."[7] Correspondingly, in the *Defence* Shelley writes that poetry redeems from decay the visitations of "the divinity *in* Man" (137); that poetry is stamped "with the image of the divinity *in* man" (119); that the evanescent revelations are only "as it were the interpenetration of a diviner nature through our own" (136); that the power which awakens the mind to transitory illuminations arises "from within" (135); and that poets are "compelled to serve the Power which is seated upon the throne of their own soul" (140).

When Shelley elsewhere describes the transcendent Power he conceives of it as "creative" in the restricted sense of a Demiurge compelling what exists into the most nearly perfect form possible, the perfect unitary Power being its own model. Its plastic stress compels "All new successions to the forms they wear;/Torturing th'unwilling dross that checks its flight/To its own likeness" (*Adonais*, 381–5). The word "God" Shelley interpreted as "the Power which models, as they pass, all the elements of this mixed universe to the purest and most perfect shape which it belongs to their nature to assume."[8] Analogously, since the mind possesses a particle of the Power, this divinity within man sporadically "inspires" the imagination with momentary apprehension of the one ideal form; and the imagination, acting as a plastic stress, drives the thoughts within the mind into organic order according to the mind's inherent principles of integration. The immediate result is an integral thought "containing within itself the principle of its own integrity" (109) and synthesized of component thoughts by the organizing imagination, which takes its model from the absolute oneness suddenly flaring within it, just as a "fading coal" flares into brilliance through the "invisible influence" of an inconstant wind, or, better, as color, evolving "from within," suffuses a flower and then fades simultaneously with the flower's growth and decay (135). Everyone, by definition, possesses the source of such an inward experience, and in Shelley's terminology everyone is a poet in the widest sense whenever such an experience occurs through an "excess" of the intuition of the perfect form, independently of expression and regardless of the nature of the thoughts so organized. Manifest poetry, as distinct from poetic conception, is "the expression of the imagination" (109); but between conception and expression must fall the shadow of the mortal condition.

If this has been an accurate account of Shelley's premises, they obviously constitute so idiosyncratic a form of Platonism that to refer the *Defence* to Platonism or any of its orthodox variants for clarification can result only in distortion.

II

For the moment it is essential to note that for Shelley the imagination is entirely an organizing principle and nothing else, and that his poetics everywhere resolves itself into the problems and consequences of integral form: the recurrent key words of the *Defence* are "order," "combination," "arrangement," "relation," "harmony," and "rhythm," or order in a temporal sequence. The essence of the poetic conception is that it is a whole, not by virtue of some *a priori* formula on whose validity it must depend or of some transcendent form which it imitates, but because, under the compulsion of the plastic stress, it is "consistent with itself,"[9] contains "within itself the principle of its own integrity" (109), and therefore is self-sustaining. Being self-contained, "time and place and number" are irrelevant to it, and hence, like the poet, it "participates in the eternal, the infinite, and the one" (112). Thus in the verbal expression of the conceived unity the "grammatical forms which express the moods of time, and the difference of persons, and the distinction of place" (112), although imposed by human limitations and the nature of language, are not limiting: other tenses, persons, and places may be substituted without affecting the integrity and universal relevance of the poem. Any diminution of this universality is also a breach in the formal integrity; for a mere "story," an inorganic "catalogue of detached facts, which have no other bond of connexion than time, place, circumstance, cause and effect," is a "mirror which obscures and distorts that which should be beautiful" (115), whereas a "poem," the union of whose elements is not dependent upon these merely discursive relationships, transforms such distortions into an eternal and universal form by mirroring them as a "beautiful" unity. Since Shelley, like Hume, consistently defined cause-and-effect as only "a constant conjunction of events" (119), it belongs with the other transient, limiting, and inorganic connectives. On the contrary, the principles creative of organic wholeness are the associative laws of "equality, diversity,[10] unity,[11] contrast, mutual dependence" (110), which, by interweaving elemental thoughts, annihilate time, space, and circumstance, and organize groups of thoughts into a single thought, a self-sustaining approximation of the intuited perfect unity. True poetic expression therefore "defeats the curse which binds us to be subjected to the accident of surrounding impressions" (137) by creating a cosmos in which everything is integral and integrated, relevant and interrelated, a "being within our being" (137). The temporal world outside poetry is experienced as "tumult" (121), "chaos" (126, 137), and "anarchy" (125), and the thoughts of men are to the imagination as "bewildered armies" to their commanding general (125). Since a poem, by virtue of form, is universal and eternal, time "for ever develops new and wonderful applications of the eternal truth which it contains" (115). And since its universality contains all potentials, it is inexhaustible to interpretation and application: "Veil after veil may be undrawn, and the inmost naked beauty of the meaning never exposed . . . and after one person and one age has exhausted all its divine effluence which their peculiar relations enable them to share, another and yet another succeeds, and new relations are ever developed . . ." (131).

But one might counter Shelley's claim for universality by insisting on the poem's necessary ties to a particular time and culture: surely the materials, customs, beliefs, and ideals incorporated in and expressed by a work of art are temporal and local. Shelley assents but denies that these constitute part of the definition of a poem or significantly limit it as poetry. Every poet is confined to his own time, place, and culture and to their inherent imperfections, everything in the mutable and "seeming" world being necessarily imperfect and transient; and these are the materials with which he is constrained to realize his intuition of the One. But the organic form which these transient views and circumstantial materials embody in poetry is outside time and flux, so that its "eternal proportions" are evident through its "temporary dress" (117), its "thin disguise of circumstance" (121). Not that Shelley is divorcing eternal poetic form from transitory content, however much he may be distinguishing them: the form "communicates" itself to the "accidental vesture," which in turn reveals the hidden form by the "manner in which it is worn" (117). Moreover, although *sub specie aeternitatis* (which is the ideal vision of poetry) the temporal materials are a clog that poetry must subdue to its own ends, it is crucial to the immediate culture that "eternal proportions" be imparted to materials bearing particularly on the contemporary "condition"; and the Romans, for example, were wrong to separate their life from their poetry by creating general art bearing only on "the universal constitution of the world" (125). Although poetry *qua* poetry is eternally relevant, it must be continuously re-created in man's successive transient conditions; it must not only be "produced" but also "sustained," for the poet "participates in the divine nature as regards providence, no less than as regards creation" (123).

Yet the fact remains that a poem is seemingly flawed in its universality by being tied to imperfect transitory conditions and values for its materials, however necessary that may be to the perfecting of the contemporary culture. Shelley's reply is to admit that the revenge motif in Homer, for example, is the mistaken ideal of a semi-barbarous age, but to insist that this vice of disharmony only gave temporal clothing to the "eternal proportions," or ideal relations, that Homer shaped as "the truth and beauty of friendship, patriotism, and persevering devotion to an object" (116). Homer's works are poems and therefore are eternal and universally relevant by virtue of their formal approximation to the intuited One, their aspiration to the order in which thoughts *should* be interwoven, not by virtue of their accidental stuff. Shelley therefore has freed himself from the trap of those who would include in critical evaluation the ethical status of the materials (the "accidental vesture") or the poet's moral judgments or his overt theme, all of which belong to discourse, not poetry: a poem should not mean, but be. Indeed, although it is frequently claimed that by identifying the One with not only the Beautiful, but also the True and the Good, Shelley has confused aesthetic with moral and ontological judgments, he has in fact freed his poetics of what we usually mean by moral judgments, since the Beautiful, the True, and the Good are only perceptions of the One in different limited perspectives; criticism in any of these contexts is only a biased consideration of the same form. Therefore any specific ethical theme, being limited to time, place, and circumstance, is a blemish and a misapplication of poetry. Men like Camillus and Regulus, Shelley claims, did not act from specific ideas of right and wrong; their imagination, beholding the beauty of such a "rhythm and order" of action, "created it out of itself according to its own idea" (125) for the sake of expressing that formal "beauty." Correspondingly, instead of dictating necessarily temporary ethical doctrines, what a poem truly expresses and communicates to the reader's imagination is its "eternal proportions," that eternal harmony which is virtue or beauty or truth, depending on the perspective in which it is considered, but which in itself is only perfect form.

However occult Shelley's definition of the poet as prophet may appear, it also is rendered intelligible by his conception of the universality and atemporality of poetry. Above all, Shelley specifically denies that the poet has any mystical gift for foretelling events. What he does say is that the poet "beholds the future in the present" (112)[12] and in that sense mirrors "the gigantic shadows which futurity casts upon the present" (140): confined to the present for his materials the poet, as "legislator," compels them into conformity with the "laws" according to which they "ought to be ordered" (112), those "eternal proportions" which prophetically include futurity. Thus "prophet" is but the temporal term for "legislator"; the poet does not combine these characters, he "unites" them (112). Because the poet apprehends the eternal order—the order that ought to be,—when he clothes this extra-temporal vision with time he not only beholds the present ideally ordered but apprehends the "spirit"[13] of futurity in it, not in addition to it. Hence the paradoxical metaphor which makes the poet's thoughts "the germs of the flower and the fruit of the latest time" (112): being eternal, they are both that out of which temporal events are spun and that in which all temporal events culminate.[14] Shelley is able to write that prophecy is "an attribute of poetry" (112) because futurity is present in eternity; as he immediately adds, time is in fact non-existent with respect to the poet's conceptions.

III

The mind, then, has an impulse to unity; and it is in part because Shelley conceives of the unity of the work of art as organic that he must attribute this impulse to a divine power within the mind acting intermittently and independently of will and consciousness. Willfully motivated and consciously controlled acts,

Shelley assumes, can be only aggregative, sequential; they can, he says, produce logic, not poetry (138), a mosaic, not a painting (136). For if a work of art contains within itself the principle whereby it is one whole, it is not a mechanical assembly of discrete finished parts, but is of the order of an organism: translation cannot produce poetry because the "plant must spring again from its seed" (114), and "a great statue or picture grows under the power of the artist as a child in the mother's womb" (136). Since a poem evolves biologically out of its indwelling genetic principle, instead of being an inert mechanical arrangement of parts, in so far as it is poetry it is not a successive accumulation of units according to a conscious external plan nor the result of a series of decisions, but an embryonic growth at all points to its organic wholeness. Therefore not only must the apprehension of the One arise within the mind outside the will and consciousness, but composition must take place under the same circumstances, the fading insight into the One and the desire to retain it operating as the compelling motive that everywhere draws the component thoughts to their perfect form; just as the sculptor does not assemble finished segments to form a statue, but instinctively and intuitively causes it to grow through various embryonic stages toward its final shape without being able to account consciously for the intent of any of his steps or for the nature of the over-all process. As Shelley insists, awareness and the will are not "the necessary conditions of all mental causation" (139); and, without denying that organic order is mentally caused, he finds them incapable of producing it. Possibly no other critical theorist has made holistic form so central to his definition of poetry or has given it such inclusive value.

To reverse the coin and consider the same problem from the point of view of critical norms: by attributing to the divinity within the mind the impulse to organic unity Shelley has transferred to theology the insoluble ultimate problem of aesthetics. Without that theology Shelley's argument would run as follows in its simplest terms: since we do, with considerable agreement, experience the greatness of a work of art and since its being a work of art is its having integral form, the minds of men must have an inward apprehension of the ideal form that all poetry aspires to. If the essential criterion of a work of art is its organic wholeness, the palpable facts are that poetics itself cannot account for our desire to experience and create organic wholeness and that although we find one unexceptionable work of art greater than another, poetics alone cannot account for the difference. We may point to the internal interrelationships; but there can be no demonstrable formula for determining that a group of thoughts has been so arranged and combined that they constitute one thought containing its own integrative principle. And if there were, we would still lack a yardstick for valuing one integral unity above another. The problem remains with us and continues to beset those critics for whom organic unity—or paradox or texture or the Coleridgean omnibus of relations—is both the definition and criterion of poetry. How does one measure the complexity of interrelations? At what point of integrity does the *claritas* shine through? Or at what point does the full potential of the materials get realized? Even if we find the answer on psychological grounds, we have to assume an intuitive and ineffable constant in man. Hence the normative role of the random apprehensions of the ideal unity which Shelley defines as "the visitations of the divinity in man." Although man cannot will such visitations or define their pure revelations, the mind can and does experience such moments; and Shelley is attempting to account for the fact. If it seems objectionable that he has abandoned poetics to the mystery of religion, it would be more accurate to say that he has identified religion with the mysteries of poetry.[15] It is the very identification of poetic conception with the divinity in man that allows Shelley to set off poetry as a unique human act, for if poetic conception is the apprehension of the perfect form and if that perfect form is the character of the divine, then to claim that man continuously apprehends or has access to it would be to claim that he is perfect and free from mutability. The presence of a capacity to apprehend ideal form accounts for man's potential; the intermittence of this apprehension is accounted for by his earthly limitations and locates the special significance and overriding relevance of poetry.

Shelley does not, however, claim that the mind lacks the principles of form unless it is "inspired." The imagination, or synthesizing power, is innate and naturally seeks to organize the mind's data. Although true poetic conception occurs only in the extraordinary moments when some invisible and unexplainable influence from within enflames the "fading coal" of the mind, the coal is a continuously burning spark. The power behind this spark is the portion of "divinity" continuously present to the synthesizing imagination so that even in his ordinary activities man may give to his otherwise chaotic or, at any rate, discursive experiences a degree of self-containing form. There is no conflict, then, between Shelley's doctrine of extraordinary "inspiration" and his postulating a natural formal principle within the human being which, instead of merely experiencing the melodic succession of impressions, creates a harmonic organization by an "internal adjustment" (109) of the media of expression to the impressions which excite the expressions. In this sense the child at play is a rudimentary poet when it expresses with sound and gesture its delight in impressions, the sounds and gestures being internally adjusted to bear a harmonic proportion to the pleasurable impressions (110); and language itself is poetry since, being metaphoric, it marks relationships and is created by the normal synthesizing principles of the mind without benefit of the extraordinary apprehension of absolute form (111–12). Indeed, Shelley provides a variety of natural grounds for the synthesizing capacity. Not only are some men, being more sensitive and delicately "organized," more susceptible to the intuition of the absolute unitary form, but the frequent recurrence of this apprehension may produce a natural "habit of order and harmony" (139). Experience with poetic expression "enlarges the circumference of the imagination" and strengthens it "in the same manner as exercise strengthens a limb" (118). And at the lowest level one may simply impose upon his expressions the traditional forms of harmony (114). But poetry in its true sense requires the flaming coal, not the glowing spark; an apprehension of absolute and unitary form, not merely a harmonizing power, however strengthened or artificially aided. Shelley's theory of the nature and informative sources of the imagination provides for both a synthesizing act in normal mental life and an extraordinary access to the oneness which is the criterion and motive for all forms; but the difference between the spark and the glowing coal is so great that the two states are different in kind rather than in degree. In the intervals between "inspiration" the poet "becomes a man, and is abandoned to the sudden reflux of the influences under which others habitually live" (139).

IV

Before proceeding, it is necessary to face the supposed contradiction in Shelley's defining poetry variously as expression (of imagination, of emotions, and of "the influence of society or nature" on the mind) and as imitation (of life and of the world).[16] Above all, it is clear that, in speaking of the child and the savage as expressing emotions, Shelley is not proposing anything so naïve as Blair's theory that poetry is strong passions flowing out as emotive language or that the fundamental purpose of poetry is to communicate feeling. The most rudimentary and primitive cause for imitating or expressing impressions, Shelley is saying, is the pleasure they have imparted and the consequent desire to prolong it; and only in this sense of cause and manifestation can poetry be considered merely an "expression" of the emotions: the child expresses itself because it is delighted by the impressions, and the expression gives evidence of that delight. Moreover, even here Shelley has not confined himself to the concept of "expression": the child's expression of its delight is the "reflected image," that is, imitation, of its pleasurable impressions (110). Even though Shelley then adds that the savage "expresses the emotions produced in him by surrounding objects," he is speaking of emotion as the dominant motive and as but one of the elements of the consequent expression; for he then defines the expression as the reflection or "image of the combined effect of those objects, *and of his apprehension of them*" (110), and not merely of his emotional responses. Under any condition, in context the main purpose of these passages is to prepare for the statement that the mind, having colored its impressions "with its own light," adjusts them to form a harmony by the order in which it apprehends them, which is different from the random order in which they are received by the senses (110). This is not to say that poetry does *not* express emotions: society produces a class of emotions, Shelley writes, in addition to those produced by nature, and hence "an augmented treasure of expressions" (110). But poetry expresses all the contents of the mind: emotions, thoughts, however produced, and the associative laws of the imagination. Even ideal poetry, which is Shelley's central concern, can be spoken of as an "expression" of delight; for man, in the fullest development of his nature, receives the purest and most intense delight from the highest degree of form (116). To him not only "beauty in art" but even "pleasure in sensation" is constituted by the internal relations of "equality, diversity, unity, contrast, mutual dependence" because the most intense and purest pleasure is inextricably bound up with the experience of the absolute order which it is the purpose of the highest poetry to approximate (110, 111).

Indeed, "imitation" and "expression," however central, as Meyer Abrams has made clear they are, to the development of eighteenth-century aesthetics, are inadequate terminological instruments for analysing Shelley's poetics and only confuse the issue by oversimplifying it and by superimposing on his poetics alien systems and expectations. Because the terms describe only partial supplementary phases of his poetics he uses them almost indiscriminately. For example, he can say that a poem is an imitation, a "very image" of life, but it is that image *"expressed* in its eternal truth," that is, given the form that approximates the "unchangeable" form existing in the poet's mind (115). Poetry represents, it is true, but it "reproduces all that it represents" (117)[17] by reorganizing and combining thoughts in a beautiful and indestructible order instead of following the accidental sequence of impressions. Briefly, although poetry *imitates* external impressions and *expresses* the emotions and "internal impressions" (109), it is not poetry by virtue of these acts, which merely account for the relation of poetic matter to its sources. Consequently Shelley's poetics does not resolve itself into a theory of imitation or a psychology of expression, for poetry is the imparting of an "indestructible order" to thoughts, whether externally or internally produced and however "colored" by such mental attributes as the emotions.

On the other hand, the ground for such orderings of thoughts is the fact that "things" do have inherent and non-contingent relations because "nature"—the one plastic stress or power, of which each individual human spirit is a derivative particle—impresses the same footsteps "upon the various subjects of the world" (111), that is, compels everything towards its own likeness.[18] Conse-

quently it is consistent with Shelley's ontology that he can conceive
of the poetic act indifferently as either a creation of ideal order or a
kind of discovery of it; because the order created by the mind is the
order that truly subsists in reality beneath the veil of appearance
and mutability, these are only different ways of describing the
same creative—not mimetic—act of the mind. By creating the ideal
organization the mind can "see" the order beneath the apparent
reality. Poetic language, for example, is a creation of the imagination, and yet it "marks the before unapprehended relations of
things" (111); poetry transmutes forms into incarnations of its
spirit, and yet it reveals the spirit within nature's forms (137). And
it is a matter of indifference whether poetry is defined as spreading
over the apparent world "its own figured curtain" fashioned by the
mind's internal apprehension of form or as withdrawing "life's
dark veil from before the scene of things" (137) to reveal the hidden
order pressed on the world by the One. The superficial "familiar
world" (137), which exists in our mere random impressions, is a
chaos; and since the mind possesses a particle of that plastic stress
which organizes the true world, it is only a shift of perspective, not
of aesthetic premises, to say on the one hand that the imagination
purges "the film of familiarity" and "strips the veil of familiarity
from the world and lays bare the naked and sleeping beauty"
(137)[19] or on the other that it "reproduces," that is, reconstitutes or
"creates anew the universe, after it has been annihilated in our
minds by the recurrence of impressions blunted by reiteration"
(137), just as language must be reconstituted when the integral
relations it designates are lost through familiarity and it has become signs of atomistic "portions or classes of thought" (111). To
demand that Shelley choose between a mimetic and an expressive
theory is to misunderstand not only his poetics but also the ontology and metaphysics in which it is grounded.

V

The integral thought synthesized of thoughts into a formal approximation of the fleeting vision of the One can be expressed, in
accordance with the laws of the mind, upon various media to become palpable poetry, whether the media are words, matter, sound,
color, gestures, or personal and social conduct. But although Shelley

postulates a unitary—and therefore unobtainable—formal ideal for all poetry, he does not, as the objection generally runs, dissolve all verbal poems into one and destroy the distinctions among genres, among poems, or among the parts of a poem. The One is, of course, ineffable, not only because the human intuition of it is transient, but because it is pure form by virtue of being indivisibly one; and the human mind must work with multiplicity.[20] But Shelley is careful to distinguish between poetry as conception and as expression, and the expression of the synthesized thought can be analysed in terms of the integrative laws of the imagination, the kinds of thoughts synthesized, the degree of synthesis, the nature of the various media, and the degree and kind of pleasure the poem produces. In brief, he has provided instruments for poetic analysis. All expression is "subject to the laws of that from which it pro-ceeds" (110), and it is clear that by "laws" are meant the integrative principles of association.[21] Although Shelley aspires, as his *Epipsychidion* testifies, to embody the ineffable One, which is all thought in indivisible unitary form, the human mind "cannot be considered pure," and diversity is essential to its existence. But the imagination is governed by certain laws—equality, diversity, unity, contrast, mutual dependence—whereby, under the impulse of the intuited oneness, it integrates the necessary diversity of the mind's thoughts into an approximation of the One. "The most astonishing combinations of poetry, the subtlest deductions of logic and mathe-matics, are no other than combinations which the intellect makes of sensations according to its own laws."[22] There is, then, no inconsistency between Shelley's so-called "Platonism" and an associational psychology; they complement each other to compose a coherent system.

Moreover, just as the one Spirit's plastic stress can compel each mass to only that degree of form which its limited nature permits, so each class of expression (or mimetic representation), such as dance, music, and verbal poetry, has its own peculiar supreme order or rhythm. In Aristotelian terms, each mode has its highest poten-tial which the artist attempts to actualize; in Platonic terms, the eternal idea is diminished in proportion to the limitations inherent in the medium or mode of expression. Each mode aspires to a special kind of ideal configuration, the criterion of which is the degree of pure, or disinterested, pleasure imparted by that form; and the faculty which judges the degree to which the formal pleasure afforded by a work of art approximates the intuitively apprehended highest pleasure of which its mode is capable as form is called "taste" (111), that is, the "inspired" imagination operating as a critical instead of creative faculty. Each mode of expression is directed and limited by the "materials, instruments, and conditions" of its medium, for these "have relations among each other, which limit and interpose between conception and expression" (113). Colors, like marble or sound, for example, have inherent intra-relations which must be satisfied regardless of the highest order to which they are compelled, and the criterion of excellence is the degree to which these intra-relations of the materials have been exploited or overcome. Language, therefore, is the supreme material of expression because, being "arbitrarily produced by the imagination," it has "relation to thought alone" and therefore is "more plastic" (113) than other materials and less resistant to the impress of the imagination. But sound inheres in language (the imagination, in forming language, presumably having chosen those sounds bearing true relation to what they represent), and since sounds "have relation both between each other and towards that which they represent" (114), verbal poetry requires not only an ideal integration of thoughts, but, organically integrated with it, both the harmony of sounds as sounds and the harmonic relation of these sounds to the thoughts.

Correspondingly, Shelley's poetics implies that every literary genre, tragedy, epic, comedy, and lyric, each being distinguished by the kind of thoughts it employs, has its own special harmony, and that they form a hierarchy of approximations to the ideal unitary order. Consequently the "most perfect and universal form" (120), drama, was the supreme mode when it once employed not only language and action, but also music, painting, dance, and religious institutions, each of these kinds of expression being developed to its own highest order and all of them organized "into a beautiful proportion and unity one towards another" (119). In brief, the goal Shelley obviously had set himself in *Prometheus Unbound*. Such a harmonious fusion of individual harmonies transcends the simpler order of the drama of action and language and, by permitting more complex synthesis, approaches more closely the ideal form revealed to the imagination. For the same reason, the harmonizing of comedy with tragedy is greater than either of the component genres. In the farthest extension of this concept of infinite harmonies of harmonies reaching more closely to the One, Shelley considers all poems "episodes to that great poem, which all poets, like the co-operating thoughts of one great mind, have built up since the beginning of the world" (124).

However, Shelley's exalted conception of the nature and role of poetry involves him in difficulty with some aspects of tragedy and some kinds of comedy. Since poetry should produce "pleasure in its highest sense" (132), which derives from the highest formal approximation to the One, he remains baffled by the fact that "sorrow, terror, anguish, despair," instead of love, friendship, admiration of nature, and the perception of poetry, "are often the chosen expressions of an approximation to the highest good" (133). The paradox has been a familiar and fertile one in critical theory, but Shelley's premises force him into the unsatisfactory conclusion that an "inexplicable defect of harmony in the constitution of human nature" connects the pain of our affections with intellectual pleasure (132–3). In other words, he resolves the problem as he does that of the transitory and imperfect materials shaped by poetry into eternal form: the sources of tragic pleasure, like vicious temporary ideals, are indigenous to the imperfection of the mortal condition, but, shaped by the imagination, they can express "that ideal perfection and energy which every one feels to be the internal type of all that he loves, admires, and would become" (121). But Shelley is clearly not in control of his argument, and he lays over this explanation not only the principle of tragic catharsis but also his own doctrine of Necessity to claim that in tragedy "crime is disarmed of half its horror and all its contagion by being represented as the fatal consequence of the unfathomable agencies of nature; error is thus divested of its wilfulness; men can no longer cherish it as the creation of their choice" (121). Here Shelley seems merely to be explaining tragedy away by recourse to the Necessitarianism which denies free will and explains actions as the inexorable fulfillment of the strongest motives. On the other hand, he is consistent with his literary premises in placing outside the limits of poetry that comedy which causes laughter from "self-complacency" (122); in Shelley's terms it is anti-poetry since, instead of fashioning a harmony that will evoke "sympathetic merriment," it distorts in order that through laughter we may congratulate ourselves for avoiding such ugliness. The end of such comedy is not that we may sympathetically identify ourselves with it, but that we may complacently claim to have repudiated it.

Shelley's doctrines preclude the possibility that verbal poetry exists for the willful purpose of communication. Denied the purpose of communicating explicit ethical ideals, the poem attains its final cause, although not its final effect, simply by coming into existence; and the poetic transaction involves only the poet and his poem, not an audience. The unwilled and unconsciously motivated process of expression is compelled only by the poet's desire to prolong his apprehension of the One, to sustain the pure delight in the organically rhythmic or integrated form generated among a group of thoughts. He is therefore a nightingale that "sings to cheer its own solitude with sweet sounds" (116). Yet of course the audience that overhears the song is significantly affected as a consequence of experiencing approximations of the ideal order, and the ultimate effect of the poem is endless. Shelley explains this effect of the poem in terms of sympathy, but there are no grounds for the occasional complaint that he thereby superimposes incoherently upon his conception of the organizing imagination the unrelated concept of the sympathetic imagination.[23] Although Shelley's predecessors and contemporaries did customarily assign to the imagination the power to identify oneself with others, Shelley obviously did not, but made it an aspect of love. Hence the "great instrument of moral good is the imagination" (118), not because it is the faculty of sympathy, but because it creates the beautiful; and the beautiful awakens the observer's sympathetic love. It is love, not the imagination, that Shelley explicitly defines as the "going out of our own nature, and an identification of ourselves with the beautiful which exists in thought, action, or person, not our own" (118). The ultimate effect of poetry therefore is the moral good of the observer because by his sympathetically identifying himself with the beautiful his own imagination attains an approximation of the ideal order and assimilates all other thoughts to that order, out of which the good arises.

VI

In 1830, eight years after Shelley's death, there appeared in the *New Monthly Magazine and Literary Journal* an account of a conversation reported to have taken place, presumably in 1822, between Shelley and Byron on the literary merits of *Hamlet*. Although the contributor did not identify himself or explain how he had managed to record the dialogue, the external and internal evidence make it difficult not to believe that in some fashion it is authentic, if indeed it had not been written by Shelley himself.[24]

The *Defence of Poetry* is not intended, of course, as a treatise in practical criticism, even though one can discern in it detailed implications of criteria, categories, and procedures for critical analysis. As a defense, it is concerned with the synthesizing imagination, not the analytic reason, which "regards the relations of things, simply as relations; considering thoughts, not in their integral unity, but as the algebraical representations which conduct to certain general results" (109). But the analysis of *Hamlet* is explicitly centered in the reason, since all the relationships in a work of art, it asserts, "depend" upon this relation-perceiving faculty and in it "live and move, and have their being."[25] Assuming that the dialogue is authentic, it permits insight into how, by substituting reason for imagination, Shelley can transform the principles of the *Defence* into practical criticism.

Although fascinated by Hamlet and self-involved, the Byron of the dialogue is depressed by the aimlessness of life that he understands the play to express through the inconsistency and futility of the characters and their actions. He can only conclude that Shakespeare was an "uncultivated genius" uttering "wild rhapsodies" and incapable of "consistency or art" (423). This view would seem to correspond to Shelley's doctrine of the inspired poet whose creative acts are not motivated by consciousness or the will. But we have seen that the doctrine, far from implying randomness and disorder, is grounded in the assumption of a compelling absolute order and finds the intelligible ordering process of expression in the relational laws of the mind. Consequently Shelley can mock Byron with a doctrine that seems drawn directly from the *Defence*: "Are you then so orthodox in any thing as to think Shakespeare a man of no art or thought—a prophet of poetry, possessed by a spirit unintelligible to himself?" (423). For his purpose is to assert both "inspiration" and analysable art which is not conscious calculation and contrivance, but the consequence of the principles of the mind and the nature and requirements of the medium. Defining "art" as whatever it is that makes a work "good," he analyses a passage of the play for its richly interactive and unified complexity, adding, "I don't say that a poet must necessarily be conscious of all this, no more than a lady is conscious of every graceful movement" (425). The motive for the creative act and for the stages of the process lies outside the will and consciousness, but the process is nevertheless mental and therefore entails art as Shelley has defined it. Even though the poet is not conscious of the motives and functions of each of his synthesizing acts, nevertheless, Shelley insists, "they all depend upon reason" (425), the faculty which perceives relations as relations and not the integral unity. The function of the critic is to employ the analytic reason to discover relevance and relationship and bring them out "into the light of distinct consciousness" (425).

It is precisely his failure to perceive such relationships that disturbs aesthetically and morally the Byron of the dialogue: the plot is stagnant, and everything is episodic, functionless; Fortinbras, Ophelia, and Polonius do not "conduce to the main of the story"; and mob-pleasing Shakespeare, "of great genius but no art," merely threw together incoherently *"quantum suff.* of courtiers, players, grave-diggers, clowns, and such like stuff" (423). Committed to organic unity as the poetic criterion and insisting that the extra-conscious imaginative synthesis depends upon "art" and therefore is susceptible to analysis by the reason, Shelley answers by unfolding the unity of the line, "How sweet the moonlight sleeps upon this bank." The analysis is a practical application of the theory in the *Defence* of the harmonic interrelation of the complex harmonies of thought and of verbal sounds: "Sounds as well as thoughts have relation both between each other and towards that which they represent, and a perception of the order of those relations has always been found connected with a perception of the order of those relations of thoughts" (114). Because his explication adumbrates the analytic techniques Shelley would apply to a poem as a whole, it deserves full quotation:

Is not a line, as well as your outspread heroics, or a tragedy, a whole, and only as a whole, beautiful in itself? . . . we perceive that all the parts are formed in relation to one another, and that it is consequently a whole. "Sleep," we see, is a reduplication of the pure and gentle sound of sweet; and as the beginning of the former symphonizes with the beginning *s* of the latter, so the *l* in moonlight prepares one for the *l* in sleep, and glides gently into it; and in the conclusion, one may perceive that the word "bank" is determined by the preceding words, and that the *b* which it begins with is but a deeper intonation of the two p's which come before it; sleeps upon this slope, would have been effeminate; sleeps upon this rise, would have been harsh and inharmonious . . . [The metaphor of the sleeping moonlight] also is very beautiful. In every single line, the poet must organize many simultaneous operations, both the meaning of the words and their emphatic arrangement, and then the flow and melting together of their symphony; and the whole must also be united with the current of the rhyme. . . . To represent the tranquility of moonlight is the object of the line; and the sleep is beautiful, because it gives a more intense and living form of the same idea; the rhyme beautifully falls in with this, and just lets the cadence of the emphasis dwell upon the sound and sense of the sweet word "sleep"; and the alliteration assimilates the rest of the line into one harmonious symmetry. This line, therefore, is it not altogether a work of art? (424–5)

Applying these procedures loosely to *Hamlet* as a whole, Shelley seeks the internal organizing principle in terms of which "the whole would appear a beautiful whole," for if *Hamlet* is one of Shakespeare's most famous plays (the poet's jury, Shelley had written in the *Defence*, "must be impanneled by Time from the selectest of the wise of many generations," 116), then he was "probably not so blind"—that is, artless—as Byron would make him (426). This integrative principle Shelley finds in Hamlet as the embodiment of the "contemplative and ideal" mind's tragically solipsistic tendency to translate the outward world into thought and thus to be paralyzed. The nature of tragedy still disturbs Shelley's definition of poetry as aspiring to perfect form and therefore to perfect beauty, truth, and goodness; and he here offers yet another rationale: "since the mind's eye is so dull and blinded . . . as not by intuition to recognise the beauty of virtue," tragedy reveals it by displaying its contrary, just as "there is but one

demonstration of the excellence of health, and that is disease"
(426). Nevertheless, as poetry tragedy displays the contrary of the
beauty of virtue by being a "beautiful whole," and Shelley sets out
to explain the functional relevance or functional antithesis of
many of the events and characters to the organizing principle of the
play. As an extreme instance of this functional analysis Shelley's
explanation of Hamlet's verses after the mousetrap episode merits
mention:

> For thou dost know, O Damon dear,
>   This realm dismantled was
> Of Jove himself; and now reigns here,
>   A very, very—pajock.

"You might have rhymed," says Horatio. But in his paralysis,
Shelley explains, Hamlet "recoils and swerves from action; and it
is an instinctive feeling of this sort that makes him impatient even
of the necessities of versification,—any thing necessary he feels a
disposition to resist or avoid . . . there is the same lame and impotent conclusion in every thing he does" (430). Having hurriedly
indicated in this fashion the functional relevance of a series of such
elements, Shelley concludes with words that echo the *Defence* on
the self-sustaining integrity effected by the mind's synthesizing
principles: *Hamlet* "is, in itself, a complete and reasonable whole,
composed in a harmonious proportion of difference and similitude,
into one expressive unity" (432).

NOTES

1. "The Zucca," 26–9.

2. Bodleian MS. Shelley adds. e. 19, pp. 4–5 (reproduced in *Verse and Prose
from the Manuscripts of Percy Bysshe Shelley*, ed. Shelley-Rolls and Ingpen,
London, 1934, pp. 17–18).

3. Ibid. 6.

4. Ibid.

5. All references to the *Defence of Poetry* are to *The Complete Works of P. B.
Shelley*, ed. R. Ingpen and W. E. Peck, vol. VII (hereafter referred to as Julian ed.).

6. Not, as many commentators have thought, God the Creator. Shelley consistently denied a Creator God in the sense of creation *ex nihilo* and insisted that the universe is eternal and without origin. In his vocabulary "create" means "organize," and although in Shelley's inclusive system the organizing act of the poet is identical in kind with the shaping stress of the One Spirit on the universe, the *Defence* makes it unnecessary that the former be referred to the latter as a model. There is a source within the mind that reveals to the organizing, or "creative," imagination the one "indestructible order" (112), or "eternal proportions" (117), without any necessary reference to the organization to which nature is being compelled by the One; and the universal consent given to expressions of this indestructible order results, not from the fact that poetry repeats or imitates the primal act of creation by a Creator God, but from the fact that the poet's mind is the "image of all other minds."

7. Julian ed., VII. 239. "Inspired and possessed" (ἔνθεοι ὄντες καὶ κατεχόμενοι) is altered to "in a state of inspiration, and, as it were, possessed by a spirit not their own" (p. 238); and "inspired and put out of his senses" (ἔνθεος . . . καὶ ἔκφρων), to "inspired, and, as it were, mad" (p. 238).

8. Julian ed., VI. 235.

9. Ibid. VII. 225.

10. Not to be confused with inequality, Shelley points out (129).

11. In Bod. MS. adds. d. 1 Shelley wrote, more suggestively, "flowing together" before substituting "unity."

12. Bod. MS. Shelley adds. d. 1 reads: "he beholds the future ⟨& the past⟩ in the present."

13. Shelley repeatedly identifies "spirit" with the "eternal proportions," or "indestructible order," that can be infused by the imagination in things or events. The poet-prophet foretells the "spirit" of events, not their "forms" (112); harmony is the "spirit" of the traditional "forms" of metre (114); and poetry lays bare the beauty of nature, which is the "spirit of its forms" (137).

14. Cp. *Prometheus Unbound*, I, 690–91, etc.: "the prophecy/Which begins and ends in thee [i.e., Prometheus]." Being eternal, Prometheus is, with respect to time, both efficient and final cause.

15. Cp. "Coleridge has said that every poet was religious, the converse, that every religious man must be a poet was more true" (Julian ed., VII. 336).

16. I find no evidence that Shelley speaks of poetry as *imitative* of the transcendent One; and certainly it is not imitative, as some commentators believe, of the Platonic Forms, Essences, or Ideas, which I do not find to enter into Shelley's thought at all. The statement that the imagination "has for its objects those forms which are common to universal nature and existence itself" (109) cannot mean, as Meyer H. Abrams believes, that the imagination "intuits" the eternal Forms (*The Mirror and the Lamp*, New York, 1953, p. 130) but merely means that the elements on which it performs its synthesizing act are common and not special. Nor does Shelley say that "poetry strips the veil

from the forms of the world" (ibid.), implying that the "objects imitated by the great poet are the eternal Forms discerned through the veil of fact and particularity" (ibid. 127). What he does write is that poetry "strips the veil of familiarity from the world, and lays bare the naked and sleeping beauty, which is the spirit of its forms" (137); that is, that it reveals (not "imitates"), beneath the interference of mutability and appearance, the one perfect harmony towards which the One Spirit's plastic stress compels all entities. See above, n. 13.

17. I.e., reconstitutes all that it imitates. Cp. the statement that poetry "reproduces the common Universe" (137), which explicates Shelley's plea for "the creative faculty to imagine that which we know" (134). "As to imitation, poetry is a mimetic art. It creates, but it creates by combination and representation. Poetical abstractions are beautiful and new, not because the portions of which they are composed had no previous existence in the mind of man or in nature, but because the whole produced by their combination has some intelligible and beautiful analogy with those sources of emotion and thought, and with the contemporary condition of them" (Pref. to *Prometheus Unbound*).

18. Bod. MS. Shelley adds. d. 1 reads: "Nor are these similitudes arbitrary and conventional: but they are the vestiges of ⟨nature⟩ power over form." In a cancelled passage in the same MS., Shelley wrote of "that analogy & even unity in all thoughts & objects of thought, the perception of which is poetry. . . ."

19. It unveils "the permanent analogy of things" (115) and "lifts the veil from the hidden beauty of the world, and makes familiar objects be as if they were not familiar" (117).

20. Although multiplicity, Shelley once wrote, is an illusion, an unreality, it is an illusion indispensable to the human condition: "diversities are events or objects, and are essential, considered relatively to human identity, for the existence of the human mind. For if the inequalities, produced by what has been termed the operations of the external universe were leveled by the perception of our being, uniting, and filling up their interstices, motion and mensuration, and time, and space; the elements of the human mind being thus abstracted, sensation and imagination cease. Mind cannot be considered pure" (Julian ed., VII. 61).

21. Bod. MS. Shelley adds. e. 8: "Association is, however, rather the law according to which this power [i.e., the imagination] is exerted than the power itself."

22. Julian ed., VII. 59.

23. M. Abrams, op. cit. pp. 130, 331.

24. In *Shelley, His Life and Work* (Boston and New York, 1927), II, 421–35, W. E. Peck reprinted the somewhat abbreviated version that appeared in *The Polar Star*, V (1830), excerpted from the *New Monthly Mazagine and Literary Journal* (not, as Peck reports, the *New Monthly and London Journal*). Peck incorrectly implies that his version is from the *New Monthly* and that the original appeared in *The Polar Star*.

The conversation, most of which takes place after dinner, is reported to have begun during a walk in the woods of the Grand Duke's palace, obviously in Pisa, where we know Byron and Shelley held frequent meetings from November 1821 to April 1822. In his *Table Talk* Samuel Rogers reported having once attended (with Trelawney, he implies) a Pisan dinner discussion of Shakespeare between Byron ("rude") and Shelley ("meek yet resolute") during which Byron, whose disapproval of Shakespeare's artistry is well known, ran down the dramatist against Shelley's defense. This precisely corresponds to the *New Monthly* dialogue, which ends with Shelley looking up, after reading aloud an earnest essay, to find Byron fast asleep.

The authors mentioned by "Shelley" in the dialogue, Spinoza, Goethe, and Schlegel, were among the poet's favorites. His misquoting a line from *The Cenci* lends a suggestion of authenticity. The quotation "dream of a shadow" comes from Pindar's Pythian odes, VIII, 95–6, which Shelley copied into one of his notebooks (Bod. MS. Shelley adds. e. 6, p. 143). The words "while he wanders in the wilderness of thought" suggest Sophocles' "Coming to many ways in the wanderings of careful thought," of which Shelley wrote, "What a picture does this line suggest of the mind as a wilderness of intricate paths" (quoted from another of Shelley's notebooks by Mary Shelley in her note on *Prometheus Unbound*).

In the dialogue Shelley's manner of questioning Byron and his dialectic procedure are often markedly Socratic; and in one of his notebooks (Bod. MS. Shelley adds. e. 8, p. 72), directly before a fragment related to the *Defence,* he began composing a similar critical dialogue on the subject of Keats's poetry. The *New Monthly* dialogue has Shelley finding in the theme of *Hamlet* a Necessitarianism that corresponds to his own. Byron's attributing to him there a belief that in the presence of "great genius" one feels "calmness and grandeur" seems to echo the statement in the *Defence* that poetry extends over all thoughts and actions a "gentle and exalted content" (117). (Bod. MS. Shelley adds. d. 1 of the *Defence* states that through the pure delight of poetry all the faculties gather "into a more calm repose.") But of course the most telling evidence of authenticity is the correspondence of the dialogue to Shelley's known critical ideas.

25. Peck, *Shelley, His Life and Work,* II, 425. All references to the dialogue will be to the text in this work.

Keats and the Embarrassments
Of Poetic Tradition

———•———

HAROLD BLOOM

ONE of the central themes in W. J. Bate's definitive *John Keats* is the "large, often paralyzing embarrassment . . . that the rich accumulation of past poetry, as the eighteenth century had seen so realistically, can curse as well as bless."[1] As Mr. Bate remarks, this embarrassment haunted Romantic and haunts post-Romantic poetry, and was felt by Keats with a particular intensity. Somewhere in the heart of each new poet there is hidden the dark wish that the libraries be burned in some new Alexandrian conflagration, that the imagination might be liberated from the greatness and oppressive power of its own dead champions.

Something of this must be involved in the Romantics' loving struggle with their ghostly father, Milton. The role of wrestling Jacob is taken on by Blake in his "brief epic" *Milton,* by Wordsworth in *The Recluse* fragment, and in more concealed form by Shelley in *Prometheus Unbound* and Keats in the first *Hyperion.* The strength of poetical life in Milton seems always to have appalled as much as it delighted; in the fearful vigor of his unmatched exuberance the English master of the sublime has threatened not only poets, but the values once held to transcend poetry:

> . . . the Argument
> Held me a while misdoubting his Intent,
> That he would ruin (for I saw him strong)
> The sacred Truths to Fable and old Song
> (So *Sampson* grop'd the Temple's Posts in spite)
> The World O'erwhelming to revenge his sight.

The older Romantics at least thought that the struggle with Milton had bestowed a blessing without a crippling; to the younger ones a consciousness of gain and loss came together. Blake's audacity gave him a Milton altogether fitted to his great need, a visionary prototype who could be dramatized as rising up, "unhappy tho' in heav'n," taking off the robe of the promise, and ungirding himself from the oath of God, and then descending into Blake's world to save the later poet and every man "from his Chain of Jealousy." Wordsworth's equal audacity allowed him, after praising Milton's invocatory power, to call on a greater Muse than Urania, to assist him in exploring regions more awful than Milton ever visited. The prophetic Spirit called down in *The Recluse* is itself a child of Milton's Spirit that preferred, before all temples, the upright and pure heart of the Protestant poet. But the child is greater than the father, and inspires, in a fine Shakespearean reminiscence:

> The human Soul of universal earth,
> Dreaming on things to come.

Out of that capable dreaming came the poetic aspirations of Shelley and of Keats, who inherited the embarrassment of Wordsworth's greatness to add to the burden of Milton's. Yielding to few in my admiration for Shelley's blank verse in *Prometheus,* I am still made uneasy by Milton's ghost hovering in it. At times Shelley's power of irony rescues him from Milton's presence by the argument's dissonance with the steady Miltonic music of the lyrical drama, but the ironies pass and the Miltonic sublime remains, testifying to the unyielding strength of an order Shelley hoped to overturn. In the lyrics of *Prometheus* Shelley is free, and they rather than the speeches foretold his own poetic future, the sequence of *The Witch of Atlas, Epipsychidion* and *Adonais.* Perhaps the turn to Dante, hinted in *Epipsychidion* and emergent in *The Triumph of Life,* was in part caused by the necessity of finding a sublime antithesis to Milton.

With Keats, we need not surmise. The poet himself claimed to have abandoned the first *Hyperion* because it was too Miltonic, and his critics have agreed in not wanting him to have made a poem "that might have been written by John Milton, but one that was unmistakably by no other than John Keats."[2] In the Great Odes and *The Fall of Hyperion* Keats was to write poems unmistakably his own, as *Endymion* in another way had been his own. Individuality of style, and still more of conception, no critic would now deny to the odes, Keats's supreme poems, or to *The Fall of Hyperion,* which was his testament, and is the work future poets may use as Tennyson, Arnold and Yeats used the odes in the past.

That Keats, in his handful of great poems, surpassed the Milton-haunted poets of the second half of the eighteenth century is obvious to a critical age like our own, which tends to prefer Keats, in those poems, to even the best work of Blake, Wordsworth and Shelley, and indeed to most if not all poetry in the language since the mid-seventeenth century. Perhaps the basis for that preference can be explored afresh through a consideration of precisely how Keats's freedom of the negative weight of poetic tradition is manifested in some of his central poems. Keats lost and gained, as each of the major Romantics did, in the struggle with the greatness of Milton. Keats was perhaps too generous and perceptive a critic, too wonderfully balanced a humanist, not to have lost some values of a cultural legacy that both stimulated and inhibited the nurture of fresh values.

Mr. Bate finely says, commenting on Keats's dedication sonnet to Leigh Hunt, that "when the imagination looks to any past, of course, including one's own individual past, it blends memories and images into a denser, more massive unit than ever existed in actuality."[3] Keats's confrontation with this idealized past is most direct from the *Ode to Psyche* on, as Mr. Bate emphasizes. Without repeating him on that ode, or what I myself have written elsewhere, I want to examine it again in the specific context of Keats's fight against the too-satisfying enrichments with which tradition threatens the poet who seeks his own self-recognition and expressive fulfillment.

Most readers recalling the *Ode to Psyche* think of the last stanza, which is the poem's glory, and indeed its sole but sufficient claim to stand near the poet's four principal odes. The stanza expresses a wary confidence that the true poet's imagination cannot be impoverished. More wonderfully, the poet ends the stanza by opening the hard-won consciousness of his own creative powers to a visitation of love. The paradise within is barely formed, but the poet does not hesitate to make it vulnerable, though he may be condemned in consequence to the fate of the famished knight of his own faery ballad. There is triumph in the closing tone of *To Psyche,* but a consciousness also I think of the danger that is being courted. The poet has given Psyche the enclosed bower nature no longer affords her, but he does not pause to be content in that poet's paradise. It is not Byzantium which Keats has built in the heretofore untrodden regions of his mind but rather a realm that is precisely not far above all breathing human passion. He has not assumed the responsibility of an expanded consciousness for the rewards of self-communing and solitary musing, in the manner of the poet-hero of *Alastor,* and of Prince Athanase in his lonely tower. He seeks "love" rather than "wisdom," distrusting a reality that must be approached apart from men. And he has written his poem, in however light a spirit, as an act of self-dedication and of freedom from the wealth of the past. He will be Psyche's priest and rhapsode in the proud conviction that she has had no others before him, or none at least so naked of external pieties.

The wealth of tradition is great not only in its fused massiveness, but in its own subtleties of internalization. One does poor service by sandbagging this profoundly moving poem, yet even the heroic innovators but tread the shadowy ground their ancestors found before them. Wordsworth had stood on that ground, as Keats well knew, and perhaps had chosen a different opening from it, neither toward love nor toward wisdom, but toward a plain recognition of natural reality and a more sublime recognition-by-starts of a final reality that seemed to contain nature. Wordsworth never quite named that finality as imagination, though Blake had done so and the young Coleridge felt (and resisted) the demonic temptation to do so. Behind all these were the fine collapses of the Age of Sensibility, the raptures of *Jubilate Agno* and the *Ode on the Poetical Character,* and the more forced but highly impressive tumults of *The Bard* and *The Progress of Poesy.* Farther back was the ancestor of all such moments of poetic incarnation, the Milton of the great invocations, whose spirit I think haunts the *Ode to Psyche* and the *Ode to a Nightingale,* and does not vanish until *The Fall of Hyperion* and *To Autumn.*

Hazlitt, with his usual penetration, praises Milton for his power to absorb vast poetic traditions with no embarrassment whatsoever: "In reading his works, we feel ourselves under the influence of a mighty intellect, that the nearer it approaches to others, becomes more distinct from them."[4] This observation, which comes in a lecture Keats heard, is soon joined by the excellent remark that "Milton's learning has the effect of intuition." The same lecture, in its treatment of Shakespeare, influenced Keats's conception of the Poetical Character, as Mr. Bate notes.[5] Whether Keats speculated sadly on the inimitable power of Milton's positive capability for converting the splendor of the past into a private expressiveness we do not know. But the literary archetype of Psyche's rosy sanctuary is the poet's paradise, strikingly developed by Spenser and Drayton, and brought to a perfection by Milton. I am not suggesting Milton as a "source" for Keats's *Ode To Psyche*. Poets influence poets in ways more profound than verbal echoings. The paradise of poets is a recurrent element in English mythopoeic poetry, and it is perhaps part of the critic's burden never to allow himself to yield to embarrassment when the riches of poetic tradition come crowding in upon him. Poets need to be selective; critics need the humility of a bad conscience when they exclude any part of the poetic past from "tradition," though humility is never much in critical fashion. Rimbaud put these matters right in one outburst: "On n'a jamais bien jugé le romantisme. Qui l'aurait jugé? Les Critiques!!"

Milton, "escap't the *Stygian* pool," hails the light he cannot see, and reaffirms his ceaseless wanderings "where the Muses haunt/ clear Spring, or shady Grove," and his nightly visits to "*Sion* and the flow'ry Brooks beneath." Like Keats's nightingale, he "sings darkling," but invokes a light that can "shine inward, and the mind through all her powers/Irradiate." The light shone inward, the mind's powers were triumphant, and all the sanctities of heaven yielded to Milton's vision. For the sanctuary of Milton's psyche is his vast heterocosm, the worlds he makes and ruins. His shrine is built, not to the human soul in love, but to the human soul glorious in its solitude, sufficient, with God's aid, to seek and find its own salvation. If Keats had closed the casement, and turned inward, seeking the principle that could sustain his own soul in the darkness, perhaps he could have gone on with the first *Hyperion,* and become a very different kind of poet. He would then have courted the fate of Collins, and pursued the guiding steps of Milton only to discover the quest was:

> In vain—such bliss to one alone
> Of all the sons of soul was known,
> And Heav'n and Fancy, kindred pow'rs,
> Have now o'erturned th'inspiring bow'rs,
> Or curtain'd close such scene from ev'ry future view.

Yeats, in the eloquent simplicities of *Per Amica Silentia Lunae,* saw Keats as having "been born with that thirst for luxury common to many at the outsetting of the Romantic Movement," and thought therefore that the poet of *To Autumn* "but gave us his dream of luxury."[6] Yeats's poets were Blake and Shelley; Keats and Wordsworth he refused to understand, for their way was not his own. His art, from *The Wanderings of Oisin* through the *Last Poems and Plays,* is founded on a rage against growing old, and a rejection of nature. The poet, he thought, could find his art only by giving way to an anti-self, which "comes but to those who are no longer deceived, whose passion is reality."[7] Yeats was repelled by Milton, and found no place for him in *A Vision,* and certainly no poet cared so little as Milton to express himself through an anti-self. In Blake's strife of spectre and emanation, in Shelley's sense of being shadowed by the *alastor* while seeking the epipsyche, Yeats found precedent for his own quest towards Unity of Being, the poet as daimonic man taking his mask from a phase opposite to that of his own will. Like Blake and Shelley, Yeats sought certainty, but being of Shelley's phase rather than Blake's, he did not find it. The way of Negative Capability, as an answer to Milton, Yeats did not take into account; he did not conceive of a poet "certain of nothing but of the holiness of the Heart's affections and the truth of Imagination." (There is, of course, no irritable reaching after mere fact and reason in Yeats: he reached instead for everything the occult sub-imagination had knocked together in place of fact and reason. But his motive was his incapability "of being in uncertainties, mysteries, doubts," and the results are more mixed than most recent criticism will admit.)

Keats followed Wordsworth by internalizing the quest toward finding a world that answered the poet's desires, and he hoped to follow Shakespeare by making that world more than a sublime projection of his own ego. Shakespeare's greatness was not an embarrassment to Keats, but the hard victories of poetry had to be won against the more menacing values of poetic tradition. The advance beyond the *Ode to Psyche* was taken in the *Ode to a Nightingale,* where the high world within the bird's song is an expansion of the rosy sanctuary of Psyche. In this world our sense of actuality is heightened simultaneously with the widening of what Mr. Bate terms "the realm of possibility."[8] The fear of losing actuality does not encourage the dull soil of mundane experience to quarrel with the proud forests it has fed, the nightingale's high requiem. But to be the breathing garden in which Fancy breeds his flowers is a delightful fate; to become a sod is to suffer what Belial dreaded in that moving speech Milton himself and the late C. S. Lewis have taught too many to despise.

Milton, invoking the light, made himself at one with the nightingale; Keats is deliberate in knowing constantly his own separation from the bird. What is fresh in this ode is not I think a sense of the poet's dialogue with himself; it is surprising how often the English lyric has provided such an undersong, from Spenser's *Prothalamion* to Wordsworth's *Resolution and Independence.* Keats wins freedom from tradition here by claiming so very little for the imagination in its intoxicating but harsh encounter with the reality of natural song. The poet does not accept what is as good, and he does not exile desire for what is not. Yet, for him, what is possible replaces what is not. There is no earthly paradise for poets, but there is a time of all-but-final satisfaction, the fullness of lines 35 to 58 of this ode.

I do not think that there is, before Keats, so individual a setting-forth of such a time, anywhere in poetic tradition since the Bible. The elevation of Wordsworth in *Tintern Abbey* still trembles at the border of a theophany, and so derives from a universe centered upon religious experience. The vatic gift of Shelley's self to the elements, from *Alastor* on, has its remote but genuine ancestors in the sibylline frenzies of traditions as ancient as Orphism. Blake's moments of delight come as hard-won intervals of rest from an intellectual warfare that differs little if at all from the struggles towards a revelatory awareness in Ezekiel or Isaiah, and there is no contentment in them. What Keats so greatly gives to the Romantic tradition in the *Nightingale* ode is what no poet before him had the capability of giving—the sense of the human making choice of a human self, aware of its deathly nature, and yet having the will to celebrate the imaginative richness of mortality. The *Ode to a Nightingale* is the first poem to know and declare, wholeheartedly, that death is the mother of beauty. The *Ode to Psyche* still glanced, with high good humor, at the haunted rituals of the already-written poems of heaven; the *Ode to a Nightingale* turns, almost casually, to the unwritten great poem of earth. There is nothing casual about the poem's tone, but there is a wonderful lack of self-consciousness at the poem's freedom from the past, in the poem's knowing that death, our death, is absolute and without memorial.

The same freedom from the massive beliefs and poetic stances of the past is manifested in the *Ode on a Grecian Urn*, where the consolations of the spirit are afforded merely by an artifice of eternity, and not by evidences of an order of reality wholly other than our own. Part of this poem's strength is in the deliberate vulnerability of its speaker, who contemplates a world of values he cannot appropriate for his own, although nothing in that world is antithetical to his own nature as an aspiring poet. Mr. Bate states the poem's awareness of this vulnerability: "In attempting to approach the urn in its own terms, the imagination has been led at the same time to separate itself—or the situation of man generally —still further from the urn."[9] One is not certain that the imagination is not also separating itself from the essential poverty of man's situation in the poem's closing lines. Mr. Bate thinks we underestimate Keats's humor in the Great Odes, and he is probably right, but the humor that apparently ends the *Grecian Urn* is a grim one. The truth of art may be all of the truth our condition can apprehend, but it is not a saving truth. If this is all we need to know, it may be that no knowledge can help us. Shelley was very much a child of Miltonic tradition in affirming the moral instrumentality of the imagination; Keats is grimly free of tradition in his subtle implication of a truth that most of us learn. Poetry is not a means of good; it is, as Wallace Stevens implied, like the honey of earth that comes and goes at once, while we wait vainly for the honey of heaven.

Blake, Wordsworth, and Shelley knew in their different ways that human splendors had no sources but in the human imagination, but each of these great innovators had a religious temperament, however heterodox, and Keats had not. Keats had a clarity in his knowledge of the uniqueness and finality of human life and death that caused him a particular anguish on his own death-bed, but gave him, before that, the imagination's gift of an absolute originality. The power of Keats's imagination could never be identified by him with an apocalyptic energy that might hope to transform nature. It is not that he lacked the confidence of Blake and of Shelley, or of the momentary Wordsworth of *The Recluse*. He felt the imagination's desire for a revelation that would redeem the inadequacies of our condition, but he felt also a humorous skepticism toward such desire. He would have read the prose testament of Wallace Stevens, *Two Or Three Ideas,* with the wry approval so splendid a lecture deserves. The gods are dispelled in mid-air, and leave "no texts either of the soil or of the soul." The poet does not cry out for their return, since it remains his work to resolve life in his own terms, for in the poet is "the increasingly human self."[10]

Part of Keats's achievement is due then to his being perhaps the only genuine forerunner of the representative post-Romantic sensibility. Another part is centered in the *Ode on Melancholy* and *The Fall of Hyperion,* for in these poems consciousness becomes its own purgatory, and the poet learns the cost of living in an excitement of which he affirms "that it is the only state for the best sort of Poetry—that is all I care for, all I live for." From this declaration it is a direct way to the generally misunderstood rigor of Pater, when he insists that "a counted number of pulses only is given to us of a variegated, dramatic life," and asks: "How may we see in them all that is to be seen in them by the finest senses?"[11] Moneta, Keats's veiled Melancholy, counted those pulses, while the poet waited, rapt in an apprehension attainable only by the finest senses, nearly betrayed by those senses to an even more premature doom than his destined one. What links together *The Fall of*

Hyperion and its modern descendants like Stevens's *Notes toward a Supreme Fiction* is the movement of impressions set forth by Pater, when analysis of the self yields to the poet's recognition of how dangerously fine the self's existence has become. "It is with this movement, with the passage and dissolution of impressions, images, sensations, that analysis leaves off—that continual vanishing away, that strange, perpetual weaving and unweaving of ourselves."[12]

Though there is a proud laughter implicit in the *Ode on Melancholy,* the poem courts tragedy, and again makes death the mother of beauty. Modern criticism has confounded Pater with his weaker disciples, and has failed to realize how truly Yeats and Stevens are in his tradition. The *Ode on Melancholy* is ancestor to what is strongest in Pater, and to what came after in his tradition of aesthetic humanism. Pater's "Conclusion" to *The Renaissance* lives in the world of the *Ode on Melancholy:*

> Great passions may give us this quickened sense of life, ecstasy and sorrow of love, the various forms of enthusiastic activity, disinterested or otherwise, which come naturally to many of us. Only be sure it is passion—that it does yield you this fruit of a quickened, multiplied consciousness.[13]

The wakeful anguish of the soul comes to the courter of grief in the very shrine of pleasure, and the renovating powers of art yield the tragedy of their might only to a strenuous and joyful seeker. Keats's problem in *The Fall of Hyperion* was to find again the confidence of Milton as to the oneness of his self and theme, but with nothing of the Miltonic conviction that God had worked to fit that self and theme together. The shrines of pleasure and of melancholy become one shrine in the second *Hyperion,* and in that ruin the poet must meet the imaginative values of tradition without their attendant credences, for Moneta guards the temple of all the dead faiths.

Moneta humanizes her sayings to our ears, but not until a poet's courteous dialectic has driven her to question her own categories for mankind. When she softens, and parts the veils for Keats, she reveals his freedom from the greatness of poetic tradition, for the vision granted has the quality of a new universe, and a tragedy different in kind from the tragedy of the past:

> Then saw I a wan face,
> Not pined by human sorrows, but bright-blanch'd
> By an immortal sickness which kills not;
> It works a constant change, which happy death
> Can put no end to; deathwards progressing
> To no death was that visage; it had pass'd
> The lily and the snow; and beyond these
> I must not think now, though I saw that face.
> But for her eyes I should have fled away.
> They held me back with a benignant light,
> Soft mitigated by divinest lids
> Half closed, and visionless entire they seem'd
> Of all external things—

Frank Kermode finds in this passage a prime instance of his "Romantic Image," and believes Moneta's face to be "alive only in a chill and inhuman way," yet Keats is held back from such a judgment by the eyes of his Titaness, for they give forth "a benignant light," as close to the saving light Milton invokes as Keats can ever get.[14] Moneta has little to do with the Yeatsian concept of the poetic vision, for she does not address herself to the alienation of the poet. M. H. Abrams, criticizing Mr. Kermode, points to her emphasis on the poet as humanist, made restless by the miseries of mankind.[15] Shelley's Witch of Atlas, for all her playfulness, has more to do with Yeats's formulation of the coldness of the Muse.

Moneta is the Muse of mythopoeia, like Shelley's Witch, but she contains the poetic and religious past, as Shelley's capricious Witch does not. Taking her in a limited sense (since she incarnates so much more than this), Moneta does represent the embarrassments of poetic tradition, a greatness it is death to approach. Moneta's perspective is close to that of the Rilkean Angel, and for Keats to share that perspective he would have to cease to depend on the visible. Moneta's is a perfect consciousness; Keats is committed still to the oxymoronic intensities of experience, and cannot unperplex joy from pain. Moneta's is a world beyond tragedy; Keats needs to be a tragic poet. Rilke dedicated himself to the task of describing a world regarded no longer from a human point of view, but as it is within the angel.[16] Moneta, like this angel, does not regard external things, and again like Rilke's angel she both comforts and terrifies. Keats, like Stevens, fears the angelic imposition of any order upon reality, and hopes to discover a possible order in the human and the natural, even if that order be only the cyclic rhythm of tragedy. Stevens's definitive discovery is in the final sections of *Notes towards a Supreme Fiction;* Keats's similar fulfillment is in his perfect poem, *To Autumn.*

The achievement of definitive vision in *To Autumn* is the more remarkable for the faint presence of the shadows of the poet's hell that the poem tries to exclude. Mr. Bate calls the *Lines to Fanny* (written, like *To Autumn,* in October 1819) "somewhat jumbled as well as tired and flat,"[17] but its nightmare projection of the imagination's inferno has a singular intensity, and I think considerable importance:

> Where shall I learn to get my peace again?
> To banish thoughts of that most hateful land,
> Dungeoner of my friends, that wicked strand
> Where they were wreck'd and live a wrecked life;
> That monstrous region, whose dull rivers pour,
> Ever from their sordid urns unto the shore,
> Unown'd of any weedy-haird gods;
> Whose winds, all zephyrless, hold scourging rods,
> Iced in the great lakes, to afflict mankind;
> Whose rank-grown forests, frosted, black, and blind,
> Would fright a Dryad; whose harsh herbag'd meads
> Make lean and lank the starv'd ox while he feeds;
> There bad flowers have no scent, birds no sweet song,
> And great unerring Nature once seems wrong.

This may have begun as a fanciful depiction of an unknown America, where Keats's brother and sister-in-law were suffering, yet it develops into a vision akin to Blake's of the world of experience, with its lakes of menace and its forests of error. The moss-lain Dryads lulled to sleep in the forests of the poet's mind in his *Ode to Psyche,* can find no home in this natural world. This is Keats's version of the winter vision, the more powerful for being so unexpected, and clearly a torment to its seer, who imputes error to Nature even as he pays it his sincere and accustomed homage.

It is this waste land that the auroras of Keats's *Autumn* transform into a landscape of perfecting process. Does another lyric in the language meditate more humanly "the full of fortune and the full of fate"? The question is the attentive reader's necessary and generous tribute; the critical answer may be allowed to rest with Mr. Bate, who is moved to make the finest of claims for the poem: "Here at last is something of a genuine paradise."[18] The paradise of poets bequeathed to Keats by tradition is gone; a tragic paradise of naturalistic completion and mortal acceptance has taken its place.

There are other Romantic freedoms won from the embarrassments of poetic tradition, usually through the creation of new myth, as in Blake and Shelley, or in the thematic struggle not to create a myth, as in the earlier work of Wordsworth and Coleridge. Keats found his dangerous freedom by pursuing the naturalistic implications of the poet's relation to his own poem, and nothing is more refreshing in an art so haunted by aspirations to surpass or negate nature. Shelley, still joined to Keats in the popular though not the critical consciousness, remains the best poet to read in counterpoint to the Great Odes and *The Fall of Hyperion*. There is no acceptance in Shelley, no tolerance for the limits of reality, but only the outrageous desire never to cease desiring, the unflagging intensity that goes on until it is stopped, and never is stopped. Keats did what Milton might have done but was not concerned to do; he perfected an image in which stasis and process are reconciled, and made of autumn the most human of seasons in consequence. Shelley's ode to autumn is his paean to the West Wind, where a self-destroying swiftness is invoked for the sake of dissolving all stasis permanently, and for hastening process past merely natural fulfillment into apocalyptic renewal. Whether the great winter of the world can be relieved by any ode Keats tended to doubt, and we are right to doubt with him, but there is a hope wholly natural in us that no doubt dispels, and it is of this hope that Shelley is the unique and indispensable poet.

NOTES

1. Walter Jackson Bate, *John Keats* (Cambridge, Mass., 1963), p. 73.

2. Keats to Severn, as quoted by Bate, p. 612.

3. Bate, p. 144.

4. *The Collected Works of William Hazlitt,* ed. Waller and Glover (London, 1902), Vol. V, "Lectures on the English Poets," p. 58.

5. Bate, p. 260.

6. W. B. Yeats, *Mythologies* (New York, 1959), p. 329.

7. Ibid. p. 331.

8. Bate, p. 509.

9. Bate, p. 513.

10. Wallace Stevens, *Opus Posthumous,* ed. Samuel French Morse (New York, 1957), pp. 206–7.

11. *The Works of Walter Pater* (London, 1900), vol. I, *The Renaissance,* "Conclusion," p. 236.

12. Pater, p. 236.

13. Pater, p. 238.

14. Frank Kermode, *Romantic Image* (London, 1961), p. 10.

15. M. H. Abrams, review of Kermode's *Romantic Image,* in *Victorian Studies,* September 1958, p. 76.

16. Rilke, letter of 27 October 1915, to Ellen Delp. Most readily available, in English, in *Selected Letters of Rainer Maria Rilke,* ed. H. T. Moore (Garden City, 1960), p. 193.

17. Bate, p. 617.

18. Bate, p. 581.

Structure and Style
In the Greater Romantic Lyric

M . H . ABRAMS

T HERE is no accepted name for the kind of poem I want to talk about, even though it was a distinctive and widely practiced variety of the longer Romantic lyric and includes some of the greatest Romantic achievements in any form. Coleridge's "Eolian Harp," "Frost at Midnight," "Fears in Solitude," and "Dejection: An Ode" exemplify the type, as does Wordsworth's "Tintern Abbey," his "Ode: Intimations of Immortality," and (with a change in initial reference from scene to painting) his "Elegiac Stanzas Suggested by a Picture of Peele Castle in a Storm." Shelley's "Stanzas Written in Dejection" follows the formula exactly, and his "Ode to the West Wind" is a variant on it. Of Keats's odes, that to a Nightingale is the one which approximates the pattern most closely. Only Byron, among the major poets, did not write in this mode at all.

These instances yield a paradigm for the type. Some of the poems are called odes, while the others approach the ode in having lyric magnitude and a serious subject, feelingfully meditated. They present a determinate speaker in a particularized, and usually a localized, outdoor setting, whom we overhear as he carries on, in a fluent vernacular which rises easily to a more formal speech, a sustained colloquy, sometimes with himself or with the outer scene, but more frequently with a silent human auditor, present or absent. The speaker begins with a description of the landscape; an aspect or change of aspect in the landscape evokes a varied but integral process of memory, thought, anticipation, and feeling which remains closely intervolved with the outer scene. In the course of this meditation the lyric speaker achieves an insight, faces up to a tragic loss, comes to a moral decision, or resolves an emotional problem. Often the poem rounds upon itself to end where it began, at the outer scene, but with an altered mood and deepened understanding which is the result of the intervening meditation.

What shall we call this Romantic genre? To label these poems simply nature lyrics is not only inadequate, but radically misleading. We have not yet entirely recovered from the earlier critical stress on Wordsworth's statement that "I have at all times endeavored to look steadily at my subject," to the neglect of his repeated warnings that accurate natural description, though a necessary, is an inadequate condition for poetry. Like Blake and Coleridge, Wordsworth manifested wariness, almost terror, at the threat of the corporeal eye and material object to tyrannize over the mind and imagination, in opposition to that normative experience in which

> The mind is lord and master—outward sense
> The obedient servant of her will.[1]

In the extended lyrics we are considering, the visual report is invariably the occasion for a meditation which turns out to constitute the *raison d'être* of the poem. Romantic writers, though nature poets, were humanists above all, for they dealt with the non-human only insofar as it is the occasion for the activity which defines man: thought, the process of intellection.

"The descriptive-meditative poem" is a possible, but a clumsy term. *Faute de mieux*, I shall call this poetic type "the greater Romantic lyric," intending to suggest, not that it is a higher achievement than other Romantic lyrics, but that it displaced what neo-classical critics had called "the greater ode"—the elevated Pindaric, in distinction to "the lesser ode" modeled chiefly on Horace—as the favored form for the long lyric poem.

The repeated out-in-out process, in which mind confronts nature and their interplay constitutes the poem, is a remarkable phenomenon in literary history. If we don't find it strange, it is because our responses have been dulled by long familiarity with such a procedure not only in the Romantic poets, but in their many successors who played variations on the mode, from Matthew Arnold and Walt Whitman—both "Dover Beach" and "Crossing Brooklyn Ferry," for example, closely follow the pattern of the greater Romantic lyric—to Wallace Stevens and W. H. Auden. But at the beginning of the nineteenth century this procedure in the lyric was part of a new and exciting poetic strategy, no less epidemic than Donne's in his day, or T. S. Eliot's in the period after the first World War. For several decades poets did not often talk about the great issues of life, death, love, joy, dejection, or God without talking at the same time about the landscape. Wordsworth's narrative of Michael emerges from a description of the scene around "the tumultuous brook of Green-head Ghyll," to which in the end it returns:

> and the remains
> Of the unfinished Sheep-fold may be seen
> Beside the boisterous brook of Green-head Ghyll.

Coleridge's great, neglected love-poem, "Recollections of Love," opens with a Quantock scene revisited after eight years have passed, and adverts suddenly to the River Greta at the close:

> But when those meek eyes first did seem
> To tell me, Love within you wrought—
> O Greta, dear domestic stream!
>
> Has not, since then, Love's prompture deep,
> Has not Love's whisper evermore
> Been ceaseless, as thy gentle roar?
> Sole voice, when other voices sleep,
> Dear under-song in clamor's hour.

Keats's first long poem of consequence, though it is his introduction to an *ars poetica*, represents what he saw, then what he thought, while he "stood tiptoe upon a little hill." Shelley treats the theme of permanence in change by describing the mutations of a cloud, defines the pure Idea of joy in a meditation on the flight and song of a skylark, and presents his ultimate concept of the secret and impersonal power behind all process in a description of Mont Blanc and the Vale of Chamouni. Wordsworth's *Prelude* can be viewed as an epic expansion of the mode of "Tintern

Abbey," both in overall design and local tactics. It begins with the description of a landscape visited in maturity, evokes the entire life of the poet as a protracted meditation on things past, and presents the growth of the poet's mind as an interaction with the natural milieu by which it is fostered, from which it is tragically alienated, and to which in the resolution it is restored, with a difference attributable to the intervening experiences; the poem ends at the time of its beginning.

What I have called "the greater lyric," then, is only a special instance of a very widespread manner of proceeding in Romantic poetry; but it is of great interest because it was the earliest Romantic formal invention, which at once demonstrated the stability of organization and the capacity to engender successors which define a distinct lyric species. New lyric forms are not as plenty as blackberries, and when one turns up, it is worth critical attention. Suppose, therefore, that we ask some questions about this one: about its genesis, its nearest literary antecedents, and the reasons why this way of proceeding, out of the alternatives in common lyric practice, should have appealed so powerfully to the Romantic sensibility. Inquiry into some probable causes of the structure and style of the greater lyric will take us not only to the evolution of certain descriptive genres in the seventeenth and eighteenth centuries, but also to contemporary developments in philosophy and in theology, and to the spiritual posture in which many poets, as well as philosophers, found themselves at the end of the Enlightenment.

I

COLERIDGE AND WORDSWORTH

In this investigation Coleridge must be our central reference, not only because he had the most to say about these matters in prose, but because it was he, not Wordsworth, who inaugurated the greater Romantic lyric, firmly established its pattern, and wrote the largest number of instances. Wordsworth's first trial in the extended lyric was "Tintern Abbey," which he composed in July 1798. Up to that time his only efforts in the long descriptive and reflective mode were the schoolboy effort, "The Vale of Esthwaite," and the two tour-poems of 1793, "An Evening Walk" and "Descriptive Sketches." The first of these was written in octosyllabic and the latter two in heroic couplets, and all differ in little but merit and the detail of single passages from hundreds of eighteenth-century predecessors.[2] Coleridge, however, as early as 20 August 1795, composed a short first version of "The Eolian Harp," and in 1796—two years before "Tintern Abbey"—expanded it to fifty-six lines which established, in epitome, the ordonnance, materials, and style of the greater lyric.[3] It is in the dramatic mode of intimate talk to an unanswering auditor in easy blank-verse paragraphs. It begins with a description of the peaceful outer scene; this, in parallel with the vagrant sounds evoked from a wind-harp, calls forth a recollection in tranquillity of earlier experiences in the same setting and leads to a sequence of reflections which are suggested by, and also incorporate, perceptual qualities of the scene. The poem closes with a summary reprise of the opening description of "PEACE, and this COT, and THEE, heart-honour'd Maid!"

Between the autumn of 1796 and the spring of 1798 Coleridge composed a number of variations on this lyric type, including "Reflections on Having Left a Place of Retirement," "This Lime-tree Bower," "Fears in Solitude," and "The Nightingale." To these writings Professor G. M. Harper applied the term which Coleridge himself used for "The Nightingale," "conversation poems"; very aptly, because they are written (though some of them only intermittently) in a blank verse which at its best captures remarkably the qualities of the intimate speaking voice, yet remains capable of adapting without strain to the varying levels of the subject-matter and feeling. And within this period, in February of 1798, Coleridge produced one of the masterpieces of the greater lyric, perfectly modulated and proportioned, but so successful in the quiet way that it hides its art that it has only recently attracted its meed of critical admiration. The poem is "Frost at Midnight," and it follows, but greatly enlarges and subtilizes the pattern of "The Eolian Harp." What seems at first impression to be the free association of its central meditation turns out to have been called forth, qualified, and controlled by the opening description, which evokes the strangeness in the familiar surroundings of the solitary and wakeful speaker: the "secret ministry" of the frost, the "strange and extreme silentness" of "sea, and hill, and wood," the life of the sleeping village "inaudible as dreams," and the film that flutters on the grate "the sole unquiet thing." In consonance with these elements, and directed especially by the rhythm of the seemingly unnoticed breathing of a sleeping infant, the meditative mind disengages itself from the physical locale, moves back in time to the speaker's childhood, still farther back, to his own infancy, then forward to express, in the intonation of a blessing, the hope that his son shall have the life in nature that his father lacked; until, in anticipating the future, it incorporates both the present scene and the results of the remembered past in the enchanting close—

> Whether the eave-drops fall
> Heard only in the trances of the blast,
> Or if the secret ministry of frost
> Shall hang them up in silent icicles,
> Quietly shining to the quiet Moon.

In the original version this concluding sentence trailed off in six more verse-lines, which Coleridge, in order to emphasize the lyric rondure, later excised. Plainly, Coleridge worked out the lyric device of the return-upon-itself—which he used in "Reflections on Having Left a Place of Retirement" and "Fears in Solitude," as well as in "The Eolian Harp" and "Frost at Midnight"—in a deliberate endeavor to transform a segment of experience broken out of time into a sufficient aesthetic whole. "The common end of all *narrative*, nay, of *all*, Poems," he wrote to Joseph Cottle in 1815, "is to convert a *series* into a *Whole*: to make those events, which in real or imagined History move on in a *strait* Line, assume to our Understandings a *circular* motion—the snake with it's Tail in its Mouth."[4] From the time of the early Greek philosophers, the circle had been the shape of perfection; and in occult philosophy the *ouroboros,* the tail-eating snake, had become the symbol for eternity and for the divine process of creation, since it is complete, self-sufficient, and endless. For Coleridge the perfect shape for the descriptive-meditative-descriptive poem was precisely the one described and exemplified in T. S. Eliot's "East Coker," which begins: "In my beginning is my end," and ends: "In my end is my beginning;" another modern writer who knew esoteric lore designed *Finnegans Wake* so that the headless sentence which begins the book completes the tailless sentence with which it ends.

Five months after the composition of "Frost at Midnight," Wordsworth set out on a walking tour with his sister. Reposing on a high bank of the River Wye, he remembered this among others of Coleridge's conversation poems—the dramatic mode of address to an unanswering listener in flexible blank verse; the opening description which evolves into a sustained meditation assimilating perceptual, personal, and philosophical elements; the free movement of thought from the present scene to recollection in tranquillity, to prayer-like prediction, and back to the scene; even some of Coleridge's specific concepts and phrases—and in the next four or five days' walk, worked out "Lines Composed a Few Miles above Tintern Abbey" and appended it forthwith to *Lyrical Ballads,* which was already in press.

To claim that it was Coleridge who deflected Wordsworth's poetry into a channel so entirely congenial to him is in no way to derogate Wordsworth's achievement, nor his powers of invention. "Tintern Abbey" has greater dimension and intricacy and a more various verbal orchestration than "Frost at Midnight." In its conclusion Wordsworth managed Coleridge's specialty, the return-upon-itself, with a mastery of involuted reference without match in the poems of its begetter. "Tintern Abbey" also inaugurated the wonderfully functional device Wordsworth later called the "two consciousnesses": a scene is revisited, and the remembered landscape ("the picture of the mind") is superimposed on the picture before the eye; the two landscapes fail to match, and so set a problem ("a sad perplexity") which compels the meditation. Wordsworth played variations on this stratagem in all his later trials in the greater lyric, and in *The Prelude* he expanded it into a persisting double awareness of things as they are and as they were, and so anticipated the structural principle of the most influential masterpiece of our own century, Proust's *À la recherche du temps perdu.*

II

THE LOCAL POEM

What was the closest poetic antecedent of this controlled and shapely lyric genre? It was not the ancient lyric formula, going back to the spring-songs of the troubadors, which set forth an ideal spring scene (the *Natureingang*) and then presented a human experience in harmony or contrast—a formula which survived in Burns's

> Ye flowery banks o' bonie Doon,
> How can ye blume sae fair?
> How can ye chant, ye little birds,
> And I sae fu' o' care?

Nor was it Thomson's *Seasons,* that omnibus of unlocalized description, episodic narration, and general reflection, in which the pious observer moves from Nature to Nature's God with the help of Isaac Newton's *Principia.* And certainly it was not the formal descriptive poem such as Collins's "Ode to Evening," which adapted Pindar's ceremonial panegyric to landscape mainly by the device of transforming descriptive and meditative propositions into a sequence of tableaux and brief allegories—a mode which Keats revitalized in his "Ode to Autumn."[5] The clue to the provenance of the greater Romantic lyric is to be found in the attributes of the opening description. This landscape is not only particularized; it is in most cases precisely localized, in place, and sometimes in time as well. Critics have often remarked on Wordsworth's scrupulosity about specifying the circumstances for his poems, but his fellow-poets were often no less meticulous in giving their greater lyrics an exact locality. We have "The Eolian Harp, Composed at Clevedon, Somersetshire" (the first versions also appended to the title a date, 20 August 1795); "This Lime-Tree Bower My Prison," subtitled: "In the June of 1797 . . . the author's cottage. . . . Composed . . . in the garden-bower"; "Fears in Solitude written April, 1798. . . . The Scene, the Hills near Stowey";[6] "Lines Written a Few Miles above Tintern Abbey . . . July 13, 1798"; "Elegiac Stanzas Suggested by a picture of Peele Castle, in a Storm"; "Stanzas Written in Dejection, Near Naples." Even when its setting is not named in the title, the poem usually has an identifiable local habitation, such as the milieu of Coleridge's cottage at Nether Stowey for "Frost at Midnight," or the view from Coleridge's study at Keswick in "Dejection: An Ode." To his "Ode to the West Wind," Shelley was careful to add the note: "Written in a wood that skirts the Arno, near Florence. . . ."

There existed in the eighteenth century a well-defined and

immensely popular poetic type, in which the title named a geographical location, and which combined a description of that scene with the thoughts that the scene suggested. This was known as the "local" or "loco-descriptive" poem; Robert A. Aubin, in his compendious and amusing survey of *Topographical Poetry in XVIII-Century England,* lists almost two thousand instances of the form. "Local poetry," as Dr. Johnson concisely defined it in his life of John Denham, was

a species of composition . . . of which the fundamental subject is some particular landscape, to be poetically described, with the addition of such embellishments as may be supplied by historical restrospection or incidental meditation.[7]

The evidence, I think, makes it clear that the most characteristic Romantic lyric developed directly out of one of the most stable and widely employed of all the neoclassic kinds.

By general consent Sir John Denham, as Dr. Johnson said, was the "author" of the genre, in that excellent poem, "Cooper's Hill," of which the first version was written in 1642. In it the poet inventories the prospect of the Thames valley visible from the hilltop, with distant London on one side and Windsor Castle on the other. As Earl Wasserman has shown, the poem is a complex construction, in which the topographical elements are selected and managed so as to yield concepts which support a Royalist viewpoint on the eve of the Civil Wars.[8] But if, like Dr. Johnson, we abstract and classify Denham's incidental meditations, we find that some are historical and political, but that others are broadly sententious, and are achieved by the device of adducing to a natural object a correspondent moral idea. Thus the "aery Mountain" (lines 217–22), forced to endure the onslaught of winds and storms, instances "The common fate of all that's high or great," while the Thames (lines 163–4) hastens "to pay his tribute to the Sea,/Like mortal life to meet Eternity."

This latter procedure is worth dwelling on for a moment, because for many of Denham's successors it displaced history and politics to become the sole meditative component in local poems, and it later evolved into the extended meditation of the Romantic lyric. The *paysage moralisé* was not invented as a rhetorical device

by poets, but was grounded on two collateral and pervasive concepts in medieval and Renaissance philosophy. One of these was
the doctrine that God has supplemented the Holy Scriptures with
the *liber creaturarum,* so that objects of nature, as Sir Thomas
Browne said, carry "in Stenography and short Characters, something of Divinity"[9] and show forth the attributes and providence
of their Author. The second concept, of independent philosophic
origin but often fused with the first, is that the divine Architect has
designed the universe analogically, relating the physical, moral, and
spiritual realms by an elaborate system of correspondences. A
landscape, accordingly, consists of *verba visibilia* which enable
pious interpreters such as Shakespeare's Duke in *As You Like It* to
find "books in the running brooks,/Sermons in stones, and good in
everything."

The metaphysic of a symbolic and analogical universe underlay
the figurative tactics of the seventeenth-century metaphysical poets
who were John Denham's predecessors and contemporaries. The
secular and amatory poems exploited unexpected correspondences
mainly as display rhetoric, positing the analogue in order to show
the author's wit in supporting an argument and to evoke in the
reader the shock of delightful discovery. In their devotional
poems, however, the poets put forward their figures as grounded
in the divine plan underlying the universe. Thus Henry Vaughan,
musing over a waterfall, was enabled by the guidance of its
Creator to discover its built-in correspondences with the life and
destiny of man:

> What sublime truths and wholesome themes,
> Lodge in thy mystical deep streams!
> Such as dull man can never find
> Unless that spirit lead his mind
> Which first upon thy face did move,
> And hatched all with his quick'ning love.

In 1655, the year in which Vaughan published "The Waterfall,"
Denham added to his enlarged edition of "Cooper's Hill" the
famous pair of couplets on the Thames which link description to
concepts by a sustained parallel between the flow of the stream and
the ideal conduct of life and art:

O could I flow like thee, and make thy stream
My great example, as it is my theme!
Though deep, yet clear, though gentle, yet not dull,
Strong without rage, without o'erflowing, full.

The metaphysical device and ingenuity are still apparent, but we can see why this became the best-known and most influential passage in the poetry of neoclassicism—a model not only for its versification, but also for some of its most characteristic ideas and rhetorical devices. In these lines the metaphysical wit has been tamed and ordered into the "true wit" which became the eighteenth-century ideal; Denham's "strength" (which Dr. Johnson defined as "much meaning in few words"), so universally admired, has replaced the "strong lines" (the compressed and hyperbolic ingeniousness) of John Donne; while the startling revelation of *discordia concors* between object and idea has been smoothed to a neoclassic decency, moulded to the deft play of antitheses around the caesura, and adapted to the presentation of the cardinal neoclassic norm of a mean between extremes.[10]

In the enormous number of eighteenth-century local poems the organization of "Cooper's Hill" around a controlling political motif was soon reduced mainly to the procedure of setting up parallels between landscape and moral commonplaces. The subtitle of Richard Jago's long "Edge Hill" (1767) neatly defines the double-function: "The Rural Prospect Delineated and Moralized"; while the title of an anonymous poem of 1790 reveals how monstrous this development could be: "An Evening's Reflection on the Universe, in a Walk on the Seashore." The literal belief in a universe of divine types and correspondences, which had originally supported this structural trope, faded,[11] and the coupling of sensuous phenomena with moral statements came to be regarded as a rhetorical device particularly apt to the descriptive poet's double aim of combining instruction with delight. John Dyer's "Grongar's Hill" (1726) was justly esteemed as one of the most deft and agreeable of prospect poems. Mounting the hill, the poet describes the widening prospect with a particularity beyond the call of the moralist's duty. Yet the details of the scene are duly equated with *sententiae;* and when he comes to moralize the river (always, after Denham's passage on the Thames, the favorite item

in the topographic inventory), Dyer echoes the great theological
concept of a typological universe lightly, as a pleasant conceit:

> And see the rivers how they run . . .
> Wave succeeding wave, they go
> A various journey to the deep,
> Like human life to endless sleep!
> Thus is nature's vesture wrought,
> To instruct our wand'ring thought;
> Thus she dresses green and gay,
> To disperse our cares away.

Thomas Gray's "Ode on a Distant Prospect of Eton College"
(1747) provides significant evidence that the local poem evolved
into the greater Romantic lyric. It is a hill-poem, and its setting
—Windsor heights and the Thames valley—is part of the very
prospect which Denham had described. The topographical form,
however, has been adapted to the Horatian ode, so that the focus
of interest is no longer in the analogical inventory of scenic detail,
but in the mental and emotional experience of a specific lyric
speaker. The meditation becomes a coherent and dramatic sequence
of thought, triggered by what was to become Wordsworth's favorite
device of *déja vu:* the scene is a scene revisited, and it evokes in
memory the lost self of the speaker's youth.

> I feel the gales that from ye blow
> A momentary bliss bestow,
> As, waving fresh their gladsome wing,
> My weary soul they seem to soothe,
> And, redolent of joy and youth
> To breathe a second spring.

As he watches the heedless schoolboys at their games, the speaker's
first impulse is to warn them of the ambuscades which the "minis-
ters of human fate" are even now laying for them: "Ah, tell them
they are men!" But a new thought leads to a reversal of intention,
for he suddenly realizes that since life's horrors are inescapable,
forewarning is a useless cruelty.

We are a long way, however, from the free flow of consciousness,
the interweaving of thought, feeling, and perceptual detail, and
the easy naturalness of the speaking voice which characterize the

Romantic lyric. Gray deliberately rendered both his observations and reflections in the hieratic style of a formal odic *oratio*. The poet's recollection of times past, for example, is managed through an invocation to Father Thames to tell him "Who foremost now delight to cleave/With pliant arm thy glassy wave," and the language throughout is heightened and stylized by the apostrophe, exclamation, rhetorical question, and studied periphrasis which Wordsworth decried in Gray—"more than any other man curiously elaborate in the structure of his . . . poetic diction."[12] Both reminiscence and reflection are depersonalized, and occur mainly as general propositions which are sometimes expressed as *sententiae* ("where ignorance is bliss/'Tis folly to be wise"), and at other times as propositions which, in the standard artifice of the contemporary ode, are converted into the tableau-and-allegory form that Coleridge derogated as Gray's "translations of prose thoughts into poetic language."[13] Gray's poem is structurally inventive, and excellent in its kind, but it remains distinctly a mid-century period piece. We need to look elsewhere for the immediate occasion of Coleridge's invention of the greater Romantic lyric.

III

COLERIDGE AND BOWLES

I have quoted Coleridge's derogation of Gray from the first chapter of the *Biographia Literaria,* in which Coleridge reviewed his own early development as a poet. To Gray's style he opposed that of three poems, the only contemporary models he mentioned with approval; and all three, it is important to note, were of a type which combines local description with associated meditation. One was William Crowe's conventional prospect poem, *Lewesdon Hill* (1788) and another was Cowper's *The Task,* which incorporated a number of episodic meditations evoked by the environs of the river Ouse. Both these poems, however, he read later—*The Task,* he says, "many years" later—than a publication which at once seized irresistibly upon his sensibility, William Lisle Bowles's *Sonnets* of 1789. By these poems he was "year after year . . . enthusiastically delighted and inspired," and he worked zealously to win "proselytes" to his poetic divinity by buttonholing strangers and friends alike, and by sending out as gifts more than forty copies of Bowles's volume, which he had himself transcribed.[14]

Coleridge mentioned also Bowles's "Monody Written at Mat-lock" (1791), which is a long prospect-poem written in blank verse. But most of Bowles's poems of 1789 were obvious adaptations of this local-meditative formula to the sonnet form. As in both the local poems and the Romantic lyric, a number of Bowles's titles specify the place, and even the time: "To the River Wens-beck"; "To the River Itchin Near Winton"; "On Dover Cliffs. July 20, 1787"; "Written at Ostend. July 22, 1787." The whole was "Written," as the title of 1789 points out, "Chiefly on Picturesque Spots, during a Tour," and constitutes a sonnet-sequence uttered by a latter-day wandering *penseroso* who, as the light fades from the literal day, images his life as a metaphoric tour from its bright morning through deepening shadow to enduring night. Within this over-arching equation, the typical single poem begins with a rapid sketch of the external scene—frequently, as in so many of Denham's progeny, a river scene—then moves on to reminiscence and moral reflection. The transition is often man-aged by a connecting phrase which signalizes the shift from objects to concepts and indicates the nature of the relation between them: "So fares it with the children of the earth"; "ev'n thus on sorrow's breath/A kindred stillness steals"; "Bidding me many a tender thought recall/Of summer days"; "I meditate/On this world's passing pageant."

Bowles wrote in a Preface of 1805, when his poems had already achieved a ninth edition, that his sonnets "describe his personal feelings" during excursions taken to relieve "depression of spirits." They exhibit "occasional reflections which naturally rose in his mind" and were

in general suggested by the scenes before them; and wherever such scenes appeared to harmonise with his disposition at the moment, the sentiments were involuntarily prompted.[15]

The local poem has been lyricized. That is, Bowles's sonnets pre-sent a determinate speaker, whom we are invited to identify with the author himself, whose responses to the local scene are a spon-taneous overflow of feeling and displace the landscape as the center of poetic interest; hence the "occasional reflections" and "sentiments," instead of being a series of impersonal *sententiae* linked to details of the setting by analogy, are mediated by the particular temperament and circumstances of the perceiving mind, and tend to compose a single curve of feelingful meditation. "To the River Itchin, Near Winton"—which so impressed Coleridge that he emulated it in his sonnet "To the River Otter"—will represent Bowles's procedure, including his use of the recollection of an earlier visit to stimulate the meditation:

> Itchin, when I behold thy banks again,
>> Thy crumbling margin, and thy silver breast,
>> On which the self-same tints still seem to rest,
> Why feels my heart the shiv'ring sense of pain?
>> Is it—that many a summer's day has past
> Since, in life's morn, I carol'd on thy side?
> Is it—that oft, since then, my heart has sigh'd,
>> As Youth, and Hope's delusive gleams, flew fast?
> Is it—that those, who circled on thy shore,
> Companions of my youth, now meet no more?
>> Whate'er the cause, upon thy banks I bend
> Sorrowing, yet feel such solace at my heart,
>> As at the meeting of some long-lost friend,
>> From whom, in happier hours, we wept to part.

Why Coleridge should have been moved to idolatry by so slender, if genuine, a talent as that of Bowles has been an enigma of literary history. It is significant, however, that Bowles's *Sonnets* of 1789 had an impact both on Southey and Wordsworth which was also immediate and powerful. As Wordsworth later told Samuel Rogers:

I bought them in a walk through London with my dear brother. . . . I read them as we went along; and to the great annoyance of my brother, I stopped in a niche of London Bridge to finish the pamphlet.[16]

And if we take into account Coleridge's intellectual preoccupations between the ages of seventeen and twenty-five, as well as his growing discontent with current modes of poetry, including his own, we find a sufficiency of reasons to explain the power of Bowles over his sensibility and his practice as a poet. Some of these are literary reasons, pertaining to Bowles's characteristic subjects and style, while others concern the philosophy of mind and its place in nature which, Coleridge believed, was implicit in Bowles's habitual manner of proceeding.

Bowles's sonnets represent the lonely mind in meditation, and their *fin de siècle* mood of weary and self-pitying isolation—what Coleridge called their "lonely feeling"[17]—proved irresistible to a vigorous young newcomer to poetry. Of much greater and more enduring importance, however, as Coleridge emphasized in his *Biographia,* was the revelation to him of the possibility of a style "so tender and yet so manly, so natural and real, and yet so dignified and harmonious, as the sonnets etc. of Mr. Bowles!"[18] Even while he was absorbedly reading and tentatively imitating Bowles, Coleridge himself in his major efforts was primarily the poet "To turgid ode and tumid stanza dear," of Byron's unadmiring comment. In his poetic volume of 1796, as enlarged in 1797, the most ambitious undertakings were the "Religious Musings" and "Ode on the Departing Year." Of this publication Coleridge said in the *Biographia* that though, even then, he clearly saw "the superiority of an austerer and more natural style" than his own obscure and turgid language, he failed to realize his ideal, partly out of "diffidence of my own comparative talent," and "partly owing to a wrong choice of subjects, and the desire of giving a poetic colouring to abstract and metaphysical truths, in which a new world then seemed to open upon me."[19] In the turbulence and crises of the early period of the French Revolution, he had been obsessed with the need to give public voice to his political, religious, and philosophical beliefs, and he had tried to poetize such materials in the fashion current in the 1790's.[20] That is to say, he had adopted a visionary and oracular persona—in accordance, as he said in the Dedication to his "Ode on the Departing Year," with the practice of the ancients, when "the Bard and the Prophet were one and the same character"[21]—and had compounded Biblical prophecy, the hieratic stance of Milton, and the formal rhetoric, allegorical tactics, and calculated disorder of what he called "the sublimer Ode" of Gray and Collins, in the effort to endow his subjects with the requisite elevation, passion, drama, and impact. As Coleridge wrote to Southey in December of 1794, while Bowles's poems were his "morning Companions," helping him, "a thought-bewilder'd

Man," to discover his own defects: "I am so habituated to philos-
ophizing, that I cannot divest myself of it even when my own
Wretchedness is the subject."

And I cannot write without a *body* of *thought*—hence my *Poetry* is
crowded and sweats beneath a heavy burthen of Ideas and Imagery! It
has seldom Ease.[22]

This "Ease" Coleridge had early discovered in Bowles. And as
he said in the *Biographia,* the example of Bowles—together with
Cowper the first of the living poets who, in the style "more sustained and elevated" than in Percy's collection of popular ballads,
"combined natural thoughts with natural diction; the first who
reconciled the heart with the head"—rescued him from the unnatural division between intellect and feeling, and consonantly,
from his use of "a laborious and florid diction"; but only, as he
adds, "gradually."[23] The reason for the delay in making, as he put
it, his "practice" conform to his "better judgment" is, I think,
plain. Coleridge succeeded in emulating Bowles's ease only after he
learned to adopt and commit himself to the lyric persona which
demands such a style. That is, in place of philosophical, moral, and
historical pronouncements translated into allegoric action by Pindaric artifice and amplified for public delivery in a ceremonious
bardic voice, Bowles's sonnets opened out to Coleridge the possibilities in the quite ordinary circumstances of a private person in a
specific time and place whose meditation, credibly stimulated by
the setting, is grounded in his particular character, follows the
various and seemingly random flow of the living consciousness, and
is conducted in the intimate yet adaptive voice of the interior
monologue. (Bowles's style, as Coleridge said, unites the possibilities both of colloquialism and elevation—it is "natural and real,
and yet . . . dignified and harmonious.") It was in "the compositions of my twenty-fourth and twenty-fifth years," Coleridge goes
on to say, including "the shorter blank verse poems"—that is, the
poems of 1796–97, beginning with "The Eolian Harp," which
established the persona, idiom, materials, and ordonnance of the
greater Romantic lyric—that he achieved his "present ideal in
respect of the general tissue of the style."[24] No doubt the scholars
are right who claim some influence on these poems of the relaxed

and conversational blank verse of Cowper's *The Task*,[25] in the recurrent passages, within its mock-Miltonic manner, of serious description or meditation. I see no reason, however, to doubt Coleridge's repeated assertion that Bowles's sonnets and blank-verse poems were for him the prior and by far the pre-eminent models.

So much for the speaker and voice of Bowles's sonnets. Now what of their central structural trope, by which, as Coleridge described it in 1796, "moral Sentiments, Affections, or Feelings, are deduced from, and associated with, the scenery of Nature"? Even so early in his career Coleridge was an integral thinker for whom questions of poetic structure were inseparable from general philosophic issues, and he at once went on to interpret this device as the correlate of a mode of perception which unites the mind to its physical environment. Such compositions, he said,

create a sweet and indissoluble union between the intellectual and the material world. . . . Hence the Sonnets of BOWLES derive their marked superiority over all other Sonnets; hence they domesticate with the heart, and become, as it were, a part of our identity.[26]

This philosophical and psychological interpretation of Bowles's lyric procedure was not only, as Coleridge indicates, a cardinal reason for his early fascination with Bowles, but also the chief clue to his later disenchantment, and it merits attention.

IV

THE COALESCENCE OF SUBJECT AND OBJECT

In the opening chapter of his *Literary Life*, Coleridge introduces Bowles's sonnets not on their own account, but as representing a stage in his total intellectual development—"as introductory to the statement of my principles in Politics, Religion, and Philosophy, and an application of the rules, deduced from philosophical principles, to poetry and criticism."[27] Hence he moves from his account of the shaping influence of Bowyer, Bowles, and Wordsworth into a summary review of the history of philosophy, as preliminary to establishing his own metaphysical and critical premises, of which the culmination was to be the crucial distinction between fancy and imagination.

In the course of his survey of the dominant philosophy of the preceding age, it becomes clear that Coleridge found intolerable two of its main features, common both to philosophers in the school of Descartes and in the school of Locke. The first was its dualism, the absolute separation between mind and the material universe, which replaced a providential, vital, and companionable world by a world of particles in purposeless movement. The second was the method of reasoning underlying this dualism, that pervasive elementarism which takes as its starting point the irreducible element or part and conceives all wholes to be a combination of discrete parts, whether material atoms or mental "ideas."

Even in 1797, while Coleridge was still a Hartleian associationist in philosophy, he had expressed his recoil from elementarist thinking. The fault of "the Experimentalists," who rely only on the "testimony of their senses," is that "they contemplate nothing but *parts*—and all *parts* are necessarily little—and the Universe to them is but a mass of *little things*." "I can contemplate nothing but parts, & parts are all *little*—!—My mind feels as if it ached to behold & know something *great*—something *one & indivisible*. . . ."[28] And he wrote later in *The Friend* about that particular separation between part and part which divides mind from nature:

The ground-work, therefore, of all true philosophy is the full apprehension of the difference between . . . that intuition of things which arises when we possess ourselves, as one with the whole . . . and that which presents itself when . . . we think of ourselves as separated beings, and place nature in antithesis to the mind, as object to subject, thing to thought, death to life.[29]

As to Coleridge, so to Wordsworth in 1797–98, "solitary objects . . . beheld/In disconnection" are "dead and spiritless," and division, breaking down "all grandeur" into successive "littleness," is opposed to man's proper spiritual condition, in which "All things shall live in us and we shall live/In all things that surround us."[30] Absolute separation, in other words, is death-dealing—in Coleridge's words, it is "the philosophy of Death, and only of a dead nature can it hold good"[31]—so that the separation of mind from nature leads inevitably to the conception of a dead world in which the estranged mind is doomed to lead a life-in-death.

To the Romantic sensibility such a universe could not be endured, and the central enterprise common to many post-Kantian
German philosophers and poets, as well as to Coleridge and
Wordsworth, was to join together the "subject" and "object" that
modern intellection had put asunder, and thus to revivify a dead
nature, restore its concreteness, significance, and human values,
and re-domiciliate man in a world which had become alien to him.
The pervasive sense of estrangement, of a lost and isolated existence in an alien world, is not peculiar to our own age of anxiety,
but was a commonplace of Romantic philosophy. According to
Friedrich Schelling, the most representative philosopher of that
age, division from unity was the fall of man consequent upon his
eating the fruit of the tree of knowledge in the Enlightenment.
The guilt of modern men must be

ascribed to their own will, which deviated from unity. . . . [This is] a
truly Platonic fall of man, the condition in which man believes that
the dead, the absolutely manifold and separated world which he conceives, is in fact the true and actual world.[32]

Long before he read Schelling, and while at the height of his
enthusiasm for Bowles, Coleridge had included in his visionary
"Religious Musings" (1794) an outline of human history in which
mankind's highest good had been "to know ourselves/Parts and
proportions of one wondrous whole"; the present evil was defined
as a fall into an anarchic separation in which each man, "dis-
herited of soul," feels "himself, his own low self the whole"; and
man's redemption at the Second Coming was anticipated as a
reintegration into his lost unity by a "sacred sympathy" which
makes "The whole one Self! Self, that no alien knows! . . . all of all
possessing!"[33] And in 1815 Coleridge recalled that the plan of
Wordsworth's projected masterpiece, *The Recluse,* as he had
understood it, had also been to affirm "a Fall in some sense, as a
fact," to be redeemed by a

Reconciliation from this Enmity with Nature . . . by the substitution
of Life, and Intelligence . . . for the Philosophy of mechanism which in
every thing that is most worthy of the human Intellect strikes *Death.*[34]

In the *Biographia Literaria,* when Coleridge came to lay down
his own metaphysical system, he based it on a premise designed to

overcome both the elementarism in method and the dualism in theory of knowledge of his eighteenth-century predecessors, by converting their absolute division between subject and object into a logical "antithesis," in order to make it eligible for resolution by the Romantic dialectic of thesis-antithesis-synthesis. The "primary ground" of his theory of knowledge, he says, is "the coincidence of an object with a subject" or "of the thought with the thing," in a synthesis, or "coalescence," in which the elements lose their separate identities. "In the reconciling, and recurrence of this contradiction exists the process and mystery of production and life."[35] And the process of vital artistic creation reflects the process of this vital creative perception. Unlike the fancy, which can only re-arrange the "fixities and definites" of sense-perception without altering their identity, the "synthetic and magical power" of the secondary imagination repeats the primal act of knowing by dissolving the elements of perception "in order to recreate" them, and "reveals itself in the balance or reconciliation of opposite or discordant qualities"—including the reconciliation of intellect with emotion, and of thought with object: "the idea, with the image."[36]

In short, the reintegration of the divided self (of "head and heart") and the simultaneous healing of the breach between the ego and the alien other (of "subject and object") was for Coleridge a profound emotional need which he translated into the grounds both of his theory of knowledge and his theory of art. How pivotal the concept of human-nonhuman reconciliation came to be for Coleridge's aesthetics is apparent in his essay "On Poesy or Art," in which he specifically defined art as "the reconciler of nature and man . . . the power of humanizing nature, of infusing the thoughts and passions of man into every thing which is the object of his contemplation." It is "the union and reconciliation of that which is nature with that which is exclusively human."[37]

*   *   *

Perhaps now, to return at last to the sonnets of Bowles, we can understand better why those seemingly inconsequential poems made so powerful an impact on Coleridge, in their materials as well as their structure and style. Bowles's primary device by which sentiments and feelings "are deduced from, and associated with, the scenery of Nature" had seemed to Coleridge evidence of a poetry which not only "reconciled the heart with the head," but also united the mind with nature; in the terms available to him in 1796, it created "a sweet and indissoluble union between the intellectual and the material world." Through the next half-decade, however, Coleridge carried on his own experiments in the descriptive and meditative lyric, came to know the early poetry of Wordsworth, had his introduction to German metaphysics, and, in intense and almost fevered speculation, groped his way out of the mechanism and associationism of David Hartley and other English empiricists. Increasingly in the process he became dissatisfied with the constitution of Bowles's poems, and the reasons came sharply into focus in 1802, at about the time he was recasting his verse "Letter to [Asra]" into his highest achievement in the greater Romantic lyric, "Dejection: An Ode." On 10 September he wrote a letter to William Sotheby which shows that his working his way through and beyond Bowles was an integral part of his working his way toward a new poetry, a new criticism, and a new world view. The letter is a preliminary sketch for the *Biographia Literaria,* for like that work it moves from a critique of Bowles through a view of the relation of mind to nature in perception to a theory of poetic production, and culminates in Coleridge's first explicit distinction between the elementaristic fancy and the synthetic imagination.

Bowles had just published a new edition of his sonnets, supplemented by several long poems in blank verse which reverted to a process of scenic inventory and incidental meditation very close to the eighteenth-century local poem. Bowles's second volume, Coleridge begins, "is woefully inferior to it's Predecessor."

There reigns thro' all the blank verse poems such a perpetual trick of *moralizing* every thing—which is very well, occasionally—but never to see or describe any interesting appearance in nature, without connecting it by dim analogies with the moral world, proves faintness of Impression. Nature has her proper interest; & he will know what it is, who believes & feels, that every Thing has a Life of it's own, & that we are all *one Life.* A Poet's *Heart & Intellect* should be *combined, intimately* combined & *unified,* with the great appearances in Nature—& not merely held in solution & loose mixture with them, in the shape of formal Similes. . . . The truth is—Bowles has indeed the *sensibility* of a poet; but he has not the *Passion* of a great Poet. . . . He has no native Passion, because he is not a Thinker.[38]

Bowles's exaggeration in his later poems of his earlier devices has opened out to Coleridge his inherent failings. Bowles is able to reconcile the heart with the head, but only because of an equality of weakness in the antagonist powers of intellect and passion. And what Coleridge had earlier described as an "indissoluble union between the intellectual and material world" now turns out to be no better than "a loose mixture," in which the separate parts, instead of being *"intimately* combined & *unified,"* are merely held together by the rhetorical expedient of "formal Similes." In other words, what to Coleridge, the Hartleian associationist, had in 1796 appeared to be an adequate integration of mind and its milieu reveals itself—when he has learned to think of all higher mental processes in terms of a synthesis of contraries—to be what he later called the "conjunction-disjunctive" of neoclassic unity by a decorum of the parts.

In the letter to Sotheby, Coleridge goes on to draw a parallel distinction between the treatment of nature in Greek mythology and in the Hebrew poets, and ends by assigning the former type to the collocative process of the lower productive faculty, or Fancy. To the Greek poets

all natural Objects were *dead*—mere hollow Statues—but there was a Godkin or Goddessling *included* in each. . . . At best it is but Fancy, or the aggregating Faculty of the mind—not *Imagination,* or the *modifying,* and co-adunating Faculty. . . . In the Hebrew Poets each Thing has a Life of it's own, & yet they are all one Life.

Bowles's poems, it becomes apparent, remain in the mode of the Fancy because they fail to overcome the division between living mind and a dead nature by that act of the coadunating Imagination which fuses the two into "one Life"; for when Bowles joins the parts *a* and *b* they form an aggregate *ab,* instead of "interpenetrating" (in terms of Coleridge's critique of elementarist thinking) to "generate a higher third, including both the former," the product *c*.[39] For the "mystery of genius in the Fine Arts," as Coleridge said in "On Poesy or Art," is

so to place these images [of nature] . . . as to elicit from, and to super-
induce upon, the forms themselves the moral reflexions to which they
approximate, to make the external internal, the internal external, to
make nature thought, and thought nature.[40]

The shift in Coleridge's theory of descriptive poetry corresponded with a change in his practice of the form; and in the sequence of sonnets and conversation poems that he wrote under
Bowles's influence we can observe him in the process of converting
the conjunction of parts, in which nature stays on one side and
thought on the other, into the Romantic interfusion of subject and
object. W. K. Wimsatt has acutely remarked that Coleridge's sonnet
"To the River Otter"—though written in express imitation of
Bowles's "To the River Itchin," perhaps so early as 1793—has begun to diverge from Bowles's "simple association . . . simply
asserted" by involving the thought in the descriptive details so that
the design "is latent in the multiform sensuous picture."[41] "The
Eolian Harp" (1795–96) set the expanded pattern of the greater
lyric, but in it the meditative flight is a short one, while the thought
is still at times expressed in the mode of *sententiae* which are
joined to the details of the scene by formal similes. We sit

> beside our Cot, our Cot o'ergrown
> With white-flower'd Jasmin, and the broad-leav'd Myrtle,
> (Meet emblems they of Innocence and Love!)
> And watch the Clouds, that late were rich with light,
> Slow-sadd'ning round, and mark the Star of eve
> Serenely brilliant (such should WISDOM be!)
> Shine opposite.

In "Frost at Midnight," however, written two years later, the
images in the initial description are already suffused with an unstated significance which, in Coleridge's terms, is merely "elicited"
and expanded by the subsequent reflection, which in turn "super-
induces" a richer meaning upon the scene to which it reverts.
"Fears in Solitude," a few months after that, exemplifies the sustained dialogue between mind and landscape which Coleridge describes in lines 215–20 of the poem: the prospect of sea and fields

> seems like society—
> Conversing with the mind, and giving it
> A livelier impulse and a dance of thought!

And "Dejection: An Ode," on which Coleridge was working in 1802 just as he got Bowles's poems into critical perspective, is a triumph of the "coadunating" imagination, in the very poem which laments the severance of his community with nature and the suspension of his shaping spirit of imagination. In unspoken consonance with the change of the outer scene and of the responsive wind-harp from ominous quiet to violent storm to momentary calm, the poet's mind, momentarily revitalized by a correspondent inner breeze, moves from torpor through violence to calm, by a process in which the properties earlier specified of the landscape—the spring rebirth, the radiated light of moon and stars, the clouds and rain, the voice of the harp—reappear as the metaphors of the evolving meditation on the relation of mind to nature; these culminate in the figure of the one life as an eddy between antitheses:

> To her may all things live, from pole to pole,
> Their life the eddying of her living soul!

On Coleridge's philosophical premises, in this poem nature is made thought and thought nature, both by their sustained interaction and by their seamless metaphoric continuity.

The best Romantic meditations on a landscape, following Coleridge's examples, all manifest a transaction between subject and object in which the thought incorporates and makes explicit what was already implicit in the outer scene. And all the poets testify independently to a fact of consciousness which underlay these poems, and was the experiential source and warrant for the philosophy of cognition as an interfusion of mind and nature. When the Romantic poet confronted a landscape, the distinction between self and not-self tended to dissolve. Coleridge asserted that from childhood he had been accustomed to "unrealize . . . and then by a sort of transfusion and transmission of my consciousness to identify myself with the Object"; also that

in looking at objects of Nature while I am thinking . . . I seem rather to be seeking, as it were *asking*, a symbolical language for something within me that already and forever exists, than observing any thing new.

So with Wordsworth: "I was often unable to think of external things as having external existence, and I communed with all that

I saw as something not apart from, but inherent in, my own im-
material nature." Shelley witnessed to "the state called reverie,"
when men "feel as if their nature were dissolved into the surrounding universe, or as if the surrounding universe were absorbed into
their being. They are conscious of no distinction." Even Byron's
Childe Harold claimed that "I live not in myself," but that mountains, waves, and skies become "a part/Of me, and of my soul, as I
of them." Keats's experience differs, but only in the conditions
that, instead of assimilating the other to the self, the self goes out
into the other, and that the boundary of self is "annihilated" when
he contemplates, not a broad prospect, but a solid particular
endowed with outline, mass, and posture or motion. That type of
poet of which "I am a Member . . . has no self" but "is continually
[informing] and filling some other Body"—a moving billiard ball,
a breaking wave, a human form in arrested motion, a sparrow, an
urn, or a nightingale.[42]

V

THE ROMANTIC MEDITATION

The greater Romantic lyric, then, as established by Coleridge,
evolved from the descriptive-meditative structure of the eighteenth-
century local poem, primarily through the intermediate stage of
Bowles's sequence of sonnets. There remains, however, a wide disparity between the Romantic lyric and its predecessors, a disparity
in the organization and nature of the meditation proper. In local
poetry the order of the thoughts is the sequence in which the
natural objects are observed; the poet surveys a prospect, or climbs
a hill, or undertakes a tour, or follows the course of a stream, and
he introduces memories and ideas intermittently, as the descriptive
occasion offers. In Bowles's sonnets, the meditation, while more
continuous, is severely limited by the straitness of the form, and
consists mainly of the pensive commonplaces of the typical late-
century man of feeling. In the fully developed Romantic lyric, on
the other hand, the description is structurally subordinate to the
meditation, and the meditation is sustained, continuous, and
highly serious. Even when the initial impression is of the casual
movement of a relaxed mind, retrospect reveals the whole to have
been firmly organized around an emotional issue pressing for

resolution. And in a number of the greatest lyrics—including Coleridge's "Dejection," Wordsworth's "Intimations," Shelley's "Stanzas Written in Dejection" and "West Wind," Keats's "Nightingale"—the issue is one of a recurrent state often called by the specialized term "dejection." This is not the pleasing melancholy of the eighteenth-century poet of sensibility, nor Bowles's muted self-pity, but a profound sadness, sometimes bordering on the anguish of terror or despair, at the sense of loss, dereliction, isolation, or inner death, which is presented as inherent in the conditions of the speaker's existence.

In the English literary tradition these Romantic meditations had their closest analogue in the devotional poems of the seventeenth century. In his study *The Poetry of Meditation* Professor Louis Martz has emphasized the importance, for the religious poets we usually class as "metaphysical," of the numerous and immensely popular devotional handbooks which undertook to discipline the casual flow of ordinary consciousness by setting down a detailed regimen for evoking, sustaining, and ordering a process of meditation toward resolution. A standard sub-department was the "meditation on the creatures" (that is, on the created world) in order, as the title of Robert Bellarmine's influential treatise of 1615 put it, to achieve *The Ascent of the Mind to God by a Ladder of Things Created*. The recommended procedure, as this became stabilized at the turn of the century, tended to fall into three major divisions. The first involved what Loyola called the "composition of place, seeing the spot"; that is, envisioning in vivid detail the person, object, or scene which initiates the meditation. The second, the meditation proper, was the analysis of the relevance to our salvation of this scene, interpreted analogically; it often included a turn inward to a close examination of conscience. The last specified the results of this meditation for our affections and will, and either included, or concluded with, a "colloquy"—usually a prayer, or discourse with God, although as St. Francis de Sales advises, "while we are forming our affections and resolutions," we do well to address our colloquy also "to ourselves, to our own hearts . . . and even to insensible creatures."[43]

Few seventeenth-century meditative poems accord exactly with the formulas of the Catholic or Anglican devotional manuals, but many of them unmistakably profited from that disciplining of fluid thought into an organized pattern which was a central enterprise in the spiritual life of the age. And those poetic meditations on the creatures which envision a natural scene or object, go on, in sorrow, anguish, or dejection, to explore the significance for the speaker of the spiritual signs built into the object by God, and close in reconciliation and the hope of rebirth, are closer to the best Romantic lyrics in meditative content, mood, and ordonnance than any poem by Bowles or his eighteenth-century predecessors. Good instances of the type are Vaughan's "The Waterfall," "Regeneration," "Vanity of Spirit," and "I walkt the other day (to spend my hour,)/Into a field"—an hour being a standard time set aside for formal meditation. "Regeneration," for example, begins with a walk through a spring landscape which stands in sharp contrast to the sterile winter of the poet's spirit, finds its resolution in a sudden storm of wind which, as *spiritus*, is the material equivalent both of the breath of God and the spirit of man, and ends in a short colloquy which is a prayer for a spiritual dying-into-life:

> Here musing long, I heard
>   A rushing wind
> Which still increas'd, but whence it stirr'd
>   No where I could not find. . . .
> Lord, then said I, on me one breath,
> And let me die before my death!

The two key figures of the outer and inner seasons and of the correspondent, regenerative wind later served as the radical metaphors in a number of Romantic poems, including Coleridge's "Dejection" and Shelley's "Ode to the West Wind."[44]

Or consider the meditation on a creature which—at least in his later life—was Coleridge's favorite poem by one of his favorite lyrists, George Herbert's "The Flower."[45] Reflecting upon the annual death and rebirth of the plant, the poet draws a complex analogy with his own soul in its cycles of depression and joy, spiritual drouth and rain, death and springlike revival, alienation from God and reconcilement; in the concluding colloquy he also (as Coleridge and Shelley were to do) incorporates into the analogy the sterility and revival of his poetic powers:

And now in age I bud again,
After so many deaths I live and write;
I once more smell the dew and rain,
And relish versing. Oh, my only light,
It cannot be
That I am he
On whom thy tempests fell all night.[46]

Herbert is describing the state of inner torpor through alienation from God known in theology as accidie, dejection, spiritual dryness, interior desolation; this condition was often analogized to circumstances of the seasons and weather, and was a matter of frequent consideration in the devotional manuals. As St. Francis de Sales wrote, in his section "Of Spiritual Dryness and Sterility":

Sometimes you will find yourself so deprived and destitute of all devout feelings of devotion that your soul will seem to be a fruitless, barren desert, in which there is no . . . water of grace to refresh her, on account of the dryness that seems to threaten her with a total and absolute desolation. . . . At the same time, to cast her into despair, the enemy mocks her by a thousand suggestions of despondency and says: "Ah! poor wretch, where is thy God? . . . Who can ever restore to thee the joy of His holy grace?"[47]

Coleridge, during the several years just preceding "Dejection: An Ode," described in his letters a recurrent state of apathy and of the paralysis of imagination in terms which seem to echo such discussions of spiritual dryness: "My Imagination is tired, down, flat and powerless. . . . As if the *organs* of Life had been dried up; as if only simple BEING remained, blind and stagnant!" "I have been . . . undergoing a process of intellectual *exsiccation*. . . . The Poet is dead in me."[48]

The Romantic meditations, then, though secular meditations, often turn on crises—alienation, dejection, the loss of a "celestial light" or "glory" in experiencing the created world—which are closely akin to the spiritual crises of the earlier religious poets. And at times the Romantic lyric becomes overtly theological in expression. Some of them include not only colloquies with a human auditor, real or imagined, and with what De Sales called "insensible creatures," but also with God or with a Spirit of Nature, in the mode of a formal prayer ("Reflections on Having Left a

Place of Retirement," "Ode to the West Wind"), or else of a terminal benediction. Thus Coleridge's "Frost at Midnight" falls into the ritual language of a blessing ("Therefore all seasons shall be sweet to thee")—a tactic which Wordsworth at once picked up in "Tintern Abbey" ("and this prayer I make. . . . Therefore let the moon/Shine on thee in thy solitary walk") and which Coleridge himself repeated in *Dejection* ("Visit her, gentle Sleep! with wings of healing. . . . To her may all things live, from pole to pole").

We must not drive the parallel too hard. There is little external evidence of the direct influence of the metaphysical poem upon the greater Romantic lyric; the similarity between them may well be the result of a common tradition of meditations on the creatures—a tradition which continued in the eighteenth century in so prodigiously popular a work as James Hervey's *Meditations and Contemplations* (1746–47).[49] And there is a very conspicuous and significant difference between the Romantic lyric and the seventeenth-century meditation on created nature—a difference in the description which initiates and directs the process of mind. The "composition of place" was not a specific locality, nor did it need to be present to the eyes of the speaker, but was a typical scene or object, usually called up, as St. Ignatius and other preceptors said, before "the eyes of the imagination,"[50] in order to set off and guide the thought by means of correspondences whose interpretation was firmly controlled by an inherited typology. The landscape set forth in Vaughan's "Regeneration," for example, is not a particular geographical location, nor even a literal setting, but the allegorical landscape common to the genre of spiritual pilgrimages, from the *Divine Comedy* to *Pilgrim's Progress*. And Herbert's flower is not a specified plant, described by the poet with his eye on the object, but a generic one; it is simply the class of all perennials, in which God has inscribed the invariable signatures of his providential plan. In the Romantic poem, on the other hand, the speaker merely happens upon a natural scene which is present, particular, and almost always precisely located; and though Coleridge occasionally alludes to it still as "that eternal language, which thy God utters,"[51] the primary meanings educed from the scene are not governed by a public symbolism, but have been brought to it by the private mind which perceives it. But we know already that these attributes also had a seventeenth-century origin, in a poet who inherited the metaphysical tradition yet went on, as Dryden and many of his successors commented,[52] to alter it in such a way as to establish the typical meter, rhetoric, and formal devices of neoclassic poetry. The crucial event in the development of the most distinctive of the Romantic lyric forms occurred when John Denham climbed Cooper's Hill and undertook to describe, in balanced couplets, the landscape before his eyes, and to embellish the description with incidental reminiscence and meditation.

NOTES

1. *The Prelude* (1850), XII, 222–3. Even Keats, though he sometimes longed for a life of sensations rather than of thought, objected to the poems of John Clare that too often "the Description overlaid and stifled that which ought to be the prevailing Idea." (Letter to John Clare from John Taylor, 27 September 1820, quoted by Edmund Blunden, *Keats' Publisher* [London, 1936], p. 80).

2. *Descriptive Sketches* (1793) drew from a contemporary reviewer the cry: "More descriptive poetry! Have we not yet enough? . . . Yes; more, and yet more: so it is decreed." *The Monthly Review*, 2d series, XII (1793), 216–17; cited by Robert A. Aubin, *Topographical Poetry in XVIII-Century England* (New York, 1936), p. 255; see also pp. 217–19.

3. Perhaps that is the reason for Coleridge's later judgment that "The Eolian Harp" was "the most perfect poem I ever wrote." (Quoted by J. D. Campbell, ed., *The Poetical Works of S. T. Coleridge*, London, 1893, p. 578). The first version of the poem and a manuscript version of 1797 (Coleridge then entitled it "Effusion") are reproduced in *The Complete Poetical Works*, ed. E. H. Coleridge (2 vols.; Oxford, 1912), II, 1021–3. For an account of the revisions of the poem, see H. J. W. Milley, "Some Notes on Coleridge's 'Eolian Harp,' " *Modern Philology*, XXXVI (1938–39), 359–75.

4. *Collected Letters*, ed. Earl Leslie Griggs (Oxford, 1956–   ), IV, 545.

5. Keats used a different figure for the poetic return. In a letter of Dec. 1818–Jan. 1819, he transcribed "Ever let the Fancy roam" and "Bards of Passion and of Mirth," in which the last lines are variants of the opening lines, and said: "These are specimens of a sort of rondeau which I think I shall become partial to" (*The Letters*, ed. H. E. Rollins, 2 vols., Cambridge, Mass., 1958, II, 21–6). In the next few months he exemplified the rondeau form in "The Eve of St. Agnes" and "La Belle Dame sans Merci," as well as in the descriptive-meditative lyric, "Ode to a Nightingale."

6. So titled in the Dowden MS. in the Morgan Library; see Carl R. Woodring, *Politics in the Poetry of Coleridge* (Madison, Wisconsin, 1961), p. 255, note 16.

7. *The Works of Samuel Johnson,* ed. Arthur Murphy (12 vols.; London, 1824), IX, 77.

8. *The Subtler Language* (Baltimore, 1959), Chap. III.

9. *Works,* ed. Geoffrey Keynes (6 vols.; London, 1928), I, 17.

10. The opening eight lines of "Cooper's Hill," despite some approximation to neoclassic neatness and dispatch, are much closer to Donne's couplets, in the cramped syntax of their run-on lines, which deploy a tortuous analogical argument to demonstrate a paradox that inverts and explodes a mythological cliché:

> Sure there are Poets which did never dream
> Upon *Parnassus,* nor did taste the stream
> Of *Helicon,* we therefore may suppose
> Those made no Poets, but the Poets those.
> And as Courts make not Kings, but Kings the Court,
> So where the Muses and their train resort,
> *Parnassus* stands; if I can be to thee
> A Poet, thou Parnassus are to me.

Compare the opening of Andrew Marvell's "Upon the Hill and Grove at Billborow" (probably written in the early 1650's) for the jolting movement, the doughty hyperbole, and witty shock-tactics of the thoroughly metaphysical management of a local hill-poem.

11. See Earl R. Wasserman, "Nature Moralized: The Divine Analogy in the Eighteenth Century," *ELH,* XX (1953), 39–76. For commentators on the local poem, the chief structural problem was how to establish easy, just, yet varied connections between its two components, the *visibilia* and the *moralia.* Joseph Warton's observation is typical, that "it is one of the greatest and most pleasing arts of descriptive poetry, to introduce moral sentences and instructions in an oblique and indirect manner." *An Essay on the Genius and Writings of Pope,* 1756 (London, 1806), I, 29.

12. Preface to *Lyrical Ballads, The Poetical Works of William Wordsworth,* ed. E. de Selincourt (5 vols.; Oxford, 1949), II, 391.

13. *Biographia Literaria,* ed. J. Shawcross (2 vols.; Oxford, 1907), I, 13.

14. Ibid. pp. 8–16.

15. *The Poetical Works of William Lisle Bowles,* ed. George Gilfillan (2 vols.; Edinburgh, 1855), I, 1.

16. *Recollections of the Table-Talk of Samuel Rogers* (New York, 1856), p. 258, note. For Bowles's effect on Southey see William Haller, *The Early Life of Robert Southey* (New York, 1917), pp. 73–6. As late as 1806–20, in *The River Duddon,* Wordsworth adopted Bowles's design of a tour represented in a sequence of local-meditative sonnets.

17. Coleridge, Introduction to his "Sheet of Sonnets" of 1796, *The Complete Poetical Works,* II, 1139. As early as November of 1797, however, Coleridge as "Nehemiah Higginbottom" parodied "the spirit of *doleful egotism*" in the

sonnet. See *Biographia Literaria*, I, 17, and David Erdman, "Coleridge as Nehemiah Higginbottom," *Modern Language Notes*, LXXIII (1958), 569–80.

18. *Biographia Literaria*, I, 10.

19. Ibid. pp. 2–3, and pp. 203–4, note. Coleridge's claim that he had recognized the defects of the "swell and glitter" of his elevated style, even as he employed it, is borne out by his Preface to the Poems of 1797, *Complete Poetical Works*, II, 1145.

20. See M. H. Abrams, "English Romanticism: The Spirit of the Age," in *Romanticism Reconsidered*, ed. Northrop Frye (New York, 1963), pp. 37–72.

21. *Complete Poetical Works*, II, 1113–14; see also p. 1145.

22. 11 December 1794, *Collected Letters*, I, 133–7.

23. *Biographia Literaria*, I, 10, 15–16.

24. Ibid. p. 16.

25. See, for example, Humphry House, *Coleridge* (London, 1953), Chap. III; George Whalley, "Coleridge's Debt to Charles Lamb," *Essays and Studies* (1958), pp. 68–85; and Max F. Schulz, *The Poetic Voices of Coleridge* (Detroit, 1963), Chap. 5. A comment of Lamb to Coleridge in December 1796 substantiates Coleridge's own statements about the relative importance for him of Bowles and Cowper: "Burns was the god of my idolatry, as Bowles of yours. I am jealous of your fraternising with Bowles, when I think you relish him more than Burns or my old favourite, Cowper." *The Works of Charles and Mary Lamb*, ed. E. V. Lucas (7 vols.; London, 1903–5), VI, 73.

26. Introduction to the "Sheet of Sonnets" of 1796, *Complete Poetical Works*, II, 1139.

27. *Biographia Literaria*, I, 1.

28. *Collected Letters*, I, 354, 349. See also ibid. IV, 574–5, and *The Notebooks of Samuel Taylor Coleridge* (New York, 1957), II, note 2151.

29. *The Friend* (3 vols.; London, 1818), III, 261–2.

30. *The Ruined Cottage*, addendum to MS. B (1797–98), *The Poetical Works*, V, 402.

31. *Theory of Life*, ed. Seth B. Watson (London, 1848), p. 63.

32. Schelling, *Sämmtliche Werke* (Stuttgart and Augsburg, 1857), Pt. I, Vol. VII, 81–2.

33. "Religious Musings," ll. 126–58, *Complete Poetical Works*, I, 113–15.

34. To Wordsworth, 30 May 1815, *Collected Letters*, IV, 574–5.

35. *Biographia Literaria*, I, 174–85.

36. Ibid. I, 202; II, 12. See *The Friend*, III, 263–4, on the "one principle which alone reconciles the man with himself, with other [men] and with the world."

37. In *Biographia Literaria*, II, 253–5. Though "On Poesy or Art" takes its departure from Schelling's "On the Relation of the Plastic Arts to Nature," the quoted statements are Coleridge's own.

38. 10 September 1802, *Collected Letters*, II, 864.

39. *Theory of Life*, p. 63.

40. In *Biographia Literaria*, II, 258.

41. "The Structure of Romantic Nature Imagery," in *The Verbal Icon* (New York, 1958), pp. 106–10.

42. Coleridge, *Collected Letters*, IV, 974–5, and *The Notebooks*, II, 2546; Wordsworth, *Poetical Works*, IV, 463; *Shelley's Prose*, ed. David Lee Clark (Albuquerque, 1954), p. 174; Byron, *Childe Harold*, III, lxxii, lxxv; Keats, *The Letters*, I, 387.

43. *Introduction to the Devout Life*, translated by John K. Ryan (Garden City, N. Y., 1955), p. 88.

44. See M. H. Abrams, "The Correspondent Breeze: A Romantic Metaphor," in *English Romantic Poets: Modern Essays in Criticism* (New York, 1960), pp. 37–54.

45. Coleridge's comments on Herbert are gathered in *Coleridge on the Seventeenth Century*, ed. Roberta Florence Brinkley (Duke University Press, 1955), pp. 533–40.

46. Coleridge wrote his later poem of aridity in a spring landscape, "Work Without Hope" (1825), expressly "in the manner of G. HERBERT." See *Complete Poetical Works*, II, 1110–11.

47. *Introduction to the Devout Life*, pp. 256–7; on "spiritual desolation," see also Loyola's *Spiritual Exercises*, ed. Orby Shipley (London, 1870), pp. 139–40.

48. *Collected Letters*, I, 470; II, 713–14; also I, 643.

49. In the *Meditations and Contemplations* (7th ed., 2 vols.; London, 1750), II, xv–xvii, Hervey describes his aim to "exhibit a Prospect of still *Life,* and grand *Operation*" in order "to *open* the *Door* of Meditation," and show how we may "*gather up* the unstable, fluctuating *Train* of Fancy; and collect her fickle Powers into a consistent, regular, and useful Habit of Thinking."

50. See Louis L. Martz, *The Poetry of Meditation* (New Haven, 1954), pp. 27–8.

51. "Frost at Midnight," ll. 58–62; cf. "This Lime-Tree Bower," ll. 39–43, and "Fears in Solitude," ll. 22–4. In Coleridge's "Hymn before Sunrise" (1802), unlike his greater lyrics, the meditation moves from the creatures to the Creator by a hereditary symbolism as old as Psalm 19: "The heavens declare the glory of God; and the firmament sheweth his handywork."

52. Dr. Johnson listed Denham among the metaphysical poets, then added, in the great commonplace of neoclassical literary history, that he "and Waller sought another way to fame, by improving the harmony of our numbers." (*The Life of Cowley, Works*, IX, 23.)

SELECTED BIBLIOGRAPHY
OF
FREDERICK A. POTTLE

I. Books
1923
1. *Shelley and Browning; a Myth and Some Facts.* Foreword by William Lyon Phelps. Chicago, Pembroke Press, 1923.

1927
2. (With Chauncey B. Tinker.) *A New Portrait of James Boswell.* Cambridge, Mass., Harvard University Press, 1927.

1929
3. *The Literary Career of James Boswell, Esq., being the Bibliographical Materials for a Life of Boswell.* Oxford, Clarendon Press, 1929.

4. *Stretchers, the Story of a Hospital on the Western Front.* New Haven, Yale University Press; London, H. Milford, Oxford University Press, 1929.

5. (Ed.) *The Officers and Nurses of Evacuation Eight,* by Arthur M. Shipley and Agnes T. Considine, with a complete Roster of all who served in the Unit. A Supplement to *Stretchers.* New Haven, Yale University Press; London, H. Milford, Oxford University Press, 1929.

1930
6. (Ed. with Geoffrey Scott.) *Private Papers of James Boswell from Malahide Castle in the Collection of Lt.-Colonel Ralph Heyward Isham.* Privately Printed, 1928–34, 18 vols. (Geoffrey Scott edited vols. 1–6.)

1931
7. (With Marion S. Pottle.) *The Private Papers of James Boswell from Malahide Castle in the Collection of Lt.-Colonel Ralph Heyward Isham.* A Descriptive Catalogue. London and New York, Oxford University Press, 1931.

1936
8. (Ed. with Charles H. Bennett.) *Boswell's Journal of a Tour to the Hebrides with Samuel Johnson, LL.D., now first published from the Original Manuscript, with Preface and Notes.* New York, Viking Press; London, Heinemann, 1936.

1937
9. (With Joseph Foladare, John P. Kirby, and Others.) *Index to the Private Papers of James Boswell from Malahide Castle in the Collection of Lt.-Colonel Ralph Heyward Isham.* London and New York, Oxford University Press, 1937.

10. *Boswell and the Girl from Botany Bay.* New York, Viking Press, 1937; London, Heinemann, 1938.

1941
11. *The Idiom of Poetry.* Ithaca, Cornell University Press, 1941. (Messenger Lectures at Cornell.)

1946
12. Revised Edition of No. 11, with three additional Essays. Ithaca, Cornell University Press, 1946.

1950
13. (Ed.) *Boswell's London Journal, 1762–63.* New York, McGraw-Hill; London, Heinemann, 1950.

1951
14. *Boswell's London Journal, 1762–63, together with Journal of My Jaunt, Harvest 1762.* London, Heinemann, 1951. (Enlarged deluxe edition of No. 13, with additional illustrations. Completely reset.)

1952
15. (Ed.) *Boswell in Holland, 1763–64.* New York, McGraw-Hill; London, Heinemann.

16. (Ed.) *James Boswell, Andrew Erskine, and George Dempster, Critical Strictures on the New Tragedy of Elvira, written by Mr. David Malloch, 1763.* Los Angeles, Augustan Reprint Society, 1952.

1953
17. (Ed.) *Boswell on the Grand Tour: Germany and Switzerland, 1764.* New York, McGraw-Hill; London, Heinemann, 1953.

1955
18. (Ed. with Frank Brady.) *Boswell on the Grand Tour: Italy, Corsica, and France, 1765–66.* New York, McGraw-Hill; London, Heinemann.

1956
19. (Ed. with Frank Brady.) *Boswell in Search of a Wife, 1766–69.* New York, McGraw-Hill, 1956; London, Heinemann, 1957.

1958
20. (Ed. with William K. Wimsatt, Jr.) *Boswell for the Defence, 1769–74.* New York, McGraw-Hill, 1959; London, Heinemann, 1960.

1961
21. New edition of No. 8, with revised introduction and additional notes by Frederick A. Pottle. New York, McGraw-Hill, 1961; London, Heinemann, 1963.

1963
22. (Ed. with Charles Ryskamp.) *Boswell: The Ominous Years, 1774–76.* New York, McGraw-Hill; London, Heinemann, 1963.

23. (Paperback of No. 12.) *The Idiom of Poetry.* Bloomington, Indiana University Press, 1963. (Photographic reprint, new introduction.)

II. Major Articles

1923
24. "Aldi Discipulus Americanus." Literary Review of the *New York Evening Post*, 29 December 1923 (4.410).

1925
25. "Bozzy and Yorick." *Blackwood's Magazine*, March 1955 (217.297–313).

26. "The Incredible Boswell." *Blackwood's Magazine*, August 1925 (218.149–65).

27. "Three New Legal Ballads by James Boswell." *Juridical Review*, September 1925 (37. 201–11).

28. "The Part played by Horace Walpole and James Boswell in the quarrel between Rousseau and Hume." *Philological Quarterly*, October 1925 (4.351–63).

29. Preface to *The Singing Swan, an Account of Anna Seward*, by Margaret Ashmun. Yale University Press, 1931.

30. "'Naes gīt yfel wīf' in the Old English Apollonius." *Journal of English and Germanic Philology*, January 1931 (30.21–5).

1933
31. "Printers' Copy in the Eighteenth Century." *Papers of The Bibliographical Society of America*, 1933 (27.65–73).

1942
32. (With Charles H. Bennett.) "Boswell and Mrs. Piozzi." *Modern Philology*, May 1942 (39.421–30).

1945
33. "The Power of Memory in Boswell and Scott." In *Essays on the Eighteenth Century* presented to David Nichol Smith in Honour of his Seventieth Birthday. Oxford, Clarendon Press, 1945, pp. 168–89.

1946
34. "The Life of Boswell." *Yale Review*, March 1946 (n.s. 35.445–60).

1948
35. "Wordsworth and Freud, or the Theology of the Unconscious." *Bulletin of The General Theological Seminary*, June 1958 (34.18–27).

1949
36. "James Boswell, Journalist." In *The Age of Johnson*, Essays Presented to Chauncey Brewster Tinker. New Haven, Yale University Press, 1949, pp. 15–25.

1951
37. "The Eye and the Object in the Poetry of Wordsworth." In *Wordsworth: Centenary Studies* presented at Cornell and Princeton Universities, ed. by Gilbert T. Dunklin. Princeton, Princeton University Press, 1951, pp. 23–42.

38. "Catharsis." *Yale Review*, June 1951 (40.621–41).

1952

39. "The Case of Shelley." *Publications of the Modern Language Association of America*, September 1952 (67. 589–608). Also in *English Romantic Poets*, ed. by M. H. Abrams. New York, Oxford University Press, 1960.

1953

40. "The New Critics and the Historical Method." *Yale Review*, September 1953 (43.14–23).

1959

41. "The Dark Hints of Sir John Hawkins and Boswell," in *New Light on Dr. Johnson: Essays on the Occasion of his 250th Birthday*, ed. by Frederick W. Hilles. New Haven, Yale University Press, 1959, pp. 153–62.

1960

42. "Modern Criticism of *The Ancient Mariner*." In *Essays on the Teaching of English*, ed. by Edward J. Gordon and Edward S. Noyes. New York, Appleton-Century-Crofts, Inc., 1960 (Publication of the National Council of Teachers of English), pp. 261–9.

1961

43. "A Method for Teaching." In *Art and the Craftsman, the Best of The Yale Literary Magazine*, 1836–1961, ed. by Joseph Harned and Neil Goodwin. New Haven, Yale Literary Magazine: Carbondale, Southern Illinois University Press, 1961, pp. 283–91.

1962

44. "Notes on the Importance of Private Legal Documents for the Writing of Biography and Literary History." In *Proceeding of The American Philosophical Society*, August 1962 (106.327–34).

1963

45. "Boswell as Icarus." In *Restoration and Eighteenth-Century Literature: Essays in Honor of Alan Dugald McKillop*, ed. by Carroll Camden. Published for William Marsh Rice University by the University of Chicago Press, 1963, pp. 389–406.

1964

46. "Boswell Revalued." In *Literary Views: Critical and Historical Essays*, ed. by Carroll Camden. Published for William Marsh Rice University by The University of Chicago Press, pp. 79–91.

III. Minor Articles, Notes, Letters to the Editor

1924

47. "An early Use of the Word 'Romantic.'" *Notes and Queries*, 16 February 1924 (146–116).

48. "A North Briton Extraordinary." *Notes and Queries*, 11 October, 6 December 1924 (147.249–61, 403–4).

1925

49. "Burke on the Sublime and Beautiful." *Notes and Queries,* 31 January 1925 (148.80).

50. "Two Notes on Ben Jonson's 'Staple of News.'" *Modern Language Notes,* April 1925 (40.223–6).

51. "James's Powders." *Notes and Queries,* 4 July 1925 (149.11–12).

52. "James Boswell the Younger." *Notes and Queries,* 18 July 1925 (149.49).

53. "Boswellian Myths I, II, III, IV." *Notes and Queries,* 4 July, 11 July, 18 July, 15 August 1925 (149.4–6, 21–2, 41–2, 120).

54. "Boswellian Notes:" 1. "Reflections on the late alarming bankruptcies in Scotland"; 2. "A Lost Publication by Boswell"; 3. "The Letters of Lady Jane Douglas"; 4. "The Irish Edition of An Account of Corsica," *Notes and Queries,* 15, 22 August; 12, 26 September 1925 (149. 113–14, 131–2, 184–6, 222).

55. "Bozzy was a bold young Blade." *New York Times* Book Review, 23 August 925 (30. No. 34.1, 13).

1928

56. "Liste des articles en prose et en verse relatifs à la querelle entre Rousseau at Hume, et trouvés dans le St. James's Chronicle, avril à décembre 1766" (translated by Albert Schinz). *Annales de la Société Jean Jacques Rousseau,* 1926, pub. 1928 (17.48–51).

57. The Scott-Croker Correspondence in the Yale University Library." *Yale University Library Gazette,* January 1928 (2.33–45).

1930

58. "The 'Character of Dr. Johnson'" (London) *Times Literary Supplement,* 22 May 1930 (29.434).

1936

59. "Shelley and Wordsworth." (London) *Times Literary Supplement,* 20 June 1936 (35.523).

1938

60. "Queries from Boswell." *Notes and Queries,* 17 September 1938 (175.208).

1939

61. "A Blank in Boswell's Journal." *Notes and Queries,* 29 July 1939 (177.80).

1940

62. "Boswell's Life of Johnson: Translations." *Notes and Queries,* 20 January 1940 (178.50–51).

1944

63. "Browning's 'A Toccata of Galuppi's.'" *The Explicator,* February 1944 (2. item 25).

64. "Arnold's 'Dover Beach.'" *The Explicator,* April 1944. (2. item 45).

1950
65. "Blake's 'The Tiger.' " *The Explicator*, March 1950 (8. item 39).

1953
66. "Auden's 'Fugal Chorus.' " *The Explicator*, April 1953 (11. item 40).

67. "Wordsworth's Ode: Intimations of Immortality from Recollections of Early Childhood, 61." *The Explicator*, February 1955 (13. item 23).

1956
68. "The Christian Teaching of Literature." *Faculty Papers, 3d Series, Christian Perspectives in University Life*. Episcopal Church, The National Council, 1956.

1957
69. "Shelley's Use of 'Recall.' " (London) *Times Literary Supplement*, 15 February 1957 (56. No. 2868, p. 97).

1958
70. "The Meaning of Shelley's 'Glirastes.' " *Keats-Shelley Journal*, Winter 1958 (7.6–7).

71. "Wordsworth's 'Lines Composed a Few Miles above Tintern Abbey,' " *The Explicator*, March 1958 (16. item 36).

INDEX